Handbook of Value

Handbook of Value

Perspectives from economics, neuroscience, philosophy, psychology, and sociology

Edited by

Tobias Brosch and David Sander

Associate editors

Fabrice Clement

Julien A. Deonna

Ernst Fehr

Patrik Vuilleumier

OXFORD
UNIVERSITY PRESS

OXFORD
UNIVERSITY PRESS

Great Clarendon Street, Oxford, OX2 6DP,
United Kingdom

Oxford University Press is a department of the University of Oxford.
It furthers the University's objective of excellence in research, scholarship,
and education by publishing worldwide. Oxford is a registered trade mark of
Oxford University Press in the UK and in certain other countries

First Edition published in 2016

Impression: 1

Published in the United States of America by Oxford University Press
198 Madison Avenue, New York, NY 10016, United States of America

British Library Cataloguing in Publication Data

Data available

Library of Congress Control Number: 2015944344

ISBN 978–0–19–871660–0

Printed and bound by
CPI Group (UK) Ltd, Croydon, CR0 4YY

Contents

Contributors

Editors

Tobias Brosch, Department of Psychology, and Swiss Center for Affective Sciences, University of Geneva.

David Sander, Department of Psychology, and Swiss Center for Affective Sciences, University of Geneva.

Associate editors

Fabrice Clement, Department of Sociology, University of Neuchatel.

Julien A. Deonna, Department of Philosophy, and Swiss Center for Affective Sciences, University of Geneva.

Ernst Fehr, Department of Economics, University of Zurich.

Patrik Vuilleumier, University Medical Center, University of Geneva.

Contributors

Elvira Basevich, Department of Philosophy, City University of New York.

Diana Boer, Institute of Psychology University of Koblenz-Landau.

Klaus Boehnke, Bremen International Graduate School of Social Sciences (BIGSSS) Jacobs University Bremen.

Eric S. Dickson, Department of Politics, New York University.

Thomas Dietz, Environmental Science and Policy Program and Department of Sociology, Michigan State University.

Dan-Mikael Ellingsen, Massachusetts General Hospital, Harvard Medical School.

Rajna Gibson, Geneva Finance Research Institute, University of Geneva and Swiss Finance Institute.

Paul Glimcher, Center for Neural Science, New York University.

Geoffrey Haddock, Department of Psychology, Cardiff University.

E. Tory Higgins, Department of Psychology, Columbia University.

Gabriela M. Jiga-Boy, Department of Psychology, Swansea University.

John T. Jost, Department of Psychology, New York University.

Morten Kringelbach, Department of Psychiatry, Oxford University.

Siri Leknes, Department of Psychology, University of Oslo.

Jerrold Levinson, Department of Philosophy, University of Maryland.

Dino Levy, Recanati Business School and Sagol School of Neuroscience, Tel Aviv University.

Gregory R. Maio, Department of Psychology, Cardiff University.

Jorge Moll, D'Or Institute for Research and Education (IDOR), Rio de Janeiro.

Sharareh Noorbaloochi, Department of Psychology, New York University.

Ricardo de Oliveira-Souza, D'Or Institute for Research and Education (IDOR), Rio de Janeiro.

Adam C. Pelser, Department of Philosophy, United States Air Force Academy.

Elizabeth A. Phelps, Department of Psychology, New York University.

Wlodek Rabinowicz, Department of Philosophy, Lund University and Department of Philosophy, Logic and Scientific Method, London School of Economics.

Robert C. Roberts, Department of Philosophy, Baylor University.

Raffaele Rodogno, Department of Philosophy and History of Ideas, Aarhus University.

Toni Rønnow-Rasmussen, Department of Philosophy, Lund University.

Mauro Rossi, Department of Philosophy, University of Quebec in Montreal (UQAM).

Christian von Scheve, Department of Sociology, Freie Universität Berlin.

Shalom H. Schwartz, Department of Psychology, Hebrew University of Jerusalem, Israel, and International Laboratory of Socio-cultural Research, National Research University-Higher School of Economics, Moscow, Russia.

Peter Sokol-Hessner, Department of Psychology, New York University.

Carmen Tanner, Leadership Excellence Center Zeppelin, Zeppelin University, and Department of Banking and Finance, University of Zurich.

Katy Tapper, Department of Psychology, City University London.

Christine Tappolet, Department of Philosophy, University of Montreal.

Fabrice Teroni, Department of Philosophy and Swiss Centre for Affective Sciences, University of Geneva.

Alexander F. Wagner, Department of Banking and Finance, University of Zurich and Swiss Finance Institute.

Roland Zahn, Institute of Psychiatry, King's College London.

"All the sciences have now to pave the way for the future task of the philosopher; this task being understood to mean, that he must solve the problem of value, that he has to fix the hierarchy of values."
Friedrich Nietzsche

Taken from Nietzsche, F. W., Zur Genealogie der Moral, translated by Horace B. Samuel, English: The Genealogy of Morals, Boni and Liveright, New York, 1913.

Section 1

What is value? Where does it come from?

Chapter 1

What is value? Where does it come from? A philosophical perspective

Christine Tappolet and Mauro Rossi

Introduction

A philosopher loves a distinction as much as any other theorist. When asked what value is, philosophers are likely to point out that this question splits into several distinct ones depending on what is considered. In common parlance, talk of values is often about what is deemed good, such as when we say that knowledge or justice are values, which ought to be promoted. Talk about values is also often talk about ideals that guide one's actions, such as when we maintain that democracy and autonomy are Western values, or when we speak of reliability and integrity as someone's personal values. Ideals, things that are considered to be good and, more generally, substantive claims about values, are important topics in philosophy and ethics, but they are far from the only ones. The prime focus in the philosophy of values is on more abstract questions. Philosophers commonly distinguish between evaluative concepts, evaluative judgments, evaluative sentences, and evaluative facts. These are the items at the heart of philosophical debates about values. For each of these, there is room for asking what it is, and there are no grounds for expecting that the answers to the question about their nature should be exactly the same. This simply follows from the fact that concepts, judgments, sentences, and facts are very different kinds of things, so that even if the questions they raise are connected, they cannot but be distinct.

Suppose we agree that pain is bad. Is there an objective fact of the matter as to whether this is so or is the badness of pain a purely subjective matter? This question, which concerns the nature of evaluative facts, is the topic of this chapter. As will become apparent, however, there are important connections between this question and the issues concerning evaluative concepts, evaluative judgments, and evaluative sentences. We will proceed as follows. Our main aim is to present the arguments for and against the claim that there are objective evaluative facts (see Anti-realism vs. realism: the arguments). In the last section (Perspectives), we will sketch what seems a promising account, according to which evaluative facts are fully objective, and yet closely tied to subjective responses. Put in a nutshell, the suggestion is that evaluative concepts are response-dependent, although they aim at picking out an objective evaluative reality. Before we launch into the arguments, we will start with a bit of groundwork. We will begin with a sketch of the different questions that are raised by the several items that need to be distinguished within the domain of values

(The many questions). On the basis of these distinctions, we will then present the main debates in the philosophy of values (The main debates). These two sections will allow us to introduce the fundamental concepts in the philosophy of values. They will also help clarify what it as stake in the controversy about the nature of evaluative facts.[1]

The many questions

To begin with, consider evaluative concepts, such as the concepts of the good, the desirable, the admirable, the courageous, the generous, and the kind, on the positive side, and the concepts of the bad, the shameful, the despicable, the disgusting, the coward, and the malevolent, on the negative side. Quite generally, concepts, and the propositions they form, are what we have in mind when we think; they constitute the contents of our thoughts. Concepts are often considered the main objects of interest for philosophers. Thus, many philosophers use thought experiments and other similar tools with the aim of establishing conceptual (or analytical) truths regarding our concepts.

A number of questions are raised by evaluative concepts and their relation to other concepts. What are concepts such as *good, desirable*, and *admirable*? How do they differ from other kinds of concepts, such as color or shape concepts? What is required to possess evaluative concepts? And how are they related to other kinds of concepts? A question that has been central in philosophical discussions is that of the relation between evaluative concepts and natural concepts. Natural concepts can be defined as the ones in which natural sciences, as well as—on a liberal conception of natural concepts—social and human sciences, including psychology, are couched (Moore 1903: 92; Smith 1994: 17). Insofar as concepts such as *approbation, desire*, or *admiration* are considered to be natural concepts, the question of how to conceive of the relation between evaluative concepts and emotion concepts is a question that raises the broad question of *naturalism*, that is, the question of how values fit into the natural world. As many have noted, there seems to be a tight connection between evaluative concepts and concepts picking out affective states (Mulligan 1998). It seems difficult to deny that *admirable* and *shameful*, for instance, must be closely related to the concepts of admiration and shame, respectively. After all, there is no doubt that the terms used to pick out the evaluative concepts are lexically connected to terms referring to emotions. The question of how to conceive the exact relation between evaluative concepts and emotion concepts has thus been one of the foremost questions in the philosophy of values. It is noteworthy that these questions regarding evaluative concepts are

[1] Our focus will be on the nature of evaluative facts, rather than on their origin. Two reasons explain our choice. First, in order to ask where something comes from, it is important to know what that thing is. Put differently, the question of the origin depends on the question of the nature of the thing under consideration. Second, depending on the account of what something is, the question of the origin can turn out to be irrelevant. For instance, even if one might ask what the origin of our concept of shape is, it seems irrelevant to ask where shapes come from. On most accounts, shapes are there in the world, instantiated by ordinary objects; they do not go anywhere and they do not come from anywhere in any philosophically interesting sense.

analogous to, but distinct from, questions about the relation between evaluative properties and affective states, to which we will turn shortly.[2]

A distinct but related set of questions concern judgments like the judgments that knowledge is good, that Sarah is admirable, or that cheating is shameful.[3] Such judgments clearly mobilize evaluative concepts. While concepts specify the content of judgments or, more generally, the content of thoughts, judgments are usually considered to be mental acts. Evaluative judgments raise the following questions. What is the nature of such judgments and do they differ from other types of judgments? Can evaluative judgments be assessed in terms of truth? More generally, can they be considered to be cognitive, in the sense that they are on a par with judgments regarding matters of fact? How do they relate to other psychological entities, such as other types of judgments, as well as emotions, moods, desires, intentions, and decisions? In particular, a question that has been central in philosophical debates is whether it is true that evaluative judgments have a tight relation to motivation and action. If this is the case, what relation is it, exactly?[4] As we will explain, this question is important because many have argued that the close relation between evaluative judgments and motivation sets them apart from other sorts of judgments.

Similar questions arise about evaluative language, that is, evaluative words and the sentences they compose. Since the way we use evaluative language is easily observable—in particular, it is easier to observe than concepts and mental acts—the study of evaluative sentences and words has often been considered the best way to make progress in the philosophy of values. The central question regarding evaluative language is that of the meaning, or more generally, the function of terms such as "good," "admirable," and "shameful," and more generally of sentences involving such terms, like "knowledge is good," "she is admirable," or "what you did is shameful." How does the function of evaluative sentences compare to the function of sentences such as "this is red" and "this is triangular," which appear to aim at describing how things are, and which can be assessed in terms of truth? If evaluative sentences do not aim at describing things and are not genuinely truth-assessable, for what other purposes do we use them? Do we aim at expressing positive and negative emotions, such as when we use interjections like "hurrah" or "boo"? Or do we recommend or even prescribe courses of actions, such as when we use imperatives? On both these accounts, one would have a ready explanation of why the sincere assertion of evaluative sentences is closely connected to motivation.

Finally, philosophers have also been interested in the nature of what could make evaluative sentences true, on the assumption that such sentences can be true. In consequence, philosophers have been questioning the nature of evaluative properties, such as the property of being good or that of being admirable, and the corresponding evaluative facts. The

2 See Deonna and Teroni, 2015, for a discussion of the relation between evaluative properties and emotions.

3 These are what psychologists call "valuations."

4 See Sokol-Hessner and Phelps, this volume, and Jiga-Boy et al., this volume, for this question.

debate about naturalism, which we have mentioned, is one that mainly concerns evaluative properties and facts. Hence, an important question in the philosophy of values is whether one can make room for such items in the natural world, and if this is not the case, whether it is a problem to postulate non-natural entities. However, the question that has worried philosophers most is whether there are objective evaluative properties that, when instantiated by things, would constitute genuinely objective evaluative facts, i.e., facts that are part of the fabric of the world. On the face of it, it might well seem that talk of evaluative properties and facts is entirely wrongheaded. Values, it is often believed, are in our head, not in the world.

Philosophers are not likely to rest content with these distinctions. They will underline that questions regarding value split even further because, even if one keeps to one of the categories we have outlined, other distinctions still need to be made. For the sake of simplicity, let us illustrate this with respect to evaluative concepts. A common distinction is that between the most general evaluative concepts, that is, *good* and *bad*, and what appear to be more specific evaluative concepts, such as *admirable, shameful, courageous*, or *cruel*. As we noted, the lexical connection between terms used to pick out concepts such as *admirable* and *shameful* and emotions terms, "admiration" and "shame" in this instance, suggests that some of the more specific concepts have a tight relation to affective states. This is less clear of other specific concepts, such as *courageous* and *cruel*, which are considered to be paradigm cases of what philosophers, after Bernard Williams (1985: 128–130), call "thick concepts." By contrast with *thin concepts*, such as *good*, which are taken to be purely evaluative or normative, *thick concepts* are thought to involve both an evaluative and a descriptive or natural aspect. For example, the concept *courageous* is such that when we apply it (say) to an action, we not only evaluate the action positively, but we also attribute some specific natural properties, such as being performed in the face of risk.[5] The question of the relation between thin and thick concepts is debated, but most agree that at least ordinarily, if something falls under a thick concept, then it also falls under a thin concept of the same valence. For example, what is considered courageous or generous, is ordinarily considered good. Given these distinctions among evaluative concepts and the corresponding distinctions among different types of evaluative judgments, sentences, and facts, if there are such things as evaluative facts, the different questions we have spelt out divide even further. And again, one should be alert to the possibility that the answers might differ, depending on exactly what is considered.

But what is value, one might insist? Is there nothing general that can be said to demarcate what could be called the "domain of values"? To put the question differently, what do evaluative concepts, evaluative judgments, evaluative sentences, and evaluative facts have in common? There seems to be no way to shed light on what the evaluative is without presupposing some familiarity with it. What can be said, for instance, is that evaluative

[5] For further distinctions among thin concepts, such as intrinsic vs. extrinsic values, see Ronnow-Rasmussen and Rabinowicz, this volume.

concepts are used to assess the worth of things, or that evaluative judgments express such assessments. But of course, to assess the worth of things is nothing but to evaluate things. What can be done, additionally, is to specify the relations between evaluative concepts and other kinds of concepts, such as emotion concepts. However, it is far from clear that by doing so, it is possible to spell out a definition of the evaluative that does not presuppose a prior grasp of that category. Not only is the exact relation between evaluative concepts and other types of concepts extremely controversial, but the most promising attempts to draw the relation between evaluative concepts and other types of concepts are openly circular. For instance, it seems a truism that something is good if and only if it makes some positive reaction appropriate, or that it is such as to give reasons to have a positive reaction toward it. However, it is notoriously difficult to say what it is to make a positive reaction appropriate without invoking the concept of the good. And the same appears true of the idea of reasons to have a positive reaction. How could one explain what it is to give reasons to have a positive reaction without making use of the notion of goodness? Given this, it appears that, by contrast to what is sometimes proposed, accounts of this kind cannot aim at reducing evaluative concepts to different kinds of concepts. The best way to understand such accounts is rather to see them as shedding light on evaluative concepts by spelling out the relations between evaluative concepts and other kinds of concepts. Put differently, what such accounts propose, on this interpretation, are not reductions of any sorts, but conceptual elucidations.[6]

On a more positive note, what can be done to further our understanding of the domain of values is to contrast this domain with other domains. A point that is generally acknowledged is that the evaluative is part of the *normative*, where the normative is understood as concerning what we *ought* to do, in contrast with what *is* the case (see Dancy 2000, *inter alia*). Moral claims regarding what we morally ought to do, but also claims about what an agent should do all things considered, are paradigmatic examples of normative claims. In so far as the evaluative is taken to be part of the normative, it thus falls on the *ought* side of the divide between the *is* and the *ought*. The evaluative is often taken to constitute a particular class within the normative. Thus, philosophers usually distinguish between the evaluative and the deontic (from the Greek *deon*, what is binding), a category to which concepts such as *obligatory*, *permitted*, and *forbidden* belong. An important question is how the evaluative is related to the deontic, and, more generally, what unifies the normative domain. To put it differently, how do judgments about what is good or bad relate to judgments about what we ought to do? Most would agree that what we ought to do depends on what is good or bad, in the sense that we ought to do what is best, but there are deep disagreements as to how to interpret this intuitive idea, on the assumption that it has to be taken at face value. Indeed, one can understand the debates in normative ethics, which concern what agents ought

6 That said, it must be noticed that the claim that evaluative concepts can be fully reduced to other kinds of normative concepts has its advocates. It is typically defended by those who adhere to a reductivist interpretation of the so-called fitting-attitude analysis of value (see, for instance, Danielsson and Olson (2007)).

to do, and which oppose consequentialists, deontologists, and virtue ethicists, as turning around this very question. Finally, let us mention another set of distinctions that is important within the normative domain. These are the broad categories of the moral, the prudential, the epistemic, and the esthetic, to name but the most important ones.[7] Interestingly, these broad distinctions cut across the deontic–evaluative distinction. Think, for instance, of the obligation not to harm an innocent person, on the deontic side, and of the shamefulness that is involved in cheating, on the evaluative side. Both this obligation and this evaluative property clearly fall within the moral.

With these distinctions in hand, let us turn to the main debates in the philosophy of values.

The main debates

The most fundamental questions about the evaluative are divided into four fields, which importantly overlap with the distinctions within the evaluative domain sketched in the previous section. These are the *ontological questions*, which concern the nature of evaluative facts, the *semantic questions* regarding evaluative sentences, the *epistemological questions*, which focus on whether or not there can be knowledge in the evaluative domain, and finally what could be called, in analogy with the term "moral psychology," the questions regarding *evaluative psychology*, such as that of the relation between evaluative judgments and motivation.[8] Hotly debated controversies mark each of these fields.

The central question concerning the ontology of the evaluative is whether evaluative facts and the properties that constitute them are objective, in the sense that they exist independently of what we think and feel. Put differently, objectives facts are not constituted by our thoughts or by our feelings, unless what is evaluated is something psychological. There are three main answers to this question in the literature. According to the first one, which characterizes what we will call *value realism*, evaluative properties, or "values" for short, are objective, and so, of course, are evaluative facts. Values are part of the fabric of the world as much as shapes or protons are. Value realists split into different subgroups, for they disagree among themselves concerning the relation between values and natural properties. According to some, values are reducible to natural properties (Railton 1986). Another possibility is to maintain that, while values are natural, since evaluative theories—or more generally normative theories—are on a par with natural sciences, values are nonetheless not reducible to any other natural properties. The claim is that the methods used in normative theorizing are not essentially different from the ones used in physics or biology, for instance, so that the entities postulated by both normative theories and natural sciences have to be considered to be of the same kind, though not reducible to one another (see Boyd 1988; Brink 1989; Sturgeon 1984). Even if they disagree about the reasons why values have to be considered natural, and about the way in which they are natural, both kinds of realist subscribe to *naturalism*. Naturalism is not accepted by all realists, however. Thus,

7 See Section 2 of this volume for discussions of different kinds of values.

8 These are the divisions that characterize metaethics. See, for instance, Shafer-Landau 2003.

non-naturalist realists argue that values are *sui generis* properties that are distinct from natural properties (Moore 1903; Oddie 2009; Shafer-Landau 2003). As we mentioned in the previous section, the question that non-naturalist realists have to address is whether one can make sense of the idea of properties that are non-natural. If one defines the natural as what is postulated by natural and social sciences, this question amounts to whether there can be things in the world that are not postulated by natural and social sciences.

All these different versions of value realism can be contrasted with *value anti-realism*, a stance that is characterized by the rejection of the thesis that there are objective values. There is again a variety of options for anti-realists. A prominent anti-realist view, sometimes called *simple subjectivism*, is that values are relative to how people feel. Thomas Hobbes thus writes: "But whatsoever is the object of any man's appetite or desire; that is it which he for his part calleth *good*: and the object of this hate, and aversion, *evil*; and of his contempt, *vile* and *inconsiderable*. For these words of good, evil, and contemptible, are ever used with relation to the person that useth them: there being nothing simply and absolutely so; nor any common rule of good and evil, to be taken from the nature of the objects themselves." (1651, Chapter VI; see also: Prinz 2007; Westermack 1906). According to simple subjectivism, being good is nothing but to be approved by someone, whether approbation is considered to be a specific emotion or a disposition to undergo a number of positive emotions. Such an account entails *relativism* about values, for what you approve might well be different for what someone else approves. Moreover, nothing would be good as such, for goodness would depend on whether or not people have the reaction of approbation or not. There are other ways to spell out anti-realist accounts; for instance, by appealing to the reactions or conventions of specific social groups. Thus, one could claim that to be good depends on what a specific social group agrees upon. Again, this claim entails relativism about values, since different groups might agree on different conventions.

By contrast with what one might expect, realism and anti-realism are not the only options. There is a third main approach in evaluative ontology, *value constructivism*, which rejects both realism and anti-realism. Constructivists claim that both adversaries in this debate falsely assume that objectivity and subjectivity are incompatible. What constructivism holds is that evaluative facts, or at least evaluative truths, are constructs that are both objective, in the sense of being at least to a certain extent independent of human thought and feelings, and subjective, in the sense of being constituted by human activity. Again, there are different ways to spell out this idea. One possibility is to claim that being good is being approved by ideal observers, which are fully knowledgeable and impartial (Brandt 1954; Firth 1952). Another possibility is to argue that to be good is to be what would be approved after an idealized process of deliberation. Such a constructivist account, which many trace back to Immanuel Kant, has been mainly developed in the moral domain (Korsgaard 1996; Rawls 1980). Remarkably, David Hume, a philosopher whose approach could not be more opposed to that of Kant, has also been seen as an early advocate of a Humean kind of constructivism, which has been contrasted with Kantian constructivism (Street 2010). The main difference between the two kinds of constructivism concerns the relativity of normative claims, the Kantian constructivist advocating the universality of moral claims, while the Humean constructivist accepts that moral claims are relative to the specific standpoints of particular agents.

Value realism is commonly paired with specific stances in semantic, epistemology, and evaluative psychology. These are: (a) *cognitivism* about evaluative sentences, (b) *rationalism* regarding evaluative knowledge, and (c) *externalism* with respect to the relation between evaluative judgments and motivation. According to cognitivism, evaluative sentences have the same function as sentences about natural facts. Thus, when we say that cheating is shameful, for instance, we aim at saying something true, just as when we say that the cat is on the mat. Cognitivism thus holds that evaluative sentences aim at describing facts and are truth-assessable. Even though cognitivism fits well with how evaluative sentences appear to be used, *non-cognitivism* has had (and still has) a great many advocates. The main non-cognitivist account about evaluative sentences, *expressivism*, holds that the function of evaluative sentences is to express positive and negative emotions or, alternatively, attitudes such as desires and aversions (Ayer 1936; Blackburn 1984; Gibbard 1990; Stevenson 1937). In the former case, evaluative sentences would be of the same kind as "boo!" or "hurrah!," two interjections we use to express our positive and negative feelings, respectively. By contrast with a sentence that attributes feelings to persons, such as "you disapprove of cheating," such interjections and, more generally, expressions of feelings do not aim at describing states of affairs, and they fail to be truth-assessable. Another possibility is to opt for *prescriptivism*, a thesis that usually concerns moral sentences, and according to which the function of such sentences is to express imperatives or prescriptions (Hare 1952). On this suggestion, the sentence "cheating is bad," for instance, would have the same function as the imperative "do not cheat!," so that it could not be considered to have genuine truth-conditions. This is why both expressivism and prescriptivism are considered to be non-cognitive accounts of evaluative language.

It should be underlined here that the distinction between cognitivism and non-cognitivism is often pitched at the psychological rather than the semantic level. Cognitivism about evaluative judgments is the claim that such judgments, like the corresponding sentences, are genuinely truth-assessable, a claim that is denied by non-cognitivism about evaluative judgments. This contrast is sometimes expressed in terms of cognitive states, such as, paradigmatically, beliefs. Accordingly, cognitivism about evaluative judgments amounts to the thesis that such judgments are on a par with beliefs, while non-cognitivism denies this and stresses the analogies with motivational states, such as, paradigmatically, desires.

Let us get back to value realism. In general, value realists tend to reject *skepticism*; they are in fact optimistic about the prospect of evaluative knowledge. Most often, realists have been, and are still tempted, to argue that knowledge about evaluative facts is obtained by the exercise of reason, thus subscribing to *rationalism* regarding the epistemology of values. According to an important strand of rationalism about evaluative knowledge, *intuitionism*, such knowledge is grounded on intuitions (Audi 1997; Moore 1903; Shafer-Landau 2003). Intuitions are often conceived as states that are immediately justified, in the sense that their justification is independent of other states. Thus, they are believed to constitute the foundation of justification and knowledge. Rationalists have other options, however. They can follow the move made by some moral realists, and argue that evaluative knowledge, or at least epistemic justification, depends not on the availability of foundational beliefs, but on the possibility of developing a coherent set of beliefs (Brink 1989; Daniels 1979; Rawls 1971). According to *coherentism* about evaluative beliefs, an evaluative belief would be justified on condition that it belongs to a fully coherent set of beliefs.

Let us make a terminological point here. Rationalism is not merely a claim regarding evaluative knowledge. Quite generally, moral (as well as evaluative) rationalism contrasts with sentimentalism. Rationalism about the evaluative can be characterized, very roughly, as the claim that evaluative judgments are grounded in reason. Kant is without doubt the foremost advocate of moral rationalism in the history of philosophy (Kant 1785, 1788). By contrast, sentimentalism about evaluative judgments not only denies that evaluative judgments are grounded in reason, but also claims that the ground of the evaluative lies in the sentiments. Thus, Hume, the most prominent moral sentimentalist, famously states that "morality [...] is more properly felt than judg'd of" (*Treatise*, book 3, part 1, section 2) and argues that moral distinctions are not derived by reason. Because they take sentiments and emotions to be non-cognitive states that are opposed to reason, sentimentalists most often reject value realism and doubt that there can be knowledge in the relevant domain (Nichols 2004; Prinz 2007). As we shall argue, however, this association between anti-realism and sentimentalism can and needs to be resisted.

What about the relation between evaluative judgments and motivation? Value realists tend to argue against *internalism*, i.e., the claim that there is an internal or necessary connection between evaluative judgments and motivation. Internalism is particularly attractive in the case of first-person moral judgments of the deontic kind (Hare 1952; Smith 1994). It appears plausible that if an agent judges that she ought to perform some action, she will be motivated to do so, or at least that, if she fails to be motivated accordingly, she can be accused of some kind of rationality failure. What is often claimed is that if an agent is not motivated in accordance with her moral judgments, she manifests practical irrationality, such as weakness of will. If this were indeed true of moral judgments, such judgments would be importantly different from judgments about natural facts, which have no particular connection to motivation. This is why many moral realists have been tempted by externalism (Brink 1989; Railton 1986). Transposed to the case of evaluative judgments, the question is whether a judgment like the judgment that this action is the best, say, is one that a fully rational agent could make without having any motivation to perform the action. As we shall argue, externalism may be more plausible in the case of evaluative judgments than in the case of judgments regarding what I ought to do.

What we have, then, are standard options that characterize realists and anti-realists. The standard realist package comprises cognitivism, rationalism, and externalism, while the standard anti-realist package is constituted by non-cognitivism, sentimentalism, and internalism.[9] There are clear affinities between these different claims, and indeed, there

9 Indeed, moral realism and anti-realism are often defined in conjunctive terms (see, for instance: Railton 1996; Sayre-McCord 1988; Sturgeon 1984).

are also a number of logical inferences between specific claims. For instance, if there are no evaluative facts, it follows that there will be nothing we can know, so that evaluative knowledge is excluded. Nevertheless, it has to be underlined that there are many more combinations than there might seem to be at first sight. Some moral realists have, for instance, argued that their account is compatible with internalism (Shafer-Landau 2003). Moreover, as John Mackie (1977) has made clear in the moral case, one can well defend both anti-realism and cognitivism. According to the so-called *error theory* that Mackie advocated, moral judgments are fully cognitive, but since there are no objective moral facts, they fail to correspond to any reality (Joyce 2001; Olson 2014). Similarly, it could be argued that even if evaluative judgments have the sole function of expressing positive and negative feelings, this does not entail that there are no evaluative facts. Sadly enough, we would simply not be able to refer to such facts. Further possibilities will emerge when we discuss the arguments for and against the objectivity of evaluative facts. In particular, we shall argue that it is possible to develop an account of the evaluative that is both sentimentalist and fully realist.

Anti-realism vs. realism: the arguments

There are at least three ways to defend a realist stance about values (cf. Shafer-Landau 2003). The first consists in offering some positive argument in support of value realism. The second consists in arguing that all anti-realist positions face problems so big as to be ultimately unappealing. The third consists in rejecting the objections against value realism raised by its opponents. Obviously, these strategies are far from incompatible; indeed, it is to be expected that a full defense of value realism will combine elements from the three of them. In what follows, we shall consider the main arguments pertaining to each of these strategies.

One straightforward argument in favor of value realism is based on the *phenomenology* of evaluative judgments (Brink 1989). First, when making an evaluative judgment, we seem to express some sort of cognitive state that does not appear to differ, in nature, from ordinary beliefs, such as the belief that the cat is on the mat. Second, our evaluative judgments seem to be about an objective evaluative reality, which exists independently of our own attitudes. This is evidenced by the fact that disagreement about value presents itself as genuine disagreement, one that can be positively resolved by figuring out how things really are. This contrasts with the implications of most anti-realist theories, for instance non-cognitivism, which depict evaluative disagreement as some kind of spurious disagreement. According to the value realist, these features of our experience should be taken at face value. This means that, unless we have overwhelming reason to think otherwise, we should admit that there really are objective evaluative facts and properties, which our evaluative judgments attempt to capture. Anyone wishing to defend an anti-realist position must either provide an account that accommodates the appearances or explain such appearances away.

Another important consideration that favors value realism comes from linguistic evidence. As is widely acknowledged, evaluative predicates, such as "is good" or "is admirable," behave like ordinary predicates. Thus, the structure of "Sarah is admirable" appears in no way different from that of "The ball is round." Both types of sentences can be evaluated in terms of truth, for we can ask "Is it true that Sarah is admirable?" just as we can wonder whether the ball is round. Thus, the two types of sentences appear to have cognitive contents that are genuinely truth-assessable. Since this is just what is to be expected if value realism holds, it provides us with a reason to embrace the claim that there are objective evaluative facts. Whether this consideration is conclusive depends on whether the anti-realist can satisfactorily account for these features of evaluative discourse.

The second strategy to defend value realism consists in casting doubt on rival accounts. Consider the most prominent non-cognitivist account, *expressivism*. Expressivism offers a clear account of the meaning of evaluative expressions when they appear in assertoric contexts. According to this view, the sentence "The cat is amusing" expresses an attitude of amusement toward the cat. However, this cannot be the full story. In fact, the same evaluative expressions are often embedded in more complex sentences, such as conditionals, negations, and so on, where no attitude seems to be positively expressed. If so, non-cognitivists owe us an explanation of the meaning of evaluative expressions when they occur in such non-assertoric contexts. More specifically, non-cognitivism must explain how the meaning of complex evaluative sentences derives from the meaning of their parts and to do this in a way that preserves and explains the semantic properties of such sentences. This task has proven to be quite difficult. Indeed, one often-rehearsed objection against non-cognitivism, the so-called *Frege–Geach problem*, is that the view is incapable of successfully explaining how arguments featuring evaluative statements can be logically valid (Geach 1960, 1965). Consider, for example, the following train of thought: the cat is wet; if the cat is wet, it is funny; hence, the cat is funny. There is little doubt that this is a valid inference, in the sense that the conclusion is bound to be true if the premises are.[10] The problem is that it is difficult to see how this can be so if we assume, with expressivism, that the conclusion merely expresses the attitude of amusement. No attitude appears to be expressed when we utter "If the cat is wet, it is funny," for in this context, "The cat is funny" is not asserted. So, strictly speaking the conclusion cannot follow from the premises. Insofar as value realism is committed to cognitivism, it is immune from this problem and, consequently, appears to be a more plausible position.[11]

Value realists have, however, to deal with a battery of objections from the anti-realist camp. Drawing partly on Hume (1739–41), John Mackie (1977) has provided a classic statement of several of these objections, so it may be useful to start our presentation from there. Mackie's first argument, which is known as *the argument from disagreement*, targets value realism's capacity to account for the phenomenon of radical and persistent evaluative

[10] As shown by Tappolet (1997), such inferences thus make for a problem for those who claim that moral truth is distinct from ordinary truth.

[11] See Schroeder (2007) for a recent extensive discussion of the Frege–Geach problem and the attempts made by expressivists to overcome it.

disagreement. It seems evident to many that the evaluative judgments made by different individuals or groups present a large degree of variation, both historically and interculturally. By itself, this is no reason to conclude that value realism is false. After all, there has been, and there still is, disagreement about scientific theories. This is generally not regarded as a reason to think that there is no fact of the matter capable of adjudicating between such theories. However, the alleged disagreement about values is supposed to present a more significant problem for value realism when it is combined with the view that the evaluative and the scientific domains are relevantly disanalogous. In order to characterize this disanalogy more precisely, some point out that there exists no method for deciding cases of evaluative disagreement comparable to the method used in science to resolve cases of scientific disagreement (Ayer 1936; Sturgeon 1984, 2006). Others claim that, supposedly unlike scientific disagreement, evaluative disagreement may persist under idealized conditions. According to this line of thought, it is a genuine possibility that different, perfectly rational and well-informed agents may fail to converge on the same evaluative judgments, through no fault of their own (Blackburn 1981; Shafer-Landau 2003). The next step of the argument consists in claiming that the best explanation of the disagreement in the evaluative domain is that there is no objective evaluative fact to be discovered. Rather, the observed disagreement seems to reflect the fact that values are inherently subjective, in that they depend on the perspective, culture or ways of life in which the individuals are immersed.

Mackie's second argument is the so-called *argument from queerness* (Mackie 1977). As Mackie points out, this argument has two parts: one metaphysical (or ontological) and one epistemological. He claims that "[i]f there were objective values, they would be entities or qualities or relations of a very strange sort, utterly different from anything else in the universe. Correspondingly, if we were aware of them, it would have to be by some special faculty of moral perception or intuition, utterly different from our ordinary ways of knowing everything else" (Mackie 1977: 38). According to Mackie, objective evaluative facts provide "the knower with both a direction and an overriding motive; something's being good both tells the person who knows this to pursue it and makes him pursue it" (Mackie 1977: 40). Since ordinary facts appear to lack the same action-guidingness and motivational force, objective values look "queer."

Let us elaborate on Mackie's argument, starting with its epistemological part. Mackie specifically targets moral intuitionism. His idea is that our knowledge of evaluative facts could not come from any of our ordinary perceptual or rational faculties, but only from some mysterious faculty of intuition or evaluative perception. However, the appeal to such a faculty seems suspect. Indeed, if our commitment to value realism forces us to adopt such an account, we would do better to revise our commitment. Mackie's worry is sometimes spelt out in terms of epistemic access. Accordingly, if values exist independently of us and if they are different from ordinary facts in the way that Mackie assumes, then it is unclear by what means we could acquire knowledge of, or justified beliefs about, them. Alternatively, the challenge for value realists is to offer an account of how we can form justifiable evaluative judgments about a supposedly independent evaluative reality, in a way that does not look like a miraculous coincidence and that is consistent with what we know about ourselves and about how our evolutionary history from other scientific disciplines (Street 2006).

Consider now the second part of Mackie's argument. For reasons of space, we shall simply focus on the relation between values and motivation. That there is such an intimate relation between the two is often considered a platitude in the philosophical literature, a claim already made by Hume (1739–41: book 3, part 1, section 1). As we have seen, many think that values and motivation are linked by an internal or necessary relation. More precisely, the claim is that, by conceptual necessity, if someone judges that an item is characterized by some positive value, then she will somehow be motivated to pursue it. For instance, R. M. Hare argues that if someone assents to a moral judgment and is sincere, then she will act accordingly, unless she is not free to do that (Hare 1952). Hare's formulation has the defect of rendering cases of weakness of will (or *akrasia*) seemingly impossible. Indeed, if Hare is right, it is simply impossible for an agent to freely act against her moral judgments. Similarly, if judging that an action is the best necessarily entails performing that action, then it is impossible for the agent to freely act against that evaluative judgment. This strong form of internalism is often taken to contrast too drastically with our ordinary experience. In order to make room for cases of weakness of will, some authors have thus proposed to weaken Hare's formulation. What we should say, according to them, is simply that if an agent sincerely judges that an item is characterized by some positive value, then she will be motivated to pursue it, *unless* she is practically irrational (Smith 1994). Put differently, the agent who is not motivated to follow her evaluative judgment suffers from weakness of will or other kinds of practical rationality failure. Be that as it may, Mackie's worry is that if our value judgments reliably track an objective evaluative reality, then they reveal to us that such an objective evaluative reality has the power of directly motivating those who have access to it (or at least those who have access to it and are rational). This appears quite extraordinary. How could some objective facts, which exist independently of our attitudes, engage our will in such a direct way? This feature seems to demarcate evaluative facts from all other ordinary facts with which we are acquainted.

This argument can actually be transformed into a positive argument in favor of non-cognitivism, when it is combined with the so-called *Humean theory of motivation* (see Smith 1994 for this argument). The central idea of the Humean theory of motivation is that, conceived of as purely cognitive states, beliefs alone cannot motivate one to act. Some non-cognitive attitudes—typically, desires—must always be present in order for one to be motivated to act. However, if we accept this account, together with the idea that evaluative judgments are necessarily motivating, it immediately follows that evaluative judgments cannot express beliefs. If they did, they would not motivate a rational agent necessarily, but only contingently, that is, in combination with some external motivational state. Thus, if we want to preserve an internalist conception of evaluative judgments, it appears that we have no choice but to abandon the cognitivist understanding of evaluative judgments and, with it, value realism.

Another anti-realist argument challenges the value realist's capacity to explain how evaluative facts depend on natural facts. Speaking in terms of normative facts, Mackie presents the challenge thus: "What is the connection between the natural fact that an action is a piece of deliberate cruelty—say, causing pain just for fun—and the moral fact that it is wrong? It cannot be an entailment, a logical or semantic necessity. Yet it is not merely that the two features occur together. The wrongness must somehow be 'consequential' or 'supervenient': it is wrong because it is a piece of deliberate cruelty. But just what in the world is signified by this 'because'?" (Mackie 1977: 44). Value realists are, indeed, typically committed to the *supervenience thesis*, according to which it is impossible for two items to have the same natural properties but not the same evaluative properties. The idea is that evaluative properties are fixed by natural properties, in such a way that if two items have the same natural properties, they have also the same evaluative properties. The supervenience thesis is generally held to be a conceptual truth. Thus, one cannot possibly judge, of two qualitatively identical things, that one is, for example, admirable, while the other is not, without manifesting some sort of conceptual confusion.

According to its opponents, however, value realism has a hard time in explaining why the supervenience relation holds. The source of the problem lies in the value realists' commitment to an additional thesis, namely, the *lack of entailment thesis*. According to it, no set of natural truths entails a corresponding set of evaluative truths. In other words, evaluative statements cannot be logically derived from natural statements. The motivation for adopting the lack of entailment thesis comes primarily from Moore's rejection of naturalism or, more precisely, from the rejection of *analytic naturalism*. Moore's argument, which has become known as *the open question argument*, is that it is always possible for one to doubt whether some item possessing some natural property, say the property of promoting biological fitness, also possesses an evaluative property, say the property of being good, without manifesting any conceptual confusion. Moore takes this to be evidence that evaluative concepts cannot be reduced to natural concepts. Put differently, evaluative concepts resist analysis in terms of natural concepts. In the absence of conceptual entailment based on such an analysis, however, it is difficult to explain why the supervenience relation holds. Indeed, there should be no reason to think that a "mixed world," in which two items have the same grounding (or subvenient) properties, but not the same evaluative properties, is conceptually impossible.

By contrast, anti-realist theories seem to have less trouble in explaining the supervenience of the evaluative on the natural. In fact, some have thought that the argument from supervenience especially favors non-cognitivism. Blackburn, for one, has argued that the purpose of evaluative discourse is not to describe an evaluative reality, but "to guide desires and choices among the natural features of the world" (Blackburn 1993: 137). Now, according to Blackburn, if it were possible to judge that two items possess the same natural properties, but not the same evaluative properties, then evaluative discourse would completely lose its point; that is, it would be incapable of fulfilling its action-guiding function. Thus, supervenience holds no mystery. One can explain it simply by pointing out the role of evaluative concepts in guiding behavior.

Like some of the previous anti-realist arguments, Blackburn's argument from supervenience is an instance of a more general strategy against value realism, which has been powerfully defended by Gilbert Harman (1977). The idea is simple. According to Harman, we have reasons to believe in the existence of some property only if that property figures in one of our best explanations of some phenomena in the world. However, evaluative properties do not seem to play any role in our best explanations. Therefore, we have no reason to believe in their existence.

Harman emphasizes the difference between ethics and science. He considers the following example. When seeing a vapor cloud in a cloud chamber, a physicist immediately utters: "There goes a proton!" The physicist's underlying judgment can be partly explained by the fact that she endorses a specific physical theory, which causes her to form the immediate belief that there is a proton. However, Harman thinks that our explanation can proceed even further. More specifically, Harman believes that the fact that there *really* was a proton is part of a more complete and powerful explanation of why the physicist made that judgment. In other words, according to Harman, the truth of the theory is part of the best explanation of the physicist's observation in the cloud chamber.

Modifying Harman's own example so as to fit the present discussion, consider now the case of an evaluative observation. Suppose that an individual watching the antics of a wet cat exclaims: "How amusing!" We can certainly explain the individual's judgment by reference to the standards of amusement that she more or less consciously endorses, and that cause her to judge that the cat is amusing. Can we go beyond that? Can we infer that the cat really possesses the objective property of being amusing? Harman is skeptical. According to him, the existence of mind-independent evaluative properties does not play any role in the best explanation of the individual's judgment. In fact, postulating an objective property of amusement is completely irrelevant. This is so because there is a better explanation of the individual's judgment, which appeals to her psychological make-up, her social and cultural upbringing, and so on, rather than to the existence of an objective evaluative reality.

Perspectives

Given these different arguments, defending value realism might seem to be a tall order. A promising line, however, is to explore possibilities that fall outside of the standard realist package we presented in the Section "The main debates." As we explained, value realism is commonly paired with rationalism regarding evaluative knowledge. In this last section, we will consider a defense of value realism, which combines value realism and sentimentalism, and which we shall call "sentimental realism."

The central claim of sentimental realism concerns evaluative concepts. As we mentioned, concepts such as *admirable, shameful*, or *disgusting* have obviously a tight connection to emotions. Such value concepts appear essentially related to specific responses. A plausible way to spell out the *response-dependence* of such concepts is by formulating equivalences like the following:

> *x* is admirable if and only if feeling admiration is appropriate in response to *x*.

It is of course easy to formulate similar equivalences regarding the amusing, the disgusting, the shameful, and so forth. Let us make clear that according to the most plausible interpretation of such equivalences, they are not to be taken as proposing conceptual or ontological reductions.[12] The best way to interpret such equivalences is to read them as proposing conceptual elucidations. The equivalence would express the thought that the concept *admirable* is conceptually connected to the concept *admiration*, but none of the concepts should be considered to be more fundamental. On such a no-priority view, the grasp of the two concepts would be interdependent. A second important issue is that, on the most plausible understanding of such equivalences, appropriateness has to be taken to be a matter of correct representation. Put differently, an appropriate emotion would be one that is correct from the epistemic point of view, in the sense that it represents things as they are, evaluatively speaking.[13] According to such an account, something is admirable if and only if it is such that feeling admiration is correct in response to it, and this is so only if it is admirable.[14]

Now, what has to be underlined is that this account of evaluative concepts is entirely compatible with value realism. It is perfectly possible to claim that evaluative concepts are response-dependent in the sense that the envisaged equivalences are true of such concepts, while also maintaining that there are objective evaluative properties, which we try to pick out when making evaluative judgments. Indeed, while the proposed interpretation of the equivalences is compatible with anti-realism, it goes best with a realist account of values, according to which our evaluative judgments can correctly represent evaluative facts.

In addition to these claims regarding evaluative concepts and properties, sentimental realism subscribes to a specific epistemology of values. Indeed, the main virtue of the proposed account is that it is grounded on what is arguably a plausible account of emotions, the so-called *perceptual theory of emotions*, according to which emotions are perceptual experiences of a particular kind.[15] What is specific about emotions, on this account, is that they represent things as having evaluative properties. Thus, an emotion of admiration with respect to a friend will be correct just in case the friend is really admirable. An important

[12] In this, sentimental realism differs from the so-called fitting attitude analysis. See Deonna and Teroni (2015).

[13] See Tappolet (2011).

[14] One might worry that such an account would not be illuminating enough to be of interest. It appears that what is proposed is simply that something is admirable just in case it is admirable. However, there is reason to think that in spite of its circularity, the resulting equivalence is of interest. As will become apparent, what it underlines is the crucial epistemic role that emotions play in our grasp of affective concepts. As David Wiggins (1987) suggested, the important point to keep in mind is that there is nothing more fundamental to appeal to than admiration when we try to find out whether or not something is admirable, and the same can be said about other evaluative concepts of the same kind.

[15] See: de Sousa 1987, 2002; Deonna 2006; Döring 2007; Goldie 2009; Johnston 2001; Meinong 1917; Prinz 2004, 2006; Tappolet 1995, 2000, 2012; Tye 2008. For critical discussions, see: Brady 2013; Deonna and Teroni 2012.

point here is that on this account, emotions have representational, albeit not conceptually articulated, content.[16] Emotions represent their object as having specific evaluative properties, that is, as being fearsome or disgusting, and so on, even though the agent who undergoes the emotion need not possess the relevant evaluative concepts (the concepts *fearsome, disgusting*, etc.).

With these claims in hand, it is easy to see how one can defend sentimental realism against some of the objections to realism that we mentioned. There is no need to elaborate on the point that if emotions are perceptual experiences of values, then we have a ready answer to the epistemological worries raised by Mackie. Moreover, given that emotions normally come with related motivations, sentimentalist realism is also in a position to handle the challenges related to internalism. Even though making an evaluative judgment does not necessarily involve a motivation to act, it will normally be accompanied by such a motivation, given that such judgments are grounded in the corresponding emotional reactions. If so, it is not necessary to postulate objective entities possessing magical motivational properties, in order to account for the motivational force of evaluative judgments.

While these points make the proposed account promising, a note of caution is in order. As spelt out, this account concerns only evaluative concepts that are explicitly related to emotions. So, the question arises as to how sentimental realism can be extended to the more general concepts of good and bad, as well as to thick evaluative concepts, such as *courageous* or *generous*, which might be thought to be more independent from emotions. Moreover, while sentimental realism brings in new resources in defense of value realism, it does not have a specific answer to all of the objections discussed in the previous section. This is not to say that it has no answer, but only that, with respect to some objections, sentimental realism will share its responses with alternative value realist accounts.

Consider the objection from supervenience. The sentimental realist may choose between several available options. One possibility is to argue that evaluative properties are identical to natural properties. To give just one example, a sentimental realist may claim that the property of being admirable is identical to a complex natural property, which can be correctly represented by the reaction of admiration. If this account is adopted, the puzzle of supervenience immediately disappears. Indeed, if two items possess the same natural properties, then they will necessarily have the same evaluative properties, simply because the latter are identical to (a subset of) the former. Given the variety of the natural features on which the value property supervenes, the question is whether these natural features really constitute a genuine natural property.[17] Alternatively, the sentimental realist may deny that the supervenience relation is a conceptual truth (see Harrison 2013). For instance, one may retreat to the idea that the supervenience relation holds only by metaphysical necessity, i.e., it is true in all possible worlds, but not in virtue of the very meaning

[16] For non-conceptual contents, see *inter alia*: Evans 1982; Peacocke 1992. For critical discussion, see: Brady 2013; Deonna and Teroni 2012; Deonna and Teroni (2015); Dokic and Lemaire 2013.

[17] See Deonna and Teroni (2015).

of evaluative concepts. If this is the case, there is indeed no conceptual ban on "mixed worlds" in which two items have the same natural properties, but not the same evaluative properties, even though such worlds are metaphysically impossible. This is because metaphysical necessity is weaker than conceptual necessity, i.e., it is possible for one to conceive of things that are false in all possible worlds.

What about the issue of the explanatory role of evaluative properties? To begin with, the sentimental realist may notice that Harman's challenge can be understood in different ways. According to one reading, the reason why evaluative facts do not play any role in our best explanations is that they are causally inefficacious. In response, the sentimental realist may argue, on the one hand, that evaluative facts, such as the fact that someone is admirable, are typically cited as causes of some events, such as the response of admiration of a person in normal conditions; and, on the other hand, that the causal requirement is too strong, since it excludes too many necessary entities or properties (e.g., numbers, scientific laws, etc.) from our best explanations. According to a second reading, the gist of Harman's argument is that the positing of evaluative facts violates a methodological principle of explanatory parsimony, according to which one should avoid postulating further entities or properties unless they are explanatory useful. In response, the sentimental realist may either argue that evaluative facts are needed in order to explain at least some phenomena in the world or maintain that evaluative facts, though explanatorily redundant, are nevertheless deliberatively indispensable. The idea is that we cannot but postulate such facts when we reason about what to do (Enoch 2011). The existence of evaluative facts would thus be justified through an inference to the best justification, rather than through an inference to the best explanation (Sayre-McCord 1988).

These are only some examples of how sentimental realism can deal with the remaining anti-realist objections. By way of conclusion, what needs to be kept in mind is that, while sentimental realism is on a par with other realist accounts of value in the way it addresses the latter objections, it appears at the same time to offer a more intuitive account of evaluative concepts and a naturalistically more attractive response to the arguments from epistemology and motivation. Of course, more needs to be said in order to provide a full defense of sentimental realism. What we hope to have shown here, however, is that sentimental realism must be taken very seriously in future debates about values.[18]

References

Audi, R. (1997). *Moral Knowledge and Ethical Character*. New York: Oxford University Press.

Ayer, A. J. (1936). *Language, Truth, and Logic*. London: Gollancz, 2nd edition, 1946.

Blackburn, S. (1981). Reply: rule-following and moral realism. In S. H. Holtzman and C. M. Leich (eds), *Wittgenstein: To Follow a Rule*, pp. 163–187. London: Routledge and Kegan Paul.

Blackburn, S. (1984). *Spreading the Word*. Oxford: Oxford University Press.

Blackburn, S. (1993). *Essays in Quasi-Realism*. Oxford: Oxford University Press.

[18] We wish to thank Julien Deonna and Fabrice Teroni for their helpful comments.

Boyd, R. (1988). How to be a moral realist. In G. Sayre-McCord (ed.), *Essays in Moral Realism*, pp. 181–228. Ithaca: Cornell University Press.

Brady, M. (2013). *Emotional insight*. Oxford: Oxford University Press.

Brandt, R. (1954). The definition of an "ideal observer" in ethics. *Philosophy and Phenomenological Research*, **15**, 407–413.

Brink, D. (1989). *Moral Realism and the Foundations of Ethics*. Cambridge MA: Cambridge University Press.

Dancy, J. (2000). Editor's introduction. In J. Dancy (ed.), *Normativity*. Oxford: Blackwell.

Daniels, N. (1979). Wide reflective equilibrium and theory acceptance in ethics. *Journal of Philosophy*, **76** (5), 256–282.

Danielsson, S. and Olson, J. (2007). Brentano and the buck-passers. *Mind*, **116**, 511–522.

Deonna, J. (2006). Emotion, perception and perspective. *Dialectica*, **60** (1), 29–46.

Deonna, J. and Teroni, F. (2012). *The Emotions: A Philosophical Introduction*. New York: Routledge.

de Sousa, R. (1987). *The Rationality of Emotion*. Cambridge MA: MIT Press.

de Sousa, R. (2002). Emotional truth. *Proceedings of the Aristotelian Society*, Suppl. Vol. **76**, 247–263.

Dokic, J. and Lemaire, S. (2013). Are emotions perceptions of value? *Canadian Journal of Philosophy*, 43 (2), 227–247.

Döring, S. (2007). Seeing what to do: affective perception and rational motivation. *Dialectica*, **61** (3), 361–394.

Enoch, D. (2011). *Taking Morality Seriously. A Defense of Robust Realism*. Oxford: Oxford University.

Evans, G. (1982). *The Varieties of References*. Oxford: Clarendon.

Firth, R. (1952). Ethical absolutism and the ideal observer. *Philosophy and Phenomenological Research*, **12**, 317–345.

Geach, P.T. (1960). Ascriptivism. *Philosophical Review*, **69** (2), 221–225.

Geach, P. (1965). Assertion. *Philosophical Review*, **74**, 449–465.

Gibbard, A. (1990). *Wise Choices, Apt Feelings*. Cambridge MA: Harvard University Press.

Goldie, P. (2009). *The Emotions. A Philosophical Exploration*. Oxford: Clarendon.

Hare, R. (1952). *The Language of Morals*. Oxford: Clarendon.

Harman, G. (1977). *The Nature of Morality*. Oxford: Oxford University Press.

Harrison, G. (2013). The moral supervenience thesis is not a conceptual truth. *Analysis*, **73** (1), 62–68.

Hobbes, T. (1651). *Leviathan*. R. Tuck (ed.). Cambridge: Cambridge University Press, 1996.

Hume, D. (1739–41). *A Treatise of Human Nature*. D. F. Norton and M. J. Norton (eds). Oxford: Oxford University Press, 2000.

Johnston, M. (2001). The authority of affect. *Philosophy and Phenomenological Research*, **53**, 181–214.

Joyce, R. (2001). *The Myth of Morality*. Cambridge: Cambridge University Press.

Kant, I. (1785). *Groundwork for the Metaphysics of Morals*. M. Gregor and J. Timmermann (eds and trans.). Cambridge: Cambridge University Press, 2012.

Kant, I. (1788). *Critique of Practical Reason*. M. Gregor (ed. and trans.). Cambridge: Cambrige University Press, 1997.

Korsgaard, C. (1996). *The Sources of Normativity*. Cambridge: Cambridge University Press.

Mackie, J. L. (1977). *Ethics. Inventing Right and Wrong*. London: Penguin.

Meinong, A. (1917). *On Emotional Presentation*. Trans. with intro by Marie-Luise Schubert Kalsi. Evanston Ill.: Northwestern University Press.

Moore, G. (1903). *Principia Ethic*a. Cambridge: Cambridge University Press, revised edition 1993.

Mulligan, K. (1998). From appropriate emotions to values. *The Monist*, **81** (1), 161–188.

Nichols, S. (2004). *Sentimental Rules: On the Natural Foundations of Moral Judgment*. New York: Oxford University Press.

Oddie, G. (2009). *Value, Reality, and Desire*. New York: Oxford University Press.

Olson, J. (2014). *Moral Error Theory: History, Critique, Defence*. Oxford: Oxford University Press.

Peacocke, C. (1992). *A Study of Concepts*. Cambridge MA: MIT.

Prinz, J. (2004). *Gut Reactions: A Perceptual Theory of Emotion*. New York: Oxford University Press.

Prinz, J. (2006). Is emotion a form of perception? In L. Faucher and C. Tappolet (eds), *The Modularity of Emotions, The Canadian Journal of Philosophy*, supp. Vol. **32**, 137–160.

Prinz. J. (2007). *The Emotional Construction of Morals*. New York: Oxford University Press.

Railton, P. (1986). Moral Realism, *Philosophical Review*, **95**, 163–207.

Railton, P. (1996). Moral realism: prospect and problems. In W. Sinnott-Armstrong and M. Timmons (eds), *Moral Knowledge?* New York: Oxford University Press.

Rawls J. (1971). *A Theory of Justice*. Cambridge MA: Harvard University Press, 2nd edition 1999.

Rawls, J. (1980). Kantian constructivism in moral theory. *Journal of Philosophy*, **77**, 515–572.

Sayre-McCord, G. (1988). Moral theory and explanatory power. In P.A. French, T.E. Uehling, and H. Wettstein, H. (eds), *Midwest Studies in Philosophy*, pp. 433–456. Minneapolis: Minneapolis University Press.

Schroeder, M. (2007). *Being For: Evaluating the Semantic Program of Expressivism*. New York: Oxford University Press.

Shafer-Landau, R. (2003). *Moral Realism: A Defence*. Oxford: Oxford University Press.

Smith, M. (1994). *The Moral Problem*. Oxford: Blackwell.

Stevenson, C.L. (1937). The emotive meaning of ethical terms. *Mind*, **46**, 14–31.

Street, S. (2006). A Darwinian dilemma for realist theories of value. *Philosophical Studies*,**127**, 109–166.

Street, S. (2010). What is constructivism in ethics and metaethics. *Philosophy Compass*, **4**, 363–384.

Sturgeon, N. (1984). Moral explanation. In D. Copp and D. Zimmerman (eds), *Morality, Reason, and Truth*. Totowa N.J.: Rowman and Allenheld.

Sturgeon, N. (2006). Ethical naturalism. In D. Copp (ed.), *The Oxford Handbook of Ethical Theory*, pp. 91–121. Oxford: Oxford University Press.

Tappolet, C. (1995). Les émotions et les concepts axiologiques. In P. Paperman and R. Ogien (eds), *La Couleur des Pensées*, thematical volume, *Raison Pratique*, 4, 237–257.

Tappolet, C. (1997). Mixed inferences: a problem for pluralism about truth predicates. *Analysis*, **57** (3), 209–210.

Tappolet, C. (2000). *Emotions et Valeurs*. Paris: Presses Universitaires de France.

Tappolet, C. (2011). Values and emotions: the prospects of neo-sentimentalism. In C. Bagnoli (ed.), *Morality and the Emotions*. Oxford: Oxford University Press.

Tappolet C. (2012). Emotions, perceptions, and emotional illusions. In C. Calabi (ed.), *Perceptual Illusions: Philosophical and Psychological Essays*. Houndsmill: Palgrave-Macmillan.

Tye, M. (2008). The experience of emotion: an intentionalist theory. *Revue Internationale de Philosophie*, **243**, 25–50.

Westermarck, E. (1906). *The Origin and Development of Moral Ideas*, Vol. 1. London: MacMillan and Co.

Wiggins, D. (1987). A sensible subjectivism. In *Needs, Values, Truth: Essays in the Philosophy of Value*. Oxford: Basil Blackwell Press.

Williams, B. (1985). *Ethics and the Limits of Philosophy*. London: Fontana.

Chapter 2

Value taxonomy

Wlodek Rabinowicz and Toni Rønnow-Rasmussen

Value taxonomy: introduction

Classical taxonomies, such as Linnaeus's classification of plants or Mendeleev's periodic table of elements, help us to structure reality into fundamental types—be they types of plants or atoms. But a value taxonomy is not necessarily about entities understood in a realistic sense. Value taxonomies need not take a stand on the realism/irrealism issue. In many contexts, what is of interest is not so much what is the case but what is believed to be the case. In empirical studies, such as, for example, the European Values' Study and the World Values' Survey, the focus tends to be on what people implicitly or explicitly believe to be valuable, or on what they like or prefer. Studies of this kind endeavor to supply social scientists and policy makers with data about people's preferences and views about what they believe to be significant (in their lives or more generally). While such studies are of great interest, we shall, in what follows, focus on other matters: Our target is conceptual analysis.

Circumventing metaphysical issues and setting empirical studies aside does not lead to arbitrariness about value taxonomy. In what follows we outline the core conceptual distinctions that underlie much of modern philosophical thinking about value. After some introductory remarks, we address in the next section ("Good and good-for") the relation between value and value-for—an issue that is attracting increasing attention in contemporary philosophical value theory. This issue concerns the distinction between what is good (impersonally good, or good, period) and what is good for someone, or—more generally—good for some entity. The divide between these two value notions shapes much of modern ethics.

The notion of good, period, has over the years been subjected to many analyses, above all when it is understood to be a gloss on what is *good in itself* or *good for its own sake* (in contrast to what is good for the sake of something else). The section "Final and non-final values" focuses on some novel analyses of these concepts, which have attracted considerable attention. In this section we also briefly consider such notions as unconditional and non-derivative value. Finally, in the section "Value relations", we will have a look at comparative values, or—to put it differently—at value relations (such as being better/worse/equally good/on a par). Recent discussions suggest that we might have to considerably extend traditional taxonomies of value relations.

First, however, some introductory remarks are in order. Our focus is on conceptual distinctions between value types, such as, for example, the distinction between final and instrumental values or a distinction between value for a person and value period. But a value taxonomy might also be substantive. That is, it might distinguish between different types of things that are thought to possess value (for their own sake); for example, between pleasure, freedom, equality, and so on. There is a need for the latter kind of classification if one's substantive theory of value is of a pluralistic kind. Since Parfit (1984: 493–502), it is customary to distinguish between three main kinds of substantive views about value. The first two are monistic: Hedonism identifies what's good (or good-for) with a positive balance of pleasure over pain,[1] while desire theories identify value with the satisfaction of desires.[2] The third kind of substantive theory is explicitly pluralistic: It is the so-called objective list view, which ascribes value to a variety of different types of things (e.g., to friendship, love, freedom, etc.) Such a list may, but need not, include pleasure or desire-satisfaction.[3]

This is not the place to survey the substantive accounts. However, they all aim at the systematization and justification of value judgments—both general judgments of this kind and specific ones. For example, judgments like the following ones:

(1) Pleasure is good and pain is bad.

(2) Drugs are not good for you.

(3) This painting by Titian is beautiful.

(4) Rescuing the girl was a courageous thing to do.

(5) Mozart was a better composer than Salieri.

(6) John is a good philosopher.

---

1 However, even a hedonist might see the need for a substantive value taxonomy if he takes the view that different pleasures may carry essentially different values. In his *Utilitarianism*, J. S. Mill (1998 [1861]) famously distinguished between higher pleasures (coming from such noble pursuits as poetry or philosophical contemplation) and lower pleasures (of sensual nature). Not surprisingly, he suggested that the former are radically superior to the latter.

2 Desire theories admit of two fundamentally different versions (see Rabinowicz and Österberg 1996). On the "satisfaction" version, what is of value is the satisfaction of our desires. On the "object" version, the value accrues to what is being desired. The objects we desire can be heterogeneous in nature, which allows for a pluralistic substantive theory of value. It is only the satisfaction version that can naturally be seen as a monistic value theory. Note that the object version can easily be generalized: On that view value might be ascribed not only to the objects of desire, but also to the objects of other kinds of pro-attitudes. This opens for value pluralism on the ontological, and not merely substantive, level: While it is arguable that the objects of desire must be states of affairs, this restriction to states of affairs as the only bearers of value disappears if one ascribes value to the objects of other pro-attitudes as well.

3 Sometimes the items on the "objective list" are themselves called values, but we prefer a different terminology, according to which these items *possess* value, or *are* valuable. The former use would make anti-realism about value an utterly implausible position. Surely, it is uncontroversial that there are such things as friendship, love, or pleasure. What is questioned by the anti-realist is whether there exists any value property that these things, or anything else for that matter, can possess.

(1) Mentions a positive and a negative general value; (2) refers to a relational value, "good-for"; (3) is about an aesthetic value; (4) mentions a specific value property; (5) states a value relation; and (6) is an example of an "attributive" use of value predicates, as opposed to their "predicative" usage in such statements as (1), for example. In the attributive usage, "good" is a category modifier ("a good philosopher," "a good knife," etc.), while in the predicative usage, it stands on its own. Sometimes it is unclear from the surface grammar how a given term is being used. Compare "*x* is a gray building" with (6). Unlike the former sentence, (6) cannot be read conjunctively: That *x* is a gray building means that *x* is gray and that it is a building. Thus, "gray" is used predicatively in this context. But that John is a good philosopher does not entail that John is good. "Good" here modifies "a philosopher," instead of standing on its own.

That statements like (1)–(6) make evaluative claims is a view deeply rooted in a loose set of ideas about how such judgments differ from (purely) descriptive claims such as, for example, "pleasure is a mental state"; "some people are addicted to drugs"; "this painting weighs five kilograms." But value claims should also be distinguished from the so-called deontic statements, such as "You ought to keep your promises" or "We must come to her rescue." While both the deontic and the evaluative statements are contrasted with the descriptive ones, there is "prescriptivity" and an action-guidingness in the area of the deontic[4] that is at least not explicitly present in the area of the evaluative. Whether the prescriptive aspect is implicit in the latter is a matter of controversy. According to the so-called fitting-attitude analysis of value (FA-analysis), which has recently been much discussed and which is going to play an important role in this chapter as a test for distinctions and theories we are going to consider, an object is valuable if and only if it is fitting (appropriate, warranted, required, etc.) to favor it. Here, "favor" is a place-holder for a pro-attitude toward the object. Depending on the nature of the fitting pro-attitude (desire, preference, admiration, respect, care, etc.) we get different kinds of value (desirability, preferability, admirability, and so on). Apart from the suggested conceptual linkage between value and attitudes, what is distinctive for this approach is that it treats deontic concepts as prior to value notions: Value is explicated in terms of the stance that *ought* to be taken toward the object. That it is fitting to have a pro-attitude, that the attitude in question is appropriate, required or called for, are different ways of expressing the deontic (i.e., explicitly normative) component in FA-analysis.[5] On some versions, the FA-approach is meant to be a meaning analysis of value terms; on other versions it is rather a so-called "real" definition: an account of what value or goodness consists in.

---

4 To be sure, not only prescriptions, but also permissions belong to the deontic area. However, one might argue that they do so simply because they are denials of prescriptions.

5 On a version of FA-analysis that is due to Scanlon (1998), for an object to be good or valuable is for it to have properties that provide reasons to respond to it in various positive ways. On this account, it is the notion of a reason that is the normative component in the analysis. Since the role of the reason-provider is here transferred from the value of the object to other properties (the ones that make the object valuable), this version of the analysis has been called "the buck-passing account of value."

The history of FA-analysis can be traced back at least to Henry Sidgwick (in the 3rd edition of his *Methods of Ethics* from 1884) and Franz Brentano (1969 [1889]).[6] An important advantage of FA-analysis is that it to some extent *demystifies* values (see Rabinowicz and Rønnow-Rasmussen 2004). It makes their normative authority unproblematic. On the FA-account, there is no mystery in values being "intrinsically prescriptive," to use J. L. Mackie's terminology (Mackie 1977: 35). An object's value simply consists in it being such that one ought to take an appropriate stance toward it. To what extent, if at all, this undermines Mackie's famous "argument from queerness" is another matter. What makes values queer on his view is not just that they are essentially prescriptive, but that they are at the same time supposed to be objective—independent of our actual attitudes toward the objects we value. Such objective prescriptivity was for Mackie inconceivable. Whether value objectivism is an unacceptable position and whether Mackie was right in his suggestion that our ordinary value judgments commit us to objectivism about value are, however, debated issues. FA-analysis as such does not take a stand on these questions.

The list of examples of value judgments that has been given may also serve as an illustration of certain conceptual distinctions that have bearing on value taxonomies. "Good" and "bad" seem to be predicates that are quite different from, say, "beautiful" or "courageous." To judge something to be good offers much less (if any) specific information about that thing than if we had judged it to be beautiful or if we had judged someone to be courageous. "Good" and "bad" have been referred to as *thin concepts* because of their lack of descriptive content; more specific value concepts have accordingly been called *thick* (Williams 1985: 140–43). The nature of this distinction between thin and thick evaluative concepts is a much debated matter.[7] In modern times, philosophical work has been mainly done on the former concepts, not least because of their greater generality, which gives them a much broader application. In what follows, therefore, the focus will be on the thin value notions rather than on the thick ones. Our taxonomical suggestions are meant to primarily apply to the former, but some of them might also apply to the latter.

Thus, in particular, although values sometimes are ordered into domains such as moral, aesthetic, prudential, political, economic—to mention some of the most common ones—in

6 For the history of this approach see: Dancy 2000; Rabinowicz and Rønnow-Rasmussen 2004; Rabinowicz 2013.

7 See: Kirchin 2013. Mulligan (2010) contains the following list of thick value categories: "There are the *aesthetic* properties of being beautiful, elegant, or sublime. There are the *cognitive* value-properties of which clarity, distinctness, illusion, error, knowledge, truth and falsity are the bearers and the property of being foolish. There are the *ethical* properties of being evil and good, and the properties corresponding to different ethical virtues and vices, for example, the property of being a coward. There are the properties of being right, just and unjust. There are the *religious* properties of being holy or sacred and profane. There are the *vital* value-properties of which health, life, and illness are the bearers. And the *sensory* value-properties of being pleasant and unpleasant." Whether all the items on Mulligan's list are thick value-properties can, of course, be discussed. Some of them might instead be classified as value-making features (truth, pleasantness), while some others seem to be thin rather than thick (rightness).

this chapter we shall focus on the conceptual distinctions that can be made independently of which of the areas of value one is interested in.

In an influential paper, Geach (1956) argued that predicative uses of "good" do not make sense, unlike its attributive uses. The apparent predicative uses, of the form "*a* is good," are on this view incomplete expressions that need to be filled out with a specification of the appropriate object category to which *a* is supposed to belong and within which it is taken to be an exemplary specimen. Thus, "John is good" is short for "John is a good man [or 'a good person'?]," "The Tour Eiffel is majestic" is short for "The Tour Eiffel is a majestic building [or 'a majestic tower'?]," and so on.[8] This all-encompassing attributivism about "good" is a controversial position. Many value theorists accept it, but at least as many reject it. It might also turn out that an acceptable form of attributivism will have to be so diluted that it will no longer clearly differ from predicativism. If one takes statements such as, say, "that *p* is the case is good/bad," which ascribe goodness or badness to states of affairs, as being elliptic for attributive statements of the form "that *p* is the case is a good/bad state of affairs," then predicativists might have no problems with accepting such attributive re-descriptions.[9]

We have discussed two distinctions in value theory: the one between thick and thin values and the other between the attributive and the predicative usages of value terms. In the next section we shall consider another important distinction: the one between impersonal and personal values.

Good and good-for

In his seminal *Methods of Ethics* (1874/1907), Henry Sidgwick argued at length that as rational agents we face a choice: we can do what (we believe) is good for us or we can do what (we believe) is good per se, i.e., what is impersonally good or as we shall also say, good, period. This choice becomes an acute problem when maximizing the good does not maximize the good for the agent. The insight that practical rationality must choose between securing what is impersonally good (acting morally) or making sure you get what is good for you (acting in your own interest) was something Sidgwick believed distinguished modern ethics from the ethics of ancient Greeks (cf. Crisp 2004: 106). By understanding what is good in terms of what is good for the agent, Greek philosophy failed in his view to properly appreciate the nature of this problem, and so it did not grasp the "dualism of practical reason": the existence of two independent ultimate objectives that we have reasons to

8 Other philosophers sympathetic to this idea have in important ways nuanced the Geachian view. See, for example, Thomson (1992) who argues that if something is good it is always good "in a way" (but not necessarily, as Geach thought, good of its kind, which is a special form of being good in a way).

9 Cf. Schroeder (2012). Geach would have claimed that categories such as "state of affairs," "event," "thing," etc., are too general to play the role of category-fillers in value statements: They do not provide standards that allow us to identify their exemplary representatives. Cf. Geach (1956). See also Thomson (2008) who explicitly rules out states of affairs from what she refers to as "goodness fixing kinds."

strive for. Whether Sidgwick was right in his claims about ancient Greek philosophy is a debated matter (for a criticism, see, for example, Brewer 2009: 200). That modern ethics turns around this divide is clear.[10,11]

One early objection against the notion of good period was based on the idea that this notion presupposes a highly questionable objectivist view that goodness can accrue to objects independently of the attitudes of the subjects.[12] On value objectivism, we must postulate that the world contains some very "queer" facts, to use Mackie's terminology: facts that possess a normative force, without there being any subjects from whom this force originates. To be sure, this would not be especially surprising if the normative force of value facts would be reducible to some features of the world that can be characterized in purely descriptive terms, but such naturalism about normativity is a highly contested position. On the other hand, a value objectivist might be tempted by a converse objection that we should give up on "good for" since *that* notion presupposes the subjectivist conception of value that he rejects. On the subjectivist view value somehow gets constituted or created by attitudes of the subjects, but it is not at all easy to clarify the nature of this constitutive process.

Such a polarization of the two concepts of goodness appears misconceived, however. It is by no means obvious that impersonal goodness is an essentially objectivist notion, while personal goodness is a subjectivist one. In recent years, there have emerged suggestions about how to understand the value subjectivism/objectivism distinction in a way that implies that both notions, good period and good-for, are available to subjectivist and to objectivist approaches alike (Rabinowicz and Österberg 1996; Rønnow-Rasmussen 2011). The subjectivist idea that value is dependent on the attitudes of a subject is not

---

10 See Crisp (2004: 112), who points out that Sidgwick's own analyses of good-for and good, period, were versions of the FA-analysis. Thus, according to Sidgwick, the "ultimate good on the whole for me" is "what I should practically desire if my desires were in harmony with reason, assuming my own existence alone to be considered" (Sidgwick 1874/1907: 112). We get the analysis of good, period, if we remove the last clause in this definition.

11 Often, when we try to clarify what we have in mind when we speak about what is good for someone, we say that it is a component of a person's well-being, or that it is something that benefits the person, or makes his or her life go better. One might agree with such paraphrases but still wonder how "well-being," "better life," or "benefit" should be understood. As Richard Kraut has pointed out, saying that what is *good for* someone consists in it "being beneficial, advantageous, and so on" is not really helpful; the latter expressions "are not conceptually prior to and explanatory of the relation of being good for someone" (Kraut 2011: 69).Sometimes "good for" refers not to an element in a person's well-being but to what promotes the latter. In this usage, "good for" refers to an instrumental value, i.e., value as a means for something else (Bradley 2013; Rønnow-Rasmussen 2002). We shall return to the distinction between instrumental and final (non-instrumental) value in the next section, but here it is important to keep in mind that the ongoing debate about good vs. good-for primarily concerns the issue whether there are one or two kinds of non-instrumental goodness (Cf. Kraut 2011; Rønnow-Rasmussen 2011, 2013, Rosati 2008, 2009, Zimmerman 2009).

12 See Hobbes, who in some places gives voice to this sort of objection: "one cannot speak of something as being simply good; since whatsoever is good, is good for someone or other" (*De Homine*. XI, 4, 47).

to be understood as an account of goodness-for but rather as a claim that all goodness is *goodness-relative-to* a subject. But that notion should not be confused with the notion of good-for. Thus, to illustrate, some of the things that are supposed to be good-relative-to *x*, i.e., things that are objects of *x*'s pro-attitudes, need not be good *for x*—they need not be conducive to *x*'s well-being in any way. This applies, for example, to various noble causes that *x* might devote her energy to. (For a discussion and criticism of the notion of relative goodness, see: Schroeder 2007. Cf. also Smith 2003.)

G. E. Moore's response in his major work *Principia Ethica* (1903) to the dualism problem highlighted by Sidgwick was different, but equally radical. Moore's Gordian cut consisted in the argument that the very notion of someone's good was nonsensical if it referred to a sort of private goodness, a positive value property that somehow was the subject's possession (which he believed egoism assumed):

> What then is meant by "my own good"? In what sense can a thing be *good for me*? It is obvious, if we reflect, that the only thing which can belong to me, which can be mine, is something which is good, and not the fact that it is good (Moore 1903: 150).

Moore's discussion paved the way for a position in contemporary value theory that reduces good-for to what is good period. Let us refer to such a reductive view as moorean monism. Moore's own, positive suggestion was that "When . . . I talk of anything I get as my own good, I must mean either that the thing I get is good, or that my possessing it is good. In both cases it is only the thing or the possession of it which is *mine*, and not *the goodness* of that thing or that possession" (Moore 1903: 150). Moorean monists often suggest that claims about what is good for someone are claims to the effect that some fact involving the person whose good we are considering, is good period. Of course, not all versions of moorean monism are inspired by Moore. Consider the so-called perfectionist views that understand what is good for a person in terms of what contributes to the excellence of that person or to the flourishing of the person's life. Such views do not directly take a stand on the "good period/good for" issue. However, they can be seen as forms of moorean monism: A dyadic predicate—"good for"—is analyzed in terms of a monadic one: "excellence" or "flourishing" (both of which may be regarded as species of goodness period).[13]

In recent years, there have been various attempts to formulate or further develop versions of moorean monism (e.g., Campbell 2013; Fletcher 2012; Regan 2004; Hurka 1987).[14]

---

[13] There is another and perhaps historically more adequate way of looking at perfectionist proposals, though. If the gist of such proposals is that what is good for an agent is what contributes to his having a *good life* or to him being an excellent person, then this kind of analysis seems to reduce good-for to an attributive usage of "good," in which that predicate does not stand on its own.

[14] Cf., for instance, the so-called locative analysis of good in Fletcher (2012): "G is non-instrumentally good for X if and only if (i) G is non-instrumentally good, (ii) G has properties that generate, or would generate, agent-relative reasons for X to hold pro-attitudes toward G for its own sake, (iii) G is essentially related to X" (p. 3). This is a straightforward example of how what is non-instrumentally good for someone is reduced to what is non-instrumentally good. Campbell (2013: 1) proposes a revisionist analysis of what is good for you in terms of what is "contributing to the appeal or desirability of being in

However, this view is challenged by an influential alternative line of thought according to which moorean monists get it fundamentally wrong: it is good-for, rather than good period, that is conceptually prior. In other words, it is good period that should be analyzed in terms of good-for—either as good for some (group of) subject(s) (Thomson 1992) or perhaps as good for "man" in general (see Campbell 1935)—and not the other way round. The idea of, say, beauty or knowledge being good quite independent of whether they are good for anyone, as, for instance, Moore thought, is rejected by the proponents of this view. This position seems especially appealing to value subjectivists who conflate goodness for with relative goodness, i.e., with goodness relative to a subject's attitudes, and who view with suspicion the notion of good period unless that notion can also somehow be reduced to subject-relative goodness.

Being a moorean monist or a good-for monist are obviously the radical options. The dualist view, according to which there is room for both good period and good-for as mutually irreducible notions, has many defenders (see, for example, Darwall 2002; Rønnow-Rasmussen 2011).

In light of the discussion between monists and dualists, the value taxonomist faces a challenge that presently is unresolved: should there be one or two value taxonomies? That is, must our value taxonomy branch out into two distinct directions—one concerning good period and another concerning good-for?

Final and non-final values

Let us now turn to another demarcation line within value theory, namely the distinction between what is intrinsically good, i.e., good in itself, and what is finally good, i.e., good for its own sake. In what follows, we focus on how this distinction is drawn within the area of good period, rather than in the area of good-for. However, the pattern of analysis we are going to employ to deal with the distinction can also be applied, *mutatis mutandis*, in the latter area.

In the *Republic*, Plato distinguished between three kinds of goods: (1) goods that we desire for their own sake, (2) goods that we desire both for their own sake and for the sake of their consequences, and finally (3) goods that we desire only for their consequences.[15] To put it somewhat anachronistically, then, Plato's taxonomy turns on the notions of "good for its own sake" and "good for the sake of something else." It should be noted, however, that for Plato things are good for their own sake in virtue of the direct benefits they bring to their possessor (Plato 1992: 367 b–e). His examples of such things include sight, hearing,

---

your position." Hurka thinks that "'good for' is fundamentally confused, and should be banished from moral philosophy. The problem is not that the expression can be given no clear sense. It can, indeed, be given too many senses, none of which is best expressed by 'good for'" (Hurka 1998: 72). The senses listed by Hurka are either purely descriptive or rely on the impersonal concept of "good."

15 Plato (1992: 357b–c).

intelligence, and health, along with justice and enjoyment. His distinction thus concerns things that are *good-for* a person.[16]

Much of the recent debate revolves around an approach to final value that goes back to G. E. Moore. For Moore (1922: 260), the ultimate value was "intrinsic" and he took an object to be intrinsically valuable insofar as its value was grounded in its "intrinsic nature." The properties that together form the intrinsic nature of an object are internal to the object in question. In addition, they are necessary to that object (Moore 1922: 260ff.). Moore was probably led to this requirement of necessity by his belief that things that are good in themselves are good independently of circumstances. Since circumstances can affect contingent properties of an object, the object's intrinsic value can only depend on those of its properties that aren't contingent. In post-Moorean discussions, however, this necessity requirement was often relinquished. On this later view, it is possible for the intrinsic value of an object to be grounded in some of its contingent properties, as long as these properties are internal to the object in question. Thus, for example, an intrinsically valuable life might derive its value from some of its experiential components, which it might not have contained if the circumstances had been different. (We will have reason to return to the necessity requirement in what follows, when we consider Kant's idea of unconditional value.)

Moore assumed that nothing can be good for its own sake unless it is intrinsically good, good "in itself." But he questioned the converse: Thus, in *Ethics* (1965 [1912]: 30–32), he suggested that an object is good for its own sake only if all of its parts are intrinsically good. If only some part of the object is intrinsically good, then this can often make the object as a whole intrinsically good, but then this object is good for the sake of its part and not for its own sake. This Moorean restriction on the use of "good for its own sake" has, however, not been followed in the later debates.

Several philosophers (e.g., Beardsley 1965; Kagan 1998; Korsgaard 1983; O'Neill 1992; Rabinowicz and Rønnow-Rasmussen 2000) have argued for the possibility that Moore excluded: What is finally valuable need not always be intrinsically valuable in the Moorean sense. Something can be valuable for its own sake in virtue of an external property it possesses—in virtue of its relation to some external object or objects. Thus, for example, a pen that was used by Abraham Lincoln might be valued for its own sake precisely because of its connection to a famous person (Kagan 1998). Or, an object might be valuable for its own sake partly in virtue of its rarity or uniqueness (Beardsley 1965). This means that final value might in some cases be extrinsic rather than intrinsic.

Korsgaard's distinction between final intrinsic and final extrinsic goodness turns on whether the "source of goodness" is located in or outside the valuable object. The term

---

[16] It is arguable that Plato considered these things to be good period, though at the same time localized to a given person (see Brewer 2009: 200). Thus, they are good-for in a Moorean sense, so to speak. It should also be noted that Plato's distinction differs from the modern one: For him, we desire something for its own sake if it directly benefits us, whether it is a constituent of our final good (as is the case with virtue) or one of its direct partial causes (sight, intelligence). In the latter case, a modern philosopher would say that we are talking about goodness as a (direct) means rather than goodness for its own sake.

"source," however, is ambiguous: it might refer to the value-making features of the object (the "supervenience base" of value) or to the subject (or some other "source") that constructs value—that bestows or projects the value onto the object. It has been questioned whether drawing the distinction in terms of the source of value is felicitous (Dancy 2004; Hussein and Shah 2006; Rabinowicz and Rønnow-Rasmussen 2000; Tannenbaum 2010. Cf. Langton 2007). In particular, the second interpretation of the notion of the source appears to be irrelevant to the issue at hand. One doesn't need to be a subjectivist or a constructivist about value in order to recognize the existence of final extrinsic values.

The words "final" and "sake" call for caution. They can be understood in different ways. In this chapter, the expressions "valuable for its own sake" and "final value" are used to make clear that the value we are talking about is not one that accrues to some *x* in virtue of *x* being conducive to, or necessary for, something else that is of value. Thus, final value should be contrasted with value as a means or value as an essential part of some valuable thing or as its necessary precondition (see next paragraph). On this interpretation, values are "final" in the sense of being "ultimate": their status as values does not require that some other things are valuable. This has an advantage over a narrower interpretation according to which final value is equated with value as an end, i.e., as an ultimate objective (some state of affairs) that we should strive to realize. The former interpretation gives the notion of final value a broader reach: It allows (but, of course, does not necessitate) ascriptions of such value to a broad range of different kinds of things (pens, stamps, persons, etc.), and not only to objects that can be ends or objectives (i.e., not only to states of affairs and the like). A concrete object such as, say, a painting, should not be confused with a state of affairs involving that object; for example, the state that this painting is located in the Louvre. And it seems that the value of concrete objects is not easily reducible to the value of states of affairs. Thus, a painting might possess a final value that is not reducible to the value of some state of affairs such as that this painting exists or continues to exist.

Objects that are finally valuable, i.e., valuable for their own sake, are standardly contrasted with instrumentally valuable things, i.e., objects that are valuable as means to something else that is valuable. Instrumentally valuable items are examples of things that are valuable *for the sake of something else* and not necessarily for their own sake. Note, however, that value for the sake of something else (i.e., non-final value) is a broad category. In particular, it also comprises so-called contributive values. An object is contributively valuable if it has value as a part—if it is a constituent of something that by the presence of this constituent is made more valuable than it would otherwise had been.

The notions of instrumental value or contributive value are to some extent problematic. For instance, it is not clear that a means to something valuable is a genuine value in the first place (cf. Lewis 1946: 384–385; Moore 1903: 24; Rønnow-Rasmussen 2002).[17] However,

[17] As far as we understand, Moore denied this. For him, being instrumentally good was simply being a means to something good and not being good in virtue of being such a means. He took an analogous view of contributive value: "To have value merely as a part is equivalent to having no value at all, but merely being a part of that which has it" (Moore 1903: 35).

FA-analysis, on which to be valuable is to be a fitting object of a pro-attitude, allows to explain in what sense instrumental values are genuine values. On that analysis, *x* possesses an instrumental value to the extent it is fitting to favor *x* on account of its instrumental role. The analysis admits of two interpretations of instrumental value—a stronger and a weaker one. On the weaker version, instrumental value accrues to *x* if, and only if, it is fitting to favor *x* on account of it being a means to some y. (Contrast this with the FA-definition of final value: such value accrues to an object if, and only if, it is fitting to favor it for its own sake.) On the stronger version, it is additionally required that *y* itself must be valuable, i.e., that it must be fitting to favor *y*. As is easily seen, it is only on the stronger version that an instrumental value must always be a means to value.

Note that, given these definitions, the existence of instrumental value (on either interpretation) does not automatically imply the existence of final values. But a value theory that allows for the former without postulating the latter would be very strange indeed.

Some further important value notions should next be considered. Sometimes certain values are described as being unconditional. A value is conditional if it accrues to an object only if a certain condition is satisfied. An unconditional value is a value something has under all possible conditions. Thus, Kant in the *Groundwork of a Metaphysics of Morals* famously argued that good will is the only unconditional value. There is an extensive amount of scholarly work on Kant's ideas about good will and his related claim that persons are "ends in themselves." It has been pointed out (Bradley 2006) that while Mooreans stress that value is something that should be promoted, it is for Kantians something that requires respect. Arguably, this contrast—which goes back to Pettit (1989)—is somewhat oversimplified. Although respect is supposed to be the core response toward good will, even for Kant promoting good will was an important goal, as may be seen from the role he gave to moral education. The idea that different kinds of value call for different kinds of appropriate responses is well in line with FA-analysis of value. This suggests that there might be a way to combine Moorean and Kantian values within the confines of the same value theory.

The notion of unconditional value appears to be easily interpretable in terms of final value. It seems to be a certain kind of final value, namely final value that accrues to an object in virtue of the latter's essential features, i.e., in virtue of features that the object in question must possess under all possible circumstances, as long as it exists. Thus, for instance, hedonism is often characterized as a view on which only pleasure carries this kind of final value. In whatever context we find pleasure, it will be valuable for its own sake in virtue of its nature. That is, it is unconditionally valuable on the hedonist view. Note that pleasure is not only finally but also intrinsically valuable. It is an open question whether there could exist an extrinsic final value that is unconditional: This would require that the extrinsic properties on which such a value is based are essential to the value bearer. Whether this is possible might well be disputed. A related but different distinction is the one between derivative and non-derivative values. Objects carrying derivative value are described as owing their value to the value of something else. Instrumental values are sometimes described in this way: "An instrumentally valuable object owes its value to the final value of whatever it is a means to" (Olson 2005: 45; as we have seen, this is not the only way of understanding instrumental values). However, even final values might be derivative. An example would be a diamond ring that possesses a final value (an intrinsic one) which exclusively derives from the value of its diamond. Also, many sentimental or personal values might be of this kind. An otherwise useless item might carry an engraving made by your beloved spouse, making it valuable to you (cf. Rønnow-Rasmussen 2011). Thus, the distinction between non-derivative and derivative is orthogonal to the distinction between final and non-final.

Value relations

This section deals with value relations.[18] It is an area of value theory that is of central importance. Value comparisons are essential to our lives: They play a crucial role in deliberation and choice. Is this alternative better than that one? Is this goal more worthy of pursuit than that goal? All such comparisons consist in determining the value relations that obtain between the items that are being compared. It is, therefore, somewhat surprising that the subject of value relations has only recently received serious attention. Consequently, there is a relatively limited literature dealing with these matters and many contributions tend to be fairly technical.

Let us say that two items are *commensurable* if one is better, worse, or equally as good as the other. In several publications, Ruth Chang has argued that two items might be *comparable* in value even though they are incommensurable in the sense already introduced (i.e., even though neither is better than, worse than, or equally as good as the other). Instead of being related in one of these standard ways, they may be on a *par*, as she puts it (see Chang 2002b; cf. also Chang 1997, 2002a, 2005).[19] Thus, consider, say, Mozart (x) and Michelangelo (y). They are comparable in their excellence as artists, but intuitively neither of them is better than the other.

What about the possibility that they are equally good? Chang dismisses this possibility using what she calls "the Small-Improvement Argument." We are asked to envisage a third artist, x^+, who is slightly better than but otherwise similar to x. x^+ is a fictional figure—a slightly improved version of Mozart—perhaps Mozart who managed to compose yet another *Requiem* and a couple of additional operas. Now, the idea is that x^+ is a better artist than x without thereby being better than y. This would have been

[18] This section draws to a large extent on Rabinowicz (2008, 2009a).

[19] The notion of parity as a fourth form of comparability, along with the standard three relations of "better," "worse," and "equally good," has predecessors in philosophy. Thus, Griffin (1986: 81, 96ff) introduced a similar notion of "rough equality," while Parfit (1984: 431) suggested using the term "rough comparability" for this relation.

impossible if x and y had been equally good: Anything that's better than one of them would have to be better than the other. Indeed, it seems that x^+ and y are on a par, just as x and y.[20]

Just as equal goodness, parity is a symmetric relation, but—unlike equal goodness—this relation is not transitive. In the example above, x is on a par with y, y is on a par with x^+, but x is not on a par with x^+: x^+ is better than x. Again, unlike equal goodness, parity is irreflexive: No item is on a par with itself.

So, x and y in our example aren't equally good, nor is any of them better than the other. That they nevertheless are comparable in value is something Chang (2002b) tries to establish by "the Unidimensional Chaining Argument." Envisage an item y_0 that is worse than both x and y, while being similar in kind to, say, y. Suppose y_0 is a sculptor, like Michelangelo (y), but not in the same league as the latter. We are asked to imagine a finite sequence of items starting with y_0 that goes all the way up to y, in which every successive item in one respect slightly improves on its immediate predecessor, while being equal to it in other respects. Respects in which improvements are made may vary as one moves up in the sequence. But in every step in the sequence there is, we assume, a small change in one respect only. For example, one sculptor in the sequence might differ from the preceding one only in being slightly more proficient in realistically portraying the ears of the model. Now, Chang suggests that such a small "unidimensional" improvement cannot affect comparability: It cannot take us from an item that is comparable with x to one that is no longer comparable. Since the first element in the sequence is comparable with x (by hypothesis, y_0 is worse than x), the same should therefore apply—by induction—to each element that follows, up to and including the last element, y.

That a small unidimensional improvement cannot make comparability disappear is a controversial assumption. Chang's chaining argument is too *sorites*-like[21] to allay the suspicion that it exploits potential indeterminacy (vagueness) in our judgments of

[20] This argument was proposed by several philosophers prior to Chang. In particular, Raz (1986: 326) calls the possibility of such a "one-sided" improvement "the mark of incommensurability." On his view, if each item can be "one-sidedly" improved, then this is a sufficient (but not necessary) test that two items are incommensurable, i.e., such that it is neither the case that one of them is better than the other, nor that they are of equal value. Note that two incommensurable items may be on a par, but they do not have to be.

[21] Sorites, i.e., the paradox of the heap, is a classic problem that arises for vague predicates. "Being a heap of sand" is an example of such a predicate. If one assumes that removing a single grain of sand does not turn a heap into a non-heap, consider what happens when the process is repeated many times: Is a single remaining grain of sand still a heap? Chang's assumption that a small unidimensional improvement cannot make comparability disappear is like the assumption that removing one grain of sand never turns a heap into a non-heap. One might deny both these assumptions, while insisting that due to the vagueness of the predicates in question there is no precise point at which comparability disappears or a heap turns into a non-heap.

comparability.[22, 23] The possibility of vagueness also threatens the small improvement argument.[24] Chang admits that the argument for parity as a fourth type of value comparability remains incomplete until it is shown, as she indeed tries to do (see Chang 2002b), that parity phenomena cannot be explained away as instances of vagueness, or perhaps as mere gaps in our evaluative knowledge.

Assuming, however, that parity exists, how should this value relation be analyzed? Joshua Gert (2004) proposes to elucidate it by an appeal to FA-analysis: The main idea is that value comparisons can be seen as normative assessments of preference. Thus, one item is better than another if, and only if, preferring the former to the latter is required. Two items are equally good if, and only if, what is required is to be indifferent between them, i.e., to equi-prefer them both.

The novelty of Gert's approach, as compared with the traditional versions of FA-analysis, rests on the observation that there are two levels of normativity—the stronger level of requirement ("ought") and the weaker level of permission ("may"). It is the availability of permission—the weaker level of normativity—that makes conceptual room for parity: x and y can be said to be on a par if, and only if, it is permissible to prefer x to y *and* permissible to have the opposite preference. (For this definition, cf. Rabinowicz 2008; Gert's own definition of parity is much more demanding: too demanding, in fact, as shown by Rabinowicz.)

Intuitively, cases of parity can arise when value comparisons are based on several value-relevant dimensions or respects (and perhaps only in such circumstances). The overall preference we arrive at will then depend on how we weigh the relevant dimensions vis-à-vis each other. If different ways of weighing are admissible, they can give rise to different permissible overall preferences, and thereby to cases of parity in value.[25]

---

22 The starting point of the sequence (y_0) might be determinately comparable with x, the endpoint (y) might be determinately non-comparable with x, and we might have cases of indeterminate comparability somewhere in-between. This could be the reason for the apparent absence of a sharp break in the sequence.

23 Indeed, Broome (1997) has argued for a more radical claim, namely that allowing for vagueness in the threshold cases of value comparisons is outright incompatible with the postulation of (determinate) incommensurabilities. If this is right, then there is no room for parity in the presence of vagueness. However, Broome's argument is based on a controversial assumption, the so-called Collapsing Principle, which has been criticized by other philosophers (cf. Carlson 2004;, Gustafsson 2013a; Elson 2014). Rabinowicz (2009b) shows how to accommodate both vagueness and parity in the same formal modeling.

24 It might be that it is indeterminate whether x is better than, worse than, or equally as good as y, but determinate that one of these three relations does obtain between these two items. This is compatible with x^+ being determinately better than x while not being determinately better than y.

25 A different analysis of parity, which is not based on FA-analysis, is provided by Carlson (2010), who defines parity in terms of betterness: Two items are on a par if neither is better than the other, nor are they equally good, and they have appropriate betterness relations to other items in the domain. (For the details, see Carlson's paper.) However, this definition can be plausible only if the domain of items is rich enough. Otherwise, there might well exist two items that intuitively are incomparable but that come out as being on a par on the definition under consideration.

Parity is a form of comparability in value. What about incomparability? Rabinowicz (2008) makes the following suggestion. Preference and indifference are different kinds of preferential attitudes: To be indifferent between two items is to be equally prepared to make either choice. But for some pairs of items we might *lack* a fixed preferential attitude. In such a case, if we need to choose, we typically experience the choice situation as internally conflicted. We can see reasons on either side, but we cannot (or do not) balance them off. Or we waver without taking a definite stand. We make a choice if we have to, but without the conflict of reasons being resolved. This possibility of a fixed preferential attitude being absent allows us to accommodate incomparabilities in the FA-analytic framework. More precisely, if the absence of a (fixed) preferential attitude with regard to a pair of items is required, then the items can be said to be incomparable. That is, x and y are incomparable if, and only if, it is impermissible to either prefer one to the other or to be indifferent.

Isn't this definition too demanding? Shouldn't it be enough for incomparability that the absence of a preferential attitude is *permissible* rather than required? Well, such a lenient criterion would seem awkward. We do not say that something is undesirable if it is merely permissible not to desire it. It is undesirable only if desiring it is *im*permissible in some sense. By analogy, we shouldn't say that two items are incomparable if it is merely permissible not to have a preferential attitude as far as they are concerned. However, if we wish, we can introduce this weaker relation by a stipulative definition: x and y are weakly incomparable if, and only if, it is permissible neither to prefer one to the other nor to be indifferent.

While incomparability is defined in terms of what is being required, comparability in value could be understood either in permissive terms, as the contradictory of incomparability (i.e., as the relation that obtains between x and y if, and only if, it is permissible to have a preferential attitude with respect to x and y), or in requiring terms, as the contradictory of weak incomparability (i.e., as the relation that obtains between x and y if, and only if, it is required to have a preferential attitude with respect to x and y). One might refer to the latter, stronger concept as "full comparability."

Rabinowicz (2008) suggests that one might work with the following "intersection modeling" to account for these different relations in a more general and more formal way. Suppose we focus on a domain D of items. Let K be the class of all permissible preference orderings of the items in D. K is non-empty, i.e., at least one preference ordering of the items in the domain is permissible. The orderings in K need not be complete, i.e., they might contain gaps. In a complete preference ordering, for every pair of items in the domain, either one item is preferred to the other or they are both equi-preferred. Since we need to make room for incomparabilities, and thus need to allow for gaps in preferential attitudes, completeness cannot be assumed. What can be assumed, however, is that all the orderings in K are well-behaved at least in the following sense: In every such permissible ordering, weak preference (i.e., preference-or-indifference) is a quasi-order, i.e., it is a transitive and reflexive relation.

In terms of K, the relation of betterness between items can now be defined as the *intersection* of permissible preferences:

(**B**) x is *better* than y if and only if x is preferred to y in every ordering in K.

This is another way of saying that x is *better* than y if and only preferring x to y is required.

Moving now to other value relations, it is easily seen how equality in value, parity, incomparability, etc. are definable in this modeling:

(**E**) Two items are *equally good* if, and only if, they are equi-preferred in every ordering in K.

(**P**) x and y are *on a par* if, and only if, K contains two orderings such that x is preferred to y in one and y is preferred to x in the other.

(**I**) x and y are *incomparable* if, and only if, every ordering in K contains a gap with regard to x and y.

And so on.[26]

The intersection model allows us to derive formal properties of value relations from the corresponding conditions on permissible preference orderings. Thus, one can now *prove* that betterness is a transitive and asymmetric relation, that equal goodness is an equivalence relation (i.e., that it is transitive, symmetric, and reflexive), and that whatever is better than, worse than, on a par with, or incomparable with one of the equally good items must have exactly the same value relation to the other item. Thus, the modeling does some work.

Indeed, this feature of the modeling might give one pause. To give an example, consider betterness. That this relation is transitive is, many would say, a conceptual truth. (Many, but not all; for an opposing view, see Temkin 1996, 2012.) But in the intersection modeling this transitivity condition on betterness comes from the transitivity of preference orderings in K. Transitivity might seem to be a very plausible condition on permissible preference orderings. But is it as firmly established as the corresponding condition on betterness? Similar remarks apply to other formal features of value relations that are derivable in the modeling. This might be seen as a weakness of the proposal under consideration. Another weakness has to do with the very notion of preference. If preference is conceptually tied

---

26 Gert (2004) provides a different model, which is framed in terms of the assignments of intervals of permissible strengths to items in the domain. For an item x, we can denote this interval by $[x^{min}, x^{max}]$, with x^{min} standing for the interval's lower bound and x^{max} for its upper bound. Then x is said to be better than y if and only if $x^{min} > y^{max}$, i.e., if, and only if, the weakest permissible preference for x is stronger than the strongest permissible preference for y. For x and y to be on a par, their intervals must overlap, which means that there is a permissible preference for x that is stronger than some permissible preference for y and vice versa: there is a permissible preference for y that is stronger than some permissible preference for x. Gert's interval model is criticized in Chang (2005) and Rabinowicz (2008). The main objection is that the model lacks constraints on *combinations* of permissible preferences: any permissible preference for one item can be combined with any permissible preference for the other item. It can be shown that this leads to counter-intuitive results: Certain structures of value relations cannot be represented by the interval modeling.

to potential choice, analyzing value relations in terms of permissible preferences restricts the domain of such relations to objects between which a choice is possible. Since objects of choice at bottom are options at an agent's disposal, this appears to be a problematic limitation: After all, we want to make value comparisons also between other things (works of art, persons, states of the world, etc.). For a suggestion how to deal with these problems without giving up the basic contours of the intersection model, see Rabinowicz (2012).

But let us move on. We now have all we need for a general taxonomy of binary value relations.

In Table 2.1, each column describes one type of a value relation, by specifying all the preferential positions that are permissible with regard to a pair of items. There are four such positions to consider: preference ($\succ$), indifference ($\approx$), dispreference ($\prec$), and gap (/). There is a plus sign in a column for every position that is permissible in a given value type. Since for any two items at least one preferential position must be permissible (if K is non-empty), the number of columns equals the number of ways one can pick a non-empty subset out of the set of four positions. For example, in type 7, all preferential positions except for the gap are permissible, while in type 15, which corresponds to incomparability (**I**), the gap is the only permissible position. In type 1, which corresponds to betterness (**B**), the only permissible position is preference, i. e., preferring one item to the other is required. And so on.

The columns in the table correspond to *atomic* types of value relations. Collections of atomic types, such as parity (**P**, types 6–9, i.e., all types in which there are plus signs in the first and the third rows), comparability (types 1–14), or weak incomparability (types 8–15), form types in a broader sense of the word. While Chang was right to suggest that parity is a form of comparability, it is not an atomic type. In this respect, it differs from the three traditional value relations: better (**B**), worse (**W**), and equally good (**E**).

The fifteen atomic types listed in Table 2.1 are all *logically* possible. But some of them might not represent "real" possibilities. For example, it might seem that both indifference and preferential gaps with regard to items that are on a par should always be permissible. This would exclude types 6, 7, and 8. In result, only type 9 would be left for parity, which would mean that parity after all does boil down to an atomic type of value relation. Note that extra requirements of this kind importantly differ from such conditions as, say,

Table 2.1 Taxonomy of binary value relations

	1	2	3	4	5	6	7	8	9	10	11	12	13	14	15
$\succ$	+			+		+	+	+	+	+	+				
$\approx$		+		+	+		+		+		+	+	+		
$\prec$			+		+	+	+	+	+				+	+	
/								+	+	+	+	+	+	+	+
	B	**E**	**W**			**P**	**P**	**P**	**P**						**I**

transitivity of preference or symmetry of indifference. The latter impose constraints on each ordering in *K*. The extra requirements instead impose constraints on class *K* taken as a whole: They state that *K* must contain orderings of certain kinds if it contains orderings of certain other kinds.

Rabinowicz's modeling of value relations has not been left unopposed. For one thing, it has been pointed out that this account presupposes FA-analysis of value, which might well be questioned. And, in any case, its reliance on FA-analysis makes it less general than would be desirable (cf. Carlson 2010; for some general criticisms of FA-analysis see Bykvist 2009; Rabinowicz and Rønnow-Rasmussen 2004). At the same time, the account in question appeals to two levels of normativity, while the classic FA-analysis mentions just one level (fittingness). Gustafsson (2013b) argues that the account is unacceptable because it violates what he calls value-preference symmetry, i.e., the condition to the effect that for every value relation there is a corresponding preference relation, and vice versa. To preserve the symmetry, Gustafsson suggests, we should introduce parity not just as a value relation but also as a *sui generis* preference relation. On his account, then, two items are on a par in value if, and only if, it is fitting to hold them preferentially on a par.

Obviously, the discussions on this subject, as on several other subjects in the theory of value, have not reached a point where consensus is in sight. Given the ever-questioning nature of philosophical investigation, it is possible that this point will never be reached.

Acknowledgment

This research was supported by grants from the Swedish Research Council.

References

Beardsley, M. C. (1965). Intrinsic value. *Philosophy and Phenomenological Research*, **26**, 1–17.

Bradley, R. (2006). Two concepts of intrinsic value. *Ethical Theory and Moral Practice*, **9**, 111–130.

Bradley, B. (2013). Instrumental value. In H. LaFollette (ed.), *The International Encyclopedia of Ethics*. Wiley-Blackwell. DOI: 10.1002/9781444367072.wbiee432. http://onlinelibrary.wiley.com/book/10.1002/9781444367072

Brentano, F. (1969 [1889]). *The Origin of Our Knowledge of Right and Wrong*. Transl. by R. M. Chisholm. London and Henley: Routledge and Kegan Paul.

Brewer, T. (2009). *The Retrieval of Ethics*. Oxford: Oxford University Press.

Broome, J. (1997). Is incommensurability vagueness?. In R. Chang (ed.), *Incommensurability, Incomparability, and Practical Reason*. Cambridge, Mass. and London: Harvard University Press, pp. 68–69.

Bykvist, K. (2009). No good fit: why the fitting attitude analysis of value fails. *Mind*, **118**, 1–30.

Campbell, C. A. (1935). Moral and non-moral values: a study in the first principles of axiology. *Mind*, **54**, 273–299.

Campbell, S. M. (2013). An analysis of prudential value. *Utilitas*, **25**, 334–354.

Carlson, E. (2004). Broome's argument against value incomparability. *Utilitas*, **16**, 220–224.

Carlson, E. (2010). Parity demystified. *Theoria*, **76**, 119–128.

Chang, R. (1997). Introduction. In R. Chang (ed.), *Incommensurability, Incomparability and Practical Reason*. Cambridge, MA: Harvard University Press, pp. 1–34.

Chang, R. (2002a). *Making Comparisons Count*. London: Routledge.

Chang, R. (2002b). The possibility of parity. *Ethics*, **112**, 659–688.

Chang, R. (2005). Parity, interval value, and choice. *Ethics*, **115**, 331–350.

Crisp, R. (2004). "Sidgwick's hedonism." In P. Bucolo, R. Crisp and B. Schultz (eds), *Proceedings of the World Congress on Henry Sidgwick; Happiness and Religion*. Università degli Studi di Catania, Dipartimento di Scienze Umane, 104–157.

Dancy, J. (2000). Should we pass the buck?. In A. O'Hear (ed.), *Philosophy, the Good, the True and the Beautiful*. Cambridge: Cambridge University Press, pp. 159–175.

Dancy, J. (2004). *Ethics without Principles*. Oxford: Oxford University Press.

Darwall, S. (2002). *Welfare and Rational Care*. Princeton: Princeton University Press

Elson, L. (2014). Borderline cases and the collapsing principle. *Utilitas* **26**, 51–60.

Fletcher, G. (2012). The locative analysis of *good for* formulated and defended. *Journal of Ethics and Social Philosophy*, **6**, 1–26.

Geach, P. (1956). Good and evil. *Analysis*, **17**, 33–42.

Gert, J. (2004). Value and parity. *Ethics*, **114**, 492–510.

Griffin JP (1986). *Well-being: Its Meaning, Measurement and Moral Importance*. Oxford: Clarendon Press

Gustafsson, J. E. (2013a). Indeterminacy and the small-improvement argument. *Utilitas*, **25**, 433–445.

Gustafsson, J. E. (2013b). Value-preference symmetry and fitting-attitude accounts of value relations. *The Philosophical Quarterly*, **63**, 476–491.

Hurka, T (1987). "Good" and "good for." *Mind*, **96**, 71–73.

Hussein, N. J. Z., and Shah, N. (2006). Misunderstanding metaethics: Korsgaard's rejection of realism. In R. Shafer-Landau (ed.), *Oxford Studies in Metaethics 1*. Oxford: Clarendon Press, pp. 265–294.

Kagan, S. (1998). Rethinking Intrinsic value. *The Journal of Ethics* **2**, 277–297.

Kant, I. (1998 [1785]). *Groundwork of the Metaphysics of Morals*, tr. Mary J. Gregor. Cambridge, U.K.; New York: Cambridge University Press.

Kirchin, S. (ed.), (2013). *Thick Concepts*. Oxford: Oxford University Press.

Korsgaard, C. (1983). Two distinctions in goodness. *Philosophical Review*, **92**, 169–195.

Kraut, R. (2011). *Against Absolute Goodness*. New York: Oxford University Press.

Langton, R. (2007). Objective and unconditioned value. *Philosophical Review*, **116**, 157–185.

Lewis, C. I. (1946). *An Analysis of Knowledge and Valuation*. La Salle, Illinois: Open Court.

Mackie, J. L. (1977). *Ethics: Inventing Right and Wrong*. London: Penguin Books.

Mill, J. S. (1998 [1861]). *Utilitarianism*. R. Crisp (ed.), Oxford: Oxford University Press.

Moore, G. E. (1965 [1912]). *Ethics*. Oxford: Oxford University Press.

Moore, G. E. (1993 [1903]). *Principia Ethic*a. Cambridge: Cambridge University Press.

Moore, G. E. (1922). *Philosophical Studies*, London: Routledge and Kegan Paul.

Mulligan, K. (2010).Emotions and values. In P. Goldie (ed.), *The Oxford Handbook of Philosophy of Emotion*, Oxford: Oxford University Press, pp. 475–500.

Olson, J. (2005). *Axiological Investigations*. Uppsala: Acta Universitatis Upsaliensis.

O'Neill, J. (1992). The varieties of intrinsic value. *The Monist*, **75**, 119–137.

Parfit, D. (1984). *Reasons and Persons*. Oxford: Clarendon Press.

Pettit, P. (1989). Consequentialism and respect for persons. *Ethics*, **100**, 116–126.

Plato (1992). *Republic*, (trans. G. M. A. Grube and C. D. C. Reeve). Indianapolis: Hackett Publishing Co.

Rabinowicz, W. (2008). Value relations. *Theoria*, **74**, 18–49.

Rabinowicz, W. (2009a). Values compared. *Polish Journal of Philosophy*, **3**, 73–96.

Rabinowicz, W. (2009b). Incommensurability and vagueness. *Proceedings of the Aristotelian Society*, Suppl. Vol., 83, 71–94.

Rabinowicz, W. (2012). Value relations revisited. *Economics and Philosophy*, **28**, 133–164.

Rabinowicz, W. (2013). Value, fitting-attitude account of. In H. LaFolette (ed.), *The International Encyclopedia of Ethics*. Wiley-Blackwell DOI: 10.1002/9781444367072.wbiee311. http://onlinelibrary.wiley.com/book/10.1002/9781444367072

Rabinowicz, W. and Rønnow-Rasmussen, T. (2000). A distinction in value: intrinsic and for its own sake. *Proceedings of the Aristotelian Society*, **100**, 33–51.

Rabinowicz, W. and Rønnow-Rasmussen, T. (2004). The strike of the demon: on fitting pro-attitudes and value. *Ethics*, **114**, 391–423.

Rabinowicz, W. and Österberg, J. (1996) Value based on preferences. *Philosophy and Economics*, **12**, 1–27.

Raz, J. (1986). Incommensurability. In J. Raz, *The Morality of Freedom*. Oxford: Oxford University Press, pp. 321–368.

Regan, D. H. (2004). Why am i my brother's keeper? In R. J. Wallace, P. Pettit, S. Scheffler, and M. Smith (eds), *Reason and Value: Themes from the Moral Philosophy of Joseph Raz*. Clarendon Press, pp. 202–230.

Rønnow-Rasmussen, T. (2002). Instrumental values: strong and weak. *Ethical Theory and Moral Practice*, **5**, 23–43.

Rønnow-Rasmussen, T. (2011). *Personal Value*. Oxford University Press.

Rønnow-Rasmussen, T. (2013). Good and Good For. In H. LaFolette (ed.), *The International Encyclopedia of Ethics*, Wiley-Blackwell, DOI: 10.1002/9781444367072.wbiee386. http://onlinelibrary.wiley.com/book/10.1002/9781444367072.

Rosati, C. (2008). Objectivism and relational good. *Social Philosophy and Politics*, **25**, 314–349.

Rosati, C. (2009). Relational good and the multiplicity problem. *Philosophical Issues*, **19**, 205–234.

Scanlon, T. (1998). *What We Owe to Each Other*. Cambridge, Mass.: Belknap Press.

Schroeder, M. (2007). Teleology, agent-relative value, and "good." *Ethics*, **117**, 265–295.

Schroeder, M. (2012). Value theory. *Stanford Encyclopedia of Philosophy*, http://plato.stanford.edu/entries/value-theory/

Sidgwick, H. (1874/1884). *The Methods of Ethics*. London: Macmillan, 3rd edition.

Sidgwick, H. (1874/1907). *The Methods of Ethics*. London: Macmillan, 7th edition.

Smith, M. (2003). Neutral and relative value after Moore. *Ethics* **113**, 576–598.

Tannenbaum, J. (2010). Categorizing goods. In R. Shafer-Landau (ed.), *Oxford Studies in Metaethics 5*. New York: Oxford University Press.

Temkin, L. (1996). A continuum argument for intransitivity. *Philosophy and Public Affairs*, **25**, 175–210.

Temkin, L. (2012). *Rethinking the Good: Moral Ideals and the Nature of Practical Reasoning*. Oxford: Oxford University Press.

Thomson, J. J. (1992). On some ways in which a thing can be good. In E. F. Paul, F. Miller, and J. Paul (eds). *The Good Life and the Human Good*. Cambridge: Cambridge University Press.

Thomson, J. J. (2008). *Normativity*. Chicago: Open Court.

Williams, B. (1985). *Ethics and the Limits of Philosophy*. London: Fontana.

Zimmerman, M. J. (2009). Understanding what's good for us. *Ethical Theory and Moral Practice*. **12**, 429–439.

Zimmerman, M. J. (2010). Intrinsic vs. extrinsic value. In E. N. Zalta (ed.), *The Stanford Encyclopedia of Philosophy* (Winter 2010 Edition). http://plato.stanford.edu/archives/win2010/entries/value-intrinsic-extrinsic/.

Chapter 3

What is value? Where does it come from? A psychological perspective

E. Tory Higgins

Introduction

To understand why people do what they do, why they feel what they feel, psychologists need to know what matters to them, what they want and don't want. A central concept concerned with "mattering" and "wanting" is *value*. Indeed, Allport (1961: 543) suggested that value priorities were the "dominating force in life." The more an object or activity has value to us, the more we prefer it over alternative objects or activities. We want to have the object or do the activity. But what gives an object or activity its value? *Where does value come from?* This chapter considers several psychological mechanisms that confer value on something. Some of these mechanisms, such as satisfying a need or giving us hedonic pleasure, are well-known to be desired results that would confer value. Other mechanisms, as we will see, are less well-known and even surprising.

Let us begin at the beginning—the *hedonic principle*. The term "hedonic" derives from the Greek term for "sweet," and it means relating to, or characterized by, pleasure (Webster's Ninth New Collegiate Dictionary 1989). From the time of the Greeks, hedonic experiences have been linked to the classic motivational principle that people *approach pleasure and avoid pain*. Jeremy Bentham made an influential and explicit early statement on the importance of hedonic experiences to both ethical and non-ethical value (Bentham 1781/1988: 1): "Nature has placed mankind under the governance of two sovereign masters, *pain* and *pleasure*. It is for them alone to point out what we ought to do, as well as to determine what we shall do. On the one hand the standard of right and wrong, on the other the chain of causes and effects, are fastened to their throne." So, apparently, we have our answer: Value comes from having pleasure and not having pain (see: also Ellingsen et al., this volume).

But hold on! Let us go back even further and consider the beginning of the beginning—the Genesis story of Adam and Eve in the Garden of Eden as told in the *Bible*:

> And out of the ground made the Lord God to grow every tree that is pleasant to the sight, and good for food; the tree of life also in the midst of the garden, and the tree of knowledge of good and evil. . . . And the Lord God commanded the man, saying, Of every tree of the garden thou mayest freely eat: But of the tree of the knowledge of good and evil, thou shalt not eat of it: for in the day that thou eatest thereof thou shalt surely die.
>
> Genesis 2: 8–9, 16–17 (King James Version)

What I find remarkable about the Genesis story is that Adam and Eve chose to go against God's command. They chose to eat the fruit from the *tree of knowledge*. What could possibly motivate them to make this choice when, by making it, they would "surely die" (or at minimum be banished from paradise)? By making this choice, they would lose paradise, lose an everlasting life of pleasure and no pain—everlasting because they *were* allowed to eat the fruit from the tree of life. If the hedonic principle is correct, if what people really want is to maximize pleasure and minimize pain, why would Adam and Eve have made this choice? What is this story telling us about human motivation?

I believe the answer lies in the fruit being from the *tree of knowledge*. The tree of *knowledge* is the tree of *truth* and a central motivation of humans is to *establish what's real*, to distinguish between truth and falsehood, between reality and fantasy. This motivation for the truth can be as important to humans as life itself (see: Higgins 2007, 2012). Moreover, the tree of knowledge is not just any knowledge—it is the "*tree of the knowledge of good and evil.*" This means that eating the fruit of this tree also satisfies another central human motivation—the motivation to *manage what happens*, the motivation to *control* our lives. Humans can only be in control of their lives when they have the knowledge of what is good and what is evil. And when you combine truth and control—when truth and control *work together* as in the tree of the knowledge of good and evil—then humans can live a life in which they "*go in the right direction.*"

It is notable that Adam and Eve's life in the Garden of Eden had little need for truth or control because everything was provided for them in this paradise. This would be fine if what people really valued was having pleasure and no pain. But people want a life in which *they* go in the right direction and for this to happen they must be effective at having truth and control (see: Higgins 2012). This is why they needed to eat from the tree of the knowledge of good and evil. What the Genesis story captures is that there is more to what humans value that just having pleasure, just having desired outcomes. As Carl Rogers said, "The good life is a process, not a state of being. It is a direction, not a destination" (Rogers 1995/1961).

When people are effective in truth and control, their *engagement* in goal pursuits is strengthened. Stronger engagement in goal pursuits makes people "feel alive" and contributes to well-being. And it does something else as well. It intensifies the value experience itself. It makes attractive things even more attractive, and it makes repulsive things even more repulsive. Not only is the journey itself more worthwhile, but stronger engagement impacts the value intensity of *the destination itself*. This is the major takeaway message of this chapter. But before I discuss how regulatory engagement works psychologically and provide evidence for its impact on value, I need to review other psychological mechanisms that impact whether something is experienced as being positive or negative to begin with. This important part of the story concerns where *valence* comes from.

Where does valence come from?

The basic psychological mechanisms that have been proposed traditionally as underlying whether something is experienced as positive or negative are: valence from need satisfaction; valence from shared beliefs about desirable objectives and procedures; valence from relating our current selves to personal standards; valence from making evaluative inferences; and valence from hedonic experience. In this section, I will briefly review each of these psychological contributors to valence (for more extensive reviews, see: Brendl and Higgins 1996; Higgins 2007, 2012).

Valence from need satisfaction

At the turn of the twentieth century, psychologists with theoretical perspectives ranging from behavioristic to Gestalt to psychodynamic proposed that need satisfaction is the basic mechanism that confers value to objects and activities. Specifically, something has positive value if it contributes to satisfying physical needs, reduces drives or deficiencies, or increases an individual's survival in the world. If it does the opposite, it has negative value. Behavior is directed toward controlling deficits of specific substances in the body, and value derives from homeostatic responses to tissue deficits and physiological equilibrium (see: Weiner 1972). Drives were manifest in behavior, had physiological correlates, and naturally gave rise to man's desires (see: Woodworth 1918).

Using operant or classical conditioning to change attitudes, social-psychological research during the 1950s provided a broader version of the need satisfaction viewpoint, including need for approval. In one paradigm, for example, while the participants were talking to the experimenter, the experimenter casually responded positively to one set of linguistic forms the participants used, such as plural nouns, with approving head movements or expressions like "mm-hmmm" and did not respond positively to other linguistic forms, such as singular nouns. Over time, without participants' awareness, the approved linguistic forms were produced more frequently than the non-approved forms—as if those linguistic forms had increased in value (for a review of such studies, see: Eagly and Chaiken 1993).

Valence from people's shared beliefs about desirable objectives and procedures

A very different mechanism that confers value is people's *shared beliefs* about which ends or objectives, and which means or procedures for attaining these ends, are or are not generally desirable. This is the kind of value that people have in mind when they say that they value "freedom" or "equality." Although these values are personal in the sense of being internalized, they are acquired within a social context and are shared with others (Schwartz 1992). Milton Rokeach describes values as "shared prescriptive or proscriptive beliefs about ideal modes of behavior and end-states of existence" (see: Rokeach 1980: 262). Similarly, Robert Merton (1957: 133) notes that: "Every social group invariably couples its cultural objectives with regulations, rooted in the mores or institutions, of allowable procedures for moving toward these objectives."

The "shared beliefs" mechanism for conferring value includes *norms* about what goals are worth pursuing and what moral principles or standards of conduct one should live by. As captured in the concept of "procedural justice" (see: Tyler and Lind 1992; Thibaut and Walker 1975), for example, people in many societies value the fairness of decision procedures independent of decision outcomes, such as employees wanting their managers to follow fair procedures in determining raises independent of whether they end up with a higher or lower raise themselves (see: Brockner 2010). Given the importance of shared cultural or socialized values as a mechanism that confers value for humans on the objects and activities in their lives, it is not surprising that such values have received special attention in social psychology (e.g., Rokeach 1973; Schwartz and Bilsky 1987; Seligman et al. 1996).

Valence from people relating themselves to standards

Shared beliefs can be considered not only at the broader societal level where the values apply to people in general, but also at the more interpersonal level where significant others apply values to a specific person. Whereas values from shared beliefs at the societal level are usually treated as social values, values from a person's shared beliefs with a significant other (e.g., mother, partner) are usually treated as personal standards. Historically, control process models have treated personal standards in terms of the relation between a current state of the self and some end-state functioning as a standard of reference. The value of the current self-state depends on the extent to which it approaches a desired end-state or avoids an undesired end-state (see: Carver and Scheier 1981, 1990; Miller et al. 1960; Powers 1973; Wiener 1948).

For human motivation, the desired and undesired end-states that function as reference points or guides for self-regulation are typically acquired from interactions with significant others. Developmentally, children learn their caretakers' hopes and aspirations for them (their *ideals*) or their caretakers' beliefs about their duties and responsibilities (their *oughts*). When children become capable of having their own standpoint on ideals and oughts, they can adopt their caretakers' ideals and oughts for them as their own, thereby creating a *shared reality* about desired end-states, which are *internalized* (or identified) *self-guides*. Ideal self-guides relate to the promotion system that is concerned with accomplishments and advancement, and ought self-guides relate to the prevention system that is concerned with safety and security (see: Higgins 1997). An actual-self attribute that is congruent with (matches) an ideal or ought self-guide has positive value, whereas an actual-self attribute that is discrepant from (mismatches) an ideal or ought self-guide has negative value (see: Higgins 1987, 1991; James, 1890/1948; Moretti and Higgins 1999; Rogers 1961).

Value is conferred by two different mechanisms in these systems. First, the person's ideal and ought standards of excellence are shared beliefs with significant others about which end-states have positive value and which have negative value. Second, the actual self-states that are congruent with, or discrepant from, the ideal and ought self-guides themselves have positive or negative values, respectively. It is this second mechanism of conferring value on actual self-states that uniquely characterizes this viewpoint on value. It introduces the notion of value from monitoring one's success or failure in meeting self-guides—value from the answer to "how am I doing?" (see: Bandura 1986; Boldero and Francis 2002; Carver and Scheier 1990; Duval and Wicklund 1972; Higgins 1987, 1996).

Valence from hedonic experience

As I mentioned earlier, interest in hedonic experiences as a mechanism conferring value has continued over the centuries. From the ancient Greeks to seventeenth- and eighteenth-century British philosophers, to twentieth-century psychologists (see: Kahneman et al. 1999), the hedonic principle that people are motivated to approach pleasure and avoid pain has dominated our understanding of people's motivation. It is the basic motivational assumption of theories across all areas of psychology, including theories of emotion in psychobiology (e.g., Gray 1982), conditioning in animal learning (e.g., Mowrer 1960; Thorndike 1935), decision-making in cognitive psychology (e.g., Edwards 1955; Kahneman and Tversky 1979), consistency in social psychology (e.g., Festinger 1957; Heider 1958), and achievement motivation in personality (e.g., Atkinson 1964). Even in *Beyond the Pleasure Principle,* when Freud (1920/1950) assigned a motivational role to the ego's reality principle, he made it clear that the reality principle "at bottom also seeks pleasure although a delayed and diminished pleasure" (p. 365). More recently, Kahneman (2000) has distinguished "decision utility," where utility is inferred from observed choices (i.e., revealed in behavior), from "experienced utility" that involves experiences of pleasure and pain. Kahneman argues that the best way to measure actual experienced utility is by moment-based methods where experienced utility of an episode is derived from real-time measures of the pleasure and pain that an individual experienced during that episode.

The motivation for pleasure can be so important that it can even trump the motivation to satisfy basic biological needs. It has been known for over half a century that animals will choose on the basis of hedonic experiences independent of any biological need being satisfied (Eisenberger 1972). There are early studies, for example, showing not only that sweet water with saccharin is preferred to regular water, but also that animals prefer sweet food to a physiologically better food, such as a food that is more beneficial for an animal given its vitamin deficiency (for a review of these early studies, see: Woodsworth and Schlosberg 1954). There are also classic studies by James Old and Peter Milner showing that rats will work to press a bar that activates the pleasure area in the brain but does not satisfy any biological need (Olds and Milner 1954). In the original and follow-up studies, metallic electrodes were implanted in certain regions of the lateral hypothalamus and some rats would push the lever up to five-thousand times an hour, even to the point of collapsing. In a T-maze, with both arms baited with food mash, the rat would stop at a point halfway down the runway to self-stimulate, never going to the food at all. Some mother rats even abandoned their newborn pups—despite the biological imperative of mothers' caring for their infants—in order to press the lever thousands of times per hour.

At this point you might be telling yourself, "So I guess the Greeks had it right all along. Maximizing pleasure is the answer to what people really want." Well, I do believe that it *is* part of the answer. But I also believe that it only *part* of the answer, and given this, I believe that there is a problem with its being anointed for centuries as being *the* answer. For too long it has dominated thinking about where value comes from. It has taken attention away from other contributions to the value of things. In the remainder of this chapter I will discuss four of these contributions: value from distinctly different ways to approach pleasure and avoid pain (i.e., promotion vs. prevention); value from being effective in establishing what's real (truth) and managing what happens (control); value from a fit between different ways of being effective (i.e., working together effectively); and value intensification from strengthening engagement.

Promotion and prevention as value beyond pleasure and pain

Where does the positive experience of success come from? Where does the negative experience of failure come from? You might think the answers are obvious: success is pleasant and failure is painful. But feeling relaxed after success is very different from feeling joyful after success. And feeling anxious after failure is very different from feeling sad. These are very different positive and negative value experiences and the hedonic principle is silent on these differences. Research testing self-discrepancy theory (see: Higgins 1987, 1989) found that these different positive and negative value experiences depended on whether the success or failure was in relation to people's personal ideals or personal oughts. Success or failure in relation to personal ideals produced emotions along the cheerfulness–dejection dimension (e.g., joyful–sad), whereas success or failure in relation to personal oughts produced emotions along the quiescence–agitation dimension (e.g., relaxed–anxious).

According to self-discrepancy theory, these different value experiences are produced by different psychological situations. When events are related to our ideals, we experience success as the presence of a positive outcome (a gain), which is a joyful experience, and we experience failure as the absence of positive outcomes (a non-gain), which is a sad experience. However, when events are related to our oughts, we experience success as the absence of a negative outcome (a non-loss), which is a relaxing experience, and we experience failure as the presence of a negative outcome (a loss), which is an anxious experience (see: Higgins and Tykocinski 1992; Strauman 1992).

Self-discrepancy theory was concerned with chronic personality differences in value experiences. But situations and events themselves can create different psychological situations that produce different kinds of positive value experiences and different kinds of negative value experiences. Regulatory focus theory (Higgins 1997, 1998) was developed to include these situational effects on value experiences and to try to understand more deeply the distinct ways that people experience positive value and negative value when they self-regulate within these different systems (as well as to examine other motivational effects of these different systems of self-regulation).

A transition point from self-discrepancy theory to regulatory focus theory occurred when Miguel Brendl and I began working on a chapter (for Mark Zanna's *Advances in Experimental Social Psychology* series) that addressed the question, "What makes events positive or negative?" (Brendl and Higgins 1996). I remember Miguel coming in to my office with an air of excitement and telling me about a critical factor for understanding the nature of valence. His insight was that the nature of valence depended on the nature of neutrality: *to understand valence, you needed to understand "0."*

A critical principle for judging valence is *the principle of goal supportiveness,* which refers to the degree to which an event is judged to support or impede the satisfaction of a set goal, with goal support producing positive valence and goal impediment producing negative valence. This principle has a long history. Lewin, Dembo, Festinger, and Sears (1944), for example, assumed that a goal separates positively valenced events from negatively valenced events, or an area of success from an area of failure, with the former being approached and the latter being avoided. More recent theories of emotion also assume that reaching versus frustrating a goal (Lazarus 1993; Ortony et al. 1988; Roseman 1984) is experienced positively versus negatively. Brendl and Higgins (1996) considered what this meant for the difference between the (promotion) ideal system and the (prevention) ought system. We proposed that given the nature of ideal and ought goals, "0" in these systems was *not* neutral. Moreover, "0" had *a different valence* for (promotion) ideal and (prevention) ought goal pursuit.

For (promotion) ideal goal pursuit, successfully attaining a positive outcome supports the goal pursuit, because it represents the presence of a positive outcome, and as such it has positive valence. Not attaining a positive outcome impedes (promotion) ideal goal pursuit, because it represents the absence of a positive outcome, and as such has negative valence. This means that simply maintaining a status quo "0" is *not* experienced as neutral in the (promotion) ideal system of goal pursuit; instead, it has *negative* valence, because it fails to attain a positive outcome (fails to advance; a non-gain). In contrast, for (prevention) ought goal pursuit, maintaining a status quo "0" has *positive* valence, because it represents the absence of a negative outcome (a non-loss). Thus, once again, "0" is *not* experienced as neutral. But for (prevention) ought goal pursuit, "0" has positive valence rather than negative valence as for promotion ideal goal pursuit. What has negative valence for (prevention) ought goal pursuit is failing to maintain a status quo "0," which represents the presence of a negative outcome.

Many subsequent studies have supported these proposed valence differences between the promotion and prevention systems (for a recent review, see: Higgins 2014). What this means is that the hedonic principle alone is *not* sufficient to understand where valence comes from. The distinction between promotion and prevention systems of self-regulation must be taken into account.

The distinction between promotion and prevention goal pursuit also has implications for understanding the nature of moral or ethical value (see also Moll et al., 2015). Moral foundations' theory (Haidt and Graham 2007) proposes that moral judgments can be explained in terms of five moral foundations: "Harm/Care," "Fairness/Reciprocity," "Ingroup/Loyalty," "Authority/Respect," and "Purity/Sanctity." Ingroup/Loyalty is said to underlie our feelings of loyalty to groups to which we belong (such as the nation or family), Authority/Respect to our feelings that certain individuals deserve our respect and to the endorsement of hierarchy, and Purity/Sanctity to our feelings that associate nobility with purity and the moral element of our feelings of disgust. They are considered "*binding*" foundations, because they generally involve the binding of individuals to larger institutions or groups such as a family, a nation, or a religious organization. Cornwell and Higgins (2013) have found that for both chronic and situationally induced focus, binding foundation endorsement is stronger for participants with a stronger prevention focus and is weaker for participants with a stronger promotion focus (independent of participants' political identification). This is consistent with previous evidence that a prevention focus, with its emphasis on duties and responsibilities, is more strongly associated with an interdependent (vs. independent) self-construal than is a promotion focus (Lee et al. 2000).

Truth and control as value beyond pleasure and pain

To return to the beginning of the beginning, the story of Adam and Eve in the Garden of Eden suggests that what matters to humans must be more than just having all pleasure and no pain. They want to be effective at establishing what's real (truth) and managing what happens (control) that is part of life's journey (Higgins 2012).

In answering the question of what is it that people want, what is it that they value, it is critical to go beyond pleasure and pain.[1] This is well illustrated by the value people assign to activities that often involve hardship and even intense suffering. Almost thirty years before Tenzing Norgay (from Nepal) and Edmund Hillary (from New Zealand) successfully climbed Mount Everest on May 29, 1953, British mountain climber George Mallory (in 1924) decided that he would attempt to climb Mount Everest, despite knowing the extreme dangers and hardships involved in such a climb. In fact, he and his climbing partner, Andrew Irvine, disappeared on the way to the summit. Given our common beliefs in "survival" and "pleasure" as what people really want, it is not surprising that, before he left on this dangerous venture, he was asked why he wanted to climb Mount Everest. His famous answer was, "Because it's there." It's not just about survival or just about pleasure. It's about succeeding at something—in this case succeeding at something that is extremely challenging.

George Mallory was not the first to engage in an extreme sport activity. And he was certainly not the last. Now we can even watch televised programs of people engaging in extreme sports, such as the X Games. But unlike the athletes in the X Games, most of those who engage in extreme sports are not competing against other athletes but are just competing against environmental obstacles and challenges. The sports are considered extreme

[1] In this chapter I will use the term "value" as a synonym for the more general term "worth" or "worthwhile." In my 2012 book, I have a more restricted meaning of "value" as "being effective at having desired results." Value is then distinguished from "being effective at establishing what's real' (truth) and "being effective at managing what happens" (control). Because the present Handbook is concerned with value in the more general sense of "worth" or "worthwhile," I have chosen here to discuss value in this more general sense as well. In this more general sense, being effective in truth and in control also have value.

precisely because the environmental weather and terrain conditions are inherently uncontrollable, such as a sudden storm, and need to be dealt with on the spot. The athletes in these sports say that what they value in these sports is testing their ability to master difficult environments. As one example, a famous paraglider pilot, Bob Drury, is quoted as saying, "We do these things not to escape life, but to prevent life escaping us."

The value from control, from managing to make something happen, is independent from being just a means for obtaining desired outcomes (i.e., instrumental value). Consider, for example, a study with rats that learned that by pressing a lever they could make a food pellet fall into a food tray where they could eat it. In one experimental condition, a food dish containing the exact same food pellets was placed in the cage, which meant that the rats could obtain the same food pellets for free (i.e., without having to work for them). On occasion a rat would accidentally push the free food dish in front of the food tray. Despite the fact that they could effortlessly attain the food from the free food dish in front of them, the rats actually pushed the food dish *out of the way* (not eating from it), and then pressed the lever to make a food pellet fall into the food tray where they ate it (Carder and Berkowitz 1970). This is not just instrumental behavior. If it were, the rats would eat from the free food dish, thereby maximizing the benefits/costs ratio given that it would be the same beneficial food for less cost in effort.

This is the value that derives from control, from managing to make something happen, even if it is painful to do so. There are similar examples of people suffering for the sake of the truth, taking on pain and suffering for the sake of establishing what's real and fighting for what's real. A well-known movie example occurs in the movie *The Matrix*. In this movie, the reality perceived by humans is actually a *simulated* reality—the Matrix—that provides people with a hedonically positive life to pacify them. Morpheus, the leader of the rebels, gives Neo a choice between a blue pill that will keep him in this comfortable simulated reality or a red pill that offers only the truth. Morpheus tells Neo, "All I'm offering is the truth, nothing more." Neo chooses the red pill.

For decades social psychologists have studied all the different ways that people value and seek the truth. The value of truth is reflected in people wanting to know "what" is happening (social judgments) and "why" it is happening (attributions), make sense of the relations among their beliefs, attitudes, and choices (consistency), and create norms and shared realities with others to establish agreement regarding what to feel and believe about the world (for reviews, see: Higgins 2012, 2013). What they want is the truth, "even if it hurts."

For an intuitive understanding of the value of truth and control over hedonic outcomes, consider the thought experiment offered by Robert Nozick in his book *Anarchy, State and Utopia* (Nozick 1974). He asks us to imagine an experience machine that could give us whatever pleasurable experiences we could possibly want. If you get into this machine, your pleasant experiences will be fully convincing; you would not be able to tell that they were not veridical. The inventor promises that for the rest of your life in the machine you will have a fully convincing experience of a life that is better than whatever would have happened to you outside the machine. Most people choose *not* to get into the machine.

This does not make sense if hedonic outcomes are all that we value. But people value truth and they consider what happens inside the machine to be an illusion rather than reality, inauthentic rather than authentic. And they value control, and inside the machine their life of successful outcomes occurs because of the *inventor's* control rather than *their* control. Thus, although they know that better outcomes will occur inside the machine, it will not be self-determined and it will not be authentic.

Value from fit

Earlier in this chapter I discussed how people value "going in the right direction," which involves control and truth working together effectively. One example of this is the value that individuals place on control when they are in the goal pursuit state of *locomotion* where they want to get "going" and keep "going," and the value that they place on truth when they are in the goal pursuit state of *assessment* where they want to do what's "right"; when they fit together we "go in the right direction." This value from fit has been shown to translate into effective performance, where the highest performance is found when individuals are high in both locomotion and assessment (Kruglanski et al. 2000).

Value from fit is also created when there is a fit between individuals' regulatory focus orientation (promotion; prevention) and their manner of goal pursuit (eager; vigilant). Manner of goal pursuit concerns effectively managing to make it happen (control). There is evidence that when there is fit (promotion–eager; prevention–vigilant) people "feel right" about, i.e., value, what they are doing. When there is non-fit (promotion–vigilant; prevention–eager) people "feel wrong" about what they are doing. Moreover, the "feel right" experience from fit in the goal pursuit activity can change the value of the goal object itself, intensifying its attractiveness (Higgins 2000).

In an early test of such value transfer from fit (Higgins et al. 2003), undergraduates at Columbia decided whether they preferred a Columbia coffee mug or an inexpensive pen. The manner in which they made this decision was manipulated by giving them different instructions prior to making their choice. Half of them were told to think about what they would *gain by choosing* the mug and what they would gain by choosing the pen—an *eager* manner of making a choice. The other half were told to think about what they would *lose by not choosing* the mug or what they would lose by not choosing the pen—a *vigilant* manner of making a choice. This manner of making a choice did not in itself influence their choice—almost all of them preferred the Columbia coffee mug over the pen—nor did it influence the perceived value of the mug (as reflected in what they were willing to pay to buy it). However, it created fit and non-fit conditions with the participants who were either predominant promotion or predominant prevention. Predominant promotion participants who made their decision eagerly and predominant prevention participants who made their decision vigilantly offered much more money to buy the mug than predominant promotion participants who made their decision vigilantly and predominant prevention participants who made their decision eagerly—almost 70 percent more money for the exact same mug!

Value from strength of engagement

When people pursue goals in a manner that fits their goal pursuit orientation, they not only "feel right" about what they are doing. They also become more strongly engaged in what they are doing. Other conditions of goal pursuit also influence how strongly people are engaged in what they are doing. As I mentioned in the beginning of this chapter, this impacts value in a couple of ways. To begin with, people "feel alive" when they are strongly engaged in what they are doing. This itself contributes to well-being in humans and other animals (for a review, see: Franks and Higgins 2012). It makes life's journey more worthwhile. But that is not all. It also changes the value of the destination itself by intensifying it. In this last section I will distinguish the contribution of engagement strength to value experiences from the contribution of hedonic experience, and I will present evidence for different sources of engagement strength that impact value.

Figure 3.1 provides an overall illustration of what *regulatory engagement theory* proposes as contributors to value experience (for a fuller discussion of regulatory engagement theory, see: Higgins 2006; Higgins and Scholer 2009). Hedonic experience is one contributing factor but there are other factors as well, including those like need satisfaction and standards that contribute to value experience through their impact on engagement strength. In discussing this proposal, I begin with the value experience itself on the far right side of Fig. 3.1. What exactly is the nature of this value experience?

For Lewin (1951), value related to *force*, which has direction and intensity. Lewin's concept of "force" can be extended to personal experiences that have direction and intensity.

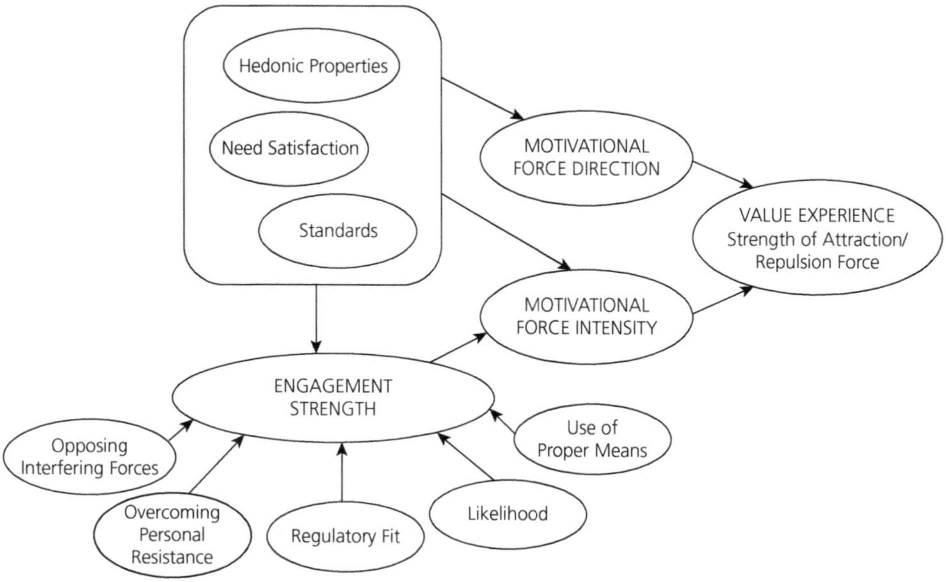

Fig. 3.1 Illustration of proposed relations among variables contributing to the value experience.

Experiencing something as having positive value corresponds to experiencing a force of attraction toward it, and experiencing something as having negative value corresponds to experiencing a force of repulsion from it. Value experiences vary in intensity. The experience of a force of attraction toward something can be relatively weak or strong (low or high positive value), and the experience of a force of repulsion from something can be relatively weak or strong (low or high negative value).

The factor of engagement strength is shown on the bottom left of Fig. 3.1. The state of being engaged is to be involved, occupied, and interested in something. Strong engagement is to concentrate on something, to be absorbed or engrossed with it (Higgins 2006). Strength of engagement alone does not make something attractive or repulsive; that is, it does not have direction. Instead, strength of engagement contributes to intensifying the force of attraction toward something or the force of repulsion away from something.

As illustrated in Fig. 3.1, value creation mechanisms such as need satisfaction, hedonic experience, and standards of different kinds all contribute to the direction of the motivational force, to whether the value force is positive attraction or negative repulsion. These mechanisms also contribute to the intensity of the motivational force, to how attractive or how repulsive something is. In contrast, strength of engagement, as illustrated in Fig. 3.1, only contributes to the intensity of the value experience. However, this contribution can be important. Different truth and control factors can contribute to the intensity of the value experience through their impact on engagement strength, including regulatory fit (which I have already discussed), use of proper means, opposing interfering forces, and likelihood (for fuller reviews, see: Higgins 2007, 2012).

Strengthening engagement by using proper means

Regulatory fit represents one kind of control effectiveness that strengthens engagement—effective use of a manner of goal pursuit that sustains one current goal orientation (e.g., eager manner for a promotion orientation). Another kind of control effectiveness that strengthens engagement is the use of proper or appropriate means when pursuing a goal—pursuing the goal in the *right way*. There are common maxims that suggest that pursuing goals in the right way contributes to value beyond the pains and pleasures of goal pursuit outcomes: "It is not enough to do good; one must do it in the right way" or "What counts is not whether you win or lose, but how you play the game." But the use of proper means need not involve behaving in a moral or ethical way in order for it to contribute to value. For example, James March (1994), a major figure in organizational decision-making, has proposed that pursuing goals in an appropriate or proper way has its own relation to value creation, separate from just hedonic outcomes.

Consider, for instance, what happens when individuals choose between a coffee mug and a pen. Some people might believe that the proper or right way to make this choice would be to list the positive and negative properties of the mug, then list the positive and negative properties of the pen, look over each list, and then make the choice. Making the choice in this way would not traditionally be considered a moral or ethical issue. But it does involve our doing something in a proper or right way, and this can strengthen engagement in what we are doing. This stronger engagement in turn can intensify our attraction toward our ultimate choice—independent of the inherent properties of that choice. In recent studies we have investigated this possibility (see: Higgins et al. 2008).

Columbia undergraduates were asked to express their preference between a Columbia coffee mug and an inexpensive pen. As in our regulatory fit mug and pen study described earlier, we were only concerned with those participants who made the *same* choice—overwhelmingly the coffee mug. In one study, before the participants actually made their choice, they were randomly assigned to two different conditions that varied in what was emphasized about the decision. One condition emphasized the "Right Way"; it began with the title, "Making Your Decision in the RIGHT WAY!" and then continued as follows: "You need to make your decision in the *right way*. The right way to make a decision is to think about which choice has the better consequences. Think of the positive and negative consequences of choosing the mug. Think of the positive and negative consequences of choosing the pen. Please write down your thoughts on the lines below." The second condition emphasized the "Best Choice"; it began with the title, "The BEST CHOICE!" and then continued as follows: "The *best choice* is the choice with the better consequences. Think of the positive and negative consequences of owning the mug. Think of the positive and negative consequences of owning the pen. Please write down your thoughts on the lines below." Note that in both conditions the specific behaviors requested of the participants were exactly the same. What varied was whether those behaviors were perceived by the participants as making their decision in the right way (process) or as leading to the best future outcomes (outcome).

After considering the two options and expressing their preference, the participants were given the opportunity to buy the mug that they preferred. The study found that the participants in the *Right Way* condition offered much more money to buy the same chosen mug than participants in the *Best Choice* condition. But that was not all. This study also asked participants how much they agreed with three cultural maxims concerning the importance of pursuing goals in a proper way: "The end does not justify the means"; "What counts is not whether you win or lose, but how you play the game."; and (reverse coded) "To do it this way or that, it does not matter– results are all that count." Stronger engagement in the *Right Way* condition should only happen for those participants with strong beliefs in pursuing goals in a proper way. Indeed, for those participants with only weak beliefs, there was no significant difference between the *Right Way* and *Best Choice* conditions. But for participants with strong beliefs in pursuing goals in a proper way, the money offered to buy the mug was much higher in the *Right Way* condition than the *Best Choice* condition—$6.35 in the *Right Way* condition versus $2.61 in the *Best Choice* condition. Other findings also supported the conclusion that pursuing goals in the right way strengthens engagement in what we are doing, which intensifies attraction toward a positively valued object.

Strengthening engagement by opposing interfering forces

There is a third kind of control effectiveness that can strengthen engagement and intensify value—*opposing interfering forces*. My collaborators and I investigated this mechanism by examining different ways of dealing with adversity. It is common for people to confront difficulties while they pursue their goals. Obstacles in the path toward a goal have to be removed. Forces pushing back from the goal have to be resisted. Aversive background conditions must be dealt with. Higgins, Marguc, and Scholer (2012) investigated whether the direction of change in the value of a positive goal pursuit object (more attractive *vs.* less attractive) would depend on how people dealt with an adversity.

When people encounter adversity in goal pursuit, they can either redouble their focus on the task at hand—the kind of response to difficulty that Woodworth (1940) described as resistance, as illustrated by leaning into a wind that is impeding one's forward progress—or they can direct their attention away from the task at hand and attend instead to something else, such as their unpleasant feelings. More specifically, one way of dealing with an unpleasant background noise is to represent it as something that is interfering with the goal pursuit and must be opposed in order to succeed on the focal task. This "*opposing an interference*" response should strengthen engagement with the focal task activity, which would *increase* attraction toward a positive goal object. Alternatively, one could treat the background noise as something producing unpleasant feelings that must be coped with. This "*coping with a nuisance*" response should weaken engagement with the focal task, which would *decrease* attraction toward a positive goal object.

Supposedly to simulate real-world conditions in which people have to deal with unpleasant ambient noise while they are working, participants worked in the presence of an aversive background noise to solve enough anagrams to receive a prize. The noise was the same for everyone and consisted of a series of different animal sounds (e.g., birds, sheep, horse, bear). Participants in the "*opposing*" condition were told, "the background noise is something you will have to overcome in order to attend to the task," and "to do well on the task, you will need to overcome the distraction and oppose its interference." Participants in the "*coping*" condition were told, "the background noise is a bit of a nuisance to cope with. It is something that may cause you to feel a bit unpleasant—a feeling that you'll need to cope with." All participants won the lottery ticket for the prize. Participants then indicated how much they valued this prize.

At the end of the study, there was a surprise recognition task for the content of the background noise. This measure checked on whether the participants followed the instructions on what to attend to during the task. The more attention they paid to dealing with the adversity as instructed (whether it was opposing or coping), the worse their memory would be for the content of the background noise. For those participants who did pay attention as instructed, the value of the prize changed in opposite directions (as predicted): for those who paid attention to opposing the background noise as an interfering force (strengthening engagement in the focal anagram task), the positive value of the prize increased (intensified attraction); for those who paid attention to coping with the unpleasant feelings created by the background noise (weakening engagement in the focal anagram task), the positive value of the prize decreased (deintensified attraction).

What this research highlights is that adversities, although unpleasant, do not necessarily make positive things in life less positive. Adversities can have this diminishing effect when people deal with them by disengaging from what they are doing in order to cope with the unpleasant feelings produced by the adversities. Such disengagement would decrease the positivity of positive things. But if people instead oppose adversities as interfering forces and redouble their focus on what they are doing, i.e., strengthen their engagement, then dealing with adversities can actually make positive things in life even more positive. These findings extend current models of how obstacles affect value by providing evidence that *how* adversity is dealt with plays a critical role in whether adversity increases or decreases the value of something.

Strengthening engagement by using high likelihood expressions

Thus far I have considered how mechanisms of *control* effectiveness can intensify (or deintensify) the positive value of something through strengthening (or weakening) engagement. In this section I will describe how a mechanism of *truth* effectiveness can both intensify the positive value of a positive object *and* intensify the negative value of a negative object by strengthening *preparatory engagement* for something that will *really* happen.

The concept of likelihood holds a special place in psychology and other disciplines studying judgment and decision-making. In psychology and economics, the concept of likelihood is perhaps best known for its role within the model of *subjective expected utility* (SEU). This model assumes that the possible outcomes from taking some action are disjunctive; that is, the outcomes are *mutually exclusive* alternatives, joined by "or." In addition, the outcomes are *exhaustive*, capturing all of the possible outcomes. In the simple case of succeeding or failing on a task, success and failure as outcomes are mutually exclusive and exhaustive. There is a subjective probability of success and a subjective probability of failure, summing to 100 percent (see: Atkinson 1957).

In a SEU model, beliefs about the probability of a specific outcome are important because of the information they communicate about whether a particular future outcome is likely to occur, with the only *motivating* force (the pull) coming from the subjective value of that future outcome. In the SEU model, for example, when there are two possible future outcomes—"I will have cereal instead of eggs this morning" and "I will have eggs instead of cereal this morning"—a high probability of one outcome (e.g., 80 percent likelihood of having cereal) is *equivalent* to a low probability of the alternative outcome (e.g., 20 percent likelihood of having eggs). In this model, it is the future outcome that matters, and the probabilities are providing the *same information* about what will happen in the future; i.e., my having cereal is more likely to happen than my having eggs.

But what if subjective likelihood has a motivational force *in its own right* because it concerns another way of being effective—truth effectiveness? What if, as James (1948/1890) suggested, high subjective likelihood establishes something as real rather than imaginary?

If this were the case, then a subjective likelihood about a future event could contribute to value not only by providing information about whether *that* specific outcome is likely to happen in the future, but also by affecting strength of engagement *now—preparatory engagement for a future reality*. And this preparatory engagement could affect the value of something *else* in the *present* by intensifying current evaluative reactions. When individuals experience high likelihood, future outcomes feel real. And because they need to prepare now for something that will *really* happen, their engagement in what they are doing in the present is strengthened. And stronger engagement will intensify evaluative reactions to what they are doing now.

From this perspective, then, experiencing high likelihood of some future outcome, by strengthening engagement now, could affect the value of something else in the present. A recent research program investigated these implications (Higgins et al. 2013). In one study, undergraduates believed that they were participating in a marketing study for a new dairy company that was trying to decide what would become their newest flavor of yogurt. In the first part of the study, they tasted two different types of yogurt flavors (labeled A and B). One type of yogurt flavor was pre-tested to be good-tasting (flavored with sugar and nutmeg) and the other was pre-tested to be bad-tasting (flavored with clove). The participants were also told that in the second part of the study they would try either more concentrations of just type A yogurt or more concentrations of just type B yogurt. It will be either A or B.

The likelihood of later trying just Type A or just Type B was expressed using either a *high likelihood expression* (80 percent chance) or a *low likelihood expression* (20 percent chance). For example, if it was probable that participants would later try more concentrations of the good-tasting yogurt A, the high likelihood expression condition said "You have an 80 percent likelihood of later tasting concentrations of yogurt A," whereas the low likelihood expression condition said "You have a 20 percent likelihood of later tasting concentrations of yogurt B"—*different likelihood expressions* (80 percent A vs. 20 percent B) for the *same future probable event* (i.e., it is probable that they will later taste concentrations of yogurt A rather than yogurt B).

Regardless of whether the probability was about tasting the good yogurt in the future or the bad yogurt in the future, describing the future activity as a 80 percent likelihood intensified evaluative reactions to both yogurts in the present more than describing the future activity as a 20 percent likelihood—the good yogurt tasted even better and the bad yogurt tasted even worse when the future was expressed as an 80 percent likelihood of something happening. When the future is expressed as being likely to happen, people prepare for it in the present, and such preparation strengthens engagement in present activities, which intensifies evaluative responses to those activities (both positive and negative responses).

Conclusion

As a psychologist, I believe it is best to think of value as the experience of a force of attraction toward something or repulsion from something. Historically, this experience would be tied to the hedonic experiences of approaching pleasure and avoiding pain. But this hedonic viewpoint alone is problematic for three major reasons. First, what people find attractive or repulsive is not restricted to experiences of pleasure and pain. Indeed, they will take on pain for the sake of establishing what's real (truth) and managing what happens (control). Second, the hedonic viewpoint is silent on the critical difference between how the promotion and prevention systems approach pleasure and avoid pain, and this difference even changes whether the status quo "0" is experienced as positive or negative. Third, and perhaps most important, the hedonic viewpoint provides a very limited understanding of where value comes from. It fails to appreciate the importance for value of the fit or non-fit between different ways of being effective, and it ignores the contribution of engagement strength to the intensity of positive and negative value. Indeed, it cannot account for how a source of engagement strength that is hedonically unpleasant for everyone, such as an unpleasant background noise, can either decrease *or increase* the positive value of an object depending on whether the way of dealing with the adversity weakens or strengthens engagement in the object-related activity. Because of engagement strength, a person can currently feel good or bad and yet the value of *something else* can be intensified in the opposite direction of how they feel.

Acknowledgment

The research by the author and his collaborators that is reported in this chapter, as well as the writing of this chapter, was supported by Grant 39429 from the National Institute of Mental Health to E. Tory Higgins.

References

Atkinson, J. W. (1957). Motivational determinants of risk-taking behavior. *Psychological Review*, **64**, 359–372.

Atkinson, J. W. (1964). An introduction to motivation. Princeton, N. J.: D. Van Nostrand.

Bandura, A. (1986). *Social foundations of thought and action: A social cognitive theory*. Englewood Cliffs, N.J.: Prentice-Hall.

Bentham, J. (1988). *The principles of morals and legislation*. Amherst, New York: Prometheus Books. (Originally published, 1781)

Boldero, J. and Francis, J. (2002). Goals, standards, and the self: Reference values serving different functions. *Personality and Social Psychology Review*, **6**, 232–241.

Brendl, C. M. and Higgins, E. T. (1996). Principles of judging valence: What makes events positive or negative? In M. P. Zanna (ed.), *Advances in experimental social psychology* (vol. 28, pp. 95–160). New York: Academic Press.

Brockner, J. (2010). *A contemporary look at organizational justice: Multiplying insult times injury*. New York: Routledge.

Carder, B. and Berkowitz, K. (1970). Rats' preference for earned in comparison with free food. *Science*, **167**, 1273–1274.

Carver, C. S. and Scheier, M. F. (1981). *Attention and self-regulation: A control-theory approach to human behavior*. New York: Springer-Verlag.

Carver, C. S. and Scheier, M. F. (1990). Origins and functions of positive and negative affect: A control-process view. *Psychological Review*, **97**, 19–35.

Cornwell, J. F. M. and Higgins, E. T. (2013). Morality and its relation to political ideology: The role of promotion and prevention concerns. *Personality and Social Psychology Bulletin*, **39**, 1164–1172.

Duval, S., and Wicklund, R. A. (1972). *A theory of objective self-awareness*. New York: Academic Press.

Eagly, A. H. and Chaiken, S. (1993). *The psychology of attitudes*. New York: Harcourt Brace Jovanovich.

Edwards, W. (1955). The prediction of decisions among bets. *Journal of Experimental Psychology*, **51**, 201–214.

Eisenberger, R. (1972). Explanation of rewards that do not reduce tissue needs. *Psychological Bulletin*, **77**, 319–339.

Festinger, L. (1957). *A theory of cognitive dissonance*. Evanston, Ill.: Row, Peterson.

Franks, B. and Higgins, E. T. (2012). Effectiveness in humans and other animals: A common basis for well-being and welfare. M. P. Zanna and J. M. Olson (eds), *Advances in Experimental Social Psychology*, **46**, pp. 285–346. New York: Academic Press.

Freud, S. (1950). *Beyond the pleasure principle*. New York: Liveright. (Original work published 1920.)

Gray, J. A. (1982). *The neuropsychology of anxiety: An enquiry into the functions of the septo-hippocampal system*. New York: Oxford University Press.

Haidt, J. and Graham, J. (2007). When morality opposes justice: Conservatives have moral intuitions liberals may not recognize. *Social Justice Research*, **20**, 98–116.

Heider, F. (1958). *The psychology of interpersonal relations*. New York: Wiley.

Higgins, E. T. (1987). Self-discrepancy: A theory relating self and affect. *Psychological Review*, **94**, 319–340.

Higgins, E. T. (1989). Self-discrepancy theory: What patterns of self-beliefs cause people to suffer? In L. Berkowitz (ed.), *Advances in experimental social psychology* (vol. 22, pp. 93–136). New York: Academic Press.

Higgins, E. T. (1991). Development of self-regulatory and self-evaluative processes: Costs, benefits, and tradeoffs. In M. R. Gunnar and L. A. Sroufe (Eds.), *Self processes and development: The Minnesota symposia on child psychology*, Volume **23**, (pp. 125–165) Hillsdale, N.J.: Erlbaum.

Higgins, E. T. (1996). The "self digest": Self-knowledge serving self-regulatory functions. *Journal of Personality and Social Psychology*, **71**, 1062–1083.

Higgins, E. T. (1997). Beyond pleasure and pain. *American Psychologist*, **52**, 1280–1300.

Higgins, E. T. (1998). Promotion and prevention: Regulatory focus as a motivational principle. In M. P. Zanna (Ed.), *Advances in experimental social psychology* (vol. 30, pp. 1–46). New York: Academic Press.

Higgins, E. T. (2000). Making a good decision: Value from fit. *American Psychologist*, **55**, 1217–1230.

Higgins, E. T. (2006). Value from hedonic experience *and* engagement. *Psychological Review*, **113**, 439–460.

Higgins, E. T. (2007). Value. In A. W. Kruglanski and E. T. Higgins (eds), *Social psychology: Handbook of basic principles*, 2nd edition (pp. 454–472). New York: Guilford.

Higgins, E. T. (2012). *Beyond pleasure and pain: How motivation works*. New York: Oxford University Press.

Higgins, E. T. (2013). Truth motivation. In K. D. Markman, T. Proulx, and M. J. Lindberg (ed.), *The psychology of meaning* (pp. 91–114). Washington D. C.: American Psychological Association.

Higgins, E. T. (2014). Promotion and prevention: How "0" can create dual motivational forces. In J. Sherman, B. Gawronski, and Y. Trope (eds), *Dual-process theories of the social mind*. New York: Guilford Press.

Higgins, E. T., Camacho, C. J., Idson, L. C., Spiegel, S., and Scholer, A. A. (2008). How making the same decision in a "proper way" creates value. *Social Cognition*, **26**, 496–514.

Higgins, E. T., Franks, B., Pavarini, D., Sehnert, S., and Manley, K. (2013). *Expressed* likelihood as motivator: Creating value through engaging what's real. *Journal of Economic Psychology*, **38**, 4–15.

Higgins, E. T., Idson, L. C., Freitas, A. L., Spiegel, S., and Molden, D. C. (2003). Transfer of value from fit. *Journal of Personality and Social Psychology*, **84**, 1140–1153.

Higgins, E. T., Marguc, J., and Scholer, A. A. (2012). Value from adversity: *How* we deal with adversity matters. *Journal of Experimental Social Psychology*, **48**, 965–967.

Higgins, E.T. and Scholer, A. A., (2009). Engaging the consumer: The science and art of the value creation process. Journal of Consumer Psychology. , **19**, 100–114.

Higgins, E. T. and Tykocinski, O. (1992). Self-discrepancies and biographical memory: Personality and cognition at the level of psychological situation. *Personality and Social Psychology Bulletin*, **18**, 527–535.

James, W. (1948). *The principles of psychology*. New York: The World Publishing Company. (Original publication, 1890.)

James, W. (1948). *Psychology*. New York: The World Publishing Company. (Original publication, 1890.)

Kahneman, D. (2000). Experienced utility and objective happiness: A moment-based approach. In D. Kahneman and A. Tversky (eds), *Choices, values, and frames* pp. (673–692). New York: Cambridge University Press.

Kahneman, D., Diener, E., and Schwarz, N. (1999). *Well-being: The foundations of hedonic psychology*. New York: Russell Sage.

Kahneman, D. and Tversky, A. (1979). Prospect theory: An analysis of decision under risk. *Econometrica*, **47**, 263–291.

Kruglanski, A. W., Thompson, E. P., Higgins, E. T., Atash, M. N., Pierro, A., Shah, J. Y., and Spiegel, S. (2000). To "do the right thing" or to "just do it": Locomotion and assessment as distinct self-regulatory imperatives. *Journal of Personality & Social Psychology*, **79**, 793–815.

Lazarus, R. S., (1993). From psychological stress to the emotions: A history of changing outlooks, **44**, 1–21.

Lee, A. Y., Aaker, J. L., and Gardner, W. L. (2000). The pleasures and pains of distinct self-construals: The role of interdependence in regulatory focus. *Journal of Personality and Social Psychology*, **78**, 1122–1134.

Lewin, K. (1951). *Field theory in social science*. New York: Harper.

Lewin, K., Dembo, T., Festinger, L., and Sears, P. S. (1944). Level of aspiration. In J. McHunt (Ed.), *Personality and the behavior disorders* (Vol. **1**, pp. 333–378). New York: Ronald Press.

March, J. G. (1994). *A primer on decision making: How decisions happen*. New York: Free Press.

Merton, R. K. (1957). *Social theory and social structure*. Glencoe, Ill.: The Free Press.

Miller, G. A., Galanter, E., and Pribram, K. H. (1960). *Plans and the structure of behavior*. New York: Holt, Rinehart, and Winston.

Moretti, M. M. and Higgins, E. T. (1999). Own versus other standpoints in self-regulation: Developmental antecedents and functional consequences. *Review of General Psychology*, **3**, 188–223.

Mowrer, O.H. (1960). *Learning theory and behavior*. New York: John Wiley.

Nozick, R. (1974). *Anarchy, state, and utopia*. New York: Basic Books.

Olds, J. and P. Milner (1954). Positive reinforcement produced by electrical stimulation of septal area and other regions of rat brain. *Journal of Comparative and Physiological Psychology*. **47**, 419–427.

Ortony, A., Clore, G. L., and Collins, A. (1988). *The cognitive structure of emotions*. New York: Cambridge University Press.

Powers, W. T. (1973) *Behavior: The control of perception*. Chicago: Aldine.

Rogers, C. R. (1961). *On becoming a person*. Boston: Houghton Mifflin Company.

Rokeach, M. (1973). *The nature of human values*. New York: Free Press.

Rokeach, M. (1980). Some unresolved issues in theories of beliefs, attitudes, and values. In H. E. Howe, Jr. and M. M. Page (eds), *1979 Nebraska symposium on motivation*. Lincoln: University of Nebraska Press.

Roseman, I. J. (1984). Cognitive determinants of emotion: A structural theory. *Review of Personality and Social Psychology*, **5**, 11–36.

Schwartz, S. H. (1992). Universals in the content and structure of values: Theoretical advances and empirical tests in 20 countries. In M. P. Zanna (ed.), *Advances in experimental social psychology* (vol. 25, pp. 1–65). New York: Academic Press.

Schwartz, S. H. and Bilsky, W. (1987). Toward a universal structure of human values. *Journal of Personality and Social Psychology*, **53**, 550–562.

Seligman, C., Olson, J. M., and Zanna, M. P. (1996). *The psychology of values: The Ontario Symposium*, vol. 8. Mahwah, New Jersey: Lawrence Erlbaum Associates.

Thibaut, J. W. and Walker, L. (1975). *Procedural justice: A psychological analysis*. Hillsdale, NJ: Erlbaum.

Thorndike, E. L. (1935). *The psychology of wants, interests, and attitudes*. New York: Appleton-Century-Crofts.

Tyler, T. R. and Lind, E. A. (1992). A relational model of authority in groups. In M. P. Zanna (ed.), *Advances in experimental social psychology* (vol. 25, pp. 115–192). New York: Academic Press.

Webster's Ninth New Collegiate Dictionary (1989). Springfield, MA: Merriam-Webster.

Weiner, B. (1972). *Theories of motivation: From mechanism to cognition*. Chicago: Rand McNally.

Wiener, N. (1948). *Cybernetics: Control and communication in the animal and the machine*. Cambridge, MA: M.I.T. Press.

Woodworth, R. S. (1918). *Dynamic psychology*. New York: Columbia University Press.

Woodworth, R. S. (1940). *Psychology*, 4th edition. New York: Henry Holt and Company.

Woodworth, R. S. and Schlosberg, H. (1954). *Experimental psychology*, revised edition. New York: Holt, Rinehart, and Winston.

Chapter 4

Basic individual values: sources and consequences

Shalom H. Schwartz

Introduction

Values have been a central concept in the social sciences since their inception. For both Durkheim (1893) and Weber (1905), values were crucial for explaining social and personal organization and change. Values play an important role not only in sociology, but in psychology, anthropology, and related disciplines as well. Values are used to characterize societies and individuals, to trace change over time, and to explain the motivational bases of attitudes and behavior.

Despite the widespread use of values, many different conceptions of this construct have emerged (e.g., Boudon 2001; Inglehart 1997; Kohn 1969; Parsons 1951; Rokeach 1973). Application of the values construct in the social sciences has suffered, however, from the absence of an agreed-upon conception of basic values, of the content and structure of relations among these values, and of reliable empirical methods to measure them (Hitlin and Piliavin 2004; Rohan 2000).

This chapter presents the current, dominant theory of individual differences in values in social psychology and sociology that has addressed these issues (Schwartz 1992). For this and related theories, value is in the eye of the beholder, not in the object of perception (Inglehart 1997; Rokeach 1973). Values are broad, motivational constructs that express what is important to people. Based on their values, individuals view different acts, objects, people, and events as more or less valuable. People's values are central to their identities and concepts of self (Hitlin 2003; Rokeach 1973).

The Schwartz theory concerns the basic or core values that people in all cultures recognize. It defines values as desirable, trans-situational goals, varying in importance, that serve as guiding principles in people's lives (cf. Kluckhohn 1951; Rokeach 1973). It identifies ten motivationally distinct values and specifies the dynamic relations among them. Some values conflict with one another (e.g., stimulation and security), whereas others are compatible (e.g., conformity and tradition). The "structure" of values refers to these relations of conflict and congruence among values. Values are structured in similar ways across culturally diverse groups. This suggests that there is a universal organization of human motivations. Although the nature of values and their structure may be universal, individuals and groups differ substantially in the relative importance they attribute to the values. That is, individuals and groups have different value "priorities" or "hierarchies."

This chapter explicates the theory of personal values and describes the distinct values it identifies. It examines why the pattern of relations among different values may be universal. It discusses mechanisms through which values influence decisions and behavior, brings examples of the relations of value priorities to behavior and attitudes, and provides an overview of the origins of individual differences in values and of value change.

The theory of value contents and structure

Defining basic values

When we think of our values, we think of what is important to us in life. Each person holds numerous values (e.g., achievement, security, benevolence) with varying degrees of importance. A particular value may be very important to one person but unimportant to another. The value theory adopts a conception of values that specifies six main features implicit in the writings of many theorists:

(1) *Values are beliefs* linked inextricably to affect. When values are activated, they become infused with feeling. People for whom independence is an important value become aroused if their independence is threatened, despair when they are helpless to protect it, and are happy when they can enjoy it.

(2) *Values refer to desirable goals* that motivate action. People for whom social order, justice, and helpfulness are important values are motivated to pursue these goals.

(3) *Values transcend specific actions and situations.* Obedience and honesty, for example, are values that may be relevant at work, in school, in the family, in sports, business, or politics. This feature distinguishes values from narrower concepts like norms and attitudes that usually refer to specific actions, objects, or situations.

(4) *Values serve as standards or criteria.* Values guide selection and evaluation of actions, policies, people, and events. People decide what is good or bad, justified or illegitimate, worth doing or avoiding, based on possible consequences for their cherished values. But the impact of values in everyday decisions is rarely conscious. Values enter awareness when the actions or judgments one is considering have conflicting implications for different values one cherishes.

(5) *Values are ordered by relative importance.* People's values form an ordered system of priorities that characterize them as individuals. Do they attribute more importance to freedom or equality, to novelty or tradition? This hierarchical feature also distinguishes values from norms and attitudes.

(6) *The* relative *importance of multiple values guides action.* Any attitude or behavior typically has implications for more than one value. For example, attending church might express and promote tradition, conformity, and security values at the expense of hedonism and stimulation values. The tradeoff among relevant, competing values guides

attitudes and behaviors (Schwartz 1992, 1996; cf. Lewin 1947). Values contribute to action to the extent that they are relevant in the context (hence likely to be activated) and important to the actor.

The above are features of *all* values. These features tell us nothing, however, about the substantive content of values—what different types of values there are. What distinguishes one value from another is the type of goal or motivation that the value expresses. Dictionaries include thousands of specific value concepts. There are, therefore, significant theoretical and practical advantages to identifying a limited set of basic values that various human groups recognize and use to form priorities. The value theory defines ten broad values according to the motivation that underlies each one. Presumably, these values encompass the range of motivationally distinct values recognized across cultures. According to the theory, these values are likely to be universal because they are grounded in one or more of three universal requirements of human existence with which they help to cope. These requirements are needs of individuals as biological organisms, requisites of coordinated social interaction, and survival and welfare needs of groups.

People cannot cope successfully with these requirements of human existence alone. To cope with them, people must articulate appropriate goals, communicate with others about them, and gain cooperation in their pursuit. Values are the socially desirable concepts used to represent the goals mentally and the vocabulary used to express them in social interaction. From an evolutionary viewpoint (Buss 1986), these goals and the values that express them have crucial survival significance.

The motivational content of basic values

I next define ten basic values in terms of the broad goals they express, note their grounding in universal requirements, and mention related value concepts. To make the meaning of each value more concrete and explicit, I list in parentheses a few of the value items used to measure it.

- *Security*: safety, harmony, and stability of society, of relationships, and of self. Security values derive from individual and group survival requirements (cf. Kluckhohn 1951; Maslow 1965; Williams 1968). There are two subtypes of security values. One serves primarily individual interests (e.g., avoiding danger), the other wider group interests (e.g., strong country); (social order, personal safety, national security).
- *Conformity*: restraint of actions, inclinations, and impulses likely to upset or harm others and violate social expectations or norms. Conformity values derive from the requirement to inhibit inclinations that might disrupt and undermine smooth interaction and group functioning. Virtually all value analyses mention conformity (e.g., Freud 1930; Kohn and Schooler 1983; Morris 1956; Parsons 1951); (obedience, politeness, honoring parents and elders).
- *Tradition*: respect, commitment, and acceptance of the customs and ideas that one's culture or religion provides. All groups develop practices, symbols, ideas, and beliefs that represent their shared experience and fate. These become sanctioned as valued

traditions that symbolize the group's solidarity, express its unique worth, and contribute to its survival (Durkheim 1912/1954; Parsons 1951). They often take the form of religious rites, beliefs, and norms of behavior; (respect for tradition, humble, devout).

Tradition and conformity values are especially close motivationally, sharing the goal of subordinating the self in favor of socially imposed expectations. They differ primarily in the objects to which one subordinates the self. Conformity entails subordination to persons with whom one is in frequent interaction—parents, teachers, bosses. Tradition entails subordination to more abstract objects—religious and cultural customs and ideas.

- *Benevolence*: preserving and enhancing the welfare of those with whom one identifies personally (the "in-group"). Benevolence values derive from the basic requirement for smooth group functioning (cf. Kluckhohn 1951; Williams 1968) and from the organismic need for affiliation (cf. Korman 1974; Maslow 1965). Most critical are relations within the family and other primary groups. Benevolence values emphasize voluntary concern for others' welfare; (helpfulness, honesty, loyalty, love).

Benevolence and conformity values both promote cooperative social relations. However, benevolence values provide an internalized motivational base for such behavior. In contrast, conformity values promote cooperation in order to avoid negative outcomes for self. Both values may motivate the same helpful act, separately or together.

- *Universalism*: understanding, appreciation, tolerance, and protection for the welfare of *all* people and for nature. This contrasts with the in-group focus of benevolence values. Universalism values derive from survival needs of individuals and groups. Recognizing these needs only ensues after encountering others beyond the extended primary group and after becoming aware of the scarcity of natural resources. People may then realize that failure to accept others who are different and to treat them justly can lead to life-threatening strife and that failure to protect the natural environment can lead to the destruction of the resources on which life depends. Universalism values entail concern for the welfare of those in the larger society and world and for nature; (justice, equality, world peace, protecting the environment).
- *Self-direction*—independent thought and action—choosing, creating, exploring. Self-direction values derive from organismic needs for control and mastery (e.g., Bandura 1977; Deci 1975) and interactional requirements of autonomy and independence (e.g., Kluckhohn 1951; Kohn and Schooler 1983; Morris 1956); (creativity, freedom, curious, independent).
- *Stimulation*: excitement, novelty, and challenge in life. Stimulation values derive from the organismic need for variety and stimulation in order to maintain an optimal, positive, rather than threatening, level of activation (e.g., Berlyne 1960). This need probably relates to the needs underlying self-direction values (cf. Deci 1975); (variety, excitement, adventure).
- *Hedonism*: pleasure or sensuous gratification. Hedonism values derive from organismic needs and the pleasure associated with satisfying them. Theorists from many

disciplines (e.g., Freud 1933; Morris 1956; Williams 1968) mention hedonism; (pleasure, enjoying life, fun).[1]

- *Achievement*: personal success through demonstrating competence according to social standards. Competent performance that generates resources is necessary for individuals to survive and for groups and institutions to reach their objectives. Many sources mention achievement values (e.g., Maslow 1965; Rokeach 1973). My conceptualization of achievement values emphasizes competence as defined by prevailing cultural standards, thereby obtaining social approval; (ambitious, successful, capable, influential).[2]
- *Power*: control or dominance over people and resources. The functioning of social institutions apparently requires some degree of power differentiation (Parsons 1951). Most empirical analyses of interpersonal relations, both within and across cultures, yield a dominance/submission dimension (Lonner 1980). To justify this fact of social life and to motivate group members to accept it, groups must treat power as a value. Power values may also be transformations of individual needs for dominance and control (Korman 1974); (authority, wealth, social power).

Both power and achievement values promote maintaining or gaining advantage for self. However, achievement values seek the prestige or status that others confer in response to performance, whereas power values seek control of resources to exercise influence independent of others (cf. Hays 2013). Achievement values (e.g., ambition) emphasize actively demonstrating successful performance in concrete interaction, whereas power values (e.g., authority) emphasize attaining or preserving a dominant position within the more general social system.

The dynamic structure of value relations

The central postulate of the value theory is that values represent a circular continuum of related motivations, like the circular continuum of colors, rather than a set of discrete motivations. Figure 4.1 portrays the circular structure of relations among the values. Each value is a fuzzy set that blends gradually into the adjacent values. Substantial evidence supports dividing the motivational circle into ten values (e.g., Bilsky, Janik, and Schwartz 2011; Fontaine et al. 2008; Schwartz 1994; Schwartz and Boehnke 2004), but doing so is actually a scientific convenience. It is sometimes more effective to divide the circle into four broader values or into as many as nineteen more narrowly defined values (Schwartz et al. 2012). Research in over eighty countries, using five different measuring instruments, largely confirms the circular motivational continuum (Cieciuch et al. 2013b), although it is not always possible to discriminate all of the values (e.g., Davidov et al. 2008).

---

1 Happiness is not included as a basic value, despite its importance, because its motivational direction is not distinct. People pursue happiness through seeking to attain whichever distinct goals they value highly (Sagiv and Schwartz 2000).

2 Achievement values differ from McClelland's (1961) achievement motivation. Achievement motivation concerns meeting internal standards of excellence. It is expressed in self-direction values.

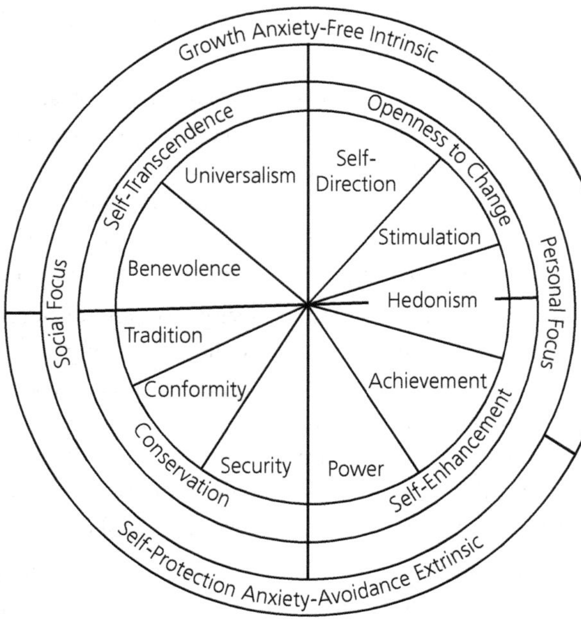

Fig. 4.1 The circular motivational continuum of ten values in the Schwartz (1992) theory.

Why do values form this [near-] universal structure? There are several dynamic sources. A first organizing principle is that actions in pursuit of any value have consequences that conflict with some values but are congruent with others. For example, pursuing novelty and change (stimulation values) typically conflicts with preserving time-honored customs (tradition values). In contrast, pursuing tradition values is congruent with pursuing conformity values. Both motivate actions of submission to external expectations.

Actions in pursuit of values have practical, psychological, and social consequences. Practically, choosing an action alternative that promotes one value (e.g., participating in a cultic rite—stimulation) may literally contravene or violate a competing value (obeying religious precepts—tradition). Psychologically, the person choosing between such actions may also sense that the alternative actions are cognitively dissonant. And social sanctions may ensue when others point to practical and logical inconsistencies between an action and other values the person professes. Of course, people can and do pursue competing values, but not in a single act. Rather, they do so through different acts, at different times, and in different settings.

Viewing values as organized along two bipolar dimensions lets us summarize the oppositions between competing values. The second circle from the center of Fig. 4.1 shows these dimensions. The "*openness to change*" versus "*conservation*" values dimension captures the conflict between values that emphasize independence of thought, action, and feelings and readiness for change (self-direction, stimulation) and values that emphasize order, self-restriction, preservation of the past, and resistance to change (security, conformity, tradition). The "*self-enhancement*" versus "*self-transcendence*" values dimension captures the conflict between values that emphasize concern for the welfare and interests of others (universalism, benevolence) and values that emphasize pursuit of one's own interests and relative success and dominance over others (power, achievement). Hedonism shares elements of both openness to change and self-enhancement, but it is typically closer to openness to change.

A second principle that organizes the value circle is the interests that value attainment serves. Values on the left of Fig. 4.1 primarily regulate how one expresses personal interests and characteristics. Values on the right primarily regulate how one relates socially to others and affects their interests.

Relations of values to anxiety are a third organizing principle. Values in the bottom part of the circle are based in the need to avoid or control anxiety and threat and to protect the self (Schwartz 2006, 2010). Conservation values (bottom left) emphasize avoiding conflict, unpredictability, and change by submission and passive acceptance of the status quo. Power values (bottom right) emphasize overcoming anxiety by actively controlling threat. In contrast, values in the top part of the circle are relatively anxiety free, expressing growth and self-expansion. Self-transcendence values (top left) emphasize promoting the welfare of others. Openness to change values (top right) emphasize autonomous, self-expressive experience. Achievement values do both: Achieving may control anxiety by meeting social standards and may affirm one's sense of competence and express the self.

This third aspect of the value structure relates to Higgins' (1997) two basic self-regulation systems. One system regulates avoidance of punishment and focuses people on preventing loss. Security needs, obligations, and the threat of loss trigger this system. Values in the bottom part of the circle, most centrally security and conformity, motivate this type of self-regulation. The second system regulates pursuit of rewards and focuses people on promoting gain. Nurturance needs, ideals, and opportunities to gain trigger this system. Values on the top of the circle, most centrally self-direction, motivate this type of self-regulation.

This aspect of the value structure also relates to the distinction between intrinsic and extrinsic motivation (e.g., Ryan and Deci 2000). Values in the bottom part of Fig. 4.1 largely express extrinsic motivation: Attainment of these values is contingent on obtaining social approval and material rewards (power and part of achievement), on meeting the expectations of others and avoiding the sanctions they may impose (conformity, tradition), or on receiving protection and care (security). Values on the top largely express intrinsic motivation: Behavior based on these values is rewarding in itself, providing satisfaction or pleasure through expressing autonomy and competence (openness) or nurturance and relatedness (self-transcendence).

Evidence is beginning to accumulate that a biological substratum underlies the psychological processes that account for the motivational value circle. Research by Brosch et al. (2011) suggests that basic neural reward mechanisms may mirror decision-making on the two major value dimensions of self-transcendence vs. self-enhancement and of openness to change vs. conservation. When individuals engaged in a donation task or a GO/NOGO task, activation of different parts of the brain reflected individual differences in value priorities on each dimension.

Relating value priorities to other variables

Most past research on antecedents and consequences of values examined empirical relations between a few target values and a particular background variable, attitude, or behavior (e.g., obedience and social class—Alwin 1984; equality and civil rights—Rokeach 1973). The value theory enables us to treat peoples' value systems as coherent structures and, thus, to systematically relate the full set of values to other variables. Conceiving values as organized in a circular motivational structure implies that any background variable, behavior, or attitude that is especially congruent with one basic value (e.g., military intervention with power) should also be relatively congruent with the adjacent values (security and achievement) but conflict with the opposing values (universalism, benevolence, and self-direction). Thus, the entire integrated structure of values relates systematically to other variables.

A second implication of the circular motivational structure of values is that associations of values with other variables should decrease monotonically in both directions around the circle from the most positively to the most negatively (or least positively) associated value. That is, the order of associations for the whole set of ten values follows a predictable pattern. If a background variable, trait, attitude, or behavior correlates most positively with one value and most negatively with another, the circular value structure largely determines the pattern of associations with all other values.

The data in Table 4.1, based on representative national samples from twenty-seven countries, illustrate this pattern. The table lists the values in their order around the circular structure of value relations (cf. Fig. 4.1). The correlations for age, gender, and education exhibit both features of value relations. Adjacent values have similar associations with the background variables and the associations of the values tend to decrease monotonically in both directions around the circle from the most positively to the most negatively associated value. The integrated structure of values facilitates theorizing about relations of the whole set of value priorities to other variables. If theory identifies the values likely to relate most and least positively to a variable, the circular motivational structure suggests the specific pattern of positive, negative, and zero associations for the remaining values.[3]

The integrated structure provides a template that reveals "deviations" from the expected pattern. For example, security values relate more strongly to gender than expected based on the circular order. An evolutionary explanation of this deviation might suggest that women differ more from men in their priority for security than for the other conservation values because women need to protect themselves and their infants during the vulnerable period of early child rearing. This maximizes their return on their heavy investment in pregnancy, nursing, and caring for infants. A social role explanation might suggest that women's smaller size, lower status, and greater dependence on others' support in most societies make them more vulnerable than men and raises security concerns. Deviations are

[3] See Schwartz (2006) for theorizing about relations of values to age, gender, and education.

Table 4.1 Correlations of values with age, gender, and education in representative national samples from the twenty-seven countries in rounds 1 and 2 of the European Social Survey

Value	**Age (N = 79,700)**	**Gender (Female) (N = 80,050)**	**Years of Education (N = 79,200)**
Security	0.25 (27)	0.12 (27)	−0.20 (27)
Conformity	0.33 (27)	0.03 (17)	−0.18 (27)
Tradition	0.34 (27)	0.09 (27)	−0.25 (27)
Benevolence	0.13 (26)	0.16 (27)	0.01 (6)†
Universalism	0.17 (27)	0.12 (27)	0.07 (21)
Self-direction	−0.08 (25)	−0.06 (25)	0.23 (27)
Stimulation	−0.38 (27)	−0.09 (27)	0.16 (27)
Hedonism	−0.32 (27)	−0.07 (22)	0.10 (27)
Achievement	−0.27 (27)	−0.12 (27)	0.10 (27)
Power	−0.10 (26)	−0.13 (25)	−0.02 (17)

All correlations differ from zero, $p<0.001$, 2-tailed, except benevolence x years of education.

The number of countries whose correlation is in the signed direction appears in parentheses.

Due to missing data, the number of respondents varies slightly around the indicated *N*s.

especially interesting because they direct us to search for special conditions that enhance or weaken relations of a variable with values (Schwartz 1996).

Mechanisms linking values to behavior

Although many factors typically influence any specific behavior, values are often an important contributing factor. Several mechanisms link values to behavior (Bardi and Schwartz 2003; Schwartz 2010). First, in order for values to exert influence they must be activated. Values that are more accessible are more likely to be activated. Because values that are more important are more accessible (Bardi 2000), they are more often activated and exert more influence. Activation experiments are particularly important because they show that values can *cause* behavior (cf. Sagiv et al. 2011).

Second, values must be experienced as relevant to the behavior in question. Because basic values are abstract, their relevance is often not obvious. People may see equality, for example, as relevant to discrimination based on gender but not on weight. Abstract values relate more consistently to people's behavior if they know specific ways to express them in real-life situations (Maio 2010). Experiments show that values influence behavior more strongly when people have previously thought about tangible or typical applications of those values.

Third, values influence behavior because they motivate people to pursue valued goals. For example, people vote for parties whose platforms facilitate attaining the values they cherish and against parties whose platforms threaten these values (Caprara et al. 2006). Put differently, people's values determine the valence they assign to the consequences of any action. Actions are more attractive to the extent that they promote or protect valued goals. High-priority values are central to the self-concept. Sensing an opportunity to attain them sets off an automatic, positive, affective response to actions that will serve them. Sensing a threat to value attainment sets off a negative affective response.

Value-based assessments of potential choices typically occur outside conscious awareness. They tend to enter awareness when the alternatives entail high costs or have conflicting implications for values one cherishes. "Value-expressive behaviors" are behaviors primarily compatible with one value and incompatible with the opposing values in the circle (Bardi and Schwartz 2003). Values predict them well. Power values predict manipulative behaviors and stimulation values predict risky behaviors, for example. But values predict "value-ambivalent behaviors," behaviors compatible with mutually conflicting values, more poorly (Lönnqvist et al. 2013). For example, the conflicting values of conformity and stimulation might both motivate agreeing to friends' pressuring to skydive, making it difficult to predict.

Fourth, value importance influences behavior through planning (Gollwitzer 1996). The more important a value, the more likely people are to form action plans to express it. Planning focuses people on the pros of desired actions rather than the cons. It increases people's belief in their ability to reach a valued goal, their persistence in the face of obstacles and distractions, and their belief in the desirability of the goal. By promoting planning, value importance increases value-consistent behavior.

Finally, values influence behavior by affecting what people attend to and perceive, and how they interpret situations. People attend more to the aspects of situations that threaten or offer opportunities to attain cherished values. Depending on their value priorities, they may perceive a job offer as an opportunity for greater self-direction or as a threat to security. They may interpret such an offer as a chance to help their family or a chance to gain power. Each value-based perception or interpretation promotes a different line of action.

Values as predictors of behavior and attitudes

The circular value structure implies that, if values on one side of the circle motivate a behavior or attitude, values on the other side of the circle oppose it. A study of voting in the Italian national elections of 2001 illustrates this. Two main coalitions, center-right and center-left, contested the election. The center-right emphasized policies compatible with power and security values—entrepreneurship, the market economy, security, and family and national values. These policies conflicted with the opposing universalism values that call for promoting the welfare of others, such as the weak and poor, those most likely to suffer from market-driven policies. In contrast, the center-left advocated policies compatible with universalism values—social welfare, social justice, equality, and tolerance, even of groups that might disturb the conventional social order—policies incompatible with pursuing individual power and security values.

For citizens who recognized these policy differences, the political choice was a tradeoff between power and security values on the right and universalism values on the left. Supporting the center-right vs. center-left should therefore correlate most positively with people's priority for power and security values and most negatively with their priority for universalism values. The value circle implies an integrated pattern of correlations that should decline from most positive for power and security values to most negative for universalism values in both directions around the circle (cf. Fig. 4.1). This pattern was confirmed in a sample of adults from the Rome region.

Column 1 of Table 4.2 lists the point-biserial correlations of voting for the center right with the ten values, controlling gender, age, income, and education. The correlations were most positive with power values and most negative with universalism values and decreased going around the circle from power to universalism in both directions. Figure 4.2 portrays the pattern for voting graphically, a sinusoidal curve that reflects the motivational continuum of values. To put the strength of these correlations in perspective, note that individuals' income, occupation, education, gender, marital status, and age all correlated less than 0.08 with voting. Moreover, values explained almost three times as much variance in voting as did the Big Five personality traits (Caprara et al. 2006).

Numerous studies of observed behavior in laboratory games also illustrate the tradeoffs between competing values in guiding behavioral choice. Typically, the consequences of a behavior promote the expression or attainment of one set of values at the expense of the opposing values in the circle. To understand and predict the behavior, we must consider the importance of the values the behavior thwarts, as well as those it promotes. Whether a behavior occurs depends on the relative priority of the competing values that a person experiences as relevant.

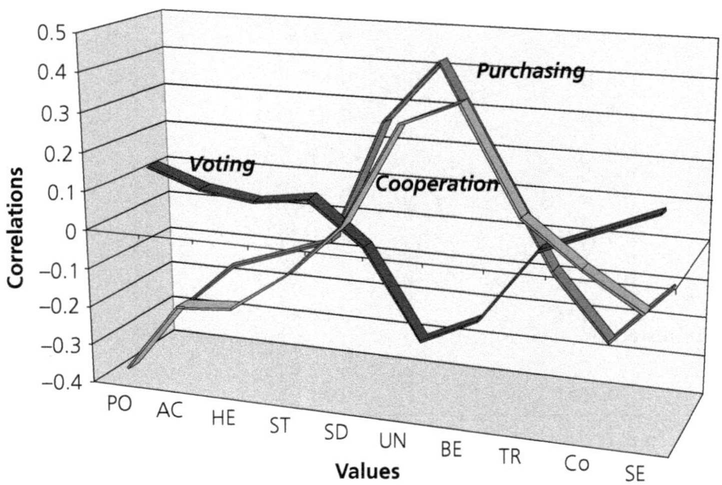

Fig. 4.2 Correlations between value priorities and three behaviors. (See Plate 1.)

In the first published laboratory game that applied the value theory (Schwartz 1996), pairs of participants chose among three alternatives for allocating money between self and a partner. Each received the amount of money they allocated to self plus the amount their partner allocated to them. The cooperative choice entailed sacrificing a little of what they could gain and giving the maximum possible to their partner. The other two choices were not cooperative. They entailed maximizing either one's own absolute or relative gain.

Both players were from the same group, but did not know their partner's identity. Benevolence values were more relevant to cooperation than universalism values in this setting because cooperation was more a matter of decency and thoughtfulness than of commitment to social justice. Power values, opposed in the circle, were most relevant to noncooperation because they emphasize competitive advantage and legitimize maximizing own gain at the expense of others. The correlations for cooperation in column 2 of Table 4.2 and in Fig. 4.2 reveal the expected pattern. Benevolence correlated most positively with cooperation, power most negatively, and correlations with the other values showed the sinusoidal pattern corresponding to their order around the value circle.

Another way of analyzing the data demonstrates clearly that tradeoffs among competing values guided behavior. Splitting the sample at the medians on benevolence and on power values and crossing these subsamples yielded four groups. In the group that valued benevolence highly and gave low importance to power values, 87% cooperated. This was twice the rate in any other group (35–43%). Thus, in order to elicit a high level of cooperation,

Table 4.2 Correlations of value priorities with behavior

	Vote for center-right vs. center-left Italy	**Cooperation in a laboratory game Israel**	**Behavior across ontexts Israel self-report other-report**	
Values[a]	***N* = 2849[b]**	***N* = 90**	***N* = 293**	***N* = 141**
Power	0.14**	–0.37**	0.52**	0.25**
Achievement	0.08**	–0.19*	0.38**	0.20**
Hedonism	0.01	–0.18*	0.55**	0.29**
Stimulation	–0.03	–0.08	0.64**	0.35**
Self-direction	–0.08**	0.06	0.47**	0.29**
Universalism	–0.28**	0.32**	0.51**	0.24**
Benevolence	–0.18**	0.38**	0.43**	0.18*
Tradition	0.07**	0.12	0.70**	0.42**
Conformity	0.10**	0.01	0.40**	0.18*
Security	0.20**	–0.08	0.31**	0.10

[a]Values are corrected for scale use (see text).

[b]*N*s vary slightly due to missing data.

** $p < 0.01$, * $p < 0.05$, 1-tailed.

both high priority for values that promote cooperation (benevolence) and low priority for values that oppose it (power) were required.

Lönnqvist et al. (2013) reviewed relations of values to prosocial behavior in monetarily incentivized strategic interaction games in forty-two samples from China, Finland, Germany, Israel, and the West Bank. The games included prisoner's dilemma, ultimatum, trust, gift exchange, and dictator games. Participants were randomly paired with an unknown other. The researchers expected universalism values to predict higher levels and power values to predict lower levels of prosocial behavior. They also expected these effects to be stronger for the roles in which the prosocial option was clearly value-expressive (cooperator, trustee, and dictator roles) rather than value-ambivalent (proposer, responder, and truster). The value–behavior correlations confirmed these expectations across the forty-two studies, although only universalism was a significant predictor in the regressions. In the dictator game, they measured the refined values (Schwartz et al. 2012) in order to clarify the aspects of universalism and power values that influenced prosocial behavior. This revealed that the narrowly defined "universalism–concern" and "power–resources" predicted more strongly than the broader universalism and power values.

Next, I describe one study that examined the consequences of individual differences in value hierarchies on various self-reported and other-reported behaviors. I then provide an overview of the wide variety of other studies that reveal how tradeoffs between opposing values shape behavior and attitudes. Bardi and Schwartz (2003) investigated everyday behavior among young Israeli adults in three studies. They generated ten sets of 6–10 behaviors that they presumed would express each one of the ten basic values (e.g., sunbathe for hedonism, watch thrillers for stimulation). Participants rated how frequently they had performed each behavior in the past year, relative to their opportunities to perform it. In studies 2 and 3, intimate partners or close peers also rated participants' behavior. The behavior indexes were the averaged frequency ratings of the behaviors expected to express each value.

Column 3 of Table 4.2 lists the value–behavior correlations for the ten values. The mean correlation across values was 0.49 (sd = 0.11) for self-reported behavior and 0.25 (sd = 0.09) for other-reported behavior. Although almost all correlations were significant, the magnitude of the correlations varied considerably. Correlations were weakest in the security, conformity, benevolence, and achievement domains. The values in these domains were either especially important or the behaviors were especially frequent in the sample. Value importance or behavior frequency might produce normative pressure to conform to the values and behaviors. Correlations were strongest for tradition and stimulation, domains in which the values were relatively unimportant and the behaviors infrequent in this sample. Bardi and Schwartz (2003) interpreted these findings as suggesting that yielding to normative pressure, even when a behavior opposes one's own values, weakens value–behavior relations.

According to the value theory, basic values underlie and shape virtually all voluntary attitudes and behaviors. Attitudes or behaviors grounded positively in (i.e., motivated by) values on one side of the motivational circle and negatively in values on the opposing side should be predictable by the tradeoff between these opposing values. Table 4.3 presents a sampling of the heterogeneous assortment of behaviors whose relations to values have been studied. Table 4.4 presents a sampling of attitude–value relations in the literature. The tables specify the opposing values implicated in the tradeoff that guides each behavior or attitude and the number of different countries or cultures in which the topic has been studied.

To clarify the tables and illustrate the reasoning used to understand or predict the observed value tradeoffs, I explicate the first behavior in Table 4.3, political activism. Data

Table 4.3 Significant value tradeoffs underlying behavior

Behavior[a]	**# Countries or cultures studied**	**Positively related values**	**Negatively related values**
Political activism (7 actions: e.g., boycotting)	26	UN/SD/ST[b]	CO/TR/SE[c]
Participation in sports (in last 12 months)	18	ST/HE	SE/TR/CO
Attendance religious services	30	TR/CO	SD/ST/HE
Work for voluntary/charitable organization	23	BE/SD/UN	SE/PO/CO
Environmentally friendly behavior	11	UN/BE	PO
Drug use frequency	6	ST/HE	BE/CO
Risky sexual behavior (multiple partners, no condom)	5	HE/PO/ST	UN/BE/SE
Choosing economics or business major	2	PO/AC	BE
Delinquent behavior	3	ST/HE	BE/CO
Choice of medical specialty—general practice	2	BE	PO
Adopting technological innovations	2	ST/SD	SE/TR/CO
Prosocial behavior	3	UN/BE	PO
Creative behavior (artistic, verbal)	2	SD/UN/ST	SE/TR/CO
Consumer choices: red meat	1	PO	UN
fair trade products	1	UN/SD	PO/AC/SE
Interpersonal violence	2	PO/HE	UN/BE/CO

SD = self-direction, ST = stimulation, HE = hedonism, AC = achievement, PO = power, SE = security, CO = conformity, TR = tradition, BE = benevolence, UN = universalism

[a]Sources available from the author.

[b]Values are ordered from most to least positive.

[c]Values are ordered from most to least negative.

Table 4.4 Significant value tradeoffs underlying attitudes

Attitude[a]	# Countries or cultures studied	Positively related values	Negatively related values
Opposition to accepting immigrants	28	SE/CO[b]	UN/SD[c]
Interpersonal trust	30	BE/UN	SE/PO
Importance of work in life	20	AC/PO	TR/BE/UN
Subjective political efficacy	20	SD/ST	SE/CO/TR
Importance high income in choosing job	26	PO/AC	UN/BE
Importance job security in choosing job	26	SE	ST/SD
Importance promotion chances in choosing job	26	AC/PO	UN/BE
Importance chances for initiative in choosing job	26	SD/ST	CO/TR
Readiness to work with out-groups: majority group	1	UN/SD	TR/SE/CO
Right-wing authoritarianism	3	SE/CO/TR/PO	UN/SD
Egalitarian gender attitudes	1	UN/SD/BE	PO/TR
Worry about meaning in life	4	UN/BE/TR	ST/HE
Music preferences (jazz and rock vs. pop)	1	UN/BE	SE/CO/TR
Preference for community sharing vs. market pricing social relationships	1	BE/UN	PO/AC
Identifying with one's nation	3	TR/CO/SE	SD/ST/HE

SD = self-direction, ST = stimulation, HE = hedonism, AC = achievement, PO = power, SE = security, CO = conformity, TR = tradition, BE = benevolence, UN = universalism

[a]Sources available from the author.

[b]Values are ordered from most positive.

[c]Values are ordered from most negative.

were from representative national samples in twenty-six countries that participated in the first three rounds of the European Social Survey (2002–07). Individuals reported whether they had taken each of seven political actions during the past year (e.g., contacted a politician, signed a petition, participated in a demonstration, boycotted a product). The index of political activism was the number of actions taken. A hierarchical linear modeling analysis, controlling key socio-demographic variables, revealed that the strongest positive value predictor of activism was universalism, followed by self-direction and stimulation. The strongest negative predictor was conformity, followed by tradition and security. The last two columns of Table 4.3 present this tradeoff, ordering the values by their importance.

What was the rationale for this tradeoff? During this period, the main ideological goals of European activism were social justice, tolerance, protecting the environment, and peace, goals central to universalism values. Self-direction values promote independent thought and action and therefore active pursuit of one's principles. Activism also expresses stimulation values through opportunities for challenge and risk. Conformity, security, and tradition values oppose political activism because they call for preserving the status quo, accepting normative expectations, and avoiding risk and change. Activism most directly contravenes conformity values in its challenge to conventional or established practices. Both the order of the value circle and reasoning about the motivations for activism support the observed order of associations.

In the case of risky sexual behavior, the values involved in the tradeoff deviate somewhat from the expected pattern. This merits comment because such deviations point to complexities in the motivation for a specific behavior or attitude. Goodwin et al. (2002) asked respondents in five East European countries whether they had engaged in sex with multiple partners during the past six months without using condoms. Hedonism, stimulation, and the non-adjacent power values correlated most positively with such behavior. Universalism, benevolence, and non-adjacent security values correlated most negatively. Moreover, power and security values, which are adjacent in the circle, related to risky sexual behavior in opposite directions.

This set of findings identifies two independent value tradeoffs that might motivate risky sexual behavior. For some, deciding whether to engage in risky sexual behavior involves the tradeoff of pleasure and excitement (hedonism and stimulation) versus risk to their own safety (security). For others, it involves a tradeoff of dominating others (power) versus concern for their dignity and welfare (universalism). For still others, both tradeoffs may influence their decision. When, as here, adjacent values relate to an attitude or behavior in opposite ways or non-adjacent values relate to them in similar ways, we can infer that the attitude or behavior has multiple, independent consequences.

Origins and change of value priorities

When do children begin to discriminate the ten basic values and organize them into the motivational value circle? And when do group differences in value priorities (e.g., education, religion, sex) begin to emerge (see also Boer and Boehnke, this volume)? Several studies have shown that the adult patterns are quite well-established by adolescence (e.g., Daniel et al. 2012; Schwartz 2012) and even, to a large extent, in late childhood (e.g., Bilsky et al. 2013; Cieciuch et al. 2013a). A recently developed picture-based method to measure the ten basic values (Döring et al. 2010) makes it possible to address these questions with children as young as seven years old.

Döring, et al. (in press) analyzed values' data from over 3000 children from six countries. Regarding the value structure, the sample in every country differentiated the four higher order values and ordered them as adults do. Moreover, at least seven of the ten values were differentiated in all but one country. Values that were not differentiated were intermixed with adjacent values in the motivational circle. Thus, children apparently experience the motivational compatibilities and incompatibilities among the values in much the same way as adults do, but the more detailed structure is still in the process of emerging. Note that the value structures observed among children and among adults refer to the group level. They do not characterize every individual.

Regarding value hierarchies, the pan-cultural location of benevolence and universalism as most important in adult samples and power as least important (Schwartz and Bardi 2001) also emerged in the children's samples. Regarding sex differences, in all countries, girls attributed higher priority to self-transcendence values and boys to self-enhancement values, paralleling adult differences around the world (Schwartz and Rubel 2005). Sex differences for conservation and openness to change values were smaller and less consistent, also as found among adults. Whether sex differences mainly reflect evolutionary or socialization and social role effects is uncertain, but they already emerge in childhood.

What do individual differences in value priorities come from? Initial evidence suggests that inborn sensitivities affect some values. Hibbing et al. (2014) bring evidence that political conservatives, who consistently prioritize conservation values (Piurko et al. 2011), exhibit heightened sensitivity to negative stimuli. Tritt, Inzlicht, and Peterson (2014) argue, instead, that conservatives are particularly responsive to arousal in general. Thus, those who give higher priority to conservation versus openness to change values may be more physiologically sensitive to negative or arousing features of the environment (Schwartz 2014). Both Rokeach (1973) and Schwartz (1992) view some values as transformations of needs into goals that can be regulated cognitively. Individual differences in temperament or in the intensity of needs might therefore give rise to differences in value priorities.

There is also some evidence for genetic influences on basic values. In a study of adult twins in Australia, Schermer et al. (2008) obtained reliable heritability estimates for the importance of conformity (0.38), tradition (0.38), and benevolence (0.28) values, but not for the importance of the other seven values. Knafo and Spinath (2011) examined genetic influences on value priorities for two bipolar dimensions of values in seven- to eleven-year-old German same-sex twins. They estimated heritability of 0.49 for power/achievement vs. benevolence values and of 0.34 for conformity/security vs. self-direction/stimulation values for both sexes. These estimates based on children may underestimate the importance of genetic influences on value priorities because heritability often increases with age (Plomin et al. 2001). Reliably establishing the genetic influences on the ten basic values demands further research.

Both genetics and continuity in people's experiences may contribute to the relative stability of value priorities over time. In adult samples, stability of value importance averages about 0.6 over a year (summarized in: Bardi and Goodwin 2011; Schwartz 2005) and stability of value hierarchies (profiles) averages 0.59 over eight years (unpublished data). Yet, value priorities do change. Race, ethnicity, gender, social class, education, occupation, family characteristics, age cohort, religion, immigrant status, economic and political systems all affect value priorities (Hitlin and Piliavin 2004; Schwartz 2007; Schwartz et al.

2000). These sources produce value change by influencing people's life experiences and the opportunities their life circumstances afford.

Adaptation to different life experiences and circumstances leads to value change and through it to value differences among individuals and groups. Typically, people upgrade the importance they attribute to values they can readily attain and downgrade the importance of values whose pursuit is blocked (Schwartz and Bardi 1997). For example, people in jobs that afford freedom of choice increase the importance of self-direction values at the expense of conformity values (Kohn and Schooler 1983). Upgrading attainable values and downgrading thwarted values applies to most, but not to all values. The reverse occurs with values that concern material well-being and security. When such values are blocked, their importance increases; when they are easily attained, their importance drops. For example, people who suffer economic hardship and social upheaval attribute more importance to power and security values than those who live in relative comfort and safety (Inglehart 1997). However, people often choose the circumstances they experience (careers, majors, spouses, etc.) based on their value priorities. These value-compatilble, circumstances do not promote value change (Bardi et al. 2014).

Socialization intentionally shapes life experiences to induce value change. Socializers, in families and organizations, seek to transmit their own or their preferred values. The success of their efforts depends on the target no less than on the socializer (Knafo and Schwartz 2008). Desired value changes are more likely to occur if the target perceives them accurately and identifies with the socializer. Several socializer characteristics affect whether the experiences they shape will influence targets' values. These include socializers' warmth, the clarity and consistency of their expectations, and the example they provide. As central aspects of the self, however, basic values tend to resist change.

Conclusion

The value theory identifies ten basic, motivationally distinct values that people in virtually all cultures implicitly recognize. The theory applies to adults and children from around the world, though we do not know whether it applies in isolated tribal groups. Especially striking is the emergence of the same circular structure of relations among values across countries and measurement instruments. People everywhere experience conflict between the values at the poles of the higher order values, openness to change values versus conservation and self-transcendence versus self-enhancement. Conflicts between specific values are also near universal. The dynamic processes suggested to account for the observed circular structure may point the way toward a unifying theory of human motivation.

Values influence most, if not all, motivated behavior, though people are often unaware of this influence. I have identified various mechanisms that link values to behavior. The magnitude of influence by values can be substantial for value-expressive behaviors and in the absence of normative pressure in the environment. It is trivial for value-ambivalent behaviors and under strong normative pressure. The value theory makes clear that behavior entails a tradeoff between competing values. Behaviors typically have positive implications for expressing, upholding, or attaining some values, but negative implications for values across the circle in opposing positions. People tend to behave in ways that balance their opposing values. Consequently, the order of positive and negative associations between any specific behavior and the ten values tends to follow the order of the value circle. The theory provides a framework for relating the integrated motivational system of ten values to behavior that enriches analysis, prediction, and explanation of value-behavior relations.

This chapter presents many examples of the relations of value priorities to a wide variety of behaviors and attitudes. The literature contains many more examples (see also Jiga-Boy et al., this volume). Value priorities also relate systematically to other personality variables. Among those studied are social desirability, authoritarianism, social dominance, subjective well-being, and the Big Five personality traits. The proliferation of behavior, attitude, and personality studies testifies to the fruitfulness of the values theory.

Little is known about possible genetic and biological underpinnings of value priorities. The circular motivational structure of values emerges during childhood, but we have yet to learn how early this occurs and what factors influence its emergence. These are among the more challenging topics for future research.

Acknowledgment

Preparation of this chapter was partly supported by the HSE Basic Research Program (International Laboratory of Sociocultural Research).

References

Alwin, D.F. (1984). Trends in parental socialization values: Detroit, 1958–1983. *American Journal of Sociology*, **90**, 359–382.

Bandura, A. (1977). Self efficacy: toward a unifying theory of behavioral change. *Psychological Review*, **84**, 191–215.

Bardi, A. (2000). *Relations of values to behavior in everyday situations*. Unpublished doctoral dissertation. The Hebrew University, Jerusalem.

Bardi, A. and Goodwin, R. (2011). The dual route to value change: individual processes and cultural moderators. *Journal of Cross-Cultural Psychology*, **42**, 271–287.

Bardi, A. and Schwartz, S.H. (2003). Values and behavior: strength and structure of relations. *Personality and Social Psychology Bulletin*, **29**, 1207–1220.

Bardi, A., Buchanan, K.E., Goodwin, R., Slabu, L., and Robinson, M. (2014) Value stability and change during self-chosen life transitions: Self-selection versus socialization effects. *Journal of Personality and Social Psychology*, **106**, 131–147.

Berlyne, D.E. (1960). *Conflict, Arousal and Curiosity*. New York: McGraw-Hill.

Bilsky, W., Döring, A.K., van Beeck, F., et al. (2013) Assessment of children's value structures and value preferences: testing and expanding the limits. *Swiss Journal of Psychology*, **72**, 123–136

Bilsky, W., Janik, M., and Schwartz, S.H. (2011). The structural organization of human values—evidence from three rounds of the European Social Survey (ESS). *Journal of Cross-Cultural Psychology*, **42**, 759–776.

Boudon, R. (2001). *The Origins of Values: Essays in the Sociology and Philosophy of Beliefs*. New York: Transaction Publishers.

Brosch, T., Coppin, G., Scherer, K.R. Schwartz, S., and Sander, D. (2011). Generating value(s): psychological value hierarchies reflect context-dependent sensitivity of the reward system. *Social Neuroscience*, **6**, 198–208.

Buss, D.M. (1986). Can a social science be anchored in evolutionary biology? Four problems and a strategic solution. *Revue Européenne des Sciences Sociales*, **24**, 41–50.

Caprara, G.V., Schwartz, S.H., Capanna, C., Vecchione, M., and Barbaranelli, C. (2006). Personality and politics: values, traits, and political choice. *Political Psychology*, **27**, 1–28.

Cieciuch, J., Döring, A.K., and Harasimczuk, J. (2013a). Measuring Schwartz's values in childhood: multidimensional Scaling across instruments and cultures. *European Journal of Developmental Psychology*, **10**, 625–633.

Cieciuch, J., Schwartz, S.H., and Vecchione, M. (2013b). Applying the refined values theory to past data: what can researchers gain? *Journal of Cross-Cultural Psychology*, **44**, 1213–1232.

Daniel, E., Schiefer, D., Möllering, A, Benish-Weisman, M., Boehnke, K., and Knafo, A. (2012). Value differentiation in adolescence: the role of age and cultural complexity. *Child Development*, **83**, 322–336.

Davidov, E., Schmidt, P., and Schwartz, S.H. (2008). Bringing values back in: the adequacy of the European Social Survey to measure values in 20 countries. *Public Opinion Quarterly*, **72**, 420–445.

Deci, E.L. (1975). *Intrinsic Motivation*. New York: Plenum.

Döring, A.K., Blauensteiner, A., Aryus, K., Drögekamp, L., and Bilsky, W. (2010). Assessing values at an early age: the picture-based value survey for children. *Journal of Personality Assessment*, **92**, 439–448.

Döring, A.K., Schwartz, S.H., Cieciuch, J., et al. (in press). Cross-cultural evidence for universals in value structures and priorities in childhood. *British Journal of Psychology*

Durkheim, E. (1893/1964). *The Division of Labor in Society*. Glencoe, IL.: Free Press.

Durkheim, E. (1912/1954). *The Elementary Forms of Religious Life*. Glencoe, IL.: Free Press.

Fontaine, J., Poortinga, Y.H., Delbeke, L., and Schwartz, S.H. (2008). Structural equivalence of the values domain across cultures: distinguishing sampling fluctuations from meaningful variation. *Journal of Cross-Cultural Psychology*, **39**, 345–365.

Freud, S. (1930). *Civilization and its Discontents*. London: Hogarth.

Freud, S. (1933). *New Introductory Lectures in Psychoanalysis*. New York: Norton.

Gollwitzer, P.M. (1996). The volitional benefits of planning. In: P.M. Gollwitzer and J.A. Bargh (eds.), *The Psychology of Action*. New York: Guilford.

Goodwin, R., Realo, A., Kwiatkowska, A., Kozlova, A., Nguyen-Luu, L.A., and Nizharadze, G. (2002).Values and sexual behaviour in Central and Eastern Europe. *Journal of Health Psychology*, **7**, 45–56.

Hays, N.A. (2013). Fear and loving in social hierarchy: sex differences in preferences for power versus status. *Journal of Experimental Social Psychology*, **49**, 1130–1136.

Hibbing, J.R., Smith, K.B., and Alford, J.R. (2014). Differences in negativity bias underlie variations in political ideology. *Behavioral and Brain Sciences*, **37**, 297–350.

Higgins, E.T. (1997). Beyond pleasure and pain. *American Psychologist*, **52**, 1280–1300.

Hitlin, S. (2003).Values as the core of personal identity: drawing links between two theories of self. *Social Psychology Quarterly*, **66**, 118–137.

Hitlin, S. and Piliavin, J.A. (2004). Values: reviving a dormant concept. *Annual Review of Sociology*, **30**, 359–393.

Inglehart, R. (1997). *Modernization and Postmodernization*. Princeton, NJ: Princeton University Press.

Kluckhohn, C. (1951). Values and value-orientations in the theory of action: an exploration in definition and classification. In: T. Parsons and E. Shils (eds), *Toward a General Theory of Action* (pp. 388–433). Cambridge, MA: Harvard University Press.

Knafo, A. and Schwartz, S.H. (2008). Accounting for parent-child value congruence: theoretical considerations and empirical evidence. In: U. Schönpflug (ed.), *Perspectives on Cultural Transmission* (pp. 240–268). New York: Cambridge University Press.

Knafo, A. and Spinath, F.M. (2011). Genetic and environmental influences on girls' and boys' gender-typed and gender-neutral values. *Developmental Psychology*, **47**, 726–731.

Kohn, M.L. (1969). *Class and Conformity*. Homewood, IL.: Dorsey.

Kohn, M.L. and Schooler, C. (1983). *Work and Personality*. Norwood, NJ: Ablex.

Korman, A. (1974). *The Psychology of Motivation*. Englewood Cliffs, NJ: Prentice-Hall.

Lewin, K. (1947). Frontiers in group dynamics: concept, method and reality in social science; social equilibria and social change. *Human Relations*, **1**, 5–41.

Lonner, W.J. (1980). The search for psychological universals. In: H.C. Triandis and W.W. Lambert (eds), *Handbook of Cross-Cultural Psychology. Perspectives*: vol. 1. Boston: Allyn and Bacon.

Lönnqvist, J-E., Verkasalo, M., Wichardt, P.C., and Walkowitz. G. (2013). Personal values and prosocial behaviour in strategic interactions: Distinguishing value-expressive from value-ambivalent behaviours. *European Journal of Social Psychology*, **43**, 554–569.

Maio, G. R. (2010). Mental representations of social values. In M. Zanna (ed.), *Advances in Experimental Social Psychology* (vol. 42, pp. 1–43). New York: Elsevier.

Maslow, A.H. (1965). *Eupsychian Management*. Homewood, IL: Dorsey.

Morris, C.W. (1956). *Varieties of Human Value*. Chicago: University of Chicago Press.

Parsons, T. (1951). *The Social System*. Glencoe, IL.: Free Press.

Piurko, Y., Schwartz, S.H., and Davidov, E. (2011). Basic personal values and the meaning of left-right political orientations in 20 countries. *Political Psychology*, **32**, 537–561.

Plomin, R., DeFries, J.C., McClearn, G.E., and McGuffin, P. (2001). *Behavioral Genetics*, 4th edition. New York: Worth Publishers.

Rohan, M.J. (2000). A rose by any name? The values construct. *Personality and Social Psychology Review*, **4**, 255–277.

Rokeach, M. (1973). *The Nature of Human Values*. New York: Free Press.

Ryan, R.R. and Deci, E.L. (2000). Intrinsic and extrinsic motivations: classic definitions and new directions. *Contemporary Educational Psychology*, **25**, 54–67.

Sagiv, L. and Schwartz, S.H. (2000). Value priorities and subjective well-being: direct relations and congruity effects. *European Journal of Social Psychology*, **30**, 177–198.

Sagiv, L., Sverdlik, N., and Schwarz, N. (2011). To compete or to cooperate? Values' impact on perception and action in social dilemma games. *European Journal of Social Psychology*, **41**, 64–77.

Schermer, J.A., Feather, N.T., Zhu, G., and Martin, N.G. (2008). Phenotypic, genetic, and environmental properties of the portrait values questionnaire. *Twin Research*, **5**, 531–537.

Schwartz, S.H. (1992). Universals in the content and structure of values: theory and empirical tests in 20 countries. In M. Zanna (ed.), *Advances in Experimental Social Psychology* (vol. 25, pp. 1–65). New York: Academic.

Schwartz, S.H. (1994). Are there universal aspects in the content and structure of values? *Journal of Social Issues*, **50**, 19–45.

Schwartz, S.H. (1996). Value priorities and behavior: applying a theory of integrated value systems. In: C. Seligman, J.M. Olson, and M.P. Zanna (eds), *The Psychology of Values: The Ontario Symposium*, (vol. 8, pp. 1–24). Hillsdale, NJ: Erlbaum.

Schwartz, S.H. (2005). Robustness and fruitfulness of a theory of universals in individual human values. In: A. Tamayo and J.B. Porto (eds.), *Valores e Comportamento nas Organizações* [Values and Behavior in Organizations] pp. 56–95. Petrópolis, Brazil: Vozes.

Schwartz, S.H. (2006). Les valeurs de base de la personne: théorie, mesures et applications [Basic human values: theory measurement and applications]. *Revue Francaise de Sociologie*, **47**, 929–968.

Schwartz, S.H. (2007). Cultural and individual value correlates of capitalism: a comparative analysis. *Psychological Inquiry*, **18**, 52–57.

Schwartz, S. H. (2010). Basic values: How they motivate and inhibit prosocial behavior. In M. Mikulincer and P. Shaver (Eds.), *Prosocial motives, emotions, and behavior: The better angels of our nature* (221–241). Washington: American Psychological Association Press.

Schwartz, S.H. (2012). Values and religion in adolescent development: cross-national and comparative evidence In: G. Tromsdorff and X. Chen (eds), *Values, Religion, and Culture in Adolescent Development*, pp. 97–122. New York: Cambridge University Press.

Schwartz, S.H. (2014). Negativity bias and basic values. *Behavioral and Brain Sciences*, **37**, 328–329.

Schwartz, S.H. and Bardi, A. (1997). Influences of adaptation to communist rule on value priorities in Eastern Europe. *Political Psychology*, **18**, 385–410.

Schwartz, S.H. and Bardi, A. (2001). Value hierarchies across cultures: taking a similarities perspective. *Journal of Cross Cultural Psychology*, **32**, 268–290.

Schwartz, S.H. and Boehnke, K. (2004). Evaluating the structure of human values with confirmatory factor analysis. *Journal of Research in Personality*, **38**, 230–255.

Schwartz, S.H. and Rubel, T. (2005) Sex differences in value priorities: cross-cultural and multi-method studies. *Journal of Personality and Social Psychology*, **89**, 1010–1028.

Schwartz, S.H., Bardi, A., and Bianchi, G. (2000). Value adaptation to the imposition and collapse of Communist regimes in Eastern Europe. In: S.A. Renshon and J. Duckitt (eds), *Political Psychology: Cultural and Cross Cultural Perspectives*, pp. 217–237. London: Macmillan.

Schwartz, S.H., Cieciuch, J., Vecchione, M., et al. (2012). Refining the theory of basic individual values. *Journal of Personality and Social Psychology*, **103**, 663–688.

Tritt, S.M., Inzlicht, M., and Peterson, J.B. (2014). Commentary on Hibbing, Smith, and Alford: confounding valence and arousal: what really underlies political orientation? *Behavioral and Brain Sciences*, **37**, 330—331.

Weber, M. (1905/1958). *The Protestant Ethic and the Spirit of Capitalism*. New York: Scribner's.

Williams, R.M., Jr. (1968). Values. In: E. Sills (ed.), *International Encyclopedia of the Social Sciences*. New York: Macmillan.

Chapter 5

Common value representation—a neuroeconomic perspective

Dino Levy and Paul Glimcher

When we talk mathematics, we may be discussing a secondary language built on the primary language of the nervous system.
As quoted in John Von Neumann, 1903–57 *(1958) by John C. Oxtoby and B. J. Pettis, p. 128.*

Background

Economics is a wonderful discipline. It is based on clear and precise definitions, axioms, and mathematical formulas. In many cases, economic theory has been successfully used to inform policy, predict human behavior and structure the financial system. In the last 300 years there has been a tremendous advancement in economic theory; from the revolutionary ideas of Daniel Bernoulli, David Ricardo, and Adam Smith through the theories of Vilfredo Pareto, Paul Samuelson, John von Neumann, and Oskar Morgenstern, to the more recent approaches of Herbert Simon, Daniel Kahneman, and Amos Tversky, and many others. However, one of the most fundamental notions in economics is that the basic aim of economic theory is to make predictions. Economists acquire observable behavioral data and through well-defined theories create predictions. What they care about is how well they can predict. As a discipline they are not interested in understanding the underlying mechanisms of *why* the predictions were at a certain level in a given situation. Although they acknowledge that human behavior is a result of neural activity, they remain agnostic to the actual mechanism within the nervous system responsible for those behaviors. Similar to the behaviorism community in psychology in the 1940s, economists in general are not interested in the "black box."

On the other hand we, as neuroeconomists, are very much interested in the "black box" and we want to understand what is the underlying neural mechanism for the instantiation of value and choice. We strongly believe that taking this approach offers certain advantages. First and foremost, having more data than less is always beneficial in trying to understand any given mechanism. Second, understanding the neural mechanisms of value and choice will set physiological boundaries on any economic theory. A theory that does not take into consideration these boundaries will be a priori false, at least at some level of analysis. Moreover, adding these boundaries into the current economic theories will, we believe, make the theories more accurate in their predictions. Third, if the instantiation of all behavior rests in neural activity, then understanding the underlying mechanisms of choice will help us build novel theories that are based not upon arbitrary axioms but natural axioms that are the result of the general and basic physiological principles governing neural activity and hence behavior.

The general neuroeconomic theory of value and choice is only in its infancy, and there are plenty of unknowns. It might even be the case that the general theory will soon be very far from its current form. However, we believe that not pursuing the goal of developing a general theory of value and choice using neural activity (and dismissing its relevance to economics) is both short-sighted and goes against the very spirit of scientific inquiry. Finally, and perhaps most importantly, there can be no doubt that ultimately, a physiologically realistic model of how we make decisions will have better predictive power than an unrealistic one—especially in domains where we have very little behavioral data. This is because models that lack a mechanistic foundation ("non-structural models" in the language of economics) simply cannot outperform models that make novel predictions based on an understanding of underlying mechanism when predicting "out of sample."

The idea of a common currency representation at a purely theoretical level is, of course, hardly new. The core principal of economic rational choice theories is *utility maximization*, which assumes that choosers act consistently to maximize an internal measure of satisfaction, or utility. By definition, utility is an ordinal entity having arbitrary units on a unified scale. In theory, this allows one to compare options on the basis of comparing the utilities of the options, which are on a common scale.

The foundation for utility theory can be traced to early work in probability theory, as scholars who sought to reconcile mathematical models of choice and human behavior. Initial work proposed that decisions should be guided by the multiplicative combination of outcome probability and magnitude, or *expected value*. However, such simple models failed to describe how human choosers actually behave, particularly concerning large rewards and small probabilities (i.e., the St. Petersburg paradox). Rather than expected value, which is by definition an objective formulation, Daniel Bernoulli proposed that choosers instead transform *expected value* to an internal *subjective* representation of value, which is a quantity incorporating an individual's subjective aversion to risk (Bernoulli 1738). This notion is very similar to the well-known *Weber–Fechner* transformation of objective sensory stimuli to the subjective perception of the stimuli in psychology.

More recently, a body of mathematical work by Samuelson and others developed the modern axiomatic approach to examining choice behavior (Samuelson 1947). These models revolutionized economics by defining rationality; describing the properties of choices consistent with maximizing an ordered, internal representation of value, termed *utility*. In normative theories of economics, *consistency* is defined by a set of several mathematical axioms, which in essence are testing how consistent an individual is in her choices. Violations of the axioms result in inconsistent or *non-rational* behavior.

Why is rational behavior so important to economic normative theories? First and foremost, the economist Paul Samuelson and his colleagues (Samuelson 1947) proved almost a century ago that any decision-maker who is internally consistent in their choices behaves, during the period in which they are consistent, exactly "as if" they were employing a single fixed common scale for the representation of value. That is, if a chooser is rational, there is at least one utility function (the function that states how the objective value is transformed to internal subjective value representation that guides the choices of that particular individual) that can describe her choices. Second, if a decision-maker demonstrates non-consistent preferences, i.e., behaves in a non-rational way, one could exploit this by taking away money from the non-rational chooser, even when the chooser carefully and precisely makes decisions with full information.[1]

Of course, the assumption that a chooser is consistent is not a necessary condition for a common currency representation.[2] But since Samuelson's proof, nearly all theories of decision, from expected utility theory (Von Neumann and Morgenstern 1944) through prospect theory (Kahneman and Tversky 1979) and even to modern reinforcement learning algorithms (Sutton and Barto 1998) have shared the notion that in order to choose, the different attributes of each option must at some point be converged, however idiosyncratically, incompletely and imperfectly, into a single value for the actual process of comparison.

In this chapter we review current knowledge about the neural representation of value and choice using human brain imaging studies. Although there are ample data and wonderful insights from studies on non-human animals, we focus on human data for the sake of brevity. Throughout this essay we have tried to answer one simple but fundamental question which may inform the general theory of value and choice: Is there evidence for a brain area/neural network that represents value and choice for any given reward type in any situation using a single *common neural currency*?

The main question

At a neurobiological level how does a thirsty animal choose between one or two milliliters of water? How does the human brain choose between one apple or two apples? In principle this seems fairly straightforward. If we assume that "more is better" under these conditions, then we simply need to represent and compare quantities. But what happens in the brain when we need to choose between a large amount of water and a single apple? Or a small amount of water and two apples? The options we face in these situations are

---

[1] Imagine that a chooser prefers apples to oranges, oranges over pears *but* pears over apples, i.e., demonstrating non-consistent preferences. If that person had a pear and we offered to sell her an orange for her pear plus one cent. She accepts. We then offer her an apple for the orange we just sold her plus one more cent. According to her preferences, she accepts. Then we offer to sell her back her original pear for the apple plus one more cent. She accepts. At the end of these trades she has lost three cents, has her original pear in hand, and considers each trade as a good trade.

[2] Although under some conditions it may be necessary for a fixed monotonic common currency representation (e.g., (Houthakker 1950).

different, and our answers depend on the reward types, the quantities of each of those rewards, and our internal metabolic states. So critically: just counting will not help. What we need to do is to take into consideration many different attributes of each option (like color, size, taste, health benefits) and of ourselves (like how hungry or thirsty we are), assess the value of each of the attributes, and combine all of these attributes into one coherent value representation that allows comparison with any other possible option. What we need, at least in principle, is a single (perhaps context dependent) common currency of valuation for comparing options of many different kinds. In as much as our choices are consistent and lawful, the brain must behave as if it represents the values of many different kinds of rewards on a common scale for comparison and choice.

Over the course of the last decade there has been a wealth of studies suggesting that activity in a small number of brain areas encodes reward quantities during decision-making tasks. Areas like the parietal cortex appear to encode how many milliliters of juice an action will yield to a thirsty monkey. Areas like the ventral striatum and the medial prefrontal cortex appear to encode the amount of money an option will yield. Indeed, there is now broad consensus in the neuroscience of decision-making community that reward magnitude is represented in a small number of well-identified areas. In this chapter we will describe some of the main findings supporting the notion that there are a few brain areas that represent various aspects related to valuation and choice. We will focus on evidence from human functional magnetic resonance imaging (fMRI) studies conducted over the last decade, which suggests that one of these reward magnitude encoding areas, the ventromedial prefrontal cortex/orbital frontal cortex (vmPFC/OFC),[3] can be thought of as representing the value of nearly all reward-types on a single common scale that predicts behaviorally observed comparison and choice. Of course, this does not mean that common currency representations occur only in this area, but available fMRI evidence clearly indicates the existence of a common currency network at least in this area.

Perhaps the first common currency representation experiment was conducted while recoding from monkey parietal cortex (Deaner et al. 2005; Klein et al. 2008) and related work has also indicated that the midbrain dopamine neurons employ a common currency for reward representation in monkeys (Matsumoto and Hikosaka 2009). For the purposes of this review, however, we restrict ourselves to the rapidly growing human fMRI literature on this subject in the frontal cortex so as to focus our analysis on the best understood structural features of the human brain related to this class of representation.

[3] Throughout the chapter we use the combined term vmPFC/OFC rather then either of the brain areas separately because there is some inconsistency in the literature regarding what are the authors' anatomical definitions of the vmPFC and/or OFC. In general, we refer to this single area with this combined acronym to highlight the generality of findings across hundreds of studies and to emphasize the importance of this brain area. Most of the studies reviewed in this chapter refer to either the vmPFC or OFC if the activity identified is mainly within Brodmann areas 11, 10, 13, 14, and in some cases 32 (for anatomical reviews see: Ongur et al. 2003; Ongur and Price 2000; Price and Drevets 2010). An anatomical plot of the area we are discussing can be found in two closely related meta-studies (Bartra et al. 2013; Levy and Glimcher 2012).

Monetary rewards

Over the course of the last decade there have been a huge number of studies that have related the magnitude of monetary rewards, and the idiosyncratic values subjects place on those rewards, to brain activations in humans. In a typical study of this kind, subjects either receive, or choose between, monetary rewards of different sizes during a scanning session. The study then searches for correlations between either the size of the reward or subject's subjective valuations of reward magnitudes and the BOLD signal throughout the brain. Perhaps surprisingly, these studies have yielded a very homogenous result. Essentially all of them identify the medial prefrontal cortex, the ventral striatum, and the posterior cingulate cortex (PCC) as correlated with these reward magnitudes. In addition, a subset of these studies reveal correlations in the amygdala, the insula and the posterior parietal cortex (PPC) (for reviews of this literature see: Grabenhorst and Rolls 2011; Kable and Glimcher 2009; Padoa-Schioppa 2011; Platt and Huettel 2008; Rushworth 2008; Wallis 2011).

Delgado and colleagues (Delgado et al. 2000), for example, used a magnitude evaluation task with monetary rewards to show that activity in the ventral striatum was correlated with monetary gains and losses. Rebecca Elliot and her colleagues, at the same time, showed that ventral striatal activity correlates with the magnitude of cumulative rewards (Elliott et al. 2000) and Brian Knutson showed, again at essentially the same time, that activity in this area correlates with the anticipation of reward (Knutson et al. 2001). Subsequent studies have clearly supported these early findings; monetary reward expectation (Breiter et al. 2001), monetary reward receipt (Elliott et al. 2003), the expected values of rewards (Knutson et al. 2005), potential monetary reward magnitude and loss magnitude (Tom et al. 2007) and discounted reward value at delays ranging from minutes to months (Kable and Glimcher 2007) are all correlated with activity in the ventral striatum—to cite just a tiny fraction of the relevant literature.

A similar story seems to hold in the medial prefrontal cortex and to a lesser degree in the posterior cingulate cortex. Activity in these areas correlates with monetary reward magnitude (Knutson et al. 2001; Knutson et al. 2003), the expected values of monetary lotteries (Knutson et al. 2005), the subject-specific valuations of gains and losses (Tom et al. 2007), and subject-specific discounted reward value (Kable and Glimcher 2007). To summarize a huge literature, activity in these areas seems extremely well correlated with how good a reward outcome will be and this is true even when the notion of "how good" must incorporate subject-specific subjective evaluations like the tradeoffs between how long one has to wait for a reward and how large is that reward (Kable and Glimcher 2007; McClure et al. 2004).

Primary rewards

It has also been demonstrated that the vmPFC/OFC, striatum and other value-related areas represent value-related signals of primary rewards per se, not the sensory stimuli that are associated with those rewards. For example, O'Doherty and colleagues (O'Doherty et al.

2000) demonstrated that activity within the vmPFC/OFC decreased in response to the odor of a food that was eaten to satiety when compared to the response when that food had not yet been consumed (here satiety is an indication of reduced reward value, usually termed *sensory specific satiation*). In another study, O'Doherty and colleagues (O'Doherty et al. 2001) showed that the vmPFC/OFC and the amygdala represent both pleasant and unpleasant tastes, suggesting that these areas code for both positive and negative values as is required for a brain area to be considered part of a general network representing values for all reward types along the entire subjective scale. Interestingly, in a later study O'Doherty and colleagues (O'Doherty et al. 2002) demonstrated that only the vmPFC/OFC represented both the expectation of reward and actual reward receipt, further strengthening the notion that the vmPFC/OFC represents value on a common scale.

In non-choice tasks, desirable food rewards also produce increased activity in the vmPFC/OFC (Kringelbach et al. 2003) and, as described in the previous paragraph, the actual consumption of palatable foods also results in a greater activation of the vmPFC/OFC (O'Doherty et al. 2002). Administration of pleasant tastes activates this area (O'Doherty et al. 2001; Zald et al. 2002) and meal consumption has been shown to be associated with increased neuronal activity in the vmPFC/OFC (Del Parigi et al. 2002). The striatum has also been shown to respond to the anticipation of primary rewards (O'Doherty et al. 2002), and activity here is correlated with juice preferences (O'Doherty et al. 2006), meal pleasantness ratings (Small et al. 2003), subjective preferences of goods (Knutson et al. 2007), and food craving (Pelchat et al. 2004).

Even the sight of food cues has been shown to activate the vmPFC/OFC and striatum (Goldstone et al. 2009; Killgore et al. 2003; Siep et al. 2009; Simmons et al. 2005). Studies involving choice tasks also demonstrate the involvement of the vmPFC/OFC and striatum in primary reward value coding. Using food items as rewards, the activity in the vmPFC/OFC was correlated with how much a subject was willing to pay (Hare et al. 2009; Plassmann et al. 2007) both for appetitive and aversive objects (Plassmann et al. 2010), reported experienced pleasantness (Plassmann et al. 2008), decision values (Hare et al. 2008), and the subjective value of delayed juice rewards (McClure et al. 2007), while the striatum was correlated with food reward prediction errors (Hare et al. 2008).

Abstract rewards

An immediate question that comes to mind is whether the neural value representations in the value-related brain areas identified using monetary and primary rewards also represent values for even more abstract non-monetary and non-primary rewards. In the last decade or so it has been shown that almost all studies that have used these kinds of rewards in value-related tasks, revealed the existence of value-related activity in the vmPFC/OFC and to a lesser extent in the striatum, anterior cingulate cortex (ACC), PCC, PPC, lateral intraparietal cortex (LIP), amygdala, and insula (Glimcher 2011; Glimcher et al. 2008).

For example, Kawabata and Zeki (2004) asked subjects to rate paintings as ugly, neutral, or beautiful while lying inside the scanner. They then contrasted the activity measurements obtained during viewing of ugly and beautiful paintings and found higher neural activation in the medial prefrontal cortex for the beautiful versus ugly paintings. O'Doherty and colleagues (2003) looked for brain areas that tracked attractiveness ratings of human faces. To do this, they first acquired attractiveness ratings of human faces from an independent group of subjects. They then presented, to a different group of subjects, the most attractive and the least attractive faces, while subjects were inside the scanner conducting an irrelevant task (stating whether the face was male or female). They demonstrated once again that a subregion of the vmPFC/OFC was more active for the attractive faces as compared to the non-attractive faces. Other studies have showed increased activity in the ventral striatum and vmPFC/OFC when subjects actively rate attractive faces as opposed to non-attractive faces from the opposite gender (Cloutier et al. 2008).

In a similar manner, Yue and colleagues (2007) asked subjects to view pictures of various natural scene pictures while inside the fMRI scanner. Subjects had to rate their preferences (on a scale from 1 to 8) regarding each of the environments presented in the pictures. They found that activity in the ventral striatum was stronger for the scenes with a high preference score as compared to the scenes with a low preference score. In yet another related finding, it has been demonstrated that activity in the ventral striatum correlates with the monetary amount that subjects are willing to bid in an auction paradigm when they listen to novel songs inside the fMRI scanner (Salimpoor et al. 2013). Furthermore, these authors demonstrated increased functional connectivity between the ventral striatum and other value-related areas such as the vmPFC/OFC and amygdala and it has even been shown that the valuation of music (see also Levinson, this volume) evidenced in the ventral striatum is associated with an increase in dopamine in this region (Salimpoor et al. 2011).

In another study, Sharot and colleagues (2009) examined the neural correlates of hedonic value (see also Ellingsen et al., this volume). They asked subjects to estimate how much they thought they would enjoy each of a set of possible vacations, sometime in the future. The authors found increased activity in the caudate nucleus (a nucleus that is part of the striatum) previously associated with reward expectancy (Gottfried et al. 2003; Knutson et al. 2001), when considering more desirable vacations. The left amygdala and pregenual anterior cingulate cortex, both previously shown to be associated with representation of monetary valuation (Glimcher et al. 2008), also showed this relationship.

A very recent study showed that when subjects viewed affective images and reported their level of positive or negatives emotions, the activity in the vmPFC/OFC predicted the experienced emotional value of the affective images (Winecoff et al. 2013). This study nicely demonstrated that the vmPFC/OFC encodes both negative and positive subjective emotional value in a similar manner to monetary or primary rewards. In related studies, it has been shown that activity in the vmPFC/OFC also tracks moral judgments (Greene et al. 2001; Moll et al. 2002; see also Moll et al., 2015).

Hence, abstract valuations, such as attractiveness ratings for faces or scenes, emotional value, or even hedonic values, are all represented within the vmPFC/OFC and striatum. Another interesting study demonstrated that the vmPFC/OFC represented preference ratings of simple moving visual stimuli (Zeki and Stutters 2012). This suggests that the vmPFC/OFC represents values even for very basic low level sensory stimuli and that the spectrum of value representations are very broad and general and do not relate only to rewards that we either consume or from which we derive notable aesthetic or hedonic pleasure.

Bargaining, charitable giving, reciprocal situations, and morality

In the previous sections we have focused on value representations in conditions where the choices an individual had to make were made in isolation and had direct impact only on one's own self. However, in many cases, the choices we make influence other peoples' well-being and other peoples' choices will influence our well-being. The question that arises is whether value representations in both of these cases are located within the same neural value networks, and specifically, is there evidence that the vmPFC/OFC represents values in social and interactive situations?

One of the early studies in this domain came from the work of Sanfey and colleagues (2003b) in which they measured subjects' neural activity while inside the fMRI scanner when they had to decide whether to accept or reject fair and unfair offers in the ultimatum game (UG). They found that the anterior insula correlated with the unfairness of an offer. That is, the more the offer was unfair, the higher the activity within the anterior insula. It was also shown that the activity in the anterior insula could be used to predict subjects' propensity to accept or reject an unfair offer (Sanfey et al. 2003b; Tabibnia et al. 2008). Importantly, the anterior insula has been identified in many other value-related studies as negatively correlated with reward values (for a review see: Levy and Glimcher 2012). It is well known that the anterior insula gets direct inputs from the vicera and is associated with feelings of disgust (Beissner et al. 2013). Hence, it was hypothesized that the feelings of unfair economics offers triggers negative emotions similar to the feelings of disgust.

Subsequent studies have demonstrated that all the main brain areas mentioned in the previous sections that represent the various aspects of valuations as measured in non-social tasks, also represent the various aspects of social-related values such as reward from mutual cooperation, empathy for recipient, aversive response to unreciprocated cooperation, etc. (for a review see: Rilling and Sanfey 2011). For example, it has been shown that reciprocated cooperation in the trust game is associated with activation in the caudate nucleus, which is part of the striatum (Delgado et al. 2005; Rilling et al. 2002; Rilling et al. 2004) and the vmPFC/OFC (Rilling et al. 2002; Rilling et al. 2004). Importantly, the level of neural activity in the caudate nucleus can even be used to predict the tendency to co-operate (King-Casas et al. 2005; Rilling et al. 2002). We direct readers who are interested in a more in-depth analyses of the neural value representations of social interactions to some excellent reviews (Rilling et al. 2008; Rilling and Sanfey 2011; Ruff and Fehr 2014).

In a similar manner to reciprocal interactions, there are several other human behaviors that also require the ability to prefer others' benefits and increased utility at the expense of one's own benefit. These kinds of behaviors are collectively known either as altruistic behaviors or other-regarding preferences, and in many cases there are driven by moral beliefs. When people engage in these sort of decision problems they must evaluate and compare the costs of giving something away, which could be a material reward, time, or even physical work, to the value they derive from the abstract notion of doing something good or preventing something bad from happening to other people or, in some cases, the value derived is in the form of an abstract goal, principle, or belief. The question again is whether there is evidence that the same core valuation areas represent the values of these very abstract and non-materialistic values.

One of the classical paradigms used for examining these kinds of choices is charitable donation. In these kinds of tasks, subjects usually have the option to decide either to donate money to some charitable organization (which would be considered an example of an altruistic or other-regarding behavior) or to keep the money to themselves. Several studies have indeed demonstrated that some parts of the vmPFC/OFC and striatal regions, represent value-related signals while subjects were evaluating and deciding whether or not to donate to a charitable organization or cause (Harbaugh et al. 2007; Moll et al. 2006; Waytz et al. 2012). In yet other related altruistic tasks, similar patterns of activity were observed (Dawes et al. 2012; de Quervain et al. 2004). (For reviews see: Fehr and Camerer 2007; Forbes and Grafman 2010; Moll et al. 2008.)

Lesions

Lesion studies are an excellent tool to examine the importance of a brain area in given situations and tasks. Lesion studies were amongst the earliest demonstrations of the importance of the vmPFC/OFC in decision-making. It is widely accepted that patients with lesions in the vmPFC/OFC show poor social and individual decision-making skills and abnormal anticipatory emotional responses. The early studies showed that lesioned patients demonstrate abnormalities in their choice behavior, their ability to correctly estimate winning probabilities, or deal with uncertainties (Bechara et al. 1999; Bechara et al. 1997; Rogers et al. 1999), or to solve real-world problems such as financial planning and other problem-types involving planning and look-ahead components (Bechara et al. 1994; Bechara et al. 2000; Goel et al. 1997). Patients with damage to the PFC even show a tendency for riskier decision-making and an apparent disregard for negative consequences of their actions (Rahman et al. 2001).

Later studies also showed that damage to this area leads to difficulties in choosing between options with uncertain outcomes, whether in the form of risk or ambiguity (Camille et al. 2011; Fellows and Farah 2005; Hsu et al. 2005; Manes et al. 2002; Sanfey et al. 2003a; Valentin and O'Doherty 2009), and to difficulties in adjusting responses when the reinforcement value of stimuli change, as demonstrated in impaired reversal learning tasks (Fellows and Farah 2003; Hornak et al. 2004). Lesion studies also demonstrated the crucial role that the vmPFC serves in social valuation. For example, vmPFC-lesioned patients rejected unfair offers more often than controls (Koenigs and Tranel 2007).

A main question that arises from these lesion studies is whether the vmPFC/OFC is necessary for representing values per se or is necessary only when there are choices that involve uncertainty, ambiguity, or the need to update value during a learning task. Two very elegant studies demonstrated that damage to the vmPFC/OFC resulted in less consistent choices during simple preference judgment tasks (Camille et al. 2011; Fellows and Farah

2007). All of these data thus suggest that an intact vmPFC/OFC is crucial for basic value representations and for obeying the fundamental axioms of economic rationality.

It has also been shown that patients with vmPFC/OFC lesions do not report any feelings of regret and they do not anticipate possible negative consequences that might occur as a result of their choices (Bechara 2004). Hence, the data suggest that the vmPFC/OFC is also mediating the role of counterfactual thinking in valuation. That is, it is not just representing values of the actual choices but it is also representing the values of other possible options that we did not take but could have taken (for a review see: Walton et al. 2011). This is an important aspect of learning the values of options in the environment and updating them for future choices.

More than one reward type

However, in all of the studies described above, only a single reward-type and a single task-type were used to examine the neural representation of value. While these studies clearly identified important areas that participate in value representation and choice, they can only provide circumstantial evidence for the notion of a single neural common currency that represents values across reward types. The more direct evidence for this notion that serves as the main claim for this chapter arises from studies that search specifically for a common representation of value across different choice tasks or across different reward types measured within individual subjects.

Different choice tasks within an individual

One of the first studies to use more than one behavioral task to search for the neural representation of a single reward-type, in this case a monetary reward, was a 2009 study by Glascher and colleagues. In that experiment, subjects completed two versions of a monetarily rewarded decision-making task while in an fMRI scanner. In the first version, subjects chose between two different visual stimuli that were associated with two different probabilistic monetary rewards. They hypothesized that under these conditions the visual cues would come to be associated with monetary values and it was those stimulus-based value representations that they hoped to identify. In the other version, subjects made choices between two different motor responses in the absence of visual cues, each of which was also associated with a probabilistic monetary reward. They hypothesized that under these conditions the motor actions would come to be associated with the monetary rewards and it was the neural representation of these action-values that they hoped to identify. They found that the activity of a subregion of the medial prefrontal cortex—a region that had been identified previously in the single-task and single-reward studies mentioned above—correlated with expected future reward in both task versions.

A closely related paper by Peters and Buchel (2009) searched for brain areas that represent the subjective values of delayed monetary rewards and the subjective values of risky monetary lotteries. Their main finding was, again, that a subregion of the medial prefrontal cortex, which they referred to as the OFC, tracked the subjective value of both delayed and probabilistic rewards. They also found that the ventral striatum showed this same pattern of activity. Levy and colleagues (2010), in a similar vein, searched for neural representations of both risky (when the probabilities are known) and ambiguous (when the probabilities are unknown) monetary lotteries. Again they found both of those representations in the medial prefrontal cortex and the ventral striatum. Basten and colleagues (2010) even showed that when subjects must integrate information about both monetary gains (benefit) and monetary losses (cost), activity in this same medial frontal area is correlated with the integrated difference between these two properties. In a related study, Treadway and colleagues (2012) showed that dopamine function (measured using PET) within the vmPFC/OFC and striatum correlated positively across subjects, and the insula correlated negatively with the willingness to invest effort for the opportunity to win larger rewards. This study nicely links the activity within some of the main value-related areas with dopamine function in cost–benefit calculations of values. However, note that Croxson and colleagues (2009) observed that cost–benefit representations of net value was evident in the striatum and not in the vmPFC/OFC but rather in an adjacent area; the dorsal anterior cingulate cortex (ACC)—an area in which there is significant ongoing inquiry.

Another recent study examined whether value representations of empathic choice, to choose on behalf of others in order to maximize their well-being, is located in the same brain areas that represent values when one chooses for oneself (Janowski et al. 2013). In two separated scanning sessions, subjects made monetary bids for DVDs; either for themselves or for other subjects. In agreement with the studies described above, activity within the vmPFC/OFC correlated with the amount of money the subjects bid for themselves *and for others*. Therefore, this study demonstrates that when we value items or options that do not benefit us directly, we employ similar brain mechanisms and brain areas.

From these studies, and a host of others, it seems clear that a subregion of the vmPFC/OFC appears to encode subjective monetary value signals of almost every kind and it suggests that these different kinds of monetary values may be represented on a common scale, irrespective of task details. But much more compelling evidence of a common currency for reward comparison would be the demonstration that, within an individual, value representations for fundamentally different reward types arise in exactly the same areas.

Multiple reward types in the same task

FitzGerald and colleagues (2009) were the first to conduct such a study. They searched for value-related representations of money and consumer goods like mugs, boxes of chocolate, and universal serial bus (USB) keys. Subjects had to choose between receiving (or giving up) some amount of money and receiving (or giving up) a few of these consumer goods. The authors found that activation in the vmPFC/OFC (and also in the PCC, and the insula—which showed a negative correlation) was correlated with the difference between the subjective values of the two available options. Importantly, they showed that this was true for both gains and losses. Soon afterwards, Chib and colleagues (2009) made this argument in a more fundamental way when they explored the neural representation of three different reward types using a within-subject design. They explored the value-associated representation of money, snack foods, and CalTech novelty items like hats (trinkets) in single individuals. Their design was organized into two scanning sessions. In the first, subjects chose on each trial between a certain monetary gain and a probability of winning a snack food or trinket. In the second session these same kinds of choices were made, but this time between the certain win of a fixed snack food and probability of winning a trinket or a given amount of money. Once again, they found that a subregion in the vmPFC/OFC represented the subjective values of all three reward types.

Ishizu and Zeki (2011) examined whether the experience of perceiving beauty derived from different sources would result in similar neural value representations. In their study, subjects rated how beautiful both auditory and visual stimuli were while inside the fMRI scanner. The auditory stimuli were classical and modern excerpts of music and the visual stimuli were paintings. The authors found a subregion within the vmPFC/OFC that tracked value ratings of both auditory and visual stimuli, suggesting that activity within the vmPFC/OFC tracks subjective valuation not just for different reward types but also for the valuation of sensory events that originate from different sensory modalities.

In line with these studies, Kim and colleagues (2011) examined brain activity while subjects made a forced choice between visual cues associated with positive/negative amounts of money and appetitive/aversive fluids delivered orally while in the scanner. They found that a subregion of the vmPFC/OFC tracked the expectation of receiving both monetary and fluid offers—showing increasing BOLD activity for positively valued fluids and monetary events and decreasing activity when either of those was of negative value. Interestingly, they also found that the right anterior insula had a negative correlation with increasing expected reward value for both money and juice. Another study demonstrated that neural activity within the dorsal striatum represented a value-teaching signal (a *reward prediction error*) while subjects learned the values of monetary and juice rewards (Valentin and O'Doherty 2009).

Talmi and colleagues (2009), in yet another related study, examined the interaction between monetary rewards and physical pain. Subjects in that study chose between two stimuli, each associated with either a high or low probability (75 and 25 per cent, respectively) of earning money and a high or low probability of experiencing pain (thus creating a 2×2 stimulus design). Thus when subjects faced a possible monetary gain they had to take into consideration the "cost" of receiving possible pain when making their choices. What the authors found was that the cost-benefit value signals converged in an interactive manner: Activity in the insula was correlated with the behavioral impact of the pain on their choices, and this insula activation was inversely correlated with activity in the vmPFC/OFC. The greater the perceived cost of the pain, the lower the activity in the vmPFC/OFC, and this effect appeared to be modulated through the level of activity in the insular region they examined. Another study also examined how humans integrate the value of monetary rewards and physical pain (Park et al. 2011). In that study subjects had to decide whether to accept or reject offers that were combinations of some amount of money and some amount of physical pain (low current electrical stimulation applied to the finger) while lying inside the fMRI scanner. Again, the authors found that the activity within the vmPFC/OFC correlated with the subjective values of the combined monetary and pain rewards.

Izuma and colleagues (2008) expanded the domain of reward studies of this kind when they examined the neural representation of both social and monetary rewards. In their experiment, subjects engaged in a monetary task and a social reputation task. Acquiring positive reputation and gaining monetary rewards both activated the same area in the left striatum, suggesting that monetary rewards and social rewards are represented in a similar manner in the striatum. Lin and colleagues (2012) also examined the interaction between monetary and social values in a probabilistic choice task. On some trials, subjects had to choose between two uncertain social rewards and on other trials between two uncertain monetary rewards. Again, they found that activity in a subregion of the vmPFC/OFC correlated with both monetary and social subjective values.

In many decision-making studies of this kind, however, the choices subjects make are hypothetical and do not result in real payment. This is a source of some concern, particularly in the economic community. For many scholars it is important to examine the neural mechanism for representing gains and losses when subjects are conducting a choice task using hypothetical rewards and when they are using real rewards. Fortunately, Min Jeong Kang and colleagues (2011) examined these questions while subjects earned both real and hypothetical rewards inside the fMRI scanner. They found that subregions of the ventral striatum and the vmPFC/OFC tracked the value of various goods in both real and hypothetical choice conditions.

Common currency representation

These studies all suggest that the vmPFC/OFC, and perhaps the ventral striatum, represent the values of rewards of many different, and perhaps all, kinds. But in order to demonstrate that these representations exist in a single common currency appropriate for computing the tradeoffs that guide choice, one must also show that the activity level in these areas is equivalent whenever subjects report that offers of two different kinds of rewards are equally desirable. There are two papers that have done that, finding that equal behavioral value equates to equal BOLD signal in the vmPFC/OFC; evidence for a neural *common currency*. The BOLD signal, however, is not actually a direct measure of neural activity but rather a measure of the metabolic demand, and thus only a proxy for the actual neural activity (Huettel et al. 2008). Thus while our current understanding of fMRI strongly indicate the existence of neural activity encoding value in a common currency, the final proof that neural activity encodes value on a common scale will ultimately have to be made electrophysiologically (and to some degree already has been made in monkeys; Deaner et al. 2005). With that important caveat, we turn to those two studies.

The first study to provide evidence for a common currency representation in the BOLD signal was by Smith and colleagues (2010). In that study, male subjects performed two tasks while being brain scanned: A forced-choice task in which subjects could either win or lose money while watching female faces that ranged from very attractive to very unattractive, and a second task in which subjects had to decide how much money they were willing to spend to view a female face at a given level of attractiveness. This allowed them to establish an explicit exchange rate between viewing female faces and money, and then to scan face/money combinations, thus establishing a common neural representation of value for both reward types. They found that a specific subregion in the anterior parts of the vmPFC/OFC tracked the subject-specific values for each of the reward types. More importantly though, they found a subregion in the posterior part of the vmPFC/OFC that predicted the exchange rate between money and faces, established in the second task, across subjects. This is important because their data suggest that this particular area tracks the subject-specific values of faces and money in a single common neural currency.

The second study that used this strategy came from our labs (Levy and Glimcher 2011). We had very similar results using a different task that examined the neural representation of the value of food items and money. In that study, hungry subjects made choices between certain and risky rewards of money or foods (either chocolate M&Ms or Ritz crackers) inside the fMRI scanner. Out of the scanner we also had subjects make choices between fixed monetary offers and probabilistic lotteries over foods in order to establish the exchange rate between food and money for each subject. From this paradigm we were able to identify, as have the many previous studies mentioned above, that subregions of the vmPFC/OFC and the striatum tracked the subjective values for both money and food. We then asked whether the activation levels of these subregions that tracked the values of both food and money could be used to predict the exchange rate for food and money identified behaviorally outside of the scanner. Our data indicated that in the vmPFC/OFC region that represented both reward types, activity levels predict the exchange rate between money and food.

A third recent study also merits discussion in this regard, although it employed a different strategy to answer the same question of whether we can find strong evidence for a common currency representation in the vmPFC/OFC (McNamee et al. 2013). Similar to the Chib and colleagues (2009) study, the authors of this study first measured subjects' willingness to pay for three different reward types (money, snack foods, and trinkets) while inside the fMRI scanner. However, instead of only employing a standard univariate analysis, they used a multi-voxel pattern analyses method (for a review of this method, see: Haynes and Rees 2006; Norman et al. 2006) to relate neural activity to subjects' willingness-to-pay. First, they looked for subregions within the vmPFC/OFC that specifically tracked the value of only one reward-type, which they termed category-dependent value signals. For this, they developed an algorithm that searched for voxels encoding one stimulus category only and then determined if activity in these same voxels could be used to decode the value of independent items from that same category and *not* items from other categories. Second, they looked for subregions within the vmPFC/OFC that tracked values irrespective of reward type, which they termed category-independent value signals. They found subregions in the more ventral parts of the vmPFC/OFC representing category-dependent values (but only for food and trinkets). More importantly, they found a more dorsal area of the vmPFC/OFC (in an area that is closely related to those found in the previous overlapping studies described in the previous sections) a category-independent value representation (McNamee et al. 2013). This is a finding that, again, strengthens the notion that there is a subregion within the vmPFC/OFC that represents values on a common currency irrespective of the reward type.

From these studies we can conclude a few things. First, there is compelling evidence that a subregion of the vmPFC/OFC represents the subject-specific subjective value of multiple reward-types, across various tasks, and in a common neural currency appropriate for guiding choice. Second, there is some evidence—although this is much less certain—that suggests the insula may also represent subjective value in a common currency under some conditions, but in a negative manner, and finally there is evidence that the striatum may also represent subjective value.

Conclusions about the striatal representation are complicated by two factors. First, single-unit studies in the monkey (Lau and Glimcher 2008; Samejima et al. 2005) report a robust subjective value signal in the dorsal striatum, which has rarely been observed in human fMRI. This disparity may be due to the fact that the value-encoding neurons in the dorsal striatum are diffusely distributed (Kawagoe et al. 1998; Lau and Glimcher 2008) and thus difficult to image using fMRI. Using fMRI, however, value-related signals have been very widely observed in the ventral striatum (see references throughout this chapter), an observation, which has only begun to be confirmed with single unit recording methods.

Meta-analyses

When we last reviewed studies of value representation and choice (Kable and Glimcher 2009) there was a tremendous amount of evidence suggesting that the vmPFC/OFC region played a critical role. Literally dozens of studies available at that time pointed toward this area as critical. Since that time, not only have many other single-reward studies continued to point toward that area as critical, but a host of fMRI studies have now converged on the vmPFC/OFC as the site of a common neural currency for value representations. With all of this apparent convergence it seems important to ask whether it is really the same area that is active in these many studies by many different labs. Put another way, how strong is the evidence for an anatomically localized subregion in the human frontal cortex that tracks subjective values on a common currency for all previously studied reward-types?

In order to answer this question we and others have conducted meta-analytic studies. In our meta-analysis (Levy and Glimcher 2012) we used data from thirteen principle studies that used more than one reward-type and/or one task. We took the coordinates specified in those studies of the voxel that was most active (peak voxel) for the value-related signals measured (mainly based on conjunction analyses between reward types or tasks). We marked these coordinates on a single brain template (using Montreal Neurological Institute coordinates). As can be seen very clearly in Fig. 5.1, the coordinates describing the peak voxels are in the vmPFC/OFC and in nearly all of these studies are strikingly similar.

The other meta-analyses have come to very similar conclusions. Bartra and colleagues (2013) conducted a meta-analysis on 206 value-related fMRI studies. As can be seen in

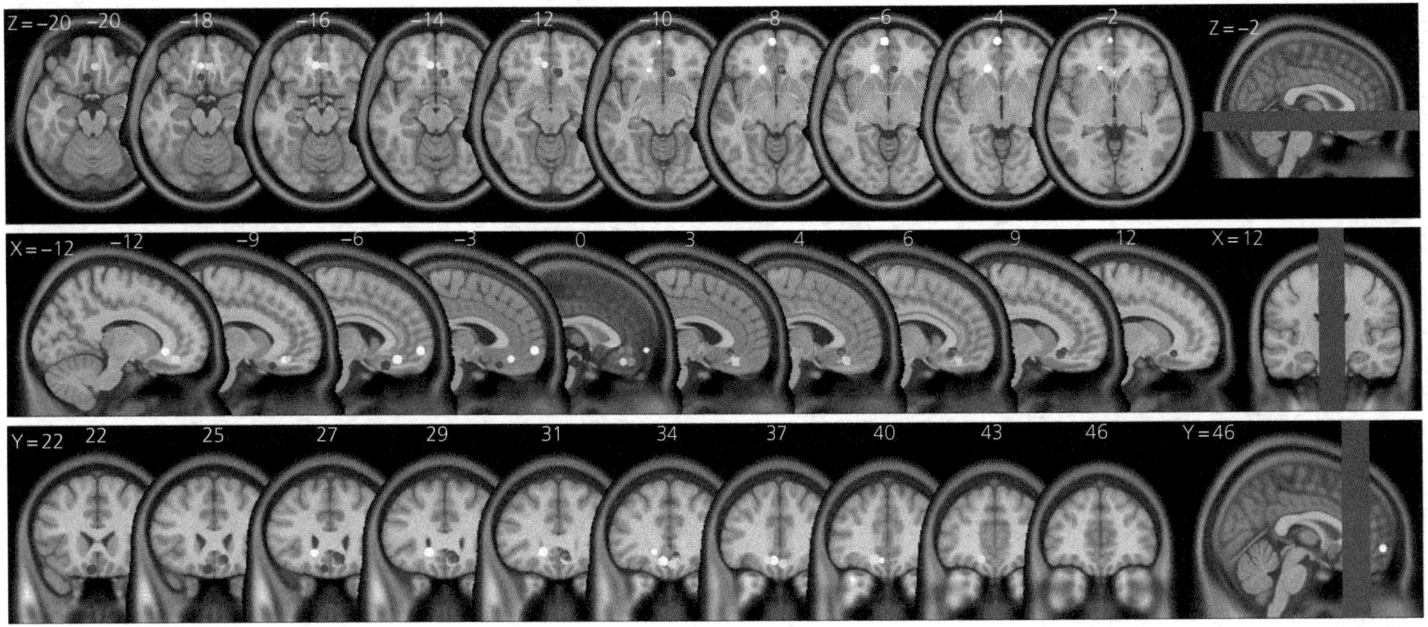

Fig. 5.1 Peak voxels in the subregion of the vmPFC/OFC representing value-related signals from thirteen studies that used more than one reward type and/or one task as described in (Levy and Glimcher 2012). The coordinates of the peak voxels were taken from the original studies and are detailed in Levy and Glimcher (2012). Brain images are the T1 MNI-152 template. (See Plate 2.)

Reprinted from *Current Opinion in Neurobiology*, 22(6), pp, 1027–1038. Levy, D. J., and Glimcher, P. W. The root of all value: a neural common currency for choice, (2012), with permission from Elsevier.

5-way Conjunction: [Positive > Negative] and Decision and Receipt and Monetary and Primary

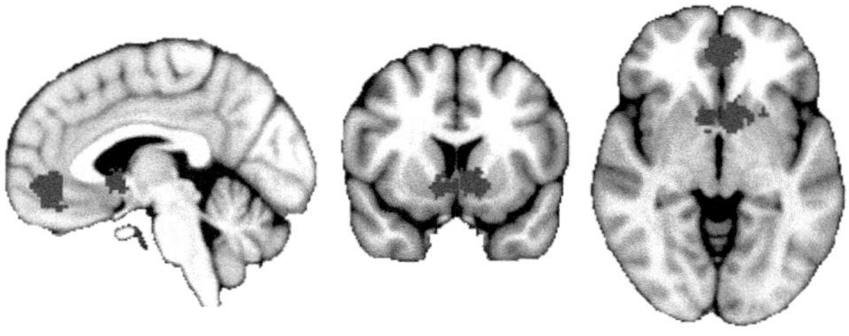

Fig. 5.2 A five-way conjunction analysis, designed to identify brain areas that represent subjective value irrespective of reward type. The conjunction analysis was conducted on voxels that showed significantly greater density for positive than negative effects, and showed high activity for positive events at both the decision and receipt stages, as well as for both monetary and primary reward types. (See Plate 3.)

Reprinted from *NeuroImage*, Volume 76, 1 August 2013, pp. 412–427, Bartra, O., McGuire, J. T., and Kable, J. W. The valuation system: a coordinate-based meta-analysis of BOLD fMRI experiments examining neural correlates of subjective value, (2013) with permission from Elsevier.

Fig. 5.2, they found that across all studies and irrespective of the reward type used, activity in the vmPFC/OFC, the PCC, and the anterior-ventral striatum were positively correlated with subjective value. They also found that the dorsal and posterior striatum (a different part than the striatal area associated with the common unified system), thalamus, anterior insula, and the dorsomedial PFC, have a quadratic relationship with value as opposed to the more linear positive correlation observed in the general value-related brain areas. They suggested that the quadratic pattern probably represent an arousal or a salience signal, while the linear relationship found in the vmPFC/OFC, PCC, and ventral striatum is indicative of a general unified value-related system.

Sescousse and colleagues (2013) conducted an activation likelihood estimation meta-analysis on eighty-seven fMRI studies that examined monetary, primary, and erotic rewards. They came to very similar conclusions: that the vmPFC/OFC, anterior insula, and striatum represent subjective values irrespective of reward type. Interestingly they also identified the amygdala and medio-dorsal thalamus as part of this value network. In a similar manner, Peters and Buchel (2010) demonstrated in a meta-analysis that the vmPFC/OFC area represents various value types such as outcome values, goal values, and decision values. Interestingly, another meta-analysis demonstrated that the vmPFC/OFC and ventral striatum probably do not represent identical value-related signals (Diekhof et al. 2012). They showed that the vmPFC/OFC area was more active during reward outcome, while the ventral striatum was more active during reward anticipation, strengthening the notion of the striatum's role in value learning and expectations.

In the most recent study of this kind, Clithero and Rangel (2013) conducted a meta-analysis on eighty-one different studies and replicated the results from the previous meta-analytic studies. That is, they showed that the vmPFC/OFC, ventral striatum, and PCC are representing various aspects of subjective values across a wide range of tasks, reward types, and choice stages. However, they extended the previous findings by showing that there are several networks that were co-activated with subareas within the vmPFC/OFC suggesting a possible parcellation of information; although questions remain about what exact information is represented within each subnetwork, and how it contributes to the global value signal. Finally the authors found some evidence that suggests a posterior-to-anterior gradient of value representations within the vmPFC/OFC. That is, the more abstract a reward is, the more anterior would be its neural value representation within the vmPFC/OFC.

This strengthens the main conclusion we hoped to convey in this chapter, that the vmPFC/OFC and striatum are principal nodes of one general and unified value-based neural system and that there is a small subregion in the vmPFC/OFC that tracks subjective value on a common currency appropriate for guiding choices between different kinds of rewards. Indeed, these data seem to suggest that the subregions within the vmPFC/OFC and striatum can be used as a basis for constructing an unbiased region of interest (ROI) for further studies of reward and valuation. Because there is now ample data demonstrating that areas in the vmPFC/OFC and striatum correlate with value signals, it now seems appropriate to conclude that research can begin to advance from using whole-brain analyses of fMRI data to a more focused approach reminiscent of the strategy used in electrophysiological studies. This could lead to more concrete and testable predictions, rather than relying on whole-brain analyses aimed only at the cerebral localization of value. The data suggest, in essence, that fMRI studies of value have now advanced beyond the point of whole-brain analyses driven only toward cerebral localization and to a point where the high-resolution physiology of valuation can become a tractable goal.

Predictions

In fact, several human fMRI studies have now employed this more focused approach and directly used neural activity in specific value-related areas of human subjects to try and predict future choices. Lebreton and colleagues (2009) extracted the neural activity from the vmPFC/OFC, striatum, hippocampus, and PCC while subjects rated how pleasant different reward types were, such as faces, houses, and paintings. They then used these neural activations to successfully predict subjects' preferences for these reward-types as measured in a binary choice task outside the scanner. The most interesting part of that study was that they were able to predict subjects' preferences, even when subjects conducted the binary choice task a month after the fMRI session. This suggests that it is possible to use neural activations from the common value areas to successfully predict subjects' subsequent choices and that these neural activations can be, in some situations, stable enough to make predictions regarding choices made relatively far in the future.

In a subsequent study, Anita Tusche and colleagues (2010) used multi-voxel pattern analysis to determine whether they could predict subjects' subsequent propensity to (hypothetically) buy cars by analyzing subjects' brain activity while they were watching the same cars inside the scanner. Interestingly, in that study there were two experimental groups. Subjects in the first group (high-attention group) were requested to consciously attend the cars and to think how much they liked the car they were currently reviewing and to report their answer on a four-point scale. Subjects in the second group (low-attention group) were asked to perform a demanding fixation task. The task was intended to distract subjects from consciously paying attention to the cars, which they did not have to consciously evaluate. After scanning, subjects from both groups were requested to imagine that they were in a store and had to choose a new car. They were shown each of the cars presented before in the scanner and were asked to answer "No/Not sure/Yes" to the question: "Would you buy this car?" The important thing to note here is that subjects did not know during scanning that they would be asked this question during the second phase outside the scanner. The authors successfully used activation in the insula and in the vmPFC/OFC in order to decode subjects' subsequent choices. An interesting part of this study was that the authors could predict subsequent choices in both experimental groups. This suggests that value representations within the vmPFC/OFC and other value-related areas are present even when subjects do not consciously evaluate an item. This suggests that valuation is an ongoing non-stop mechanism that operates always and is not dependent on conscious awareness or on attention (although it might be modulated and affected by them).

In a related study, Levy and colleagues (2011) measured the neural activations in the vmPFC and striatum while subjects passively viewed twenty different goods inside the scanner. Thereafter, outside the scanner, they conducted a binary choice task for all possible pairwise comparisons of the same twenty items. From the choices, they constructed an ordinal preference ranking of the twenty items. They then used the measured neural activations to successfully predict subjects' subsequent choices. Importantly, the authors also constructed an ordinal neural ranking of the twenty items and showed that the two ordinal rankings (behavioral and neural) were significantly correlated across subjects and that the prediction accuracy was a function of the neural ordinal distance. That is, the greater the "neural distance," the better the prediction power (the maximum accuracy in this study was 82–83 percent). First, this study demonstrated again that one could use the neural activations from the common value areas to predict choice. Second, it demonstrated that the same brain areas are representing value during active choice and during passive evaluation of goods.

Quite a few studies have thus now demonstrated that a subregion of the vmPFC/OFC represents subject-specific reward value in a common neural currency, the *expected subjective value* of neuroeconomic theory (Glimcher 2011). This remarkably small area in both right and left vmPFC/OFC is activated in a way that parametrically correlates with the subjective values subjects attribute to nearly every kind of reward that has ever been studied in the scanner. The data indicate that when two disparate kinds of rewards are equally desirable to a subject, then activity in this area will be of equal magnitude for these two rewards in that individual. This is strong evidence supporting the claim that a subregion in the vmPFC/OFC tracks subjective value in a single common currency of the kind first described by economic theory hundreds of years ago. Using the insights from all the

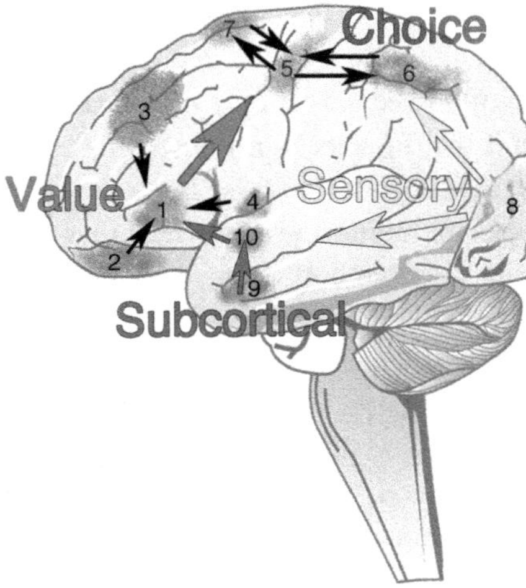

Fig. 5.3 One possible schema for understanding the decision-making networks of the human brain. Current evidence suggests that information from cortical and subcortical structures converges toward a single common value representation before passing on to the choice-related motor control circuitry. Modulatory inputs play a critical role in establishing this final common representation with those inputs carrying signals related to arousal, internal state (satiety, thirst, hormonal levels, etc.) and emotional intensity. In this schema, sensory information from all modalities carries, among other things, the identity and location of the options. We use visual signals in this diagram to stand for information from all sensory modalities. (1) vmPFC, (2) OFC, (3) DLPFC, (4) insula, (5) primary motor cortex (M1), (6) posterior parietal cortex, (7) frontal eye fields, (8) visual cortex, (9) amygdala, (10) striatum. (See Plate 4.)

Reprinted from *Current Opinion in Neurobiology*, 22(6), pp. 1027–1038. Levy, D. J., and Glimcher, P. W. The root of all value: a neural common currency for choice, (2012), with permission from Elsevier.

reviewed studies in this chapter we have previously generated a diagram (Levy and Glimcher 2012) that is a suggested possible schema for understanding the decision-making networks of the human brain (Fig. 5.3).

A recent study provided supporting evidence for this possible schema (Lim et al. 2013). In that study, subjects had to evaluate T-shirts that varied in their visual esthetic, by varying color or font type and in semantic meaning (the meaning of the logo on a printed T-shirt). Subjects had to rate how much they liked the esthetic appearance of the logo words on the T-shirt, and in another rating how much they liked the semantic meaning of the words. The authors found that activity in the fusiform gyrus, an area associated with the processing of visual features, correlated with the value of the visual esthetic attributes, but not with the value of the semantic attributes. In contrast, activity in posterior superior temporal gyrus, an area associated with the processing of semantic meaning, exhibited the opposite pattern. Interestingly, they also found that both areas exhibited functional connectivity with a subregion of the vmPFC/OFC that tracked the overall stimulus values at the time of decision. This study again supports the notion that some of the different attributes related to a given item are represented in different and specific brain areas but that the neural information of these attributes converge into the vmPFC/OFC (probably to other areas as well) to form a general and combined value representation of a given good.

It is important to note, however, that there is no evidence to support the claim that the neural common currency of value arises only in this subregion of the vmPFC/OFC. Any common currency observed in the brain must reflect the activation of multiple brain areas. It is almost certainly the case that other local and network activations lie beneath the resolution of the techniques used in these studies. Indeed, the evidence reviewed here suggests that portions of the striatum, the PCC, and perhaps the insula also participate in this process.

Another very relevant brain area that is hypothesized to be part of the valuation network is the ACC. First, it has strong anatomical connections with the vmPFC/OFC and other cortical and subcortical areas (Rushworth et al. 2011). Second, it has been shown that the ACC is monitoring several aspects of valuation and choice. It has been shown that it tracks erroneous choices (Rushworth et al. 2004; van Veen and Carter 2002), that it uses current and long-term reward information to guide appropriate choices (Boorman et al. 2013; Kolling et al. 2014), cost–benefit representations of net value (Croxson et al. 2009), and that it is coding the difficulty posed by conflict between competing choices (Botvinick 2007; Botvinick et al. 2001; Pochon et al. 2008; Shenhav et al. 2014). It is beyond the scope of this chapter to fully describe and discuss the different possible roles that the ACC might have in the common valuation network. We also want to note that the ACC is not a homogeneous area and it could be split into several smaller subregions that subserve somewhat different aspects of valuation (Beckmann et al. 2009; Torta and Cauda 2011). All we want to emphasize here is that it is probably an important part of the common valuation network. We guide the readers for several excellent reviews discussing the role of the ACC in valuation and choice (Noonan et al. 2011; Rushworth et al. 2011; Rushworth et al. 2012; Vassena et al. 2014).

Conclusion

An important point that needs to be considered is that the vmPFC/OFC has long been associated with functions other than decision-related valuation (Schoenbaum et al. 2011; Viskontas et al. 2007; Zald and Andreotti 2011). Factors ranging from emotion (Bechara 2004; Diekhof et al. 2011; Mitchell 2011; Sabatinelli et al. 2011), to social behavior (Viskontas et al. 2007), learning and memory (Corcoran and Quirk 2007; Gilboa 2004; Nieuwenhuis and Takashima 2011; Petrides 2007), through mental disorders such as depression (Lorenzetti et al. 2009; Pizzagalli 2011), post-traumatic stress disorder (Koenigs and Grafman 2009), obsessive–compulsive disorder (Del Casale et al. 2011; Zald and Kim 1996a, b), and psychopathy (Blair 2004, 2010) have all been identified in this brain region. This general area has also been associated with theory of mind (Abu-Akel and Shamay-Tsoory 2011; Lewis et al. 2011; Sebastian et al. 2012) and with the default network (Buckner et al. 2008). Given this host of functional associations, how should one interpret the wealth of data linking a subregion in this area to a function as specific as encoding a common neural currency for decision-making? Of course it is the case that the vmPFC/OFC is a fairly large area and not all of these functions will be mapped to the precise subregion we identify here, but there is enough overlap that this problem cannot be overlooked. And thus the observed overlap of these functions raises the fundamental question of whether we can consolidate all these functions into a unified theory of what this brain area is doing.

An excellent meta-analytic study and review paper tried to address exactly this question (Roy et al. 2012). In that paper, the authors conducted a meta-analysis of thousands of imaging studies using Neurosynth (www.neurosynth.org), which enables one to examine neural activations based on terms frequently used in manuscripts. They examined the relationship between the activation maps of various domains such as memory and "default mode" function, self-reflection, social cognition and mentalizing, emotion, reward, and autonomic and endocrine changes. They found a striking overlap for all these "meaning-related" constructs in the vmPFC/OFC, very similar to the area identified in value-related meta-analyses described in this chapter (see Fig. 5.4). They then conducted a factor analysis of all the various construct-maps they have identified and found two main subsystems that only overlapped in the vmPFC/OFC. They suggested that one system could be termed the "affect generation" system and the other system could be termed the "simulation system." Interestingly, they also suggested that, based on both these functional subsystems and on anatomical connectivity analyses, the vmPFC/OFC region is a unique area that integrates high-level cognitive signals with signals involved in the most basic forms of affective experience and physiological regulation.

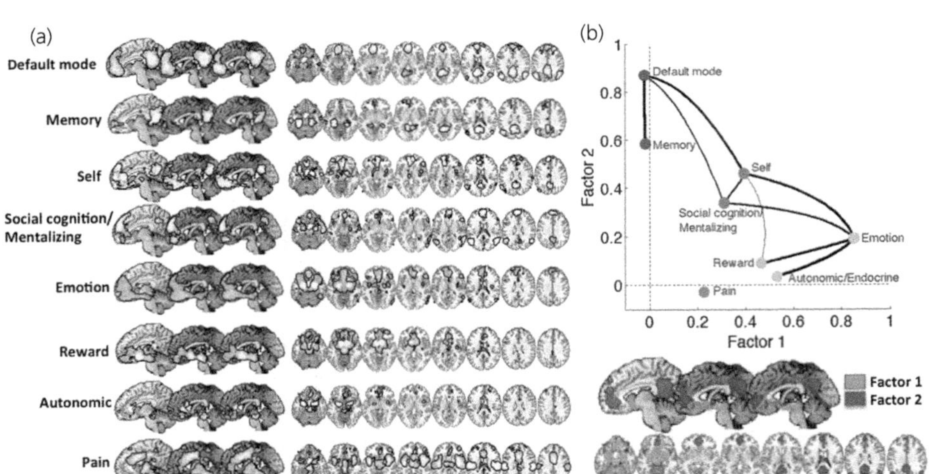

Fig. 5.4 The authors conducted a meta-analysis across various domains ranging from the default mode to reward and pain (see panel (a) for specific domains). They then conducted a factor analysis (with two main factors) across all the functional maps identified for the individual domains. Note that there is an overlap of both factors in the vmPFC/OFC area. For full details please refer to the original manuscript (Roy et al., 2012). (See Plate 5.)

Reprinted from *Trends in Cognitive Science*, 16 (3), pp. 147–156. Mathieu Roy, Daphna Shohamy, Tor D. Wager. Ventromedial prefrontal-subcortical systems and the generation of affective meaning, (2012), with permission from Elsevier.

We quote their conclusion of what they suggest as the main common role of the vmPFC/OFC: "... the functional role of the vmPFC is not reducible to any one of these functional categories [mentioned in the previous paragraph]. Rather, it serves as a hub that connects systems involved in episodic memory, representation of the affective qualities of sensory events, social cognition, interoceptive signals, and evolutionarily conserved affective physiological and behavioral responses. As such, it plays a unique role in representing conceptual information relevant for survival and in transducing concepts into affective behavioral and physiological responses." They termed this process or role of the vmPFC/OFC "affective meaning." They continue and explain that: "... meaning centered view of vmPFC predicts that vmPFC and its subcortical connections are not essential for simple forms of affect, valuation, and affective learning, but are essential when conceptual information drives affective physiological and behavioral responses." They conclude that the vmPFC/OFC may be considered as a system of systems that integrates signals from many other systems to generate an affective meaning of a situation.

One possibility is that this brain area is associated with many functions in different contexts and states. This possibility, although appealing, does not describe a fundamental and parsimonious principal of how the brain works. One might also hypothesize that a unifying feature of this area might be the notion that this area is representing some kind of value-related signal in each of these contexts. Presumably, what drives and directs much neural activity and subsequent behavior is value maximization in some form and it may be that this is one of several common threads relating the many findings in this brain region.

To resolve these issues more detailed anatomical measurements will be required that can map subregions to specific loci in the brain, ideally at a within-subject level. Given that higher anatomical resolution studies, and studies with causal methods, will be required to relate activation in these brain areas to specific functions any reconciliation would be purely speculative at this stage. The BOLD signal in a subregion of the vmPFC/OFC clearly represents the values of choice objects on a single common neural scale appropriate for guiding choice behavior. What that means for a larger functional assessment of the vmPFC/OFC area remains to be determined. Another open question is: What is the exact functional role in valuation and choice of each subregion within the vmPFC/OFC, based on the specific cytoarchitectonic organization and anatomical connections with other cortical and non-cortical areas? As described above, a recent meta-analysis addressed this question and has suggested some interesting hypotheses (Clithero and Rangel 2013).

Neuroeconomic and decision-making studies in the last decade have revealed some basic notions about the neural circuitry with which we make choices and represent value in our brains. There have been great advances in our understanding of how we learn and store new values in the brain and how these values influence our expectations and future behavior. In this exciting time, scientists from many fields are working to develop a unified theory of value and choice. This fast-growing area of inquiry will help us not just understand some of the basic principles of how the brain works, but should also help us understand and treat pathologies of choice such as addiction, pathological gambling and obesity.

References

Abu-Akel, A. and Shamay-Tsoory, S. (2011). Neuroanatomical and neurochemical bases of theory of mind. *Neuropsychologia*, **49**(11), 2971–2984. DOI: S0028-3932(11)00336-8 [pii] 10.1016/j.neuropsychologia.2011.07.012

Bartra, O., McGuire, J. T., and Kable, J. W. (2013). The valuation system: a coordinate-based meta-analysis of BOLD fMRI experiments examining neural correlates of subjective value. [Research Support, N.I.H., Extramural Research Support, Non-U.S. Gov't]. *Neuroimage*, **76**, 412–427. DOI: 10.1016/j.neuroimage.2013.02.063

Basten, U., Biele, G., Heekeren, H. R., and Fiebach, C. J. (2010). How the brain integrates costs and benefits during decision making. *Proc Natl Acad Sci USA*, **107**(50), 21767–21772. DOI: 0908104107 [pii]10.1073/pnas.0908104107

Bechara, A. (2004). The role of emotion in decision-making: evidence from neurological patients with orbitofrontal damage. *Brain Cogn*, **55**(1), 30–40. DOI: 10.1016/j.bandc.2003.04.001 S0278262603002859 [pii]

Bechara, A., Damasio, A. R., Damasio, H., and Anderson, S. W. (1994). Insensitivity to future consequences following damage to human prefrontal cortex. [Research Support, Non-U.S. Gov't Research Support, U.S. Gov't, P.H.S.]. *Cognition*, **50**(1–3), 7–15.

Bechara, A., Damasio, H., Tranel, D., and Damasio, A. R. (1997). Deciding advantageously before knowing the advantageous strategy. [Comparative Study Research Support, U.S. Gov't, P.H.S.]. *Science*, **275**(5304), 1293–1295.

Bechara, A., Damasio, H., Damasio, A. R., and Lee, G. P. (1999). Different contributions of the human amygdala and ventromedial prefrontal cortex to decision-making. [Comparative Study Research Support, Non-U.S. Gov't Research Support, U.S. Gov't, P.H.S.]. *J Neurosci*, **19**(13), 5473–5481.

Bechara, A., Damasio, H., and Damasio, A. R. (2000). Emotion, decision making and the orbitofrontal cortex. [Research Support, Non-U.S. Gov't Research Support, U.S. Gov't, P.H.S. Review]. *Cereb Cortex*, **10**(3), 295–307.

Beckmann, M., Johansen-Berg, H., and Rushworth, M. F. (2009). Connectivity-based parcellation of human cingulate cortex and its relation to functional specialization. [Research Support, Non-U.S. Gov't]. *J Neurosci*, **29**(4), 1175–1190. DOI: 10.1523/JNEUROSCI.3328–3308.2009

Beissner, F., Meissner, K., Bar, K. J., and Napadow, V. (2013). The autonomic brain: an activation likelihood estimation meta-analysis for central processing of autonomic function. [Meta-Analysis Research Support, N.I.H., Extramural Research Support, Non-U.S. Gov't Review]. *J Neurosci*, **33**(25), 10503–10511. DOI: 10.1523/JNEUROSCI.1103–1113.2013

Bernoulli, D. (1738). Specimen theoriae novae de mensura sortis. *Commentarii Academiae Scientiarum Imperialis Petropolitanae*(5), 175–192.

Blair, R. J. (2004). The roles of orbital frontal cortex in the modulation of antisocial behavior. *Brain Cogn*, **55**(1), 198–208. DOI: 10.1016/S0278–2626(03)00276–8 S0278262603002768 [pii]

Blair, R. J. (2010). Psychopathy, frustration, and reactive aggression: the role of ventromedial prefrontal cortex. *Br J Psychol*, **101**(Pt 3), 383–399. DOI: bjp604 [pii] 10.1348/000712609X418480

Boorman, E. D., Rushworth, M. F., and Behrens, T. E. (2013). Ventromedial prefrontal and anterior cingulate cortex adopt choice and default reference frames during sequential multi-alternative choice. [Randomized Controlled Trial Research Support, Non-U.S. Gov't]. *J Neurosci*, **33**(6), 2242–2253. DOI: 10.1523/JNEUROSCI.3022–3012.2013

Botvinick, M. M. (2007). Conflict monitoring and decision making: reconciling two perspectives on anterior cingulate function. [Research Support, N.I.H., Extramural Review]. *Cogn Affect Behav Neurosci*, **7**(4), 356–366.

Botvinick, M. M., Braver, T. S., Barch, D. M., Carter, C. S., and Cohen, J. D. (2001). Conflict monitoring and cognitive control. [Research Support, Non-U.S. Gov't Research Support, U.S. Gov't, P.H.S.]. *Psychol Rev*, **108**(3), 624–652.

Breiter, H. C., Aharon, I., Kahneman, D., Dale, A., and Shizgal, P. (2001). Functional imaging of neural responses to expectancy and experience of monetary gains and losses. *Neuron*, **30**(2), 619–639. DOI: S0896-6273(01)00303-8 [pii]

Buckner, R. L., Andrews-Hanna, J. R., and Schacter, D. L. (2008). The brain's default network: anatomy, function, and relevance to disease. *Ann N Y Acad Sci*, **1124**, 1–38. DOI: 1124/1/1 [pii] 10.1196/annals.1440.011

Camille, N., Griffiths, C. A., Vo, K., Fellows, L. K., and Kable, J. W. (2011). Ventromedial frontal lobe damage disrupts value maximization in humans. [Comparative Study Research Support, N.I.H., Extramural Research Support, Non-U.S. Gov't]. *J Neurosci*, **31**(20), 7527–7532. DOI: 10.1523/JNEUROSCI.6527-6510.2011

Chib, V. S., Rangel, A., Shimojo, S., and O'Doherty, J. P. (2009). Evidence for a common representation of decision values for dissimilar goods in human ventromedial prefrontal cortex. *J Neurosci*, **29**(39), 12315–12320. DOI: 29/39/12315 [pii] 10.1523/JNEUROSCI.2575-2509.2009

Clithero, J. A. and Rangel, A. (2013). Informatic parcellation of the network involved in the computation of subjective value. *Soc Cogn Affect Neurosci*. DOI:10.1093/scan/nst106

Cloutier, J., Heatherton, T. F., Whalen, P. J., and Kelley, W. M. (2008). Are attractive people rewarding? Sex differences in the neural substrates of facial attractiveness. [Comparative Study Research Support, N.I.H., Extramural Research Support, Non-U.S. Gov't]. *J Cogn Neurosci*, **20**(6), 941–951. DOI: 10.1162/jocn.2008.20062

Corcoran, K. A. and Quirk, G. J. (2007). Recalling safety: cooperative functions of the ventromedial prefrontal cortex and the hippocampus in extinction. *CNS Spectr*, **12**(3), 200–206.

Croxson, P. L., Walton, M. E., O'Reilly, J. X., Behrens, T. E., and Rushworth, M. F. (2009). Effort-based cost-benefit valuation and the human brain. [Comparative Study Research Support, Non-U.S. Gov't]. *J Neurosci*, **29**(14), 4531–4541. DOI: 10.1523/JNEUROSCI.4515-4508.2009

Dawes, C. T., Loewen, P. J., Schreiber, D., Simmons, A. N., Flagan, T., McElreath, R., and Paulus, M. P. (2012). Neural basis of egalitarian behavior. [Research Support, Non-U.S. Gov't]. *Proc Natl Acad Sci USA*, **109**(17), 6479–6483. DOI: 10.1073/pnas.1118653109

Deaner, R. O., Khera, A. V., and Platt, M. L. (2005). Monkeys pay per view: adaptive valuation of social images by rhesus macaques. *Curr Biol*, **15**(6), 543–548. DOI: S0960-9822(05)00093-X [pii] 10.1016/j.cub.2005.01.044

Del Casale, A., Kotzalidis, G. D., Rapinesi, C., Serata, D., Ambrosi, E., Simonetti, A., and Girardi, P. (2011). Functional neuroimaging in obsessive-compulsive disorder. *Neuropsychobiology*, **64**(2), 61–85. DOI: 000325223 [pii] 10.1159/000325223

Del Parigi, A., Gautier, J. F., Chen, K., Salbe, A. D., Ravussin, E., Reiman, E., and Tataranni, P. A. (2002). Neuroimaging and obesity: mapping the brain responses to hunger and satiation in humans using positron emission tomography. *Ann N Y Acad Sci*, **967**, 389–397.

Delgado, M. R., Nystrom, L. E., Fissell, C., Noll, D. C., and Fiez, J. A. (2000). Tracking the hemodynamic responses to reward and punishment in the striatum. *J Neurophysiol*, **84**(6), 3072–3077.

Delgado, M. R., Frank, R. H., and Phelps, E. A. (2005). Perceptions of moral character modulate the neural systems of reward during the trust game. [Comparative Study Research Support, N.I.H., Extramural Research Support, Non-U.S. Gov't]. *Nat Neurosci*, **8**(11), 1611–1618. DOI: 10.1038/nn1575

de Quervain, D. J., Fischbacher, U., Treyer, V., Schellhammer, M., Schnyder, U., Buck, A., and Fehr, E. (2004). The neural basis of altruistic punishment. [Research Support, Non-U.S. Gov't]. *Science*, **305**(5688), 1254–1258. DOI: 10.1126/science.1100735

Diekhof, E. K., Geier, K., Falkai, P., and Gruber, O. (2011). Fear is only as deep as the mind allows: a coordinate-based meta-analysis of neuroimaging studies on the regulation of negative affect. *Neuroimage*, **58**(1), 275–285. DOI: S1053-8119(11)00598-2 [pii] 10.1016/j.neuroimage.2011.05.073

Diekhof, E. K., Kaps, L., Falkai, P., and Gruber, O. (2012). The role of the human ventral striatum and the medial orbitofrontal cortex in the representation of reward magnitude—an activation likelihood estimation meta-analysis of neuroimaging studies of passive reward expectancy and outcome processing. [Meta-Analysis Review]. *Neuropsychologia*, **50**(7), 1252–1266. DOI: 10.1016/j.neuropsychologia.2012.02.007

Elliott, R., Friston, K. J., and Dolan, R. J. (2000). Dissociable neural responses in human reward systems. *J Neurosci*, **20**(16), 6159–6165. DOI: 20/16/6159 [pii]

Elliott, R., Newman, J. L., Longe, O. A., and Deakin, J. F. (2003). Differential response patterns in the striatum and orbitofrontal cortex to financial reward in humans: a parametric functional magnetic resonance imaging study. *J Neurosci*, **23**(1), 303–307. DOI: 23/1/303 [pii]

Fehr, E. and Camerer, C. F. (2007). Social neuroeconomics: the neural circuitry of social preferences. [Review]. *Trends Cogn Sci*, **11**(10), 419–427. DOI: 10.1016/j.tics.2007.09.002

Fellows, L. K. and Farah, M. J. (2003). Ventromedial frontal cortex mediates affective shifting in humans: evidence from a reversal learning paradigm. [Research Support, Non-U.S. Gov't Research Support, U.S. Gov't, Non-P.H.S. Research Support, U.S. Gov't, P.H.S.]. *Brain*, **126**(Pt 8), 1830–1837. DOI: 10.1093/brain/awg180

Fellows, L. K. and Farah, M. J. (2005). Different underlying impairments in decision-making following ventromedial and dorsolateral frontal lobe damage in humans. [Research Support, Non-U.S. Gov't Research Support, U.S. Gov't, Non-P.H.S. Research Support, U.S. Gov't, P.H.S.]. *Cereb Cortex*, **15**(1), 58–63. DOI: 10.1093/cercor/bhh108

Fellows, L. K. and Farah, M. J. (2007). The role of ventromedial prefrontal cortex in decision making: judgment under uncertainty or judgment per se? [Research Support, N.I.H., Extramural Research Support, Non-U.S. Gov't]. *Cereb Cortex*, **17**(11), 2669–2674. DOI: 10.1093/cercor/bhl176

FitzGerald, T. H., Seymour, B., and Dolan, R. J. (2009). The role of human orbitofrontal cortex in value comparison for incommensurable objects. *J Neurosci*, **29**(26), 8388–8395. DOI: 29/26/8388 [pii] 10.1523/JNEUROSCI.0717-09.2009

Forbes, C. E. and Grafman, J. (2010). The role of the human prefrontal cortex in social cognition and moral judgment. [Research Support, N.I.H., Intramural Review]. *Annu Rev Neurosci*, **33**, 299–324. DOI: 10.1146/annurev-neuro-060909-153230

Gilboa, A. (2004). Autobiographical and episodic memory—one and the same? Evidence from prefrontal activation in neuroimaging studies. *Neuropsychologia*, **42**(10), 1336–1349. DOI: 10.1016/j.neuropsychologia.2004.02.014 S0028393204000636 [pii]

Glascher, J., Hampton, A. N., and O'Doherty, J. P. (2009). Determining a role for ventromedial prefrontal cortex in encoding action-based value signals during reward-related decision making. *Cereb Cortex*, **19**(2), 483–495. DOI: bhn098 [pii] 10.1093/cercor/bhn098

Glimcher, P. W. (2011). *Foundations of neuroeconomic analysis*. New York: Oxford University Press.

Glimcher, P. W., Camerer, C., C., Fehr, E., and Poldrack, R. A. (2008). *Neuroeconomics: Decision making and the brain* (1st edn). London, U.K.: Academic Press.

Goel, V., Grafman, J., Tajik, J., Gana, S., and Danto, D. (1997). A study of the performance of patients with frontal lobe lesions in a financial planning task. [Research Support, Non-U.S. Gov't]. *Brain*, **120**(Pt 10), 1805–1822.

Goldstone, A. P., de Hernandez, C. G., Beaver, J. D., Muhammed, K., Croese, C., Bell, G., and Bell, J. D. (2009). Fasting biases brain reward systems toward high-calorie foods. *Eur J Neurosci*, **30**(8), 1625–1635. DOI: EJN6949 [pii] 10.1111/j.1460-9568.2009.06949.x

Gottfried, J. A., O'Doherty, J., and Dolan, R. J. (2003). Encoding predictive reward value in human amygdala and orbitofrontal cortex. [Research Support, Non-U.S. Gov't]. *Science*, **301**(5636), 1104–1107. DOI: 10.1126/science.1087919

Grabenhorst, F. and Rolls, E. T. (2011). Value, pleasure and choice in the ventral prefrontal cortex. *Trends Cogn Sci*, **15**(2), 56–67. DOI: S1364-6613(10)00256-1 [pii] 10.1016/j.tics.2010.12.004

Greene, J. D., Sommerville, R. B., Nystrom, L. E., Darley, J. M., and Cohen, J. D. (2001). An fMRI investigation of emotional engagement in moral judgment. [Research Support, Non-U.S. Gov't Research Support, U.S. Gov't, Non-P.H.S.]. *Science*, **293**(5537), 2105–2108. DOI: 10.1126/science.1062872

Harbaugh, W. T., Mayr, U., and Burghart, D. R. (2007). Neural responses to taxation and voluntary giving reveal motives for charitable donations. [Research Support, N.I.H., Extramural Research Support, U.S. Gov't, Non-P.H.S.]. *Science*, **316**(5831), 1622–1625. DOI: 10.1126/science.1140738

Hare, T. A., O'Doherty, J., Camerer, C. F., Schultz, W., and Rangel, A. (2008). Dissociating the role of the orbitofrontal cortex and the striatum in the computation of goal values and prediction errors. *J Neurosci*, **28**(22), 5623–5630. DOI: 28/22/5623 [pii] 10.1523/JNEUROSCI.1309-1308.2008

Hare, T. A., Camerer, C. F., and Rangel, A. (2009). Self-control in decision-making involves modulation of the vmPFC valuation system. *Science*, **324**(5927), 646–648. DOI: 324/5927/646 [pii] 10.1126/science.1168450

Haynes, J. D. and Rees, G. (2006). Decoding mental states from brain activity in humans. [Research Support, Non-U.S. Gov't Review]. *Nat Rev Neurosci*, **7**(7), 523–534. DOI: 10.1038/nrn1931

Hornak, J., O'Doherty, J., Bramham, J., Rolls, E. T., Morris, R. G., Bullock, P. R., and Polkey, C. E. (2004). Reward-related reversal learning after surgical excisions in orbito-frontal or dorsolateral prefrontal cortex in humans. [Comparative Study Research Support, Non-U.S. Gov't]. *J Cogn Neurosci*, **16**(3), 463–478. DOI: 10.1162/089892904322926791

Houthakker, H. S. (1950). Revealed preference and the utility function. *Economica*, **17**, 159–174.

Hsu, M., Bhatt, M., Adolphs, R., Tranel, D., and Camerer, C. F. (2005). Neural systems responding to degrees of uncertainty in human decision-making. *Science*, **310**(5754), 1680–1683. DOI: 310/5754/1680 [pii] 10.1126/science.1115327

Huettel, S. A., Song, A. W., and McCarthy, G. (2008). *Functional magnetic resonance imaging* (2nd edn). Sunderland, Mass.: Sinauer Associates.

Ishizu, T. and Zeki, S. (2011). Toward a brain-based theory of beauty. [Research Support, Non-U.S. Gov't]. *PLoS One*, **6**(7), e21852. DOI: 10.1371/journal.pone.0021852

Izuma, K., Saito, D. N., and Sadato, N. (2008). Processing of social and monetary rewards in the human striatum. *Neuron*, **58**(2), 284–294. DOI: S0896-6273(08)00266-3 [pii] 10.1016/j.neuron.2008.03.020

Janowski, V., Camerer, C., and Rangel, A. (2013). Empathic choice involves vmPFC value signals that are modulated by social processing implemented in IPL. [Research Support, Non-U.S. Gov't Research Support, U.S. Gov't, Non-P.H.S.]. *Soc Cogn Affect Neurosci*, **8**(2), 201–208. DOI: 10.1093/scan/nsr086

Kable, J. W. and Glimcher, P. W. (2007). The neural correlates of subjective value during intertemporal choice. *Nat Neurosci*, **10**(12), 1625–1633. DOI: nn2007 [pii] 10.1038/nn2007

Kable, J. W. and Glimcher, P. W. (2009). The neurobiology of decision: consensus and controversy. *Neuron*, **63**(6), 733–745. DOI: S0896-6273(09)00681-3 [pii] 10.1016/j.neuron.2009.09.003

Kahneman, D. and Tversky, A. (1979). Prospect theory—analysis of decision under risk. *Econometrica*, **47**(2), 263–291.

Kang, M. J., Rangel, A., Camus, M., and Camerer, C. F. (2011). Hypothetical and real choice differentially activate common valuation areas. [Research Support, Non-U.S. Gov't]. *J Neurosci*, **31**(2), 461–468. DOI: 10.1523/JNEUROSCI.1583-1510.2011

Kawabata, H. and Zeki, S. (2004). Neural correlates of beauty. [Comparative Study Portraits Research Support, Non-U.S. Gov't]. *J Neurophysiol*, **91**(4), 1699–1705. DOI: 10.1152/jn.00696.2003

Kawagoe, R., Takikawa, Y., and Hikosaka, O. (1998). Expectation of reward modulates cognitive signals in the basal ganglia. *Nat Neurosci*, **1**(5), 411–416. DOI: 10.1038/1625

Killgore, W. D., Young, A. D., Femia, L. A., Bogorodzki, P., Rogowska, J., and Yurgelun-Todd, D. A. (2003). Cortical and limbic activation during viewing of high- versus low-calorie foods. *Neuroimage*, **19**(4), 1381–1394. DOI: S1053811903001915 [pii]

Kim, H., Shimojo, S., and O'Doherty, J. P. (2011). Overlapping responses for the expectation of juice and money rewards in human ventromedial prefrontal cortex. *Cereb Cortex*, **21**(4), 769–776. DOI: bhq145 [pii] 10.1093/cercor/bhq145

King-Casas, B., Tomlin, D., Anen, C., Camerer, C. F., Quartz, S. R., and Montague, P. R. (2005). Getting to know you: reputation and trust in a two-person economic exchange. [Research Support, Non-U.S. Gov't Research Support, U.S. Gov't, P.H.S.]. *Science*, **308**(5718), 78–83. DOI: 10.1126/science.1108062

Klein, J. T., Deaner, R. O., and Platt, M. L. (2008). Neural correlates of social target value in macaque parietal cortex. *Curr Biol*, **18**(6), 419–424. DOI: S0960-9822(08)00233-9 [pii] 10.1016/j.cub.2008.02.047

Knutson, B., Adams, C. M., Fong, G. W., and Hommer, D. (2001). Anticipation of increasing monetary reward selectively recruits nucleus accumbens. *J Neurosci*, **21**(16), RC159. DOI: 20015472 [pii]

Knutson, B., Fong, G. W., Bennett, S. M., Adams, C. M., and Hommer, D. (2003). A region of mesial prefrontal cortex tracks monetarily rewarding outcomes: characterization with rapid event-related fMRI. *Neuroimage*, **18**(2), 263–272. DOI: S1053811902000575 [pii]

Knutson, B., Taylor, J., Kaufman, M., Peterson, R., and Glover, G. (2005). Distributed neural representation of expected value. *J Neurosci*, **25**(19), 4806–4812. DOI: 25/19/4806 [pii] 10.1523/JNEUROSCI.0642-05.2005

Knutson, B., Rick, S., Wimmer, G. E., Prelec, D., and Loewenstein, G. (2007). Neural predictors of purchases. *Neuron*, **53**(1), 147–156. DOI: S0896-6273(06)00904-4 [pii] 10.1016/j.neuron.2006.11.010

Koenigs, M. and Grafman, J. (2009). Posttraumatic stress disorder: the role of medial prefrontal cortex and amygdala. *Neuroscientist*, **15**(5), 540–548. DOI: 1073858409333072 [pii] 10.1177/1073858409333072

Koenigs, M. and Tranel, D. (2007). Irrational economic decision-making after ventromedial prefrontal damage: evidence from the Ultimatum Game. [Comparative Study Research Support, N.I.H., Extramural]. *J Neurosci*, **27**(4), 951–956. DOI: 10.1523/JNEUROSCI.4606-4606.2007

Kolling, N., Wittmann, M., and Rushworth, M. F. (2014). Multiple neural mechanisms of decision making and their competition under changing risk pressure. [Research Support, Non-U.S. Gov't]. *Neuron*, **81**(5), 1190–1202. DOI: 10.1016/j.neuron.2014.01.033

Kringelbach, M. L., O'Doherty, J., Rolls, E. T., and Andrews, C. (2003). Activation of the human orbitofrontal cortex to a liquid food stimulus is correlated with its subjective pleasantness. *Cereb Cortex*, **13**(10), 1064–1071.

Lau, B. and Glimcher, P. W. (2008). Value representations in the primate striatum during matching behavior. *Neuron*, **58**(3), 451–463. DOI: S0896-6273(08)00175-X [pii] 10.1016/j.neuron.2008.02.021

Lebreton, M., Jorge, S., Michel, V., Thirion, B., and Pessiglione, M. (2009). An automatic valuation system in the human brain: evidence from functional neuroimaging. [Research Support, Non-U.S. Gov't]. *Neuron*, **64**(3), 431–439. DOI: 10.1016/j.neuron.2009.09.040

Levy, D. J. and Glimcher, P. W. (2011). Comparing apples and oranges: using reward-specific and reward-general subjective value representation in the brain. *J Neurosci*, **31**(41), 14693–14707. DOI: 31/41/14693 [pii] 10.1523/JNEUROSCI.2218-2211.2011

Levy, D. J. and Glimcher, P. W. (2012). The root of all value: a neural common currency for choice. [Review]. *Curr Opin Neurobiol*, **22**(6), 1027–1038. DOI: 10.1016/j.conb.2012.06.001

Levy, I., Snell, J., Nelson, A. J., Rustichini, A., and Glimcher, P. W. (2010). Neural representation of subjective value under risk and ambiguity. *J Neurophysiol*, **103**(2), 1036–1047. DOI: 00853.2009 [pii] 10.1152/jn.00853.2009

Levy, I., Lazzaro, S. C., Rutledge, R. B., and Glimcher, P. W. (2011). Choice from non-choice: predicting consumer preferences from blood oxygenation level-dependent signals obtained during passive viewing. [Research Support, N.I.H., Extramural]. *J Neurosci*, **31**(1), 118–125. DOI: 10.1523/JNEUROSCI.3214-3210.2011

Lewis, P. A., Rezaie, R., Brown, R., Roberts, N., and Dunbar, R. I. (2011). Ventromedial prefrontal volume predicts understanding of others and social network size. *Neuroimage*, **57**(4), 1624–1629. DOI: S1053-8119(11)00518-0 [pii] 10.1016/j.neuroimage.2011.05.030

Lim, S. L., O'Doherty, J. P., and Rangel, A. (2013). Stimulus value signals in ventromedial PFC reflect the integration of attribute value signals computed in fusiform gyrus and posterior superior temporal gyrus. [Research Support, N.I.H., Extramural Research Support, U.S. Gov't, Non-P.H.S.]. *J Neurosci*, **33**(20), 8729–8741. DOI: 10.1523/JNEUROSCI.4809-4812.2013

Lin, A., Adolphs, R., and Rangel, A. (2012). Social and monetary reward learning engage overlapping neural substrates. *Soc Cogn Affect Neurosci*. DOI: nsr006 [pii] 10.1093/scan/nsr006

Lorenzetti, V., Allen, N. B., Fornito, A., and Yucel, M. (2009). Structural brain abnormalities in major depressive disorder: a selective review of recent MRI studies. *J Affect Disord*, **117**(1–2), 1–17. DOI: S0165-0327(08)00476-X [pii] 10.1016/j.jad.2008.11.021

Manes, F., Sahakian, B., Clark, L., Rogers, R., Antoun, N., Aitken, M., and Robbins, T. (2002). Decision-making processes following damage to the prefrontal cortex. [Research Support, Non-U.S. Gov't]. *Brain*, **125**(Pt 3), 624–639.

Matsumoto, M. and Hikosaka, O. (2009). Two types of dopamine neuron distinctly convey positive and negative motivational signals. *Nature*, **459**(7248), 837–841. DOI: nature08028 [pii] 10.1038/nature08028

McClure, S. M., Ericson, K. M., Laibson, D. I., Loewenstein, G., and Cohen, J. D. (2007). Time discounting for primary rewards. *J Neurosci*, **27**(21), 5796–5804. DOI: 27/21/5796 [pii] 10.1523/JNEUROSCI.4246-4206.2007

McClure, S. M., Laibson, D. I., Loewenstein, G., and Cohen, J. D. (2004). Separate neural systems value immediate and delayed monetary rewards. *Science*, **306**(5695), 503–507. DOI: 306/5695/503 [pii] 10.1126/science.1100907

McNamee, D., Rangel, A., and O'Doherty, J. P. (2013). Category-dependent and category-independent goal-value codes in human ventromedial prefrontal cortex. [Randomized Controlled Trial Research Support, Non-U.S. Gov't]. *Nat Neurosci*, **16**(4), 479–485. DOI: 10.1038/nn.3337

Mitchell, D. G. (2011). The nexus between decision making and emotion regulation: a review of convergent neurocognitive substrates. *Behav Brain Res*, **217**(1), 215–231. DOI: S0166-4328(10)00715-1 [pii] 10.1016/j.bbr.2010.10.030

Moll, J., de Oliveira-Souza, R., Bramati, I. E., and Grafman, J. (2002). Functional networks in emotional moral and nonmoral social judgments. *Neuroimage*, **16**(3 Pt 1), 696–703.

Moll, J., Krueger, F., Zahn, R., Pardini, M., de Oliveira-Souza, R., and Grafman, J. (2006). Human fronto-mesolimbic networks guide decisions about charitable donation. [Research Support, N.I.H., Intramural Research Support, Non-U.S. Gov't]. *Proc Natl Acad Sci USA*, **103**(42), 15623–15628. DOI: 10.1073/pnas.0604475103

Moll, J., De Oliveira-Souza, R., and Zahn, R. (2008). The neural basis of moral cognition: sentiments, concepts, and values. [Review]. *Ann N Y Acad Sci*, **1124**, 161–180. DOI: 10.1196/annals.1440.005

Nieuwenhuis, I. L. and Takashima, A. (2011). The role of the ventromedial prefrontal cortex in memory consolidation. *Behav Brain Res*, **218**(2), 325–334. DOI: S0166-4328(10)00807-7 [pii] 10.1016/j.bbr.2010.12.009

Noonan, M. P., Mars, R. B., and Rushworth, M. F. (2011). Distinct roles of three frontal cortical areas in reward-guided behavior. [Comparative Study Randomized Controlled Trial Research Support, Non-U.S. Gov't]. *J Neurosci*, **31**(40), 14399–14412. DOI: 10.1523/JNEUROSCI.6456-6410.2011

Norman, K. A., Polyn, S. M., Detre, G. J., and Haxby, J. V. (2006). Beyond mind-reading: multi-voxel pattern analysis of fMRI data. *Trends Cogn Sci*, **10**(9), 424–430. DOI: 10.1016/j.tics.2006.07.005

Ongur, D., and Price, J. L. (2000). The organization of networks within the orbital and medial prefrontal cortex of rats, monkeys and humans. [Research Support, U.S. Gov't, P.H.S. Review]. *Cereb Cortex*, **10**(3), 206–219.

Ongur, D., Ferry, A. T., and Price, J. L. (2003). Architectonic subdivision of the human orbital and medial prefrontal cortex. [Research Support, U.S. Gov't, P.H.S.]. *J Comp Neurol*, **460**(3), 425–449. DOI: 10.1002/cne.10609

Oxtoby, J. C., Pettis, B. J., and Price, G. B. (1958). John von Neumann 1903–1957 in *Bulletin of the American Mathematical Society*, **64**(3), 128.

O'Doherty, J. P., Buchanan, T. W., Seymour, B., and Dolan, R. J. (2006). Predictive neural coding of reward preference involves dissociable responses in human ventral midbrain and ventral striatum. *Neuron*, **49**(1), 157–166. DOI: S0896-6273(05)00960-8 [pii] 10.1016/j.neuron.2005.11.014

O'Doherty, J., Rolls, E. T., Francis, S., Bowtell, R., McGlone, F., Kobal, G., and Ahne, G. (2000). Sensory-specific satiety-related olfactory activation of the human orbitofrontal cortex. [Research Support, Non-U.S. Gov't]. *Neuroreport*, **11**(2), 399–403.

O'Doherty, J., Rolls, E. T., Francis, S., Bowtell, R., and McGlone, F. (2001). Representation of pleasant and aversive taste in the human brain. *J Neurophysiol*, **85**(3), 1315–1321.

O'Doherty, J. P., Deichmann, R., Critchley, H. D., and Dolan, R. J. (2002). Neural responses during anticipation of a primary taste reward. *Neuron*, **33**(5), 815–826. DOI: S0896627302006037 [pii]

O'Doherty, J., Winston, J., Critchley, H., Perrett, D., Burt, D. M., and Dolan, R. J. (2003). Beauty in a smile: the role of medial orbitofrontal cortex in facial attractiveness. [Research Support, Non-U.S. Gov't]. *Neuropsychologia*, **41**(2), 147–155.

Padoa-Schioppa, C. (2011). Neurobiology of economic choice: a good-based model. *Annu Rev Neurosci*, **34**, 333–359. DOI: 10.1146/annurev-neuro-061010-113648

Park, S. Q., Kahnt, T., Rieskamp, J., and Heekeren, H. R. (2011). Neurobiology of value integration: when value impacts valuation. [Research Support, Non-U.S. Gov't]. *J Neurosci*, **31**(25), 9307–9314. DOI: 10.1523/JNEUROSCI.4973-4910.2011

Pelchat, M. L., Johnson, A., Chan, R., Valdez, J., and Ragland, J. D. (2004). Images of desire: food-craving activation during fMRI. *Neuroimage*, **23**(4), 1486–1493. DOI: S1053-8119(04)00484-7 [pii] 10.1016/j.neuroimage.2004.08.023

Peters, J. and Buchel, C. (2009). Overlapping and distinct neural systems code for subjective value during intertemporal and risky decision making. *J Neurosci*, **29**(50), 15727–15734. DOI: 29/50/15727 [pii] 10.1523/JNEUROSCI.3489-3409.2009

Peters, J. and Buchel, C. (2010). Neural representations of subjective reward value. [Review]. *Behav Brain Res*, **213**(2), 135–141. DOI: 10.1016/j.bbr.2010.04.031

Petrides, M. (2007). The orbitofrontal cortex: novelty, deviation from expectation, and memory. *Ann N Y Acad Sci*, **1121**, 33–53. DOI: annals.1401.035 [pii] 10.1196/annals.1401.035

Pizzagalli, D. A. (2011). Frontocingulate dysfunction in depression: toward biomarkers of treatment response. *Neuropsychopharmacology*, **36**(1), 183–206. DOI: npp2010166 [pii] 10.1038/npp.2010.166

Plassmann, H., O'Doherty, J., and Rangel, A. (2007). Orbitofrontal cortex encodes willingness to pay in everyday economic transactions. *J Neurosci*, **27**(37), 9984–9988. DOI: 27/37/9984 [pii] 10.1523/JNEUROSCI.2131-2107.2007

Plassmann, H., O'Doherty, J. P., and Rangel, A. (2010). Appetitive and aversive goal values are encoded in the medial orbitofrontal cortex at the time of decision making. *J Neurosci*, **30**(32), 10799–10808. DOI: 30/32/10799 [pii] 10.1523/JNEUROSCI.0788-10.2010

Plassmann, H., O'Doherty, J., Shiv, B., and Rangel, A. (2008). Marketing actions can modulate neural representations of experienced pleasantness. *Proc Natl Acad Sci USA*, **105**(3), 1050–1054. DOI: 0706929105 [pii] 10.1073/pnas.0706929105

Platt, M. L. and Huettel, S. A. (2008). Risky business: the neuroeconomics of decision making under uncertainty. *Nat Neurosci*, **11**(4), 398–403. DOI: nn2062 [pii] 10.1038/nn2062

Pochon, J. B., Riis, J., Sanfey, A. G., Nystrom, L. E., and Cohen, J. D. (2008). Functional imaging of decision conflict. [Research Support, N.I.H., Extramural Research Support, Non-U.S. Gov't]. *J Neurosci*, **28**(13), 3468–3473. DOI: 10.1523/JNEUROSCI.4195-4107.2008

Price, J. L. and Drevets, W. C. (2010). Neurocircuitry of mood disorders. [Research Support, N.I.H., Extramural Review]. *Neuropsychopharmacology*, **35**(1), 192–216. DOI: 10.1038/npp.2009.104

Rahman, S., J. Sahakia B, N. Cardinal R., Rogers, R., Robbins, T. (2001). Decision making and neuropsychiatry. *Trends Cogn Sci*, **5**(6), 271–277.

Rilling, J. K. and Sanfey, A. G. (2011). The neuroscience of social decision-making. [Review]. *Annu Rev Psychol*, **62**, 23–48. DOI: 10.1146/annurev.psych.121208.131647

Rilling, J., Gutman, D., Zeh, T., Pagnoni, G., Berns, G., and Kilts, C. (2002). A neural basis for social cooperation. [Research Support, Non-U.S. Gov't Research Support, U.S. Gov't, P.H.S.]. *Neuron*, **35**(2), 395–405.

Rilling, J. K., Sanfey, A. G., Aronson, J. A., Nystrom, L. E., and Cohen, J. D. (2004). Opposing BOLD responses to reciprocated and unreciprocated altruism in putative reward pathways. [Comparative Study Research Support, Non-U.S. Gov't]. *Neuroreport*, **15**(16), 2539–2543.

Rilling, J. K., King-Casas, B., and Sanfey, A. G. (2008). The neurobiology of social decision-making. [Review]. *Curr Opin Neurobiol*, **18**(2), 159–165. DOI: 10.1016/j.conb.2008.06.003

Rogers, R. D., Owen, A. M., Middleton, H. C., Williams, E. J., Pickard, J. D., Sahakian, B. J., and Robbins, T. W. (1999). Choosing between small, likely rewards and large, unlikely rewards activates inferior and orbital prefrontal cortex. [Research Support, Non-U.S. Gov't]. *J Neurosci*, **19**(20), 9029–9038.

Roy, M., Shohamy, D., and Wager, T. D. (2012). Ventromedial prefrontal-subcortical systems and the generation of affective meaning. [Research Support, N.I.H., Extramural Research Support, Non-U.S. Gov't Review]. *Trends Cogn Sci*, **16**(3), 147–156. DOI: 10.1016/j.tics.2012.01.005

Ruff, C. C. and Fehr, E. (2014). The neurobiology of rewards and values in social decision making. [Research Support, Non-U.S. Gov't Review]. *Nat Rev Neurosci*, **15**(8), 549–562. DOI: 10.1038/nrn3776

Rushworth, M. F. (2008). Intention, choice, and the medial frontal cortex. *Ann N Y Acad Sci*, **1124**, 181–207. DOI: 1124/1/181 [pii] 10.1196/annals.1440.014

Rushworth, M. F., Walton, M. E., Kennerley, S. W., and Bannerman, D. M. (2004). Action sets and decisions in the medial frontal cortex. [Research Support, Non-U.S. Gov't Review]. *Trends Cogn Sci*, **8**(9), 410–417. DOI: 10.1016/j.tics.2004.07.009

Rushworth, M. F., Noonan, M. P., Boorman, E. D., Walton, M. E., and Behrens, T. E. (2011). Frontal cortex and reward-guided learning and decision-making. [Research Support, Non-U.S. Gov't Review]. *Neuron*, **70**(6), 1054–1069. DOI: 10.1016/j.neuron.2011.05.014

Rushworth, M. F., Kolling, N., Sallet, J., and Mars, R. B. (2012). Valuation and decision-making in frontal cortex: one or many serial or parallel systems? [Research Support, Non-U.S. Gov't Review]. *Curr Opin Neurobiol*, **22**(6), 946–955. DOI: 10.1016/j.conb.2012.04.011

Sabatinelli, D., Fortune, E. E., Li, Q., Siddiqui, A., Krafft, C., Oliver, W. T., and Jeffries, J. (2011). Emotional perception: meta-analyses of face and natural scene processing. *Neuroimage*, **54**(3), 2524–2533. DOI: S1053-8119(10)0130313-0 [pii] 10.1016/j.neuroimage.2010.10.011

Salimpoor, V. N., Benovoy, M., Larcher, K., Dagher, A., and Zatorre, R. J. (2011). Anatomically distinct dopamine release during anticipation and experience of peak emotion to music. [Research Support, Non-U.S. Gov't]. *Nat Neurosci*, **14**(2), 257–262. DOI: 10.1038/nn.2726

Salimpoor, V. N., van den Bosch, I., Kovacevic, N., McIntosh, A. R., Dagher, A., and Zatorre, R. J. (2013). Interactions between the nucleus accumbens and auditory cortices predict music reward value. [Research Support, Non-U.S. Gov't]. *Science*, **340**(6129), 216–219. DOI: 10.1126/science.1231059

Samejima, K., Ueda, Y., Doya, K., and Kimura, M. (2005). Representation of action-specific reward values in the striatum. *Science*, **310**(5752), 1337–1340. DOI: 310/5752/1337 [pii] 10.1126/science.1115270

Samuelson, P. A. (1947). *Foundations of economic analysis*. Cambridge MA: Harvard University Press.

Sanfey, A. G., Hastie, R., Colvin, M. K., and Grafman, J. (2003a). Phineas gauged: decision-making and the human prefrontal cortex. *Neuropsychologia*, **41**(9), 1218–1229.

Sanfey, A. G., Rilling, J. K., Aronson, J. A., Nystrom, L. E., and Cohen, J. D. (2003b). The neural basis of economic decision-making in the Ultimatum Game. [Research Support, Non-U.S. Gov't]. *Science*, **300**(5626), 1755–1758. DOI: 10.1126/science.1082976

Schoenbaum, G., Takahashi, Y., Liu, T. L., and McDannald, M. A. (2011). Does the orbitofrontal cortex signal value? *Ann N Y Acad Sci*, **1239**, 87–99. DOI: 10.1111/j.1749-6632.2011.06210.x

Sebastian, C. L., Fontaine, N. M., Bird, G., Blakemore, S. J., Brito, S. A., McCrory, E. J., and Viding, E. (2012). Neural processing associated with cognitive and affective Theory of Mind in adolescents and adults. *Soc Cogn Affect Neurosci*, **7**(1), 53–63. DOI: nsr023 [pii] 10.1093/scan/nsr023

Sescousse, G., Caldu, X., Segura, B., and Dreher, J. C. (2013). Processing of primary and secondary rewards: a quantitative meta-analysis and review of human functional neuroimaging studies. *Neurosci Biobehav Rev*, **37**(4), 681–696. DOI: 10.1016/j.neubiorev.2013.02.002

Sharot, T., De Martino, B., and Dolan, R. J. (2009). How choice reveals and shapes expected hedonic outcome. [Research Support, Non-U.S. Gov't]. *J Neurosci*, **29**(12), 3760–3765. DOI: 10.1523/JNEUROSCI.4972-4908.2009

Shenhav, A., Straccia, M. A., Cohen, J. D., and Botvinick, M. M. (2014). Anterior cingulate engagement in a foraging context reflects choice difficulty, not foraging value. *Nat Neurosci*, **17**(9), 1249–1254. DOI: 10.1038/nn.3771

Siep, N., Roefs, A., Roebroeck, A., Havermans, R., Bonte, M. L., and Jansen, A. (2009). Hunger is the best spice: an fMRI study of the effects of attention, hunger and calorie content on food reward processing in the amygdala and orbitofrontal cortex. *Behav Brain Res*, **198**(1), 149–158. DOI: S0166-4328(08)00597-4 [pii] 10.1016/j.bbr.2008.10.035

Simmons, W. K., Martin, A., and Barsalou, L. W. (2005). Pictures of appetizing foods activate gustatory cortices for taste and reward. *Cereb Cortex*, **15**(10), 1602–1608. DOI: bhi038 [pii] 10.1093/cercor/bhi038

Small, D. M., Jones-Gotman, M., and Dagher, A. (2003). Feeding-induced dopamine release in dorsal striatum correlates with meal pleasantness ratings in healthy human volunteers. *Neuroimage*, **19**(4), 1709–1715. DOI: S1053811903002532 [pii]

Smith, D. V., Hayden, B. Y., Truong, T. K., Song, A. W., Platt, M. L., and Huettel, S. A. (2010). Distinct value signals in anterior and posterior ventromedial prefrontal cortex. *J Neurosci*, **30**(7), 2490–2495. DOI: 30/7/2490 [pii] 10.1523/JNEUROSCI.3319-3309.2010

Sutton, R. S. and Barto, A. G. (1998). *Reinforcement learning: an introduction*. Cambridge, Mass.: MIT Press.

Tabibnia, G., Satpute, A. B., and Lieberman, M. D. (2008). The sunny side of fairness: preference for fairness activates reward circuitry (and disregarding unfairness activates self-control circuitry). [Research Support, Non-U.S. Gov't]. *Psychol Sci*, **19**(4), 339–347. DOI: 10.1111/j.1467-9280.2008.02091.x

Talmi, D., Dayan, P., Kiebel, S. J., Frith, C. D., and Dolan, R. J. (2009). How humans integrate the prospects of pain and reward during choice. *J Neurosci*, **29**(46), 14617–14626. DOI: 29/46/14617 [pii]10.1523/JNEUROSCI.2026-2009.2009

Tom, S. M., Fox, C. R., Trepel, C., and Poldrack, R. A. (2007). The neural basis of loss aversion in decision-making under risk. *Science*, **315**(5811), 515–518. DOI: 315/5811/515 [pii] 10.1126/science.1134239

Torta, D. M. and Cauda, F. (2011). Different functions in the cingulate cortex, a meta-analytic connectivity modeling study. [Meta-analysis]. *Neuroimage*, **56**(4), 2157–2172. DOI: 10.1016/j.neuroimage.2011.03.066

Treadway, M. T., Buckholtz, J. W., Cowan, R. L., Woodward, N. D., Li, R., Ansari, M. S., and Zald, D. H. (2012). Dopaminergic mechanisms of individual differences in human effort-based decision-making. [Research Support, N.I.H., Extramural]. *J Neurosci*, **32**(18), 6170–6176. DOI: 10.1523/JNEUROSCI.6459-6411.2012

Tusche, A., Bode, S., and Haynes, J. D. (2010). Neural responses to unattended products predict later consumer choices. [Comparative Study Research Support, Non-U.S. Gov't]. *J Neurosci*, **30**(23), 8024–8031. DOI: 10.1523/JNEUROSCI.0064-10.2010

Valentin, V. V. and O'Doherty, J. P. (2009). Overlapping prediction errors in dorsal striatum during instrumental learning with juice and money reward in the human brain. *J Neurophysiol*, **102**(6), 3384–3391. DOI: 91195.2008 [pii] 10.1152/jn.91195.2008

van Veen, V. and Carter, C. S. (2002). The anterior cingulate as a conflict monitor: fMRI and ERP studies. [Review]. *Physiol Behav*, **77**(4–5), 477–482.

Vassena, E., Krebs, R. M., Silvetti, M., Fias, W., and Verguts, T. (2014). Dissociating contributions of ACC and vmPFC in reward prediction, outcome, and choice. [Research Support, Non-U.S. Gov't]. *Neuropsychologia*, **59**, 112–123. DOI: 10.1016/j.neuropsychologia.2014.04.019

Viskontas, I. V., Possin, K. L., and Miller, B. L. (2007). Symptoms of frontotemporal dementia provide insights into orbitofrontal cortex function and social behavior. *Ann N Y Acad Sci*, **1121**, 528–545. DOI: annals.1401.025 [pii] 10.1196/annals.1401.025

Von Neumann, J. and Morgenstern, O. (1944). *Theory of games and economic behavior*. Princeton, New Jersey Princeton Univ. Press.

Wallis, J. D. (2011). Cross-species studies of orbitofrontal cortex and value-based decision-making. *Nat Neurosci*, **15**(1), 13–19. DOI: nn.2956 [pii]10.1038/nn.2956

Walton, M. E., Behrens, T. E., Noonan, M. P., and Rushworth, M. F. (2011). Giving credit where credit is due: orbitofrontal cortex and valuation in an uncertain world. [Research Support, Non-U.S. Gov't Review]. *Ann N Y Acad Sci*, **1239**, 14–24. DOI: 10.1111/j.1749-6632.2011.06257.x

Waytz, A., Zaki, J., and Mitchell, J. P. (2012). Response of dorsomedial prefrontal cortex predicts altruistic behavior. [Research Support, N.I.H., Extramural Research Support, Non-U.S. Gov't]. *J Neurosci*, **32**(22), 7646–7650. DOI: 10.1523/JNEUROSCI.6193-6111.2012

Winecoff, A., Clithero, J. A., Carter, R. M., Bergman, S. R., Wang, L., and Huettel, S. A. (2013). Ventromedial prefrontal cortex encodes emotional value. [Randomized Controlled Trial Research Support, N.I.H., Extramural]. *J Neurosci*, **33**(27), 11032–11039. DOI: 10.1523/JNEUROSCI.4317-4312.2013

Yue, X., Vessel, E. A., and Biederman, I. (2007). The neural basis of scene preferences. [Research Support, U.S. Gov't, Non-P.H.S.]. *Neuroreport*, **18**(6), 525–529. DOI: 10.1097/WNR.0b013e328091c1f9

Zald, D. H. and Andreotti, C. (2011). Neuropsychological assessment of the orbital and ventromedial prefrontal cortex. *Neuropsychologia*, **48**(12), 3377–3391. DOI: S0028-3932(10)00366-0 [pii] 10.1016/j.neuropsychologia.2010.08.012

Zald, D. H. and Kim, S. W. (1996a). Anatomy and function of the orbital frontal cortex, I: anatomy, neurocircuitry; and obsessive-compulsive disorder. *J Neuropsychiatry Clin Neurosci*, **8**(2), 125–138.

Zald, D. H. and Kim, S. W. (1996b). Anatomy and function of the orbital frontal cortex, II: Function and relevance to obsessive-compulsive disorder. *J Neuropsychiatry Clin Neurosci*, **8**(3), 249–261.

Zald, D. H., Hagen, M. C., and Pardo, J. V. (2002). Neural correlates of tasting concentrated quinine and sugar solutions. *J Neurophysiol*, **87**(2), 1068–1075.

Zeki, S. and Stutters, J. (2012). A brain-derived metric for preferred kinetic stimuli. [Research Support, Non-U.S. Gov't]. *Open Biol*, **2**(2), 120001. DOI: 10.1098/rsob.120001

Chapter 6

The neural underpinnings of moral values

Jorge Moll, Roland Zahn,
and Ricardo de Oliveira-Souza

Introduction

Watching friends and relatives disputing political, ideological, or even fortuitous personal preferences is often a source of amusement and bewilderment. At the core of such debates lie differences, frequently subtle ones, concerning hierarchies of values, which nonetheless often bring about fierce disputes. Values, as abstract as they may be, have sat at the center stage of human deliberation for millennia and are a powerful source of motivation and self-identity (Blasi 1980; Rokeach 1973). But what are values, why are they important, and what has neuroscience to say about them?

A vast literature on psychology, philosophy, anthropology, and sociology concurs that values are criteria by which we judge our own and others' ideas and actions (Hitlin and Piliavin 2004). From a strict neuropsychological standpoint, values are motivational constructs that determine what we consider important and which goals we choose to pursue (Rohan 2000). Therefore, the primary content of a value is the particular goal or motivational concern that it expresses. Cross-cultural research has shown that human values are universal, although different cultures and, for that matter, individuals, attribute different priorities, or hierarchies, to sets of values (Han et al. 2013; Schwartz 1992, see also Schwartz, this volume). Currently, value theory recognizes ten motivationally distinct value orientations, and the dynamics of conflict (e.g., benevolence and power) and congruence among them (e.g., conformity and security) (Schwartz 2006). This universality concurs with the strong heritability of values (Waller et al. 1990). Cultural and inter-individual differences in value hierarchies can be conveniently described within a value space with two main orthogonal dimensions (Inglehart and Baker 2000). One dimension spans the range between the pursuit of self-interest (i.e., self-enhancement) and self-transcendence/benevolence (which includes altruistic goals), while the other covers the range between openness to change and tradition/conservation).

The orthogonal selfish–altruistic dimension of the circumplex value space is akin to the core moral dimension of selfishness–altruism, thus supporting the claim that morality is inherent to the value construct itself (de Oliveira-Souza et al. 2015). Humans possess a remarkable capacity to behave malleably toward others on a continuum that ranges from extreme antisociality (selfishness) to extreme prosociality (altruism). Most people fall within the median region of this prosocial–antisocial continuum—in ordinary life, we sometimes gladly give our seat to an elderly woman, while at other times we may feel so tired that we just pretend not to see her. Besides morality, the structure of values and personality are also closely related, since altruism comprises a facet of the agreeableness dimension of the Big Five model (Costa and McCrae 2010). However, critical differences in the respective constructs of personality traits and value hierarchies must be kept in mind, since traits are enduring dispositions, while values are enduring goals (Hitlin 2003). Clearly, further studies are needed to assess the multiple associations among morality, values, and personality and how they are represented in the brain.

Moral values

Moral values comprise one of the two axial dimensions of the core values construct, which corresponds to at least one facet of the circumplex Big Five model of personality. Moral values are assimilated during development as part of a multistage socialization process; eventually, they become instrumental in the guidance of adult behavior. Vygotsky (1962) was one of the first to investigate this process of socialization in a series of ingenuous experiments. He claimed that the individual assimilation of socially rooted and historically developed symbols and values distinguishes the human from the nonhuman mind. He described this "internalization of higher psychological functions" as consisting of a lengthy developmental process by which an operation that initially represents an external activity shared with significant others, such as parents and siblings (interpersonal), is reconstructed and begins to occur autonomously in the mind of the child (intrapersonal). Internalization is the vehicle for the transmission and continuity of cultural values and social order across generations. This shift from external to internal regulation of behavior is the hallmark of socialization and its completion is reflected in two major indexes of moral maturity—the ability of the individual to regulate his actions according to self-generated ideas and goals, and to anticipate the consequences of his actions onto others and be held responsible for them, i.e., to be a "moral agent" (Bell and Deater-Deckard 2007).

Developmental psychologists have further worked out the internalization of values over the past decades. The characteristics of moral internalization of values were expanded to indicate that it depends on the concomitant activation of particular emotions that act as "somatic markers" for the acquisition and future retrieval of moral values as the situation calls for moral decision-making. Fear, guilt, and disgust play a major role in the formation of moral character. During development, the fearful anticipation of punishment by parents, teachers, and peers reinforces the wrongful nature of transgressions (Kochanska 1994). Another set of interpersonal emotions that is critical for laying down moral values is represented by the empathy-based emotions (Eisenberg 2000), especially when empathy is viewed as the aversive arousal experienced by perceiving the distress in others caused by acts that violate their welfare or rights (Blair et al. 1995).

The laborious nature of moral learning did not go unnoticed to philosophers. Aristotle, for example, likened moral development to the slow practice needed to develop virtuosity on a musical instrument (Aristotle 1941). As stated by modern researchers, "the characteristic developmental trajectory in the moral domain is a movement from crude, global judgments articulated using a small number of innate moral intuitions to highly sophisticated and differentiated perceptions, beliefs, emotional responses and judgments" (Haidt and Joseph 2007). By the time maturity is achieved, moral judgment and reasoning have become largely intuitive (Bargh and Ferguson 2000), similarly to what is proposed to be the case with the "managerial knowledge units" that make up the scripts and schemes of everyday life (Grafman 1989).

Several lines of research have revealed the superordinate status of the moral values construct. Since values are themselves conceived as a broad motivational construct, moral motivations and moral sentiments naturally lie at the core of the concept. There is agreement among philosophical schools that motivations that oppose our self-interests are at the core of moral actions. By definition, then, moral motivations are altruistic (Zahn et al. 2011). As such, they can drive behavior through the experience of moral sentiments, such as pity/sympathy, or of moral values, such as honesty and generosity. Moral values are the symbolic expression of distinctively human motivational-emotional experiences and behaviors that promote social adjustment through adherence to norms, rules, and customs. However, the road that leads from moral sentiments to moral values may not be straightforward. Damasio (2005) has suggested that once an "emotionally competent stimulus," like witnessing the perpetration of an injustice, is perceived, it triggers an emotional experience and a corresponding propensity to act accordingly. Cognitively, this experience comes to mind as a moral intuition that over time becomes amenable to translation into linguistic and iconic means, and fine-tuned to cultural symbols transmitted across generations through oral and written tradition. Eventually, the whole process is codified as social conventions, systems of justice, and ethical canons. The ultimate mission of the neuroscientist is to explore how such complex phenomena are organized in the human brain.

The neural underpinnings of moral valuation

The neural underpinnings of moral valuation have concerned neuroscientists for a long time (Delgado 2000), but only recently have the technical means to probe them objectively become available. However, despite the enormous literature on the neural correlates of moral emotions, judgment, and reasoning, relatively few studies have addressed the issue of the neural representation of moral values. One outstanding finding in this regard is the verification that the universal value dimensions of self-enhancement and openness to change are reflected in the basal forebrain mechanisms of reward (Kim et al. 2011). In a paradigm of donation to charitable organizations, individuals scoring high on self-interest values sacrificed less money for charitable donations and showed higher activation of the ventral striatum and the amygdala when receiving monetary rewards (Brosch et al. 2011).

The amount of money donated to charity, in turn, was inversely proportional to ventral striatal activation, a finding similar to what is observed in financial losses in monetary experiments (Delgado 2007). Using a go/no-go task previously adapted by Amodio et al. (2007), Brosch et al. (2011) also found that the openness dimension was differentially related to engagement of the head of the right caudate nucleus. This study provides initial evidence for the neural representation of individual differences in value hierarchies and their sensitivity to context, thus bridging the gap between the concepts of core and economic values. However, because other potentially relevant brain regions were not assessed, information is lacking on the expected activation of brain structures implicated in altruistic behaviors, such as the subgenual cortex (Moll et al. 2006) and the septo-hypothalamic area (Moll et al. 2012), in value-guided decisions.

To date, relatively few studies have been performed on normal volunteers and patients with brain damage to address the cerebral organization of morality as related to individual core values. Nevertheless, many current investigations dealing with morality often touch on the construct of core values, even if only implicitly or tangentially. With little modification, these studies might pose testable questions and furnish paradigms for the specific study of core values and morality.

Drawing on clinical observations that degenerative diseases of the anterior temporal cortex may lead to severe impairments in social conduct, Zahn et al. (2007) showed that the right anterior temporal cortex plays a key role in social cognition by representing abstract conceptual knowledge of social behaviors, and that these representations are independent of emotional valence and context. Incidentally, several such concepts, such as loyal and loyalty, are value items of the Schwartz Value Survey scale. In a complementary investigation, Zahn et al. (2009) showed that social values emerge from the co-activation of stable abstract (context-independent) social conceptual representations in the anterior temporal cortex and the context-dependent moral sentiments encoded in frontobasal regions. Studies in patients with strategic brain lesions indicate that fronto-temporo-insular integration is necessary for the tuning of abstract social knowledge to concrete situations, especially when they are the agents of moral transgressions (Ciaramelli et al. 2007; Saver and Damasio 1991). Different regions within this broad fronto-temporo-insular region probably perform complementary roles in the attribution of moral values to ideas and events. For example, whereas damage to the ventromedial prefrontal cortex increases utilitarian moral judgments (Koenigs et al. 2007), damage to the amygdala impairs the sensory–affective dimension of value judgments (Gupta et al. 2011). This contextual contribution of the amygdala to moral judgment concurs with its dense connections with the prefrontal and anterior temporal cortices, as well as with its central role as a recipient of visceroendocrine and higher order sensory projections from the hypothalamus and heteromodal cortices, respectively (Barbas 2007).

An ensemble of typically human emotions called "moral sentiments" affords a major dimension of moral evaluation. Moral sentiments are tied to abstract values described by social concepts such as "honesty." Moral sentiments are emotions that are "linked to the interests or welfare either of society as a whole or at least of persons other than the judge or agent" (Haidt 2003). These sentiments, which comprise a host of emotional experiences, such as guilt, embarrassment, and compassion, are typically elicited by interpersonal transactions. Contrary to the "basic" emotions, which have been debated since the nineteenth century (Darwin 1872), the moral sentiments have become objects of active investigation by neuroscientists only recently (Gray and Wegner 2011). In morally mature individuals, moral sentiments constitute a rapid and effortless means of attributing moral values to ordinary conduct, events and circumstances. It is increasingly clear that the cerebral localization of discrete moral sentiments differs according to their nature. In a study on normal volunteers using fMRI, the right anterior temporal lobe was equally activated irrespective of the type of moral sentiment (guilt, pride, gratitude, indignation) associated with socio-moral concepts, whereas different frontal-subcortical regions were associated with the different moral sentiments (Zahn et al. 2009). The neurological literature has also touched on acquired changes in core values in cases of focal brain damage and epilepsy. For example, patients with frontotemporal dementia, showing impairments in the prosocial sentiments of guilt and pity, show a reduction of metabolism in the frontopolar cortex and septal nuclei, whereas impairments in the other-critical sentiments of anger and disgust are differentially associated with metabolic decrease in the amygdala and superomedial prefrontal cortex (Moll et al. 2011). Departing from William James' (1890) conception of the tripartite self into material, social, and spiritual selves, Miller et al. (2001) described seven patients who presented a dramatic change in their previous political, social, or religious values as a result of degeneration of the frontal lobes. In six, the degeneration selectively involved the right (nondominant) frontal lobe. One of the clearest examples of a change in core values due to neurologic disease is given by cases of religious conversion in patients with temporolimbic epilepsy. Howden (1872–73) was one of the first to describe a case of religious conversion after an epileptic fit. The patient believed he had been in Heaven and that God had made him fully aware of the real meaning of "true peace." Cases of religious conversion have also been described in severe depression, schizophrenia, and following recovery from deadly neurological illness (Alexander 2012; Hoffmann 2009). Many of them emerge from their illness with a lasting change in personal values with far-reaching impact on their lives, friends, and relatives. At least in cases of temporolimbic epilepsy, chronic subliminal seizure activity in the temporal lobe leads to an enhancement of experiences that ultimately change the way that the patient experiences the world of values (Bear 1979; Dewhurst and Beard 1970). This "sensory-limbic hyperconnection" may underlie many cases of the "epileptic personality" of the early authors, which is characterized by an increased concern for religious, moral and philosophical issues, hypergraphia, interpersonal viscosity, and circumstantiality (Geschwind 1983). Evidence for the causal role of the epileptogenic lesion in the personality changes is further provided by their remission following temporal lobectomy (Falconer 1973).

The foregoing observations raise the possibility that what is commonly referred to in the literature as a "personality change" (Barrash et al. 2011) may, at least in some cases, primarily reflect a disease-related change of core values instead of an alteration of personality traits. This view lends support to a distinction between the concepts of values and traits

(Roccas et al. 2002), and the need to take into account the role played by value, in contrast to trait, changes in behavioral alterations due to brain disease. Truly, both personality traits and core values are stable constructs that predetermine behavior in the long-term, and their interdependencies and neural underpinnings are still in the early stages of scientific exploration.

A final dimension of values that has been underestimated is the dimension of attachment, especially the human forms of attachment. The inclination to form affective bonds is one major driving force behind the behavior of social mammals. The affiliative bonds that are set up between mother and child even before birth illustrate this motivation for attachment. This tie is present in all mammals (MacLean 1985) and provides a mold for the subsequent affective bonds that will be established throughout life. In humans, attachment extends to abstract ideas and concepts providing the affective-motivational "glue" that binds people to values and beliefs (Moll and de Oliveira-Souza 2009; Moll and Schulkin 2009).

Conclusions and prospects

This selective review indicates several pitfalls in the neuroscience of values and means of experimentally tackling them. First, as aptly put by Brosch et al. (2011), different disciplines use the term "value" to refer to different theoretical constructs. For example, strictly speaking, the concept of core values as used by Schwartz school differs from the concept of "moral values" (Moll et al. 2005), which are internalized abstract social norms or rules against which the appropriateness of one's behavior is evaluated and which are often disobeyed. In contrast to norm-based representations, core values are representations to which one willingly attaches and which comprise an important part of the self. Second, whereas the neural underpinnings of personality traits have been fairly well studied, the same is not true for the core values. In part, this may be due to the lower awareness by neuroscientists of the conceptual structure of core values. Third, little evidence on the neurological underpinnings of core values indicate that a distributed network of regions encompassing the prefrontal and temporopolar cortices, along with their subcortical connections with the amygdala and basal forebrain, are critical in this regard; accordingly, we recently suggested that moral values, as moral emotions, arise from the co-activation of these structures as "event–feature–emotion complexes" (Moll et al. 2005). Finally, neuroscientific research should consider including in its study agenda the stable constructs that predetermine behavior in the long-term in complex investigations such as those involving morality, neuroeconomics, and core values. At a minimum, these constructs should distinguish personality traits and types, long-term (in contrast to short-term) needs, core values, and adherence to norms.

References

Alexander, E. (2012). *Proof of Heaven: A Neurosurgeon's Journey into the Afterlife*. New York: Simon *and* Schuster.

Amodio, D.M., Jost, J.T., Master, S.L., and Yee, C.M. (2007). Neurocognitive correlates of liberalism and conservatism. *Nature Neuroscience*, **10**, 1246–1247.

Aristotle. (1941). Nichomachean ethics (W.D. Ross, Transl.). In: R. McKeon (ed.). *The Basic Works of Aristotle*. New York: Random House, pp. 927–1112. (Original work c. 350BCE.).

Barbas, H. (2007). Flow of information for emotions through temporal and orbitofrontal pathways. *Journal of Anatomy*, **211**, 237–249.

Bargh, J.A. and Ferguson, M.J. (2000). Beyond behaviorism: on the automaticity of higher mental processes. *Psychological Bulletin*, **126**, 925–945.

Barrash, J., Asp, E., Markon, K., Manzel, K., Anderson, S.W., and Tranel, D. (2011). Dimensions of personality disturbance after focal brain damage: Investigation with the Iowa Scales of Personality Change. *Journal of Clinical and Experimental Neuropsychology*, **33**, 833–852.

Bear, D.M. (1979). Temporal lobe epilepsy: a syndrome of sensory-limbic hyperconnection. *Cortex*, **15**, 357–384.

Bell, M.A. and Deater-Deckard, K. (2007). Biological systems and the development of self-regulation: integrating behavior, genetics, and psychophysiology. *Journal of Developmental and Behavioral Pediatrics*, **28**, 409–420.

Blair, R.J.R., Jones, L., Clark, F., and Smith, M. (1995). Is the psychopath "morally insane"? *Personality and Individual Differences*, **19**, 741–752.

Blasi, A. (1980). Bridging moral cognition and moral action: a critical review of the literature. *Psychological Bulletin*, **88**, 1–45.

Brosch, T., Coppin, G., Scherer, K.R., Schwartz, S.H., and Sander, D. (2011). Generating value(s): Psychological value hierarchies reflect context-dependent sensitivity of the reward system. *Social Neuroscience*, **6**, 198–208.

Ciaramelli, E., Muccioli, M., Ladavas, E., and di Pellegrino, G. (2007) Selective deficit in personal moral judgment following damage to ventromedial prefrontal cortex. *Social Cognitive and Affective Neuroscience*, **2**, 84–92.

Costa, P.T. and McCrae, R.R. (2010). *NEO PI-R. Inventário de Personalidade NEO Revisado*. São Paulo: Vetor.

Damasio, A.R. (2005). The neurobiological grounding of human values. In: J.-P. Changeux, A.R. Damasio, W. Singer, and Y. Christen (eds) *Neurobiology of Human Values*. Heidelberg: Springer, pp. 47–56.

Darwin, C. (1872). *The Expression of the Emotions in Man and Animals*. New York: Oxford University Press.

Delgado, J.M.R. (2000). Neuronal imprinting of human values. *International Journal of Psychophysiology*, **35**, 237–246.

Delgado, M.R. (2007). Reward-related responses in the human striatum. *Annals of the New York Academy of Sciences*, **1104**, 70–88.

de Oliveira-Souza, R., Zahn, R., and Moll, J. (2015). The neuropsychiatry of social behaviour and the cerebral organization of morality. In: S. M. Liao (ed.) *Moral Brains: The Neuroscience of Morality*. Oxford: Oxford University Press.

Dewhurst, K. and Beard, A.W. (1970). Sudden religious conversions in temporal lobe epilepsy. *British Journal of Psychiatry*, **117**, 497–507.

Eisenberg, N. (2000). Emotion, regulation, and moral development. *Annual Review of Psychology*, **51**, 665–697.

Falconer, M.A. (1973). Reversibility by temporal-lobe resection of the behavioral abnormalities of temporal lobe epilepsy. *New England Journal of Medicine*, **289**, 451–455.

Geschwind, N. (1983). Interictal behavioral changes in epilepsy. *Epilepsia*, **24**, suppl. 1, S20–S30.

Grafman, J. (1989). Plans, actions, and mental sets: managerial knowledge units in the frontal lobes. In: E. Perecman (ed.) *Integrating Theory and Practice in Clinical Neuropsychology*. Hillsdale, N.J.: Lawrence Erlbaum, pp. 93–138.

Gray, K. and Wegner, D.M. (2011). Dimensions of moral emotions. *Emotion Review*, **3**, 258–260.

Gupta, R., Koscik, T.R., Bechara, A., and Tranel, D. (2011). The amygdala and decision-making. *Neuropsychologia*, **49**, 760–766.

Haidt, J. (2003). The moral emotions. In: R.J. Davidson, K.R. Scherer, and H.H. Goldsmith (eds) *Handbook of Affective Sciences*. Oxford, UK: Oxford University Press, pp. 852–870.

Haidt, J, and Joseph, C. (2007). The moral mind: how five sets of innate intuitions guide the development of many culture-specific virtues, and perhaps even modules. In: P. Carruthers, S. Laurence, and S. Strich (eds) *The Innate Mind*, **volume 3**. New York: Oxford University Press, pp. 367–391.

Han, S., Northoff, G., Vogeley, K., Wexler, B.E., Kitayama S., and Varnum, M.E.W. (2013). A cultural neuroscience approach to the biosocial nature of the human brain. *Annual Review of Psychology*, **64**, 335–359.

Hitlin, S. (2003). Values as the core of personal identity: drawing links between two theories of self. *Social Psychology Quarterly*, **66**, 118–137.

Hitlin, S. and Piliavin, J.A. (2004). Values: reviving a dormant concept. *Annual Review of Sociology*, **30**, 359–393.

Hoffmann, A. (2009). *LSD My Problem Child. Reflections on Sacred Drugs, Mysticism and Science*, 4th edition. Sarasota, FL: Multidisciplinary Association for Psychedelic Studies.

Howden, J.C. (1872/3). The religious sentiments in epileptics. *Journal of Mental Science*, **18**, 491–497.

Inglehart, R. and Baker, W.E. (2000). Modernization, cultural change, and the persistence of traditional values. *American Sociological Review*, **65**, 19–51.

James, W. (1890). *Principles of Psychology*. Boston: Harvard University Press.

Kim, H., Shimojo, S., and O'Doherty, J.P. (2011). Overlapping responses for the expectation of juice and money rewards in human ventromedial prefrontal cortex. *Cerebral Cortex*, **21**, 769–776.

Kochanska, G. (1994). Beyond cognition: Expanding the search for the early roots of internalization and conscience. *Developmental Psychology*, **30**, 20–22.

Koenigs, M., Young, L., Adolphs, R., Tranel, D., Cushman, F., Hauser, M., and Damasio, A. (2007). Damage to the prefrontal cortex increases utilitarian moral judgements. *Nature*, **446**, 908–911.

MacLean, P.D. (1985). Brain evolution relating to family, play, and the separation call. *Archives of General Psychiatry*, **42**. 405–417.

Miller, B.L., Seeley, W.W., Mychack, P., Rosen, H.J., Mena, I., and Boone, K. (2001). Neuroanatomy of the self. Evidence from patients with frontotemporal dementia. *Neurology*, **57**, 817–821.

Moll, J., Bado, P., de Oliveira-Souza, R., Bramati, I.E., Lima, D.O., Paiva, F.F., Sato, J.R., Tovar-Moll, F., and Zahn, R. (2012). A neural signature of affiliative emotion in the human septohypothalamic area. *Journal of Neuroscience*, **32**, 12499–12505.

Moll, J. and de Oliveira-Souza, R. (2009). "Extended attachment" and the human brain: Internalized cultural values and evolutionary implications. In: J. Verplaetse, J.D. Schrijver, S. Vanneste, and J. Braeckman (eds). *The Moral Brain. Essays on the Evolutionary and Neuroscientific Aspects of Morality*. Heidelberg: Springer, pp. 69–85.

Moll, J., Krueger, F., Zahn, R., Pardini, M., de Oliveira-Souza, R., and Grafman, J. (2006). Human fronto-mesolimbic networks guide decisions about charitable donation. *Proceedings of the National Academy of Sciences of the United States of America*, ***103***, 15623–15628.

Moll, J. and Schulkin, J. (2009). Social attachment and aversion in human moral cognition. *Neuroscience and Biobehavioral Reviews*, **33**, 456–465.

Moll, J., Zahn, R., de Oliveira-Souza, R., Krueger, F., and Grafman, J. (2005). The neural basis of human moral cognition. *Nature Reviews Neuroscience*, **6**, 799–809.

Moll, J., Zahn, R., de Oliveira-Souza, R., Bramati, I.E., Krueger, F., Tura, B., Cavanagh, A.L., and Grafman, J. (2011). Impairment of prosocial sentiments is associated with frontopolar and septal damage in frontotemporal dementia. *NeuroImage*, **54**, 1735–1742.

Roccas, S., Sagive, L.S.S.H., Schwartz, S.H., and Knafo, A. (2002). The big five personality factors and personal values. *Personality and Social Psychology Bulletin*, **28**, 789–801.

Rohan, M.J. (2000). A rose by any name? The values construct. *Personality and Social Psychology Review*, **4**, 255–277.

Rokeach, M. (1973). *The Nature of Human Values*. New York: Free Press.

Saver, J. and Damasio, A.R. (1991). Preserved access and processing of social knowledge in a patient with acquired sociopathy due to ventromedial frontal damage. *Neuropsychologia*, **29**, 1241–1249.

Schwartz, S.H. (1992). Universals in the content and structure of values: theory and empirical tests in 20 countries. In: M. Zanna (ed.), *Advances in Experimental Social Psychology*, **volume 25**. New York: Academic Press, pp. 1–65.

Schwartz, S.H. (2006). Les valeurs de base de la personne: Théorie, mesures et applications. *Revue Française de Sociologie*, **42**, 249–288.

Vygotsky, L.S. (1962). *Thought and Language*. (E. Hanfmann and G. Vakar, trans.) New York: The MIT Press. (Original work published 1934.)

Waller, N.G., Kojetin, B.A., Bouchard, T.J., Lykken, D., and Tellegen, A. (1990). Genetic and environmental influences on religious interests, attitudes, and values: a study of twins reared apart and together. *Psychological Science*, **1**, 138–142.

Zahn, R., de Oliveira-Souza, R., and Moll, J. (2011). The neuroanatomical basis of moral cognition and emotion. In: R. Ebstein, S, Shamay-Tsoory, and S.H. Chew (eds) *From DNA to Social Cognition*. New York: John Wiley *and* Sons, pp. 123–138.

Zahn, R., Moll, J., Paiva, M.M.F., Garrido, G., Krueger, F., Huey, E.D., and Grafman, J. (2009). The neural basis of human social values: evidence from functional MRI. *Cerebral Cortex*, **19**, 276–283.

Chapter 7

What are values? Where do they come from? A developmental perspective

Diana Boer and Klaus Boehnke

Introduction

Values play a central role in human development. They serve as motivational goals transcending situations and contexts. Hence, once they develop, values become part of our identity; they guide our behaviors and attitudes, impact on our understanding of morality and on the quality of our interpersonal relations. As values form and develop in interaction with close others, as well as with the surrounding environment, variability across cultures and the change of value preferences across time are important aspects to consider beyond individual value preferences. In this chapter we aim to provide answers to the question of how values develop. We focus primarily on personal development but subsequently also on cultural value change, because values encapsulate personal and cultural continuity and change, which are interlinked.

This chapter construes value development from various perspectives (see Fig. 7.1). Looking at individual value development, we first link values to central developmental theories and we elaborate on value theories and their functions for development, before describing instruments for the measurement of value preferences during childhood. Then we consider two important phases of value development: development during childhood and adolescence via vertical and horizontal transmission processes, and value development during the lifespan. We close our chapter with a look at societal values and cultural value change.

Values and their development within individuals

Values in developmental theories

Values are relatively abstract ideas about desired or desirable states or ways of doing things (Hitlin and Piliavin 2004). Their abstractness necessitates some level of cognitive capabilities and social learning skills that children need to achieve in order to form values. Value development is also part of identity formation and personality development processes. Hence, value development can be conceived within frameworks of cognitive development, identity formation, social learning, and personality development.

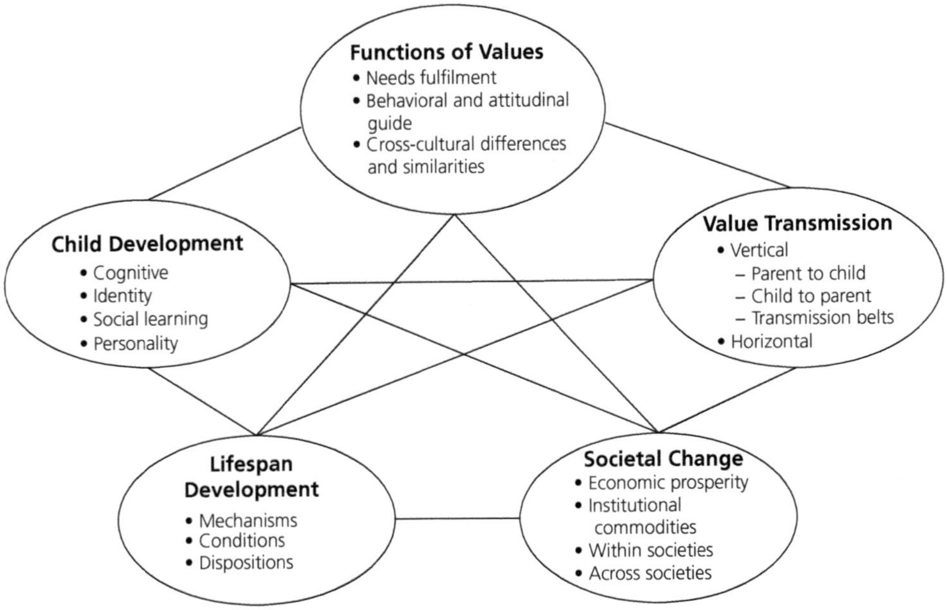

Fig. 7.1 Aspects of value development.

Cognitive development

Value development is a core developmental task. While Kohlberg's moral stages entail the development of conformity and group-oriented values already from Stage 3 (good boy/girl attitude; interpersonal concordance), higher stages postulate the development of more differentiated moral, autonomous, and individualistic values. Simpson (1976) argued that Kohlberg's stages converge with Maslow's needs sequence in that the more opportunistic, conforming, and reward/punishment orientation at Kohlberg's lower levels corresponds with Maslow's survival and belongingness needs at lower and middle levels. Furthermore, Kohlberg's less self-involved values in higher stages then correspond with Maslow's need for self-actualization at the top of the needs hierarchy. According to those two developmental theories, conformity and group-oriented values may develop earlier and relate to lower level needs and their fulfillment, while self-direction and autonomous values may emerge later based on higher order needs.

In Piaget's stage of concrete operations, children already hold basic conceptions of desirable stable goals, which align closely to definitions of personal values (Döring et al. 2010). Hence, an intuitive understanding of values is likely to be available at this stage. In the formal operational stage, individuals develop more conscious cognitive control over moral judgments and decisions, including justice and the differentiation between action and intent, leading to a more differentiated and conscious understanding of values. Piaget's and Kohlberg's theories relate closely to other forms of cognitive developments, including the development of cognitive structures. Perspective taking is one core capacity for developing values as motivational guides (Kohlberg 1976). Social and cultural learning of values requires imitating behavior, the distinctions between goal-directed and irrelevant behavior, and therefore the recognition of persons as actors who direct their actions toward goals (Tomasello 2001). The cognitive prerequisites for perspective taking are acquired very early, while the actual understanding of values as motivational and behavioral guides is gained somewhere after entry into primary school, when children begin comprehending more complex perspectives and intentions (cf. Tomasello et al. 1993).

The development of a worldview that influences a person's behavior is among the eight developmental tasks proposed in Havighurst's (1948) developmental system. Here individual goals and values are seen as part of the self, which is defined as a driving force for an active development. Hence, identity development seems an important aspect in the development of values.

Identity development

During adolescence individuals develop their "I" identity in an active search for a definition and construction of the self (Erikson 1950, 1968). This identity includes the feeling of continuity and unity with oneself being developed in a (lifelong) process of interacting with others. The acquired identity is not fixed and constant, but a dynamic process involving social and group processes. Marcia (1966, 1980) further stated that identity entails a clear self-definition, including goals, values, and beliefs, that a person considers as important and binding. His typology of identity statuses involves the two activities (1) exploration of, and (2) commitment to goals, values, and beliefs, which can result in the four statuses: identity achievement (successful exploration and commitment), diffusion (no exploration, no commitment), foreclosure (commitment without exploration), and moratorium (exploration without commitment). More recently, Hitlin (2003) argued that values act as a driving force of identity formation that cohesively link one's various social identities. He describes their role in identity as "values at the core of the self that produce our sense of personal identity are distal influences on action [. . .] values are cognitive-emotional frameworks that constitute the self-as-agent" (Hitlin 2003: 125).

Social learning

Socialization is a lifelong process of individuals engaging in interaction with their social environment and adapting to the social and societal requirements. Socialization is seen as an active participatory, rather than passive learning, process in which social values are learned first as a frame of reference for desirable states. Social learning is facilitated by the observation of models and the imitation of their (verbal and non-verbal) action (e.g., Bandura 1977). For instance, children observe their parents and caregivers very closely and imitate their value-driven behaviors. By the time they are cognitively able to understand the value intentions in these behaviors, children are likely to transfer value intents to other behaviors. The social learning perspective postulates that values are acquired in such an active learning process.

Personality development

Personality entails attributes that characterize a person including behavioral tendencies, temperament as well as values. Developmental perspectives on personality explain where inter-individual differences originate, how continuity is achieved, and how personality changes (Caspi 1997; Caspi and Roberts 2001). These are important aspects for value development, although research focuses mostly on personality traits. There is ample evidence from behavior-genetic studies for a considerable heritability of personality (traits). At the same time, environmental forces do influence personality characteristics. This suggests that genetic roots interact with shared and non-shared environments to give shape to an individual's personality. Interestingly, already at the age of three years, temperament characteristics can be observed, which are moderately stable and predictive of personality traits throughout early adulthood (Caspi and Silva 1995).

Srivastava and colleagues (2003) investigated the stability versus plasticity of traits and found little support for the stability hypothesis: most traits develop further after age thirty. These findings appeal to life-trajectory interpretations suggesting a concurrent adaptation to changing demands and life situations. Despite a moderate continuity and stability of personality, traits do not become fixed at any age and change is possible until old age (Caspi and Roberts 2001). Similar trajectories have been suggested for value development across the lifespan and findings from trait development may apply closely to value development. However, the theorizing and empirical testing of personality and value development have so far been conducted in isolation (cf. Fischer and Boer 2014; Parks-Leduc et al. 2015).

This overview of developmental theories showed that these theories cover value development rather implicitly than explicitly. We will turn to value theories more specifically now looking at the functions of values for individual development.

Value theories

Most definitions of personal values in psychology and sociology elaborate on the functions that values serve in people's lives. One family of value definitions focuses more on needs-based functions of values, while another family contains behavioral and attitudinal guidance functions of values, and a third family construes values in terms of societal and cultural challenges leading to cross-cultural differences in value orientations. We briefly summarize these three (broad and non-exclusive) families of value theories and their developmental connotations.

Values as indicators of needs' fulfillment

The first family of value research provides a political science perspective on human needs (Maslow 1970, 1999) and their satisfaction or deprivation. From Inglehart's (1977) analysis of societal change followed a theory of value orientations claiming two positions: (1) values are formed in early socialization and their development concludes during late adolescence, and (2) individuals' value priorities focus on those life aspects that were deprived or showed some deficiencies in needs' fulfillment during childhood or adolescence. Those basic assumptions lead to the differentiation between survival values vs. self-expression values in Inglehart's (1997) value taxonomy. An additional value dimension distinguishes traditional vs. secular orientations toward authority. This value dimension is premised on security needs and their fulfillment. Norris and Inglehart's (2004) security thesis argues that in contexts of high insecurity (e.g., in developing countries), people turn to traditional religious values, since religious institutions provide security and uncertainty management, whereas in highly developed, secure contexts, individuals rely more on secular values. Hence, value priorities seem closely related to fundamental human needs and their fulfillment within specific macro-contextual and social environments.

Values as behavioral and attitudinal guides

One influential psychological theory of personal values developed by Shalom H. Schwartz goes back to Milton Rokeach (1973) and Clyde Kluckhohn (1951). Rokeach (1968, 1973) distinguished between terminal and instrumental values in his value–attitude–behavior pyramid. He argued that terminal values (encompassing desirable end states) facilitate instrumental values (encompassing desirable ways of doing things), which in turn impact on attitudes that then determine behavioral intentions. Developing this idea further, Schwartz (1992) differentiated a comprehensive set of values that relate systematically to each other, comprising a consistent system of complementary and conflicting values that serves as guiding principle in people's lives (see also Schwartz, this volume).

Schwartz argues that the human values' system by and large serves three requirements of human life: biological needs, the coordination of social interactions, and the survival of the group. Most importantly, these requirements need to be negotiated against each other by reconciling and prioritizing one's values as behavioral guides. The guidance functions of values have been summarized by Rohan (2000) in terms of what type of judgments they influence: (1) as guides for survival, (2) as guides for goodness, (3) as guides for best possible living, and (4) for ordering the importance of requirements and desires. Some of these judgments point toward needs-based functions of values, which thereby also seem linked to the guidance function of values (cf. Fischer et al. 2011).

Values as cultural differences

The third family of value theories hails from research in intercultural relations, cross-cultural psychology, and cultural sociology. Geert Hofstede (1980, 2001), Harry Triandis (1995), and Shalom H. Schwartz (1994, 2004) put forward value theories that emphasize cultural value climates. Specific cultural values develop based on macro-contextual challenges that societies and cultural groups need to attend to in order to optimize conditions of collective survival and well-being. Importantly, cultural values determine general tendencies of individual value orientations and self-definitions within a given context. The three scholars—similar to Inglehart—state that cross-cultural differences in personal values proceed from differences in the socio-cultural and macro-contextual environments where individuals are embedded.

Most prominently, individualism vs. collectivism differentiates a culture's emphasis on the individual as unique and autonomous entity or on group goals as superior to individuals' goals (Hofstede 1980). Triandis and colleagues (1985; Triandis 1995) made the appropriate distinction between individualistic vs. collectivistic values as a cultural dimension vis-à-vis its individual psychological expression called idiocentrism vs. allocentrism. In individualistic societies individuals tend to hold stronger idiocentric values emphasizing autonomous decisions and goals, whereas in collectivistic societies individuals hold more allocentric values emphasizing collective goal pursuit. Referring to differences in how people construe their selves, Markus and Kitayama (1991) showed that in individualistic societies individuals tend to define their self as being independent, whereas in collectivistic societies people think of themselves in interdependence with close others. Differences in self-construals contribute to explaining major cross-cultural differences in cognition, emotion, and motivation.

In sum, values contribute to human well-functioning by offering a system for an assessment of needs fulfillment as well as for behavioral guidance leading to functional adjustment with regard to self-definitions, well-being, and social functioning. This overview of value functions and their theories indicates their importance for individuals' lives; however, from which age onward can values be validly assessed and which methods can be used that accommodate cognitive development of young children? The next section discusses value measurement in childhood. Obviously instruments for the measurement of values among adults exist also in reference to the value theories sketched out in this chapter, but as they are clearly geared toward assessing values among adults, we refrain from a detailed documentation and refer readers among others to the website of World Values Survey[1] for an assessment of value preferences along the lines of Inglehart's value theory.

Value assessment during childhood

Most value measurements have been designed to capture personal value orientations among adults and older adolescents due to the inherent abstractness of values (cf. Hitlin and Piliavin 2004). Aiming to capture values in a less abstract manner, Schwartz and colleagues (2001) developed the Portrait Values Questionnaire (PVQ) that encompasses items describing people who assert certain attitudinal and behavioral tendencies. An example item for assessing benevolence values is "It's very important to her to help the people around her. She wants to care for their well-being." Respondents[2] are then asked to indicate how similar the described person is to themselves on a rating scales ranging from 1 (not at all like me) to 6 (very much like me). The use of PVQ's vignette-style items reduces the abstractness of the assessment and the similarity-based response format is rather simplified allowing the measurement of values in younger populations. Various studies support

1 www.worldvaluessurvey.org

2 Female in this case; the PVQ has separate versions for female and male respondents.

the validity of value assessment via PVQ-style instruments in primary and secondary school children (e.g., Bilsky et al. 2013; Boehnke and Welzel 2006; Bubeck and Bilsky 2004; Cieciuch et al. 2013; Schwartz et al. 2001).

Döring and colleagues (2010) contributed an important step toward valid value assessment in young children with the development of the Picture-Based Value Survey for Children (PBVS-C). Using values (or value-laden behaviors) illustrated in pictures, children are asked to sort the pictures according to their importance for them in a form similar to a sticker album. The twenty pictures contain two pictures/stickers for each of ten Schwartz's value types. Two pictures are picked that are considered very important; two are selected that are least important; four pictures are selected that are important; and four that are not important; while the remaining eight are of indifferent importance. The PBVS-C is able to assess values in children from an age of six years onward and might even be usable with preschoolers.

The recent scale developments of PVQ and PBVS-C opened up the possibility of self-report value assessments in children. Findings reveal valid and reliable measurements of values according to Schwartz's value theory. It is important to note, however, that the differentiation between ten value types of Schwartz's value theory[3] is less distinct in younger participants. Younger children do not differentiate, for instance, universalistic from benevolent values as clearly as older children do. Nevertheless, the general structure of Schwartz's two-dimensional space is validly assessed using both PVQ and PBVS-C.

The overview of value functions and measurement during childhood indicates their importance for individuals' lives and the validity of their assessment; however, how are specific values developed, transferred from one generation to the next, and socialized within a specific context? Are values even heritable? The next sections aim to provide tentative answers to these questions.

Value transmission and socialization

Transmission and socialization encompass fundamental processes for the acquisition and development of values, both having received considerable attention by sociologists and developmental psychologists. Transmission is the process of transferring something from one person or group to another person or group (Baier and Hadjar 2004). In this process, individuals or groups become more similar in their characteristics—an important aspect of cultural maintenance (Schönpflug 2001) and socialization (Hitlin 2006). In their development, individuals receive value input mainly from their parents and families, but also from peers and significant others in their life context. We, thus, differentiate between intergenerational (vertical) and horizontal value transmission.

[3] Schwartz and colleagues (2012) have recently refined the theory into an approach that distinguishes nineteen different values that can, however, be collapsed into the ten value types distinguished in earlier work (e.g., Schwartz and Boehnke, 2004).

Vertical (intergenerational) value transmission

Parents and children align their values to some degree (e.g., Knafo and Schwartz 2009; Min et al. 2012; Roest et al. 2010). Boehnke et al. (2007) mentioned four sources of intergenerational value similarity: (1) parents' values influencing children's values, (2) parents being influenced by children's values, (3) contextual factors influencing both values, and (4) common genetic dispositions (Knafo and Spinath 2011; Schermer et al. 2008). This section covers these four aspects briefly.

Parents' influence on their children's values Parent–child value transmission evolves through a two-step process (Grusec and Goodnow 1994). First, children perceive their parents' values; second, they actively choose to accept (or reject) these values. Value congruence between parents and their child is particularly likely when the child perceives his/her parents' values correctly and then accepts them, making them his/her own. Knafo and Schwartz (2004) tested how Marcia's aforementioned identity statuses relate to children's attainment of a correct value perception and to the acceptance of parental values. They found that adolescents who are successful in identity exploration (achievement and moratorium status) perceive their parents' values more accurately. Furthermore, those who committed already to an identity (achievement and foreclosure status) accept those values of their parents more.

A longitudinal study aimed at disentangling the persistence and timing of value transmission over the life course (Min et al. 2012). Data were collected in 1971 and in 2000, assessing religious beliefs and gender role attitudes as proxies for two specific values. Intergenerational value similarity was established in 1971 (when children were adolescents) and predicted offspring values in 2000. Gender role-related values were less similar and less stable over time compared to religious values (cf. Evis and Okagakia 1999), indicating that values may not be homogenously transmitted, but that the transmission process features content-specific mechanisms. Value similarity between caregivers and children depends on the value type, and additionally societal context matters. Boehnke (2004; see also Boehnke et al. 2007) showed, for example, that for values cherished less in a society, intergenerational similarity is larger, and explained this through the greater necessity of parents and offspring to communicate about such values than it is the case for values generally cherished in a society. Contexts of value preferences and value development—like the cultural value climate—that impact on the value transmission process have been labeled transmission belts by Schönpflug (2001; 2009).

Transmission belts Considering intergenerational value transmission as one process contributing to cultural continuity, Schönpflug (2001) addresses the selectivity of which values are transferred and the conditions that facilitate or inhibit value transmission. Such transmission belts are of a relational nature (parenting styles, family cohesion, family rituals) or resource-related (education, developmental stage and age, sibling position).

A good intergenerational relationship quality supports vertical transmission (e.g., Evis and Okagakia 1999; Hitlin 2006). Here, parental support and relationship quality facilitate children's acceptance of, and alignment with, parental values. In addition to good relationships, value transmission and development is also influenced by parenting style. Alignment between Canadian children's ideal-self values and their parents' values was stronger for more authoritative parents (authoritativeness encompassing warmth and strictness) compared to less authoritative parents (Pratt and Hunsberger 2003), particularly at younger age. Baier and Hadjar (2004) found that German parents' democratic parenting style facilitates mother–child value transmission. Here, a more equal role distribution in the parenting responsibilities may lead to an enhanced impact of mothers' on their children's values. Interparental agreement on a particular value seems to strengthen transmission (Boehnke 2004) as well. Also, family routines and rituals, such as anniversaries, annual celebrations, and other special activities are whole-family events that reflect the family's identity and shared values. According to Reiss (1981), rituals are the main mechanism used by families to keep their paradigm, i.e., the shared perceptions and beliefs about the outside world and about the family's place in that world. Although no empirical research has been conducted so far with regard to value transmission within rituals, theorists in this field agree that intergenerational value transmission occurs during these special events (e.g., Fiese 2006; Reiss 1981).

Resource-related transmission belts including parents' educational and socio-economic background, the child's age and peer contacts play a central role (cf. Baier and Hadjar 2004). Contacts to siblings and peers are additional socialization agents that provide input to value development. In particular, firstborns may rely more on parent–child value transmission compared to later-born children, whereas later-born children may also align their values with their siblings' values (MacDonald 1969). However, Schönpflug's (2001) results did not find support for reduced parent–child value transmission among later-born children; neither did Boehnke et al.'s (2007), but their study showed clear evidence for horizontal transmission among siblings. Furthermore, extended contact to peers may limit parental influences on their children's values. Baier and Hadjar (2004) findings partially support this hypothesis: girls' more frequent contact to peers reduced their parent–child value congruence with regard to achievement values, whereas boys' peer contacts did not influence parent–child value transmission.

These findings open the question: What values do parents want to transmit to their kids? When mothers from Sweden, Estonia, and Russia (living in Estonia) were asked which of their own values they would like to pass on to their children, benevolence values were mentioned most frequently by all three groups of mothers (Tulviste et al. 2011). Furthermore, Swedish mothers want their kids to value self-direction and achievement, whereas mothers from Estonia aim to pass conformity and self-direction values, and Russian mothers aim to transmit conformity and achievement values. Besides the universal importance of benevolence (Schwartz and Rubel-Lifschitz 2009), cultural patterns, as well as cultural changes, seem to determine mother's value socialization goals (Tulviste et al. 2011).

Heritability Despite the persuasiveness of evidence on value transmission, recent research suggests that value orientations are similarly heritable as personality traits (Knafo and Spinath 2011; Schermer et al. 2008). Genetic similarity may be a prerequisite for facilitating value transmission. Knafo and Schwartz (2009) speculate three possible mechanisms: (1) interindividual genetic differences predispose complex traits being possible motivational anchors of values (cf. Fischer and Boer 2014), (2) gene–environment correlation may enhance parent–child value similarity due to a genetic propensity of the child to engage in and shape environments that request parents' and children's responses, and (3) certain genetic make-up may influence the susceptibility of parental influence, e.g., by enhancing the perception accuracy and acceptance of parental values.

What is the evidence on value heritability? First, Keller and colleagues (1992) showed higher similarity in work values (achievement and status orientation) among monozygotic compared to dizygotic twins. In Australian twins, nine out of ten value types had a genetic component with heritability ranging between 10.8 percent (power values) and 38 percent (conformity values) (Schermer et al. 2008), whereas achievement values were mainly explained by environmental factors. Furthermore, Knafo and Spinath (2011) assessed the heritability and environmental factors in children's values by distinguishing between gender-neutral (conservation, openness to change) and gender-stereotypical (self-transcendence, self-enhancement) values. Interestingly, gender-stereotypical values showed high (0.49) and gender-neutral values showed moderate (0.34) heritability. The gender-stereotypical values of boys and girls were explained by genetic variations, the gender-atypical values showed strong differences between boys and girls: Girls' a-typical values (self-enhancement) were largely inherited (0.76), whereas boys' a-typical values (self-transcendence) were neither inherited nor strongly shaped by the environment (0.10). This finding may be driven by the universalistic importance of self-transcendence values (cf. Schwartz and Rubel-Lifschitz 2009). This section highlights that intergenerational value transmission extends beyond socialization to genetic and environmental factors.

Children's influence on parents While parents certainly have a primary influence on their children, including their values, the nature of their relationship is bidirectional, which means that children and parents influence each other throughout time as postulated by the transactional model of development (Sameroff 2009). Kuczynski and colleagues (1997) expanded the idea of socialization to a bidirectional interactive model, where parents' as well as children's mental working models of values are interactively linked in addition to communicating with an ecology of other's value working models (school, media, other parents, peers). Such an interactive approach de-emphasizes the uni-lateral influence that parents have on their children by conceiving value transmission as an interactive ongoing process entailing negotiation, cooperation, mutual shaping, and mutual observation and modeling. By sharing their life, being supportive of each other, and open for each other's concerns and ideas, children can also impact on their parents' values. This works particularly for values that are salient in kids' lives: Values of central concern for adolescents (related to technology, tradition, and religion) were transmitted from children to their parents, which was not the case for values that become salient only later in life, as shown in Pinquart and Silbereisen's (2004) seminal study (see also: Roest et al. 2010). Children expose their caregivers to situations and interactions that in turn fine-tune parental values by drawing their attention to specific topics.

Horizontal value transmission

Irrefutably, peers (and significant others from other than the offspring generation)[4] are also important sources influencing our development, including the commitment to certain values. First, adolescents affect each other's behaviors. The strongest predictor of teen drug use and delinquency, for instance, is their peers' drug use and delinquency (Garnier and Stein 2002). At the same time, adolescents' values of tradition, achievement, humanitarianism, and egalitarianism, which were moderately influenced by maternal values, inhibited such problem behaviors to some degree. These findings support the functions of certain values for social well-functioning, i.e., preventing problem behaviors. Nevertheless, peer influences can sometimes override the guiding forces of personal values.

Peers and siblings shape their values interactively. A number of studies report strong value and ideological similarity between siblings (e.g., Rose et al. 1990). One explanation attributes this similarity to the shared environment and intense contact between siblings (an alternative explanation vis-à-vis heritability). Those twins who lived together longer and who retained close contact in adulthood showed more similarity in some traits and lifestyles (Rose et al. 1990).

Similar to sibling contact, peer contact also impacts on value development. First, peer values may have direct influences on the formation of personal values. Pratt and Hunsberger (2003) showed that peers' emphasis (in addition to parental emphasis) on moral values contributed to a stronger valuing of a moral self. This indicates peers' mutuality of value influence and interactive value development. Shared socialization environments further contribute to their common value orientations. Furthermore, it is important to consider that values play a key role in peer relations and friend selection. Value similarity facilitates friendships and social relationships (e.g., Boer et al. 2011; Solomon and Knafo 2007). When people agree on what is important in their lives, their relationship is likely to be more harmonious.

Values are acquired in interaction with families, friends, and others, while shared environments, cultural contexts, and genetic make-up contribute to an ongoing value development throughout the lifespan. In the next section we elaborate on changes in value preferences after primary value formation.

Value development throughout the lifespan

Values are considered as relatively stable personal constructs in adulthood and longitudinal data suggest that annual test–retest correlations of value preferences in mid-adulthood may be as high as $r = 0.86$ (Boehnke 2012). Still, individuals change during their lives: Their life situations, priorities, and motivations modify, amend, and adjust to current

4 Cavalli-Sforza and Feldman (1981) call this latter transmission mode "oblique transmission."

life stages and events. In younger years, fun and excitement are more important than in mid-adulthood, where success and financial security may catch up in importance, while health orientation and family cohesion may become particularly prioritized after retirement. These changes entail some shifts in value priorities. Value development can occur in three ways (Dusek and Flaherty 1981): (1) change in the structure of the value system (continuity/discontinuity), (2) stability/instability of value preferences across time points, and (3) mean shifts referring to increases and decreases in the preferences of particular values across the lifespan. In this section we elaborate on these aspects of value development, emphasizing which mechanisms they involve and under which conditions value change is particularly likely. Finally, we address some dispositional aspects of individuals' value development in adulthood.

Mechanisms of value change

The development, formation, and change of values are adaptive processes that accommodate to social and political situations or compensate deprivation. Before value preferences change in the long run, they will first have to undergo repeated temporary changes (Bardi and Goodwin 2011; Bardi et al. 2009). By repeating temporary changes, cognitive structures as mental schemas revolving around value contents can be modified. This happens via repeated reinterpretation of situations according to the new values leading to long-term changes in value orientations (Bardi and Goodwin 2011).

Psychological mechanisms that can trigger a temporary change in value preferences can be pinned down to five processes (Bardi and Goodwin 2011): priming, adaptation, identification, consistency maintenance, and direct persuasion. For instance, *priming* refers to the temporary activation of value contents, which can lead to quasi-automatic changes in value preferences—particularly if this activation occurs repeatedly. Values can be primed and activated, for instance, by environmental, situational, and social stimuli, or via media contents and cultural influences. When participants in an experiment were asked to imagine having a child, they reported stronger social (self-transcendence) and lower self-centered (self-enhancement) values than before (Maio et al. 2008; cited in Bardi and Goodwin 2011). Value change via *adaptation* refers to new life situations, which question old values, because these new stages in life are accompanied by novel environmental stimuli, events, and demands. Values that do not fit the new life stages any more are changed after being challenged repeatedly in order to accommodate the new life demands. Societal changes or historical events can initiate such adaptive value changes. The transition from communism to post-communism in the Czech Republic triggered stronger openness-to-change values. Terrorist attacks in 9/11 increased the importance of security values. Migration is another example where migrants adapt their own values to the host societies' values or to the new life situation. These are examples of mechanisms that drive value instability (priming) and mean shifts (adaptation).

Concerning the structure of values change, values do not change spontaneously and unsystematically, instead value change occurs holistically and systematically. If one value type changes, other related values also adjust in order to retain a functional and compatible intra-individual system (Bardi et al. 2009; Maio et al. 2009). This also means that changes in value preference do not occur isolated, but extend to adjunct changes in other values, attitudes, and behaviors. Value assessments across a diverse age range corroborate a similar structural alignment of values. Studies using different age-appropriate value measures confirm that values are represented according to Schwartz's (1992) value theory, indicating that values develop (and change) systematically and coherently. Next we elaborate on the conditions that facilitate value change.

Conditions of value change

Age and cohort effects Various conditions can elicit changes in value preferences. Age, new life situations, societal changes, and migration are important contributors to lifespan development in values. On the one hand, values can change according to age-related demands and needs. For example, heightened security needs increase with age, while achievement values are more important during younger years and decrease in importance after peaking during mid-adulthood (Bardi et al. 2009). Changing educational settings also co-occur with value changes that accommodate the new life situation. Research showed value changes after participants entered vocational training (Strack et al. 2008) or secondary education (Hofmann-Towfigh 2007; Sheldon 2005). For instance, students adapted their values (to a small but significant extent) to conform to the ideological culture of their new schools being religious, private, or public institutions (Hofmann-Towfigh 2007). Felson and colleagues (1994) examined the influence of violent subcultures in schools. Values of violence in schools impact on actual violent behaviors between pupils (beyond the personal values of pupils). Hence, the school contexts can contribute to violent behaviors, when it supports and legitimizes such behaviors. The contextual activation of values can override personal values and their attitudinal and behavioral influences (Daniel et al. 2012).

Interestingly, it is argued that changes in values are more likely in younger years: As values are stabilized and internalized in late adolescents or young adulthood, major changes in value preferences become less likely with increasing age (Bardi et al. 2009). Confirming this proposal, younger migrants more easily adapted to the host societies' values compared to older migrants (Marin et al. 1987). Accounting for *Zeitgeist* and generational effects, it is important to differentiate between the influence of cohort and age groups in value development, but currently there are only few longitudinal studies. Bardi and colleagues (2009) found that particularly major life events (child birth, job change, or loss of the partner) impacted on value change, whereas age played only a minor role. The diversity of life trajectories is likely to affect this finding. Looking at specific cohort effects in China and the US, Egri and Ralston (2004) found that the generations since communism (Consolidation, Cultural Revolution, Social Reform) valued openness-to-change and self-enhancement more and conservation and self-transcendence less than the generation growing up before communism (Republican Era). The younger generations of Chinese and Americans were more similar in their value orientations than the generations growing up during the closed-door policy of the PRC. This finding points toward assimilating values of citizens in these two cultural contexts being facilitated by macro-contextual factors, including changing societal values and economic developments.

Cultural and situational contexts The previous examples of migration, culture, and *Zeitgeist* already indicated that contextual factors are major sources for value activation and change. Values can be activated by situational or subcultural and macro-cultural cues. Various experimental studies showed that activated values are more coherently expressed in attitudes and behaviors (Maio and Olson 1995; Verplanken and Holland 2002). Context factors can, therefore, activate values, which in turn enhance value-consistent behaviors due to the salience of associated motivations and goal-oriented cognitive and behavioral processes. Cultural and other macro-contextual conditions are arguably the most influential sources of value activation due to their ubiquity and salience. A recent meta-analysis reporting data from thirty-one societies found, for instance, that the associations between personal conservative values and social attitudes are stronger in contexts with more collectivistic values and uncertainty avoidance (Boer and Fischer 2013). This finding supports the authors' claim that these cultural values facilitate the extent to which personal values guide social attitudes. Enhanced contextual salience of these values leads to an increased internalization of such values, which in turn affect aligned attitudes more strongly. Schiefer and colleagues (2010) found that cultural hierarchy orientation influences individual's group-based prejudice, if these values are accepted and internalized. The internalization process was found to be stronger for older adolescents compared to younger adolescents, because value internalization and formation is still in progress during mid-adolescence, leading to a stronger impact of cultural values on personal attitudes in the older age group.

Migration is a special case of changing contextual values impacting on personal values and attitudes. First-generation migrants enter a new societal context that entails many new cultural values. Schiefer (2013) proposed and found that societal values impact more strongly on social attitudes of non-migrants because non-migrants were longer socialized within the frame of societal values, while migrants grew up embedded in a society entailing other cultural values. The author argued that the influence of host societies' values will be stronger for second-generation migrants (as strong as for non-migrants) due to their socialization within the host society. Hence, generational status is an important factor for socio-cultural adaptation of migrants' values and attitudes. Recent longitudinal evidence showed that Ingrian-Finnish migrants change their values right after migration (Lönnqvist et al. 2011), but returned to their old values two years after migration indicating a rebound effect (Lönnqvist et al. 2013). These studies highlight the impact of migration and new societal values on personal values being a vital force in a globalized world characterized by massive voluntary and involuntary migration waves, as well as drastic cultural changes.

The extent to which value frames change across situations in six cultural groups has been examined by Daniel et al. (2011). The authors investigated whether value priorities differ when different contexts (family, school, and country) were the reference frame. Values were consistent in their rank order, but varied in importance ratings according to the contextual circumstance. Interestingly, minority members' value priorities were consistent across contexts in Israel, whereas in Germany, some values were negatively correlated indicating value conflict across situations. The authors concluded that cultural contextual factors (including country of residence in interaction with minority status) are relevant for the coherence in value systems. Furthermore, it becomes apparent that we live through various situational and relational contexts every day and our values may shift in order to appropriate such contexts. Additionally, intra-individual factors play an important role in value change besides contextual conditions.

Dispositional resistance to change

People vary in their general receptivity for change. Some people are receptive for changes in values and other attributes, while others are more resistant to change. One personality characteristic called dispositional resistance to change characterizes this receptivity (Oreg 2003). Individuals possessing this disposition to a high degree are, thus, unlikely to change their values, whereas individuals who are not characterized by this trait are more receptive to value changes. Furthermore, openness-to-experience as one personality trait and Schwartz's value dimension called openness-to-change are intuitively entailing enhanced individual propensity to be open for alternative explanations and to engage in situations that may trigger changes in values. In contrast, conservation values imply a strong motivation to maintain previous values and not to question them. A study across seventeen countries showed that individuals who hold traditional, conformity, and security values have a stronger dispositional resistance to change and are, therefore, less likely to change their values, whereas individuals who hold openness-to-change values reported lower resistance to change and were thought to be more receptive to value changes (Oreg et al. 2008).

Furthermore, some contexts may be more facilitative of individuals' value change. According to Bardi and Goodwin's (2011) proposal, societal values of autonomy and uncertainty avoidance are thought to be supportive of individual value changes, whereas collectivistic and hierarchy-oriented societies may rather hinder individuals' value changes. Although this proposal has not been tested empirically, it highlights the potential impact of cultural and societal values on personal values. We have already elaborated on the cross-linkage of societal values on personal value systems; however, societal values are also subject to ongoing changes. The closing section briefly describes societal value developments and links them to personal value development.

Value change within and across cultures

Changes in the modal value preferences of cultures have presumably been omnipresent throughout human history. However, the question arises: What drives changes in these modal value preferences? One of the most comprehensive approaches to explain value change across history and cultures dates back to the work of Karl Marx. Marx (e.g., 1858 [1973]) sees two mechanisms in effect. The first is related to "ownership to the means of production," i.e., who owns production sites and resources. Whenever the prevalent ownership to the means of production changes in a given society (in Marx's terms the "base"), value preferences (in his terms the "superstructure") will also change. Marx's historical materialism theory suggests that value change takes the road from purely collectivist values in primeval societies to ever more individualism in fully developed capitalism, because people tend to prefer values that guarantee the perpetuation of the modal model of ownership to the means of production prevalent in a given society.

The second "motor" of value change, according to Marx, is the "level of development of the productive forces." This concept can easily be translated into *degree of economic prosperity* being an important change agent for values cherished in a given culture. Here Marx's thinking merges well into that of modern theoreticians and empirical researchers of societal value change. As early as 1977, Inglehart suggested that the degree of—economic—need fulfillment (in the early years of life) is decisive for the values a person holds. He showed convincingly that value preferences of generations that had grown up in—economic—scarcity differed sharply from the values of generations that have grown up in relative abundance in Western publics. Those generations that had experienced scarcity, clearly expressed what Inglehart then called materialist values, whereas generations that never had experienced scarcity were more inclined to express postmaterialist value orientations. Other analyses show (e.g., Inglehart and Welzel 2005) that even concurrent changes in economic prosperity are reflected in the value preferences of the population of a given society. Mexico, for example, experienced a monotonous increase in economic prosperity since 1990. Its modal preferences of self-expression values, as defined by Inglehart, also increased monotonously during the same time period. Russia, on the other hand, decreased in prosperity during the 1990s and only increased again well after the turn of the millennium. Self-expression values followed exactly the same trend: preferences going down in the 1990s and recovering to prior scores only well into the new millennium.

Modal value preferences obviously also differ between cultures and not only across time. Cultural differences seem to follow the same logic as does value change. Cultures that experience higher levels of economic prosperity tend to also have modal value preferences dominated by self-expression values, whereas poor countries are more prone to support survival values. Studies of cultural differences in modal value preferences of societies come to amazingly similar conclusions: In the contemporary world one can distinguish some eight to nine cultural zones. This conclusion is reached by researchers regardless of their analytic approach. Inglehart and Welzel (2010) label their zones as Islamic, Africa, and South Asia, cultural zones dominated by below-average secular-rational values (SRV–; see Norris and Inglehart 2004) and below-average self-expression values (SEV–); Orthodox and Confucian (SRV+, SEV–); Catholic Europe (SRV+, average-level self-expression values, SEV±); English Speaking (SRV±, SEV+); and Protestant Europe (SRV+, SEV+). These descriptions of cultural zones closely resemble classifications offered by Schwartz (2008) and Huntington (1996). Resorting once again to Marx's terms, one can summarize that the cross-cultural variations in the modal value preferences of people have their roots in differences both of the "base" (economic prosperity) and the "superstructure." The superstructure also entails other forms of institutional mechanisms, for instance, the tightness of norms and the sanctions directed toward norm violations, which interact with societal values and their development (Gelfand et al., 2011).

Conclusion and future research

This chapter elucidated values as an essential concept for child and lifespan development, which seem interlinked with societal values and their change. Personal values emerge as part of cognitive, identity, social, and personality development. At the same time, values evolve in interaction with the environment: Their transmission and lifespan development afford a dynamic interplay of individual factors, close others, specific (family) contexts, and societal progress. Taking the genetic make-up as basic gear and the needs-fulfilling context as base camp, the individual evolves as a conscious being who formulates desired goals of living that guide behaviors and evaluations.

Value changes are inevitable for societal development. We argue that a developmental perspective adds an intriguing perspective to current theories of societal value development and change. Value change has often been construed by distinguishing age, cohort, and period effects; concerns about how to statistically disentangle these effects seem to have dominated that discussion. Above and beyond a focus on the genetic base plus cohort and period-specific socialization circumstances, a developmental perspective offers insights into *how* children are experiencing contemporary trends. By looking, e.g., at the meaning of technology for identity construction, it helps to explain on which pathways children bring change-relevant topics closer to their parents' daily experience and thereby impact on the values of their parents with regard to openness toward novel developments. Societal change from a developmental perspective, hence, adds an important component for within-cohort changes and intergenerational influences. Particularly an influence from younger to older generations (at a time when the former cannot yet exert control over societal and institutional life and developments) may steer progressive societal change as contemporary developments are readily included into existing value systems and not rejected. Such rejection could yield an inappropriate maintenance of "old" reactive values counteracting timely and dynamic societal development. The progressive inclusion of younger generations' values means that value development of older generations affords a dynamic cohort development that counterbalances ontological age-trajectories and generational stability (cf. Egri and Ralston 2004).

Future research is encouraged to bring together mechanisms of what one might call "retrogenerational" value transmission (i.e. child-to-parent-transmission) with progressive vs. regressive societal value development. Moreover, specific societal conditions that mediate the relationship between the base (economic and bio-genetic) and the superstructure (values, beliefs, and mentalities, the *Weltanschauung*, to use a well-known German term) may enact their influence as transmission belts in facilitating or inhibiting retrogenerational influences and their role in steering societal value development. Thus, institutional societal characteristics may encourage or hinder bilateral generational transmission processes and societal value change. Subsequent consequences of societal value change for societal innovativeness and economic growth seem viable and we hope to spark interest in future research that addresses societal economic and value development from—ontogenetic and phylogenetic—developmental perspectives.

References

Baier, D. and Hadjar, A. (2004). Wie wird Leistungsorientierung von den Eltern auf die Kinder übertragen? Ergebnisse einer Längsschnittstudie/How are achievement orientations transmitted from parents to children? Results of a longitudinal study. *Zeitschrift für Familienforschung*, **15**(2), 156–177.

Bandura, A. (1977). *Social learning theory*. Englewood Cliffs, NJ: Prentice-Hall.

Bardi, A. and Goodwin, R. (2011). The dual route to value change: Individual processes and cultural moderators. *Journal of Cross-Cultural Psychology*, **42**(2), 271–287. DOI:10.1177/0022022110396916

Bardi, A., Lee, J. A., Hofmann-Towfigh, N., and Soutar, G. (2009). The structure of intraindividual value change. *Journal of Personality and Social Psychology*, **97**(5), 913–929. DOI:10.1037/a0016617

Bilsky, W., Döring, A. K., van Beeck, F., Rose, I., Schmitz, J., Aryus, K., Lisa Drögekamp and Sindermann, J. (2013). Assessment of children's value structures and value preferences. *Swiss Journal of Psychology*, **72**(3), 123–136. DOI:10.1024/1421-0185/a000106

Boehnke, K. (2004). Do our children become as we are? Intergenerational value transmission and societal value change—two unlinked concepts in social research. In F. Hardt (ed.), *Mapping the world: new perspectives in the humanities and social sciences* (pp. 99–118). Tübingen: Francke.

Boehnke, K. (2012, December). Do our children become as we are? The development of children's values in cultural and social context. Invited address at the conference "Value change in childhood" [http://childrenvalues.uksw.edu.pl/index.php/en/program], Münster, Germany.

Boehnke, K. and Welzel, C. (2006). Wertetransmission und Wertewandel: Eine explorative Drei-Generationen-Studie/Value transmission and value change: An exploratory three-generation study. *Zeitschrift für Soziologie der Erziehung und Sozialisation*, **26**(4), 341–360. Retieved from http://www.pedocs.de/volltexte/2012/5654/pdf/ZSE_2006_4_Boehnke_Welzel_Wertetransmission_D_A.pdf

Boehnke, K., Hadjar, A., and Baier, D. (2007). Parent-child value similarity: the role of Zeitgeist. *Journal of Marriage and Family*, **69**(3), 778–792. DOI:10.1111/j.1741-3737.2007.00405.x

Boer, D. and Fischer, R. (2013). How and when do personal values guide our attitudes and sociality? Explaining cross-cultural variability in attitude-value linkages. *Psychological Bulletin*, **139**(5), 1113–1147. DOI:10.1037/a0031347

Boer, D., Fischer, R., Strack, M., Bond, M. H., Lo, E., and Lam, J. (2011). How shared preferences in music create bonds between people: values as the missing link. *Personality and Social Psychology Bulletin*, **37**(9), 1159–1171. DOI:10.1177/0146167211407521

Bubeck, M. and Bilsky, W. (2004). Value structure at an early age. *Swiss Journal of Psychology*, **63**(1), 31–41. DOI:10.1024/1421-0185.63.1.31

Caspi, A. (1997). Personality development across the life course. In W. Damon and N. Eisenberg (eds), *Handbook of child psychology*: Vol. 3. *Social, emotional, and personality development*, 5th edn (pp. 311–388). New York: Wiley-Blackwell Publishing Ltd.

Caspi, A. and Roberts, B. W. (2001). Personality development across the life course: the argument for change and continuity. *Psychological Inquiry*, **12**(2), 49–66. DOI:10.1207/S15327965PLI1202_01

Caspi, A. and Silva, P. A. (1995). Temperamental qualities at age 3 predict personality traits in young adulthood: longitudinal evidence from a birth cohort. *Child Development*, **66**(2), 486–498. DOI:10.1111/j.1467-8624.1995.tb00885.x

Cavalli-Sforza, L. L. and Feldman, M. (1981). *Cultural transmission and evolution*: a quantitative approach. Princeton: Princeton University Press.

Cieciuch, J., Döring, A. K., and Harasimczuk, J. (2013). Measuring Schwartz's values in childhood: multidimensional scaling across instruments and cultures. *European Journal of Developmental Psychology*, **10**(5), 625–633. DOI:10.1080/17405629.2012.707779

Daniel, E., Schiefer, D., and Knafo, A. (2011). One and not the same: the consistency of values across contexts among majority and minority members in Israel and Germany. *Journal of Cross-Cultural Psychology*, **43**(7), 1167–1184. DOI:10.1177/0022022111430257

Daniel, E., Schiefer, D., Möllering, A., Benish-Weisman, M., Boehnke, K., and Knafo, A.(2012). Value differentiation in adolescence: the role of age and cultural complexity. *Child Development*, **83**(1), 322–336. DOI:10.1111/j.1467–8624.2011.01694.x

Dusek, J. B. and Flaherty, J. F. (1981). *The development of the self-concept during the adolescent years*. Chicago: University of Chicago Press.

Döring, A. K., Blauensteiner, A., Aryus, K., Drögekamp, L., and Bilsky, W. (2010). Assessing values at an early age: the Picture-Based Value Survey for Children (PBVS-C). *Journal of Personality Assessment*, **92**(5), 439–448. DOI:10.1080/00223891.2010.497423

Egri, C. P. and Ralston, D. A. (2004). Generation cohorts and personal values: A comparison of China and the United States. *Organization Science*, **15**(2), 210–220. DOI:10.1287/orsc.1030.0048

Erikson, E. H. (1950). *Childhood and society*. New York: Norton.

Erikson, E. H. (1968). *Identity: youth and crisis*. New York: Norton.

Evis, L. and Okagakia, C. (1999). Transmission of religious values: relations between parents' and daughters' beliefs. *The Journal of Genetic Psychology: Research and Theory on Human Development*, **160**(3), 303–318. DOI:10.1080/00221329909595401

Felson, R. B., Liska, A. E., South, S. J., and McNulty, T. L. (1994). The subculture of violence and delinquency: individual vs. school context effects. *Social Forces*, **73**(1), 155–173. DOI:10.1093/sf/73.1.155

Fiese, B. H. (2006). *Family routines and rituals*. New Haven: Yale University Press.

Fischer, R. and Boer, D. (2014). Motivational basis for personality trait: A meta-analysis of value-personality correlations. *Journal of Personality*. DOI: 10.1111/jopy.12125

Fischer, R., Milfont, T. L., and Gouveia, V. V. (2011). Does social context affect value structures? Testing the within-country stability of value structures with a functional theory of values. *Journal of Cross-Cultural Psychology*, **42**(2), 253–270. DOI:10.1177/0022022110396888

Garnier, H. E. and Stein, J. A. (2002). An 18-year model of family and peer effects on adolescent drug use and delinquency. *Journal of Youth and Adolescence*, **31**(1), 45–56. DOI:10.1023/A:1014085016511

Gelfand, M. J., Raver, J. L., Nishii, L., Leslie, L. M., Lun, J., Lim, B. C., . . . Yamaguchi, S. (2011). Differences between tight and loose cultures: a 33-nation study. *Science*, **332**(6033), 1100–1104. DOI: 10.1126/science.1197754

Grusec, J. E. and Goodnow, J. J. (1994). Impact of parental discipline methods on the child's internalization of values: a reconceptualization of current points of view. *Developmental Psychology*, **30**(1), 4–19. DOI:10.1037/0012-1649.30.1.4

Havighurst, R. J. (1948). *Developmental tasks and education*. New York: David McKay.

Hitlin, S. (2003). Values as the core of personal identity: drawing links between two theories of self. *Social Psychology Quarterly*, **66**(2), 118–137. Retrieved from http://www.jstor.org/stable/10.2307/1519843

Hitlin, S. (2006). Parental influences on children's values and aspirations: bridging two theories of social class and socialization. *Sociological Perspectives*, **49**(1), 25–46. DOI:10.1525/sop.2006.49.1.25

Hitlin, S. and Piliavin, J. A. (2004). Values: reviving a dormant concept. *Annual Review of Sociology*, **30**, 359–393. DOI:10.1146/annurev.soc.30.012703.110640

Hofmann-Towfigh, N. (2007). Do students' values change in different types of schools?. *Journal of Moral Education*, **36**(4), 453–473. DOI:10.1080/03057240701688010

Hofstede, G. (1980). *Culture's consequences–international differences in work-related values*. Newbury Park: Sage.

Hofstede, G. (2001). *Culture's consequences–comparing values, behaviors, institutions, and organizations across nations*. Thousand Oaks: Sage.

Huntington, S. P. (1996). *The clash of civilizations and the remaking of world order*. New York: Simon and Schuster.

Inglehart, R. (1977). *The silent revolution*. Princeton, NJ: Princeton University Press.

Inglehart, R. (1997). *Modernization and postmodernization*. Princeton, NJ: Princeton University Press.

Inglehart, R., and Welzel, C. (2005). *Modernization, cultural change, and democracy: The human development sequence*. Cambridge, UK: Cambridge University Press.

Inglehart, R., and Welzel, C. (2010). Changing mass priorities: The link between modernization and democracy. *Perspectives on Politics*, **8**(2), 551–567. DOI:10.1017/S1537592710001258

Keller, L. M., Bouchard, T. J., Arvey, R. D., Segal, N. L., and Davis, R. V. (1992). Work values: genetic and environmental influences. *Journal of Applied Psychology*, **77**(1), 79—88.

Kluckhohn, C. (1951). Values and value-orientations in the theory of action: An exploration in definition and classification. In T. Parsons and E. Shils (Eds.), *Toward a general theory of action*. Cambridge, MA: Harvard University Press.

Knafo, A. and Schwartz, S. H. (2004). Identity formation and parent-child value congruence in adolescence. *British Journal of Developmental Psychology*, **22**(3), 439–458. DOI:10.1348/0261510041552765

Knafo, A.,and Schwartz, S. H. (2009). Accounting for parent-child value congruence: theoretical considerations and empirical evidence. In U. Schönpflug (ed.), *Cultural transmission: psychological, developmental, social, and methodological aspects* (pp. 240–268). Cambridge, UK: Cambridge University Press.

Knafo, A. and Spinath, F. M. (2011). Genetic and environmental influences on girls' and boys' gender-typed and gender-neutral values. *Developmental psychology*, **47**(3), 726–731. DOI:10.1037/a0021910

Kohlberg, L. (1976). Moral stages and moralization: the cognitive-development approach. In T. Lickona (ed.), *Moral development and behavior: theory, research and social issues* (pp. 31–53). New York: Holt, Rinehart and Winston.

Kuczynski, L., Marshall, S., and Schell, K. (1997). Value socialization in a bidirectional context. In J. E. Grusec and L. Kuczynski (eds), *Parenting and children's internalization of values: a handbook of contemporary theory* (pp. 23–50). New York: Wiley.

Lönnqvist, J.-E., Jasinskaja-Lahti, I., and Verkasalo, M. (2011). Personal values before and after migration: a longitudinal case study on value change in Ingrian-Finnish migrants. *Social Psychological and Personality Science*, **2**(6), 584–591. DOI:10.1177/1948550611402362

Lönnqvist, J.-E., Jasinskaja-Lahti, I., and Verkasalo, M. (2013). Rebound effect in personal values: Ingrian Finnish migrants' values two years after migration. *Journal of Cross-Cultural Psychology*, **44**(7), 1122–1126. DOI:10.1177/0022022113480040

MacDonald Jr, A. P. (1969). Manifestations of differential levels of socialization by birth order. *Developmental Psychology*, **1**(5), 385—399.

Maio, G. R. and Olson, J. M. (1995). Relations between values, attitudes, and behavioral intentions: The moderating role of attitude function. *Journal of Experimental Social Psychology*, **31**(3), 266–285. DOI:10.1006/jesp.1995.1013

Maio, G. R., Pakizeh, A., Cheung, W.-Y., and Rees, K. J. (2009). Changing, priming, and acting on values: effects via motivational relations in a circular model. *Journal of Personality and Social Psychology*, **97**(4), 699–715. DOI:10.1037/a0016420

Marcia, J. E. (1966). Development and validation of ego-identity status. *Journal of Personality and Social Psychology*, **3**(5), 551–558.

Marcia, J. E. (1980). Identity in adolescence. In J. Adelson (ed.), *Handbook of adolescent psychology*. New York: Wiley.

Marín, G., Sabogal, F., Marín, B. V., Oter-Sabogal, R., and Perez-Stable, E. J. (1987). Development of a short acculturation scale for Hispanics. *Hispanic Journal of Behavioral Science*, **9**(2), 183–205. DOI: 10.1177/07399863870092005

Markus, H. and Kitayama, S. (1991). Culture and the self: implications for cognition, emotion, and motivation. *Psychological Review*, **98**, 224—253. DOI:10.1037/0033-295X.98.2.224

Marx, K. (1858[1973]). *Grundrisse der Kritik der Politischen Ökonomie*. London: unpublished manuscript [published in English as Grundrisse: Foundations of the critique of political economy. Hammondsworth: Penguin, 1973].

Maslow, A. H. (1970). *Motivation and personality*. New York, NY US: Harper and Row.

Maslow, A. H. (1999). *Toward a psychology of being, 3rd edition*. New York, NY US: Wiley.

Min, J., Silverstein, M., and Lendon, J. P. (2012). Intergenerational transmission of values over the family life course. *Advances in Life Course Research*, **17**(3), 112–120. DOI:10.1016/j.alcr.2012.05.001

Norris, P., and Inglehart, R. (2004). *Sacred and secular: religion and politics worldwide*. Cambridge: Cambridge University Press.

Oreg, S. (2003). Resistance to change: developing an individual differences measure. *Journal of Applied Psychology*, **88**(4), 680–693. DOI:10.1037/0021-9010.88.4.680

Oreg, S., Bayazit, M., Vakola, M., Arciniega, L., Armenakis, A., Barkauskiene, R., . . . van Dam, K. (2008). Dispositional resistance to change: measurement equivalence and the link to personal values across 17 nations. *Journal of Applied Psychology*, **93**(4), 935–944. DOI:10.1037/0021-9010.93.4.935

Parks-Leduc, L., Feldman, G., and Bardi, A. (2015). Personality Traits and Personal Values: A Meta-Analysis. *Personality and Social Psychology Review*, **19**(1). DOI: 10.1177/1088868314538548

Pinquart, M. and Silbereisen, R. K. (2004). Transmission of values from adolescents to their parents: the role of value content and authoritative parenting. *Adolescence*, **39**(153), 83–100.

Pratt, M. and Hunsberger, B. (2003). A longitudinal analysis of personal values socialization: correlates of a moral self-ideal in late adolescence. *Social Development*, **12**(4), 563–585. DOI:10.1111/1467-9507.00249

Reiss, D. (1981). *The family's construction of reality*. Cambridge, MA: Harvard University Press.

Roest, A.M.C., Dubas, J. S., and Gerris, J. R. M. (2010). Value transmissions between parents and children: gender and developmental phase as transmission belts. *Journal of Adolescence*, **33**(1), 21–31. DOI:10.1016/j.adolescence.2009.05.017

Rohan, M. J. (2000). A rose by any name? The values construct. *Personality and Social Psychology Review*, **4**(3), 255–277. DOI:10.1207/S15327957PSPR0403_4

Rokeach, M. (1968). *Beliefs, attitudes, and values: a theory of organization and change*. San Francisco: Jossey-Bass.

Rokeach, M. (1973). *The nature of human values*. New York: Free Press.

Rose, R. J., Kaprio, J., Williams, C. J., Viken, R., and Obremski, K. (1990). Social contact and sibling similarity: facts, issues, and red herrings. *Behavior Genetics*, **20**(6), 763–778. Retrieved from http://www.ncbi.nlm.nih.gov/pubmed/2078166

Sameroff, A. J. (ed.) (2009). *The transactional model of development: how children and contexts shape each other*. Washington, DC: American Psychological Association.

Schermer, J. A., Feather, N. T., Zhu, G., and Martin, N. G. (2008). Phenotypic, genetic, and environmental properties of the portrait values questionnaire. *Twin Research and Human Genetics*, **11**(5), 531–537. DOI:10.1375/twin.11.5.531

Schiefer, D. (2013). Cultural values and group-related attitudes: a comparison of individuals with and without migration background across 24 countries. *Journal of Cross-Cultural Psychology*, **44**(2), 245–262. DOI:10.1177/0022022112444898

Schiefer, D., Möllering, A., Daniel, E., Benish-Weisman, M., and Boehnke, K. (2010). Cultural values and outgroup negativity: a cross-cultural analysis of early and late adolescents. *European Journal of Social Psychology*, **40**(4), 635–651. DOI:10.1002/ejsp.745

Schönpflug, U. E. (2001). Intergenerational transmission of values: the role of transmission belts. *Journal of Cross-Cultural Psychology*, **32**(2), 174–185. DOI:10.1177/0022022101032002005

Schönpflug, U. E. (2009). *Cultural transmission: psychological, developmental, social, and methodological aspects*. Cambridge, UK: Cambridge University Press.

Schwartz, S. H. (1992). Universals in the content and structure of values: theoretical advances and empirical tests in 20 countries. *Advances in Experimental Social Psychology*, **25**(1), 1–65.

Schwartz, S. H. (1994). Beyond individualism/collectivism: new cultural dimensions of values. In H. C. T. U. Kim, Ç. Kâgitçibasi, S. Choi, and G. Yoon (eds), *Individualism and collectivism: theory, method, and applications* (pp. 85–119). Thousand Oaks: Sage Publications.

Schwartz, S. H. (2004). Mapping and interpreting cultural differences around the world. In H. Vinken, J. Soeters, and P. Ester (eds), *Comparing cultures: dimensions of culture in a comparative perspective* (pp. 43—73). Leiden, the Netherlands: Brill.

Schwartz, S. H. (2008). *Cultural value orientations: Nature and implications of national differences*. Moscow: State University Higher School of Economics Press.

Schwartz, S. H. and Boehnke, K. (2004). Evaluating the structure of human values with confirmatory factor analysis. *Journal of Research in Personality*, **38**(3), 230–255. DOI:10.1016/S0092–6566(03)00069–2

Schwartz, S. H. and Rubel-Lifschitz, T. (2009). Cross-national variation in the size of sex differences in values: effects of gender equality. *Journal of Personality and Social Psychology*, **97**(1), 171–185. doi: 10.1037/a0015546.

Schwartz, S. H., Melech, G., Lehmann, A., Burgess, S., Harris, M., and Owens, V. (2001). Extending the cross-cultural validity of the theory of basic human values with a different method of measurement. *Journal of Cross-Cultural Psychology*, **32**(5), 519–542. DOI:10.1177/0022022101032005001

Schwartz, S. H., Cieciuch, J., Vecchione, M., Davidov E., Fischer R., Beierlein C., Ramos A, Verkasalo M, Lönnqvist JE, Demirutku K, Dirilen-Gumus O, and Konty M. (2012). Refining the theory of basic individual values. *Journal of Personality and Social Psychology*, **103**(4), 663–688. DOI:10.1037/a0029393

Sheldon, K. M. (2005). Positive value change during college: Normative trends and individual differences. *Journal of Research in Personality*, **39**(2), 209–223. DOI: 10.1016/j.jrp.2004.02.002

Simpson, E. L. (1976). A holistic approach to moral development and behavior. In T. Lickona (ed.), *Moral development and behavior* (pp. 81–106). New York: Holt, Rinehart and Winston.

Solomon, S. and Knafo, A. (2007). Value similarity in adolescent friendships. In T. C. Rhodes (ed.), *Focus on adolescent behavior research* (pp. 133–155). New York, NY: Nova Sprecher.

Srivastava, S., John, O. P., Gosling, S. D., and Potter, J. (2003). Development of personality in early and middle adulthood: Set like plaster or persistent change? *Journal of Personality and Social Psychology*, **84**(5), 1041–1053. DOI:10.1037/0022–3514.84.5.1041

Strack, M., Gennerich, C., and Hopf, N. (2008). Warum Werte?/Why values?. In E. H. Witte (Ed.). Sozialpsychologie und Werte / Social psychology and values (pp. 90–130). Lengerich: Pabst.

Tomasello, M. (2001). *The cultural origins of human cognition*. Cambridge, MA: Harvard University Press.

Tomasello, M., Kruger, A., and Ratner, H. (1993). Cultural learning. *Behavioral and Brain Sciences*, **16**(3), 495–511. DOI:10.1017/S0140525X0003123X

Triandis, H. C. (1995). *Individualism—collectivism*. Boulder, CO: Westview Press.

Triandis, H. C., Leung, K., Villareal, M., and Clack, F. (1985). Allocentric vs. idiocentric tendencies: convergent and discriminant validation. *Journal of Research in Personality*, **19**(4), 395–415.

Tulviste, T., Mizera, L., and De Geer, B. (2011). Socialization values in stable and changing societies: a comparative study of Estonian, Swedish, and Russian Estonian mothers. *Journal of Cross-Cultural Psychology*, **43**(3), 480–497. DOI:10.1177/0022022111401393

Verplanken, B. and Holland, R. W. (2002). Motivated decision making: effects of activation and self-centrality of values on choices and behavior. *Journal of Personality and Social Psychology*, **82**(3), 434–447. DOI:10.1037/0022-3514.82.3.434

Section 2

Values, emotions, and decision-making

Chapter 8

Value and emotion

Julien A. Deonna and Fabrice Teroni

Introduction

There are close links between emotions and values, or at least this is what our ordinary ways of talking suggest. For many, if not all, types of emotion it is thus possible to find a corresponding evaluative term, one often derived from the name of the emotion in question. These are for example evaluative terms such as "shameful," "offensive," "annoying," "dangerous," "contemptible," "admirable," "amusing," "exciting," "boring," and the like.[1] Starting from these linguistic observations, the philosophical task is to elucidate the nature of these links between emotions and values. Attempts at doing so have traditionally revolved around the following three questions: First, what is the role of emotions in elucidating the nature of value? For example, should dangerousness be understood in term of the fear response? Second, what is the role of emotions in our gaining access to values? For example, what may be the role of fear in becoming aware of a given animal's dangerousness? Third, what value do emotions have? For example, is fear of special value because it promotes appropriate behavior toward its object? We shall take up these questions in turn and survey the most important answers they have received in the literature. As we shall discover, answering the first question amounts to surveying a variety of theories according to which there is an *ontological relation* between values and emotions, since the former should be elucidated in terms of the latter (see "Emotions and the nature of values"). Addressing the second question consists in reviewing theories according to which there is an *intentional relation* between emotions and values because the former are apprehensions of value or evaluations (see "Emotion and access to value"). Grappling with the third question, we shall explore some reasons for thinking that emotions can *exemplify* values (see "The value of emotions").

Emotions and the nature of values

The linguistic considerations with which we started our discussion have proved a potent incentive for thinking that the existence of values somehow traces back to the fact that we react emotionally to the world. To explore this idea, we shall review some theories according to which values depend on emotions.

[1] This point is aptly emphasized by Mulligan (1998).

Before we turn our attention to these theories, however, a caveat is apposite. Although contemporary philosophers do not speak of "value" in a strictly technical sense, they use the term in a quite specific way. We are very familiar with the term "value" as it is used in connection with abstract ideals guiding the lives of people. In this sense, typical values are friendship, honesty, solidarity, freedom, etc. By contrast, philosophers mean to designate by "value" or "evaluative property" a type of property that objects, events, or situations may have. A sketch may, for example, have the value of being amusing, a given utterance that of being offensive, or a gesture that of being degrading. The idea under discussion is thus that properties of this type depend on emotional responses, in these cases, say, amusement, anger and humiliation.

Subjectivism about values

A widespread tendency consists in not taking these properties too seriously—we certainly are prone to describe the world in evaluative terms, yet many want to deny that they are "out there in the world" waiting for us to be detected. It is also observed that the question of whether they are exemplified in given circumstances often gives rise to apparently insoluble disagreements and that, in sharp contrast to other ordinary properties, they directly relate to what we ought to do. This explains why many philosophers have tried to explain values away. Now, one potentially promising approach consists in conceiving of value talk as a mere reflection of our emotional life. This is obviously a rather vague idea and those that have pursued it have unsurprisingly clashed over the more precise formulations to which it should lead.

The most radical approach is to analyze evaluative properties in terms of the actual emotional responses that the relevant entities elicit. An event's regrettable or rejoicing character consists in its eliciting regret or joy. If Sally regrets what she has done, then she has done something regrettable. And if her friend Bud does admire it, then it is admirable. This analysis in terms of actual responses straightforwardly entails that a given event may be regrettable or admirable for one subject but not for another, and for the same subject at one time but not at another. While this might be considered at first sight to be a problem, the approach under discussion is likely to embrace the idea that evaluative properties should be relativized to specific subjects and times—an act's being regrettable is analyzed in terms of the more complex property consisting in its eliciting regret in given subjects at given times. Still, we should perhaps hesitate endorsing this extreme form of subjectivism.

First, although this view is typically endorsed so as to explain the existence of never-ending disputes about values, the only way it can make sense of these disputes consists in assuming that those engaged in them are deeply confused. For observe that participants to these disputes are prone to check their reactions against those of others, to attempt to discount subjective factors that might disqualify their judgments, to appeal to general principles, or to adopt another's perspective—yet all these moves are according to radical subjectivism premised on the mistaken conviction that there is a fact of the matter as to whether a given evaluative property is exemplified. The approach simply leaves no room for the kind of disputes we believe we are often engaged in and to which we are so committed (e.g., Blackburn 1998).

A second and related implication of the view is that the very idea of improving one's epistemological standing vis-à-vis evaluative properties makes no sense. Sally could not come to realize that the deed she presently regrets has much to be said in its favor. According to radical subjectivism, the conclusion should rather be that her deed has in the process acquired a new property. The fact that Sally's emotional responses have altered simply cannot be due to the fact that she has previously failed to take into account some important considerations about the object. This is to say that the approach leaves no room for evaluative mistakes.

One may think that these problems require only slight amendments that will leave the basic picture promoted by radical subjectivism intact. The suggestion is likely to be that the problems result from appealing to *actual* emotional responses: these should be replaced by *dispositions* to elicit such responses.[2] Sally's deed being regrettable is now a function of whether or not that deed (or deeds of the relevant type) has the disposition, in given circumstances, to elicit regret in given creatures, for instance in human beings. There is an immediate benefit to be reaped by appealing to dispositions instead of actual emotional responses. This so to say increases the distance between values and emotions, leaving in this way room for possible evaluative mistakes and, consequently, for substantial disputes about them. A dispositional approach can countenance situations in which someone responds to an event with, say, admiration when this event is not in fact admirable, as well as situations in which the event is admirable despite not eliciting admiration. This mirrors the straightforward fact that something may be disposed to elicit a given sort of response despite failing, for a variety of reasons, to do so. One may fail to be indignant at a friend's misdeed (onlookers are disposed to feel indignation), or conversely be indignant at a hated rival's blameless conduct (they remain indifferent). Such a consequence holds for any approach which, like the one under discussion, detaches the exemplification of values from any particular occurrence of an emotional response and which subscribes, for that reason, to a moderate form of subjectivism.

Yet, if the problems attending the crudest form of subjectivism have been addressed, we have until now considered nothing more than a dispositionalist schema. A fully-fledged version of the approach requires that one be explicit as to which subjects should be appealed to, and, among their responses, which count as manifestations of the relevant dispositions. Does the shamefulness of a given trait depend on its disposition to cause shame in every creature who happens to instantiate it, only in those that show minimal interest in it, or perhaps only in established experts? Of course, whatever class of subjects gets elected, the fact is that some of their responses (those elicited in people who themselves exemplify the target trait, those elicited when they are moody or tired, etc.) will fail to qualify as manifestations of the relevant disposition. It has been quite usual at this juncture

[2] A recent book-length defense of this approach is Prinz (2008).

to appeal to an impartial spectator (Smith 1790/1976), this constituting one attempt—notoriously hard to work up into something more than vague hand-waving—at specifying the relevant class of subjects. Now, independently of whether or not one reaches a principled decision concerning which subjects and responses are relevant, one basic implication of dispositionalism should in our opinion lead us to refuse endorsing any specific form it might take.

For the fact that something possesses a certain evaluative property ultimately depends, according to this approach, on a brute psychological fact—this is an implication that it shares with radical subjectivism. We are thus asked to endorse the doubtful conclusion that the world could host fewer evils if future generations were to grow emotionally indifferent to torture, poverty, or slavery, which are per hypothesis evils only due to our current indignant sensitivity to them. To put the same point differently, the distance the dispositionalist approach manages to put between values and emotions is still insufficient to convincingly account for what we mean by correct and incorrect emotions. The views we are now going to discuss are all premised on the idea that the existence of a prevalent and stable disposition to elicit a given feeling is compatible with the absence of the relevant evaluative property.

Fitting attitude analysis

We should emphasize that disagreeing with the foregoing subjectivist approaches for the reasons we have presented does not mean that one is bound to deny that emotional responses can be used in a convincing analysis of values. The consequence is rather that the emotions that the relevant subjects have, or are likely to have, are not up to the job and that the responses enlisted into the analysis must fulfill further constraints. This might prompt one to pursue the influential idea that the relevant emotions must be normatively qualified (Brentano 1889/1969).

An emotion is normatively qualified when it is *required* or *appropriate* in the circumstances, i.e., when there are good reasons to endorse it. Shame toward a given trait is appropriate neither because the trait has the stable disposition to elicit shame, nor because it has the primitive property of being shameful, but rather because there is a norm or a set of norms stating that shame toward it is required or appropriate. Recall that the dispositionalist approach introduces dispositions in order to filter out the responses relevant for the analysis of values. That same role is now played by a property of the responses that they exemplify because of the existence of norms stating that they are required, appropriate, or fitting in the circumstances. This is the central contention of the Fitting Attitude analysis of value (FA-analysis).

According to this analysis, the appropriateness of a response is explanatorily prior with respect to the evaluative property: an object is valuable in virtue of a relevant response being appropriate. One of the selling points of the FA-analysis—in this respect it is comparable to subjectivist approaches—is that it helps demystify evaluative properties, while also furnishing distinctive grounds to concern ourselves with them, since evaluative properties are explained in terms of norms (Rabinowicz and Rønnow Rasmussen 2004). Yet, if we should not understand the idea of an appropriate response as that of a response whose object exemplifies the relevant value, what sort of alternative understanding should we adopt? The task here is substantial: it consists in trying to isolate a group of norms against which the appropriateness of emotions can be assessed independently of any reference to the evaluative properties of their objects. Two reasonable options come to mind.

The first option is to proceed by reference to the biological functions the emotions supposedly have: the relevant norms would be teleological in nature (e.g., Ruse and Wilson 1986). A given emotion is appropriate if it promotes the fitness of the subject undergoing it (or alternatively that of the subject's social group or some of its genes). This may then lead one to say that fear of vipers is appropriate for humans, whereas fear of blind-worms is not, since responding in this way does not correspond to the function assigned to fear by our biological make-up: avoiding physical harm. Similarly, indignation might be said to be appropriate when it deters other members of the group from taking more than their share and fosters fair interpersonal relationships, and inappropriate when it leads to destructive behavior. The approach is then premised on the idea that a specific norm corresponds to each emotion type and encapsulates the manner in which it is adaptive, thus furnishing us with a yardstick to measure the appropriateness of specific emotional occurrences. The contrast with the dispositionalist approach lies in the fact that a statistically rare response can favor biological fitness, and conversely that a widespread response can run counter to such fitness.

Now, there are obviously as many different FA-analyses of the sort under discussion as there are different opinions regarding the biological functions performed by emotional responses—and it is, of course, in the nature of the case that evidence as to these functions is hard to come by. Such a detailed investigation is obviously beyond the scope of the present discussion. This appeal to biological functions raises a more general issue, however. The main thrust of FA-analyses is to introduce normative qualifications in order to account for possible discrepancies between evaluative facts and emotional responses. Can biological functions be pressed into service to that end? There is room for doubt, since the fact that a response favors fitness is often quite divorced from the evaluative considerations that we think bear on the circumstances and that guide the way we actually measure the appropriateness of the response. It may be the case that the episodes of indignation felt toward some event by members of a given group contribute to their sense of belonging and, through it, to their fitness. Still, this is certainly not to offer any reason for viewing their indignation as appropriate—it will not be if it targets a perfectly blameless deed. For this reason, one may deny that the norms we are after are fitness-related teleological norms. This is perhaps unsurprising: they are after all not norms we invoke to measure the appropriateness of emotions, so there is bound to be a tension between their verdicts and those that a less theoretically loaded look at the situation delivers.

The second option within the FA-analysis consists precisely in elucidating the appropriateness of emotions by means of norms—rational norms—that we invoke or could invoke in their favor. Some emotions we reflectively endorse because we think that there are reasons to respond in these ways and others we discard because we think that there are none. An army general's shame after having been convicted for high treason will certainly be assessed as an appropriate response, as opposed to indignation at unavoidable budget restrictions, which we are prone to view as inappropriate. The reasons that are appealed to need not be easily accessible, and may sometimes require a complex process of determination relying on significant deliberation (Wallace 2010). The important point in the present context is the central idea that there exists a set of reasons with the requisite normative force, i.e., reasons which when available make the emotion reasonable.

It should be emphasized once more that we are considering a form of the FA-analysis according to which reasons and normativity are explanatory prior to the evaluative properties: an object exemplifies the relevant value insofar as there are reasons that make an emotion appropriate. This is to say that a trait is shameful because there are reasons to endorse shame toward it, and that one should hold in check one's inclination to say that shame is appropriate because the trait is shameful. So, on pain of rendering this variant of the FA-analysis viciously circular, the relevant reasons and norms should be specified in isolation from evaluative properties. Yet, is it possible to do so?[3] The problem is made more acute as we realize that there are different sorts of reasons for which we endorse or reject emotions, and so a variety of ways in which they can be perceived as reasonable or appropriate. To make the situation a bit dramatic, we may help ourselves of a well-known thought experiment. Suppose that we all had to feel admiration for a despicable demon reigning over us on pain of facing some horrendous torment. If such was the case, we all would have excellent reasons to admire the demon and this response would to that extent be reasonable or appropriate (Rabinowicz and Rønnow-Rasmussen 2004).

This example makes it especially salient that there are a variety of reasons and rational norms—prudential norms in the demon case—which may undergird our assessment of an emotion. However, these reasons and norms are not created equal insofar as their potential for analyzing evaluative properties is concerned: the demon certainly remains despicable, despite the presence of overwhelming reasons to endorse admiration of him. The lesson is that the analysis is defective because it fails to specify *the sense in which* a response must be reasonable when fixing the object's value. All of the mentioned responses conform to certain rational norms, yet they do not help fix the evaluative facts. We have seen that appealing to teleological norms is unsatisfying insofar as these norms are distinct from those we readily use to assess emotions; we now are reminded that a mere gesture toward "those reasons we use to assess them" falls short of the needed specification. And, of course, the goods promised by the FA-analysis cannot be delivered if it fails to bring the correct verdict in the demon case. So, is a convincing specification of the reasons and norms forthcoming within the framework of a FA-Analysis? It might well be that a slight majority of philosophers working on this issue favor a negative answer to this question. Yet, since it is a matter

[3] We shall focus here on whether the FA-analysis has the resources to discard situations in which an object does not have the relevant value despite their being reasons for the response. This is a problem of sufficiency. Some have also questioned whether the analysis provides a necessary condition. On this issue, see: Bykvisk 2009.

of ongoing and sophisticated debate, this is not the place here to embark on a detailed discussion of the various options that have been explored in the recent literature.[4]

Forms of value realism

The various attempts to analyze evaluative properties in terms of emotional responses that we had the occasion to consider in the foregoing, suffer from undeniable difficulties. This provides some grist for those who think that the unquestionable existence of intimate links between emotions and values should not lead us to endorse an analysis of the latter in terms of the former. What sort of approaches to values is available if one subscribes to that conclusion? We shall end this section with a few words on this issue.

Obviously, these approaches must be grounded on the claim that values are independent of emotional responses. This suggests that our efforts to understand these properties should rather focus on the way they relate to the natural properties of the objects exemplifying them. Now, one widespread claim is that this relation is constrained by what is called the universalizability of evaluative properties vis-à-vis natural properties: if an object with certain natural properties exemplifies a given value, then a perfect duplicate of this object will also exemplify it (Moore 1903). To illustrate: suppose that a certain distribution of wealth is fair. A distribution exemplifying the same natural properties (an identical allocation across the population, etc.) will then also be fair. In this sense, a given distribution of natural properties determines a given distribution of evaluative properties and it is customary in such a case to say that the evaluative properties *supervene* on the natural properties.

This is not yet a definite theory of what evaluative properties are but rather a sort of template that must be filled in to lead to more substantive theories. As a matter of fact, there are various forms of supervenience, and there is also no agreement as to their consequences for reducibility. Assuming that evaluative properties supervene in a given way on natural properties, does that entail that the former are identical to the latter? It should be emphasized that if the answer to this question is positive, then the sort of identity at stake holds with respect to quite peculiar natural conditions. This is because we group as a matter of course under the same evaluative label entities that appear quite dissimilar as far as their natural properties are concerned. It is difficult to see which natural property a generous deed, an haiku poem, and one of Titian's late works share, yet they are all admirable. For that reason, the natural condition on which admirableness and other evaluative properties supervene is likely to be a highly disjunctive one that can be captured by saying that to be admirable is to exemplify either a subset of the natural properties of a generous deed *or* of some haiku poems, etc.

The question is now whether highly disjunctive sets of natural conditions are natural properties. A liberal view of properties favors an affirmative answer and, as a result,

[4] For detailed discussions of some of these options, see: Rabinowicz and Rønnow-Rasmussen 2004; Louise 2009.

concludes that evaluative properties are identical to these gerrymandered natural properties. However, a stricter conception is prone to reject the idea of highly disjunctive properties, the likely conclusion being that evaluative properties are sui generis properties distinct from the natural properties on which they supervene.[5] This is, of course, not the place to adjudicate between these two forms of realism about values. We simply wanted to illustrate the sort of approach that the problems attending analyses of values in terms of emotions might lead one to embrace.

In the foregoing, we have briefly reviewed some accounts philosophers have endorsed in exploring the first issue raised by the intuitive relations between emotions and values—that regarding the role of emotions in understanding values. The likely lesson is that the former cannot be used to demystify and explain away the latter. Does this mean that ordinary language leads us astray in suggesting that emotions are closely tied to values? Perhaps not, since the relation between the two need not take this ontological form—it may be an intentional or epistemic one. This is, you will remember, the second issue with which we said we shall be concerned, and to which we now turn.

Emotion and access to value

We shall be interested now in the role emotions play in our *accessing* values, i.e., in the idea that emotions are apprehensions of value or evaluations. To address this issue, we shall first provide a preliminary sketch of how emotions can put us in an intentional relation[6] to values. We will then be in a position to survey three types of theories that attempt to build on that idea and offer a full-blown account of the intentional relation at stake.

Emotions and access to values

We can approach the matter in the following way. There are domains of properties that correspond to different senses: the textures of objects are apprehended by touch, the sounds they emit by hearing, their colors by sight, and so on. More contentiously, there are domains of properties that reason can apprehend, say the probability of certain events, or the properties of numbers. The core idea shared by the approaches according to which emotions are evaluations is nicely captured by the thought that there is another domain of properties—the evaluative properties—that emotions can apprehend. More generally, the thought is that emotions display an intentional relation to the values exemplified by the objects and events one may confront and that different types of emotions are apprehensions of as many distinct values. Accordingly, sadness, anger, and admiration are intentional relations to, respectively, loss, the offensive, and the admirable. This is meant to elucidate the

5 Two discussions of the underlying issues pointing to different conclusions are Jackson (1998) and Oddie (2005).

6 The notions of "intentionality" or "intentional relation" are simply terms of art for saying that some mental state (in this case emotions) are *about* something (in this case values), and should not be understood as saying that these are states that we *voluntarily* or *deliberatively* enter into.

intuitive appeal of the idea that there is a relation between emotions and values. What is more, it has some important theoretical virtues.

To start with, observe that the approach can provide convincing answers to three basic questions in emotion theory. Indeed, values allow for the *individuation, rationalization,* and *evaluation* of emotions. First, values can individuate emotion types insofar as they constitute something that is shared amongst the various particular objects of a given type of emotions. Episodes of admiration may be related to quite dissimilar particular objects, such as a generous deed, a haiku poem, a disinterested action, or Titian's late works—yet in all of them the subject apprehends something as admirable. In other words, the different types of emotions are unified at the level of their evaluative intentionality, and we can tell them apart by means of the values to which they relate. Second, a reference to evaluative properties puts one in a position to assess whether emotions are intelligible or not. We understand how different situations can elicit emotions of the same type once we realize that, from a subject's point of view, they each exemplify the same value. For that reason, an emotion becomes intelligible once we figure out how such a point of view is possible ("After all, she might have thought that the murderer wanted to offer his help and so got into his car with gratitude"); otherwise it remains unintelligible. Third and finally, and as has already transpired in the previous section, values take center stage when we assess the appropriateness of emotions. Insofar as our murderer's intent is malevolent, for instance, gratitude toward him is inappropriate.

These observations clarify perhaps some of the reasons why one may be attracted to the idea that emotions are intentionally related to values. Yet, in order to account for these and many other claims regarding the emotions, we need a firmer grip on a notion central in these observations, that of a *mode of apprehension of value.*

Three theories of the emotions

A fundamental distinction in the philosophy of mind is that between attitude or mode on the one hand and content on the other hand.[7] Edna may believe that her investments are safe, or she may believe that they are at risk—that is, she may have the same attitude toward different contents. Another possibility is for two different attitudes to target the same content: Suzy comes to believe that her investments are shaky immediately after having read the morning journal. Max, who secretly envies her being so well-off but has had no time to look at the financial news, only desires this to be the case. One may be quite naturally led to approach the emotions in terms of the very same contrast—in the same way as one may believe or desire that one's investments are safe, can't we hope, fear, or regret it to be

[7] In this article, we use "attitude" rather than "mode." Because emotions are in fact different attitudes we take toward the world, we think that this is the right terminological choice. Being typically used within the expression "propositional attitude," however, it may encourage the false idea that emotions are attitudes exclusively directed at propositions. This drawback is largely made up by the benefits of avoiding any confusion that might arise between the notion of "mode" and that of "modes of presentation." The latter, which has to do with distinctions amongst contents, will play no role in what is to come.

the case? Despite its intuitive character, this line of thought has been rarely pursued. As a result, philosophers have not envisaged the consequences of the idea that emotions are distinctive sorts of attitudes—in their immense majority, they have attempted to account for the emotions in terms of one or another type of already familiar attitude and, correlatively, to adjust their specific contents so as to account for what is emotional about them. We shall now consider in more detail two such attempts—the judgment of value theory and the perceptual theory.

The judgment of value theory

The fact that philosophers have attempted to understand emotions by reference to other types of attitudes is made especially manifest by a conception that was already widespread in antiquity. According to it, emotions relate to values because they are evaluative occurrent beliefs or judgments; a given type of emotions is then set apart from another thanks to the distinct values that judgments may attribute to their objects.[8] Judging that an action is admirable is to admire it, judging that one has missed an opportunity is to regret, and so on. The approach not only allows for the individuation of emotions by means of the evaluative concepts deployed in the relevant judgments, it can also draw important distinctions like those between intelligible and unintelligible or between appropriate and inappropriate emotions. Still, it is widely acknowledged that conceiving of emotions as consisting in a judgment-like attitude directed toward evaluative contents is hardly satisfactory.

The basic problem is simple: an evaluative belief is neither necessary nor sufficient for an emotion. Consider first the objection regarding necessity. The claim that emotions necessarily imply evaluative beliefs is not compelling, for at least two reasons. A first worry is that it does not only seem possible but indeed commonplace to experience an emotion without making the kind of judgment required by the theory. Mary is convinced that she has done nothing wrong, yet she is assailed with crushing guilt. Should we then, to save the theory, say that she in fact has contradictory beliefs, one of which is unacknowledged or unconscious and, in so doing, attribute to her a severe form of irrationality (Döring 2009; Tappolet 2000)? Conceiving of emotions as involving the attitude of belief, i.e., holding a proposition true, is clearly problematic. It simply seems wrong to regard those situations in which one believes that a given value is not exemplified yet one undergoes the relevant emotion as similar to situations in which one holds contradictory beliefs.

Second, attributing evaluative beliefs might be too demanding with regard to the cognitive capacities the subject is required to deploy.[9] She must at least master the concepts that figure in the propositions she holds to be true. For example, we can only attribute to

[8] This theory, which is often said to have been defended by the Stoics, has been brought back into fashion by Nussbaum (1994) and Solomon (1993).

[9] The same worry is raised by theories that, despite not requiring that the subject form evaluative beliefs, still demand of her that she masters and deploys the relevant evaluative concepts. One such theory is that developed by Roberts (2003).

Marcel the belief that the table is made of American chestnut if he has some kind of idea of what tables, chestnut trees, and America are. Likewise, if he believes that an event constitutes a loss, then he must master the concept of loss. Yet, is it really necessary that one master evaluative concepts in order to undergo emotions? The fact that we commonly attribute emotions to animals and infants clearly conflicts with such a requirement, and many would rightly prefer to drop the evaluative judgment theory rather than the idea that infants and animals partake in our emotional life.

The objection concerning sufficiency is perhaps even more decisive. The worry is that it seems not only possible but indeed commonplace to make the kind of evaluative judgment that the theory invokes without having the corresponding emotion. You may, for example, believe that you have achieved a very important and difficult task without feeling happy or proud about it. To use a colloquial expression, there are evaluative beliefs that, despite being firmly held, leave us cold. Emotions are felt and this fundamental aspect of them is something the evaluative judgment theory seems bound to overlook.

The foregoing considerations explain why it is nowadays widely accepted that, if emotions are ways of apprehending values, this should not lead us to identify them with evaluative judgments. The purpose of the so-called perceptual theory of emotions is precisely to articulate an alternative understanding of the idea of value apprehension.

The perceptual theory

The essential claim around which this theory revolves is that emotions are not judgments but *perceptions* of values (e.g., Döring 2009; Scheler 1973; Tappolet 2000). To admire something is to perceive its admirable character, to be ashamed of having acted in a given way is to perceive the shamefulness of one's action, much as having a visual experience is to perceive, say, a yellow blotch on a white sheet. According to advocates of this theory, it is no more necessary to deploy the concepts of admirableness or shamefulness to experience, respectively, admiration and shame, than it is to deploy the concept of a yellow blotch to see one. This constitutes a clear improvement over the evaluative judgment theory.

As is the case within the latter theory, the different types of emotions are individuated by means of specific values. Yet, this is now due to the fact that experiences of a perceptual nature reveal the presence of values. In this way, the perceptual theory puts itself in a position to respect the basic insight that emotions are felt, an insight on which the evaluative judgment theory stumbles. Indeed, emotions are conceived of as a form of affective perception precisely in order to do justice to the idea that they acquaint us in an experientially salient way with an array of evaluative properties. The approach also benefits from the existence of a relation between perceptual experiences and perceptual judgments that is akin to that between emotions and evaluative judgments. In the two cases, a type of experience seems to cause, and potentially to justify, the associated type of judgment. At the heart of the perceptual theory, one finds indeed the idea that the nature of emotions as experiences of values endows them with a substantial epistemological potential: that of functioning as reasons for evaluative judgments. One's admiration of a given artwork, say, constitutes a prima facie reason for believing the work is admirable, i.e., the belief is justified in the light of admiration provided no countervailing reasons are forthcoming.

By conceiving of the emotions as perceptual experiences that are distinct from, and epistemologically related to, evaluative judgments, the perceptual theory can explain the sorts of "irrational" emotions we talked about in a much more satisfying way than the evaluative judgment theory. They do not manifest any severe form of irrationality on the subject's part, since they are to be understood on the model of perceptual illusions: phobias are, for instance, persistent affective illusions. Just as one can, without the slightest inkling of irrationality, see lines as diagonal in the Zöllner illusion while being appraised of the fact that they are not, one can also, without being irrational, feel ashamed of a trait one knows not to be shameful. In each case, one is rational insofar as one resists judging while enjoying an experience of a type that typically causes the relevant judgment and would justify it in the absence of countervailing evidence. All this makes it seem as if we should be happy to endorse the claim that emotions literally are perceptions of values. One would be too quick off the mark with such identification, however, because there are essential differences between the two sorts of experiences. Let us emphasize two here.

The first one regards the variety of things emotions can target. The objects of our emotions are not fixed in a way similar to the way perceptual objects are. For instance, a variety of constraints have to be fulfilled in order for someone to see an object: one can only see concrete objects, one must be in given spatial relation to them, there must be no obstacle between one and them, certain lighting conditions must obtain, and so forth. If these conditions remain unfulfilled, no object can be seen. Things do significantly differ with the emotions. If Jonas is afraid of the snake right in front of him, then conditions identical to those holding for perception must surely be met. Still, many emotions do not target what is perceived, but rather what is believed, supposed, remembered, or imagined. The worry is then the following. In all the cases in which emotions target an object one does not perceive, how could one be, as the theory under discussion suggests, in a perceptual relation with some of its properties, i.e., its evaluative properties? The theory's power of seduction is perhaps the result of an undue and exclusive focus on situations in which emotions are about what is perceived—these cases are admittedly paradigmatic, but certainly not the only ones.

There is a second and even more significant difference between perceptual and emotional experiences, which is closely related to what we have just said. When one perceives an item, one enjoys an autonomous way of representing it in the sense that seeing, tasting and touching do not latch onto some prior apprehension of the properties or objects they give access to. In order for a subject to see the yellowness of a blotch, or feel the smoothness of a given texture, no prior access to such properties needs to be secured. This is not so in the case of the emotions. An emotion always has another psychological state as its cognitive base, which may be, as we have seen, of many distinct types (beliefs, memories, imaginative or perceptual experiences). In order to admire a melody, some representation of the melody that is logically prior to the emotion itself is required: one needs to hear it.

The foregoing observations may lead one to draw some important lessons from the undisputable fact that emotions can be about a great variety of objects. One of these is that this should lead us to challenge the idea that emotions are states susceptible of having but only one type of content—a conceptual proposition-like content according to the evaluative judgment theory or a non-conceptual one according to the perception theory. An alternative to these must be found, since emotions appear to latch on to a variety of different and cognitively more or less demanding ways of apprehending their objects. So, while the analogy between emotion and perception may be fruitful in some respects, it should not be pushed too far on pain of obscuring essential differences between the two types of mental state.[10] In our opinion, the strategy to be followed consists in preserving the idea that emotions relate to values while rejecting a claim shared by the judgment theory and the perceptual theory, namely that values are represented by the emotions. We shall now briefly present this strategy.

The attitudinal theory

We have considered some reasons why the relation that takes place between emotions and values should not be analyzed in terms of judgment-like or perception-like attitudes. All in all, these reasons may encourage the following diagnosis: the main source of the problems these approaches confront is the fact that they attempt to understand emotions in terms of other attitudes, believing and perceiving. This is problematic because these attitudes not only have nothing emotional about them, they in addition differ in some significant ways from the emotions. For that reason, the suggestion that they turn into emotions when they relate to specific evaluative contents proves unsatisfying. Now, these observations should in our opinion provoke us into thinking that the emotions do not relate to values because they represent such properties—for any such representational approach is bound to miss what is distinctive of the emotions. The idea we think should be pursued is that the difference between emotions and other types of attitudes, as well as that between different types of emotions—at least insofar as their relation to values is concerned—does not come down to their having different contents, but rather to their being different types of attitudes. This alternative way of approaching the issue has at least some intuitive appeal.

Conceiving of the different types of emotions such as admiration, shame, and fear as different attitudes rather than one and the same attitude—that of judging or that of perceiving—directed at different evaluative properties, looks after all like plain common sense. Is it not obvious that the contrast between these three types of emotions is one between different attitudes we take toward something? Is this contrast not similar to the contrast between, say, desiring, believing, and conjecturing—and is it not at the same time to be carefully distinguished from the contrast between believing a

[10] One option we shall not discuss consists in forsaking any straight identification of the emotions with *perceptions* of values, while insisting that emotions are still *experiences* of values. For a discussion of the perceptual model in its various forms, see Deonna and Teroni (2012, ch. 6). Additional criticisms can be found in Dokic and Lemaire (2013).

given proposition and believing a different one? We think that these two questions should be answered affirmatively. The difference between the emotions and other attitudes, as well as that between different types of emotions, is first and foremost one of attitudes toward that which is represented as opposed to one regarding that which is represented. Adopting this alternative approach and locating the relation between emotions and values at the level of the attitude has an additional virtue: it puts us in a position to adopt the intuitive idea that two distinct emotions can literally be about the same thing. Suppose, for instance, that John is saddened by an event about which Edna is delighted—in such a case, it seems quite likely that they are adopting different attitudes about one and the same thing.[11] The perceptual theory is ill-suited to adopt this idea, however, since it maintains that to be sad about an event is to perceive its being a loss, whereas to be delighted by it is to perceive its being delightful.

Now, as intuitive as an approach to the relation between emotions and values in terms of attitudes may be, there is no guarantee that it will prove viable. Its being so depends on whether we can give convincing answers to the following questions: What sorts of attitudes are emotional attitudes? In what sense are emotions evaluations? Although this is not the place to answer these difficult questions, we believe a case can be made for the idea that emotional attitudes should be conceived of as felt action tendencies and that this in itself is sufficient for elucidating the sense in which emotions are evaluations. For example, fear of a snake is an experience of the snake as dangerous because it consists in feeling the body's readiness to act so as to diminish its likely impact on one (flight, preemptive attack, etc.) and this felt attitude is correct only if the snake is dangerous. In the same vein, anger at someone is an experience of her as being offensive precisely because it consists in feeling the body's readiness to act so as to retaliate one way or another and this felt attitude is correct only if the person is, or has been, offensive. This is, of course, no more than a sketch of what the theory would look like, but we believe it can be developed into a promising account.[12]

The value of emotions

In the foregoing, we have first considered whether values stand in an ontological relation to emotions and, second, whether and in what way emotions stand in an intentional relation to values. It is now time to turn our attention to our last topic: do the emotions themselves have any value and, if so, of what sort?[13] As is reflected in the very organization

[11] Goldie (2004) and Gunther (2004) object to the idea that we can draw in emotion a clear demarcation line between attitude and content. The weaknesses of their respective criticisms are exposed in Herzberg (2012).

[12] A detailed presentation of such an account is offered in Deonna and Teroni (2012, ch.7) and some of its consequences are explored in Deonna and Teroni (2015).

[13] A positive answer to this question in relation to well-being can be found in Deonna and Teroni (2013).

of the present volume, there are many types of values. Among them, hedonic, moral, and epistemic values will be of particular interest to us, since we shall soon realize that emotions may be thought to exemplify values of these three types.

Let us consider *hedonic* values first. Emotions might be thought to have such value in virtue of the fact that we feel pleasures and displeasures when we undergo emotional experiences. Pleasure, or maybe the pleasantness characteristic of pleasure, is no doubt the value most discussed by philosophers, and, for many of them, it is in fact the only value.[14] Whether or not it is the only value, it is safe to assume that positive emotions are, or involve, pleasures and, assuming that pleasure is a positive value, positive emotions are for this reason good, or at least good for the person experiencing them.[15] Of course, the exact import of this statement might vary considerably depending on what one means by "pleasure." On one quite common interpretation, positive emotions are hedonically good in the sense that they are invariably accompanied by pleasant feelings or sensations. Accumulating positive emotions would be good because it increases the amount of pleasant feelings or sensations one experiences.

While appeal to such feelings or sensations is in fact the most traditional way of providing a unified explanation of what makes something a pleasure, it might in fact not be the best way to account for the unity in question. This is, in particular, the case if one's attention is to the variety of positive emotions. After all, a plausible hypothesis is that there is simply no specific feeling that is shared by all pleasant mental states. A claim to the contrary is already problematic given the variety of bodily pleasures (compare, for instance, the pleasure of wrestling to the pleasure of the subsequent massage), and even more so when we remind ourselves of how positive emotional experiences differ from one another (compare admiring a haiku, feeling proud of an achievement, and being amused by a Bollywood movie). If no unity is to be found at the level of sensations, alternative approaches must be found.

One that is nowadays quite popular consists in claiming that what pleasant mental states have in common is not a kind of sensation, but rather a kind of attitude: one consisting in welcoming or being pleased by something. This, of course, speaks to the sort of approaches to the emotions with which we have been concerned in the previous section and according to which emotions are types of evaluations. These approaches indeed encourage another understanding of what makes a variety of mental states and emotions pleasant: enjoying, admiring, amused, or delighted by are all specific ways to be pleased and are so in virtue of being evaluative mental states. Undergoing a pleasant mental state is, accordingly, not feeling a particular sensation, but rather positively evaluating an object—which can certainly be a sensation, as in the case of bodily pleasures, but need not be and most of the time indeed is not as far as emotions are concerned. This is to say that interest, admiration,

[14] For a careful discussion of various sorts of hedonism, see Feldman (2006).

[15] On the distinction between value and relational value or value for, see Rabinowicz and Rønnow-Rasmussen, this volume.

and amusement are pleasant to the extent that they evaluate their objects in terms of three distinct positive values: say, the interesting, excellence, and the comical.

Second, emotions can be argued to be of *epistemic* value in at least two distinct senses: one *instrumental*, the other *final*.[16] We shall consider these in this order. The issue of the emotions' instrumental epistemic value can be approached as follows. It should be observed that, while evaluative properties can, in principle, be accessed by us dispassionately, so to say, it is often difficult to see how we could access them if we were deprived of our emotional capacities, i.e., our dispositions or concerns to react emotionally to our surroundings, which are variously shaped by our more or less idiosyncratic developmental paths, sentiments, character traits, desires, and moral sensitivities. Given how complex our environment is, the prospects for detecting these properties without the aid of such a capacity are not very good. As has been often observed, distinct emotional sensitivities engender specific patterns of salience among the objects of experience (e.g., De Sousa 1987: 195). Consider, as an illustration, the predicament of someone deprived of any sense of beauty who is asked to latch on what may be admirable in one of Bach's motets. Or think of the subtle clues (the way others look at us, which values are at stake in the circumstances, etc.) to which our sense of shame so often responds. In addition, part of what it is to respond emotionally to the presence of an evaluative property consists in a readiness to respond to it in ways perceived to be appropriate—in fear, one is ready to avoid the danger, in anger, to retaliate, and so on.

All in all, then, emotions appear to be of instrumental epistemic value insofar as they provide a rough and ready mechanism assisting us in obtaining information about our environment that we would otherwise be likely to overlook; and, given their uncontroversial impact on motivation, they also quite literally prepare us to take the appropriate courses of action. This sort of epistemic value is clearly instrumental: it derives entirely from what the emotions contribute to achieve, since emphasis is laid on the fact that they are tools for accessing, and proper dealing with, the environment. To conclude with this first sense in which emotions are epistemically valuable, let us observe that emotions can be said to have the value in question only if their verdicts turn out to be reliable. As is well-known, emotional capacities and emotions often seriously bias the subjects having them and can make them impervious to relevant considerations. This has encouraged many to downplay, perhaps unduly, their epistemic credentials.[17]

Emotions might also have a more substantial sort of epistemic value in the sense of being of *final* value or valuable as ends. This is at least a contention that seems to be supported by their contribution to our most fundamental type of *understanding* of what it is for something to exemplify a value. The idea here is the following: if we were incapable of emotionally reacting to evaluative properties, this would put serious pressure on the claim that we can deploy evaluative knowledge when passing evaluative judgments. For, arguably, being

16 On this distinction, see also Rabinowicz and Rønnow-Rasmussen, this volume.

17 See Lacewing (2014) for a good survey of the relevant literature.

a competent user of evaluative concepts requires more than the mere ability to apply them in the right circumstances. This is why we find it so difficult to detach the categorization of an object as funny or shameful from the understanding that its properties give reasons to favor or reject it. And we should seriously wonder as to the sort of understanding of there being reasons to favor or reject an object that would outlive the relevant emotions.

If we subscribe to the idea articulated at the end of the previous section, namely that the sense in which emotions are evaluative attitudes is intimately related to their preparing us to deal in given ways with our environment, then it is tempting to pursue this line of thought as follows. It is because emotions are experiences of how given objects are to be acted on that they prove so essential to our capacity to master evaluative concepts. Someone who never felt the sort of impulse to retaliate that one feels in anger, or someone so brazen as to remain ignorant of the urge to disappear so characteristic of shame may perhaps learn to apply the concepts of offensiveness or shamefulness, but it seems difficult to maintain that he really understands what he says when applying them. A comparable claim has been endorsed by many regarding the relations between the understanding of color concepts and visual experiences as of colors; we submit that it is even more convincing in the case under discussion. This provides reasons to conclude that, insofar as one is disposed to consider evaluative knowledge as a final good, one should extend this claim to the emotional underpinnings of the conceptual abilities it relies on.[18]

Third and finally, let us turn our attention to the reasons for which emotions may be said to have *moral* value. We can again draw a distinction between the instrumental and the final reading of that claim. The issue of the emotions' instrumental moral value can once more be profitably considered from the vantage point provided by the sorts of behavior that emotions are likely to foster. There are many kinds of emotions, such as sympathy, guilt, or indignation, that are typically elicited in morally relevant circumstances and have, as any other type of emotions, important motivational consequences. Sympathy arises when fellow human beings face dire predicaments and disposes us to assist them, whereas guilt is typically the result of the conviction that one has contributed to an unjust outcome and disposes us to restore the balance. It will be unpersuasive to deny that such emotions, at least sometimes, foster behavior that is called for by the morally relevant situation they happen to be about. In this sense, these emotions promote morally good behavior and derive an instrumental moral value from the sort of behavior they help achieve.

Yet again, there are reasons for bestowing a more substantial, final moral value to the emotions. These reasons closely relate to the observations we brought to bear on the emotions' epistemic values. We said that the emotional verdicts we reach typically, if not always, result from the exercise of our emotional sensitivities, i.e., of dispositions to respond in specific ways in specific circumstances. Now, virtues and vices constitute a specific subset of such dispositions. The responses of sympathy, guilt, or indignation we

[18] These observations obviously relate to recent debates as to what explains the distinctive value we bestow upon knowledge. For an influential emphasis on the role of understanding in this wider context, see Greco (1999) and, for discussion, Pritchard et al. (2010).

have mentioned are, of course, quite often the manifestation of virtues, such as honesty, kindness, or compassion. Virtues and vices are relatively stable dispositional traits that are structured around a given value and are being manifested in very different ways depending on the circumstances (Deonna and Teroni 2009, 2012, ch. 8; Goldie 2000, ch. 6). Honesty is, for instance, a sensitivity to issues of equity that can manifest itself in feelings of outrage (when others behave inequitably), of shame (if one does so oneself), of satisfaction (when an equitable outcome is unexpectedly reached), and so on. One may even insist that, barring special explanations, the recurrent incapacity to manifest such feelings is not compatible with the existence of the relevant virtue or vice. Now, virtues and vices are certainly morally valuable or disvaluable for their own sake—and not simply as instruments to promote the good or the evil. This is manifest in the fact that we disapprove of an agent's response to her circumstances in a distinctive way if it is not only the wrong one but also, and especially, if it manifests a vice. And, if emotions count amongst the most fundamental manifestations of virtues and vices, it appears difficult to resist the conclusion that they can, for this very reason, be finally morally valuable and disvaluable.

In this final section, we have surveyed reasons for thinking that emotions have value, both instrumental and final. Emotions have final hedonic value since it is pleasant or unpleasant to have them. They have instrumental epistemic value to the extent that they help us track evaluative properties and promote behavior adapted to them. When the properties in question are moral, they sometimes help promote moral behavior. And emotions have final value because they provide a non-eliminable kind of understanding of what values are and constitute a fundamental manifestation of virtues and vices.

References

Blackburn, S. (1998). *Ruling Passions: A Theory of Practical Reasoning*. New York: Oxford University Press.

Brentano, F. (1889/1969). *The Origin of Our Knowledge of Right and Wrong*. R. Chisholm and E. Schneewind (transl.). London: Routledge.

Bykvist, K. (2009). No good fit: why the fitting attitude analysis of value fails. *Mind*, **118**.469, 1–30.

De Sousa, R. (1987). *The Rationality of Emotion*. Cambridge, Mass: MIT.

Deonna, J. and Teroni, F. (2009). Taking affective explanations to heart. *Social Science Information*, **48**.3, 359–377.

Deonna, J. and Teroni, F. (2012). *The Emotions: A Philosophical Introduction*. New York: Routledge.

Deonna, J., and Teroni, F. (in press). Emotions as attitudes. *Dialectica*

Deonna, J. and Teroni F. (2013). What role for emotions in wellbeing? *Philosophical Topics* **41**.1, 123–142.

Dokic, J. and Lemaire, J. (2013). Are emotions perceptions of value? *Canadian Journal of Philosophy*, **43**.2, 227–247.

Döring, S. (2009). The logic of emotional experience: noninferentiality and the problem of conflict without contradiction. *Emotion Review*, **1**.2, 240–247.

Feldman, F. (2006). *Pleasure and the Good Life: Concerning the Nature, Varieties and Plausibility of Hedonism*. New York: Oxford University Press.

Goldie, P. (2000). *The Emotions: A Philosophical Exploration*. Oxford: Oxford University Press.

Goldie, P. (2004). Emotion, feeling, and knowledge of the world. In: R. Solomon (ed.), *Thinking About Feeling: Contemporary Philosophers on Emotions*. New York: Oxford University Press, pp. 91–106.

Greco, J. (1999). Agent reliabilism. *Philosophical Perspectives*, **13**, 273–296.

Gunther, Y. (2004). The phenomenology and intentionality of emotion. *Philosophical Studies*, **117**.1–2, 43–55.

Herzberg, L. (2012). To blend or to compose: a debate about emotion structure. In P. Wilson (ed.), *Dynamicity in Emotion Concepts*. Bern: Peter Lang, pp. 74–94.

Jackson, F. (1998). *From Metaphysics to Ethics: A Defence of Conceptual Analysis*. New York: Oxford University Press.

Lacewing, M. (forthcoming). Moral intuitions and its development: a guide to the debate. *Topoi*.

Louise, J. (2009). Correct responses and the priority of the normative. *Ethical Theory and Moral Practice*, **12**.4, 345–364.

Moore, G. E. (1903). *Principia Ethica*. Cambridge: Cambridge University Press.

Mulligan, K. (1998). From appropriate emotions to values. *The Monist*, **81**.1, 161–188.

Nussbaum, M. (1994). *The Therapy of Desire—Theory and Practice in Hellenistic Ethics*. Princeton: Princeton University Press.

Oddie, G. (2005). *Value, Reality, and Desire*. New York: Oxford University Press.

Prinz, J. (2008). *The Emotional Construction of Morals*. New York: Oxford University Press.

Pritchard, D., Millar, A., and Haddock, A. (2010). *The Nature and Value of Knowledge: Three Investigations*. New York: Oxford University Press.

Rabinowicz, W. and Ronnow Rasmussen, T. (2004). The strike of the demon: on fitting pro-attitudes and values. *Ethics*, **114**.3, 391–423.

Roberts, R. (2003). *Emotions: An Essay in Aid of Moral Psychology*. New York: Cambridge University, Press.

Ruse, M. and Wilson, E. (1986). Moral philosophy as applied science. *Philosophy*, **61**.236, 173–192.

Scheler, M. (1916/1973). *Formalism in Ethics and Non-Formal Ethics of Values: A New Attempt Toward the Foundation of an Ethical Personalism*. M. Frings and R. Funk (transl.). Evanston, Illinois: Northwestern University Press.

Smith, A. (1790/1976). *The Theory of Moral Sentiments*. D. D. Raphael and A.L. Macfie, eds. Oxford: Clarendon Press.

Solomon, R. (1993). *The Passions: Emotions and the Meaning of Life*. Indianapolis: Hackett.

Tappolet, C. (2000). *Emotions et valeurs*. Paris: Presses Universitaires de France.

Wallace, J. (2010). Reasons, values and agent-relativity. *Dialectica*, **64**.4, 501–528.

Chapter 9

Societal origins of values and evaluative feelings

Christian von Scheve

Sociology, in a broad understanding, is traditionally concerned with two problems: explanations of social action and social order. Values and valuation have always played key roles in both domains. Although the concept of "values" today is much more frequently used in sociology, theories of "value" and "valuation" have an equally long tradition, dating back to Marx ([1867] 1976) and Simmel ([1900] 1978). Theories of value are, in most cases, concerned with the question of what individuals "value," i.e., what they deem good or desirable and seek to obtain in terms of their interests (Spillman and Strand 2013). Understandings of value in contemporary sociology are closely related to the concept of utility, as it is used in economics or rational choice theory, and primarily refer to "subjective psychological value" (Molm 1997: 14). In this view, subjective psychological value is more or less tied to basic affective responses of hedonic pleasure (e.g., Higgins 2006).

The idea that interests and subjective valuations determine individuals' actions becomes a sociological one given two basic premises. First is the idea that a host of subjective interests is shared across many, if not most, individuals in a society; for instance, basic needs related to bodily homeostasis. Hence, actions based on widely shared valuations should produce certain social structural effects, although they are equally known to lead to competition, conflict, and the disruption of order, since valued resources are usually scarce. Second, and more intriguing, is the conjecture that individual valuations manifest a genuinely social dimension when the goods and services that people value are *exchanged* between individuals. What Simmel ([1900] 1978) has argued early on in his *Philosophy of Money* has become a cornerstone of modern exchange theories (Emerson 1976): the exchange of (individually) valued goods requires their values to be compared to one another, which means that what is individually valued becomes, first, socially related, and thus, second, clearly transcends the realm of individual valuation (see also Canto Mila 2005: 164).

In contrast to individual valuations and their social ramifications, the concept of "values" in sociology explicitly focuses on the idea of socially shared beliefs and convictions that can hardly be commoditized. Traditionally, values are understood as conceptions of the desirable, as Kluckhohn (1951) famously noted: "A value is a conception, explicit or implicit, distinctive of an individual or characteristic of a group, of the desirable, which influences the selection from available modes, means, and ends of action" (p. 395). As such, values are, on the one hand, crucial ingredients to culture and symbolic social order, and many scholars have argued that values are the *essence* of culture, as reflected in Weber's figure of the "*Kulturmensch*" (cultural being) (Weber [1904] 1949; see Oakes 2003). Values are usually distinguished from a close relative, social norms, in that they are context-independent reasons for action and that they need not be (but in fact often are) backed by informal sanctions.

In addition to self-interests related to utility and individual valuation, values are, on the other hand, not only seen as conceptions of the desirable, but also as concrete motivators of social action (Parsons and Shils 1951; Weber [1921] 1978). One of the most debated issues in sociological theory is in fact the distinction between actions that are clearly based on individual interests and valuations and those that are "value rational" in the sense that they are aimed at what is deemed desirable, but what is often not actually *desired* because it is individually costly or runs counter to one's immediate interests (Weber [1921] 1978). Many instances of prosocial behavior, such as donating or volunteering (Omoto and Snyder 1995; Schokkaert 2006), can be conceived of as forms of value rational action.

Based on these two assumptions, a vast array of social science research has attended to measuring the values that people hold dear, often in large population-based surveys (e.g., Hofstede 1984; Rokeach 1973; Schwartz 1992; see overviews by: Hitlin and Piliavin 2004; Spates 1983; Wuthnow 2008). On the one hand, this research investigates associations between values and various forms of social action; for instance, voting behavior (Leimgruber 2011; Schwartz 1996), economic performance (Granato et al. 1996), gender relations (Xiao 2000), religious practices (Kim 2008), or environmental behavior (Poortinga et al. 2004). On the other hand, scholars in this tradition have studied values and how they change over time to assess and describe the "culture" of a population and its dynamics (e.g., Inglehart and Welzel 2005). The aim of these studies often is comparative in the sense of identifying differences and similarities in the value structures of societies or amongst different subgroups of a society. Although many have argued that values do not only reflect what is desirable but likewise have a motivational force (e.g., Rokeach 1973; Schwartz 1992), only very few studies have directly investigated the processes and mechanisms underlying the linkage of values and specific actions (but see Maio et al. 2003; Tao and Au 2014).

After values had become out of fashion in sociological research on action and interaction, they recently regained prominence in various areas of study (Hitlin and Piliavin 2004). One of the major debates revolves around the status of values in determining or informing action. Whereas it was long taken for granted that values somehow "cause" behavior or are direct predictors of action, more recent studies paint a markedly more nuanced picture arguing that values are often cultural "tools" that are deployed for post-hoc justifications or rationalizations of actions rather than as direct and immediate motivators (Swidler 1986; Vaisey 2009). If this was indeed the case, then the question to be asked is what principles and mechanisms bring about the observable patterns of action in situations that cannot be fully explained by (material) self-interests? A second and largely unresolved issue in sociological accounts of values is how they emerge in the first place. Although much is known about changes in values in longer terms, for instance, as a consequence of modernization or globalization (Inglehart and Welzel 2005), and about links between values and socio-demographic indicators, for example, race and ethnicity (Waters 1990), social class (Kohn et al. 1990), or age cohort (McBroom et al. 1985) (see Hitlin and Piliavin 2004, for an overview), comparably little research has directly addressed the question of where values actually "come from," i.e., what the basic mechanisms and processes are by which individual valuations become socially shared within a group (but see: Boudon 2001; Joas 2001).

In this chapter, I will address both of these topics. In particular, drawing on classical theorizing and more recent empirical evidence, I suggest that feelings and emotions lie at the heart of how values and value commitments emerge and of how they influence social action. Specifically, my goal is to show that the affective processes that contribute to the emergence and consolidation of socially shared valuations do so through their influence on social action and interaction. The conjecture that emotions are critical to values and value-driven behavior is by no means a new one and has been proposed by eminent scholars in the field; for example, Feather (1980) and Kluckhohn (1951) (see Rohan 2000). More recently, Schwartz (2012) stated that "values are beliefs linked inextricably to affect" (p. 3). Nevertheless, the "affect part" of the story has often been neglected in favor of a focus on the "cognitive structures" underlying values. I hope to add to this affective understanding of values in two respects. First, by exploring avenues of how values and affect become interlinked in the first place, and, second, by looking at the ways in which affect and values interact in social action. Although some of the current works in moral philosophy and psychology do address similar questions, my understanding of this line of inquiry is that it is primarily concerned with questions of moral judgment. Moreover, regarding the role of emotions in (moral) value judgments, my impression is that the pertinent approaches consider emotions as either closely tied to evolutionary thinking and nativist assumptions, or, if holding more relativist views, lack conceptualizations of how the social sharing of values and emotions (or evaluative feelings) actually go together. Thus, an understanding of how affect and emotion are fundamentally shaped by social and cultural processes at various levels of analysis (Rogers et al. 2014) is integral to my approach to how values emerge and influence action.

The emergence of values and evaluative feelings

The question where values come from and how they emerge and manifest within groups and societies has intrigued thinkers for centuries and produced a broad spectrum of explanations in different disciplines. In sociology, however, interest in values has ceased since World War II, as Joas (2001) contends, and innovative approaches to the question seem to be lacking. To my knowledge, only two book-length sociological treatments (and one edited volume, see Hechter et al. 1993) specifically tackling this issue have been published more recently. Joas's (2001) *The Genesis of Values* and Boudon's (2001) *The Origin of Values* are two works that could not be more antagonistic in their approach—the former standing in the pragmatist and symbolic-interactionist tradition, the latter belonging to the camp of rational choice theory. But these antithetical points of departure come in handy when reviewing the field, since they cover an exceptionally broad range of sociological thinking—both historical and contemporary—on the emergence of values. Both, however, also often delve into the realms of individual valuations, preferences, and social norms, so that I shall exclusively focus on what they have to say about the emergence of values and the role of emotions therein.

One of the major approaches to explaining the emergence of values (and value commitments) is rooted in utilitarian principles. The key assumption held by proponents of this view is that individuals subscribe to certain values because they have *good reasons* to do so, given the goal of satisfying their very own interests (Boudon 2001: 2). A problem with these theories, of course, is the constraint that the utility derived from values needs to be shared within a group or population, so that the applicability of utilitarian explanations is clearly limited to specific instances of values, i.e., those from which *everyone* benefits. This limitation has been extensively discussed along very similar lines for the problem of conformity to social norms (Elster 1989). Utilitarian notions are not necessarily identical with rational explanations of the emergence of values. This is illustrated, for example, by Weber's ([1921] 1978) distinction between instrumental and axiological (*Wertrationalität*) rationality. Boudon (2001) further shows that both Kant's and Rawls's accounts of values and value judgments rest on rational accounts that are clearly different from the purely utilitarian perspective. Both suggest that "moral feelings" are grounded in those rational principles; for example, of fairness, that can be shared by all members of a society.

Another class of theories attending to the origins of values focuses on cultural transmissions and socialization (e.g., Parsons and Shils 1951), arguing that individuals hold certain values because most actors in a group or society subscribe to these values. These views are largely insensitive to the question of how values arise in the first place, but rather presuppose a set of existing values, which are then internalized during socialization and enacted, mostly pre-reflexively and automatically, in the form of socially shared practices. Aside from assuming that values "simply exist," works in this tradition are faced with findings showing that certain values are universal across societies, whereas others are not (Brown 1991; Shweder et al. 1997). If all values were only culturally transmitted, then how can the comparably large cultural overlap in certain values be explained?

Some have suggested that these universalities in values are rooted in biological or psychological primitives; for example, regarding their adaptive significance and inclusive fitness. This perspective includes views emphasizing the links between biological drives and individual valuations or preferences that are more or less universal across the human species (Michod 1993). Others have proposed a limited set of universal domains for moral values (e.g., Graham et al. 2013) or suggested that culture itself follows evolutionary principles and therefore has certain adaptive functions to which values are a central ingredient (Richerson and Boyd 2005).

Feelings in the emergence of values

A fourth major avenue is seen in works looking at the emergence of values as primarily brought about or rooted in feelings and emotions. Although utilitarian and biological accounts also touch on this issue, emotions are much more center stage in other works. Scheler's (1973) phenomenological theory of value, for example, assumes that humans are equipped with a sense of value that is similar to other senses, like our sense of color. Insofar, we cannot but perceive anything in the world always in terms of valuation based on certain characteristics of what is perceived. Valuations, according to Scheler, are *intentional* acts of meaning making, although they are not primarily brought about by reason or intellect, but rather by the "heart," i.e., through emotions (see Davis and Steinbock 2014). This is reflected in Scheler's (1973) critical distinction between mere "feeling states" and "feelings for something" (see Joas 2001: 92). Feeling states refer to undirected moods and other kinds of affective experiences, whereas "feelings for something" have an intentional object as their referent to which they grant the kind of *value feeling* Scheler was interested in (see Joas 2001). These "feelings for something" can be categorized as belonging to "acts of love" or "acts of hate" and relate to the different hierarchically ordered value-types pleasure, utility, life, culture, and holy (from low to high) (Joas 2001; Kamolnick 2001; Kriegel 2008).

Scheler's account is, however, for the most part person-centered and aside from postulating very basic value responses has only little to say on how values become socially shared within a society. Indeed, as Joas (2001) recounts, Scheler saw no tension between his idea of a "rigid ethical absolutism and objectivism" and the broad palette of values throughout history and across cultures (Scheler 1973: xxiii, cited in Joas 2001: 94). In Joas's (2001) interpretation, his perspective on the genesis of values is that there must exist a set of "eternal values" that are brought to the forefront of behavior through social relationships with "model persons" that represent different kinds of "value essences." "Following" these model persons does not mean blind imitation of their actions, but rather a reflexive orientation toward the values they embody.

This person-centered and almost intuitionist perspective on emotions and values is widened in scope by pragmatist scholars who have related the question of how value commitments arise to intersubjectivist understandings of identity formation. Based on the works of William James, John Dewey, and Charles Taylor, Joas (2001) suggests that value commitments arise from experiences of "self-transcendence and self-formation." For most of the above mentioned thinkers, "communication, intersubjectivity, and shared experience" are critical ingredients to the process of value formation (Joas 2001: 116ff.). It is primarily the affective dimension of these extraordinary experiences, for example, in social relationships, during rituals, or in aesthetic involvement, and the communicative practices that constitute these experiences that give rise to certain value feelings.

It is interesting to note that in most cases the difference between "the desired" and "the desirable" is critical for the pragmatist endeavor. This is reflected in Taylor's (1989) approach to values and his concepts of "weak" and "strong evaluations." According to his view, weak evaluations reflect evaluations based on individual desires and preferences, whereas strong evaluations are related to the desirable. Importantly, strong evaluations are never only felt as private forms of "moral feelings," but are rather experienced as revealing some "higher" and almost objective good (see Joas 2001: 130).

Boudon (2001) identifies a further emotion-based approach to the emergence of values in Pareto's (1935) theory of "residues" and "derivations," as outlined in *The Mind and Society*. Pareto basically argued that emotions (residues) are motivators of all those actions that are not fully grounded in reasons and instrumental rationality (derivatives). However, this theory mainly tackles issues of action and decision-making and is much less concerned with actual questions of how socially shared values come to exist. Bourdon's reading of Pareto's work is nevertheless interesting because it reveals a common misconception of the role of feelings and emotions in the emergence of values. Boudon (2001) states that "feelings of value are distorted expressions of affective causes" in the sense that "I believe X is good because an instinct pushes me to feel so" (p. 34). This interpretation is misleading in that it reduces value feelings to hard-wired "instincts" rather than answering the question how these feelings and their connections to values come into existence in the first place. Although the works briefly reviewed above are clearly not as reductionist as Boudon suggests, they are equally mute or imprecise in attending to this question.

This is much less so in one of the most influential sociological works on the origins of values, namely Durkheim's theory of rituals and collective effervescence (Durkheim [1912] 1995). Although Durkheim does not use the term "values," his studies are clearly concerned with various conceptions of what is deemed "desirable" in groups and societies (cf. Boudon 2001: 5). His starting point is more collective than the individualist accounts of, for example, Scheler. Durkheim's central argument is that values emerge in rituals and through the experience of what he calls "collective effervescence," a form of heightened emotional arousal. Rituals in his understanding involve the carrying out of cooperative actions amongst members of a specific group according to a predefined structure and choreography, in most cases in close physical proximity and face-to-face contact of the individuals involved. Also, rituals critically involve the presence and use of "totems" that symbolize shared values and beliefs of the group. Durkheim argued that, in particular, pro-social values that benefit the group's welfare ("solidarity") are individually costly to follow and usually too abstract and ephemeral to influence action in everyday life. Hence, during rituals, the collective effervescence that individuals experience is attributed or associated with the group's totems and the values they represent.

This way, Durkheim argues, beliefs are infused with specific feelings and an affective meaning that grant *evaluative* qualities to these beliefs which then acquire the status of conceptions of the desirable above and beyond what is individually desired and valued. Importantly, these affective meanings transcend the immediate ritual context and become guiding or even imperative principles in mundane contexts. Durkheim was also aware of the possibility that this affective "charging" of beliefs may abate over time and thus needs to be reinforced on a regular basis through rituals and the experience of collective effervescence.

Durkheim's and Scheler's positions can to some degree be construed as opposing poles in sociological analyses of value objectivism and value relativism, both justifying their arguments by making reference to feelings and emotions. Scheler assumed a number of "eternal" or universal values from which value feelings emerge that are made salient in societies in different combinations and to different degrees, hence creating the enormous historical and cultural variability in human values we observe. In contrast, Durkheim held much less rigid assumptions regarding the existence of universal values. Instead, he emphasized that the notable variability of value feelings is brought about by social and cultural dynamics and can potentially result from more or less arbitrary belief systems.

Feelings and moral values

Recent psychological and philosophical research in particular on *moral* values has reinvigorated the long dormant idea that feelings and emotions play a critical role in moral judgment and behavior, and tallies with some of the sociological approaches outlined above. This is reflected, for example, in Haidt's (2001) "social intuitionist" account and "moral foundations theory" (see also Graham et al. 2013), in Prinz's (2007) concept of "emotionism," or in Nichols's (2004) discussion of "sentimentalism" (see also: "Deonna and Teroni (2015)" and "Moll et al. (2015)"). Although most of these works are primarily concerned with the role of emotions in moral judgment, they also make explicit assumptions on the origins of moral values. Perhaps the most prominent account in this respect is moral foundations' theory (henceforth referred to as MFT; e.g., Graham et al. 2013; Haidt and Joseph 2004). In a nutshell, MFT rests on evolutionary premises and the "nativist" assumption that the human mind is pre-organized to be responsive to issues of moral valuation and judgment in a number of specific domains. Based on extensive theorizing and research, MFT has sought to uncover these domains primarily in relation to foundational dimensions of (human) sociality. It explicitly refers to the sociological literature on the fabrics of sociality, for example, Durkheim's ([1912] 1995) concept of the "sacred" or Tönnies ([1887] 2005) concepts of "*Gemeinschaft*" and "*Gesellschaft*" (Haidt and Graham 2009), to identify these dimensions, which in the most current version of the theory are care/harm, fairness/cheating, loyalty/betrayal, authority/subversion, and sanctity/degradation (Graham et al. 2013). Although the theory takes an evolutionary standpoint, it emphasizes that the concrete manifestations of these dimensions in different cultures and societies are the product of cultural learning, socialization, and adaptation. In this view, the moral foundations do constrain the kinds of moral orders that can emerge, but do not prescribe these orders.

Moral foundations' theory is based on Haidt's (2001) social intuitionist model of moral reasoning positing that *evaluative feelings* are at the core of moral judgments and in fact precede deliberative reasoning on moral issues. MFT assumes that these feelings fall into different categories and are constitutive for the different universal moral domains. Moreover, they manifest in specific discrete emotions that are characteristic for a particular domain, such as anger in the fairness/cheating domain.

In sum, there is considerable theorizing and evidence suggesting that feelings are critical to the genesis of values. At the same time, however, there are notably different positions on, or little treatment of, the question how, precisely, feelings become related to the contents of values in the first place, in sociological theory as well as in philosophical and psychological research. Attending to this question, however, seems critical for a comprehensive understanding of how values emerge and impact social action and behavior. For Scheler, it seems to be clear that because there are eternal and universal values, they are more or less directly linked to positive or negative "feelings of something," given that the respective values have been adopted from "model" persons. For Durkheim, the links between values and emotions are clearly more collective and need to be established through specific social processes; in particular, symbols and the experience of effervescence. Pragmatists roughly hold that feelings are connected to values through social interaction and experiences of self-transcendence. Psychological research suggests that moral feelings originate in universal moral domains and are "shaped by development within a cultural context" (Graham et al. 2013: 66).

In the following, I suggest that a more comprehensive understanding of values as integral to culture and sociality—in particular with regard to their socio-historical variability—entails a corresponding understanding of the social and cultural processes that shape not only discrete emotions, but also more basic and "intuitive" affective reactions associated with values. This understanding is important not only in view of the clearly notable cross-cultural differences in value orientations, but also to better comprehend the more subtle variations of values *within* societies. In fact, given the supposed coupling of values and evaluative feelings, empirical research should be able to demonstrate systematic relationships between both factors within a population or to uncover the mechanisms by which emotions are coupled to values in the first place.

The social and cultural constitution of value feelings

Research in sociology and anthropology, as well as in some areas of psychology, has long argued that emotions are substantially shaped by the social and cultural environment within which individuals are brought-up and socialized. Countless studies have reported marked cross-national differences in how people react differentially to specific events. This includes experiencing different discrete emotions in reaction to comparable events (Matsumoto and Hwang 2012; Oishi 2002) and showing different patterns of facial expression and other behavioral components of emotion (e.g., Elfenbein et al. 2007). It also refers to the ways in which discrete emotions are conceptualized and symbolically represented (for example, in media and the arts) (Wierzbicka 1999), as well as different norms and practices related to emotions (Mesquita 2003). Likewise, it has been shown that emotions are valued to varying degrees across societies (Tsai 2007).

Cross-cultural emotion research has repeatedly demonstrated that cultural differences in emotional experience and a host of emotion-related behaviors are systematically tied to specific values that are dominant in a culture. One of the most prominent examples is differences between cultures holding "individualistic" or "collectivistic" values, a value-type first investigated by Hofstede (1984) and now widely used—although often conceptualized differently—in values research (e.g., Schwartz 1990; Triandis 1995). In emotion research, individualism and collectivism are typically ascribed to "Western" and "East Asian" societies, respectively, and are associated, for example, with notable differences in facial expressions and the recognition of emotion (Matsumoto et al. 2008), ideal affect (Tsai et al. 2006), and emotion norms (Eid and Diener 2001).

Although the relationship between values and emotions has been investigated with a range of emotions and emotion-related behaviors as dependent variables and a population's value structure as the independent variable, there is reason to believe that *evaluative feelings*, understood as basic and intuitive affective reactions toward value-relevant events or situations, are equally structured and socially shared as values are. Put another way: given that affective intuitions are integral to the emergence of values and critical for value commitments, and that values are a key part of culture and thus socially shared within a population, we should be able to demonstrate widely shared evaluative feelings within a cultural group regarding specific value-relevant issues. In fact, characteristic affective responses toward value sensitive issues' make-up an important part of a group's (emotional) culture (Thoits 2004).

Hence, in the same way as emotions have been shown to differ across cultures, it seems plausible that value feelings differ systematically across cultures, co-varying with value structures. If, indeed, as the social intuitionist component of MFT suggests, intuitive feelings precede deliberative value judgments, then these feelings—by definition—need to be shared within a cultural group in much the same way as values are. I suspect that this idea of shared evaluative feelings has put much of research on values and moral judgment on a universalist or nativist track, assuming that shared feelings are best explained by invoking evolutionary (Haidt 2001) or anthropological (Scheler 1973) principles.

Until now, the majority of cross-cultural emotion research has focused on discrete emotions, their conceptualizations, and behavioral components. In terms of values, this would include, for example, characteristic emotional reactions toward actions that are in accordance or incompatible with ethical values, often also called "moral emotions" (Mulligan 2009), such as indignation or contempt on the one hand, or admiration and awe on the other hand. Moral emotions, however, are a different breed than the "value feelings" discussed so far, since they are the complex kinds of self- or other-directed emotions that arise in view of ethical or unethical actions, often acting as reinforcement devices for normative moral obligations (see, for example, Mulligan 2009).

Here, the question rather touches on the more basic evaluative feelings that underlie (or contribute to bringing about) potentially very different kinds of values and the value structure of a society. I suggest that many of the processes involved in the social shaping of emotions also contribute to establishing links between values and evaluative feelings. Much like Scheff (2002) has described shame as a "moral gyroscope," the development of a positive or negative stance, i.e., of intuitive feelings of "goodness" or "badness" toward certain objects and conceptions, renders them "desirable." We could also say that widespread cultural practices that are reflected, for instance, in parenting and socialization styles, social institutions, political programs, ideologies, discourse, media, and the arts all contribute to the emergence of socially shared "affective dispositions" toward what is widely deemed "good" and "desirable" and thus valued in a society.

This is not the place to a give a detailed account of the processes and mechanisms involved in the social shaping of knowledge and cognitive structures, as well as more basic cognitive processes, since there is a number of abundant approaches from different disciplines dealing with these issues (e.g., in cognitive sociology: Cerulo 2002; DiMaggio 1997; social and cognitive anthropology: Shore 1996; psychology: Varnum et al. 2010). Elsewhere, I have outlined the ways in which not only knowledge and cognition become socially shared, but also emotions and more basic affective responses toward specific objects, events, and actions based on the levels of neural, cognitive, and social cultural processing (Rogers et al. 2013; von Scheve 2013). This line of argument is mirrored roughly in many ways in the sociology of emotion (Barbalet 1998; Turner 2007). Importantly, these socially structured affective reactions—that are likely to include evaluative feelings—are elicited rapidly, automatically, and largely outside conscious awareness, hence mirroring what nativist or universalist accounts ascribe to intuitive value feelings originating in universal domains of morality (Graham et al. 2013).

Acknowledging some of the critique that has been marshaled against nativist positions concerning the origins of moral values (e.g., Kelly et al. 2007; Prinz 2009, 2007; Slaby 2013; see also: von Scheve 2010), I argue that the assumption of universal "moral modules" or pre-organized "moral domains" is, first and most importantly, *not necessary* to make sense of intuitionist positions regarding moral judgments and, more generally, the existence of certain value feelings. Moreover, I agree with scholars holding that we would need more convincing evidence, in particular, at a neurophysiological level (e.g., Suhler and Churchland 2011), to posit the existence of such universal domains or modules. If the "moral mind," as Graham and colleagues (2013) put it, is merely "organized in advance of experience" and then massively susceptible to social and cultural learning, the question arises at which point in time (or if ever) it is relevant for behavior in an "unaltered" form, given the ontogenetically early onset of social learning.

Be that as it may, my argument rather is that affective dispositions are generated during socialization toward all sorts of social concepts, the ones mentioned by MFT in any case *appearing* to be universal because they are related to very basic dimensions of human sociality present in almost any known society and not necessarily because they have a special "moral" status. Hence, these kinds of evaluative feelings will likewise be elicited toward social norms and conventions as well as to non-ethical values—not only within the "moral" sphere.

Social structures and processes of evaluative feelings

Our own research has attended in somewhat different ways both to the structuring of affective responses in value relevant domains as well as to the processes that are involved in imbuing values with evaluative feelings. In one study, we used the principles of affect control theory (ACT; Heise 2007) to investigate the evaluative feelings toward two basic dimensions of human sociality: *authority* and *community*. Affect control theory is roughly compatible with positions on the origins of values as put forward by pragmatist accounts. It rests on the principles of symbolic interactionism and assumes that evaluative feelings toward concepts in general emerge during social interaction and the formation of the self. They become socially patterned because interactions are always embedded in tight networks of social institutions. ACT measures evaluative feelings toward concepts using semantic differentials to assess individuals' affective perceptions of words denoting concepts on the dimension of evaluation, potency, and activity (Heise 2007). These dimensions have been shown to be perceptual primitives that underly much of human social cognition (e.g., Scholl 2013) and tally with many dimensional understandings of human affective experience (e.g., Barrett and Bliss-Moreau 2009; Fontaine et al. 2007).

Using a quasi-representative survey of the German population, we obtained ratings for 909 words from the semantic fields of authority and community (Ambrasat et al. 2014). Although our results show a broad consensus in the affective meaning of (i.e., evaluative feelings toward) authority- and community-related concepts and thus confirm previous studies (e.g., Heise 2010), we also find notable differences between social groups, in particular socio-economic status groups. These findings are broadly in line with the presumption that values do not only exhibit notable cross-cultural differences, but are also differentially distributed within a society. At the same time our results concur with more recent findings regarding the psychology of social class (e.g., Kraus and Stephens 2012). Crucial for the argument I seek to make, the consensus finding in evaluative feelings is in line with most existing survey studies on values in German society. Likewise, looking at international studies using ACT, we find that, for example, authority-related concepts are perceived more positively by U.S.-American than by German respondents, which is mirrored in the different value structures of the two societies. Hence, the study supports the assumption that evaluative feelings exhibit structures that are similar to the value structures of a society.

A second study has investigated the mechanisms through which values may be imbued with affective feelings (von Scheve et al. 2014). We specifically looked at Durkheim's ([1912] 1995) proposition that the experience of collective effervescence during rituals is transferred to the symbols of a group and thus, ultimately, to the beliefs and values represented by those symbols. To investigate the influence of collective effervescence on the affective perception or evaluation of group-related symbols, we conducted a natural quasi-experiment in which the Football World Cup 2010 is considered the treatment. World Cups reliably elicit collective effervescence during ritual gatherings and public screenings of matches in a highly nationalized context. Our study showed that the more participants experienced collective effervescence during the tournament, the more positively they perceived national symbols after the event. There was no general, affect-independent tendency to perceive symbols more positively after the event and the effect only holds for in-group symbols. In sum, this finding supports the view that social processes are indeed critical in the genesis of evaluative feelings, although the results are confined to those symbols that presumably represent specific values.

Values and social action

In sociology, detailed analysis of the influence of values on social action is inextricably linked to the works of Weber ([1921] 1978). Weber is widely associated with methodological individualism that places primacy on social actions as the main explanatory factors in social science research. He argued that social order at least partly results from patterns of social action and stable social relationships. To make sense of such patterns and to interpretively understand actions in scientific terms, Weber ([1921] 1978) suggested four well-known ideal types of action, namely: instrumental-rational, value-rational, habitual, and affectual action. According to Weber, the first two make the most significant contributions to explaining social order. Whereas instrumental-rational action is more or less universally based on principles of deductive reasoning and means-ends relations, value-rational action accounts for much of the variation in social orders observed across cultures and societies.

Although the exact status of value-rational compared to instrumental-rational action continues to be much debated in the humanities and the social sciences (e.g., Beckermann 1985), its basic idea is straightforward. Individuals tend to act in the social world based on what is important to them, what they hold dear, what is of value to them—*irrespective* of the likelihood of success of an action, of costs that might occur, or whether other goals are negatively affected. Value-rational action in Weber's sense is solely oriented toward the "intrinsic" value of a particular kind of action—Weber uses the German phrase "*unbedingter Eigenwert*" to denote this intrinsic value of an action (Weber, [1921] 1980: 12; see also the discussion in Kroneberg 2007). Most importantly, an action is value-*rational* in that it is intentionally and purposefully oriented toward some *Eigenwert* (Kroneberg 2007).

Since Weber devoted much of his work to investigating the role of religious beliefs in the transformation of modern societies, he considered religious values in many ways "primordial," i.e., as governing behavior in almost any area of social life (see also Pelser and Roberts, this volume). His famous diagnosis of an increasing rationalization and disenchantment of the world consequently included a social-evolutionary account of "value-rationalization." Value-rationalization is a process through which value-bearing spheres of life other than religion, for example, politics and the economy, become more and more self-contained and autonomous in view of their potential to generate action guiding values that are independent of religious concern. On the one hand, these "value spheres"—religion, the economy, politics, aesthetics, the erotic, and intellectualism—guide value-rational action in many areas of social life and also inform other ideal types of action (see Oakes 2003, for a discussion). On the other hand, value spheres are elements of social order in their own right. In Weber's works and in much of contemporary sociology, they are considered *the* building blocks of culture.

This classical view of the role of values in culture and social action has been substantiated by Parsons (1937) in his works on the structure of social action and then developed into becoming the paradigmatic view in sociology of how values (and social norms) influence social action. Paramount in this perspective is that values are not primarily conceived of as external constraints, but as internalized during socialization. According to the underlying structural functionalist logic, actions oriented toward dominant values and norms then contribute to reproducing a prevailing social order.

Challenges to the prevailing view on values in action

More recently, this view has been increasingly criticized for making unrealistic assumptions on the power of values to control social action (Vaisey 2009). One of the first to voice substantial concerns was Swidler (1986), who in her now classic piece argues that we should conceive of culture (and thus of values) as a "toolkit" from which actors assemble mostly post-hoc justifications for how they act, rather than as determinants of action. Culture—and hence values—according to Swidler are much less the *ends* toward which purposeful action is oriented, but more so the *means* through which actors make sense of the world and their behavior (Swidler (1986); see also Wuthnow 2008). Part of the evidence for this skeptical view is given in Swidler's (2001) more recent work showing that people are, on a regular basis, surprisingly incapable of giving well-grounded reasons and justifications for many of their actions. Likewise, Smith et al. (2011) report results of a large interview study with U.S.-American adolescents on various issues of social life showing that these respondents are remarkably inept when it comes to thinking about morals and values. In accounting for their own actions, many of the interviewees "talked more about the power of personal gut feelings and emotions to inform their moral choices" than giving consistent reasons for why they do what they do (Smith et al. 2011: 51). Similar arguments have been developed in moral psychology and philosophy. Haidt (2001), for instance, reviews studies showing that individuals are frequently incapable of giving reasons for their moral judgments but rather rely on their gut feelings.

In discussing much of the critical sociological work on the direct motivational impact of values, Vaisey (2009) asserts that the critics, often implicitly, hold a "conception of cultural meanings as propositional, articulated, and logically coimplicated" (p. 1681). I concur with Vaisey's assessment that this view has become outdated not only in sociology, but also in many other disciplines. In sociology, it is first and foremost theories of *social practices* that have substantially challenged this account of the role of culture—and values—in social action (e.g., Giddens 1984; Turner 2002). These theories have provided various models of how culture is supposed to influence social action in a pre-reflexive, automatic, and intuitive manner. One of the most well-known concepts in this regard is Bourdieu's (1977) notion of the *habitus* as a complex set of socially and culturally embodied dispositions for thinking, feeling, and acting.

Although practice theories propose a number of "transmission" processes through which "culture" interacts with the human mind and body, and brings about shared patterns of action, such as socialization, implicit learning, and internalization, still little is known about the precise mechanisms through which this is accomplished. Vaisey (2009) and others (e.g., Ignatow 2007; Lizardo 2004) have suggested that information processing theories from the cognitive sciences could be helpful in refining sociological accounts of praxeological action. In particular, dual-process theories of reasoning (Evans 2007) have been considered useful in accounting for the pre-reflexive "patterning" of social action, as suggested by the habitus concept (Vaisey 2009).

Emotions and social practices

My argument continues this line of thought and capitalizes on dual-process models of reasoning. These models assume that there are two different systems of information processing underlying human reasoning and behavior: one characterized by "unconscious, rapid, automatic, and high capacity" processing; and another based on "conscious, slow, and deliberative" processes (Evans 2007: 256). Many proponents of dual-process models suggest that affects and emotions play an important role in the latter kind of processing and are implicated in the implicit, automatic, fast, and effortless processing in this "experiential" system (e.g., Evans 2007; MacDonald 2008). This view is adequately summarized by Epstein (1994: 716, cited from Slovic et al. 2004: 313): "The experiential system is assumed to be intimately associated with the experience of affect, . . . which refer[s] to subtle feelings of which people are often unaware. When a person responds to an emotionally significant event . . . the experiential system automatically searches its memory banks for related events, including their emotional accompaniments" (p. 716). It is precisely these dual-process models that also play a key role in research highlighting the importance of emotions in moral judgment (Greene 2007; Haidt 2001).

Although sociological works referring to these models in explaining the influence of culture and values on action do acknowledge the role of affect and emotion (Lizardo 2006; Vaisey 2009), a more systematic treatment is still needed. Sociological analyses turning to dual-process models as a cure for some of the weak spots of practice theories are confronted with a problem that is hardly relevant for the psychologists or decision-scientists who developed these models, namely that the behavioral outcomes of the automatic experiential system are *widely shared* within a social group. One way to make sense of this sharing is to rely on the workhorses of cognitive sociology and anthropology, such as cognitive structures, schemas, and scripts. Another and more fruitful way, I suggest, is to turn to the social shaping of emotions and basic affective responses—including the evaluative feelings discussed above.

Given that there is ample evidence from the sociology of emotion and cross-cultural psychology suggesting that emotions and affective responses (that are by definition evaluative) are widely influenced by culture and values and are shared within social groups, and that these affective responses are critical components of automatic and implicit information processing, we should be on safe grounds to assume that they are equally implicated in bringing about socially shared patterns of action and judgments that reflect how people value and evaluate—both implicitly and explicitly—various issues. Socially structured evaluative feelings thus become an essential link between rather abstract values as conceptions of the desirable on the one hand and social action on the other hand. In line with dual-process accounts and works in moral psychology and philosophy, these evaluative feelings intuitively motivate or constrain specific forms of action. The important sociological caveat here is that the assumption of socially shared evaluative feelings can also be applied to the ensuing patterns of social action and hence the creation and reproduction of social order, which is one of the key explanatory concerns in the social sciences.

Conclusion

In this chapter I have argued that values' research should be complemented by an account of emotions and more basic evaluative feelings as socially structured and culturally shaped. This perspective, I presume, is necessary to arrive at a more comprehensive understanding of where values and value commitments come from and how they motivate action. My suggestion is rooted in the largely uncontroversial claim that affect and values are most tightly intertwined and that emotions are integral to understanding both the emergence of values and their influence on action. An initial review of classic and contemporary sociological literature on the emergence of values has shown that there are roughly three—not entirely opposing—positions on the role of emotions in the genesis of values. The first, "universalist" position assumes that value feelings are rooted in specific and hierarchically ordered "eternal values" that operate like sensory perception (e.g., Scheler 1973). The second, "pragmatist" view emphasizes that values are generated in social-interactive contexts through notable experiences of self-transcendence (Joas 2001). The third, "collectivist" account highlights the role of rituals and collective effervescence in the emergence of values (Durkheim [1912] 1995). Turning to more recent work in moral psychology, my aim was to introduce a perspective to the sociological discussion that is, although still considered "nativist," less restrictive than universalist views in positing a number of universal "moral domains" that are shaped through culture and learning and from which evaluative feelings originate. I have voiced concerns over these theories' shortcomings regarding a proper model of how, more precisely, these evaluative feelings are shaped by culture and socially shared within a group.

In addressing this limitation, I have discussed sociological and cultural psychological approaches showing how emotions and basic evaluative feelings are socially constructed and become shared almost as a "common sense" within a population. Importantly, this pertains to feelings toward various concepts, conventions, norms, and values, not just to moral values. Hence, in my view, there is no imminent need to postulate universal moral domains. Rather, the proposed universality of some (moral) values, as in moral foundations theory (Graham et al. 2013), might be explained by the universality of certain foundational dimensions of *sociality* rather than of morality.

In a second step, I moved on to discuss the influence of values on social action. As a point of departure, I sketched Weber's classical concept of value-rational action and then briefly reviewed more recent critique that has been brought forward in some areas of cultural sociology against this direct motivating force of values for action. Alternative accounts, such as theories of social practices, emphasize the automatic and pre-reflexive nature of much of our day-to-day actions. Dual-process models of reasoning have been proposed to supplement these accounts. However, as I argue, sociologists have largely disregarded the critical role that affect and emotion play in dual-process models, in particular those concerned with moral judgment (e.g., Haidt 2001). Conversely, dual-process models show only little interest in explaining where the emotions and affective reactions actually "come from" and how they become associated to different situational cues. Drawing on extant research on the social structuration and cultural shaping of emotions and evaluative feelings, I have argued that the very affective processes that are integral to the emergence of values are likely to play a vital role in how values—or, more precisely, evaluative feelings—influence social action. Most importantly, the assumption that these feelings are socially structured and shared within a group or population makes them ideal candidates to explain regular patterns of social action that are necessary to understand social order. Some of my own studies that I have discussed provide initial but indirect evidence on this perspective on the tight coupling of values and emotion. At the same time, they show that more research is needed that directly investigates the links between socially structured and culturally shaped emotions and the values that are shared within a group.

References

Ambrasat, J., von Scheve, C., Conrad, M., Schauenburg, G., and Schröder, T. (2014). Consensus and stratification in affective meaning of human sociality. *Proceedings of the National Academy of Sciences of the USA*, 111(22), 8001–8006.

Barbalet, J. M. (1998). *Emotion, Social Theory and Social Structure*. Cambridge: Cambridge University Press.

Barrett, L. F., and Bliss-Moreau, E. (2009). Affect as a psychological primitive. In M. P. Zanna (ed.), *Advances in Experimental Social Psychology*, Vol. 41 (pp. 167–218). Burlington: Academic Press.

Beckermann, A. (1985). Value-rationality and the distinction between goal-oriented and value-oriented behavior in Weber. In G. Seebass (ed.), *Theory and Decision Library*, Vol. 43 (pp. 225–233). Dordrecht: Reidel.

Boudon, R. (2001). *The Origin of Values*. New Brunswick: Transaction.

Bourdieu, P. (1977). *Outline of a Theory of Practice*. Cambridge: Cambridge University Press.

Brown, D. E. (1991). *Human Universals*. New York: McGraw–Hill.

Canto Mila, N. (2005). *A Sociological Theory of Value*. Bielefeld: transcript.

Cerulo, K. A. (2002). Establishing a sociology of culture and cognition. In K. A. Cerulo (ed.), *Culture in Mind: Toward a Sociology of Culture and Cognition* (pp. 1–12). New York: Routledge.

Davis, Z. and Steinbock, A. (2014). Max Scheler. In E. N. Zalta (ed.), *The Stanford Encyclopedia of Philosophy*, Spring 2014 edition. Retrieved from http://plato.stanford.edu/archives/spr2014/entries/scheler/. Last accessed May 13, 2015.

Deonna, J. A., and Teroni, F. (2015). Value and emotion. In Brosch, T. and Sander, D. (eds), *Handbook of Value. Perspectives from economics, neuroscience, philosophy, psychology, and sociology* (pp. 155–173). New York: Oxford University Press.

DiMaggio, P. (1997). Culture and cognition. *Annual Review of Sociology*, **23**, 263–287.

Durkheim, E. ([1912] 1995). *The Elementary Forms of Religious Life*. New York: The Free Press.

Eid, M. and Diener, E. (2001). Norms for experiencing emotions in different cultures: Inter- and intranational differences. *Journal of Personality and Social Psychology*, **81**, 869–885.

Elfenbein, H. A., Beaupré, M., Lévesque, M., and Hess, U. (2007). Toward a dialect theory: cultural differences in the expression and recognition of posed facial expressions. *Emotion*, **7**, 131–146.

Elster, J. (1989). Social norms and economic theory. *Journal of Economic Perspectives*, **3**(4), 99–117.

Emerson, R. M. (1976). Social exchange theory. *Annual Review of Sociology*, **2**, 335–362.

Epstein, S. (1994). Integration of the cognitive and the psychodynamic unconscious. *American Psychologist*, **49**, 709–724.

Evans, J. (2007). Dual-processing accounts of reasoning, judgment, and social cognition. *Annual Review of Psychology*, **59**, 268–269.

Feather, N. T. (1980). Values in adolescence. In J. Adelson (ed.), *Handbook of Adolescent Psychology* (pp. 247–294). New York: Wiley.

Fontaine, J. R. J., Scherer, K. R., Roesch, E. B., and Ellsworth, P. C. (2007). The world of emotions is not two-dimensional. *Psychological Science*, **18**, 1050–1057.

Giddens, A. (1984). *The Constitution of Society: Outline of the Theory of Structuration*. Berkeley: University of California Press.

Graham, J., Haidt, J., Koleva, S., Motyl, M., Iyer, R., Wojcik, S., and Ditto, P. H. (2013). Moral foundations theory: the pragmatic validity of moral pluralism. *Advances in Experimental Social Psychology*, **47**, 55–130.

Granato, J., Inglehart, R., and Leblang, D. (1996). The effect of cultural values on economic development: theory, hypotheses, and some empirical tests. *American Journal of Political Science*, **40**(3), 607–631.

Greene, J. D. (2007). The secret joke of Kant's soul. In W. Sinnott-Armstrong (ed.), *Moral Psychology*, Vol. 3: *The Neuroscience of Morality Emotion Disease and Development* (pp. 35–79). Cambridge, MA: MIT Press.

Haidt, J. (2001). The emotional dog and its rational tail: a social intuitionist approach to moral judgment. *Psychological Review*, **108**, 814–834.

Haidt, J. and Graham, J. (2009). Planet of the Durkheimians, where community, authority, and sacredness are foundations of morality. In J. Jost, A. C. Kay, and H. Thorisdottir (eds), *Social and Psychological Bases of Ideology and System Justification* (pp. 371–401). New York: Oxford University Press.

Haidt, J. and Joseph, C. (2004). Intuitive ethics: how innately prepared intuitions generate culturally variable virtues. *Daedalus*, **133**(4), 55–66.

Hechter, M., Nadel, L., and Michod, R. E. (eds) (1993). *The Origin of Values*. New York: de Gruyter.

Heise, D. R. (2007). *Expressive Order: Confirming Sentiments in Social Action*. New York: Springer.

Heise, D. R. (2010). *Surveying Cultures: Discovering Shared Conceptions and Sentiments*. New York: Wiley.

Higgins, E. T. (2006). Value from hedonic experience and engagement. *Psychological Review*, **113**(3), 439–460.

Hitlin, S. and Piliavin, J. A. (2004). Values: reviving a dormant concept. *Annual Review of Sociology*, **30**, 359–393.

Hofstede, G. (1984). *Culture's Consequences: International Differences in Work-Related Values* (2nd edn). Beverly Hills, CA: Sage.

Ignatow, G. (2007). Theories of embodied knowledge: new directions for cultural and cognitive sociology? *Journal for the Theory of Social Behaviour*, **37**, 115–135.

Inglehart, R. and Welzel, C. (2005). *Modernization, Cultural Change, and Democracy*. Cambridge: Cambridge University Press.

Joas, H. (2001). *The Genesis of Values*. Chicago: University of Chicago Press.

Kamolnick, P. (2001). Simmel's legacy for contemporary value theory: a critical assessment. *Sociological Theory*, **19**(1), 65–85.

Kelly, D., Stich, S. P., Haley, K. J., Eng, S. J., and Fessler, D. M. (2007). Harm, affect and the moral/conventional distinction. *Mind and Language*, **22**, 117–131.

Kim, M. (2008). Spiritual values, religious practices, and democratic attitudes. *Politics and Religion*, **1**(2), 216–236.

Kluckhohn, C. (1951). Values and value orientations in the theory of action. In T. Parsons and E. A. Shils (eds), *Toward a General Theory of Action* (pp. 388–433). New York: Harper.

Kohn, M. L., Naoi, A., Schoenbach, C., Schooler, C., and Slomczynski, K. M. (1990). Position in the class structure and psychological functioning in the United States, Japan, and Poland. *American Journal of Sociology*, **95**, 964–1008.

Kraus, M. W. and Stephens, N. M. (2012). A road map for an emerging psychology of social class. *Social and Personality Psychology Compass*, **6**, 642–656.

Kriegel, U. (2008). Moral phenomenology: foundational issues. *Phenomenology and the Cognitive Sciences*, 7 (1), 1–19.

Kroneberg, C. (2007). Wertrationalität und das Modell der Frame-Selektion [Axiological Rationality and the Frame Selection Model]. *Kölner Zeitschrift für Soziologie und Sozialpsychologie*, **59**, 215–239.

Leimgruber, P. (2011). Values and votes: the indirect effect of personal values on voting behavior. *Swiss Political Science Review*, **17**(2), 107–112.

Lizardo, O. (2004). The cognitive origins of Bourdieu's habitus. *Journal for the Theory of Social Behaviour*, **34**, 375–401.

Lizardo, O. (2006). How cultural tastes shape personal networks. *American Sociological Review*, **71**(5), 778–807.

MacDonald, K. B. (2008). Effortful control, explicit processing and the regulation of human evolved predispositions. *Psychological Review*, **115**(4), 1012–1031.

Maio, G. R., Olson, J. M, Bernard, M. M., and Luke, M. A. (2003). Ideologies, values, attitudes, and behavior. In J. DeLamater (ed.), *Handbook of Social Psychology* (pp. 283–308). New York: Kluwer-Plenum.

Marx, K. ([1867] 1976). *Capital*, Vol. I. Harmondsworth: Penguin.

Matsumoto, D. and Hwang, H. S. (2012). Culture and emotion: the integration of biological and cultural contributions. *Journal of Cross-Cultural Psychology*, **43**(1), 91–118.

Matsumoto, D., Yoo, S. H., and Fontaine, J. (2008). Mapping expressive differences around the World: the relationship between emotional display rules and individualism versus collectivism. *Journal of Cross-cultural Psychology*, **39**, 55–74.

McBroom, W. H., Reed, F. W., Burns, C. E., Hargraves, J. L., and Trankel, M. A. (1985). Intergenerational transmission of values: a data-based reassessment. *Social Psychology Quarterly*, **48**, 150–163.

Mesquita, B. (2003). Emotions as dynamic cultural phenomena. In D. J. Davidson, K. R. Scherer, and H. H. Goldsmith (eds), *The Handbook of the Affective Sciences* (pp. 871–890). New York: Oxford University Press.

Michod, R. E. (1993). Biology and the origin of values. In M. Hecher, L. Nadel, and R. E. Michod (eds). *The Origin of Values* (pp. 261–272). New York: de Gruyter.

Moll, J., Zahn, R., and de Oliveira-Souza, R. (2015). The neural underpinnings of moral value. In Brosch, T. and Sander, D. (eds), *Handbook of Value. Perspectives from economics, neuroscience, philosophy, psychology, and sociology* (pp. 119–127). New York: Oxford University Press.

Molm, L. (1997). *Coercive Power in Social Exchange*. New York: Cambridge University Press.

Mulligan, K. (2009). Moral emotions. In D. Sander, and K. Scherer (eds), *The Oxford Companion to Emotions and the Affective Sciences* (pp. 262–264). New York: Oxford University Press.

Nichols, S. (2004). *Sentimental Rules: On the Natural Foundations of Moral Judgment*. New York: Oxford University Press.

Oakes, G. (2003). Max Weber on value rationality and value spheres. *Journal of Classical Sociology*, **3**(1), 27–45.

Oishi, S. (2002). Experiencing and remembering of well-being: a cross-cultural analysis. *Personality and Social Psychology Bulletin*, **28**, 1398–1406.

Omoto, A. M. and Snyder, M. (1995). Sustained helping without obligation: motivation, longevity of service, and perceived attitude change among AIDS volunteers. *Journal of Personality and Social Psychology*, **68**, 671–686.

Pareto, V. (1935). *The Mind and Society*. New York: Harcourt, Brace.

Parsons, T. (1937). *The Structure of Social Action*. New York: Free Press.

Parsons, T. and Shils, E. A. (1951). Values, motives, and systems of action. In T. Parsons and E. A. Shils (eds), *Toward a General Theory of Action* (pp. 47–246). New York: Harper and Row.

Poortinga, W., Steg, L., and Vlek, C. (2004). Values, environmental concern, and environmental behavior. *Environment and Behavior*, **36**(1), 70–93.

Prinz, J. (2007). *The Emotional Construction of Morals*. Oxford: Oxford University Press.

Prinz, J. (2009). Against moral nativism. In D. Murphy and M. Bishop (eds), *Stich and His Critics* (pp. 167–189). Malden, MA: Wiley-Blackwell.

Richerson, P. J. and Boyd, R. (2005). *Not by Genes Alone: How Culture Transformed Human Evolution*. Chicago: University of Chicago Press.

Rogers, K. B., Schröder, T., von Scheve, C. (2014). Dissecting the sociality of emotion: a multi-level approach. *Emotion Review*, **6**(2), 140–141.

Rohan, M. J. (2000). A rose by any name? The values construct. *Personality and Social Psychology Review*, 4(3), 255–277.

Rokeach, M. (1973). *The Nature of Human Values*. New York: The Free Press.

Scheff, T. J. (2002). Shame in self and society. *Symbolic Interaction*, **2**, 239–262.

Scheler, M. (1973). *Formalism in Ethics and Non-Formal ethics of value*. Evanston, I.L.: Northwestern University Press.

Schokkaert, E. (2006). The empirical analysis of transfer motives. In S.-C. Kolm S.-C., and J. Ythier (eds), *Handbook of the Economics of Giving, Altruism and Reciprocity*, Vol. 1 (pp. 128–180). Amsterdam: North-Holland.

Scholl, W. (2013). The socio-emotional basis of human interaction and communication: How we construct our social world. *Social Science Information*, **52**(1), 3–33.

Schwartz, S. H. (1990). Individualism-collectivism: critique and proposed refinements. *Journal of Cross-Cultural Psychology*, **21**, 139–157.

Schwartz, S. H. (1992). Universals in the content and structure of values: theory and empirical tests in 20 countries. In M. Zanna (ed.), *Advances in Experimental Social Psychology*, Vol. 25 (pp. 1–65). New York: Academic Press.

Schwartz, S. H. (1996). Value priorities and behaviour: applying a theory of integrated value systems. In C. Seligman, J. M. Olson, and M. P. Zanna (eds), *The Psychology of Values: The Ontario Symposium*, Vol. 8 (pp. 1–24). Mahwah, NJ: Erlbaum.

Schwartz, S. H. (2012). An overview of the Schwartz theory of basic values. *Online Readings in Psychology and Culture*, 2(1). http://dx.doi.org/10.9707/2307-0919.1116

Shore, B. (1996). *Culture in Mind*. Oxford: Oxford University Press.

Shweder, R. A., Much, M. C., Mahapatra, M., and Park L. (1997). The "Big Three" of morality (autonomy, community, divinity), and the "Big Three" explanations of suffering. In A. Brandt and P. Rozin (eds), *Morality and Health* (pp. 119–172). New York: Routledge.

Simmel, G. ([1900] 1978). *The Philosophy of Money*. London: Routledge and Kegan Paul.

Slaby, J. (2013). The new science of morality: a bibliographical review. *The Hedgehog Review*, **15**(1), 46–54.

Slovic, P., Finucane, M. L., Peters, E., and MacGregor, D. G. (2004). Risk as analysis and risk as feelings: some thoughts about affect, reason, risk, and rationality. *Risk Analysis*, **24**, 311–322.

Smith, C., Christoffersen, K., Davidson, H., and Herzog, P. S. (2011). *Lost in Transition: The Dark Side of Emerging Adulthood.* New York: Oxford University Press.

Spates, J.L. (1983). The sociology of values. *Annual Review of Sociology*, **9**, 27–49

Spillman, L. and Strand, M. (2013). Interest-oriented action. *Annual Review of Sociology*, **39**(1), 85–104.

Suhler, C. L. and Churchland, P. S. (2011). Can innate, modular "foundations" explain morality? Challenges for Haidt's moral foundations theory. *Journal of Cognitive Neuroscience*, **23**(9), 2103–2116.

Swidler, A. (1986). Culture in action: symbols and strategies. *American Sociological Review*, **51**(2), 273–286.

Swidler, A. (2001). *Talk of Love: How Culture Matters.* Chicago: University of Chicago Press.

Tao, L. and Au, W.-T. (2014). Values, self and other-regarding behavior in the dictator game. *Rationality and Society*, **26**(1), 46–72.

Taylor, C. (1989) *Sources of the Self.* Cambridge: Cambridge University Press.

Thoits, P. A. (2004). Emotion norms, emotion work and social order. In A. S. R. Manstead, N. H. Frijda, and A. Fischer (eds), *Feelings and Emotions* (pp. 359–378). New York: Cambridge University Press.

Triandis, H. C. (1995). *Individualism and Collectivism.* Westview: Boulder.

Tsai, J. L. (2007). Ideal affect. cultural causes and behavioral consequences. *Perspectives on Psychological Science*, **2**(3), 242–259.

Tsai, J. L., Knutson, B., and Fung, H. H. (2006). Cultural variation in affect valuation. *Journal of Personality and Social Psychology*, **90**, 288–307.

Turner, S. (2002). *Brains/Practices/Relativism: Social theory after cognitive science.* Chicago: University of Chicago Press.

Turner, J. H. (2007). *Human Emotions. A Sociological Theory.* London: Routledge.

Tönnies, F. ([1887] 2005). *Gemeinschaft und Gesellschaft. Grundbegriffe der reinen Soziologie.* [Community and Society]. Darmstadt: Wissenschaftliche Buchgesellschaft.

Vaisey, S. (2009). Motivation and justification: a dual-process model of culture in action. *American Journal of Sociology*, 114, 1675–1715.

Varnum, M. E. W., Grossmann, I., Kitayama, S., and Nisbett, R. E. (2010).The origin of cultural differences in cognition: evidence for the social orientation hypothesis. *Current Directions in Psychological Science*, **19**(1), 9–13.

von Scheve, C. (2010). Emotionen, Normkonformität und das Problem sozialer Ordnung. [Emotions, norm conformity and the problem of social order]. In M. Iorio and R. Reisenzein (eds), *Regel, Norm, Gesetz: Eine interdisziplinäre Bestandsaufnahme* [Rule, Norm, Law: An Interdisciplinary Review] (pp. 285–308). Frankfurt/Main: Lang.

von Scheve, C. (2013). *Emotion and Social Structures. The Affective Foundations of Social Order.* New York: Routledge.

von Scheve, C., Beyer, M., Ismer, S., Kozlowska, M., and Morawetz, C. (2014). Emotional entrainment, national symbols and identification: a naturalistic study around the men's football world cup. *Current Sociology*, **62**(1), 3–23.

Waters, M. C. (1990). *Ethnic Options Choosing Identities in America.* Berkeley: University of California Press.

Weber, M. ([1904] 1949). "Objectivity" in social science and social policy. In E. A. Shils and H. A. Finch (eds), *The Methodology of the Social Sciences* (pp. 49–112). New York: Free Press.

Weber, M. ([1921] 1978). *Economy and Society.* Berkeley, CA: University of California Press.

Weber, M. ([1921] 1980). Wirtschaft und Gesellschaft. Grundriss der verstehenden Soziologie. [Economy and Society. An Outline of Interpretive Sociology]. Tübingen: Mohr Siebeck.

Wierzbicka, A. (1999). *Emotions Across Languages and Cultures.* Cambridge, UK: Cambridge University Press.

Wuthnow, R. (2008). The sociological study of values. *Sociological Forum*, **23**(2), 333–343.

Xiao, H. (2000). Class, gender, and parental values in the 1990s. *Gender and Society*, **14**(6), 785–803.

Chapter 10

Affect, decision-making, and value: neural and psychological mechanisms

Peter Sokol-Hessner and Elizabeth A. Phelps

Interactions between affect and decision-making

To examine the intersection of affect, value, and decision-making, we begin with the question "What is the role of affect in decision-making?" Though appealing in its simplicity, this question is rooted in the classic dual-process models of "emotion" and "cognition" (e.g., Cohen 2005), implicitly assuming that "affect" is a singular construct with a singular role in altering "decision-making." There are three primary reasons that this question is ultimately unsatisfying.

First, the word "affect" describes a broad category that covers many phenomena different in their origins, time scale, and consequences (Scherer 2005). In fact, the definition of emotion, and emotion theory in general, is an active area of research. Some theories consider emotion to be a collection of component processes, each of which captures an objectively distinct piece of the emotional experience (e.g., bodily physiological reactions, facial expressions, subjective feelings, etc.; Scherer 2005), while others propose definitions centering on concepts of core affective responses interacting with appraisals and contexts (Barrett 2006) or take a more functionalist view (Farb et al. 2013). Regardless of the specific definition, we can certainly conclude that emotion does not live on a single axis, and is not a unitary construct. To consider emotion, we must therefore consider the *parts* or *components* of emotion.

Second, our original question, as phrased, ignores the growing neuroscience of emotion and cognition. This literature highlights the emerging understanding of both emotions and cognitive function as distributed across different brain regions. Evidence for this comes not only from neuroimaging studies (Lindquist et al. 2012), but also from lesion (Feinstein 2013) and single-neuron recording studies (Salzman and Fusi 2010). These find that cells or regions of the brain involved in "emotion" are not separate from cells or regions related to "cognitive" functions. In other words, neuroscientific data suggest that "emotion" and "cognition" are not separate systems in the brain. Rather, their shared substrates suggest that we should think in terms of interrelated networks and their functions instead of the classic, but ultimately less truthful, dichotomous labels of "emotion" and "cognition."

Third, decision-making is also multi-faceted and complex. Though this may seem a basic point, its consequence is that we should expect not a single shift in decision-making (i.e., toward the "irrational"), but rather changes in specific processes that contribute to decision-making. This logically follows from the observation that option values are not all computed in exactly the same way. Sometimes an option will entail risk; other times, weighing losses against gains; or balancing fairness in an interpersonal interaction. Especially in recent years, studies have begun to dissociate these and other processes that underlie the computation of value, and thus the ways in which different option attributes shape the choices made about those options. This means that the ways in which affect and decision-making interact will be characterized not only by the affective dimension at play, but by the computations being used in the context at hand to make a choice.

Taking these three points into account, we can re-define our question. Attempting to address the many dimensions of affect, the neuroscience suggesting that emotion and cognition are not truly separable, and an appreciation for the complexity of decision-making, we propose a revised question: "How do different components of affect and emotion represent or modulate specific decision-making processes and their neural mechanisms?" Note that this asks not how emotion changes decisions, but how components of emotion might represent and/or modulate decision processes. This is the difference between asking how drugs change a cough, and how a particular antibiotic chemically interferes with infectious bacterial growth. By being more specific in our question, we only improve our ability to answer it.

This chapter will be organized around two main approaches taken in the literature to studying the interactions between emotion and decision-making. The first, correlational approach, is to measure affect and relate it to the variables at hand and the decisions made; the second is to introduce stimuli or contexts that evoke emotional responses, and examine how choices change as a result of that intervention.

The studies we include in this chapter generally meet three criteria. First, as we are examining the neuroscience of interactions between affect, value, and decision-making, the studies must be part of a literature contributing to our understanding of the neural mechanisms underlying these interactions. Second, they include measurement or manipulation of affect. In particular, when we use the word "emotion" here, we will be doing so mostly in the sense captured in Scherer (2005)—as a collection of discrete, short-lived, coordinated responses to an event of significance. These responses could include bodily physiological responses (e.g., measurements of arousal), reported subjective feelings (like anger or disgust), emotional expressions (e.g., a fearful face), or cognitive appraisals (the interpretation of an event), among others. We will also examine moods and stress responses, which while sometimes not considered discrete "emotions" due to their longer timescales and diffuse focus (Scherer 2005), still fall under the umbrella term of affect. Third, the studies must include observations of some kind of decision over options that differ in their subjective value, or utility to the decision-maker.

In the studies we consider, we will endeavor to identify some of the roles of affect in decision-making in terms of the processes and neural mechanisms modulated by affect, and when possible, the specific ways affect contributes to the assessment of value. In domains other than decision-making, as the interactions between emotions and more classically "cognitive" processes have been investigated, a consistent pattern has emerged in which the role of emotion is one of modulation—that is, changes in emotions are linked to changes in specific processes that define those domains. For example, emotions can act in perception to sharpen or broaden attention (Phelps et al. 2006), or in memory they can enhance the subjective confidence associated with a memory (Poldrack et al. 2008) or the consolidation of the memory itself (LaBar and Cabeza 2006). As we will see, such a modulatory perspective makes sense in the context of decision-making as well (Phelps et al. 2014).

We begin by discussing "assessed emotion," a category of research largely characterized by the measurement of components of discrete emotional responses during otherwise unmanipulated decision-making tasks.

Assessed emotion

Three main types of paradigms have dominated the literature examining the links between discrete emotional responses and value-based decision-making. The first set of paradigms has focused on gambling, in the casino sense, by simulating slot machines, also known as electronic gambling machines (EGMs). Understandably, studies in this category have largely been concerned with the clinical implications of emotion's role in gambling by examining the factors that drive continued gambling despite the relative rareness of reinforcing wins. The second dominant paradigm has examined emotions in the context of what might be termed "risky decision-making." These tasks, many of which borrow from behavioral economics, generally present participants with multiple options characterized by potential gains or losses and their associated probabilities of occurrence. In contrast to the focus of EGM studies, studies of risky decision-making instead examine processes or variables related to the choice at hand (for example, loss aversion, risk, volatility, etc.), with the aim of understanding the basic motivations that drive choices under risk. Finally, the third paradigm type considers decisions in social contexts. In these studies, participants generally play simplified, highly stylized monetary games that are designed to isolate various aspects of interpersonal interactions, such as punishment, social loss, or trust. We will consider each of these dominant approaches in turn.

In neuroscience, a large and growing literature has highlighted the roles of the insula and the ventromedial prefrontal or orbitofrontal cortex in representing value, and the striatum as integrating value with action (see Bartra et al. 2013 for a review). As we will see later in this chapter, activity in these regions has been found to scale with components of emotions as well, including self-reported subjective feelings (like the desire to play a game), as well as discrete arousal responses like the skin conductance response (an increase in the electrical conductivity of the skin over several seconds driven by activity in the "fight or flight" sympathetic nervous system).

Gambling

The paradigms researching gambling behavior have used real slot machines or EGMs (Wilkes et al. 2009; Wilkes et al. 2010) or have aimed to replicate the experience of EGMs in a simpler structure (e.g., Clark et al. 2009). In a typical simulated version of these games, participants are presented with two "wheels," each with six distinct objects. Participants select one object on the left wheel, after which the right wheel spins. If the two wheels line up, participants win some amount of money (a "win"). If the wheels are one object away from lining up (a "near-miss") or more (a "full-miss"), participants do not win anything. The decision to persevere in this kind of game is of strong clinical relevance, as problem gambling is associated with clinically significant disorders that incur very real societal costs (Potenza 2006).

Studies combining EGM tasks with the measurement of emotions have found a pattern of results consistent with a role for emotional responses in reinforcing game play. There are two sources of evidence for this—discrete arousal responses, and the self-reported desire to continue playing. One of the most common measurements of arousal is the transient increase in the conductivity of the skin as the sympathetic ("fight or flight") nervous system increases sweat gland output. This brief increase in conductance is called the skin conductance response, or SCR. In EGM-like tasks, arousal responses appear focused on the positive aspects of gameplay: participants experience elevated SCRs at the time of outcome when they win, but not when they lose or miss (Lole et al. 2011; Wilkes et al. 2009; Wilkes et al. 2010) (though see Studer and Clark 2011). There may also be changes in measures like heart rate (Wilkes et al. 2009), but the evidence on this point is more mixed (Wilkes et al. 2010), and may reflect a combination of anticipation and outcomes (Lole et al. 2011). These findings suggest that when the structure of the task makes non-wins or losses less salient, responses to wins may instead dominate behavior, and could thus drive choices to continue to play.

Though objectively there are only wins and misses in EGM games, a number of studies have made a convincing case that "near-misses" also play a critical role in encouraging gambling by altering participants' reported subjective feelings. Studies that separated near-misses from full-misses and wins found that relative to wins (which increased desire to play and were rated as pleasurable), full-misses decreased desire to play and were unpleasant. However, while near-misses felt even more unpleasant than full-misses, they paradoxically increased the desire to play the game (Clark et al. 2009; Clark et al. 2012; Clark et al. 2014). Near-misses have also been found to elicit SCRs, which, while less than those to wins, are greater than those to full-misses, which result in no response at all (Clark et al. 2012). Importantly, these physiological responses to, and desire to continue playing after, near-misses appear to arise only in contexts in which participants are able to exert control—that is, when they physically participate in play (Clark et al. 2009; Clark et al. 2012; Clark et al. 2014), and may be related to an increased perceived chance of winning resulting from active choice (Clark et al. 2009; Clark et al. 2012; Clark et al. 2014; see also Langer 1975).

In probing the underlying neural mechanisms that drive EGM play and the near-miss effects, studies using functional magnetic resonance imaging (fMRI; Clark et al. 2009) and patients with focal brain lesions performing these tasks (Clark et al. 2014) have converged to suggest that the underlying neural mechanisms may include the striatum and the insula in mediating the effect of near-misses on EGM behavior. The insula's role, in particular, accords with previous research tying insula addiction to cravings in addition (Naqvi and Bechara 2010), physiological arousal responses (Critchley et al. 2000), and the sensation of internal bodily states, or "interoception" (Craig 2009; Critchley et al. 2004; Khalsa et al. 2009). The insula exhibits a salience-like signal in response to value, increasing for both greater gains and losses (Bartra et al. 2013), which may have the effect in gambling behavior of increasing the salience of positive or near-positive events, as these dominate behavior generally. However, as only a couple of studies have examined the neural correlates of EGM behavior, the precise functional roles of the insula and the striatum in mediating the responses to near-miss outcomes are as yet unclear. Future studies will hopefully deconstruct some of the processes that drive the desire to play and begin to ascribe those processes to specific underlying neural mechanisms.

Finally, there is some empirical evidence that gambling behavior in such experimental contexts is related to real-world pathology. First, measurements of insula activity during near-miss outcomes in the simulated EGM were found to correlate with a measure of participants' errant cognitions surrounding gambles (e.g., whether they felt that their active participation in a game of chance increased the probability of winning) (Clark et al. 2009; though unilateral lesions to the insula did not significantly reduce such explicit cognitions: Clark et al. 2014), suggesting that the insula may contribute to the irrational cognitions surrounding gambling behavior through altered subjective perception of probabilities and outcomes. Second, and more generally, it's possible that long-term emotional adaptation may dampen the power of emotions in problem gamblers. In a study with both recreational and problem gamblers, problem gamblers were found to exhibit blunted stress responses (as measured by the hormone cortisol) to arousing videos (one of which featured gambling, and the other of which featured rollercoasters), implying a general reduction in intensity of responses to arousing events (Paris et al. 2009). If emotional responses to discrete events encourage gambling by signaling positive outcomes (or proximity to them), blunted responses to those events may have an additive effect, encouraging more gambling in an effort to attain similar levels of physiological responses. However, the extant research on this topic is correlational in nature, making it impossible to disentangle at this time whether such decreased responses result from, or cause, pathological levels of gambling.

The role of emotion in casino-like gambling scenarios seems best characterized by a focus on positive events, mediated by insula (and maybe striatal) activity. Critically, this focus extends to objectively negative "near-miss" events that are subjectively perceived as "close" to positive events. These near-miss events may have a particularly central role in gambling behavior, as their occurrence is related to an increased desire to continue playing, relative to full-misses. Any theory of gambling behavior will benefit from incorporating this focus of emotional arousal on positive and near-positive events in explaining why people gamble with the intensity they do, and how to change it.

Risky decision-making

Despite a similar underlying mathematical structure and focus on monetary outcomes, a category of paradigms that we will call "risky decision-making" has found very different roles for emotion in contributing to value and shaping choices. The experimental paradigms in this category generally involve selections amongst multiple options with clearly defined gains and/or losses that occur with known or learned probabilities. This emphasis on value and probability is paired with meaningful choices between options with different objective attributes, and differs from EGM studies' emphasis on subjective framing effects (like near-misses), and lack of true multiple options to evaluate and decide between (e.g., different objects on a slot machine wheel do not have objectively different probabilities of success if selected). Having established that the influence of emotion in EGM tasks tends to be on positive events and continued play, we now examine how that pattern changes in "risky choice" scenarios.

One of the earliest studies to measure emotional responses during decision-making measured skin conductance responses during the classic Iowa Gambling Task (IGT; Bechara et al. 1997). Researchers found that anticipatory skin conductance responses predicted subsequent avoidance of decision options that would ultimately yield a net loss if repeatedly selected, suggesting that emotional responses served as warnings of possible negative consequences in the game. Patients with amygdala and ventromedial prefrontal cortex (VMPFC) damage failed to generate anticipatory SCRs and subsequently anticipate and avoid net negative decision options (Bechara et al. 1999), suggesting that both brain regions were necessary to integrate avoidance signals with action. More recently, other studies have used similar games and generally confirmed that differentially greater arousal to "bad" options predicts the subsequent avoidance of those options (Dunn et al. 2010). Though numerous critiques have exposed issues with the IGT (Fellows and Farah 2005; Maia and McClelland 2004) and the related somatic marker hypothesis (LeDoux and Gorman 2001), Bechara et al. (1997) remain one of the first to have objectively measured a component of emotions, the arousal response, and related it to decision-making. Unfortunately, the IGT does not allow the quantitative decomposition of decision behavior into separate processes, with the consequence that any inferences about arousal's role are limited by the multiple confounded valuation and decision processes at work. If the measure of decision behavior is only the number of risky options selected (as has been the case in many decision-making studies), then it naturally follows that anything that changes the number of risky selections (including risk, ambiguity, learning, gain–loss weighting, probability weighting, or consistency across choices, depending on the task) is unavoidably confounded, as in the IGT. The solution to this problem is a quantitative, mathematical model of the processes driving choices, combined with a decision task that allows the separation of the model's components.

Such quantitative approaches to decision-making have recently enabled precise analysis of the relationship between emotional responses and value. One set of studies using such quantitative analysis has focused on the phenomenon of loss aversion (Sokol-Hessner et al. 2009; Sokol-Hessner et al. 2013; Sokol-Hessner et al. 2015a; Sokol-Hessneret et al. 2015b), defined as an overweighting of potential losses relative to gains of equivalent size. In these experiments, participants choose between risky gambles and guaranteed alternatives. For example, in a choice between a gamble with an equal chance of receiving +\$9 or –\$6, and an alternative of \$0 (neither winning nor losing), consistently rejecting the gamble in favor of \$0 would suggest that loss dollars were weighted at least 1.5 times as much as gain dollars. That relative weighting is captured in the multiplicative parameter λ, the loss aversion coefficient (e.g., in this example, λ would be ≥ 1.5 so that -\$6 $\times$ λ would be greater in absolute magnitude than +\$9). By examining choices made over many similar options with slightly different amounts in the gamble and guaranteed alternative, it's possible to estimate each individual's unique λ. By additionally including choices between options that only contained gains (e.g., a large, risky gain versus a smaller certain gain), risk attitudes (a dislike of chance relative to certainty) can be separated from loss aversion, as risk is involved in both the former and latter kinds of choices, but loss aversion only affects the former. Finally, risk and loss aversion could be separated from noisiness in the decision process (how consistent participants are across choices) by asking participants to make many similar choices. Using this carefully constructed choice set and a model of the decision process, these studies were able to separate these easily and commonly confounded processes.

The first study to use the above task and model measured the arousal component of emotions by recording SCRs as participants won or lost money in the task (Sokol-Hessner et al. 2009). Examining SCRs to wins and losses, the authors found that the skin conductance response per dollar lost was greater than that per dollar won, and that this relative over-arousal to losses correlated with each individuals' weighting of potential losses relative to gains in their choices, as quantified by λ. Importantly, this correlation was selective—SCRs to gains and losses did not correlate with risk attitudes or choice consistency.

Neuroimaging studies of this task and a slightly different, but similar task, have found that activity in the striatum reliably reflects the subjective expected value of the gamble under consideration (Sokol-Hessner et al. 2013; Tom et al. 2007), consistent with a role of the striatum in integrating value with action. However, fMRI of the outcome period found that amygdala activity to losses relative to gains correlated with individuals' behavioral loss aversion (Sokol-Hessner et al. 2013), just as SCRs to losses relative to gains correlated with loss aversion (Sokol-Hessner et al. 2009). A case study in which patients with lesions to the amygdala performed a similar gambling task also found less loss aversion in those patients, suggesting the necessity of the amygdala to loss aversion (De Martino et al. 2010). Since the amygdala is known to mediate arousal responses in other domains (Garavan et al. 2001; Glascher and Adolphs 2003; Williams et al. 2001), and contribute to the computation of value in other regions (Rudebeck et al. 2013), these findings thus suggest the working hypothesis that amygdala-mediated arousal responses at outcome may drive striatally mediated decisions to avoid losses. This hypothesized amygdala–striatal avoidance circuit directly parallels that observed elsewhere, in which the amygdala has been found to mediate avoidance actions via its projections to the striatum (LeDoux and Gorman 2001), and modulate memory by altering activity in the striatum and hippocampus (McGaugh

2004). In the latter case, the amygdala's modulatory effects were found to rely critically on noradrenaline, such that blocking noradrenergic receptors had the effect of preventing the modulation of downstream memory systems like the striatum. To test whether a noradrenergic system also supported the relationship between the amygdala and loss aversion, Sokol-Hessner et al. (2015a) administered the noradrenergic receptor antagonist propranolol in a double-blind, within-subjects design and found that it selectively reduced loss aversion without affecting risk aversion or choice consistency. This suggests that a domain-general modulatory system exists in which amygdala-mediated arousal responses drive avoidance actions via noradrenergic projections to the striatum.

Note that this relationship between arousal and decision-making in mediating avoidance-related behavior in risky decision-making contrasts with the relationship between arousal and decision-making identified in studies using EGMs. In those studies, arousal-related responses are related to *increased* engagement, and so we should expect some divergence in their underlying neural basis (e.g., the effects of emotion may be mediated by interactions between the insula and the striatum).

To the extent to which laboratory studies benefit from being tightly controlled and designed, they are also distanced from the ecological validity associated with "real life" choices. Field studies attempt to bridge this gap. One excellent example was a study in which various physiological measurements were recorded from professional securities traders during live trading sessions (Lo and Repin 2002). The authors recorded skin conductance, cardiovascular variables, respiration, and body temperature during trader's decisions in the course of real, unplanned market fluctuations. The authors found greater cardiovascular responses and more SCRs both in response to discrete market events and during periods of heightened market volatility. While the complexity of market events leaves it unclear what precise decision-related information these physiological variables represented, this study strongly argues that emotion doesn't just play a role in naive participants' decision-making in laboratory tasks, but in the real world, with experienced decision-makers in complex contexts.

Social interactions

The emphasis of emotional responses on negative events within the context of risky decisions (and hence avoidance-related behaviors like loss aversion) appears to extend to the social domain, in which studies have found that emotional responses generally guide actions like rejection or punishment.

An early neuroimaging study scanned people using fMRI to identify regions of the brain involved in the "Ultimatum Game" (U.G.). In the U.G., "proposers" are endowed with a sum of money. They can then split that money between themselves and a "responder" who is given veto power over the split. If the responder dislikes the split and chooses to exercise their veto, neither the proposer nor the responder receives any money. Otherwise, the money is apportioned as proposed. The authors scanned responders, and found differentially greater activity in the insula, among other regions, to unfair versus fair offers—but only when that offer was made by a human proposer. This unique pattern suggests that insula activity indexes the subjective unfairness of the offer, and not just its monetary value. In line with this interpretation, greater activity in the anterior insula also correlated with the probability of offer rejection. This general pattern of insula activity has since been replicated in multiple studies (e.g., Grecucci et al. 2012; Kirk et al. 2011), and may be related to the insula's aforementioned putative role in interoception (Craig 2009; Critchley, et al. 2004; Khalsa et al. 2009) and value salience (Bartra et al. 2013).

One of the limitations of neuroimaging in the study of affect is that a change in brain activity cannot be taken as evidence of affect due to the problem of reverse inference (Poldrack 2011). In order to identify whether affect is present, affect must be measured. One of the earliest studies to do so in social interactive games used the "Ultimatum Game" (van 'T Wout et al. 2006). The authors found that SCRs were greater to unfair versus fair offers, but only if the opponent was human—just as in previous imaging findings (Sanfey et al. 2003). Responses to offers from a computer were not affected by the fairness of the offer. Critically, these arousal responses were also related to behavior: the magnitude of the differential SCR to unfair vs. fair offers was positively correlated with rejection behavior, a pattern reminiscent of avoidance behaviors in the risky choice domain (Bechara et al. 1997; Dunn et al. 2010; Sokol-Hessner et al. 2009). That there was no differential arousal when the U.G. proposer was a computer suggests that some aspects of value, and the emotional responses related to it, can be selectively and powerfully motivated by social contexts.

Social interactions are complex, not only in the structure of the interaction, but in the people interacting. While Sanfey et al. (2003) and van 'T Wout et al. (2006) examined how emotional responses to unfair offers shaped decisions, other research has focused on how our perception of others can shape the decisions we make about them (Stanley et al. 2011). In this study, individuals played a "trust game." In the classic trust game (T.G.), Player A is endowed with money and must decide how much of that money to send to Player B. Whatever money is sent to B is quadrupled in value. Player B then decides how much of that increased amount to send back to A, after which the game ends. Because the money sent from A to B increases so much in value, A has an incentive to send that money to B, so long as she trusts B to share it back. Participants in Stanley et al. (2011) played a series of one-shot games as Player A. On each trial they were matched with a different Player B, of whom they were shown a facial photo. Crucially, on the trials of interest, Player Bs were either black or white. After the T.G., participants then completed a test measuring their implicit associations with black and white races called the Implicit Association Test (IAT). In this IAT, participants faced a stream of words and faces, and had to categorize words as pleasant or unpleasant, and faces as white or black—but participants had only two buttons to do so. In one portion of the IAT, one button was used to indicate pleasant words and white faces, while the other button was used for unpleasant words and black faces; in the other portion of the IAT, one button was used for pleasant/black and one button for unpleasant/white. Empirically, people tend to sort words and faces faster and with fewer errors in the first mapping (white/pleasant and black/unpleasant) compared to the second (black/pleasant and white/unpleasant). The extent of this difference quantifies the bias in the implicit associations individuals make with these racial groups. In

Stanley et al. (2011), the authors asked whether this affective variable measuring implicit attitudes was related to how much participants chose to trust their partners in the T.G., and found a strong correlation—the more participants had an anti-black/pro-white bias, the less money they shared with black partners compared to white partners. Crucially, the authors also assessed participants' explicit beliefs and associations with both black and white racial groups (i.e., those they explicitly reported), and even when taking those beliefs into account, the relationship between the IAT and trusting behavior held. When this task was performed during fMRI, amygdala activity was found to scale with the amount of money offered, more strongly for black partners than white partners, while activity in the striatum reflected the racial difference in decisions to trust the partner (Stanley et al. 2012). This suggested a model in which the amygdala coded the racial identity of the partner while the striatum represented and integrated action with overall value, in a direct parallel to the amygdala–striatal modulatory circuit discussed above (LeDoux and Gorman, 2001; McGaugh 2004; Sokol-Hessner et al. 2013a). Clearly, when understanding value and emotion in social contexts, we must take into account not only what is happening (e.g., fairness), but who is interacting, and how they perceive one another both explicitly and implicitly. The valenced associations we hold with those individuals and with their social groups (racial group, but also age, gender, etc.) can dramatically shape how we perceive value, and how we behave toward those individuals.

Conclusion

The studies in this section have all attempted to measure some aspect of our affective experience and then connect those measures to a decision-making process or phenomenon. While studies of casino-like gambling find that emotional responses to positive events dominate, and that those responses may drive more gambling, studies of risky decision-making and interpersonal interactions both find a clear role for discrete emotions in signaling negative events and driving behaviors broadly associated with avoidance or rejection. The contrast of the findings in these areas highlights the need for more study, and the importance of contextual factors in shaping when and how emotions contribute to decision-making.

Differences aside, one recurrent theme has been the emotional response as a signal used by the decision-maker. This conceptualization suggests that the ability to clearly and accurately perceive the signal may also be a variable of interest. Perceiving one's own internal bodily state is referred to as "interoception." A number of studies have recently examined interoception and related it to decision-making. Although they do not measure affective variables *during* the decision process, studies that show correlations between interoception and decision behavior provide indirect evidence for a role for emotion. Evidence for such a relationship has emerged relating interoception to decision performance in tasks similar to the Iowa Gambling Task (Dunn et al. 2010; Werner et al. 2009), to loss aversion in risky monetary decision-making (Sokol-Hessner et al. 2015b), and to rejection behavior in the ultimatum game (Dunn et al. 2012). In some cases, better interoception has been found to mediate the relationship between arousal responses and behavior such that the relationship only exists for good interoceptors (Dunn et al. 2010; Dunn et al. 2012), while in other cases, interoception is a simple linear predictor of behavior (Sokol-Hessner et al. 2015b; Werner et al. 2009). Understanding the extent to which affective variables are not only generated but perceived is clearly going to be important in future studies of the roles of emotion in decision-making.

Introducing and changing affect

Though measuring emotional responses during unperturbed decision-making is an effective way of identifying correlations between affect and estimates of value, an alternative option is to introduce or alter affective states, stimuli, or responses, and examine how choices change. Studies taking this approach fall into three main categories. In the first, manipulations are used to create incidental affective states with long temporal timescales, on the order of minutes to tens of minutes—like sad or angry moods or stress responses. These studies often feature between-subjects designs using an induction of some kind followed by a decision task. The second category of manipulation introduces emotional primes, like angry or happy faces, that then affect other, nominally unrelated value- and decision-related processes driving the choices at hand. Both of these first two categories involve experimenter-introduced incidental affective variables. In contrast, the third and final type of manipulation leverages the central role cognitive appraisals play in affect (Ochsner and Gross 2008; Scherer 2005) to change existing affective responses, asking participants to use cognitive strategies to endogenously alter their emotional responses, and thus change their choices.

Mood

Moods are defined as diffuse affective states that typically occur on a scale of tens of minutes, have no precise focus (e.g., aren't necessarily in response to an event), and are relatively low in intensity despite their long duration (Scherer 2005). One of the most straightforward ways to induce such a state in the laboratory is to view film clips featuring emotional content. In one of the first studies to demonstrate the power of mood, participants watched film clips that led to self-reported feelings of sadness or of disgust, or a neutral clip (Lerner et al. 2004). Afterwards, participants were either given a set of highlighters and asked how much money they would require to sell them (their selling price), or asked to choose between highlighters and money (their "choosing" price). When these objectively identical questions are posed this way, the classic finding, replicated in the neutral condition, is that the selling price is higher than the choosing price (Kahneman et al. 1991). The induced moods, however, led to different price patterns. When sad, the endowment effect was reversed, leading to higher choosing prices than selling prices. The authors interpreted this as a consequence of a mood-related desire (called an "action tendency") to change participants' circumstances that selectively lowered the value of endowed goods, thereby promoting the acquisition of new things. Disgust, on the other hand, reduced both choosing and selling prices to equally low levels, a finding attributed to a global desire to expel or get rid of things that reduced the value of all objects, whether owned or not. This study was an early, but powerful example of how moods could dramatically change how participants valued everyday objects, and how much that valuation depended on the framing of the question itself.

A similar induction technique was used in a study of the Ultimatum Game (described earlier) to examine how such moods (and their attendant subjective feelings and action tendencies) related to interpersonal interactions (Harlé and Sanfey 2007). In this study, participants viewed clips that were neutral or that induced feelings of sadness or of amusement, after which they played the U.G. as the responder, deciding whether to accept the proposer's monetary split, or veto the offer and prevent anyone from receiving any money. While the amusement film clip did not change choice behavior compared to the neutral clip, participants accepted fewer unfair offers the sadder they felt in response to the sad clip. This increased rejection was interpreted as a negative attentional focus brought on by the sad mood: rather than focusing on the money they would receive if they accepted even an unfair offer, the majority of their attention was commanded by the offer's unfairness. A follow-up neuroimaging study found that the relationship between induced sadness and increased rejection behavior was statistically mediated by increases in anterior insula activity (Harlé et al. 2012), consistent with earlier work placing the insula at the center of the subjective perception of unfairness in interpersonal interactions (Sanfey et al. 2003). Notably, a separate, more recent study also examined U.G. rejection behavior in the contexts of moods, though in this case, neutral, sad, and disgust moods were induced with sequences of images. The authors found that the induced sad mood had no effect on rejection behavior, but disgust led to significantly more rejections (Moretti and di Pellegrino 2010), raising the possibility that even within a given type of mood, the exact induction approach may be a critical variable. In the context of Lerner et al. (2004), these studies generally highlight the importance of specifying the kind of decision at hand and the exact affective manipulation used when considering how something like a mood can change the actions or decisions participants make. While simple action tendencies to "change" or "expel" dominated behavior during straightforward valuation, the ability of a mood to shift attentional focus became more important in a complex, multi-attribute interaction like the U.G..

Finally, the negative affective states of fear and anger have been the focus of several studies examining risk-taking. One of the reasons for this focus is that while fear and anger share a negative valence, they differ in their consequences for action: the former emphasizes avoidance and withdrawal, and the latter, approach and engagement. Thus, if the effect of these mood states on behaviors like decision-making is due to changes in appraisals and not simple valence-contamination, then fear and anger should have different consequences for choices. In an early study, this kind of difference was indeed found (Lerner and Keltner 2001). Examining individuals' natural dispositions toward fear and anger showed that while high-fear individuals were risk averse, high-anger individuals were risk seeking. Cementing the centrality of appraisals in risk behavior, the pattern of responses for individuals disposed to anger held for those disposed to happiness (which results in similar approach and engagement appraisals). Beyond dispositions, experimental inductions using writing prompts to encourage individuals to re-experience previous fear- or anger-inducing events led to identical patterns in risk perception. Finally, statistical mediation confirmed that the differential effects of anger and fear on the perception of decision options was due to the cognitive appraisals those affective states generated. Clearly, mood has subtle effects—the valence of subjective feelings was not predictive of behavior, but one of the components of the mood state, appraisals, was closely related to the processing of risky options. More recent work has followed up on the finding linking anger to risk-taking by examining how the context of the task might make appraisals versus subjective feelings more salient (Baumann and DeSteno 2012). The study found that manipulations that emphasized appraisals over feelings confirmed the prior findings of anger leading to more risk-taking, but when the task context was shifted to emphasize feelings over appraisals, risk-taking under anger actually decreased.

The above studies provide strong evidence that when considering moods, we must understand the components of that mood (e.g., how it changes our appraisals vs. how it makes us feel), the decision at hand, and the current context, in order to predict how the mood will affect the decisions we make. Much more work remains to be done in understanding the components of moods and their relationship to decision processes, but it is already clear just how important it is to consider these dimensions.

Stress

In contrast to moods, much more is known about stress as a biological process involving different neural and hormonal systems at varying time scales. Stress can be defined as the body's response to real or implied threats induced by novel, unpredictable, or uncontrollable situations (Lupien et al. 2007). The activity of two different systems together comprises the stress response. One system consists of sympathetic nervous system responses that occur on a scale of seconds to minutes and result in increased bodily arousal and hormones like adrenaline surging through the bloodstream. The other system consists of a hormonal cascade in which each hormone triggers the release of the next, leading to a physiological response on a scale of minutes to tens of minutes. Though there is evidence that both systems are required for stress to alter behavior (Roozendaal et al. 2006; Schwabe et al. 2010), the slower-moving hormone cascade most strongly differentiates the stress response from shorter-term arousal responses. In that it involves the hypothalamus, pituitary, and adrenal glands, the system underlying the hormonal cascade is thus termed the hypothalamic–pituitary–adrenal (HPA) axis of the stress response. In practice, studies quantifying the effect of stress generally assay one of the final hormones produced by the HPA axis, cortisol. Cortisol is a glucocorticoid that can be easily and non-invasively measured using a cotton swab to collect saliva, and because of its position near the end of the hormone cascade, only peaks about 20–30 minutes after an acute stressor. Because of this delay, studies examining the effect of the HPA axis response on behavior generally administer their task during this period of peak cortisol response.

The consequences of stress in the brain are two-fold: stress impairs prefrontal cortical (PFC) regions that support executive control and top-down processing, while simultaneously potentiating reactivity in subcortical regions like the amygdala, driving bottom-up associations and attentional saliency (Arnsten 2009). In decision-making, it is thus unsurprising that the single most consistent effect of stress is a reduced reliance on structured, often intentional, cognitively complex decision mechanisms ("goal-directed" processes), and increased influence of simple action-outcome behaviors (habits or heuristics). One seminal study in rats showed that chronic stress led rats to become insensitive to changes in value (Dias-Ferreira et al. 2009). The rats were initially trained to press levers for food, and when fed to satiety on one of the food items, unstressed rats subsequently stopped pressing the specific lever for that food. In contrast, chronically stressed rats continued to press equally on all levers, showing no specific reduction in pressing related to their satiety for one of the foods. This suggests that while unstressed rats could use decision systems that linked actions with objects and objects with value, the stressed rats were disproportionately relying on simple habit systems that connected actions directly to value—and so couldn't update the value of an action when an outcome changed (e.g., when the food that action produced was no longer valuable). In other words, the effect of chronic stress on decision-making was not directly on value, in this case, but on which mechanisms were being used to act in the service of value. The authors found that stress also led to changes in the striatum (both hypertrophy and hypotrophy), a region known to link actions with values (Rangel et al. 2008) and to process surprising outcomes (Maia and McClelland 2004), suggesting that the effect of chronic stress on which system was being used to guide action might be mediated by morphological changes in the striatum.

Though using acute stress manipulations instead of chronic stress, a similar study done in humans found much the same pattern: acute stress led to insensitivity to changes in action-associated value (Schwabe et al. 2011). Additionally, this study found that propranolol, a beta-adrenergic receptor antagonist that blunts noradrenergic function, restored normal, goal-directed behavior (that is, people who took propranolol prior to stress were normally sensitive to devaluation). Propranolol's protective effect is consistent with evidence that interactions between glucocorticoid and noradrenergic systems produce the effects of stress, perhaps through glucocorticoids enhancing noradrenergic function (e.g., Roozendaal et al. 2006; Schwabe et al. 2010). More research, however, is necessary to fully understand how these two branches of the stress response interact in humans during decision-making, and to what extent the effects of stress rely on one or the other branch.

One of the limitations of Schwabe et al. (2011) was that while the dominance of habit systems under stress is the most likely explanation for the behavior, the influence of habits on behavior were not computationally dissociated or quantified relative to more goal-directed influence. To address this gap, a recent study asked participants to perform a complex task involving two stages of choices (Otto et al. 2013), designed to separately identify the contributions of two different learning mechanisms to behavior. The first mechanism, called "model-based" learning, entails building a model of the two-stage structure of the task linking actions to objects to value and relies upon the PFC (Balleine and O'Doherty 2010). The second simply involves reinforcing actions that ultimately lead to reward (linking action directly to value, such "model-free" learning is conceptually similar to habits), and is known to rely upon the striatum (Montague et al. 1996). While both mechanisms contribute to behavior under normal circumstances, the authors found that acute stress impaired the PFC-dependent model-based mechanism and did not affect the model-free mechanism. In other words, stress didn't alter habit-like model-free learning, but instead attenuated other, competing mechanisms, allowing model-free learning to dominate how participants learned about value, and thus the choices they made. Finally, the authors found that HPA axis activity (as quantified by cortisol) predicted the decrease in model-based learning, subject to the constraint that working memory capacity had a protective effect—acute stress attenuated model-based learning less for participants with high working memory capacity relative to those with lower capacity. The effect of stress was very selective, though not uniform across people.

Beyond habits and learning, the effect of stress on value and decision-making is less clear, though it may play a role in a variety of contexts. Acute stress has been shown to eliminate the success of PFC-reliant, appraisal-based emotion regulation techniques (Raio et al. 2013); it may make people less sensitive to rewards (Berghorst et al. 2013; Bogdan and Pizzagalli 2006) or punishments (Petzold et al. 2010); and stress may lead to greater impulsivity in intertemporal choices (Kimura et al. 2013), depending on contextual factors like trait perceived stress or future/present orientation (Lempert et al. 2012). However, the effects of stress in other realms of decision-making are as yet unclear. In social contexts, acute stress has been found to increase generosity while not affecting punishment behavior (von Dawans et al. 2012), while others have found stress reduces both generosity and punishment (Vinkers et al. 2013). Studies of risky decision-making have generally focused on risk aversion but their findings have been similarly inconclusive, showing that acute stress increases (Cingl and Cahlikova 2013; Porcelli and Delgado 2009), decreases (Pabst et al. 2013; Preston et al. 2007; Starcke et al. 2008), or does not affect (Delaney et al. 2014; von Dawans et al. 2012) risk aversion. Of note is that the above-mentioned research on risk attitudes has relied on coarse behavioral measures of decision-making (e.g., probability of gambling) that do not separate the processes that contribute to decisions under risk, including risk attitudes, loss aversion, and choice consistency. One recent study that did use modeling to estimate risk attitudes directly administered cortisol and found no effect of an acute administration (Kandasamy et al. 2014). This same study also administered cortisol over multiple days to a separate group of participants, and found that this "tonic" administration of cortisol led to increased risk aversion. Of course, cortisol is only one piece of the complex, multi-system neurohormonal responses that occur during stress. This may be why, for example, another recent study examining endogenous cortisol levels on a scale of months found that increased cortisol did not have any relationship to risk aversion, but instead was correlated with reduced loss aversion (Chumbley et al. 2014). These studies' different timescales (a week versus two months) and assessments or manipulations of stress (exogenously administered bursts of cortisol; quantification of endogenous stress responses via basal cortisol) may ultimately be the key to reconciling their findings.

The single clearest effect of stress discussed above is its reduction of the contribution of prefrontal cortex-dependent intentional, goal-directed, and working-memory-based computations to our estimates of value and our behavior. Though our relatively deep understanding of the biological effects of stress is a tremendous foundation from which to start in examining how it shapes decision-making, we clearly have more work to do to understand the timescales and components of stress and its effects. Stress can be acute, with responses occurring on a scale of tens of minutes, but as some of the studies we discussed have found, stress on a scale of days, weeks, or months (let alone years) may have important and divergent effects on decision-making. Timescale aside, stress is also a complex phenomenon, comprising multiple systems each with multiple components. For example, while cortisol is used to quantify endogenous stress responses as a marker of HPA axis activity, pharmacologically administering cortisol in isolation from the rest of the stress response may lead to different effects. In addition to appreciating the subtleties of stress, unraveling the effects of stress on risky monetary decision-making is going to require a high level of specificity and sophistication in analyzing the processes that compute value and use it to make decisions. Future studies using models of these processes will likely have the greatest success in identifying when and how stress changes value.

Emotional primes

Turning to a different component of the affective experience, expression, yields studies on how the perception of facial expressions can change the choices made in a variety of domains. For example, one early study presented participants with photographs of faces with different expressions just before decisions about drinks (Winkielman et al. 2005). Importantly, the faces were on the computer screen so briefly that participants did not report any awareness of their presence. Despite being perceived only at a subliminal level, the faces, which were angry, happy, or neutral, changed participants' pouring, consumption, rating, and pricing of a drink. Angry faces preceding the task resulted in less drink poured, less consumed, lower ratings, and lower dollar value given to the drink. Happy faces had the opposite effect. Because the faces were both irrelevant to the task at hand and subliminally presented, the authors concluded that participants' subtle responses to those faces contaminated affective processes contributing to their subsequent actions and judgments in the drink task.

In a study with important differences and similarities, Luo et al. (2014) asked participants to hold a fearful, happy, or neutral face in memory during an intertemporal choice task involving tradeoffs between small rewards in the present and larger rewards in the future. Each trial began with an expressive face that participants were asked to remember. Next, they chose between a smaller, sooner reward and a larger, later reward (while holding the face in memory), after which they were shown a second expressive face from the same individual and were asked if the intensity of the expression was the same as the first face. Once again, the emotional faces were irrelevant to the task at hand, but the authors found that holding happy faces in memory led to more impulsive choices relative to fearful faces, which led to more patience (Luo et al. 2014). Thus while the use of faces as an irrelevant contaminant was similar, despite differences in awareness, face emotionality, and decision task, the perception of facial emotion was able to change choice, in this case apparently contaminating the processes supporting the valuation of reward and its discounting with time. In an important caveat, other studies using either pictures or words in a similar fashion have found that the consequence of preceding an intertemporal decision with an affective stimulus can depend not only on the stimulus, but on the current affective state and the personality traits of the individual making the choices (Augustine and Larsen 2011). As with some of the research discussed earlier, while the stimulus is obviously important, these findings highlight the importance of stimulus context, including the attributes of the decision-maker themselves (Dunn et al. 2010; Sokol-Hessner et al. 2015b; Stanley et al. 2011).

One remarkably consistent factor in the studies discussed above (and others) using emotional primes is the frequent choice of social stimuli (faces) as the manipulation (Aïte et al. 2013; Luo et al. 2014; Winkielman et al. 2005). While other stimuli can certainly be used (e.g., pictures or words; Augustine and Larsen 2011), this predominance demonstrates the emotional power often found in social stimuli and serves as a reminder of the significant overlap between the social and emotional domains (Phelps and Sokol-Hessner 2012).

Cognitive regulation and strategy use

Cognitive appraisal as a component of emotion has a central role in modulating the influence of other affective components on decision-making. Recent research has shown that internally generated reinterpretive appraisals can dramatically change behavioral, physiological, and neural responses to stimuli that normally cause emotional reactions (Delgado et al. 2008; Eippert et al. 2007; Ochsner et al. 2002). In these studies, the dorsolateral prefrontal cortex (DLPFC) is generally found to increase in activity during regulation, while other regions, like the amygdala, decrease (Ochsner and Gross 2008). Because DLPFC does not have strong direct connections to regions like the amygdala, it's possible that its effects are mediated by the ventromedial (Delgado et al. 2008) or ventrolateral prefrontal cortex (Buhle et al. 2014), which do have direct subcortical projections. As noted earlier, this prefrontal dependence is one of the reasons cognitive regulation is vulnerable to stress (Raio et al. 2013). In the domain of decision-making, cognitive strategies that emphasize reinterpretation, like in classic emotion regulation paradigms, have also been shown to be effective in changing how we assess value.

One early study, portions of which we discussed earlier, examined whether such intentional cognitive strategies could change risky monetary decision-making (Sokol-Hessner et al. 2009). Participants were asked to make choices over the same set of gambles twice, allowing a within-subjects comparison of any changes in the processes underlying their decisions, including loss aversion, risk attitudes, and choice consistency. One set of choices was completed using a baseline strategy that emphasized considering each choice on its own merits, in isolation from any context. For the other set, participants were asked to consider their choices as one of many, in their greater context. When participants used this second strategy to re-appraise or contextualize their choice, they were less loss-averse. Not everything changed about their choices, though—their sensitivity to risk and their consistency across choices remained the same. This strategy also reduced participants' arousal (Sokol-Hessner et al. 2009) and amygdala hemodynamic responses (Sokol-Hessner et al. 2013) to losses, suggesting that they did, in fact, feel the weight of losses less. When using the strategy, regions of the brain, including the DLPFC and VMPFC, increased their activity, exhibiting a similar pattern as in more classic emotion-regulation studies (Ochsner and Gross 2008). Other subsequent studies using different kinds of gambles and different strategies have confirmed the power of reinterpretive strategies to alter risky monetary decision-making (Martin Braunstein et al. 2013; Martin and Delgado 2011), and even shown that habitual, every day use of cognitive strategies to regulate emotions may function as a "baseline trait" of sorts, shaping risk-taking behavior in the lab in the absence of explicit strategy instruction (Panno et al. 2013). Appraisals can alter the context within which possible gains and losses are considered and weighed. By changing the context, the resulting estimate of value is also shifted, and thus different decisions are made.

Not all decisions are exclusively about money, of course—and cognitive strategies are equally capable of changing how these other factors are interpreted; for example, altering decisions in social contexts, like the Ultimatum Game. In a follow-up to a study described earlier (van 'T Wout et al. 2006), responders were asked to reappraise the offers they received from proposers—take a more detached view of them, or imagine reasons why that offer may have been made (e.g., that the proposer was not well off and could use the money). When participants did so, rejection rates dropped, consistent with a reduction in the negative value assigned to unfair offers. Fewer rejections also had an interesting consequence down the line in a second phase of the study: after responding to offers, participants took on the role of the proposer and made their own offers. Those participants who reduced their own rejection behavior using reappraisal made more generous offers when the tables turned (van 'T Wout et al. 2010).

A subsequent fMRI study, briefly mentioned above, confirmed the basic behavioral finding of van 'T Wout et al. (2010): positive reinterpretations increased acceptance of unfair offers, while additionally showing that negative reappraisals (e.g., that the proposer was selfish and wanted all the money) could increase rejection rates (Grecucci et al. 2012). The authors also found that frontal regions increased in activity during reinterpretation, consistent with studies of the reappraisal of emotional images (Ochsner et al. 2004) and risky monetary decision-making (Sokol-Hessner et al. 2013). A similar pattern was observed in another neuroimaging study examining individual differences in U.G. rejection behavior (Kirk et al. 2011), in which individuals who accepted most unfair offers had greater DLPFC activity during those decisions, suggesting that they were spontaneously regulating their responses. These findings highlight that changing choices through changing appraisals operates very similarly to changing emotions in other, non-decision contexts: PFC regions implement regulation strategies, which can alter emotional and neural responses in other regions, and thereby change the assessment of value and the decision. Importantly, the effects of reappraisal can extend beyond the choice at hand. Especially as we consider choices in social contexts, these studies convincingly show that such reappraisals

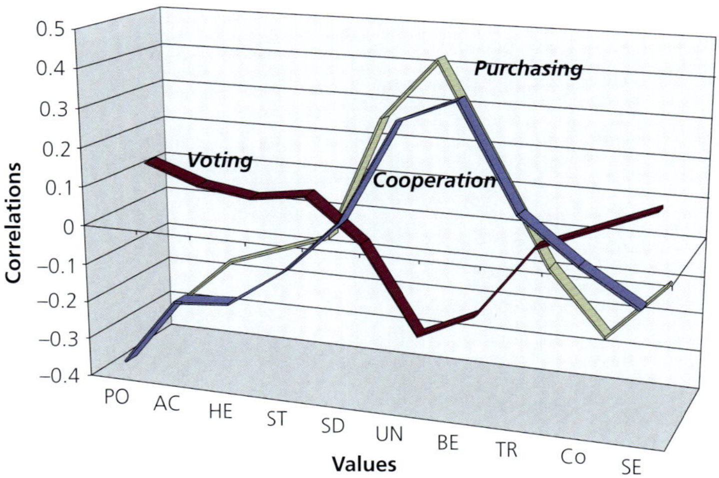

Plate 1 Correlations between value priorities and three behaviors (see Fig. 4.2.).

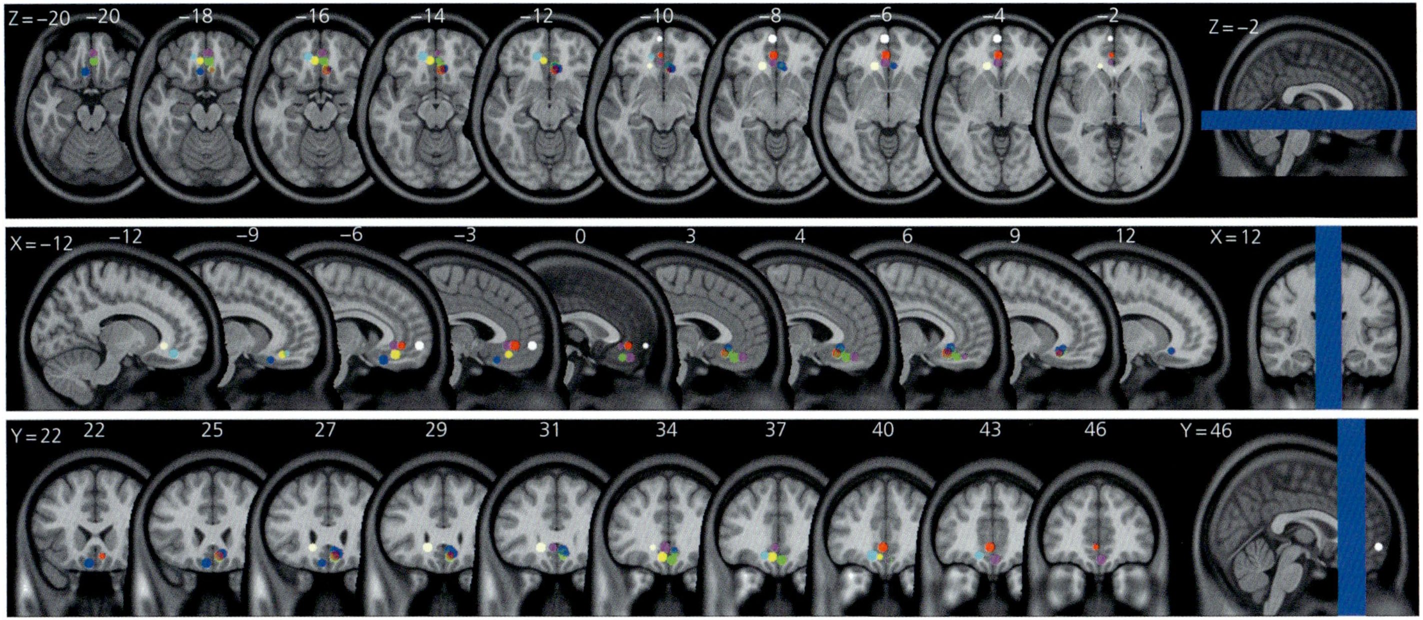

Plate 2 Peak voxels in the subregion of the vmPFC/OFC representing value-related signals from thirteen studies that used more than one reward type and/or one task as described in (Levy and Glimcher 2012). The coordinates of the peak voxels were taken from the original studies and are detailed in Levy and Glimcher (2012). Brain images are the T1 MNI-152 template. (See Fig. 5.1.)

Reprinted from *Current Opinion in Neurobiology*, 22(6), pp, 1027–1038. Levy, D. J., and Glimcher, P. W. The root of all value: a neural common currency for choice, (2012), with permission from Elsevier.

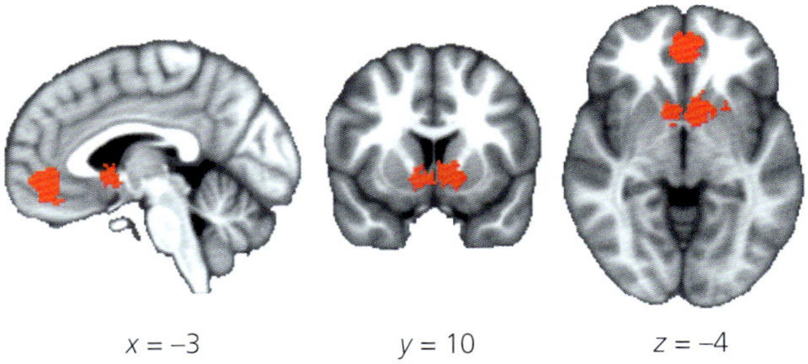

Plate 3 A five-way conjunction analysis, designed to identify brain areas that represent subjective value irrespective of reward type. The conjunction analysis was conducted on voxels that showed significantly greater density for positive than negative effects, and showed high activity for positive events at both the decision and receipt stages, as well as for both monetary and primary reward types. (See Fig. 5.2.)

Reprinted from *NeuroImage*, Volume 76, 1 August 2013, pp. 412–427, Bartra, O., McGuire, J. T., and Kable, J. W. The valuation system: a coordinate-based meta-analysis of BOLD fMRI experiments examining neural correlates of subjective value, (2013) with permission from Elsevier.

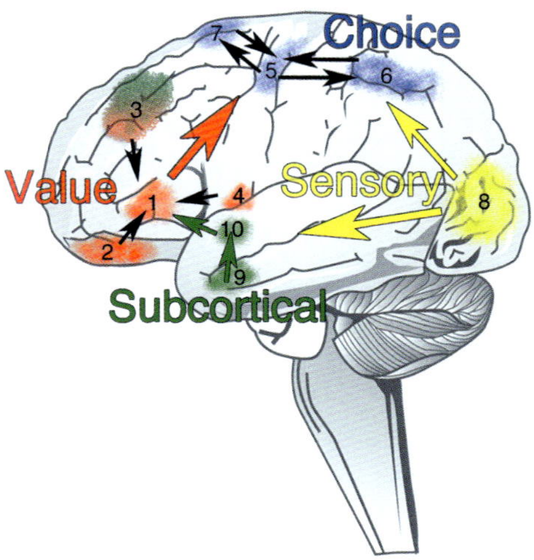

Plate 4 One possible schema for understanding the decision-making networks of the human brain. Current evidence suggests that information from cortical and subcortical structures converges toward a single common value representation before passing on to the choice-related motor control circuitry. Modulatory inputs play a critical role in establishing this final common representation with those inputs carrying signals related to arousal, internal state (satiety, thirst, hormonal levels, etc.) and emotional intensity. In this schema, sensory information from all modalities carries, among other things, the identity and location of the options. We use visual signals in this diagram to stand for information from all sensory modalities. (1) vmPFC, (2) OFC, (3) DLPFC, (4) insula, (5) primary motor cortex (M1), (6) posterior parietal cortex, (7) frontal eye fields, (8) visual cortex, (9) amygdala, (10) striatum. (See Fig. 5.3.)

Reprinted from *Current Opinion in Neurobiology*, 22(6), pp. 1027–1038. Levy, D. J., and Glimcher, P. W. The root of all value: a neural common currency for choice, (2012), with permission from Elsevier.

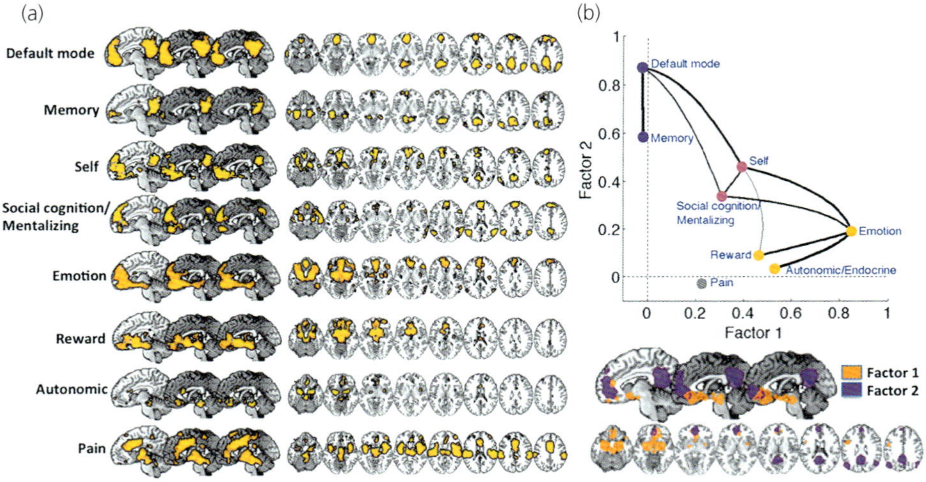

Plate 5 The authors conducted a meta-analysis across various domains ranging from the default mode to reward and pain (see panel (a) for specific domains). They then conducted a factor analysis (with two main factors) across all the functional maps identified for the individual domains. Note that there is an overlap of both factors in the vmPFC/OFC area. For full details please refer to the original manuscript (Roy et al., 2012). (See Fig. 5.4.)

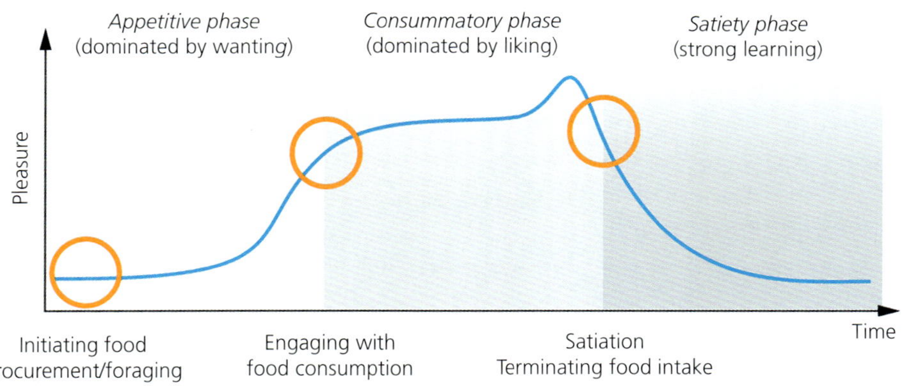

Plate 6 Pleasure cycles. Although research has mostly focused on wanting, liking, and learning aspects as separate components, it may be meaningfully to view them temporally as components of a cyclical process. The cyclical processing of rewards has classically been proposed to be associated with appetitive, consummatory, and satiety phases (Craig 1918; Sherrington 1906). Research has demonstrated that this processing is supported by multiple brain networks and processes, which crucially involves *liking* (the core reactions to hedonic impact), *wanting* (motivational processing of incentive salience), and *learning* (typically Pavlovian or instrumental associations and cognitive representations) (Berridge and Kringelbach 2011). These components wax and wane during the pleasure cycle and can co-occur at any time. Importantly, however, wanting processing tends to dominate the appetitive phase, while liking processing dominates the consummatory phase. In contrast, learning can happen throughout the cycle. (See Fig. 13.1.)

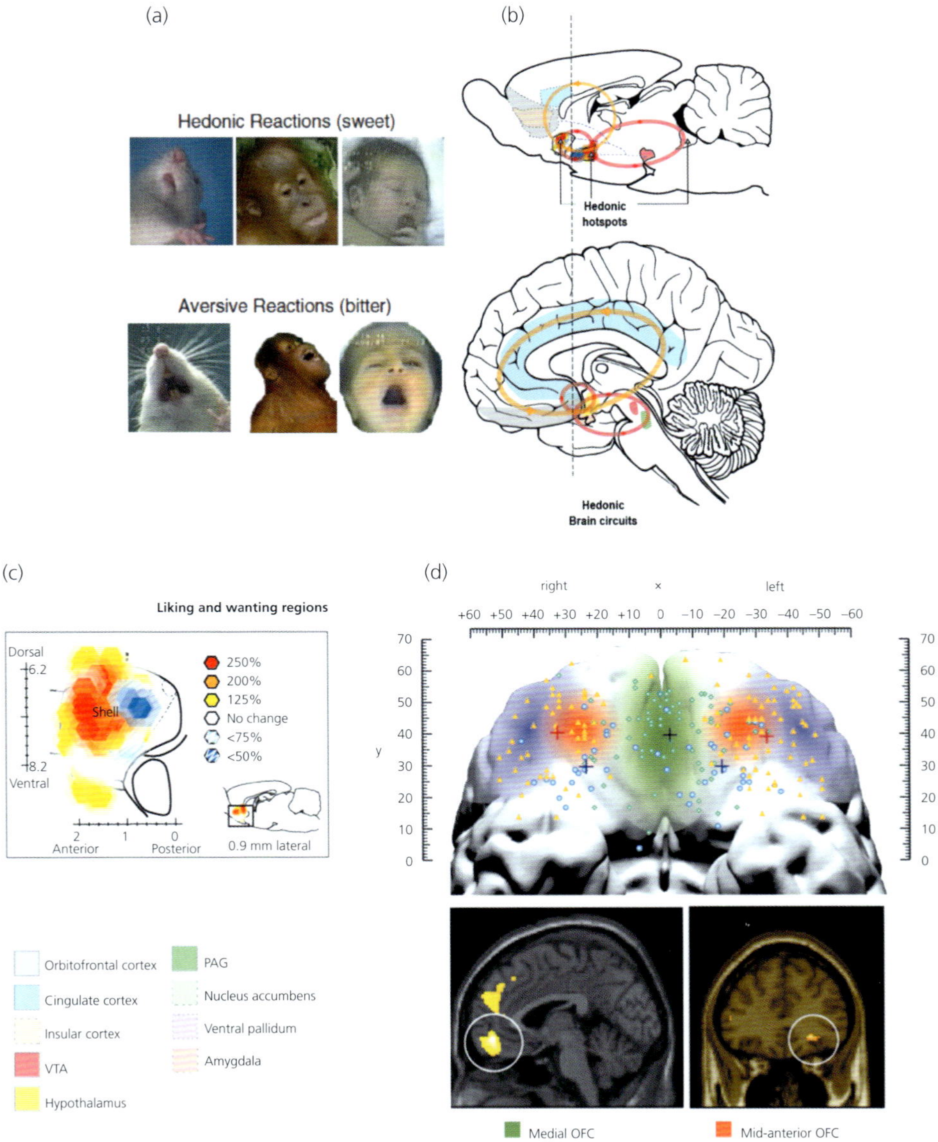

Plate 7 Brain circuitry for generating hedonic value. This schematic figure summarizes subcortical and cortical systems for generating and coding of hedonic value. (a) Typical facial reactions to sweet and bitter taste are comparable in rodents, primates and human infants, and provide a useful model for investigating "liking" and "disliking." (b) Brain circuitry involved in hedonic processing in rodents and humans. (c) Hedonic "hotspots" have been found in the nucleus accumbens shell and the ventral pallidum. Microinjection of mu opioid agonists into these locations increase "liking" responses to e.g., sweet taste. (d) Cortical hedonic coding may reach an apex in the orbitofrontal cortex, where hedonic value may be translated into subjective pleasure or displeasure. (See Fig. 13.2.)

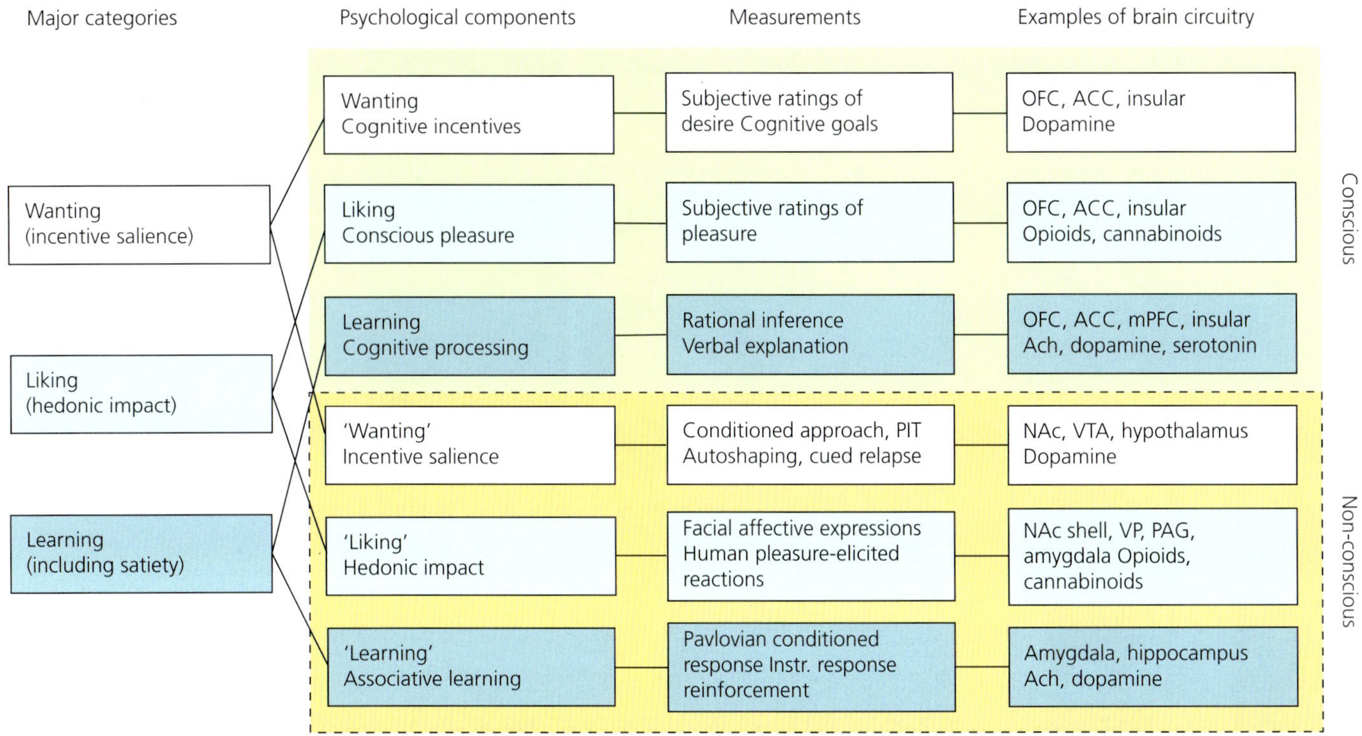

Plate 8 Measuring hedonia. Hedonic processes may be divided into at least three major neurobiologically and psychologically components: wanting or incentive salience (white), liking or hedonic impact (light blue), and learning (blue). These components have conscious aspects, which can only be investigated in humans, and non-conscious aspects, which can also be investigated in non-human animals. Types of measurements are listed in the second column, and examples of brain circuitry involved in each subcomponent are listed in the third column. (See Fig. 13.3.)

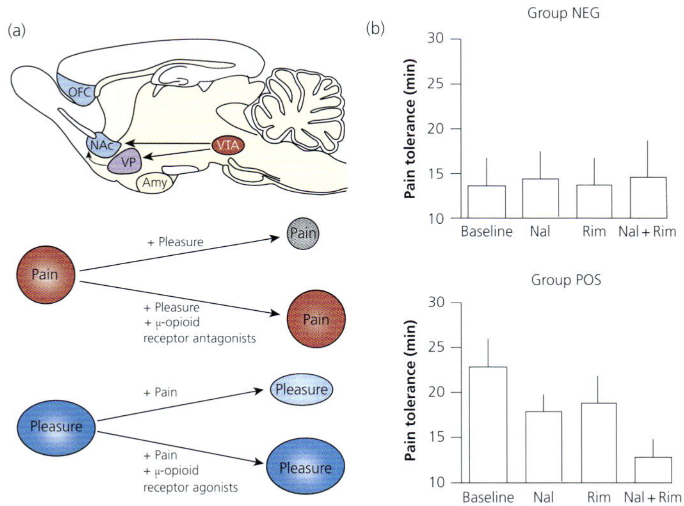

Plate 9 Opioid modulation of pleasure and pain. (a) Pleasure and pain both elicit opioid release in the orbitofrontal cortex, nucleus accumbens, ventral pallidum, and amygdala. Pleasure and pain often works in a mutually inhibitory, opioid-dependent, fashion. Mu-opioid receptor antagonists, like naloxone, can attenuate pleasure-induced analgesia. Vice versa, mu-opioid receptor agonists, like morphine, can reverse pain-related suppression of pleasure. (b) In a recent experimental study, one group of participants were told that experimental muscle pain would hurt but had therapeutic benefits (POS), while another group were only told that pain would hurt (NEG). Pain tolerance in the (POS) group was almost doubled compared to the (NEG) group. This increase in pain tolerance was partially reversed when participants were pre-treated with either naloxone (Nal) or the endocannabinoid receptor antagonist rimonabant (Rim), and completely abolished when pre-treated with both Nal and Rim. (See Fig. 13.4.)

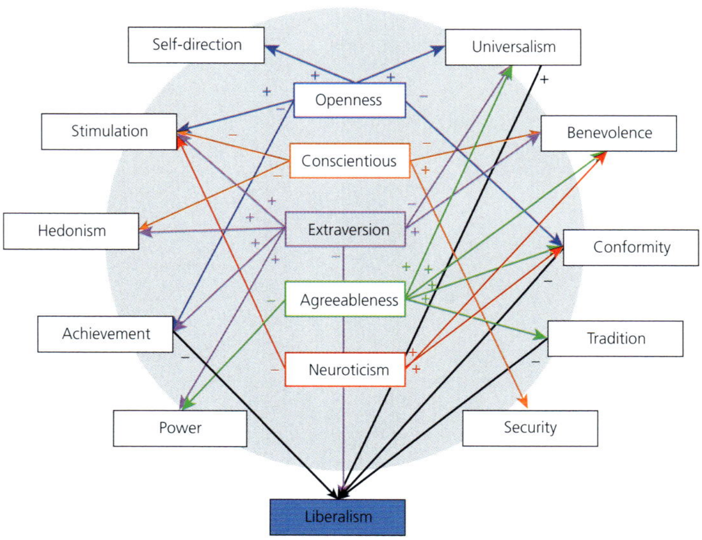

Plate 10 Path model illustrating the direct and indirect effects of "big five" personality characteristics on political ideology. (See Fig. 17.1.)

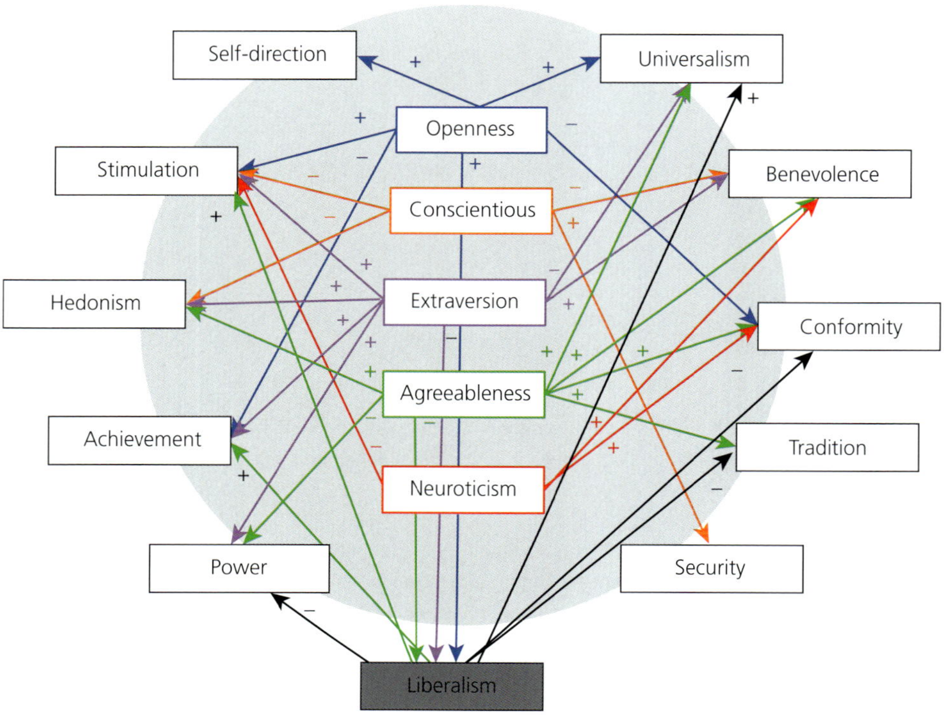

Plate 11 Path model illustrating the direct and indirect effects of "big five" personality characteristics on political orientation and value endorsement. (See Fig. 17.2.)

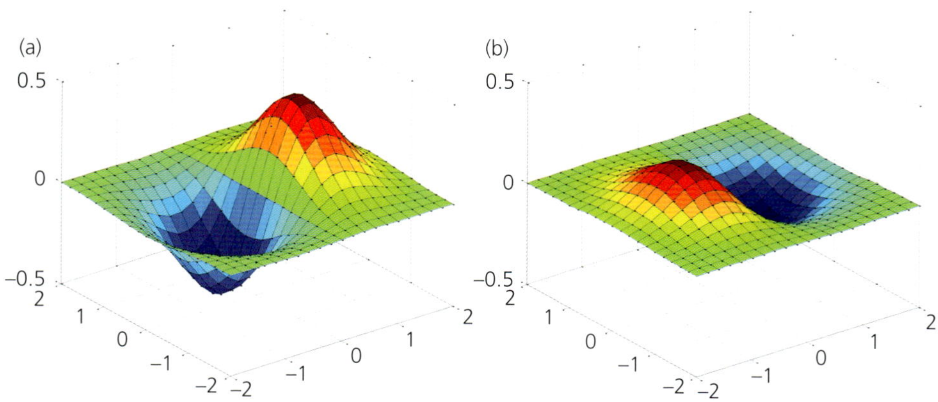

Plate 12 Two different "value fields" with zones of attraction and repulsion that define the "decision value" of different choice options located at specific positions within the field. Differences in the overall "value landscape" of two individuals may represent individual "core value" differences. (See Fig. 19.1.)

have the power to change the tone of an entire extended interaction, making appraisal a very important tool in shaping decision-making.

Because (re)appraisal is one of the most powerful and flexible ways to alter emotions, it is unsurprising that differences in appraisal habits and techniques have been related to experience and performance in real-world decision-making. Real traders' self-reports of emotional responses in the course of doing their job indicate that while all traders experience such responses, the more experienced and well-paid traders additionally report strategies for managing and using their emotions to perform their job better—less-experienced traders tend to discuss emotions only as a distraction to be minimized if at all possible (Fenton-O'Creevy et al. 2011). However, in the course of aiming to minimize the relationship between their emotions and their choices, low-performing traders ironically appear to maximize it: they have a tighter, stronger relationship between their subjective emotional experience and the day's trading events than do high-performing traders (Lo et al. 2005). While the two studies above both examine participants' self-report of their subjective emotional experience, the connection between emotions and trading extends to the physiological domain: traders with less experience have stronger autonomic responses to discrete market events and market volatility compared to more experienced traders (Lo and Repin 2002). Though these studies find that greater experience and performance is related to reduced emotional reactivity, note that emotions are reported by, and objectively measured in, *all* traders—the question is not who experiences emotions, but what they do with their emotions when they experience them. More generally, these studies make it clear that emotions have a role in value and decision-making not only in the lab, but in the real world as well.

The many ways affect and decision-making interact

As we have seen above, affect and decision-making are clearly related in their shared behavioral, physiological, and neural correlates. As we observe measures or manipulations of affect changing neural mechanisms in ways that correlate with changes in choices, the parsimonious explanation is that affect is intertwined with the computation of value across a wide variety of decision-making domains (Phelps et al. 2014). Regions like the amygdala, insula, striatum, DLPFC, and VMPFC appear repeatedly at the center of these studies. Roles may be emerging for the amygdala in mediating the effects of arousal on decision-making, the insula in mediating the subjective perception of probability, fairness, and interoception, the striatum in integrating value with action, the DLPFC in implementing intentional strategies or regulation, and the VMPFC in combining different sources of information to compute an overall value estimate. There are other portions of the affective experience whose roles don't appear as tightly linked to single regions in the brain, including stress, mood, and emotional primes, though more research will be necessary to understand their neural correlates. Critically, all of these regions are not only identified in studies manipulating or measuring affect, but are commonly found in studies examining value and decision-making generally (Bartra et al. 2013; Phelps et al. 2014; see also Levy and

Glimcher, this volume). It is likely that the construction of value consistently involves the integration of affect—the precise component of which, and the way it influences decision-making, depend on the context and the choice being made.

One important caveat is that the exact function of many of these regions is still under debate. We know neurons calculate quantities that they then pass on to other neurons, which integrate those computations with their own, ultimately culminating in the muscle movements of making a choice—the question for us is what is that computation? Unfortunately, even in commonly studied regions like the amygdala, numerous divergent theories of its computational role have been put forth. These include representing the relative stability of stochastic events (termed "associability"; Li et al. 2011), ambiguity (Hsu et al. 2005), simple Pavlovian conditioned attentional value (Seymour and Dolan 2008), or the integrated value of contexts, motivational states, stimuli, and learning (termed "state value"; Morrison and Salzman 2010). Clearly, much work remains to be done to understand the linkages between regions of the brain, the neural computations they implement, and the mapping of those computations to the component processes underlying affective phenomena—work which will require an increasing focus on computational specificity in analyzing both behavior and the brain (Behrens et al. 2009).

In the introduction, we stated our main question: "How do different components of affect and emotion represent or modulate specific decision-making processes and their neural mechanisms?" As this chapter can clearly attest, there is no single, simple answer. Affect has a very real effect on our choices, but it depends on the context of the choice, the choice target, our appraisals (instructed or induced), and who we are, among other factors. To the extent that there is a theme, it is this: affect changes the ongoing computation of value, effectively weighting different aspects of the situation in a given choice—the hallmark of a modulatory role (Phelps et al. 2014). However, as our perspective on affect and decision-making increases in complexity, so too will our challenge in neuroscience. We will likely find that the classic module-based approach to studying the brain will break down as we begin to focus more on computations and distributed representations than on discrete regions and discrete categorical factors (Salzman and Fusi 2010).

The more we understand about how aspects of what we call "affect" interact with what we call "cognition," the clearer it becomes that they are in fact not fundamentally separable. "Affective" processes are a natural part of "cognition," and vice versa—and nowhere is this more apparent than in the study of the myriad processes and factors that interact when computing value and using it to make decisions.

References

Aïte, A., Borst, G., Moutier, S. et al. (2013). Impact of emotional context congruency on decision making under ambiguity. *Emotion*, **13**, 177–182.

Arnsten, A. F. T. (2009). Stress signalling pathways that impair prefrontal cortex structure and function. *Nat Rev Neuro*, **10**, 410–422.

Augustine, A. A. and Larsen, R. J. (2011). Affect regulation and temporal discounting: Interactions between primed, state, and trait affect. *Emotion*, **11**, 403–412.

Balleine, B. W. and O'Doherty, J. P. (2010). Human and rodent homologies in action control: Corticostriatal determinants of goal-directed and habitual action. *Neuropsychopharmacology*, **35**, 48–69.

Barrett, L. F. (2006). Are emotions natural kinds? *Perspectives on Psychological Science*, **1**, 28–58.

Bartra, O., Mcguire, J. T., and Kable, J. W. (2013). The valuation system: a coordinate-based meta-analysis of BOLD fMRI experiments examining neural correlates of subjective value. *Neuroimage*, **76**, 412–427.

Baumann, J. and Desteno, D. (2012). Context explains divergent effects of anger on risk taking. *Emotion*, **12**, 1196–1199.

Bechara, A., Damasio, H., Tranel, D., and Damasio, A. R. (1997). Deciding advantageously before knowing the advantageous strategy. *Science*, **275**, 1293–1295. DOI: 10.1126/science.275.5304.1293

Bechara, A., Damasio, H., Damasio, A. R., and Lee, G. P. (1999). Different contributions of the human amygdala and ventromedial prefrontal cortex to decision-making. *The Journal of Neuroscience*, **19**, 5473–5481.

Behrens, T. E. J., Hunt, L. T., and Rushworth, M. F. S. (2009). The computation of social behavior. *Science*, **324**, 1160–1164.

Berghorst, L. H., Bogdan, R., Frank, M. J., and Pizzagalli, D. A. (2013). Acute stress selectively reduces reward sensitivity. *Frontiers in Human Neuroscience*, **7**, 1–15.

Bogdan, R. and Pizzagalli, D. A. (2006). Acute stress reduces reward responsiveness: Implications for depression. *Biological Psychiatry*, **60**, 1147–1154.

Buhle, J. T., Silvers, J. A., Wager, T. D. et al. (2014). Cognitive reappraisal of emotion: a meta-analysis of human neuroimaging studies. *Cerebral Cortex*, **24**, 2981–2990.

Chumbley, J. R., Krajbich, I., Engelmann, J. B. et al. (2014). Endogenous cortisol predicts decreased loss aversion in young men. *Psychological Science*, **25**, 2102–2105.

Cingl, L. and Cahlikova, J. (2013). Risk preferences under acute stress. *Institute of Economic Studies Working Paper*, 1–44.

Clark, L., Lawrence, A. J., Astley-Jones, F., and Gray, N. (2009). Gambling near-misses enhance motivation to gamble and recruit win-related brain circuitry. *Neuron*, **61**, 481–490.

Clark, L., Crooks, B., Clarke, R., Aitken, M. R. F., and Dunn, B. D. (2012). Physiological responses to near-miss outcomes and personal control during simulated gambling. *Journal of Gambling Studies*, **28**, 123–137.

Clark, L., Studer, B., Bruss, J., Tranel, D., and Bechara, A. (2014). Damage to insula abolishes cognitive distortions during simulated gambling. *Proceedings of the National Academy of Sciences*. DOI: 10.1073/pnas.1322295111

Cohen, J. D. (2005). The vulcanization of the human brain: a neural perspective on interactions between cognition and emotion. *Journal of Economic Perspectives*, **19**, 3–24.

Craig, A. D. B. (2009). How do you feel—now? The anterior insula and human awareness. *Nature Reviews Neuroscience*, **10**, 59–70. DOI: 10.1038/nrn2555

Critchley, H. D., Elliott, R., Mathias, C. J., and Dolan, R. J. (2000). Neural activity relating to generation and representation of galvanic skin conductance responses: a functional magnetic resonance imaging study. *The Journal of Neuroscience*, **20**, 3033–3040.

Critchley, H. D., Wiens, S., Rotshtein, P., Ohman, A., and Dolan, R. J. (2004). Neural systems supporting interoceptive awareness. *Nature Neuroscience*, **7**, 189–195. DOI: 10.1038/nn1176

De Martino, B., Camerer, C. F., and Adolphs, R. (2010). Amygdala damage eliminates monetary loss aversion. *Proceedings of the National Academy of Sciences*, **107**, 3788–3792.

Delaney, L., Fink, G., and Harmon, C. (2014). Effects of stress on economic decision-making: Evidence from laboratory experiments. *IZA Discussion Paper* No. 8060, p1–35.

Delgado, M. R., Nearing, K. I., Ledoux, J. E., and Phelps, E. A. (2008). Neural circuitry underlying the regulation of conditioned fear and its relation to extinction. *Neuron*, **59**, 829–838. DOI: 10.1016/j.neuron.2008.06.029

Dias-Ferreira, E., Sousa, J. C., Melo, I. et al. (2009). Chronic stress causes frontostriatal reorganization and affects decision-making. *Science*, **325**, 621–625.

Dunn, B., Galton, H., Morgan, R. et al. (2010). Listening to your heart: how interoception shapes emotion experience and intuitive decision making. *Psychological Science*, **21**, 1835–1844. DOI: 10.1177/0956797610389191

Dunn, B., Evans, D., Makarova, D., White, J., and Clark, L. (2012). Gut feelings and the reaction to perceived inequity: The interplay between bodily responses, regulation, and perception shapes the rejection of unfair offers on the ultimatum game. *Cognitive, Affective, and Behavioral Neuroscience*, **12**, 419–429.

Eippert, F., Veit, R., Weiskopf, N. et al. (2007). Regulation of emotional responses elicited by threat-related stimuli. *Human Brain Mapping*, **28**, 409–423.

Farb, N. A. S., Chapman, H. A., and Anderson, A. K. (2013). Emotions: form follows function. *Current Opinion in Neurobiology*, **23**, 393–398.

Feinstein, J. S. (2013). Lesion studies of human emotion and feeling. *Current Opinion in Neurobiology*, **23**, 304–309.

Fellows, L. K. and Farah, M. J. (2005). Different underlying impairments in decision-making following ventromedial and dorsolateral frontal lobe damage in humans. *Cerebral Cortex*, **15**, 58–63.

Fenton-O'creevy, M., Soane, E., Nicholson, N., and Willman, P. (2011). Thinking, feeling and deciding: the influence of emotions on the decision making and performance of traders. *Journal of Organizational Behavior*, **32**, 1044–1061.

Garavan, H., Pendergrass, J. C., Ross, T. J., Stein, E. A., and Risinger, R. C. (2001). Amygdala response to both positively and negatively valenced stimuli. *Neuroreport*, **12**, 2779–2783.

Glascher, J. and Adolphs, R. (2003). Processing of the arousal of subliminal and supraliminal emotional stimuli by the human amygdala. *The Journal of Neuroscience*, **23**, 10274–10282.

Grecucci, A., Giorgetta, C., Van 'T Wout, M., Bonini, N., and Sanfey, A. G. (2012). Reappraising the ultimatum: an fMRI study of emotion regulation and decision making. *Cerebral Cortex*, **23**, 399–410.

Harlé, K. and Sanfey, A. G. (2007). Incidental sadness biases social economic decisions in the Ultimatum Game. *Emotion*, **7**, 876–881. DOI: 10.1037/1528-3542.7.4.876

Harlé, K., Chang, L. J., Van 'T Wout, M., and Sanfey, A. G. (2012). The neural mechanisms of affect infusion in social economic decision-making: A mediating role of the anterior insula. *Neuroimage*, **61**, 32–40.

Hsu, M., Bhatt, M. A., Adolphs, R., Tranel, D., and Camerer, C. F. (2005). Neural systems responding to degrees of uncertainty in human decision-making. *Science*, **310**, 1680–1683.

Kahneman, D., Knetsch, J. L., and Thaler, R. H. (1991). Anomalies—the endowment effect, loss aversion, and status-quo bias. *Journal of Economic Perspectives*, **5**, 193–206.

Kandasamy, N., Hardy, B., Page, L. et al. (2014). Cortisol shifts financial risk preferences. *Proceedings of the National Academy of Sciences*, **111**, 3608–3613.

Khalsa, S. S., Rudrauf, D., Feinstein, J. S., and Tranel, D. (2009). The pathways of interoceptive awareness. *Nature Neuroscience*, **12**, 1494–1496. DOI: 10.1038/nn.2411

Kimura, K., Izawa, S., Sugaya, N. et al. (2013). The biological effects of acute psychosocial stress on delay discounting. *Psychoneuroendocrinology*, **38**, 2300–2308.

Kirk, U., Downar, J., and Montague, P. R. (2011). Interoception drives increased rational decision-making in meditators playing the Ultimatum Game. *Frontiers in Neuroscience*, **5**, 1–11. DOI: 10.3389/fnins.2011.00049

Labar, K. S. and Cabeza, R. (2006). Cognitive neuroscience of emotional memory. *Nature Reviews Neuroscience*, **7**, 54–64.

Langer, E. J. (1975). The illusion of control. *Journal of Personality and Social Psychology*, **32**, 311–328.

Ledoux, J. E. and Gorman, J. M. (2001). A call to action: overcoming anxiety through active coping. *American Journal of Psychiatry*, **158**, 1953–1955.

Lempert, K. M., Porcelli, A. J., Delgado, M. R., and Tricomi, E. (2012). Individual differences in delay discounting under acute stress: the role of trait perceived stress. *Frontiers in Psychology*, **3**, 1–10.

Lerner, J. S. and Keltner, D. (2001). Fear, anger, and risk. *Journal of Personality and Social Psychology*, **81**, 146–159.

Lerner, J. S., Small, D. A., and Loewenstein, G. F. (2004). Heart strings and purse strings: carryover effects of emotions on economic decisions. *Psychological Science*, **15**, 337–341.

Li, J., Schiller, D., Schoenbaum, G., Phelps, E. A., and Daw, N. D. (2011). Differential roles of human striatum and amygdala in associative learning. *Nature Neuroscience*, **14**, 1250–1252.

Lindquist, K. A., Wager, T. D., Kober, H., Bliss-Moreau, E., and Barrett, L. F. (2012). The brain basis of emotion: a meta-analytic review. *Behavioral and Brain Sciences*, **35**, 121–202.

Lo, A. W. and Repin, D. V. (2002). The psychophysiology of real-time financial risk processing. *Journal of Cognitive Neuroscience*, **14**, 323–339. DOI: 10.1162/089892902317361877

Lo, A. W., Repin, D. V., and Steenbarger, B. N. (2005). Fear and greed in financial markets: a clinical study of day-traders. *The American Economic Review*, **95**, 352–359.

Lole, L., Gonsalvez, C. J., Blaszczynski, A., and Clarke, A. R. (2011). Electrodermal activity reliably captures physiological differences between wins and losses during gambling on electronic machines. *Psychophysiology*, **49**, 154–163.

Luo, S., Ainslie, G., and Monterosso, J. (2014). The behavioral and neural effect of emotional primes on intertemporal decisions. *Social Cognitive and Affective Neuroscience*, **9**, 283–291.

Lupien, S. J., Maheu, F. S., Tu, M., Fiocco, A., and Schramek, T. E. (2007). The effects of stress and stress hormones on human cognition: implications for the field of brain and cognition. *Brain and Cognition*, **65**, 209–237.

Maia, T. V. and Mcclelland, J. L. (2004). A reexamination of the evidence for the somatic marker hypothesis: What participants really know in the Iowa gambling task. *Proceedings of the National Academy of Sciences*, **101**, 16075–16080.

Martin Braunstein, L., Herrera, S. J., and Delgado, M. R. (2013). Reappraisal and expected value modulate risk taking. *Cognition and Emotion*, **28**, 172–181.

Martin, L. and Delgado, M. R. (2011). The influence of emotion regulation on decision-making under risk. *Journal of Cognitive Neuroscience*, **23**, 2569–2581.

Mcgaugh, J. L. (2004). The amygdala modulates the consolidation of memories of emotionally arousing experiences. *Annual Review of Neuroscience*, **27**, 1–28.

Montague, P. R., Dayan, P., and Sejnowski, T. J. (1996). A framework for mesencephalic dopamine systems based on predictive Hebbian learning. *Journal of Neuroscience*, **16**, 1936–1947.

Moretti, L. and Di Pellegrino, G. (2010). Disgust selectively modulates reciprocal fairness in economic interactions. *Emotion*, **10**, 169–180.

Morrison, S. E. and Salzman, C. D. (2010). Re-valuing the amygdala. *Current Opinion in Neurobiology*, **20**, 221–230.

Naqvi, N. H. and Bechara, A. (2010). The insula and drug addiction: an interoceptive view of pleasure, urges, and decision-making. *Brain Structure and Function*, **214**, 435–450. DOI: 10.1007/s00429-010-0268-7

Ochsner, K. N. and Gross, J. J. (2008). Cognitive emotion regulation: Insights from social cognitive and affective neuroscience. *Current Directions in Psychological Science*, **17**, 153–158.

Ochsner, K. N., Bunge, S. A., Gross, J. J., and Gabrieli, J. D. E. (2002). Rethinking feelings: an fMRI study of the cognitive regulation of emotion. *Journal of Cognitive Neuroscience*, **14**, 1215–1229.

Ochsner, K. N., Ray, R. D., Cooper, J. C. et al. (2004). For better or for worse: neural systems supporting the cognitive down- and up-regulation of negative emotion. *Neuroimage*, **23**, 483–99.

Otto, A. R., Raio, C. M., Chiang, A., Phelps, E. A., and Daw, N. D. (2013). Working-memory capacity protects model-based learning from stress. *Proceedings of the National Academy of Sciences*, **110**, 20941–20946.

Pabst, S., Schoofs, D., Pawlikowski, M., Brand, M., and Wolf, O. T. (2013). Paradoxical effects of stress and an executive task on decisions under risk. *Behavioral Neuroscience*, **127**, 369–379.

Panno, A., Lauriola, M., and Figner, B. (2013). Emotion regulation and risk taking: predicting risky choice in deliberative decision making. *Cognition and Emotion*, **27**, 326–334.

Paris, J. J., Franco, C., Sodano, R., Frye, C. A., and Wulfert, E. (2009). Gambling pathology is associated with dampened cortisol response among men and women. *Physiology and Behavior*, **99**, 230–233.

Petzold, A., Plessow, F., Goschke, T., and Kirschbaum, C. (2010). Stress reduces use of negative feedback in a feedback-based learning task. *Behavioral Neuroscience*, **124**, 248–255.

Phelps, E. A. and Sokol-Hessner, P. (2012). Social and emotional factors in decision-making: appraisal and value. *In:* Sharot, T. and Dolan, R. J. (eds) *Neuroscience of Preference and Choice*.

Phelps, E. A., Ling, S., and Carrasco, M. (2006). Emotion facilitates perception and potentiates the perceptual benefits of attention. *Psychological Science*, **17**, 292–299.

Phelps, E. A., Lempert, K. M., and Sokol-Hessner, P. (2014). Emotion and decision making: multiple modulatory neural circuits. *Annual Review of Neuroscience*, **37**, 263–287.

Poldrack, R. A. (2011). Inferring mental states from neuroimaging data: from reverse inference to large-scale decoding. *Neuron*, **72**, 692–697.

Poldrack, R. A., Wagner, A. D., Phelps, E. A., and Sharot, T. (2008). How (and why) emotion enhances the subjective sense of recollection. *Current Directions in Psychological Science*, **17**, 147–152.

Porcelli, A. J. and Delgado, M. R. (2009). Acute stress modulates risk taking in financial decision making. *Psychological Science*, **20**, 278–283.

Potenza, M. N. (2006). Should addictive disorders include non-substance- related conditions? *Addiction*, **101**, 142–151.

Preston, S. D., Buchanan, T. W., Stansfield, R. B., and Bechara, A. (2007). Effects of anticipatory stress on decision making in a gambling task. *Behavioral Neuroscience*, **121**, 257–263.

Raio, C. M., Orederu, T. A., Palazzolo, L., Shurick, A. A., and Phelps, E. A. (2013). Cognitive emotion regulation fails the stress test. *Proceedings of the National Academy of Sciences*, **110**, 15139–15144.

Rangel, A., Camerer, C. F., and Montague, P. R. (2008). A framework for studying the neurobiology of value-based decision making. *Nature Reviews Neuroscience*, **9**, 545–556.

Roozendaal, B., Okuda, S., De Quervain, D. J. F., and Mcgaugh, J. L. (2006). Glucocorticoids interact with emotion-induced noradrenergic activation in influencing different memory functions. *Neuroscience*, **138**, 901–910.

Rudebeck, P. H., Saunders, R. C., Prescott, A. T., Chau, L. S., and Murray, E. A. (2013). Prefrontal mechanisms of behavioral flexibility, emotion regulation and value updating. *Nature Neuroscience*, **16**, 1140–1145.

Salzman, C. D. and Fusi, S. (2010). Emotion, cognition, and mental state representation in amygdala and prefrontal cortex. *Annual Review of Neuroscience*, **33**, 173–202.

Sanfey, A. G., Rilling, J. K., Aronson, J. A., Nystrom, L. E., and Cohen, J. D. (2003). The neural basis of economic decision-making in the ultimatum game. *Science*, **300**, 1755–1758.

Scherer, K. R. (2005). What are emotions? And how can they be measured? *Social Science Information*, **44**, 695–729. DOI: 10.1177/0539018405058216

Schwabe, L., Tegenthoff, M., Hoffken, O., and Wolf, O. T. (2010). Concurrent glucocorticoid and noradrenergic activity shifts instrumental behavior from goal-directed to habitual control. *Journal of Neuroscience*, **30**, 8190–8196.

Schwabe, L., Höffken, O., Tegenthoff, M., and Wolf, O. T. (2011). Preventing the stress-induced shift from goal-directed to habit action with a β-adrenergic antagonist. *J Neurosci*, **31**, 17317–17325.

Seymour, B. and Dolan, R. J. (2008). Emotion, decision making, and the amygdala. *Neuron*, **58**, 662–671.

Sokol-Hessner, P., Hsu, M., Curley, N. G. et al. (2009). Thinking like a trader selectively reduces individuals' loss aversion. *Proceedings of the National Academy of Sciences*, **106**, 5035–5040. DOI: 10.1073/pnas.0806761106

Sokol-Hessner, P., Camerer, C. F. and Phelps, E. A. (2013). Emotion regulation reduces loss aversion and decreases amygdala responses to losses. *Social Cognitive and Affective Neuroscience*, **8**, 341–350. DOI: doi:10.1093/scan/nss002

Sokol-Hessner, P, Lackovic, S.F., Tobe, R.H., Camerer, C.F., Leventhal, B.L., and Phelps, E.A. (2015a) Determinants of propranolol's selective effect on loss aversion. *Psychological Science*. DOI: 10.1177/0956797615582026

Sokol-Hessner, P., Hartley, C. A., Hamilton, J. R., and Phelps, E. A. (2015b). Interoceptive ability predicts aversion to losses. *Cognition and Emotion*. 29, 695–701.

Stanley, D. A., Sokol-Hessner, P., Banaji, M. R., and Phelps, E. A. (2011). Implicit race attitudes predict trustworthiness judgments and economic trust decisions. *Proceedings of the National Academy of Sciences*, **108**, 7710–7715.

Stanley, D. A., Sokol-Hessner, P., Fareri, D. S. et al. (2012). Race and reputation: Perceived racial group trustworthiness influences the neural correlates of trust decisions. *Philosophical Transactions of the Royal Society B*, **367**, 744–753.

Starcke, K., Wolf, O. T., Markowitsch, H. J., and Brand, M. (2008). Anticipatory stress influences decision making under explicit risk conditions. *Behavioral Neuroscience*, **122**, 1352–1360.

Studer, B. and Clark, L. (2011). Place your bets: psychophysiological correlates of decision-making under risk. *Cognitive, Affective, and Behavioral Neuroscience*, **11**, 144–158.

Tom, S. M., Fox, C. R., Trepel, C., and Poldrack, R. A. (2007). The neural basis of loss aversion in decision-making under risk. *Science*, **315**, 515–518.

Van 'T Wout, M., Kahn, R., Sanfey, A. G., and Aleman, A. (2006). Affective state and decision-making in the Ultimatum Game. *Experimental Brain Research*, **169**, 564–568. DOI: 10.1007/s00221-006-03463-5

Van 'T Wout, M., Chang, L. J., and Sanfey, A. G. (2010). The influence of emotion regulation on social interactive decision-making. *Emotion*, **10**, 815–821.

Vinkers, C. H., Zorn, J. V., Cornelisse, S. et al. (2013). Time-dependent changes in altruistic punishment following stress. *Psychoneuroendocrinology*, **38**, 1467–1475.

Von Dawans, B., Fischbacher, U., Kirschbaum, C., Fehr, E., and Heinrichs, M. (2012). The social dimension of stress reactivity: acute stress increases prosocial behavior in humans. *Psychological Science*, **23**, 651–660.

Werner, N., Jung, K., Duschek, S., and Schandry, R. (2009). Enhanced cardiac perception is associated with benefits in decision-making. *Psychophysiology*, **46**, 1123–1129. DOI: 10.1111/j.1469-8986.2009.00855.x

Wilkes, B. L., Gonsalvez, C. J., and Blaszczynski, A. (2009). Psychophysiological responses to win and loss events during electronic gaming machine (EGM) play: a pilot investigation. *Gambling Research*, **21**, 22–34.

Wilkes, B. L., Gonsalvez, C. J., and Blaszczynski, A. (2010). Capturing SCL and HR changes to win and loss events during gambling on electronic machines. *International Journal of Psychophysiology*, **78**, 265–272.

Williams, L., Phillips, M., Brammer, M. et al. (2001). Arousal dissociates amygdala and hippocampal fear responses: evidence from simultaneous fMRI and skin conductance recording. *Neuroimage*, **14**, 1070–1079.

Winkielman, P., Berridge, K. C., and Wilbarger, J. L. (2005). Unconscious affective reactions to masked happy versus angry faces influence consumption behavior and judgments of value. *Personality and Social Psychology Bulletin*, **31**, 121–135. DOI: 10.1177/0146167204271309

Chapter 11

Protected values and economic decision-making

Rajna Gibson, Carmen Tanner, and Alexander F. Wagner

Values in economic decision-making

The concepts of "economic value" and economic decision-making

In economics, the term value is primarily associated with goods and services and describes their economic benefit. Yet, this economic benefit has more than one origin. Indeed, ever since Adam Smith (1776, book 1, ch. 4, p 28), in a famous passage from the "Wealth of Nations," two meanings of value have been distinguished: the term "value in use" refers to the usefulness, the utility, or the "desiredness" of a given good (Bowley 1973), while the term "value in exchange" refers to the idea that the value of goods or services depends on their ability to be exchanged for a given price on the market. Importantly, as Edgeworth would write: "The value in use of a certain quantity of commodity corresponds to its total utility; the value in exchange to its marginal utility (multiplied by the quantity). The former is greater than the latter, since the utility of the final increment of commodity is less than that of every other increment" (Edgeworth 1899: 602). From there, one of the core aspects of market pricing is that any set of goods can be compared—based on their values in exchange—and that tradeoffs between competing goods are always feasible.

Besides the values-in-exchange paradigm, the standard economic choice model of the homo oeconomicus additionally rests on the related assumption that individuals make choices simply by comparing the utility—or expected discounted utility under uncertainty—of the outcomes (generally payoffs) associated with various alternatives. This paradigm underlying most economic choice modeling has had widespread applications to consumer, investor, worker, and other economic agents' decisions. It has also been widely used to derive social welfare implications. However, the standard economic choice model has, since its inception, also been subject to a number of technical and conceptual criticisms. First, economists have ever since the 1930s questioned whether utility can be cardinally or simply ordinally measured and whether interpersonal utilities could be compared. Second, and more importantly for the purpose of this chapter, the standard economic choice model is essentially consequentialist in that it only focuses on the outcomes (payoffs) associated with the various alternatives and abstracts from any notion of rightness or wrongness associated with the process leading to those various alternatives. The process by which an outcome is chosen is deemed irrelevant to the decision-making and thus makes this model ill-suited to choices involving cheating, fraud, injustice, or other immoral behaviors to generate higher payoffs. Third, in its simplest version this model offers a reductionist vision of human character in which economic agents act solely based on their self-interest and only care about their own utility irrespective of the consequences of their choices for others.

The moral foundations of economic decision-making

Do the above considerations imply that the standard economic choice model only provides a selfish and instrumental perspective of human nature (the traditional perspective) and thus is "value-neutral," a term chosen by Sandel (2013: 122), or, alternatively, that one can nevertheless reconcile this model with a more elevated sense of morality? We attempt below to provide an answer to this delicate question.

According to the Oxford dictionaries, a moral act is "concerned with the principles of right and wrong behavior." Thus, one may wonder how a choice model that is based on self-interest and on extrinsic motivations, as claimed by the traditional perspective, can bear a moral dimension. In order to identify the latter one, we have to remember that economists have been, since the eighteenth century, concerned with the implications of that standard choice model for aggregate wealth allocation purposes.

Economics has been, and remains, under the influence of utilitarian moral and political philosophies, which have been defined by Riley (2008) as considering "general utility or social welfare as the sole ethical value or good to be maximized." Early utilitarians assumed that this maximization of general utility would take place in an orderly society governed by certain rights. For Bentham, these legal rights "must include among others, a right to subsistence and, consistently with that, rights to keep or trade the fruits of one own labor and saving so as to foster abundance" (Riley 2008). Mill saw the importance of the role of justice and, as Riley (2008) points out, for him, "this complex feeling of security can be fully experienced only by cooperating with others in terms of an optimal code that distributes equal rights and correlative duties among individuals." Thus, utilitarians early on recognized the need for some basic or fundamental rights that would discipline humans' selfishness and provide for some redistribution of wealth in the economy.

More than 200 years later, the debate about the nature of the morality surrounding economics and markets is still open. Philosophers, like Sandel (2013), argue that markets are not "value-neutral" but may affect—through the "crowding out"[1] of humans' intrinsic motivations—and corrupt nonmarket norms as soon as some originally non-tradable goods or services—for instance, blood giving—become marketable. Sandel (2013: 139) thus invites modern economics to reconnect with "its origins in moral and political

[1] As an analogy, in macroeconomics, for instance, crowding out occurs when increased government borrowing, a kind of expansionary fiscal policy, reduces investment spending. The increased borrowing "crowds out" or "forces out" private investing.

philosophy." Others, like Bruni and Sugden, (2013) shed a more optimistic light on the morality of economics. Indeed, the latter authors use the methods of "virtue ethics" to show that the ultimate goal of the markets is to "facilitate mutually beneficial exchange." They further argue that in the process of accomplishing this mission, markets do possess certain fundamental virtues such as "universality, enterprise and alertness, trust and trustworthiness, acceptance of competition, self-help, non-rivalry, and reward stoicism." They conclude by asserting that these market virtues "do not, as some moral critics of the market might have expected, merely normalize egoism and instrumentality: they are genuine virtues that can be upheld with authenticity."

In parallel to this philosophical debate about the moral foundations of economics, behavioral and experimental economists and psychologists have since more than two decades, enriched the standard economic choice model, by introducing "social preferences" into the standard utility based decision-making framework. Ernst Fehr and others were pioneers who recognized that consequences for (and thus payoffs to) others also matter in terms of how individuals make individual choices; in particular, if they display a concern for altruism (Fehr and Fischbacher 2003), for reciprocity (Fehr et al. 1993), and for fairness (Fehr and Schmidt 1999; Güth et al. 1982; Kahneman et al. 1986). Decision models relying on social preferences have found support in numerous laboratory games and field experiments, and it is widely accepted nowadays that choice models relying on pure self-interest are too simple and reductionist in that they abstract from the fact that individuals are fundamentally social and heterogeneous in terms of their pro-social concerns.

More recently, other moral dimensions of economic decision-making, in particular the interest and recognition of humans' propensity to cheat or lie, entered and transformed the standard economic choice model. Indeed, several authors (Erat and Gneezy 2012; Gibson et al 2013; Gneezy 2005; Sanchez-Pagès and Vorsatz 2007; among others) recognized that some individuals are averse to lying per se and thus incur lying costs that may counteract the monetary benefits associated with the lying or cheating option. The origin of the lying costs referred to in these "extended preferences" choice models is still hard to identify and in particular it remains an open debate whether the desire to act honestly is rooted in selfish (such as signaling one's self-image) or in unselfish motivations (such as valuing truth in and of itself). This is perhaps a focus area where economics can learn a lot from the deontological foundations for morality recognized early on in philosophy and more recently in psychology.

The next section reviews research in psychology focusing on the role of deontological considerations in decision-making with a special emphasis on the features of so-called "protected values." The section titled "Honesty as an important example of moral values" starts by examining a specific moral value, namely honesty, and discusses how the literature in psychology and in economics has explained the determinants of honesty. The section next describes our own experimental evidence of the role of protected values for honesty in economic decision-making. The section titled "Some speculative thoughts on policy relevance and implications for practitioners" offers some speculative thoughts on the relevance of research on moral—and more specifically on protected values—for various business policies. Finally, the section titled "Conclusion: some open issues in research on honesty and economic decision-making" surveys some open research topics regarding the role of moral values in economic decision-making.

Deontology and protected values

While traditional research on judgment and decision-making has predominantly focused on the role of consequences, the field of normative ethics centuries ago considered deontology as another basic moral orientation in moral decision-making. Unlike consequentialism, deontology, from the Greek word *deon*, or duty, emphasizes the desirability of obligations, principles, or rights, irrespective of the consequences. It refers to morally mandated actions or prohibitions, such as the duty to keep promises or the duty not to lie. Influential examples of deontological rules are the Ten Commandments or Kant's categorical imperative (Kant 1797). It is only recently that the role of deontological orientation has also become a subject of interest in (descriptive) decision-making research (Greene 2007). In this section, we draw on a recent research line in social and cognitive psychology that reflects deontological orientations and provides evidence for values that challenges some principles of rational choice theory.

This research line has proposed that people sometimes endorse *protected values* (Baron and Spranca 1997; Ritov and Baron 1999), also called *sacred values* (Atran et al. 2007; Fiske and Tetlock 1997; Tetlock et al. 2000) or *taboo values* (Lichtenstein et al. 2007). They refer to objects or behavioral standards that people believe ought to be absolute and protected from (utilitarian) tradeoffs because they tap into moral or ethical principles or are central to one's moral identity. Such values are treated as non-compensatory, incommensurable and "not for sale." What counts as protected values, however, varies across social groups, culture, and historical periods. Importantly, protected or sacred values possess specific characteristics that go beyond simply attributing importance to specific values. We review here a few of their main features.

Tradeoff reluctance

Protected values are often associated with enhanced or even absolute *tradeoff reluctance*—the phenomenon that people deem certain tradeoffs as not permissible (Atran et al. 2007; Baron and Spranca 1997; Fiske and Tetlock 1997; Ritov and Baron 1999; Tetlock et al. 2000). For example, many people think that it is morally unacceptable to compromise freedom, love, honor, human rights, or human lives in return for other values, in particular economic benefits. Many people would never sell friendship for money—no matter how much money is offered (see also Sandel 2012, for more examples). Tradeoffs involving protected values are considered taboo, because they would erode and corrupt the inherent worth and symbolic meaning attached to such values, or undermine one's self-image and social identity as a moral being (Fiske and Tetlock 1997). Such observations are at odds with the claim of rational choice theory that *all* types of values are fungible and can be traded off. At the same time, they emphasize that more is at work than just utility maximizing based on (extrinsic) consequences. But this resistance has also further important implications: it signals that an extension of a market-pricing model to such values is deemed inappropriate. Taboo tradeoffs appear to set moral boundaries to the reach of markets (Bénabou and Tirole 2011; Fiske and Tetlock 1997; Norris and Inglehart 2004; Sandel 2012).

The belief that protected values ought to be defended from tradeoffs does not imply that individuals endorsing such values do always demonstrate absolute tradeoff reluctance (Bartels 2008; Tetlock 2003). Indeed, there is ample evidence that protected values are somewhat malleable and flexible (Iliev et al. 2009). According to Tetlock, compromising sacred values becomes acceptable in situations that pose a conflict between several sacred values (so called *tragic tradeoffs*). Imagine a hospital administrator who is faced with the problem of saving the life of one of two individuals; both need a liver transplant but due to shortage of organs, only one liver is available. Or imagine a manager who has to decide whether to improve the safety conditions of a group of employees working in the company or to solve company's widely criticized severe environmental pollution. In both scenarios, each option may involve protected values. Thus, provided no other reconciling solutions are possible, the situations require to sacrifice one of the values. Actually, studies have shown that reframing protected values in such ways, or pushing people to think of counter-arguments to protected values, increased their flexibility to compromise them (Baron and Leshner 2000; McGraw and Tetlock 2005).

The observation that commitments to taboo values can be modified has led some authors to claim that protected or sacred values are often merely *pseudo-sacred*; they may primarily serve impression management or "posturing". In negotiations, for instance, claiming to endorse protected values could be a beneficial tactic that a negotiator may use to get individually a more advantageous settlement (e.g., Thompson and Gonzalez 1997). However, despite the possibility that people sometimes only pretend to have sincere protected values, this does not imply that protected values are nonexistent. Other studies have shown that decision maker suffer emotionally from trading off protected values (e.g., Lichtenstein et al. 2007). Bartels and Medin (2007) have found that individuals endorsing protected values were more than others motivated to search for ways to maximize value protection when violations of taboo values were unavoidable. Such findings indicate that individuals' claims to have protected values can be real, even when tradeoff resistance is not expressed in its strongest version (Baron and Leshner 2000).

Negative affective reactions

Since considering tradeoffs of taboo values question the validity of the value and one's personal identity (Fiske and Tetlock 1997), forcing people to tradeoff such values or to "put a price" on them is threatening and can lead to harsh reactions. Such reactions will typically involve affective reactions, such as anger, fear, or moral outrage (Baron and Spranca 1997; Tetlock et al. 2000), increase of social and physical distance to the transgressors (Skitka et al. 2005), or even the intention to sanction the transgressors (Ginges et al. 2007). Tetlock and colleagues propose that people treat even the mere contemplation of trading of taboo values as disturbing (Tetlock 2003; Tetlock et al. 2000). Consistent with this, empirical studies have shown people were more likely to respond with negative affective and protest reactions when faced with *taboo tradeoffs* (conflicts between sacred and secular values, e.g., friendship vs. money) rather than *routine tradeoffs* (conflicts between secular values, e.g., services vs. money) (Hanselmann and Tanner 2008; Tetlock et al. 2000). Further support for the view that states of threat are induced when protected values are at risk is provided by Kouzakova and colleagues (2013) who included cardiovascular measures in their recent study. These researchers found that conflicts about values, but not conflicts about allocations of resources, raised cardiovascular threat profiles and prevention-focused motivational states.

Ginges and colleagues examined, in real-world conflicts (such as the Middle East conflict), how people respond when they are expected to compromise sacred values and to trade them off against money (Ginges and Atran 2009; Ginges et al. 2007). Providing Palestinian and Israeli participants with various deals, which could potentially have led them to compromise over core issues (e.g., giving up land in the case of Israeli settlers, or the right of return for Palestinians) in exchange for monetary incentives, they found that those participants who treated the corresponding issue *not* as a sacred value responded with less emotional outrage and support for violence. However, among those participants who attached sacred values with the issues concerned, offering money for compromising the sacred values, largely increased the level of emotional outrage and support for violence (including suicide attacks). Obviously, these findings challenge the economic view that all individuals reason in terms of maximizing monetary benefits. Moreover, they also highlight that strategies to solve disputes that involve sacred issues can even backfire.

Evidence in favor of deontology

There is mounting evidence that people who care for protected values base their decisions not on consequences solely, but on moral duties to particular behaviors (Baron and Spranca 1997; Tanner and Medin 2004). For example, one implication of deontological thinking is that it should make a difference whether outcomes derive from an act or an omission, whereas from a consequentialist perspective, this difference should be irrelevant. Consistent with this conjecture, studies revealed that individuals holding protected values were more than other people sensitive to the act–omission distinction (Tanner 2009).

Another implication of deontological thinking is that individuals should be less sensitive to the magnitude of outcomes, because they focus more on the inherent wrongness or rightness of the activity per se. Evidence for such *quantity insensitivities* has been provided by Ritov, Baron, and colleagues (Baron and Spranca 1997; Ritov and Baron 1990). For instance, when faced with the problem that the only way to prevent 1000 children from dying from a serious epidemic would be to vaccinate the children, which, however, will also cause the death of 100 children, Ritov and Baron (1990) found that a substantial number of participants holding protected values preferred not to vaccinate (even though not doing so would result in larger losses). They appeared to reject this tradeoff on the grounds that they would not want to cause the death of any single child. Ritov and Baron suggested that people holding protected values were more likely to perceive the harmful act as violating moral prohibitions, which led them to prefer the harmful omission over the harmful act. Such preferences for (more) harmful omission over (less) harmful acts are also known as the "omission bias" (Ritov and Baron 1999).

Nonetheless, despite the evidence in favor of protected values being associated with deontological rules, one should not conclude that consequences never matter. Some researchers have speculated that the observation of quantity insensitivity among people holding protected values is primarily given in contexts that prompt individuals to direct their attention to the nature of the act (e.g., as in taboo tradeoffs). But other situations may prompt individuals to focus more on balancing risks and consequences (e.g., when violations of protected values are unavoidable). In line with this, Bartels and Medin replicated quantity insensitivity among people holding protected values only in tasks that entailed a choice between a harmful omission and a (less) harmful act (similar to the vaccination task by Ritov and Baron 1990). Yet, the pattern reversed in decision tasks that entailed equal acts but associated with varying magnitudes of (harmful) consequences, thereby forcing individuals to compromise over protected values. In such situations, individuals holding protected values revealed suddenly greater quantity sensitivity and *more* consequentialism and utility-maximization than people without protected values (Bartels 2008). The findings suggest that individuals who care for the values at risk are more than other individuals motivated to find ways to achieve maximal defense of the value.

Resistance to situational influences

Related to the fact that individuals who care for protected values are generally more than other people prone to deontological thinking and value defense reactions, some research tested the idea that protected values also result in stronger resistance to *situational influences*. First evidence for this claim has been found in studies investigating *framing effects*. Framing effects stand for subtle contextual influences on decision-making (Tversky and Kahneman 1981). They refer to the effect that different but otherwise equivalent descriptions of choice problems give rise to preference reversals. Given Tversky and Kahneman's risky choice framing paradigm, the typical finding is that people are sensitive to whether the outcomes of the options are described in terms of gains (positive frame: e.g., human lives are saved) or losses (negative frame: e.g., human lives are lost): they are more risk-seeking under the negative frame and more risk-averse under the positive frame.

However, the typical framing paradigm is structured in a way that brings *only* outcomes to bear, but not a deontological focus on acts versus omissions. It is, therefore, not surprising that explanations of framing effects (Tversky and Kahneman 1981) are predominantly based on the evaluation of consequences. Yet, the findings change when the outcomes of the options are not just described either in terms of gains or losses, but *also* in terms of whether the outcomes are related either to an action or an omission. Given this slight modification, Tanner and colleagues found that participants who cared for protected values and were prone to deontological thinking (assessed separately), revealed immunity to framing effects, while framing effects were only found among people prone to consequentialist thinking (Tanner and Medin 2004; Tanner et al. 2008).

While the previous sections focused on moral and protected values in general, the next sections will focus on one specific moral value, namely "honesty."

Honesty as an important example of moral values

Honesty is a key element of ethical behavior in business. Yet, examples of dishonesty can be found everywhere. Since the turn of the century we have witnessed the deceptions that led to the economic and financial crisis, numerous accounting scandals (e.g., WorldCom, Satyam, Enron), financial fraud (e.g., Jerome Kerviel, Bernard Madoff, Kweku Adoboli), and banking scandals (e.g., the LIBOR and FX market manipulations). These cases have shocked many beyond the world of business and finance. Such recurring ethical scandals have raised questions again about the conditions and motivations underlying (dis)honest behavior (including lying, deceiving, stealing, cheating, fraud, etc.). Why do people behave honestly or dishonestly?

Research on determinants of (dis)honesty

Dishonesty is part of many business interactions, since they often provide people with the opportunity to profit (gain money) from selecting the dishonest path (or act). Such opportunities may reflect tradeoffs between taking selfish gains (by cheating, misleading others) versus acting in virtuous ways (by telling the truth). The approach predominantly taken to understand determinants of honesty is the standard economic theory with its premise that the *pursuit of self-interest* is one of the main drivers of human beings. Individuals are portrayed as opportunists who care only about maximizing their own utility of wealth; they thus will always lie when it is in their material self-interest to do so (Grover 1997; Somanthan and Rubin 2004). Certainly, standard economics provides one powerful mechanism through which honest behavior can be sustained, even when it is not in agents' immediate short-term interest: over time, through repeated interaction, cooperative equilibria can be sustained. Thus, truth-telling is incentive-compatible for an agent, even if it brings a short-run cost, as long as the agent knows that a deviation from that behavior results in the loss of long-run reputation benefits. However, in practice, reputational losses due to dishonesty do not always seem to be as dramatic as proposed in repeated games models. Therefore, some scholars have asked: why be honest when dishonesty does pay out and is rarely detected (Bhide and Stevenson, 1990)? Clearly, according to these views, strategies aimed at increasing the frequency and magnitude of truth-telling have to center around changes in the consequences. This typically means either changing the reinforcement contingencies or implementing controls and monitoring measures to increase the detection of dishonest behavior.

In contrast to such proposals, but in line with the self-interested view, several psychologists have highlighted the role of *self-control mechanisms* in restraining selfish temptations (e.g., Baumeister and Heartherton 1996; Mischel 1974). Yet, self-control is effortful and does require mental resources. It was, therefore, hypothesized that depletion of self-control resources would make one "too tired to tell the truth" (Mead et al. 2009). Consistent with this, studies demonstrated that individuals cheated less when the situation allowed for self-control, but they cheated more when individual's self-control resources were depleted by prior mental exertion (Gino et al. 2011; Mead et al. 2009).

However, in sharp contrast to the self-interest hypothesis, history and daily life provides us with numerous examples of virtuous role models (e.g., Nelson Mandela, Ghandi), whistleblowers, or journalists who seem to accept enormous costs in order to reveal the truth about the wrongdoing of organizations or political systems. In addition, there is mounting evidence from experimental studies that more people tell the truth than conventional models would predict. For example, using a simple sender–receiver game, Gneezy (2005) found that many people were not only unwilling to lie but they took also care about the well-being of others. Other studies investigating cheating in various contexts (e.g., tax evasion, cheating in classroom, and simulated business interactions) also found a substantial fraction of individuals who behaved honestly, even at the expense of financial benefits (e.g., Evans et al. 2001; Sánchez-Pagés and Vorsatz 2007; Zak 2008).

Some scholars interpreted those findings to be consistent with the existence of two groups: the *economic type* (who cares only about consequences) and the *ethical type* (who cares only about moral oughts) (Hurkens and Kartik 2009; Koford and Penno 1992). In line with the deontological approach, the ethical type conceptualizes honesty as a prescriptive norm. But other work suggests that these categories are likely to be malleable by *contextual influences*. Gibson et al. (2013) provide a simple experiment that rejects the type-based model by observing that agents do change behavior as economic costs of stating the truth change. Moreover, studies have shown that people are less likely to behave honestly in public rather than in private settings (Abeler et al. 2014), in market rather than in personal contexts (Cappelen et al. 2013), in competitive rather than in cooperative settings (Rode 2010), or when people are exposed to a social norm that approves rather than disapproves dishonesty (Gino et al 2009). Finally, other interesting research suggests that the mere exposure to material objects common to the domain of business (such as briefcases, boardroom tables, money) triggers (non-consciously) competitive behavior (Kay et al. 2004; Voh et al. 2006), whereas moral reminders (such as honor codes or the Ten Commandments) cause people to cheat less (Ariely 2012). Overall, these results lend more support to the view that individual behavior, when it comes to truth-telling, is heterogeneous.

Emphasizing moral commitments as an essential source of moral motivations, research lines referring to concepts such as *moral identity* (Aquino and Reed 2002; Blasi 1983) or *moral integrity* (Carter 1996) propose that an individual feels committed to moral oughts when moral beliefs and values are central to one's self-understanding. Indeed, (cross-cultural) studies have confirmed that strong moral commitments are associated with less cheating and corruption in business (Fine 2010). These approaches share with the approach of the *protected values* that at least some people would behave truthfully because they treat honesty as morally mandatory, even when it is associated with extrinsic costs.

Approaches of *moral self-regulation* attempt to integrate such positions into a dynamic view (e.g., Bandura 1986; Carver and Scheier 1981). They state that individuals are motivated to behave consistently with their moral standards and to maintain a positive view of themselves by exercising control over their behaviors through self-regulatory processes. Within such systems, internalized moral values serve as an internal reference by which compliance with the moral standards leads to intrinsic rewards and deviations leads to intrinsic costs of lying (Bandura 1986; Mazar et al. 2008). One advantage of the self-regulatory frameworks is that it may integrate both the deontological and consequentialist aspects. Individuals endorsing honesty as a moral duty are more than other people motivated to behave consistently with this principle (this is the deontological part), while behaving in line with this internalized standard minimizes lying costs (this is the consequentialist part).

Other developments by economic researchers have started to model moral identity management less in terms of commitments to moral oughts (as, for example, in the approach by Aquino and Reed 2002) but more in terms of "investments" into moral identity. By highlighting the notion of *self-signaling* (Bénabou and Tirole 2011), the premise is that individuals are uncertain about their moral self, and they signal their true identity to themselves through their actions (see also Bem 1972). According to this view, individuals are then primarily motivated to behave honestly, when such a behavior is more likely to reinforce a positive view of oneself as a moral being.

In sum, prior research suggests that truth-telling is likely to reflect both adherence to moral principles and regulation based on consequences. The next section describes some recent results from our own research on the interplay of these two factors.

Experimental evidence on protected values for honesty

How relevant are protected values for honesty in the realm of economic decision-making? Conceptually, treating honesty as a protected value implies a motivation to defend honesty against monetary tradeoffs, because considering such tradeoffs would threaten and undermine one's self-image as a moral being (e.g., Fiske and Tetlock 1997). We, therefore, hypothesized that the extent to which individuals consider honesty as a protected value would determine the regulatory potency of situational factors (such as monetary incentives) in affecting dishonesty. The framework and findings testing this general hypothesis are detailed in Gibson, Tanner, and Wagner (2013, 2015) and Tanner, Gibson, and Wagner (2015). To our knowledge, these studies are the first to test the relevance of the protected values' concept in situations where acting according to these values is actually financially costly. Here, we present some selected findings.

The existence of a felt obligation to behave honestly is likely to be most clearly visible in situations where living up to such a commitment entails a sacrifice. We used *earnings' management* as an example of a realistic business context that confronts people with a tradeoff between expected monetary gains and honesty. Earnings' management occurs when a manager changes reported earnings to mislead stakeholders about the accurate economic performance of the company (Healy and Wahlen 1999). Hence, earnings' management can be viewed as a form of deceit or dishonesty. Typically, a manager's salary has a fixed and variable component, while the variable one is often tied to the announced earnings. That is, managers can profit financially from behaving dishonestly. It may be important to mention that such a behavior, even though it is a case of lying, is permitted within a *legal* range, provided by generally accepted accounting standards.

These are the features that we simulated in our experiments as well. The participants were placed in the situation of a manager and asked to disclose earnings per share (EPS) of their companies in multiple-choice tasks. In each choice situation they had the option to announce the real economic performance (honest option) or not (dishonest option). The situations only varied in terms of *opportunity costs* (i.e., the benefits in terms of variable salary a person would have received when behaving dishonestly). We used *real* money as financial consequences. Crucially, participants earned less money when choosing the honest option. Standard economic models, which view individuals essentially as being self-interested and utility maximizing, would predict that people do not behave honestly in such situations.

The extent to which participants treated honesty as a protected value ($PV_{honesty}$) was assessed with the Protected Value Measure (Tanner et al. 2009) in separate steps. To illustrate: in one set of experiments, participants were provided with five choice tasks, in each of them they had to choose between announcing the true earnings per share (honest option) or announcing higher earnings per share (dishonest option). The five situations differed in terms of opportunity costs. The costs of behaving honestly (i.e., announcing the true earnings per share) differed in the five situations from CHF 0.00 (not-costly) to CHF 1.20 (costly), in steps of 30 Rappen (cents). At the end, participants got real money, the amount being dependent on their decisions.

Combining the results of several such experiments ($N = 361$), we generally found that in about 36.9% of the situations involving costs for honesty, participants preferred the honest option, foregoing monetary benefits. Participants sacrificed 31.1% of the total amount of money they could have earned. We also found that 21.3% of all the participants were displaying absolute tradeoff resistance, i.e., these individuals kept on behaving honestly, irrespective of the financial costs involved. This behavior was more often adopted by individuals stating stronger $PV_{honesty}$, as indicated in Fig. 11.1 (where for the sake of convenience, $PV_{honesty}$ is divided into low vs. high, based on a median split). As can be seen in Fig. 11.1, people stating higher levels of $PV_{honesty}$ were more likely to behave honestly—even when it was costly for them do to so. In a further study, we also found that people endorsing $PV_{honesty}$ were also more likely to resist the pressure from social norms, which suggest that dishonesty is socially approved (Gibson et al. 2015).

But let us also note that Fig. 11.1 also reveals a wide range of heterogeneity in individual behavior. Though 36.6% of individuals of the group high in $PV_{honesty}$ displayed absolute tradeoff resistance (compared to 7.4% within the group low in $PV_{honesty}$), intentions of even highly intrinsically motivated individuals (Bowles and Polania-Reyes 2012) appear to *crowd out* when higher incentives for cheating are provided.

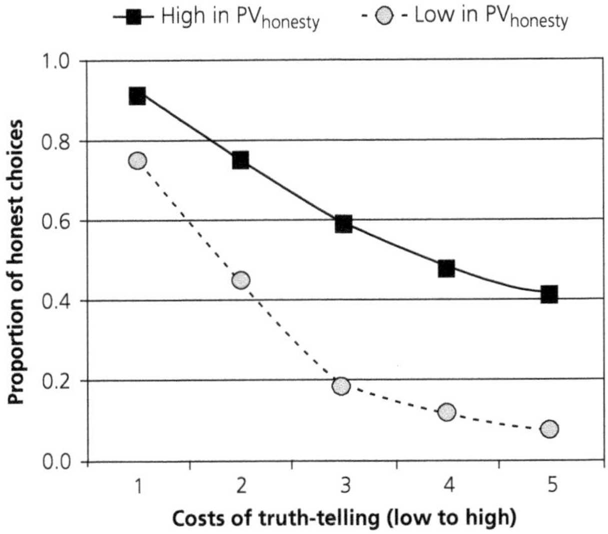

Fig. 11.1 Proportion of honest choices as a function of $PV_{honesty}$ and costs of truth-telling (varying from low to high).

One possible explanation of the difference between individuals high or low in PV may be that they differ in their skills to make tradeoffs and calculations. To examine this, we provided people in another study ($N = 261$), beyond the original *honesty task* (taboo tradeoff) also with an *effort task* (routine tradeoff). This latter task was identical to the honesty task, except that participants had to make tradeoffs between effort and monetary benefits. More specifically, participants were asked to engage in five sets of simple calculation tasks. In each of them they had the option to do one or five calculations. They could increase their payment by doing more calculations. But more payment would also imply taking more effort or time to solve calculations. Again, choice situations differed in terms of monetary compensations associated with doing one or five calculations. The costs of engaging in one calculation instead of doing five differed from not-costly to costly.

As expected, with regard to the honesty task, we found very similar findings as described in Fig. 11.1. But with regard to the effort task, we found no differences at all between people low or high in $PV_{honesty}$ (see Fig. 11.2). This finding is important, because it suggests that individuals high in $PV_{honesty}$ are not less skilled in doing standard tradeoffs. They only differ from other people when honesty comes into play.

In more recent studies, we also studied the role of $PV_{honesty}$ and perception of trustworthiness of CEOs in *investment decisions* (Tanner et al. 2015). Participants were in the situation of investors who had to decide in which of two companies (one managed by CEO A and the other by CEO B) they wanted to invest their money. For this purpose, participants were also provided with some information about the two companies, which were identical, except that CEO A and CEO B announced different earnings per share (EPS) and thus received different salaries. Based on this information, we expected that participants will infer that one CEO is more committed to honesty (since he does not engage in earnings' management) and hence is more trustworthy, while the other CEO is less committed to honesty (since he engages in earnings' management) and thus is less trustworthy.

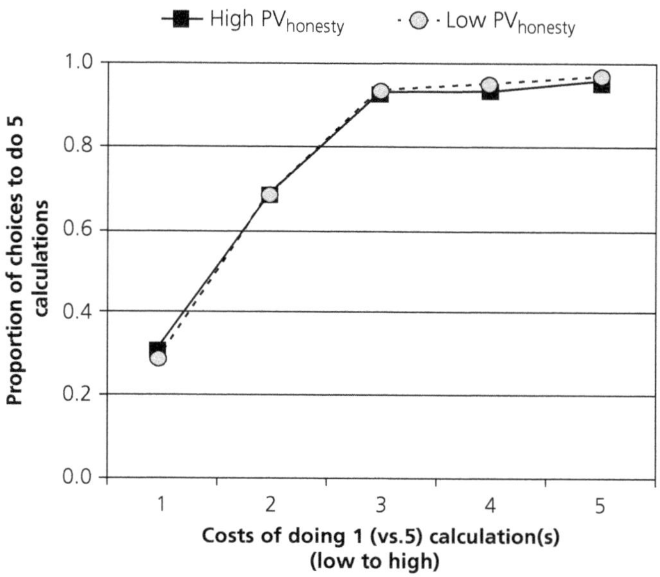

Fig. 11.2 Proportion of choices to do five calculations as a function of $PV_{honesty}$ and costs of doing one calculation (instead of five calculations) (varying from low to high).

Indeed, the studies revealed that the CEO who did not engage in earnings' management was perceived as more honest, trustworthy, and credible, and this, in turn, increased the likelihood of investing more into this CEO than into the other company. Importantly, this relation was more prominent for those investors with higher levels of $PV_{honesty}$. The results suggest that perceived honesty and trust of market participants is an essential aspect of investment decisions, but that this aspect is particularly important for some categories of investors (those with higher levels of $PV_{honesty}$).

Overall, our research provides evidence that individuals vary in their propensity to tell the truth and that some people are more likely to treat honesty as a moral mandate, which is expressed in the stronger (albeit not always absolute) resistance to trade honesty off against money. The study on investors' decisions adds to this by suggesting that the perception of other people as honest and trustworthy may economically pay off, and that this relation is moderated by individuals own level of $PV_{honesty}$. Nonetheless, what we also see from our studies, is that there is not only heterogeneity between individuals, but also much within individuals (see also Gibson et al. 2013); the intrinsic motivation among individuals claiming higher levels of moral commitments appears to crowd out when exposed to higher incentives for cheating.

Some speculative thoughts on policy relevance and implications for practitioners

It is tempting to consider—even at this early stage of research—possible implications of the research cited in the previous sections for business practices. We shall give in to this temptation and in particular speculate on how hiring decisions, corporate governance policies, remuneration policies, and the role of regulation may be affected by the previous findings. In doing so, our task is to raise hopefully interesting questions and make a few conjectures, rather than to report on firmly established evidence.

We may first conjecture that in order to establish a moral climate and ethically driven corporate governance policies, firms should hire managers and boards of directors' members who display moral values; for instance, those who possess high protected values for honesty. We have seen previously that such individuals are better able to resist tradeoffs between monetary benefits (associated with cheating) and honesty or to resist the pressure from morally (dubious) social norms. Thus, these individuals are a priori well-equipped to manage a firm in the long-run interests of all its stakeholders, since they can sacrifice short-term personal gains and resist negative social pressure for the sake of implementing corporate choices rooted in integrity. Such hiring decisions at the top of corporations, however, may raise other questions. First, will the established management hire such moral leaders at the risk of losing their own situational rents? Second, managers with high integrity may favor a cooperative climate for doing business that may not be compatible with the competitive environment under which companies have to operate. Finally, one may wonder whether individuals endorsing protected values may be less open for innovations and policies that require changes. In short, interesting tensions could be explored in further research that may, under some circumstances, lead to the conclusion that absolute protected values are optimal, whereas in other circumstances an interior solution may be optimal.

Another core lesson from the literature on honest decision-making rooted in deontological motives is that the "principal–agent" conflicts' issue may need to be revisited. Central to the corporate finance literature, it describes the type of contract that an owner, i.e. principal, will write with the agent who works for him in order to incentivize him to exercise best effort. Indeed, the hiring of virtuous leaders may resolve or mitigate this problem without relying so heavily on financial incentives to align the interests between the principals and such virtuous agents. This statement brings us to the related topic of managerial remuneration that has over the past two decades been at the heart of the corporate governance dilemmas faced by corporations. Corporate shareholders have to regularly deal with issues such as excessive managerial pay, the lack of pay for performance, misaligned incentives resulting from executive compensation packages, and even fraud on a massive scale (e.g., "the investment banking Libor scandal"). Carlin and Gervais (2009) have shown that when one hires a virtuous manager, the optimal contract is a fixed-wage contract. The key message is that high-morality individuals who are driven primarily by deontological motives need not be subject to such high financial incentives to work in the interest of their principals: they derive their satisfaction from doing the right thing without requiring extra compensation for that purpose. Despite a number of challenges, we thus believe that the favorable characteristics of leaders with high moral traits make them well-suited to promote an ethical culture and sound corporate governance principles within their organizations. When it comes to the long-term prospects, we would argue that one first needs to analyze the fitness for survival of moral leaders and whether their firm's profits are sustainable within competitive environments. Another challenge for future research would be to deepen our understanding of the possible workings, implications, and limitations of a system of governance and incentives that acknowledges protected values as one important force in economic decision-making.

Finally, it is worth considering the potential role and need for regulation to foster sound corporate governance and remuneration policies, especially in systemically risky industries, which are prone to market abuses (such as the financial industry). Preventing market abuse, protecting customers and clients, and promoting a climate of trust in the markets and in our financial institutions are all important goals that require an enforcement of individual and thus ultimately market integrity. It is, however, a matter of debate as to whether markets can, and, in fact, will, implement such enforcement goals freely (via self-regulation, whereby behavior in line with integrity gets rewarded by market participants) or whether regulation needs to be exogenously imposed. Optimal regulation represents a challenging task. While exogenous regulation is arguably needed to directly address the most egregious cases of misconduct and while it is, by design, a powerful enforcement tool, it can also come at significant direct and indirect costs, including distorted incentives. Besides direct command and control regulation, there are also approaches attempting to leverage the power of financial incentives in order to foster proper conduct by market participants. Some may worry that this, by nature, goes counter to the very notion of trying to promote moral behavior. Whether or not one shares this view, however, it is to be kept in mind that the interplay of financial incentives and intrinsic preferences is far from trivial. A significant number of studies show that financial incentives may ultimately "crowd out" the moral intentions of highly intrinsically motivated individuals. A smaller, but noteworthy set of studies shows that financial incentives can, in fact, "crowd in" intrinsic preferences (for a survey, see: Bowles and Polania-Reyes 2012). Future research must make progress in identifying the conditions under which one or the other happens.

Conclusion: some open issues in research on honesty and economic decision-making

Despite a prolific literature on the theme of moral values and, more specifically, of honesty in economic decision-making, a number of questions still remain open for future research. We have highlighted some of the more policy-oriented questions in the previous section. Here, we close with two more conceptual questions.

First, it would be interesting to explore whether reputation in repeated strategic games, complements the role of preferences for truth-telling in fostering agents' truth-telling propensity, or whether there are, in fact, substitutive effects between reputation and preferences for truth-telling. Similarly, we have ruled out from our discussion other important situational factors, such as the roles of explicit punishment, group dynamics, and loyalty considerations, in enhancing or hindering agent honesty in economic choices. Further research could investigate how these factors interact with intrinsic preferences for truth-telling.

Second, while several authors have acknowledged the existence of individuals' preferences for truth-telling, it remains unclear whether those preferences are driven by selfish (such as signaling one's identity as an honest person, for instance) or unselfish considerations or by a mixture of both. A related question is to determine whether moral economic choices rely on emotional and/or cognitive processes and the extent to which those processes are associated with different brain regions than those activated by standard economic choices. We believe that the cross-fertilization of experimental economics, neuroscience, and psychology will in the future be able to shed light on these fundamental questions.

Acknowledgment

This research was funded by the Research Priority Program Finance and Financial Markets of the University of Zurich, the NCCR FINRISK, the Swiss Finance Institute, the Swiss National Science Foundation (Grant #PP001-102845), and the ERC (FP7/2007-2013, grant agreement 249415 RMAC).

References

Abeler, J., Becker, A., and Falk, A. (2014). Representative evidence on lying costs. Journal of Public Economics, **113**, 96–104.

Aquino, K. and Reed, A. (2002). The self-importance of moral identity. *Journal of Personality and Social Psychology*, **83**, 1423–1440.

Ariely, D. (2012). *The (Honest) Truth about Dishonesty: how we Lie to Everyone—Especially Ourselves.* New York: Harper Collins Publishers.

Atran, S., Axelrod, R., and Davis, R. (2007). Sacred barriers to conflict resolution. *Science*, **317**, 1039–1040.

Bandura, A., (1986). *Social Foundations of Thought and Action*. Englewood Cliffs: Prentice-Hall.

Baron, J. and Leshner, S. (2000). How serious are protected values? *Journal of Experimental Psychology: Applied*, **3**, 183–194.

Baron, J. and Spranca, M. (1997). Protected values. *Organizational Behavior and Human Decision Process*, **70**, 1–16.

Bartels, D. M. (2008). Principled moral sentiment and the flexibility of moral judgment and decision-making. *Cognition*, **108**, 381–417.

Bartels, D. M. and Medin, D. (2007). Are morally motivated decision makers insensitive to the consequences of their choices? *Psychological Science*, **18**, 24–28.

Baumeister, R. F. and Heatherton, T. F. (1996). Self-regulation failure: an overview. *Psychological Inquiry*, **7**, 1–15.

Bem, D. J. (1972). Self-perception theory. In: L. Berkowitz (ed.). *Advances in Experimental Social Psychology*. New York: Academic Press, pp. 2–62.

Bentham, J. (1789). *An Introduction to the Principles of Morals and Legislation*. London: Athlone Press.

Bhide, A. and Stevenson, H. H. (1990). Why be honest when honesty doesn't pay? *Harvard Business Review*, **68**, 121–130.

Black, R. D. Collison (2008).Utility. In S. N. Durlauf and L. E. Blume (eds). *The new Palgrave dictionary of economics*. London: MacMillan. http://www.dictionaryofeconomics.com/article?id=pde2008_U000047

Blasi, A. (1983). Moral cognition and moral action: a theoretical perspective. *Developmental Review*, **3**, 178–210.

Blume, L. E. and Easley, D. (2008). The new Palgrave dictionary of economics. In S. N. Durlauf and L. E. Blume (eds). *Rationality*. London: MacMillan.

Bowles, S. and Polanía-Reyes, S. (2012). Economic incentives and social preferences: substitutes or complements? *Journal of Economic Literature*, **50**, 368–425.

Bowley, M. (1973). *Studies in the History of Economic Theory before 1870.* London: MacMillan.

Bruni, L. and Sugden R. (2013). Reclaiming virtue ethics for economics. *Journal of Economic Perspectives*, **27**, 141–164.

Bénabou, R. and Tirole, J. (2011). Identity, morals, and taboos: beliefs as assets. *Quarterly Journal of Economics*, **126**, 805–855.

Cappelen, A. W., Sørensen, E. Ø., and Tungodden, B., 2013. When do we lie? *Journal of Economic Behavior and Organization*, **93, 258–265.**

Carlin, B. and Gervais, S. (2009). Work ethic, employment contracts, and firm value. *Journal of Finance*, **64**, 785–821.

Carter, S. (1996). *Integrity.* New York: Harper Perennial.

Carver, C. S. and Scheier, M. F. (1981). *Attention and Self-regulation: A Control Theory Approach to Human Behavior.* New York: Springer-Verlag.

Eaton, J. and Gersowitz, M. (1981). Debt with potential repudiation: theoretical and empirical analysis. *Review of Economic Studies*, **48**, 289–309.

Edgeworth, F. Y. (1899).Utility. In R. H. Palgrave (ed.). *Dictionary of political economy.* London: MacMillan, pp. 776–779.

Erat, S. and Gneezy, U. (2012). White lies. *Management Science*, **58**, 723–733.

Evans, J., Hannan, L.R., Krishnan, R., and Moser, D. V. (2001). Honesty in managerial reporting. *Accounting Review*, **76**, 537–559.

Fehr, E. and Fischbacher, U. (2003). The nature of human altruism. *Nature*, **425**, 785–791.

Fehr, E. and Schmidt, K. M. (1999). A theory of fairness, competition, and cooperation. *The Quarterly Journal of Economics*, **114**, 817–868.

Fehr, E., Kirchsteiger, G., and Riedl, A.(1993). Does fairness prevent market clearing? An experimental investigation. *Quarterly Journal of Economics*, **108**, 437–460.

Fehr, E., Kirchsteiger, G., and Riedl, A.(1998). Gift exchange and reciprocity in competitive experimental markets. *European Economic Review*, **42**, 1–34.

Fine, S. (2010). Cross-cultural integrity testing as a marker of regional corruption rates. *International Journal of Selection and Assessment*, **18**, 251–259.

Fiske, A. P. and Tetlock, P. E. (1997). Taboo trade-offs: reactions to transactions that transgress the spheres of justice. *International Society of Political Psychology*, **18**, 255–297.

Gibson, R., Tanner, C., and Wagner, A.F. (2013). Preferences for truthfulness: heterogeneity among and within individuals. *American Economic Review*, **103**, 532–548.

Gibson, R., Tanner, C., and Wagner, A. F. (2015). Do situational social norms crowd out intrinsic preferences? An experiment regarding the choice of honesty, CEPR Discussion Paper 9880 and Swiss Finance Institute Research Paper 15-01.

Ginges, J. and Atran, S. (2009). Noninstrumental reasoning over sacred values: an Indonesian case study. In D. M. Bartels, C. W. Bauman, L. J. Skitka and D. L. Medin (eds). *Moral Judgment and Decision Making.* San Diego: Academic Press, pp. 193–206.

Ginges, J., Atran, S., Medin, D., and Shikaki, K. (2007). Sacred bounds on rational resolution of violent political conflict. *Proceedings of the National Academy of Sciences*, **104**, 7357–7360.

Gino, F., Ayal, S., and Ariely, D. (2009). Contagion and differentiation in unethical behavior. *Psychological Science*, **20**, 393–398.

Gino, F., Schweitzer, M.E., Mead, N.L., and Ariely, D. (2011). Unable to resist temptation: how self-control depletion promotes unethical behavior. *Organizational Behavior and Human Decision Processes*, **155**, 191–203.

Gino, F., Krupka, E. L., and Weber, R. A. (2013). License to cheat: voluntary regulation and ethical behavior. *Management Science*, **59**, 2187–2203.

Gneezy, U. (2005). Deception: the role of consequences. *American Economic Review*, **95**, 384–394.

Greene, J. D. (2007). The secret joke of Kant's soul. In W. Sinnott-Armstrong (ed.). *Moral Psychology*, Vol. 3: *The Neuroscience of Morality: Emotion, Brain Disorders, and Development*. Cambridge, MA: MIT Press, pp. 35–80.

Grover, S. L. (1997). Lying in organizations: theory, research, and future directions. In R. A. Giacalone, R. A. and J. Greenberg (eds). *Antisocial Behaviour in Organizations*. Thousand Oaks: Sage, pp. 68–84.

Guiso, L., Sapienza, P., and Zingales, L. (2008). Trusting the stock market. *Journal of Finance*, **63**, 2557–2600.

Güth, W., Schmittberger, R., and Schwarze, B. (1982). An experimental analysis of ultimatum bargaining. *Journal of Economic Behavior and Organization*, **3**, 367–388.

Hanselmann, M. and Tanner, C. (2008). Taboos and conflicts in decision making: sacred values, decision difficulty, and emotions. *Judgment and Decision-making*, **3**, 51–63.

Healy, P. M. and Wahlen, J. M. (1999). A review of the earnings management literature and its implications for standard setting. *Accounting Horizons*, **13**, 365–383.

Hurkens, S. and Kartik, N. (2009) Would I lie to you? On social preferences and lying aversion. *Experimental Economics*, **12**, 180–192.

Iliev, R., Sachdeva, S., Bartels, D. M., Joseph, C., Suzuki, S., and Medin, D. L. (2009). Attending to moral values. In D. M. Bartels, C. W. Bauman, L. J. Skitka and D. L. Medin (eds). *Moral Judgment and Decision Making*. San Diego: Academic Press, pp. 170–192.

Kahneman, D., Knetsch, J. L., and Thaler, R. (1986). Fairness as a constraint on profit seeking: entitlements in the market. *The American Economic Review*, **76**, 728–741.

Kant, I. (1797). *Die Metaphysik der Sitten [The Metaphysics of Morals]. 2 Teile*. Königsbert: Nicolovius.

Kay, A. C., Wheeler, C. S., Bargh, J. A., and Ross, L. (2004). Material priming: the influence of mundane physical objects on situational construal and competitive behavioral choice. *Organizational Behavior and Human Decision Processes*, **95**, 83–96.

Koford, K. and Penno, M. (1992). Accounting, principal-agent theory, and self-interested behavior. In N. E. Bowie and R. E. Freeman (eds). *Ethics and Agency Theory: An Introduction*. New York: Oxford University Press, pp. 127–142.

Kouzakova, M., Harinck, F., Ellemers, N., and Scheepers, D. (2013). At the heart of a conflict. Cardiovascular and self-regulation responses to value versus resource conflicts. *Social Psychological and Personality Science*, **5**, 35–42.

Lichtenstein, S., Gregory, R., and Irwin, J. (2007). What's bad is easy: taboo values, affect, and cognition. *Judgment and Decision-making*, **2**, 169–188.

Mazar, N., Amir, O., and Ariely, D., (2008). The dishonesty of honest people: a theory of self-concept maintenance. *Journal of Marketing Research*, **45**, 633–644.

McGraw, P. A. and Tetlock, P. E. (2005). Taboo tradeoffs, relational framing, and the acceptability of exchanges. *Journal of Consumer Psychology*, **15**, 2–15.

Mead, N. L., Baumeister, R. F., Gino, F., Schweitzer, M. E., and Ariely, D. (2009). Too tired to tell the truth: self-control resource depletion and dishonesty. *Journal of Experimental Social Psychology*, **45**, 594–597.

Mill, J.S. (1861). Utilitarianism. In J. M. Robson (ed.). *Essays on Ethics, Religion, and Society, Vol. 10 of Collected Works of John Stuart Mill*. Toronto, University of Toronto Press, 1969, pp. 203–260.

Mischel, W. (1974). Processes in delay of gratification. In L. Berkowitz (ed.). *Advances in Experimental Social Psychology*. New York: Academic Press, pp. 249–292.

Norris, P. and Inglehart, R. (2004). *Sacred and Secular: Religion and Politics Worldwide*. Cambridge: Cambridge University Press.

Riley, J., (2008). The new Palgrave dictionary of economics. In S. N. Durlauf and L. E. Blume (eds). *Utilitarianism and Economic Theory*. London: MacMillan.

Ritov, I. and Baron, J. (1990). Reluctance to vaccinate: omission bias and ambiguity. *Journal of Behavioral Decision-making*, **3**, 263–277.

Ritov, I. and Baron, J. (1999). Protected values and omission bias. *Organizational Behavior and Human Decision Processes*, **79**, 79–94.

Rode, J. (2010). Truth and trust in communication—experiments on the effect of a competitive context. *Games and Economic Behavior*, **68**, 325–338.

Sandel, M. (2012). *What Money Can't Buy: the Moral Limits of Markets*. New York: Farrar, Straus and Giroux.

Sandel, M.J. (2013). Market reasoning as moral reasoning: why economists should re-engage with political philosophy. *Journal of Economic Perspectives*, **27**, 121–140.

Skitka, L. J., Bauman, C. W., and Sargis, E. G. (2005). Moral conviction another contributor to attitude strength or something more? *Journal of Personality and Social Psychology*, **88**, 895–917.

Smith, A. (1776). *An Inquiry into the Nature and Causes of the Wealth of Nations*. Oxford: Clarendon Press.

Somanathan, E. and Rubin, P. H. (2004). The evolution of honesty. *Journal of Economic Behavior and Organization*, **54**, 1–17.

Sánchez-Pagés, S. and Vorsatz, M. (2007). An experimental study of truth-telling in a sender-receiver game. *Games and Economic Behavior*, **61**, 86–112.

Tanner, C. (2009). To act or not to act: nonconsequentialism in environmental decision-making. *Ethics and Behavior*, **19**, 479–495.

Tanner, C. Gibson, R. and Wagner, A. F. (2015). Investment decisions and protected values: The case of honesty, University of Zurich working paper.

Tanner, C. and Medin, D. L. (2004). Protected values: no omission bias and no framing effects. *Psychonomic Bulletin and Review*, **11**, 185–191.

Tanner, C., Medin, D. L., and Iliev, R. (2008). Influence of deontological vs. consequentialist orientations on act choices and framing effects: when principles are more important than consequences. *European Journal of Social Psychology*, **38**, 757–769.

Tanner, C., Ryf, B., and Hanselmann, M. (2009). Protected value measure: construction and validation of an instrument to assess sacred values. *Diagnostica*, **55**, 174–183.

Tetlock, P. E. (2003). Thinking the unthinkable: sacred values and taboo cognitions. *Trends in Cognitive Sciences*, **7**, 320–324.

Tetlock, P. E., Kristel, O. V., Elson, S. B., Green, M., and Lerner, J. S. (2000). The psychology of the unthinkable. Taboo trade-offs, forbidden base rates, and heretical counterfactuals. *Journal of Personality and Social Psychology*, **5**, 853–870.

Thompson, L. L. and Gonzalez, R. (1997). Environmental disputes: competition for scarce resources and clashing of values. In M. H. Bazerman, D. M. Messick, A. E. Tenbrunsel, and K. A. Wade-Benzoni (eds), *Environment, Ethics, and Behavior*. San Francisco: New Lexington, pp. 75–104.

Tversky, A. and Kahneman, D. (1974). Judgment under uncertainty: heuristics and biases. *Science*, **185**, 1124–1131.

Tversky, A. and Kahneman, D. (1981). The framing of decisions and the psychology of choice. *Science*, **211**, 453–458.

Vohs, K. D., Mead, N. L., and Goode, M. R. (2006). The psychological consequences of money. *Science*, ***314***, 1154–1156.

Zak, P. J. (2008). *Moral Markets: the Critical Role of Values in the Economy*. Princeton and Oxford: Princeton University Press.

Chapter 12

Values and behavior

Gabriela M. Jiga-Boy, Gregory R. Maio, Geoffrey Haddock, and Katy Tapper

Introduction

The current social, economic, and political states of our habitats reveal a pressing need to think about the values that guide our behavior. From the ongoing financial crises to national and trans-national issues such as climate change, immigration, and impending refugee emergencies, we are tempted to look for general guides that can predict how we should respond to these problems. Were there values that prompted the immense financial misdemeanors in the past, and are there values that could prevent them in the future? What values guide the way we construe immigration, and how will they orient our response to the new market laws? Will the values of equality and freedom be extended to help refugees? And how will we overcome our present tendency to overconsume, in light of the detrimental effects this has on the environment?

Such questions signal the need to find more than temporary, immediate responses; we need *trans-situational* or more *sustainable* solutions. This is where values can play a role. Longstanding social psychological theories of values stress their functioning across diverse situations (e.g., Feather 1995; Rokeach 1973; Schwartz 1992). They are ideals that can guide our responses in a way that is more stable than ad hoc solutions. For example, ideals such as fairness, tolerance, or equality could lead to a more coherent and long-term societal response to immigration than short-term solutions such as changes in government aid provisions. This premise has led scholars and lay people to naturally expect values to have a high influence on everyday behavior. After all, how can humans live without ideals that give coherence to their actions?

Extant evidence makes us broadly sympathetic to this perspective, but it also forces us to look more closely at the nature of the value–behavior link. In our opinion, the potential for values to shape behavior has elicited a somewhat artificial view that our values should be visible in *every* behavior we perform. Consequently, much of the debate in science or in domains where this matters (e.g., politics, public policy) has focused on the instances when that is not the case: instances where our behavior seems wildly discrepant from our values or instances where evidence fails to reveal associations between personal values and relevant behavior. In this review, we argue that this view is, first, an artificial stance regarding values and behavior, however popular it may be to think of a "value–behavior gap" (Maio 2011). Second, we argue that this view ignores a substantive methodological problem, namely that values and behavior reside at different levels of concreteness. Thus, we propose that the extent to which values guide our behavior depends on the *process* through which values are applied, the *types of behavior* being performed, and the *contexts* in which we look at values within behavior.

This focus entails considering diverse questions: Is the behavior that is aligned to one's values the easier option to choose? Is it the most (stereo)typical or the most normative? Is it an old, easy-to-perform action consistent with our past behaviors, or a new, challenging one? A common feature of these questions is that they tackle the relationship between values and behavior by looking more closely at *behavior*. This focus on behavior complements the focus on values that is found in abundant prior research. Together, we believe these complementary foci yield a more complete picture of the value–behavior relationship.

This chapter first addresses broad definitions and assumptions about values—what values are and are not, as they are defined within the social psychological literature. It then discusses whether values impact behavior by looking at the relationships between values and personality, and at how different values are seen in different domains: political/voting behavior, prosocial behavior and morality, environmental behavior, and consumer behavior. Finally, the chapter takes the debate about values' influence on behavior to the issue of what mechanisms or processes can account for this relationship, or for the lack of it: the congruence of values with social norms, the characteristics and mindsets of people, and the extent to which values are mindful components of one's mental space or merely cultural truisms spontaneously applied.

What are values?

Traditional conceptualizations of values within social psychology have defined them in numerous ways. Rokeach (1973) introduced a distinction between values that specify ways of behaving (instrumental values) and values that serve as desired end states (terminal values). Contemporary views define values as "abstract structures that involve the beliefs that people hold about desirable ways of behaving or about desirable end states" (Feather 1995: 1135). However, the most important aspect of values, which transcends the instrumental versus terminal distinction, is the idea that values operate as *guides for action*. Values transcend situations and have, in Feather's words, a "normative, or oughtness quality."

But rather than discussing what values actually are, research on values tends to outline the aspects that differentiate them from other psychological concepts such as needs, attitudes, norms, or traits—in other words, what values *are not*. Values are "conceptions of the desirable" (Kluckhohn 1951; Schwartz and Bilsky 1987) that capture ideals and give meaning to actions (Rokeach 1973), thus holding a "higher place in one's internal evaluative hierarchy" (Hitlin and Piliavin 2004: 361). Values are more positive and more abstract than attitudes (Hitlin and Piliavin 2004; Rokeach 1973), because while attitudes reflect an evaluation of an object on a continuum from negative to positive (Maio and Haddock 2010), values rather illustrate the desirable aspect of a behavior. Values are trans-situational, while norms are situation-based. Values elicit goals (Parks and Guay 2009; Verplanken and Holland 2002), while traits are enduring dispositions (Roccas et al. 2002).

As discussed elsewhere in this Handbook (see Schwartz, this volume), the most prominent contemporary model of values is Schwartz's universal model of human values, which focuses on motivational dynamics among values (Schwartz 1992; Schwartz and Bilsky 1987). According to this model, ten distinct values reflect an intrapsychic balancing act among biological needs, interpersonal relationships, and societal and institutional demands: self-direction, stimulation, hedonism, achievement, power, security, conformity, tradition, benevolence, and universalism. These values are arranged in a circular system capturing the similarities and differences between them alongside two principal axes: self-enhancement/self-transcendence and openness to change/conservation. Although the positions of values and the exact types have been refined recently (Schwartz et al. 2012), the key principle is that values reflecting compatible needs are adjacent and values reflecting conflicting needs are opposed. Consequently, priority given to universalist values (tolerance, concern, nature) is predicted to undermine priority given to achievement or power values (dominance, money), as the two value types are opposed in the model (Schwartz 1996, 1994). A compelling literature demonstrates that these values, and the relationships among them, are distinguishable across various cultures and languages (e.g., Cieciuch et al. 2013; Schwartz et al. 2012).

Evidence of connections between values and behavior

Research has discovered connections between values and behavior by examining links between values and broad sets of behavioral dispositions (i.e., personality) and by linking values to particular sets of actions that are important in specific applied contexts (e.g., voting, morality, environment, consumption). This section reviews both approaches.

Values and personality

If we want to analyze values' impact on behavior, we might need to record multiple situations in which values are visible (i.e., to test their "transcending" property) and to compare the values with the behaviors that express them. A useful first step entails looking at values' consistency over time and situations.

One way of looking at this consistency is by examining the correlations between values and scores on personality measures, which directly reflect behavioral tendencies across time and situations. Extant theories of personality, however, focus on dimensions of behavior that are simultaneously relevant to different values. That is, the dominant models do not posit traits that are directly linked to values in a one-to-one fashion. This is easily discernable in the most prominent model of personality, the Five-Factor model. Roccas et al. (2002; see also: Dollinger et al. 1996; Luk and Bond 1993) and Olver and Mooradian (2003) predicted that some of the five factors would be linked to values in complex patterns, not in simple, one-to-one correspondences, and that others would simply be unrelated.

In both programs of research, neuroticism was found to be nonsignificantly correlated with ten value types from Schwartz's model. This does not in itself mean that neuroticism is fully unrelated to values, but it does suggest that behaviors relevant to neuroticism are less relevant to values than behaviors relevant to other trait dimensions. Another of Roccas et al.'s (2002) predictions stated that extraversion should provide strong support for values that affirm the importance of activity, challenge, excitement, and pleasure, while being antithetical to tradition values (e.g., respect for tradition, humble, devout). Consistent with these hypotheses, participants high in extraversion attached greater importance to achievement, stimulation, and hedonism values and lower importance to tradition values than participants low in extraversion. Olver and Mooradian (2003) supported this by showing that extraversion correlated positively with power and stimulation, and negatively with universalism—a result consistent with more classic findings that extraversion would be associated with assertiveness, social visibility, dominance, and ambition (Watson and Clark 1997). In contrast, agreeableness was correlated positively with universalism, benevolence, and tradition, and negatively with power, achievement, and stimulation.

Finally, Roccas et al. (2002) suggested that, because conscientiousness often directly aids success, aspects of conscientiousness (e.g., responsibility) tend to promote a concern with prevailing norms. Their results revealed that conscientiousness is related positively to security values and negatively to stimulation values. Olver and Mooradian (2003) found further support for this personality trait: conscientiousness was indeed positively correlated with benevolence, conformity, and achievement, and negatively with stimulation. In contrast, openness to experience was correlated positively with self-direction, stimulation, and universalism, and negatively with tradition, conformity, and power.

Within this work, it is worth noting that the correlations between traits and values are frequently low, suggesting that traits and values do not measure the same thing. For example, one might have a disposition toward acting in an authoritarian manner, but due to a positive family environment, one might weakly endorse the value of authority. Values and behavior clearly overlap, but behavior is, of course, a function of varied forces. Moreover, the correlations may arise from varied processes: the trait–value relations may arise because values shape the traits, the traits influence values, or other factors (e.g., context) influence both. Furthermore, when values influence traits, they may do so through mediators that vary across contexts (e.g., goals, perceived norms), while being moderated by factors that elicit value or trait stability across situations (e.g., individual differences in consistency, habitual determinants of behaviors).

Relevant to these routes of influence, more recent work (Schermer et al. 2008; Schermer et al. 2012) has looked at the heritable aspect of values and personality and showed that part of the link between self-transcending social values (e.g., equality, a world at peace, forgiveness, helpfulness, honesty) and personality may be explained by a genetic component (63%), while achievement values seem to be better explained by common and unique environmental influences. Thus, genetic and environmental factors may help to shape the associations between values and personality, albeit to different degrees for different values.

Related to this idea, Knafo and Spinath (2011) looked at the genetic and environmental contributions to gender-typical and gender-atypical value preferences for boys and for girls. They found that gender-typed values (self-transcendence values for girls and self-enhancement values for boys) showed higher heritability (0.49) than gender-neutral values. Their results confirmed previous findings, as well as gender stereotypes, that women attach more importance to self-transcendent values, while men attach more importance to self-enhancement values.

Another possibility is that genes create special conditions that constrain the learning or the expression of social-orientation dimensions like independence or interdependence. In a recent study addressing this issue, Asian participants scored higher on scales measuring interdependent values, while European American participants scored higher on scales measuring independent mindedness, but this predictable difference was pronounced only for those who showed more dopamine signaling due to variations of the gene DRD4 (Kitayama et al. 2014).

Different values, different behavior: some recent examples

There are instances when values may underlie particular behaviors of interest in applied settings. The examples we describe in this chapter show that values can be relevant to diverse social issues, and these examples serve to highlight how the precise role of values depends on the context.

Political attitudes and voting behavior

Research has revealed key values that play important roles in explaining people's endorsement of particular political parties or candidates. Although *freedom* and *equality* were initially seen as the prominent political values (Rokeach 1973), recent research showed that center-left voters appear higher in universalism, benevolence, and self-direction, and lower in security, power, achievement, conformity, and tradition than their center-right counterparts (Caprara et al. 2006). These values are seen as an important grounding for the ideology underlining political preferences, explaining more variance in voting behavior than personality traits (such as openness, energy, or conscientiousness). Caprara et al. suggest that this predictive power of values emerges because voting behavior entails thoughtful processing of information, whereas traits reflect both deliberative and spontaneous (or automatic) behavioral patterns. An alternative possibility is that values simply line-up better with the goals that are relevant to voting; that is, the goal content of values is more relevant to political issues of the day than are abstract traits (e.g., extraversion).

But different types of values become politically relevant depending on context (Barnea and Schwartz 1998), and their potential to shape a certain behavior is relative, not absolute. When there is political debate about conflicts between national security versus equal rights and liberties as, for example, in the recent revelations of intrusive data collection by American and British governments, these values become the focus of attention, enabling them to have more of a role in structuring how citizens construe diverse political and societal issues. In contrast, if the debate revolves around the distribution of material resources, as in controversies about extreme amounts of wealth in the hands of very few, values of universalism versus benevolence come to the forefront of public thinking.

In fact, some evidence indicates that making salient particular values or changing them are two ways in which to alter relevant political attitudes, with implications for subsequent political behavior (Bernard et al. 2003a; Blankenship and Wegener 2012; Blankenship et al. 2012). For instance, participants who read a message attacking the utility of equality in society changed their attitudes toward affirmative action more (i.e., became less favorable to affirmative action) than participants who read a message questioning the value of affirmative action in society (Blankenship et al. 2012). This indirect change through values was explained by people's decreasing confidence in the value of equality and tendency to counterargue the message following the attack, illustrating values' role as part of the cognitive structure that underlies attitudes.

Prosocial behavior and morality

Social value orientations were typically linked to values such as *fairness* or *justice* (Samuelson 1993). But there are many more values that can guide such behavior, and an important additional dimension reflects how concerns for the well-being of others are balanced alongside concerns for personal well-being. In one line of work, Garling (1999) investigated the potential for values such as universalism (reflecting concerns for fairness) or benevolence (reflecting concerns for compassion) to predict more prosocial or proself actions using a game wherein participants allocated resources between themselves and unknown others. Participants who declared universalism (but not benevolence) as a priority—or an end state they attempted to achieve—acted more prosocially than proself, possibly because fairness would play a more important role in cooperation than compassion. Whether people behave more or less prosocially in resource allocation games is illustrative of the values they endorse, or of the values that are salient at that moment, but is also shaped by the context of the game (see also Ashton and Lee 2007; Hilbig and Zettler 2009).

Other research shows that participants who scored high on values related to altruism and humanitarian concerns tended to devote more time to volunteering in the twelve months prior to testing, persisted more, and participated in a bigger volume of activities (Shantz et al. 2014). Given the growing role of volunteerism in sustaining many compassionate services, this role of values is important and merits closer scrutiny. One consideration is that the values underlying different volunteering roles can vary across different types of voluntary service. Volunteers choose their domain, initiation, and length of involvement themselves, but they also need to juggle the ratio of their involvement and its personal costs alongside the unknown nature of the recipient, when the volunteering involves personal engagement with another person. For instance, the motivation to donate blood is linked mostly to social responsibility concerns, such as morality and compassion (Karacan et al. 2013). Another form of volunteering, namely providing long-term assistance and support to people (medical patients, homeless individuals, etc.), also involves a role for compassionate values, but in competition with personal motivations. Values focusing on humanitarian concern to help others are one of the five strong predictors of

AIDS volunteerism, alongside more personal motivations such as an obligation toward the community or self-interested needs (e.g., the desire to understand an issue like AIDS, to feel better about oneself, or to develop relations with the other volunteers or beneficiaries; Omoto and Snyder 1995).

An interesting question is whether volunteering is more likely to be enjoyed and pursued over the long term when it expresses a *blend* of both self-transcendent *and* self-enhancing values than either set of values alone. Some recent research suggests one possible problem with such a combination: when self-interested reasons are seen as being co-determinants of charitable behavior alongside altruistic reasons, altruism becomes "tainted". Participants evaluated a target's actions as *less moral* when its actions led to a charitable benefit that also involved a self-interested benefit, compared to actions that had no charitable benefits whatsoever (Newman and Cain 2014). Thus, it is not enough to know that values can predict volunteering behavior; knowing *which* values are being applied allows us a better understanding of people's cognitions about the behavior.

Pro-environmental behavior

There has been a growing interest in the role of values as determinants of pro-environmental behavior, as concern mounts regarding the human response to climate change (see also Dietz, this volume). Initial findings suggested *personal moral norm* as a determinant of pro-environmental behavior independently of behavioral intentions alone (Schwartz 1977). Personal moral norm refers to "strong moral obligations that people experienced for themselves to engage in pro-social behavior" (Bamberg and Möser 2007: 15). But more recent theorizing has considered how different types of values are related to different types of pro-environmental behavior. Some researchers regard pro-environmental behavior as an extension of altruism. *Environmental altruism* refers to behavior conducted to protect the natural environment, determined by an internal set of values and carried out with no expectation of reciprocity (Schultz and Zelezny 1998). Unsurprisingly, some of the relevant values are self-transcendent (universalist) values, such as protecting the environment, a world of beauty, and unity with nature (Stern et al. 1993).

Further research has focused on three value orientations specifically relevant in this context: egoistic (expecting benefits from protecting the environment for oneself), social-altruistic (protecting others), and biospheric (concerns with other species and the natural environment). Stern et al. (1993) suggested that values lead to environmental action when people believe that environmental conditions can have adverse consequences for the things they value. People's willingness to pay, in the form of gasoline or income tax, is predicted by their awareness of consequences for oneself (egoistic), but not by the other two types of values. Of interest, these tendencies are more pronounced for women than men, suggesting that women are more likely to connect consequences of environment quality to personal well-being, social welfare, and the quality of biosphere as a whole. People who cherish universalist values are also more likely to show positive attitudes toward environmental protection (as measured by the New

Environmental Paradigm, NEP; Dunlap et al. 1992, cited by Schultz and Zelezny 1999) and more "ecocentrism"—environmental concern specifically predicated on the inherent value of natural environment.

This research on values and pro-environmental behavior has led to new tangents of investigation. First, literature supports the operation of the path from values to action via awareness of consequences. Preserving the environment by choosing biofuels instead of conventional (coal, oil) resources becomes a social dilemma involving a conflict among three factors: (1) individual versus collective or societal interests, (2) short-term versus long-term consequences of current choices, and (3) egoistic (good for me) versus biospheric (good for the biosphere) motives (Khachatryan et al. 2013). How will these three dimensions interact when determining one's preference for biofuels? Values and consideration of future consequences (CFC) do overlap: Egoistic values (e.g., control over others, dominance, material possessions, money, right to lead and command) correlate positively with concerns about both immediate and future consequences. Altruistic (e.g., equality, a world at peace, social justice, and being helpful) and biospheric values (e.g., preventing pollution, respecting the earth, unity with nature), however, correlate positively with concern about future consequences but negatively with concerns about immediate consequences. Hence, participants who endorse more strongly egoistic values tend to be more oriented toward the immediate, short-term consequences of their actions, while those who endorse altruistic and biospheric values tend to be more oriented toward the future, long-term consequences. Khachatryan et al.'s (2013) results showed that people preferred corn- or cellulose-based ethanol (vs. gasoline) fuel options more if they scored higher on biospheric values and concern about future consequences. In contrast, people preferred gasoline fuels more when they scored higher on egoistic values and concern about immediate consequences.

Second, biospheric values, and values more generally, are expressed in congruent behavior (e.g., environmental preferences, intentions, and actions) only if they are activated and central to the self. Values are central to one's self when "they make up part of one's self-definition and, thus, contribute to one's sense of identity" (Verplanken and Holland 2002: 435). Participants who strongly endorsed biospheric values scored higher on items measuring energy use self-identity and a more general environmental self-identity (van der Werff et al. 2013). These participants' environmental self-identity explained how their biospheric values influenced a few environmentally friendly behaviors: they ate less meat, took shorter showers, used a more fuel-efficient driving style, intended to reduce their energy use, and expressed their support for a range of measures designed to compensate for energy consumption (e.g., support generation of green energy or extra costs for it). Moreover, participants for whom environmental values were central chose television sets that had higher environment-friendly ratings after being primed with environmental words (e.g., green, ecological, earth, nature, climate; van der Werff et al. 2013). Those participants for whom these values were less central did not display a difference between the priming conditions (environmental versus neutral primes). According to Verplanken and Holland (2002), these effects could be due to a few mechanisms, such as increased attention to value-relevant information and a motivation to restore the central values once one had to act against them.

Additionally, literature has supported earlier findings that pro-environmental behavior correlates negatively with self-enhancement values such as power, authority, wealth, or ambition (Schultz and Zelezny 1998). *Value spillover*—or the likelihood that a value applied in a certain situation leads to its application in another, similar situation—has become an important research topic precisely because values are trans-situational ideals that *should* predict aggregate sets of behavior, more than any single, isolated behavior. For example, in two studies, outlining the environmental benefits for car sharing elicited more pro-environmental action in an unrelated situation, but *adding* personal financial benefits for car sharing removed this spillover to the unrelated situation (Evans et al. 2013).

Finally, before moving to the next domain of behavior, it is worth noting that pro-environmental behavior is a good example of an important principle underlining *why* values may play a role in action. People's attitudes and behavior ultimately depend on how environmental issues are construed. A more liberal political orientation is related to viewing the environment in moral terms because environmental issues are depicted as a threat to populations (Feinberg and Willer 2013). This perspective should activate compassionate, benevolent, and universalism values more strongly than a viewpoint that sees environmental change as nonthreatening or unlikely to occur. A similar role of viewpoint should be in effect for all behaviors—the role of values should always depend on how the behaviors are construed, and this may vary between people and contexts.

Consumer behavior: symbolic and health-related goods

One important obstacle to consistency between pro-environmental values and behavior might be people's tendency to exaggerate the pleasure of indulging in a consumer lifestyle and the negativity of giving that up. Consumers with a high preoccupation toward having a successful life and deriving happiness from possessions (Richins 2004, as cited by Richins 2013) showed hedonic elevation before purchasing a product, which declined after purchase. The hedonic elevation seems to come from materialist consumers' high expectations that purchasing a desired product will transform their lives in significant and meaningful ways, when in fact the positive emotions (e.g., optimism, excitement, joy) associated with the purchase tend to decrease soon thereafter (Richins 2013). This illustrates that anticipating and desiring a product may in itself be more pleasurable than actually owning that product. This may make it difficult for people to assign lower weight to materialistic concerns when adopting pro-environmental goals (e.g., reducing one's carbon footprint by giving up a lifestyle that includes taking long-distance flights to tempting holiday destinations).

At the same time, different personal values may be linked to different types of consumerism. One domain that illustrates this link is fashion, where values guide one's choices by suggesting what aspects of clothing can best express the individual's positioning within social hierarchies. Individuals who are "socially oriented" (i.e., who endorse values such as being well respected by others, having warm relationships, and a sense of belonging) express greater needs for affiliation and group identification (Rose et al. 1994). In turn, these needs translate into higher likelihood of conforming to others' opinions. But "socially oriented" individuals are attracted not just to the display aspects of clothing (e.g., brand name or style), as we would easily predict, but also to the utilitarian aspects (durability, quality, fit) that might express a different facet of socially desirable fashion. Different patterns of consumption seem to actually reflect not just basic human needs or rational versus irrational practices, but, most importantly, how cultural values can be differently expressed. Pop music—or music more generally—also carries this same symbolic function of allowing one's very personal values to be expressed to the "outside" world (Dolfsma 1999).

Human nutrition is another consumer domain with important potential links to values. What we eat and the extent to which we use the environment's resources disclose motivations that are core to human survival. Health consciousness is the main major motive in a vegan diet and lifestyle (47%), more than religious (40%) or animal welfare (9%) motives (Dyett et al. 2013). Omnivores (versus vegans) score higher on values denoting hierarchical domination and place less importance on emotions (Allen et al. 2000). Similarly, omnivores are more likely than vegetarians to endorse authoritarian values, to accept inequality and social hierarchies, and to accept behavior directly illustrative of these values, such as exerting high control over one's subordinates in the workplace (Loughnan et al. 2014).

When should values impact behavior?

The evidence we've reviewed thus far shows that values have been connected to beliefs, judgments, emotions, and behavior in diverse settings. But because values are more akin to guiding principles than are attitudes, it has been suggested that they may be stronger imperatives that influence behavior (Ravlin and Meglino 1987). However, attempting to prove or disprove a value–behavior link by looking at instances when values appear or do not appear to guide behavior is methodologically inappropriate, because of the vast conceptual distance between the abstract ideals represented by values and more specific, contextually rich behaviors. The literature we reviewed so far would suggest that values *can be* associated with single behaviors, but we do not show these relations as *proof* of a role of values. These relations show connections between values and particular actions, but it would remain conceivable that the values show no link to other relevant actions, while perhaps even showing spurious links to other irrelevant actions. Such a broader pattern would argue against the idea of the value as a broader, cohesive abstract entity in understanding behavior.

Although, in combination, the extant evidence provides many demonstrations of instances where a psychological model that assumes a role of particular values is useful for those behaviors that were examined (in the context that they were examined), any test of the broader role of values in behavior must look for a *diversity* of value instantiations, because values transcend concrete behavioral instances. Several decades ago, Weigel and Newman (1976) provided an important but often overlooked example of this approach.

They gave residents of a small New England town surveys probing their general concern about environment protection. Three new researchers contacted the residents several months later and presented them with a *range* of different pro-environmental actions. Participants were given a chance to sign and circulate petitions, take part in a litter pick-up program, and help with a recycling scheme. The researchers found that the residents' environmental concern more strongly predicted their subsequent actions to protect the environment when the statistical analysis included *more behaviors* than when it focused on each behavior separately. For example, environmental concern explained only 1% of the residents' actual recycling in the fifth week of the program, but was fifteen times more effective at predicting recycling behavior across an eight-week period. The predictive power more than doubled again when researchers examined the association between environmental concern and all of the actions (petitioning, litter collection, and recycling), predicting 36% of environmentally-friendly action in total.

This evidence converges well with theoretical perspectives on the roles of other types of abstract psychological constructs in behavior. For example, measures of abstract attitudes better predict measures of aggregate behavior than measures of specific behavior (Ajzen and Fishbein 1977). Consequently, we might take a great risk if we choose to ignore values while working to change relevant behavior. Although we may be able to change particular behaviors without appealing to values, attempts to alter a large range of behaviors may need to consider the value or values that psychologically bind these behaviors together.

Nonetheless, values cannot possibly influence aggregated actions if they do not also influence specific actions to some degree at least. It therefore remains interesting and important to examine *how* values translate into *specific* actions.

How do values impact behavior?

There are many ways in which values might become manifest in specific behavior. Recent perspectives have proposed four distinct sequences (Verplanken and Holland 2002). First, values need to be activated. Second, values influence attention, perception, and interpretation of a situation as relevant to the value itself. Third, values may lead an individual to choose one action over others. And fourth, values activate the planning of action. Consequently, one's choices are driven in the direction of the values that are the most salient in these situations (Verplanken and Holland 2002), hence why people prefer behavioral alternatives promoting values that are higher in their personal hierarchy (Feather 1995).

Extant evidence supports the thesis that values may influence behavior by shaping situational goals, which drive the individual toward specific actions (Parks and Guay 2009). This assumption is consistent with Schwartz's (1992) emphasis on the way in which values serve to help fulfill different psychological motives—an assumption that is also present in recent alternative models (Fischer et al. 2011). It also fits recent evidence about the effects of priming values on one's actions (Maio et al. 2009b). Priming values make congruent goals more important and increases the frequency of value-congruent behavior, while decreasing the frequency of value-opposing behaviors. Moreover, according to Sheldon and

Elliott's (1999) *self-concordance model*, goals have a mediating role: individuals are better able to persist at achieving their goals when these are consistent with their core values.

In short, values are abstract principles, while behavior is concrete. Values may shape behavior via a motivational route that allows the individual to form plans as to how to act in concrete situations. A cognitive value structure may have an influence on behavior if (1) it is well established in the person's cognitive system, (2) it is activated in working memory, and (3) it is seen as relevant in the current situation (Wojciszke 1989). This process leads to questions regarding the conditions under which values give rise to goals and goals influence behavior. One such question is when do values predict behavior more strongly: when they are congruent with broader social norms *or* when they are isolated systems of individual thought? Another question is whether the impact of values on behavior is weakened by a tendency for them to function as cultural truisms? Also, does values' expression depend on person characteristics, such as one's social identity, one's mindset, or the values' centrality to the self? Finally, are there particular mindsets and mental contents that help people bridge the large gap between the abstract representations of values and actual behavior in concrete situations? In this chapter, we discuss research examining each of these questions.

When do values predict behavior more strongly: when they are congruent with broader social norms or when they are isolated systems of individual thought?

It is possible that values that are the most consistent with normative influences are more predictive of behavior than non-normative values. This might be the case for habitual, day-to-day situations, where expressing a particular value does not encounter strong barriers. Bardi and Schwartz (2003) have shown that there is large variability in the correlations between values and the behavior expressing them directly: stimulation, tradition, and hedonism values correlate with corresponding behavior (coefficients of 0.68, 0.67, and 0.62, respectively) stronger than benevolence, security, achievement, and conformity do (coefficients of 0.30, 0.32, 0.33, and 0.39, respectively). Moreover, social norms to behave in a certain way might create important situational pressure for an individual: the more normative a certain behavior, the weaker will be its relationship with the value that supposedly expresses it, because people may have the tendency to conform to norms at the expense of the values they endorse (Bardi and Schwartz 2003). Following this reasoning, we can expect stronger correlations between values and behavior when these behaviors express values unimportant to the group (i.e., when the pressure toward conformity is lower). In more exceptional life situations (such as the case for political prisoners or dissidents), less normative values might be easier to express because their expression becomes symbolic for not just the value itself, but for the purpose it serves (e.g., to oppose oppression, to affirm one's rights).

Is the impact of values on behavior weakened by values' tendency to function as cultural truisms?

Values' influence on behavior depends highly on their centrality to the self (Verplanken and Holland 2002) and on their anchoring in one's strong system of beliefs. According to the *values-as-truisms* hypothesis (Bernard et al. 1998), people often agree strongly with a value, but rarely think of reasons why it is important. Values function as truisms when they are accepted without question and held confidently. Prior research on the values-as-truisms hypothesis has tested whether values such as helpfulness and honesty possess the two defining characteristics of truisms, and found that agreement with these values was even stronger than agreement with medical truisms (e.g., "it is good to brush your teeth frequently"; McGuire 1964). The values-as-truisms hypothesis states that if people lack argumentative support for their values, then analyzing one's reasons should cause an individual to access novel, accessible thoughts (more or less supportive of values), which will cause value change. Past research indeed revealed that participants who analyzed reasons for or against social values changed their importance ratings of those values significantly more than did control participants (Bernard et al. 2003b; Maio and Olson 1998). Importantly, this effect was bidirectional (i.e., the values became either more or less important), instead of a simple polarization effect. The bidirectional shifts are vital for arguing that participants were merely accessing reasons that were accessible and easy to verbalize (Wilson et al. 1989), but not the psychologically real reasons for their values. Moreover, the effect is eliminated when participants are given a prior opportunity to build cognitive support for the values—evidence that the effect relies on the absence of accessible cognitive arguments supporting values.

More relevant to the prediction of behavior is the finding that people who thoughtfully analyze their reasons for endorsing a value are subsequently more likely to display value-consistent behavior (Maio 2010). This occurred even among individuals who downgraded the importance of the value as they developed reasons *for* the value; the new reasons nonetheless acted as *new* motivators of subsequent pro-value behavior (Maio et al. 2001), making people more perceptually ready to detect the value's relevance for subsequent behavioral options (Maio et al. 2009a).

Does values' expression depend on person characteristics?

Social class or *social status* designate important person characteristics in research on ethical behavior. Some research has found that higher social class is related to more unethical behavior such as cheating or driving ruthlessly (Piff et al. 2012). However, others have outlined nuances to these conclusions: individuals of higher socio-economic status tend to act more unethically when the payoffs for the unethical behavior, or the temptation to act as such, are greater (e.g., cheat on taxes or report a less negative attitude toward infidelity), but would be less likely to shoplift (Trautmann et al. 2013). Class differences in individuals' implicit benefit/cost analysis of moral rules or patterns of social orientation are more predictable than class differences in ethical behavior per se, and they depend largely on how we conceptualize class and the sociocultural context. In other words, social class might shape the value one gives to different ethical standards and different degrees of willingness to transgress these standards (Ariely and Mann 2013). Therefore, it might shape how one's value system is translated into personal goals and what strategies one will employ to reach these goals.

Some research suggested that the impact of values on behavior (e.g., voting) might depend on the degree to which one elaborately thinks about the topic, because values may come to the fore more strongly when action is deliberate and thoughtful than when it is spontaneous (Caprara et al. 2006). Among university-educated voters (a proxy for intellectual sophistication), values accounted for slightly more variance (0.20) in political choice than among the less-educated voters (0.16). Among the former, values alone accounted for variance in voting, while among the latter, age and gender predicted voting alongside values. Whether this effect is attributable to individual differences that pertain to depth of thinking across topics or is topic-specific remains to be seen.

Other relevant person or personality characteristics tap the likely role of social norms in behavior—for instance, some individuals rely more heavily on social norms to guide their behavior, whereas others pay more attention to values. Self-monitoring is a personality trait that reflects this distinction (Snyder 1987). High self-monitors use external cues, such as social norms, as guides to action. These individuals are pragmatic, constantly monitoring the link between themselves and the demands of the external world around them. In contrast, low self-monitors rely on internal cues, such as values, to guide their behavior. These individuals do not monitor the connection between themselves and the demands of the outer world; they act on principle. Unsurprisingly, therefore, high self-monitors exhibit less value–attitude–behavior consistency than low self-monitors (Kristiansen and Zanna 1988; Snyder and Kendzierski 1982; Zanna et al. 1980). There are likely a number of factors that may undermine value–behavior consistency of high self-monitors: they are less likely to follow through on their behavioral intentions than low self-monitors (Ajzen et al. 1982) and presumably are easily diverted from their intentions by unanticipated situational demands. It is also possible that high self-monitors' values and attitudes are less salient to themselves (Kardes et al. 1986; Mellema and Bassili 1995).

While self-monitoring refers broadly to consistency with internal dispositions, people may also vary in the extent to which they feel bound to their values and ideals, in particular. According to Wojciszke (1989), people vary in idealism, which is the extent to which self-related ideals are valued and used to determine behavior. Indeed, people scoring higher in idealism do exhibit more value–behavior consistency, illustrated in both self- and peer-ratings of value-relevant behavior (Wojciszke 1989).

Ironically, recent research has found that values themselves may moderate the impact of other values on behavior. Conformity values in particular (e.g., obedience, politeness) can play this moderating role, because people who consider conformity values to be highly important should be more motivated to adhere to salient social norms and be relatively less governed by *other* values that are important to them. Participants were asked to rate their values using Schwartz's Value Survey and friends of the participants also rated participants' altruistic behavior (Lönnqvist et al. 2006). In theory, altruistic behavior should be more likely among individuals who consider the self-transcending (universalism and benevolence) values to be important and the self-enhancement values (achievement and power) to be less important, and the pattern of correlations was consistent with this expectation. More importantly, this pattern was stronger among those who placed less importance on conformity values than among those who attached more importance to conformity. Thus, conformity values moderated the relation of the self-transcendence and self-enhancement values with altruistic behavior.

There are numerous other individual difference variables that may also determine the strength of relations between values and specific actions. For example, an interesting question is whether greater use of values is also more likely among people who possess two important constructs theoretically relevant to the use of values: higher levels of moral identity (Aquino and Reed 2002) and religiosity (Batson et al. 1993). Another question is whether values need to be seen as external guidelines for one's behavior or as something one can be aware of already. The latter possibility suggests that the consistency between one's values and the values emphasized in one's social environment matter very much for one's well-being (Sagiv and Schwartz 2000).

Such possibilities serve merely to underscore the broader point that values reside in human minds that encode diverse dispositions, goals, knowledge, and perceptual habits, and it is more powerful to examine values in combination with these characteristics than in isolation.

Does values' expression depend on mindset?

For a value to function, we must bridge the gap from the abstract representation of the value to the concrete representation of the situation. This bridging process involves recognizing a situation as a context where the value can be applied, deciding how it would be applied, whether other values are relevant, how feasible it is to act in the way compelled by that value, how effective the actions will be, and whether or not other forces in the situation are more relevant (e.g., norms, urgent goals). This is not an easy task. If a person approaches you and asks for money to get a bus home, do you decide that it is time to be helpful and give her money or decline? A myriad of questions might pass through our minds. Is the person lying? Would she misspend the money? Does she look needy or threatening? Would helping simply foster her dependence on others? Is being short of money just punishment for not being responsible? Can we afford to give? Are there others around (e.g., children) who will evaluate us based on our actions? Sometimes we have to make an immediate decision and have very little time to consider such questions and whether the importance we place on helpfulness applies in this case. When situations are concrete, we see obstacles we simply do not anticipate in the abstract.

This bridging process suggests two broad ways to line up values and specific actions. First, the actions can be made more abstract. Values are more likely to be expressed through value-congruent judgments and behaviors when people think abstractly, and not concretely, about their actions (Torelli and Kaikati 2009). Moreover, because values are abstract principles, they impact behavior more when that behavior is psychologically distant (Eyal et al. 2009), whether it is distant in time (e.g., many years from now) or place (e.g., a country far away). This effect of psychological distance presumably arises because values play a greater role when individuals think about the high-level motivations of their actions, instead of the actions' concrete details (Eyal et al. 2009), and psychological distance promotes precisely this match between the abstractness of high-level motivations and the abstractness of one's principles or values.

Second, values can be made more concrete by thinking of them in specific situations. For instance, the contemplation of reasons why a value is important or unimportant tends to draw people into considering more concrete situations where they believe the value matters (Maio et al. 2001). Short stories or scenarios can also encourage people to consider values in concrete situations. For example, a news item about discrimination can activate thoughts about the value of equality in this context (Maio et al. 2009a). More important, such concrete instantiations of a value increase the likelihood that people will express the value in their behavior immediately afterward (Maio et al. 2001, 2009a). This effect does not appear to rely on thinking about concrete instantiations that are closely relevant to the subsequent behavior, but it does rely on thought about concrete instantiations that are close to the heart of how people think about the value. When people think of situations that are fairly common examples of a value, they are more likely to spontaneously see the relevance of that value to subsequent behavior (Maio et al. 2009a). In other words, thinking of concrete, typical instantiations makes people perceptually ready to detect the relevance of the value to subsequent action.

These effects are probably just the tip of the iceberg in how values can be coupled with concrete mindsets in order to have an effect on behavior. There are many ways in which instantiations of a value can vary (e.g., extremity, vividness, complexity) and all of these variations may matter in how the value itself comes to be applied. In the real world, where values are frequently activated by concrete situations, this process may be vital to figuring out how values work.

Conclusion

The literature reviewed in this chapter supports the view that values do not have a direct translation into everyday behavior. Instead, they map onto personal traits, goals, and contextual specifications. Their influence on behavior depends on their congruence with social norms, person characteristics such as social class, the ability to engage in deeper thought about the behavior, moral identity or political orientation, and various mindsets that can help bridge values and behavior. This suggests that it might be more fruitful to pay attention to values' functions instead of values as imperfect, albeit ideal, determinants of our behavior. Knowing what values are and are not, when values impact behavior, and by what mechanisms this happens might allow us to have a more realistic expectation about how much our behavior should and could be aligned to our principles.

References

Ajzen, I. and Fishbein, M. (1977). Attitude-behavior relations: a theoretical analysis and review of empirical research. *Psychological Bulletin*, **84**, 888–918.

Ajzen, I., Timko, C., and White, J.B. (1982). Self-monitoring and the attitude–behavior relation. *Journal of Personality and Social Psychology*, **42**, 426–435.

Allen, M.W., Wilson, M., Hung NG S., and Dunne, M. (2000). Values and beliefs or vegetarians and omnivores. *The Journal of Social Psychology*, **140**, 405–422.

Aquino, K. and Reed II, A. (2002). The self-importance of moral identity. *Journal of Personality and Social Psychology*, **83**, 1423–1440.

Ariely, D. and Mann, H. (2013). A bird's eye view of unethical behavior: commentary on Trautmann et al. (2013). *Perspectives on Psychological Science*, **8**, 498–500.

Ashton, M.C. and Lee, K. (2007). Empirical, theoretical, and practical advantages of the HEXACO model of personality structure. *Personality and Social Psychology Review*, **11**, 150–166.

Bamberg, S. and Möser, G. (2007). Twenty years after Hines, Hungerford, and Tomera: new meta-analysis of psycho-social determinants of pro-environmental behavior. *Journal of Environmental Psychology*, **27**, 14–25.

Bardi, A. and Schwartz, S.H. (2003). Values and behavior: Strength and structure of relations. *Personality and Social Psychology Bulletin*, **29**, 1207–1220.

Barnea, M.F. and Schwartz, S.H. (1998). Values and voting. *Political Psychology*, **19**, 17–40.

Batson, C.D., Schoenrade, P., and Ventis, W.L. (1993). *Religion and the individual: a social-psychological perspective*. New York, NY: Oxford University Press.

Bernard, M.M., Maio, G.R., and Olson, J.M. (2003a). Effects of introspection about reasons for values: extending research on values-as-truisms. *Social Cognition*, **21**, 1–25.

Bernard, M.M., Maio, G.R., and Olson, J.M. (2003b). The vulnerability of values to attack: inoculation of values and value-relevant attitudes. *Personality and Social Psychology Bulletin*, **29**, 63–75.

Blankenship, K.L. and Wegener, D.T. (2012). Value activation and processing of persuasive messages. *Social Psychological and Personality Science*, **3**, 391–397.

Blankenship, K.L., Wegener, D.T., and Murray, R.A. (2012). Circumventing resistance: using values to indirectly change attitudes. *Journal of Personality and Social Psychology*, **103**, 606–621.

Caprara, G.V., Schwartz, S.H., Capanna, C., Vecchione, M., and Barbaranelli, C. (2006). Personality and politics: values, traits, and political choice. *Political Psychology*, **27**, 1–28.

Cieciuch, J., Schwartz, S.H., and Vecchione, M. (2013). Applying the refined values theory to past data: what can researchers gain? *Journal of Cross-Cultural Psychology*, **44**, 1215–1234.

Dolfsma, W. (1999). The consumption of music and the expression of values: a social economic explanation for the advent of pop music. *American Journal of Economics and Sociology*, **58**, 1019–1046.

Dollinger, S.J., Leong, F.T.L., and Ulicni, S.K. (1996). On traits and values: with special reference to openness to experience. *Journal of Research in Personality*, **30**, 23–41.

Dunlap, R.E., Van Liere, K., Mertig, A., and Howell, R. (1992, August). Measuring endorsement of an ecological worldview: A revised NEP scale. *Paper presented in the Annual Meeting of the Rural Sociology Society*, State College, PA.

Dyett, P.A., Sabaté, J., Haddad, E., Rajaram, S., and Shavlik, D. (2013). Vegan lifestyle behaviors. An exploration of congruence with health-related beliefs and assessed health indices. *Appetite*, **67**(C), 119–124.

Evans, L., Maio, G.R., Corner, A.J., Hodgetts, C.J., Ahmed, S., and Hahn, U. (2013). Self-interest and pro-environmental behaviour [Letter]. *Nature Climate Change*, **3**, 122–125.

Eyal, T., Sagristano, M.D., Trope, Y., Liberman, N., and Chaiken, S. (2009). When values matter: expressing values in behavioral intentions for the near vs. distant future. *Journal of Experimental Social Psychology*, **45**, 35–43.

Feather, N.T. (1995). Values, valences, and choice: the influences of values on the perceived attractiveness and choice of alternatives. *Journal of Personality and Social Psychology*, **68**, 1135–1151.

Feinberg, M. and Willer, R. (2013). The moral roots of environmental attitudes. *Psychological Science*, **24**, 56–62.

Fischer, R., Milfont, T.L., and Gouveia, V.V. (2011). Does social context affect value structures? Testing the within-country stability of value structures with a functional theory of values. *Journal of Cross-Cultural Psychology*, **42**, 253–270.

Garling, T. (1999). Value priorities, social value orientations and cooperation in social dilemmas. *British Journal of Social Psychology*, **38**, 397–408.

Hilbig, B.E. and Zettler, I. (2009). Pillars of cooperation: honesty–humility, social value orientations, and economic behavior. *Journal of Research in Personality*, **43**, 516–519.

Hitlin, S. and Piliavin, J.A. (2004). Values: reviving a dormant concept. *Annual Review of Sociology*, **30**, 359–393.

Karacan, E., Seval, G.C., Aktan, Z., Ayli, M., and Palabiyikoglu, R. (2013). Blood donors and factors impacting the blood donation decision: motives for donating blood in Turkish sample. *Transfusion and Apheresis Science*, **49**, 468–473.

Kardes, F.R., Sanbonmatsu, D.M., Voss, R.T., and Fazio, R.H. (1986). Self-monitoring and attitude accessibility. *Personality and Social Psychology Bulletin*, **12**, 468–474.

Khachatryan, H., Joireman, J., and Casavant, K. (2013). Relating values and consideration of future and immediate consequences to consumer preference for biofuels: a three-dimensional social dilemma analysis. *Journal of Environmental Psychology*, **34**(C), 97–108.

Kitayama, S., King, A., Yoon, C., Tompson, S., Huff, S., and Liberzon, I. (2014). The dopamine D4 receptor gene (DRD4) moderates cultural difference in independent versus interdependent social orientation. *Psychological Science*, **25**, 1169–1177.

Kluckhohn, C. (1951). Values and value-orientations in the theory of action. In T. Parsons and E.A. Shils (eds), *Toward a general theory of action* (pp. 388–433). New York: Harper.

Knafo, A. and Spinath, F.M. (2011). Genetic and environmental influences on girls' and boys' gender-typed and gender-neutral values. *Developmental Psychology*, **47**, 726–731.

Kristiansen, C.M. and Zanna, M.P. (1988). Justifying attitudes by appealing to values: a functional perspective. *British Journal of Social Psychology*, **27**, 247–256.

Lönnqvist, J.-E., Leikas, S., Paunonen, S., Nissinen, V., and Verkasalo, M. (2006).Conformism moderates the relations between values, anticipated regret, and behavior. *Personality and Social Psychology Bulletin*, **32**, 1469–1481.

Loughnan, S., Bastian, B., and Haslam, N. (2014). The psychology of eating animals. *Current Directions in Psychological Science*, **23**, 104–108.

Luk, C.L. and Bond, M.H. (1993). Personality variation and values endorsement in Chinese university students. *Personality and Individual Differences*, **14**, 429–437.

Maio, G.R. (2010). Mental representations of social values. In M.P. Zanna (ed.), *Advances in experimental social psychology* (**Vol. 42**, pp. 1–43). Burlington: Academic Press.

Maio, G.R. (2011). *Don't mind the gap between values and action*. Discussion Paper. Common Cause. Available at: http://valuesandframes.org/download/briefings/Value-Action%20Gap%20|%20 Common%20Cause%20Briefing.pdf.

Maio, G.R. and Haddock, G. (2010). *The psychology of attitudes and attitude change*. SAGE Social Psychology Program. London: Sage.

Maio, G.R. and Olson, J.M. (1998). Values as truisms: evidence and implications. *Journal of Personality and Social Psychology*, **74**, 294–311.

Maio, G.R., Olson, J., Allen, L., and Bernard, M. (2001). Addressing discrepancies between values and behavior: The motivating effect of reasons. *Journal of Experimental Social Psychology*, **37**, 104–117.

Maio, G.R., Hahn, U., Frost, J.-M., and Cheung, W.-Y. (2009a). Applying the value of equality unequally: Effects of value instantiations that vary in typicality. *Journal of Personality and Social Psychology*, **97**, 598–614.

Maio, G.R., Pakizeh, A., Cheung, W.-Y., and Rees, K. J. (2009b). Changing, priming, and acting on values: effects via motivational relations in a circular model. *Journal of Personality and Social Psychology*, **97**, 699–715.

McGuire, W. (1964). Inducing resistance to persuasion: some contemporary approaches. In L. Berkowitz (ed.), *Advances in experimental social psychology* (**Vol. 1**, pp. 191–229). New York: Academic Press.

Mellema, A. and Bassili, J.N. (1995). On the relationship between attitudes and values: exploring the moderating effects of self-monitoring and self-monitoring schematicity. *Personality and Social Psychology Bulletin*, **21**, 885–892.

Newman, G.E. and Cain, D.M. (2014). Tainted altruism: when doing some good is evaluated as worse than doing no good at all. *Psychological Science*, **25**, 648–655.

Olver, J.M. and Mooradian, T.A. (2003). Personality traits and personal values: a conceptual and empirical integration. *Personality and Individual Differences*, **35**, 109–125.

Omoto, A.M. and Snyder, M. (1995). Sustained helping without obligation: motivation, longevity of service, and perceived attitude change among AIDS volunteers. *Journal of Personality and Social Psychology*, **68**, 671–686.

Parks, L. and Guay, R.P. (2009). Personality, values, and motivation. *Personality and Individual Differences*, **47**, 675–684.

Piff, P.K., Stancato, D.M., Côté, S., Mendoza-Denton, R., and Keltner, D. (2012). Higher social class predicts increased unethical behavior. *Proceedings of the National Academy of Sciences*, **109**, 4086–4091.

Ravlin, E.C. and Meglino, B.M. (1987). Effect of values on perception and decision making: A study of alternative work values measures. *Journal of Applied Psychology*, **72**, 666–673.

Richins, M.L. (2004). The Material Values scale: Measurement properties and development of a short form. *Journal of Consumer Research*, **31**, 209–219.

Richins, M.L. (2013). When wanting is better than having: materialism, transformation expectations, and product-evoked emotions in the purchase process. *Journal of Consumer Research*, **40**, 1–18.

Roccas, S., Sagiv, L., Schwartz, S.H., and Knafo, A. (2002). The Big Five personality factors and personal values. *Personality and Social Psychology Bulletin*, **29**, 789–801.

Rokeach, M. (1973). *The nature of human values*. New York, NY: Free Press.

Rose, G.M., Shoham, A., Kahle, L.R., and Batra, R. (1994). Social values, conformity, and dress. *Journal of Applied Social Psychology*, **24**, 1501–1519.

Sagiv, L. and Schwartz, S.H. (2000). Value priorities and subjective well-being: direct relations and congruity effects. *European Journal of Social Psychology*, **30**, 177–198.

Samuelson, C.D. (1993). A multiattribute evaluation approach to structural change in resource dilemmas. *Organizational Behavior and Human Decision Processes*, **55**, 298–324.

Schermer, J.A., Feather, N.T., Zhu, G., and Martin, N.G. (2008). Phenotypic, genetic, and environmental properties of the portrait values questionnaire. *Twin Research and Human Genetics*, **11**, 531–537.

Schermer, J.A., Vernon, P.A., Maio, G.R., and Jang, K.L. (2012). A behavior genetic study of the connection between social values and personality. *Twin Research and Human Genetics*, **14**, 233–239.

Schultz, P.W. and Zelezny, L.C. (1998). Values and proenvironmental behavior: a five-country survey. *Journal of Cross-Cultural Psychology*, **29**, 540–558.

Schultz, P.W. and Zelezny, L.C. (1999). Values as predictors of environmental attitudes: Evidence for consistency across 14 countries. *Journal of Environmental Psychology*, **19**, 255–265.

Schwartz, S.H. (1977). Normative influence on altruism. In L. Berkowitz (ed.), *Advances in experimental social psychology* (**Vol.10**, pp. 221–279). New York: Academic Press.

Schwartz, S.H. (1992). Universals in the content and structure of values: theoretical advances and empirical tests in 20 countries. *Advances in Experimental Social Psychology*, **25**, 1–65.

Schwartz, S.H. (1994). Are there universal aspects in the structure and contents of human values? *Journal of Social Issues*, **50**, 19–45.

Schwartz, S.H. (1996). Value priorities and behavior: applying a theory of integrated value systems. In C. Seligman, J.M. Olson, and M.P. Zanna (eds), *The psychology of values: the Ontario symposium* (**Vol. 8**, pp. 1–24). Mahwah, NJ: Lawrence Erlbaum Associates.

Schwartz, S.H. and Bilsky, W. (1987). Toward a universal psychological structure of human values. *Journal of Personality and Social Psychology*, **53**, 550–562.

Schwartz, S.H., Cieciuch, J., and Vecchione, M. et al. (2012). Refining the theory of basic individual values. *Journal of Personality and Social Psychology*, **103**, 663–688.

Shantz, A., Saksida, T., and Alfes, K. (2014). Dedicating time to volunteering: values, engagement, and commitment to beneficiaries. *Applied Psychology: An International Review*, 63, 671–697.

Sheldon, K.M. and Elliot, A.J. (1999). Goal striving, need satisfaction, and longitudinal well-being: the self-concordance model. *Journal of Personality and Social Psychology*, **76**, 482–497.

Snyder, M. (1987). *Public appearances, private realities: the psychology of self-monitoring*. New York, NY: W H Freeman/Times Books/Henry Holt and Co.

Snyder, M. and Kendzierski, D. (1982). Acting on one's attitudes: procedures for linking attitude and behavior. *Journal of Experimental Social Psychology*, **18**, 165–183.

Stern, P.C., Dietz, T., and Kalof, L. (1993). Value orientations, gender, and environmental concern. *Environment and Behavior*, **25**, 322–348.

Torelli, C.J. and Kaikati, A.M. (2009). Values as predictors of judgments and behaviors: the role of abstract and concrete mindsets. *Journal of Personality and Social Psychology*, **96**, 231–247.

Trautmann, S.T., van de Kuilen, G., and Zeckhauser, R.J. (2013). Social class and (un)ethical behavior: a framework, with evidence from a large population sample. *Perspectives on Psychological Science*, **8**, 487–497.

van der Werff, E., Steg, L., and Keizer, K. (2013). The value of environmental self-identity: the relationship between biospheric values, environmental self-identity and environmental preferences, intentions and behaviour. *Journal of Environmental Psychology*, **34**, 55–63.

Verplanken, B. and Holland, R.W. (2002). Motivated decision making: effects of activation and self-centrality of values on choices and behavior. *Journal of Personality and Social Psychology*, **82**, 434–447.

Watson, D. and Clark, L.A. (1997). Extraversion and its positive emotional core. In R. Hogan, J. Johnson, and S. Briggs (eds), *Handbook of personality psychology* (pp. 767–793). New York: Academic Press.

Weigel, R.H. and Newman, L.S. (1976). Increasing attitude-behavior correspondence by broadening the scope of the behavioral measure. *Journal of Personality and Social Psychology*, **33**, 793–802.

Wilson, T.D., Dunn, D.S., Kraft, D., and Lisle, D.J. (1989). Introspection, attitude change, and attitude-behavior consistency: the disruptive effects of explaining why we feel the way we do. *Advances in Experimental Social Psychology*, **22**, 287–343.

Wojciszke, B. (1989). The system of personal values and behavior. In N. Eisenberg, J. Reykowski, and E. Staub (eds), *Social and moral values: individual and societal perspectives* (pp. 229–251). Hillsdale, NJ: Lawrence Erlbaum.

Zanna, M.P., Olson, J.M., and Fazio, R.H. (1980). Attitude–behavior consistency: an individual difference perspective. *Journal of Personality and Social Psychology*, **38**, 432–440.

Section 3

Varieties of value

Chapter 13

Hedonic value

Dan-Mikael Ellingsen, Siri Leknes, and Morten Kringelbach

Introduction

Hedonic processing of pleasure and displeasure motivates behavior, influences decision-making, and is essential for survival of both the individual and the species. While much of our behavior is geared toward seeking pleasant experiences over both the short and long run, we will also work to avoid aversive or painful experiences. The hedonic valuation of sensation helps to guide us toward which behaviors to engage in and which behaviors to avoid. The hedonic value of sensory experiences is linked to homeostatic processes. While the taste of chocolate can evoke intense feelings of pleasure, the very same stimulus can change its value and become less pleasurable after having eaten too much.

Although the subjective experience of pleasure is often what first comes so mind when thinking of reward—and pleasure and reward are sometimes used interchangeably—hedonic processing can be conceptually divided into at least three components—wanting, liking, and learning (Berridge and Kringelbach 2008; Smith et al. 2011). There is now substantial evidence that these three processes constitute partly separable neuroanatomical and neuropharmacological systems (Berridge and Kringelbach 2013; Berridge and Robinson 1998). Further, recent theorizing suggests that anhedonia, a prominent and devastating feature of a wide range of psychiatric illnesses (and chronic pain), may be related more to a disruption of the balance between these hedonic subcomponents than to a "loss of pleasure" per se (Rømer Thomsen et al., 2015). Such an imbalance can take different forms in different conditions. Addictive disorders often involve gradually increased motivation and desire for obtaining the object of addiction, while actual liking is instead reduced. In contrast, many affective disorders, like unipolar depression, are instead characterized by reductions in both motivation and actual liking.

In this chapter we discuss evidence from animal and human studies of the brain circuitry that enables the brain to create pleasure and displeasure, and how hedonic processing can be meaningfully divided into the subcomponents wanting, liking, and learning. We then discuss how the brain determines hedonic value, and review the rationale for the idea that subjective experiences can always be placed on a "hedonic continuum" with pleasure and displeasure as end-points.

The brain networks underlying hedonic processing

Pleasure and displeasure are never merely sensations—they are always "about" something—and can be conceptualized as the "hedonic gloss" that is painted onto sensations (Frijda 2010; Kringelbach 2010; Kringelbach and Berridge 2010).

Moreover, hedonic reactions can be divided into subjective and objective aspects. While subjective experiences of pleasure can be indirectly assessed experimentally through self-report in humans, only objective reactions can be studied in animals. Subjective and objective hedonic reactions are evident in both wanting, liking, and learning aspects of rewards. Implicit—or core—"wanting" can be studied by observing how hard an individual will work to obtain a reward, while explicit wanting corresponds to the subjective experience of desire and cognitive goals (Berridge and Kringelbach 2011). Correspondingly, motivational aspects of negative hedonics, like painful or disgusting events, can be studied by observing how much an individual will work to avoid a punishment (implicit), or by assessing subjective feelings of dread (explicit).

Core "liking" or "disliking" can be assessed through observation of hedonic reactions during consumption of a reward or during a punishment. This can be quantified by the intensity or frequency with which an animal licks its lips as a response to a sweet taste stimulus, or makes gapes in response to an aversive bitter taste (Steiner 1973; Steiner et al. 2001). Unfortunately, behaviors indexing core liking for non-food rewards have yet to be determined. Explicit liking or disliking corresponds to the subjective feelings of pleasure or displeasure.

Core "learning" comprises a range of processes involved in associative conditioning and implicit knowledge, while explicit learning includes the conscious updating of cognitive predictions. As we explain later in this chapter, wanting, liking, and learning of rewards can be neuroanatomically and pharmacologically decoupled/disentangled as separable yet closely interacting systems. These separable yet closely coupled aspects can be thought of as components of a cyclical process that characterizes most "normal" hedonic events (Fig. 13.1) (Berridge and Kringelbach 2011; Kringelbach et al. 2012). Disruption of this normal pleasure cycle may lead to anhedonia, the lack of normal ability to enjoy pleasures, which is a core feature of affective disorders (Rømer Thomsen et al., 2015).

Measuring subjective hedonic value in humans

Measuring hedonic value in humans can seem just a matter of asking the person how much he or she enjoys a pleasurable stimulus and get a more or less reliable answer. Functional neuroimaging studies that measure brain activity during self-reported enjoyment of rewards—be it sensory, social, or abstract rewards—have revealed many regions that play roles in pleasure processing, most notably the subcortical structures Nucleus Accumbens (NAc), ventral pallidum and the amygdala; midbrain structures Ventral Tegmental Area (VTA) and Periaqueductal Grey (PAG); and cortical structures orbitofrontal, cingulate, and insular cortices. However, since these neuroimaging techniques are correlative in nature, they cannot answer whether a brain region actually generates pleasure or if it

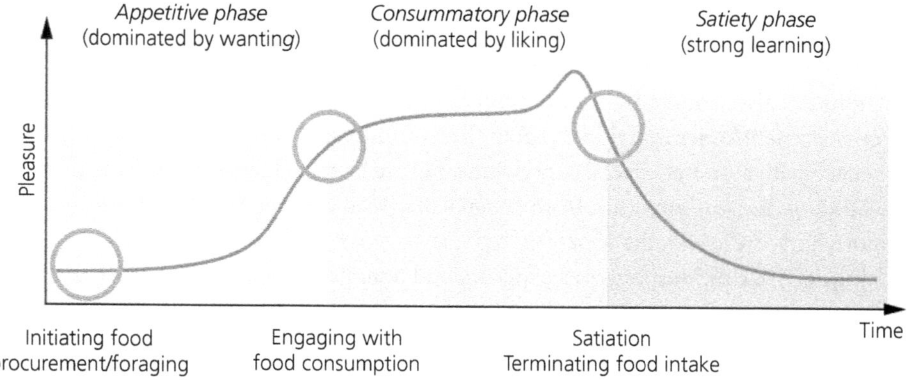

Fig. 13.1 Pleasure cycles. Although research has mostly focused on wanting, liking, and learning aspects as separate components, it may be meaningfully to view them temporally as components of a cyclical process. The cyclical processing of rewards has classically been proposed to be associated with appetitive, consummatory, and satiety phases (Craig 1918; Sherrington 1906). Research has demonstrated that this processing is supported by multiple brain networks and processes, which crucially involves *liking* (the core reactions to hedonic impact), *wanting* (motivational processing of incentive salience), and *learning* (typically Pavlovian or instrumental associations and cognitive representations) (Berridge and Kringelbach 2011). These components wax and wane during the pleasure cycle and can co-occur at any time. Importantly, however, wanting processing tends to dominate the appetitive phase, while liking processing dominates the consummatory phase. In contrast, learning can happen throughout the cycle. (See Plate 6.)
Reproduced from Berridge, K. C. and Kringelbach M. L., Building a neuroscience of pleasure and well-being, *Psychology of Well-Being: Theory, Research and Practice* 2011, 1 (3), Springer, Copyright © 2011. http://www.psywb.com/content/1/1/3.

represents a readout of hedonic value in a subsequent process that primarily serves a different function.

Moreover, self-report measures are limited for several reasons. The participant may—for various reasons—not be entirely accurate in their self-report (response bias), or they may be unable to fully describe the subjective experience verbally (especially on a one-dimensional scale assessing the intensity or magnitude of "pleasure"). Furthermore, the self-report, in form of producing a mark on a scale, is several computational steps down the line from the actual subjective experience, after monitoring, evaluation, language, and motor processes. However, self-report is the closest available estimate to assess subjective experiences, and although biased, it provides a useful tool to understand hedonic processes. To capture more complexity of the subjective experience, some researchers also employ measures of several dimensions, such as feeling "good" and "bad" simultaneously (e.g., Larsen et al. 2004).

Measuring explicit hedonic value

Nevertheless, there are also aspects of liking that are objectively observable by conspecifics, even in the absence of a verbal statement. It is relatively easy for a parent to determine whether their toddler liked or disliked a given taste, based on observation of their behavioral reaction. In human infants, facial expressions like licking the lips or making gapes are common reactions to sweet or bitter tastes, respectively (Steiner et al. 2001). These reactions are also evident in both nonhuman primates and rodents, and provide cues to the environment/other individuals about the hedonic value of the food reward. Pain is also associated with automatic facial expressions that are likely to have evolved because of their capability of drawing attention from conspecifics who can potentially provide sympathy, support, and care (Williams 2002).

Using core "liking" responses as experimental outcome measures is useful, especially in animals and pre-verbal children, where subjective experiences cannot be directly assessed. If a manipulation successfully changes an animal's "liking" response to a reward, this indicates that the manipulation altered a process responsible for generating "liking."

The brain networks generating hedonic value

For many years, the mesolimbic dopaminergic system, consisting of the ventral tegmentum, amygdala, and ventral striatum, was assumed to be responsible for pleasure processing. This idea grew from observations that rodents with microelectrode implants in mesolimbic locations (e.g., nucleus accumbens) would self-stimulate to obtain electrical stimulation from the electrode (Olds and Milner 1954; Shizgal et al. 2001; Valenstein et al. 1970). By turning the current on only at certain locations in the testing apparatus, the animals would return repeatedly to this location, sometimes preferring this location to locations where food was provided. When given the ability to turn on the current themselves by pulling a lever, they would obsessively pull the lever—sometimes up to 2,000 times per hour (Olds 1956).

Some similar experiments were even performed in human patients with mental illnesses. These patients engaged sometimes obsessively in "lever pressing" that released electrical pulses from electrode implants in various subcortical locations (Heath 1972; Portenoy et al. 1986). However, it is not clear whether they actually enjoyed these pulses, or if their behavior involved excessive wanting without much liking (Berridge and Kringelbach 2008; Green et al. 2010; Kringelbach and Berridge 2012; Smith 2010).

Blockade of dopaminergic signaling typically disrupts reward-directed and consummatory behavior in rodents (Berridge and Robinson 1998; Schultz 2002). Extensive destruction of dopaminergic neurons can completely abolish rats' interest in food, to the extent that they will starve to death unless artificially fed (Berridge and Robinson 1998). In humans, a wide range of reward-related activities has been associated with dopamine signaling (Egerton et al. 2009), e.g., anticipation and emotional reactions to pleasurable music, presentation of cocaine, drug-associated stimuli, video games, and monetary rewards (Breiter et al. 1997; Koepp et al. 1998; Salimpoor et al. 2011; Scott et al. 2007; Volkow et al. 1997).

These findings lead to the widespread idea of dopamine as a "common neural currency" for pleasant rewards (Schultz 2002). However, while manipulations of dopaminergic signaling or microinjections of dopamine into different parts of this "reward network" often increase how much the animal would work to obtain a reward, it does little to change the hedonic impact of the reward—i.e., how much animals lick their lips when consuming the sucrose (Fig. 13.2a). Although stimulation of these "pleasure centers" increases wanting of food rewards, it doesn't actually make the animals enjoy their food more, according to simultaneous measures of objective facial responses (Berridge and Valenstein 1991).

In contrast, microinjections of opioids and certain other neurochemicals into discrete locations in the ventral pallidum and the rostral part of the NAc enhance the intensity of actual "liking" (Pecina and Berridge 2005). The "hedonic hotspots," where microinjections of opioids increase "liking," are very small in size compared to locations where opioid or dopamine microinjections increase "wanting" responses (Fig. 13.2b–c). The hotspots correspond to <10% of the accumbens shell (about 1 mm^3 in rodents and 1 cm^3 in humans, if proportional) and the ventral pallidum. The hotspots in the NAc shell and ventral pallidum seem to work as a single integrated circuit in the rat brain. Opioid stimulation in the NAc hotspot increases liking reactions to sucrose and corresponding firing signals in the ventral pallidum hotspot (Smith et al. 2011). Further, pharmacological opioid blockage of either of these hotspots prevents amplification of "liking" by activation of the other, suggesting that cooperation of both hotspots is needed for improving hedonic impact (Smith and Berridge 2007). Additional potential hotspots for "liking" reactions have been discovered in rodents in a prefrontal region that may correspond to the Orbitofrontal Cortex (OFC) in humans, and in the rat homolog for the human insula (Berridge, personal communication).

Although the hedonic "hotspots" appear to be few and cover only a small fraction of brain regions that generate reward-related behaviors, this circuitry is very resilient, and there are few known human cases where basic liking reactions are completely abolished. One case report describes a patient whose life became overshadowed by anhedonia and depression, with much reduced positive affect and attenuated craving for rewards. These symptoms appeared after selective damage to the bilateral ventral pallidum, which was performed to alleviate his Parkinsonian symptoms (Miller et al. 2006).

Within the accumbens shell, μ-opioids increase liking only when microinjected within the small rostroventral hotspot. When microinjected in nearby locations, the same substance instead increases wanting without liking, suppresses aversive "disgust" reactions, or suppresses both "liking" and "disliking" reactions to sweet or bitter tastes (Figs 13.2c and 13.3). Moreover, there is recent evidence that other substances, like orexin and cannabinoids, may have comparable effects within these hotspots (Ho and Berridge 2013; Mahler et al. 2007). This may reflect a strong flexibility of this circuit, allowing other pharmacological agents to employ the role of opioids if this system is disrupted.

Opioids mediate preference for the most valuable option when several rewards are available. μ-opioid antagonism reduces consumption of palatable cookies in rats, but does not affect the consumption of standard chow (Cooper and Turkish 1989). Conversely, μ-opioid agonism enhances sexual "wanting" of estrus, but not non-estrus females (Mahler and Berridge 2012). In humans, μ-opioid agonism increases, while antagonism reduces, the relative appeal of highly attractive, over less attractive, opposite-sex faces (Chelnokova et al. 2014).

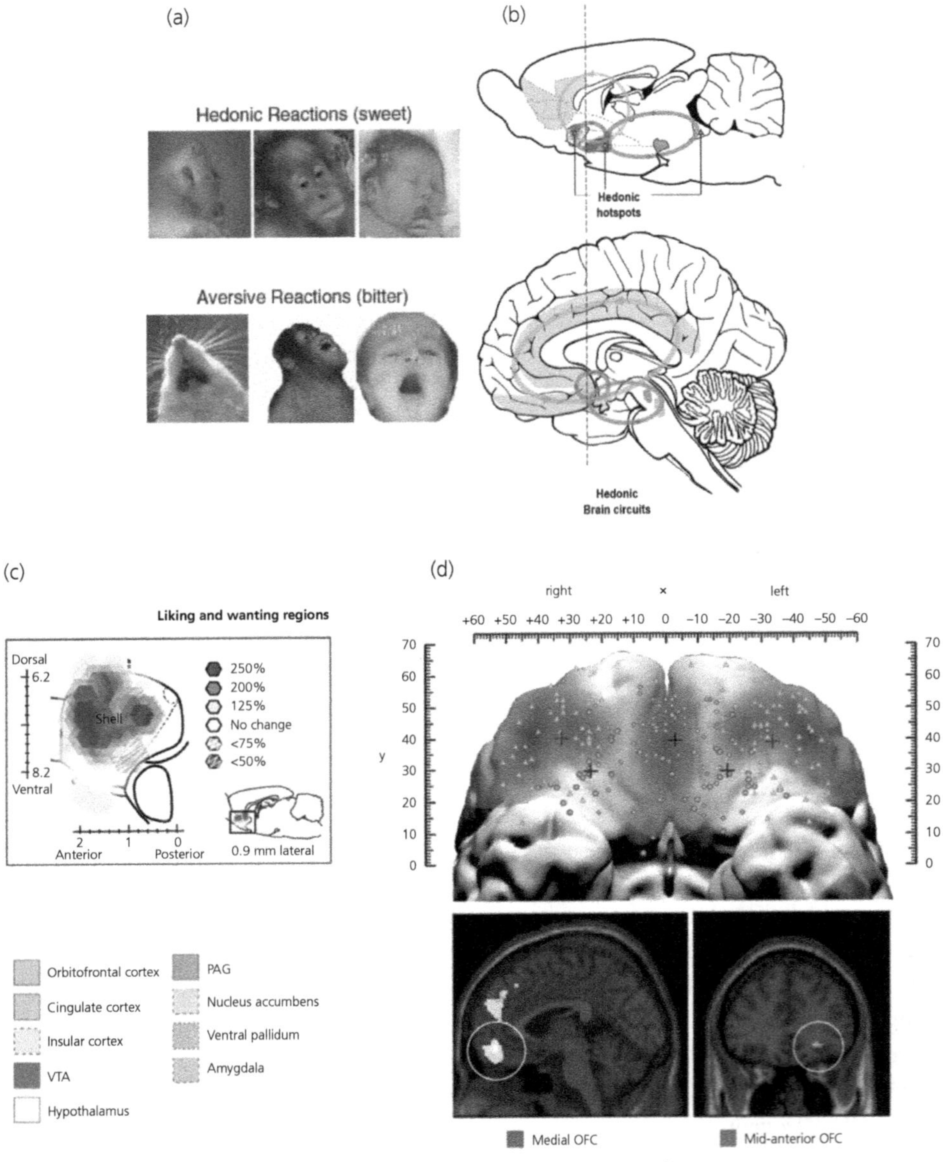

Fig. 13.2 Brain circuitry for generating hedonic value. This schematic figure summarizes subcortical and cortical systems for generating and coding of hedonic value. (a) Typical facial reactions to sweet and bitter taste are comparable in rodents, primates and human infants, and provide a useful model for investigating "liking" and "disliking." (b) Brain circuitry involved in hedonic processing in rodents and humans. (c) Hedonic "hotspots" have been found in the nucleus accumbens shell and the ventral pallidum. Microinjection of mu opioid agonists into these locations increase "liking" responses to e.g., sweet taste. (d) Cortical hedonic coding may reach an apex in the orbitofrontal cortex, where hedonic value may be translated into subjective pleasure or displeasure. (See Plate 7.)

Reprinted from *Trends in Cognitive Science*, 13 (11), pp. 479–487. Morten L. Kringelbach, Kent C. Berridge, Toward a functional neuroanatomy of pleasure and happiness, (2009), with permission from Elsevier. Reproduced from Susana Peciña and Kent C. Berridge, *The Journal of Neuroscience*, 25(50), pp. 11777–11,786, Hedonic Hot Spot in Nucleus Accumbens Shell: Where Do μ-Opioids Cause Increased Hedonic Impact of Sweetness? © 2005, The Society for Neuroscience.

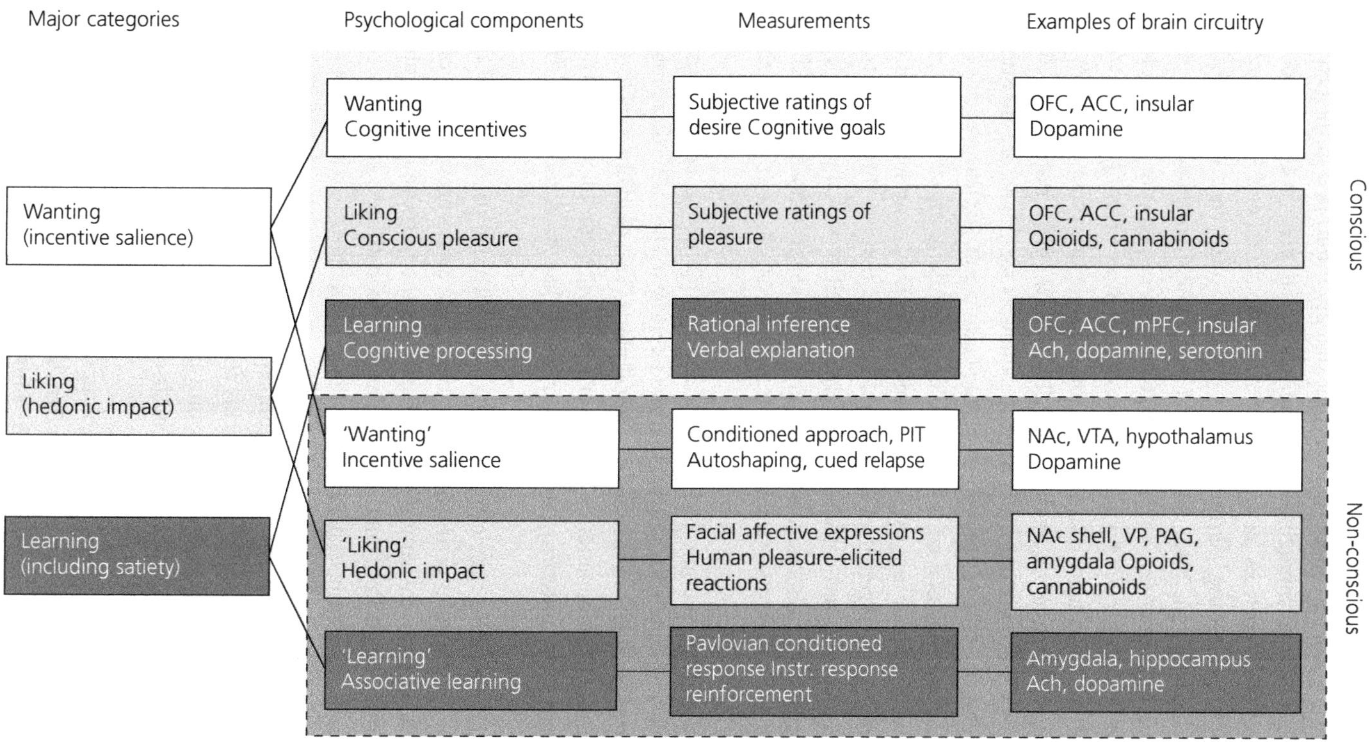

Fig. 13.3 Measuring hedonia. Hedonic processes may be divided into at least three major neurobiologically and psychologically components: wanting or incentive salience (white), liking or hedonic impact (light gray), and learning (dark gray). These components have conscious aspects, which can only be investigated in humans, and non-conscious aspects, which can also be investigated in non-human animals. Types of measurements are listed in the second column, and examples of brain circuitry involved in each subcomponent are listed in the third column. (See Plate 8.)

Reproduced from Berridge, K. C. and Kringelbach, M. L., Building a neuroscience of pleasure and well-being, *Psychology of Well-Being: Theory, Research and Practice* 2011, 1 (3), Springer, Copyright © 2011. http://www.psywb.com/content/1/1/3.

Cortical coding of pleasure

Apart from the circuitry that has been found to cause pleasure in animal experiments, there are a number of cortical and subcortical regions that are implicated in the processing of pleasure. Functional neuroimaging in humans suggest that orbitofrontal, insular, and ventromedial prefrontal cortices (as well as the amygdala, PAG, and VTA) play important roles in reward processing. Activity in this circuitry often correlates with self-reported pleasure (Ellingsen et al. 2013; Grabenhorst et al. 2008; Kringelbach 2005; Rolls et al. 2003). Although they may not be the main generators of pleasure, these regions are likely to represent hedonic value for other processes, such as learning and memory, cognitive representations, language, decisions, action, or consciousness (Berridge and Kringelbach 2013; Kringelbach and Berridge 2010). This builds on the notion that, while large-scale disruption of these regions often has consequences for the before-mentioned processes, it seldom abolishes the capacity for normal pleasure and displeasure.

Two locations in the orbitofrontal cortex seem to be particularly important for pleasure. One site in the mid-anterior and mid-lateral part of the OFC may serve as an apex of cortical pleasure coding (Kringelbach 2005) (Fig. 13.2d). Activity in this region tracks changes in subjective pleasure, and correlates strongly with self-reported pleasantness of food, touch, sexual orgasms, drugs, chocolate, and music (Blood and Zatorre 2001; Ellingsen et al. 2013; Georgiadis et al. 2006; Grabenhorst et al. 2008; McGlone et al. 2012; Small et al. 2001; Vollm et al. 2004).

Another important site for hedonic coding is located on the medial edge. Since unpleasant events mainly correlate with activation more laterally in the OFC, there may be a pleasure–displeasure "gradient" in the medial–lateral plane. This gradient may interact with a complexity gradient in the anterior–posterior plane, with complex rewards such as money being coded more anteriorly, and basic rewards like food more posteriorly (Kringelbach 2005).

Other cortical regions are also implicated in reward and affective processing. The anterior insula serves a crucial role for interoceptive awareness and representation of the "self" (Craig 2009). It seems to monitor emotional state for the purpose of maintaining homeostasis. The ventromedial Prefrontal Cortex (vmPFC) constitute a set of interconnected regions that may integrate information from episodic memory, sensory events, social cognition, and current bodily state to construct affective meaning (Roy et al. 2012). It has reciprocal projections to numerous cortical, limbic, and midbrain structures, and is a central node in the resting default network (Greicius et al. 2003; Gusnard et al. 2001). As we will see later in this chapter, the anterior insula and subregions of the vmPFC are likely to play key roles in direct hedonic value on the basis of memory processes and current homeostatic and motivational state.

Although the cortex, and in particular the OFC, appears to code hedonic value, it is possible that these regions are not necessary for experiencing pleasure. Thousands of human patients received prefrontal lobotomy in the 1950s with massive damage to the ACC and OFC. However, in spite of clear deficits in decision-making and dramatic personality changes, these patients did not seem to lose the capacity for hedonic feelings, and continued to live affective lives (Damasio 2000; Valenstein 1986). Further, case reports suggest that affective processing may be relatively intact in patients with insular damage. One patient had bilateral insular cortices completely destroyed from herpes simplex encephalitis. Although he showed massive learning deficits, and was unable to remember any new factual item for more than 45 s, he still showed differential preference for food, and reported feelings of happiness, pleasure, and pain (Damasio et al. 2012). Another case report of patients with insular damage reported intact feelings of pain, but with increased pain intensity for experimental pain stimuli (Starr et al. 2009), in line with a role for the insula in pain regulation (Craig 2009). Lastly, a case report of a 6-year-old patient with hydrocephalus, with the absence of cerebral tissue rostral to the thalamus, reported that the boy "smiled when spoken to and giggled when played with" (Shewmon et al. 1999: 366). Together, these cases suggest that, although playing important roles in the hedonic valuation, cortical nodes of hedonic processing are not necessary for hedonic experience.

Determining hedonic value

While much of the circuitry involved in valuation and reward is remarkably similar between humans and other mammals (Haber and Knutson 2010; Murray et al. 2007), there are some notable differences. For example, humans have massively expanded prefrontal cortices, reflecting greater encephalization. This is likely to be accompanied by more prefrontal influence of other brain processing via increased prefrontal connectivity to other cortical and subcortical brain regions. Compared to rats, primate orbitofrontal cortex projects more clearly defined descending connections to the hypothalamus and brainstem structures. Thus, "higher-order" cognitive and affective information may have more influence over hedonic value in humans compared to other animals/mammals.

Homeostatic utility and pleasure

Pleasure and displeasure are never sensory experiences per se, but are qualities that are imposed onto sensory experiences. Even stimuli that seem inherently "positive," like sweet taste, can become hedonically "flipped." Eating a delicious chocolate can be intensely pleasant if you are hungry for chocolate. Yet the delight turns to disgust if you keep eating it beyond satiety, although the sensory stimulus remains the same (Small et al. 2001). Introducing the concept of alliesthesia, Cabanac (1971) postulated that stimuli that serve to move the organism toward physiological or psychological homeostasis should be perceived as pleasant, while stimuli that serve to move the organism out of homeostasis should be perceived as unpleasant or painful. Rather than the inherent quality of the stimulus itself, it is the *utility* of the stimulus for the organism at the time that determines the hedonic value of the stimulus. The taste of salt at concentrations higher than seawater is usually unpleasant to humans, and causes "disliking" gape reactions in rats. However, if sodium levels are experimentally depleted, which induces a state of "salt appetite," rats will instead display "liking" reactions comparable to that of sucrose taste (Berridge et al. 1984;

Tindell et al. 2006). Moreover, this "hedonic flip" is mirrored by the firing rate of neurons in the ventral pallidum, indicating that coding of basic sensory pleasure depends on the homeostatic utility, and not merely intrinsic qualities, of the stimulus (Tindell et al. 2006).

The homeostatic utility—and consequently the hedonic value—of a stimulus is dependent on a range of factors, like other sensory input, the individual's memories, and their concurrent affective, cognitive, and physiological states. In the example before, chocolate was pleasant when it served to relieve hunger, but disgusting when this need was satiated. Similarly, while a hot bath is likely very pleasant if you just came in freezing from a winter storm, you may prefer an invigorating cold shower if you're boiling in the midst of a heat wave. The brain similarly makes use of its own predictions about the future when assigning hedonic value.

Hedonic feelings are modulated by motivational states

The brain draws on all its available sensory and internal information in order to build an internal model of the environment/world. This model is used to predict the outcome of different actions and the hedonic value of the most likely outcomes (Friston and Kiebel 2009; O'Reilly et al. 2013). Consequently, sensations are always a product of both sensory activation and top-down regulation, making the brain more of an "interpreter" than a "measuring instrument." Such sensory "bias," directed from the predicted utility of outcomes, is likely energy efficient compared to more comprehensive processing of a full range of "raw" sensory information. Moreover, it can facilitate rapid decision-making when sensory information is ambiguous or incomplete, which is an essential evolutionary advantage.

These principles have been employed to understand why pain is subject to such a vast intra-individual variability across situations. Physical pain is generally associated with displeasure and suffering, and is typically something an individual will work to avoid (however, as we will see later in this chapter, some pain experiences are perhaps equally associated with pleasure and displeasure). The motivation-decision model of pain, as proposed by Fields (2006, 2007), describes brain mechanisms that enhance or reduce the hedonic impact of events based on their relative importance at a given time. The model was initially put forward to explain modulation of pain, but the basic idea holds for all events that fall within a reward–punishment continuum. Fields postulates that—as a result of an unconscious decision-making process—any concurrent or impending event that is more important for the individual than a pain stimulus should suppress the hedonic impact of this pain. The event of superior importance may, for instance, be a greater threat or a potential reward. Likewise, anything judged as more important that an impending reward—for example, a threat or a bigger reward—should suppress the hedonic impact of this reward.

A central question is how the brain modulates this hedonic impact. Does it target the neural systems that generate pleasure or displeasure, e.g., hedonic hot and cold spots, or does it also modulate ascending sensory information that gives rise to pleasure or displeasure? If so, at which levels does this modulation take place?

There is well-established evidence that ascending nociceptive neurons in the spinal dorsal are modulated by the brain (Wall 1967; Woolf 2011). The PAG in the midbrain controls incoming nociceptive signals indirectly through the rostroventral medulla (RVM) (Fields 2004; Millan 2002). Neurons in the RVM project to the spinal dorsal horn, with inhibitory ("OFF cells") or excitatory ("ON cells") effects on nociceptive transmission (Neubert et al. 2004; Urban and Gebhart 1999). The PAG receives direct input from the limbic structures amygdala and ventral striatum, and from the prefrontal cortex, constituting a pathway by which affective or cognitive information can influence ascending sensory information already at the spinal dorsal horn (Fields 2004).

Modulation of hedonic experience by contextual meaning

Hedonic experience is modulated by context, expectations, attention, arousal, and mood. A range of neuroimaging studies in humans show that such top-down modulation of pain can alter widespread somatosensory processing in the brain (Amanzio et al. 2013; Berna et al. 2010; Ellingsen et al. 2013; Knudsen et al. 2011; Tracey and Mantyh 2007; Wager et al. 2004).

A particularly useful experimental model for probing psychological modulation of pain, but also hedonic value in general, is placebo responses. The term "placebo" is derived from the Latin stem "*placebit*" ("it will please"), and placebo responses refer to positive treatment outcomes that are not caused by the physical properties of this treatment but by the meaning ascribed to it. When people expect a placebo treatment to have analgesic effects, they often report reduced pain, which is accompanied by widespread reductions of somatosensory (pain) processing in thalamus, insula, primary and secondary somatosensory areas, and dorsal ACC (Amanzio et al. 2013; Eippert et al. 2009a; Lu et al. 2010). Further, activity in a "pain modulatory network" consisting of vmPFC, OFC, ventral striatum, amygdala, and the midbrain, is instead increased, and is thought to be responsible for the suppression of pain processing. This modulatory network is dependent on opioid processing, since administration of the opioid receptor antagonist naloxone can attenuate both the reduced pain reports (Amanzio and Benedetti 1999; Levine et al. 1978) and the reduction in pain/somatosensory processing (Eippert et al. 2009a). The modulatory network responsible for placebo analgesia may play a more general role in expectancy-induced modulation of hedonic sensations. Petrovic and colleagues (2005) used a conditioning paradigm, whereby participants were shown threatening images before and after administration of the anxiolytic drug midozalam. This drug robustly reduced self-reported unpleasantness from viewing the images. In a subsequent session, participants who were given a placebo, labeled as midozalam, reported reductions in unpleasantness comparable to the active substance. Furthermore, the placebo improvement was underpinned by increased fMRI activation in ventral striatum, rostral ACC and mid-lateral OFC, but suppressed activation in visual cortex.

Recent findings suggest that nociceptive processing at the spinal dorsal horn can be altered when people expect pain relief. Eippert et al. (2009b) recorded fMRI of the spinal segment receiving information from the arm, and found increased activity when people had received placebo treatment that also reduced their arm pain. Similarly, attentional modulation of nociceptive signals in the spinal cord has been found when people are performing a cognitively demanding working memory task, which induces analgesia (Sprenger et al. 2012). Within the framework of the motivation-decision model, this similarity between expectancy- and distraction-induced analgesia is interesting, and may reflect a more general mechanism whereby motivational states control the presence of pain. In both cases, the importance of pain is reduced, either because the brain is convinced an "analgesic" treatment will reduce pain, or because attention is focused at another, more important task. As a consequence of the brain's decision to "respond less" to pain, the individual can focus attention to other important tasks, such as reward seeking.

Nocebo hyperalgesia, the worsening of pain by negative expectations, may work by a comparable mechanism (Scott et al. 2008). fMRI studies indicate that expectancy-induced increases in pain hedonics are underpinned by amplified somatosensory responses to pain stimuli (Bingel et al. 2011; Kong et al. 2008; Rodriguez-Raecke et al. 2010). Further, a recent study investigated spinal fMRI activity during nocebo hyperalgesia, and found increased activation in the relevant spinal cord segment when people expected pain to be increased (Geuter and Buchel 2013). These studies indicate that psychological processes, in this case expectation of treatment benefit, are able to modulate sensory information along the entire sensory neural "axis" stretching from sensory circuitry in the brain to coupling stations in the spinal dorsal horn, resulting in this context in reduced or amplified pain experience. Such modulation is less studied for non-nociceptive sensory processing or positive hedonic experiences.

If boosting the pleasure of a pleasant sensation (hyperhedonia) works in a corresponding manner, we would expect sensory activity of this appetitive stimulus instead to be increased. We recently found that a placebo modulation boosting the pleasantness of gentle touch might rely on a mechanism similar to that of placebo analgesia (Ellingsen et al. 2013). We suggested to a group of healthy volunteers that a nasal spray would increase both the pleasantness of gentle touch and reduce the unpleasantness of pain. After self-administration of this nasal spray, a placebo, people reported increased touch pleasantness and reduced pain unpleasantness. The reported improvements of pleasure and pain were proportional to their prior expectations of treatment effects. While fMRI recordings during pain showed decreased somatosensory processing, recordings during gentle touch stimuli showed instead amplified activity in somatosensory areas (SI, SII, insula). Moreover, the magnitude of both hyperhedonic increases and analgesic decreases in somatosensory responses were accounted for by the individual strength of the functional coupling between medial OFC and PAG. It remains to be seen whether the modulation of pleasurable touch, like pain, involves descending modulation of cutaneous afferents in the spinal cord, perhaps via the RVM. It will also be interesting to see whether this modulation relies on opioid processing. These results cannot tell us the direction of causality. Nevertheless, this finding may suggest that, like negative hedonics such as pain, psychological modulation of pleasant sensations involves modulation of the underlying sensory processing, and not only within higher-level valuation circuitry.

A hedonic continuum?

Cognitively induced improvements of both pleasant and painful feelings are underpinned by increased activity in orbitofrontal and ventromedial prefrontal areas, ventral striatum, amygdala, and midbrain hubs PAG and VTA (Becker et al. 2012; Haber and Knutson 2010; Leknes and Tracey 2008). The extensive similarities between the brain networks and endocrinology involved in processing, and improving, pleasure and pain, pose the question of whether the brain uses a "common currency" for hedonic value (Cabanac 1992; Leknes and Tracey 2008; Ramirez and Cabanac 2003).

Pleasure and pain are often regarded as opposites, and is related to the idea that the brain places subjective experiences on a "hedonic continuum" with end-points distress and delight, and indifference in the middle (Cabanac 1979; Young 1959). This concept seems accurate in many (perhaps most) cases. Pain and pleasure are often opposing forces. Pleasant experiences like delicious food, music (Bernatzky et al. 2011), beautiful pictures, pleasant touch, and perceived support from others can dampen concurrent pain. Conversely, the occurrence of pain often suppresses positive feelings, as illustrated by the burden of depression and anhedonia that frequently accompanies chronic pain conditions (Marbach and Lund 1981; Marbach et al. 1983).

Pain–pleasure modulations may be reciprocally mediated by opioid signaling—a mu-opioid antagonist can attenuate the pain-reducing effect of pleasant experiences, while a mu-opioid agonist can attenuate the pleasure-reducing effect of pain (Fields 2007; Leknes and Tracey 2008) (Fig. 13.4a).

Mixed emotions and the benefits of pain

Although punishment is usually unpleasant and aversive, there are cases where painful experiences instead gain a positive meaning, and can even be pleasant. The often positively laden experiences of eating spicy food, burning muscle during physical exercise, or engaging in endurance sports illustrate that pain does not always carry an exclusively negative hedonic value.

All consciously perceived hedonic experiences are associated with meaning. For instance, a delicious cup of hot chocolate is often a welcome indulgence, but it can also be associated with guilt in both a positive (guilty pleasure) and a negative (I've failed to stick to my diet) manner. The meaning of pain provides another compelling illustration of the importance of meaning. While muscle pain is inevitable during a marathon run, it may nevertheless carry a certain positive value, if the pain represents a challenge rather than a threat. This change in meaning reduces the negative hedonic feeling usually associated with pain, as demonstrated in a recent study assessing the impact of positive or negative verbal instructions on the tolerance of ischemic arm pain. Participants who were told that the pain would have beneficial effects on muscle cells tolerated the pain for almost twice as long as participants who were informed only about the aversive aspects of the pain (Benedetti et al. 2013) (Fig. 13.4b).

Further, moderate pain can be "hedonically flipped" from unpleasant to pleasant if the pain represents avoidance from an even more painful stimulus (Leknes et al. 2013). This

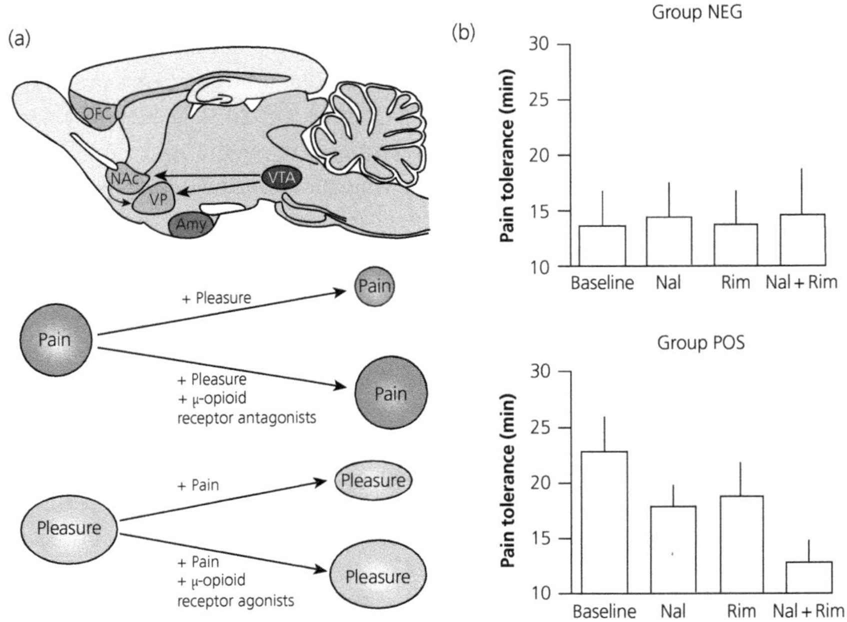

Fig. 13.4 Opioid modulation of pleasure and pain. (a) Pleasure and pain both elicit opioid release in the orbitofrontal cortex, nucleus accumbens, ventral pallidum, and amygdala. Pleasure and pain often works in a mutually inhibitory, opioid-dependent, fashion. Mu-opioid receptor antagonists, like naloxone, can attenuate pleasure-induced analgesia. Vice versa, mu-opioid receptor agonists, like morphine, can reverse pain-related suppression of pleasure. (b) In a recent experimental study, one group of participants were told that experimental muscle pain would hurt but had therapeutic benefits (POS), while another group were only told that pain would hurt (NEG). Pain tolerance in the (POS) group was almost doubled compared to the (NEG) group. This increase in pain tolerance was partially reversed when participants were pre-treated with either naloxone (Nal) or the endocannabinoid receptor antagonist rimonabant (Rim), and completely abolished when pre-treated with both Nal and Rim. (See Plate 9.)

(a) Reprinted by permission from Macmillan Publishers Ltd: *Nature Reviews Neuroscience*, 9(4), pp. 314–320, Leknes, S. and I. Tracey (2008). "A common neurobiology for pain and pleasure, © 2008, Macmillan Publishers Ltd.

(b) Reproduced from Benedetti, F., Thoen, W., Blanchard, C., Vighetti, S., Arduino, C., Pain as a reward: changing the meaning of pain from negative to positive co-activates opioid and cannabinoid systems, Pain, 154(3), pp. 361–367, © 2013, Lippincott Williams and Wilkins, Inc.

hedonic flip is underpinned by increased co-activation of the PAG with NAc and vmPFC (Leknes et al. 2013). Pain can also enhance the pleasure of reward hedonics. For example, people report greater pleasure from chocolate after undergoing a cold-pressor test, where the task is to keep ones hand dipped in a bath of cold water (~1°C) for as long as possible (Bastian et al. 2014).

A possible mechanism whereby painful experiences can be pleasant, e.g., in consumption of spicy food, is that the enhanced arousal pain causes, increases attention also to positive sensory signals, resulting in a more intense, and also pleasant, sensory experience (Bastian et al. in press; Leknes and Bastian 2014). Another possibility is that endogenous release of endorphins caused by aversive signaling accounts for the positive affect (Carstens et al. 2002). However, one study found that offset analgesia, the disproportionally large analgesic response that often follows a slight reduction in the intensity of an ongoing pain, was unaffected by administration of an opioid antagonist or an agonist (Martucci et al. 2012).

While pain is most often regarded as negative and reward is often regarded as positive, there are many examples of experiences that carry both positive and negative hedonic values. Therefore, a simple pleasure–pain dichotomy may be too simple. Pain is a multi-faceted phenomenon, which consists of more than just "displeasure." The term "algosity" refers to the unique sensation of "painfulness" that distinguishes pain from other unpleasant somatic sensations, like itch and nausea (Fields 1999). Algosity and pain unpleasantness do not necessarily go hand in hand, which is illustrated by pain asymbolia, a condition where patients report feeling pain, but not unpleasantness or suffering. It is likely that the presence of pleasure during a painful experience in most cases reduces displeasure, although the algosity may remain the same. This would be consistent with the idea of a hedonic continuum treating pleasure and displeasure as opposites.

There are nevertheless several examples of situations where feelings of pleasure and displeasure may perhaps be equally prominent, like deep pressure massage, being tickled, feelings of nostalgia, or bittersweet feelings. In one study, people engaged in a gambling game with two types of contexts. In one context there was a 50/50 chance of winning either of two amounts of money, while in the other context there was a 50/50 chance of losing either of two amounts (Larsen et al. 2004). Thus, winning the lowest amount was the worst possible outcome in the first context, while losing the least amount was the best possible outcome in the second context. Participants reported feeling both good and bad about the disappointing wins and relieving losses. Moreover, when participants indicated with two buttons whenever they felt good or bad, participants reported feeling good or bad simultaneously rather than alternating between the two, suggesting that these constituted unitary mixed emotional events.

Rozin and colleagues refer to the enjoyment of experiences that are innately aversive, but do not represent a threat, as "benign masochism" (Rozin and Schiller 1980; Rozin et al. 2013). According to this idea, when the brain judges such an aversive sensation to represent no real danger, a sense of control, or mastery, gives rise to positive affect.

There is little evidence for the preference of mixed emotions in animals. Rats display both aversive and "liking" taste reactivity responses to bittersweet foods (Doyle et al. 1993), but would likely choose a purely sweet substance over the bittersweet. Typically a stimulus is associated with either avoidance or approach behavior by the animal, not both at the same time (Rozin et al. 1979; however, see Rozin and Kennel 1983). This is in line with the notion that hedonic impact may be more influenced by top-down factors in humans compared other mammals (Berridge and Kringelbach 2013).

Although most of the studies investigating mixed emotions address explicit hedonic feelings, either through here-and-now assessments or in retrospect, they tell relatively little about how this liking or disliking relate to motivational or learning aspects of rewards. For example, although an experience can be simultaneously liked and disliked, it could still be that motivational processes follow a more either/or principle—that an event cannot be both worked for and against at the same time. More research is needed to definitely answer whether it is meaningful to classify sensations on a bipolar continuum with pleasure and displeasure as end-points, or whether they are separable processes that compete for preference in the brain, but are not mutually exclusive. Nevertheless, it seems clear that, at least humans are capable of experiencing unitary feelings that are both pleasant and unpleasant.

Conclusion

In this chapter, we have reviewed the neurocircuitry and neuropharmacology that generates hedonic value in humans and animals. There is extensive evidence from animal research that hedonic events can be disentangled into wanting, liking, and learning aspects, which may constitute a cyclical process that characterizes normal pleasure events. The hedonic value of both basic sensory and "higher order" pleasure and displeasure is often strongly dependent on homeostatic utility rather than the inherent properties of the stimuli. This is illustrated by the fact that hedonic reactions to stimuli can be flipped from pleasant to unpleasant, and vice versa, depending on the motivational or homeostatic state. Interestingly, such modulation is not only mirrored by processing in mesolimbic and prefrontal valuation circuitry, but also in corresponding modulation of sensory processing along the entire "neural axis" from central sensory networks to (at least) sensory relay stations in the spinal cord. Along with these principles, pleasure and displeasure play crucial roles in optimizing brain resources to guide survival-promoting behavior. Although pleasure and displeasure often appear opposite, there are many examples of cases where hedonic experiences can consist of both. It remains to be discovered whether pleasure and displeasure may meaningfully be viewed as opposites on a "hedonic continuum," or whether they comprise separate systems that often, but not always operate in an opposing manner.

References

Amanzio M, Benedetti F (1999) Neuropharmacological dissection of placebo analgesia: expectation-activated opioid systems versus conditioning-activated specific subsystems. *The Journal of Neuroscience: the official journal of the Society for Neuroscience* **19**:484–494.

Amanzio M, Benedetti F, Porro CA, Palermo S, Cauda F (2013) Activation likelihood estimation meta-analysis of brain correlates of placebo analgesia in human experimental pain. *Human Brain Mapping* **34**:738–752.

Bastian B, Jetten J, Hornsey MJ (2014) Gustatory pleasure and pain. The offset of acute physical pain enhances responsiveness to taste. *Appetite*, **72**:150–155.

Bastian B, Jetten Y, Hornsey MJ, Leknes S (2014) The positive consequences of physical pain: A biopsychosocial approach. *Personality and Social Psychology Review, 1088868314527831.*

Becker S, Gandhi W, Schweinhardt P (2012) Cerebral interactions of pain and reward and their relevance for chronic pain. *Neuroscience Letters* **520**:182–187.

Benedetti F, Thoen W, Blanchard C, Vighetti S, Arduino C (2013) Pain as a reward: changing the meaning of pain from negative to positive co-activates opioid and cannabinoid systems. *Pain* **154**:361–367.

Berna C, Leknes S, Holmes EA, Edwards RR, Goodwin GM, Tracey I (2010) Induction of depressed mood disrupts emotion regulation neurocircuitry and enhances pain unpleasantness. *Biological Psychiatry* **67**:1083–1090.

Bernatzky G, Presch M, Anderson M, Panksepp J (2011) Emotional foundations of music as a non-pharmacological pain management tool in modern medicine. *Neuroscience and Biobehavioral Reviews* **35**:1989–1999.

Berridge KC, Kringelbach ML (2008) Affective neuroscience of pleasure: reward in humans and animals. *Psychopharmacology* **199**:457–480.

Berridge KC, Kringelbach ML (2011) Building a neuroscience of pleasure and well-being. *Psychology of Well-being* **1**:1–3.

Berridge KC, Kringelbach ML (2013) Neuroscience of affect: brain mechanisms of pleasure and displeasure. *Current Opinion in Neurobiology* **23**:294–303.

Berridge KC, Robinson TE (1998) What is the role of dopamine in reward: hedonic impact, reward learning, or incentive salience? *Brain Research Reviews* **28**:309–369.

Berridge KC, Valenstein ES (1991) What psychological process mediates feeding evoked by electrical stimulation of the lateral hypothalamus? *Behavioral Neuroscience* **105**:3–14.

Berridge KC, Flynn FW, Schulkin J, Grill HJ (1984) Sodium depletion enhances salt palatability in rats. *Behavioral Neuroscience* **98**:652–660.

Bingel U, Wanigasekera V, Wiech K, Ni Mhuircheartaigh R, Lee MC, Ploner M, Tracey I (2011) The effect of treatment expectation on drug efficacy: imaging the analgesic benefit of the opioid remifentanil. *Science Translational Medicine* **3**:70ra14.

Blood AJ, Zatorre RJ (2001) Intensely pleasurable responses to music correlate with activity in brain regions implicated in reward and emotion. *Proceedings of the National Academy of Sciences of the United States of America* **98**:11818–11823.

Breiter HC, Gollub RL, Weisskoff RM et al. (1997) Acute effects of cocaine on human brain activity and emotion. *Neuron* **19**:591–611.

Cabanac M (1971) Physiological role of pleasure. *Science* **173**:1103–1107.

Cabanac M (1979) Sensory pleasure. *The Quarterly Review of Biology* **54**:1–29.

Cabanac M (1992) Pleasure: the common currency. *Journal of Theoretical Biology* **155**:173–200.

Carstens E, Carstens MI, Dessirier JM et al. (2002) It hurts so good: oral irritation by spices and carbonated drinks and the underlying neural mechanisms. *Food Quality and Preference* **13**:431–443.

Chelnokova O, Laeng B, Eikemo M et al. (2014) Rewards of beauty: the opioid system mediates social motivation in humans. *Molecular Psychiatry* **19**: 746–747.

Cooper SJ, Turkish S (1989) Effects of naltrexone on food preference and concurrent behavioral-responses in food-deprived rats. *Pharmacology Biochemistry and Behavior* **33**:17–20.

Craig, W. (1918) Appetites and aversions as constituents of instincts. *Biological Bulletin of Woods Hole* **34**, 91–107.

Craig AD (2009) How do you feel—now? The anterior insula and human awareness. *Nature Reviews Neuroscience* **10**:59–70.

Damasio A (2000) *The feeling of what happens: body and emotion in the making of consciousness*. New York: Houghton Mifflin Harcourt.

Damasio A, Damasio H, Tranel D (2013) "Persistence of feelings and sentience after bilateral damage of the insula." *Cereb Cortex* **23**(4):833–846.

Doyle TG, Berridge KC, Gosnell BA (1993) Morphine enhances hedonic taste palatability in rats. *Pharmacology, Biochemistry, and Behavior* **46**:745–749.

Egerton A, Mehta MA, Montgomery AJ et al. (2009) The dopaminergic basis of human behaviors: A review of molecular imaging studies. *Neuroscience and Biobehavioral Reviews* **33**:1109–1132.

Eippert F, Bingel U, Schoell ED et al. (2009a) Activation of the opioidergic descending pain control system underlies placebo analgesia. *Neuron* **63**:533–543.

Eippert F, Finsterbusch J, Bingel U, Buchel C (2009b) Direct evidence for spinal cord involvement in placebo analgesia. *Science* **326**:404.

Ellingsen DM, Wessberg J, Chelnokova O, Olausson H, Laeng B, Leknes S (2014) In touch with your emotions: oxytocin and touch change social impressions while others' facial expressions can alter touch. *Psychoneuroendocrinology* **39**:11–20.

Ellingsen DM, Wessberg J, Eikemo M et al. (2013) Placebo improves pleasure and pain through opposite modulation of sensory processing. *Proceedings of the National Academy of Sciences of the United States of America* **110**:17993–17998.

Fields HL (1999) Pain: an unpleasant topic. *Pain* Suppl **6**:S61–69.

Fields H (2004) State-dependent opioid control of pain. *Nature Reviews Neuroscience* **5**:565–575.

Fields HL (2006) A motivation-decision model of Pain: the role of opioids. In: *Proceedings of the 11th world congress on pain* (Flor, H., Kalso, E. and Dostrovsky, J.O., eds), pp. 449–459 Seattle: IASP Press.

Fields HL (2007) Understanding how opioids contribute to reward and analgesia. *Regional Anesthesia and Pain Medicine* **32**:242–246.

Frijda N (2010) On the nature and function of pleasure. In: *Pleasures of the brain* (Kringelbach, M. L. and Berridge, K. C., eds), pp 99–112 Oxford, U.K.: Oxford University Press.

Friston K, Kiebel S (2009) Predictive coding under the free-energy principle. *Philosophical Transactions of the Royal Society of London Series B, Biological Sciences* **364**:1211–1221.

Georgiadis JR, Kortekaas R, Kuipers R et al. (2006) Regional cerebral blood flow changes associated with clitorally induced orgasm in healthy women. *The European Journal of Neuroscience* **24**:3305–3316.

Geuter S, Buchel C (2013) Facilitation of pain in the human spinal cord by nocebo treatment. *The Journal of Neuroscience: the official journal of the Society for Neuroscience* **33**:13784–13790.

Grabenhorst F, Rolls ET, Bilderbeck A (2008) How cognition modulates affective responses to taste and flavor: top-down influences on the orbitofrontal and pregenual cingulate cortices. *Cerebral Cortex* **18**:1549–1559.

Green AL, Pereira EA, Aziz TZ (2010) Deep brain stimulation and pleasure. In: *Pleasures of the brain* (Kringelbach, M. L. and Berridge, K. C., eds), pp 302–319 Oxford, U.K.: Oxford University Press.

Greicius MD, Krasnow B, Reiss AL, Menon V (2003) Functional connectivity in the resting brain: a network analysis of the default mode hypothesis. *Proceedings of the National Academy of Sciences of the United States of America* **100**:253–258.

Gusnard DA, Raichle ME, Raichle ME (2001) Searching for a baseline: functional imaging and the resting human brain. *Nature Reviews Neuroscience* **2**:685–694.

Haber SN, Knutson B (2010) The reward circuit: linking primate anatomy and human imaging. *Neuropsychopharmacology: official publication of the American College of Neuropsychopharmacology* **35**:4–26.

Heath RG (1972) Pleasure and brain activity in man. Deep and surface electroencephalograms during orgasm. *The Journal of Nervous and Mental Disease* **154**:3–18.

Ho CY, Berridge KC (2013) An orexin hotspot in ventral pallidum amplifies hedonic "liking" for sweetness. *Neuropsychopharmacology: official publication of the American College of Neuropsychopharmacology* **38**:1655–1664.

Knudsen L, Petersen GL, Nørskov KN et al. (2011) Review of neuroimaging studies related to pain modulation. *Scandinavian Journal of Pain* **2**:108–120.

Koepp MJ, Gunn RN, Lawrence AD et al. (1998) Evidence for striatal dopamine release during a video game. *Nature* **393**:266–268.

Kong J, Gollub RL, Polich G et al. (2008) A functional magnetic resonance imaging study on the neural mechanisms of hyperalgesic nocebo effect. *The Journal of Neuroscience: the official journal of the Society for Neuroscience* **28**:13354–13362.

Kringelbach ML (2005) The human orbitofrontal cortex: linking reward to hedonic experience. *Nature Reviews Neuroscience* **6**:691–702.

Kringelbach ML (2010) The hedonic brain: a functional neuroanatomy of human pleasure. In: *Pleasures of the brain* (Kringelbach, M. L. and Berridge, K. C., eds), pp 202–221 Oxford, U.K.: Oxford University Press.

Kringelbach ML, Berridge KC (2010) The functional neuroanatomy of pleasure and happiness. *Discovery Medicine* **9**:579–587.

Kringelbach ML, Berridge KC (2012) The joyful mind. *Scientific American* **307**:40–45.

Kringelbach ML, Stein A, van Hartevelt TJ (2012) The functional human neuroanatomy of food pleasure cycles. *Physiology and Behavior* **106**:307–316.

Larsen JT, McGraw AP, Mellers BA, Cacioppo JT (2004) The agony of victory and thrill of defeat: Mixed emotional reactions to disappointing wins and relieving losses. *Psychological Science* **15**:325–330.

Leknes S, Bastian B (2014) The benefits of pain. *Review of Philosophy and Psychology* **5**:57–70.

Leknes S, Tracey I (2008) A common neurobiology for pain and pleasure. *Nature Reviews Neuroscience* **9**:314–320.

Leknes S, Berna C, Lee MC, Snyder GD, Biele G, Tracey I (2013) The importance of context: When relative relief renders pain pleasant. *Pain* **154**:402–410.

Levine JD, Gordon NC, Fields HL (1978) The mechanism of placebo analgesia. *Lancet* **2**:654–657.

Lu HC, Hsieh JC, Lu CL et al. (2010) Neuronal correlates in the modulation of placebo analgesia in experimentally-induced esophageal pain: a 3T-fMRI study. *Pain* **148**:75–83.

Mahler SV, Berridge KC (2012) What and when to "want"? Amygdala-based focusing of incentive salience upon sugar and sex. *Psychopharmacology (Berl)* **221**:407–426.

Mahler SV, Smith KS, Berridge KC (2007) Endocannabinoid hedonic hotspot for sensory pleasure: anandamide in nucleus accumbens shell enhances "liking" of a sweet reward. *Neuropsychopharmacology: official publication of the American College of Neuropsychopharmacology* **32**:2267–2278.

Marbach JJ, Lund P (1981) Depression, anhedonia and anxiety in temporomandibular joint and other facial pain syndromes. *Pain* **11**:73–84.

Marbach JJ, Richlin DM, Lipton JA (1983) Illness Behavior, Depression and Anhedonia in Myofascial Face and Back Pain Patients. *Psychotherapy and Psychosomatics* **39**:47–54.

Martucci KT, Eisenach JC, Tong C, Coghill RC (2012) Opioid-independent mechanisms supporting offset analgesia and temporal sharpening of nociceptive information. *Pain* **153**:1232–1243.

McGlone F, Olausson H, Boyle JA et al. (2012) Touching and feeling: differences in pleasant touch processing between glabrous and hairy skin in humans. *The European Journal of Neuroscience* **35**:1782–1788.

Millan MJ (2002) Descending control of pain. *Progress in Neurobiology* **66**:355–474.

Miller JM, Vorel SR, Tranguch AJ et al. (2006) Anhedonia after a selective bilateral lesion of the globus pallidus. *The American journal of Psychiatry* **163**:786–788.

Murray EA, O'Doherty JP, Schoenbaum G (2007) What we know and do not know about the functions of the orbitofrontal cortex after 20 years of cross-species studies. *The Journal of Neuroscience: the official journal of the Society for Neuroscience* **27**:8166–8169.

Neubert MJ, Kincaid W, Heinricher MM (2004) Nociceptive facilitating neurons in the rostral ventromedial medulla. *Pain* **110**:158–165.

Olds J (1956) Pleasure centers in the brain. *Scientific American* **195**:105–116.

Olds J, Milner P (1954) Positive reinforcement produced by electrical stimulation of septal area and other regions of rat brain. *Journal of Comparative and Physiological Psychology* **47**:419–427.

O'Reilly JX, Jbabdi S, Rushworth MF, Behrens TE (2013) Brain systems for probabilistic and dynamic prediction: computational specificity and integration. *PLoS Biology* **11**:e1001662.

Pecina S, Berridge KC (2005) Hedonic hot spot in nucleus accumbens shell: where do mu-opioids cause increased hedonic impact of sweetness? *The Journal of Neuroscience: the official journal of the Society for Neuroscience* **25**:11777–11786.

Petrovic P, Dietrich T, Fransson P, Andersson J, Carlsson K, Ingvar M (2005) Placebo in emotional processing—induced expectations of anxiety relief activate a generalized modulatory network. *Neuron* **46**:957–969.

Portenoy RK, Jarden JO, Sidtis JJ, Lipton RB, Foley KM, Rottenberg DA (1986) Compulsive thalamic self-stimulation: a case with metabolic, electrophysiologic and behavioral correlates. *Pain* **27**:277–290.

Ramirez JM, Cabanac M (2003) Pleasure, the common currency of emotions. *Annals of the New York Academy of Sciences* **1000**:293–295.

Rodriguez-Raecke R, Doganci B, Breimhorst M et al. (2010) Insular cortex activity is associated with effects of negative expectation on nociceptive long-term habituation. *The Journal of Neuroscience: the official journal of the Society for Neuroscience* **30**:11363–11368.

Rolls ET, O'Doherty J, Kringelbach ML, Francis S, Bowtell R, McGlone F (2003) Representations of pleasant and painful touch in the human orbitofrontal and cingulate cortices. *Cerebral Cortex* **13**:308–317.

Rømer Thomsen K, Whybrow PC, Kringelbach ML (2015) Reconceptualizing anhedonia: novel perspectives on balancing the pleasure networks in the human brain Frontiers in behavioral neuroscience **9**:49.

Roy M, Shohamy D, Wager TD (2012) Ventromedial prefrontal-subcortical systems and the generation of affective meaning. *Trends in Cognitive Sciences* **16**:147–156.

Rozin P, Gruss L, Berk G (1979) Reversal of innate aversions: attempts to induce a preference for chili peppers in rats. *Journal of Comparative and Physiological Psychology* **93**:1001–1014.

Rozin P, Guillot L, Fincher K, Rozin A, Tsukayama E (2013) Glad to be sad, and other examples of benign masochism. *Judgment and Decision Making* **8**:439–447.

Rozin P, Kennel K (1983) Acquired preferences for piquant foods by chimpanzees. *Appetite* **4**:69–77.

Rozin A, Schiller D (1980) The nature and acquisition of a preference for chili pepper by humans. *Motivation and Emotion* **4**:77–101.

Salimpoor VN, Benovoy M, Larcher K, Dagher A, Zatorre RJ (2011) Anatomically distinct dopamine release during anticipation and experience of peak emotion to music. *Nature Neuroscience* **14**:257–262.

Schultz W (2002) Getting formal with dopamine and reward. *Neuron* **36**:241–263.

Scott DJ, Stohler CS, Egnatuk CM, Wang H, Koeppe RA, Zubieta JK (2007) Individual differences in reward responding explain placebo-induced expectations and effects. *Neuron* **55**:325–336.

Scott DJ, Stohler CS, Egnatuk CM, Wang H, Koeppe RA, Zubieta J-K (2008) Placebo and nocebo effects are defined by opposite opioid and dopaminergic responses. Archives of *General Psychiatry* **65**:220–231.

Sherrington, C. S. (1906) *The integrative action of the nervous system*. C. Scribner's Sons: New York.

Shewmon, D.A., Holmes, G.L., and Byrne, P.A. (1999). Consciousness in congenitally decorticate children: developmental vegetative state as self- fulfilling prophecy. *Developmental Medicine and Child Neurology*, **41**, 364–374.

Shizgal P, Fulton S, Woodside B (2001) Brain reward circuitry and the regulation of energy balance. *International Journal of Obesity and Related Metabolic Disorders: journal of the International Association for the Study of Obesity* 25 Suppl **5**:S17–21.

Small DM, Zatorre RJ, Dagher A, Evans AC, Jones-Gotman M (2001) Changes in brain activity related to eating chocolate: from pleasure to aversion. *Brain: a Journal of Neurology* **124**:1720–1733.

Smith KS (2010) Hedonic hotspots: generating sensory pleasure in the brain. In: *Pleasures of the brain* (Kringelbach, M. L. and Berridge, K. C., eds), pp 27–49 Oxford, U.K.: Oxford University Press.

Smith KS, Berridge KC (2007) Opioid limbic circuit for reward: interaction between hedonic hotspots of nucleus accumbens and ventral pallidum. *The Journal of Neuroscience: the official journal of the Society for Neuroscience* **27**:1594–1605.

Smith KS, Berridge KC, Aldridge JW (2011) Disentangling pleasure from incentive salience and learning signals in brain reward circuitry. *Proceedings of the National Academy of Sciences of the United States of America* **108**:E255–264.

Sprenger C, Eippert F, Finsterbusch J, Bingel U, Rose M, Buchel C (2012) Attention modulates spinal cord responses to pain. *Current Biology* **22**:1019–1022.

Starr CJ, Sawaki L, Wittenberg GF et al. (2009) Roles of the insular cortex in the modulation of pain: insights from brain lesions. *The Journal of Neuroscience: the official journal of the Society for Neuroscience* **29**:2684–2694.

Steiner JE (1973) The gustofacial response: observation on normal and anencephalic newborn infants. In: *Symposium on Oral Sensation and Perception* (Bosma, J., ed) **4**:254–278 Oxford, U.K.: Us Government Printing Office.

Steiner JE, Glaser D, Hawilo ME, Berridge KC (2001) Comparative expression of hedonic impact: affective reactions to taste by human infants and other primates. *Neuroscience and Biobehavioral Reviews* **25**:53–74.

Tindell AJ, Smith KS, Pecina S, Berridge KC, Aldridge JW (2006) Ventral pallidum firing codes hedonic reward: when a bad taste turns good. *Journal of Neurophysiology* **96**:2399–2409.

Tracey I, Mantyh PW (2007) The cerebral signature for pain perception and its modulation. *Neuron* **55**:377–391.

Urban MO, Gebhart GF (1999) Supraspinal contributions to hyperalgesia. *Proceedings of the National Academy of Sciences of the United States of America* **96**:7687–7692.

Valenstein ES (1986) *Great and desperate cures: the rise and decline of psychosurgery and other radical treatments for mental illness*. Basic Books: New York, NY.

Valenstein ES, Cox VC, Kakolewski JW (1970) Reexamination of the role of the hypothalamus in motivation. *Psychological Review* **77**:16–31.

Volkow ND, Wang GJ, Fowler JS et al. (1997) Decreased striatal dopaminergic responsiveness in detoxified cocaine-dependent subjects. *Nature* **386**:830–833.

Vollm BA, de Araujo IE, Cowen PJ et al. (2004) Methamphetamine activates reward circuitry in drug naive human subjects. *Neuropsychopharmacology: official publication of the American College of Neuropsychopharmacology* **29**:1715–1722.

Wager TD, Rilling JK, Smith EE et al. (2004) Placebo-induced changes in FMRI in the anticipation and experience of pain. *Science* **303**:1162–1167.

Wall PD (1967) The laminar organization of dorsal horn and effects of descending impulses. *The Journal of Physiology* **188**:403–423.

Williams AC (2002) Facial expression of pain: an evolutionary account. *The Behavioral and Brain Sciences* **25**:439–455

Woolf CJ (2011) Central sensitization: implications for the diagnosis and treatment of pain. *Pain* **152**:S2–15.

Young PT (1959) The role of affective processes in learning and motivation. *Psychological Review* **66**:104–125.

Chapter 14

Prudential value or well-being

Raffaele Rodogno

The language of well-being

Kim, a high school graduate, is considering a number of rather unsurprising questions: Should I become a doctor, endure a long period of study without an income, but hopefully have a meaningful job with a good income at the end? What are my chances of succeeding? Would I enjoy my studies and then my job? And what would my life look like if I did succeed? Would I have time to keep up mountain climbing and see my friends? And would I eventually have time for a rich family life? Perhaps it would be better for me to work as a postman, take the morning shift, be finished at 2 p.m., have time to go mountain climbing after work, and meet up with my friends in the evening, if I feel like it. Surely work, of whichever kind, can never be as good for me as climbing and being with the people I care about. Or should I rather devote my life to those in need, or to intellectual and artistic achievement? Are these kinds of pursuits at all good for me?

When answering questions such as these, moral and perhaps other kinds of values may surely be at play. Yet it is at least as clear that these common questions are motivated in large part by a concern with well-being or prudential value. The idea of prudential value is often found in the literature in these terms:

> [Well-being is] what we have when our lives are going well for us, when we are living lives that are not necessarily morally good, but good *for us*.
>
> (Tiberius 2006: 493; italics in original)

Or again:

> It is commonly supposed that there is a single notion of individual well-being that . . . serves as a basis for the decisions of a single rational being, at least for those decisions in which he or she alone is concerned (that is to say, in which moral obligations and concern for others can be left aside).
>
> (Scanlon 1998: 108)

Four general points about well-being arise from these quotes.

1. The terminology of well-being. Questions about the prudential value or disvalue of lives or, alternatively, questions about what in an individual's life is of prudential value or disvalue[1]

[1] Rodogno (2014a) argues that these two questions, though connected, are distinct.

are also discussed in terms of "well-being" and "ill-being," "welfare," "benefit" and "harm," "happiness" and "misery," what is "good for" and "bad for" an agent, as well as in terms of "flourishing" or "thriving," "a person's interest," or a "person's good" or "personal good." Generally, that is, there is an assumed relation of synonymy standing among these expressions.[2] While we shall, for the most part, go along with this presumption, as we shall see in the "Well-being in philosophy" section, there are reasons not to equate conceptually "happiness" and "well-being." In fact, the pair "good for" and "bad for" also deserves special attention. These expressions are often used in connection with the good or perfect functioning of organisms and artifacts, as in "lubricant is *good for* the engine," "rust is *bad for* the car," and "smoking *is not good for* people." By these expressions, we typically mean that certain things are good or bad for the proper functioning of the organism or artifact in question. This is not the sense of "good for" and "bad for" at issue with prudential value. Or better, it is not conceptually the case that well-being is to be equated with good or perfect functioning in this sense. This latter claim, if true, needs substantive argument.[3] In the absence of that, it may well be true that smoking is bad for my organism but prudentially good for me.[4]

2. The axiological nature of prudential value. As some of the above remarks suggest, at the conceptual level, prudential value is neither moral, nor esthetic, nor perfectionist value. It is arguably a kind of value irreducible to any other kind, which may nonetheless stand in various substantive relations to them. Hence, for example, if we admit that pleasure has prudential value, the alleged truth of the claim "Evil pleasures are not good for us" cannot be conceptual and must be argued substantively. As we shall see in the "Well-being in philosophy" section, however, the claim that well-being is not reducible to other values has been the object of sustained scepticism.

3. The normativity of well-being. There is widespread agreement to the effect that well-being is, both, a descriptive and a normative concept. As Tiberius and Plakias (2010: 402) claim, the term "well-being" "aims to pick out an empirical phenomenon that can be measured, compared, and (one hopes) realized in people's lives: to achieve well-being is to enjoy a certain kind of life or set of experiences that we can investigate and influence." Yet, "well-being" also has normative significance, i.e., it involves reasons: if *A* is better for you than *B*, ceteris paribus, you have more reason to do *A*. While very few disagree with this claim,[5] growing disagreement is to be encountered with respect to the kind of normativity

---

[2] Rosati (2006: 108–109) offers reasons that relate to her specific prudential theory to prefer "personal good" over "flourishing," "welfare," and "well-being." Raz (1986: 294–295) draws a distinction between well-being and self-interest, where the former is treated as "the general term for evaluating success in life" and the latter is a largely biological notion.

[3] Substantive argument here may amount to a simple intuition to the effect that an individual's well-being consists in its perfect functioning.

[4] Rosati (2009a) contains an excellent discussion of the various meanings of "good for" and their relation to the concept of well-being.

[5] Kraut (2007: 62) is the only exception known to me.

well-being is taken to involve. The standard view is that well-being is an agent-relative value, i.e., it gives reasons to the agent whose well-being it is. Hence, if something increases *my* well-being, then *I* have reason to desire it and pursue it, and similarly for *you* and *your* well-being, *him* and *his well-being*, etc. In each case, the reason-giving fact for the agent is that *his* or *her* good would be contributed to or not diminished. It is less clear, however, what the standard view would hold with regard to the agent-neutrality of well-being. Agent-neutrality here means that everyone has reason to promote everyone's well-being, including his or her own. For every agent, the reason-giving fact is that *someone's* good would be promoted or not diminished.[6]

4. The limits of the concept of well-being. This question can be understood at the level of the subjects of well-being (Rodogno 2010)—what kinds of entities can have well-being beside human beings? Non-human animals? Plants and trees? Microbes?—or it can be understood at the level of the kinds of states, activities, or choices that can be counted as enhancing someone's well-being. One important discussion here is the interplay between well-being and self-sacrifice. One of the central features of the idea of well-being is that an individual's well-being or self-interest may well compete or come into conflict with other demands placed on the individual. Perhaps the most common conflict of this kind is the one between one's well-being or self-interest, on the one hand, and one's moral duties, on the other. When such conflicts arise, individuals may be required to self-sacrifice, to forego their self-interest, in order to fulfill their overriding moral duties. This picture does seem in line with our moral phenomenology, as when we only recalcitrantly comply with our duties. On this picture, the respective extensions of "well-being" and "self-sacrifice" exclude each other. At least on modern conceptions, it follows that any account of well-being that systematically describes as self-interested actions that are self-sacrificing will attribute to "well-being" a scope that is too wide. Such accounts are affected by a "scope problem."

With these basics in mind, we are ready to broach philosophical analyses of well-being, in the next section, and the theoretical connections between the philosophy and the psychology of well-being, in the section after that.

Well-being in philosophy

Philosophical discussion of well-being has traditionally focused on so-called *theories of well-being*. These are of two kinds: *formal* (or *explanatory*) and *substantive* (or *enumerative*).[7] A theory counts as substantive only if it directly attributes prudential value to certain

6 The claim that well-being is an agent-relative value has recently been challenged (Darwall 2002), and its agent neutrality has been more clearly defended (Darwall 2002; Reagan 2004; Rosati 2008).

7 This distinction is clearly introduced and at work in Frankena (1973: 84), Moore and Crisp (1996: 599) Crisp (2006: 102–103); and Fletcher (2013: 206). Griffin (1986: 31–34) and Sumner (1996: 16–17) present a closely connected distinction. See Brülde (2007a) for a review of the various types of common subdivisions of theories of well-being.

items (e.g. kinds of mental states, relationships, states of affairs, activities, etc.). Theories of this kind provide answers to the question: *Which things make someone's life go better for them?* A substantive hedonist, for example, is someone who claims that only pleasurable mental states are prudentially good where non-hedonists would also mention other goods (e.g., friendship, knowledge, autonomy, etc.) that are taken by them to be irreducible to pleasurable mental states.

A theory counts as formal only if it tries to identify *why* something is prudentially good, or, as some would say, only if it identifies the *prudential* or *good-for* value maker. Such a theory provides answers to the question: *What makes something good for the individual?* A formal hedonist, for example, will hold that pleasantness, and only pleasantness is what makes substantive goods what they are. Others, however, will argue that it is the satisfaction of an individual's desires that makes something prudentially good, and so on.

The two kinds of theory stand in a complementary relation. Hence a substantive hedonist will typically also be a formal hedonist, holding that pleasantness is what makes pleasure good for an individual. Yet, it is logically possible and in fact a live option to combine substantive hedonism with other formal outlooks. One may for example hold that what makes pleasurable mental states prudentially good is the fact that they fulfill one of the individual's desires.

Theories of well-being are also often categorized as being either *subjective* or *objective*. Subjectivism states that nothing can intrinsically enhance the quality of an individual's life unless that person desired or endorsed that thing, or unless the person would desire or endorse that thing under idealized conditions, i.e. perfect rationality and/or full-information (Arneson 1999; Sumner 1996). Objective theories do not include such a requirement. Hence, something may be good for an individual even in the absence of a relevant pro-attitude on his or her behalf.

Finally, theories of well-being are often divided along another dimension, which we shall call *mentalism* or, alternatively, *experientialism*. A theory is mentalist or experientialist if it states that something can affect an individual's well-being only to the extent to which the individual experiences that thing. Hence while pleasurable experiences would clearly be good candidates for mentalist views, on such views the fact that unbeknownst to me my wife is cheating on me cannot as such affect my well-being. *Non-mentalist* or *non-experientialist* accounts could in principle accommodate also such facts.

More recently, some philosophers (Darwall 2002; Rosati 2006) have moved beyond theories of well-being of the kinds described above and have focussed instead on conceptual analyses of well-being compatible with a number of such theories. While we will not have the opportunity to discuss them here, these analyses afford much needed answers to the sceptical challenge that well-being is in fact reducible to other values. In the next section, we shall turn to this challenge and provide some reason to dismiss it.[8]

[8] Scanlon (1998: 126–141) has formulated another powerful sceptical challenge to the effect that well-being is not as important in first-personal thinking as often alleged. See Rodogno (2008) for a reply.

Scepticism about well-being

In 1903, G. E. Moore challenged the idea that something can be "good for" someone, if this notion is to be understood as a value independent of what Moore calls *absolute goodness* (see also Rabinowicz and Rønnow-Rasmussen, this volume). He asks:

> In what sense can a thing be good *for me*? It is obvious, if we reflect, that the only thing which can belong to me, which can be *mine*, is something which is good, and not the fact that it is good. When therefore, I talk of anything I get as "my own good," I must mean either that the thing I get is good, or that my possessing it is good.
>
> (Moore 1993, sec. 59)

The notion of "my own good" strikes Moore as strangely proprietary and, as he goes on to argue, its proprietary nature has unwelcome effects on its normativity. Hurka (1987) and Rosati (2008) have glossed Moore's point by drawing a parallel between the expressions "good for me" and "true for me." As Rosati (2008: 314) puts it:

> Just as the latter expression suggests a kind of truth that the individual herself could have exclusive reason to believe, so the former expression suggests a kind of value that the individual herself could have exclusive reason to promote, and that, Moore evidently thought, would be no kind of value at all.

The problem, as Moore sees it, is that goodness, just like truth, cannot be relativized in the proprietary way suggested by the expression "good for." Goodness can only be absolute. Therefore:

> . . . the only reason I can have for aiming at 'my own good' is that it is *good absolutely* that what I so call should belong to me . . . . But if it is *good absolutely* that I should have it, then everyone else has as much reason for aiming at my having it, as I have myself.
>
> (Moore 1993, sec 59)

If correct, this view spells trouble for the notion of well-being or good for. As Rosati notes (2008: 315), the challenge at hand here is ultimately metaphysical. If Moore is right, the idea of a person's "own good" signifies nothing over and above the idea that the thing a person gets is good or that the state of her possessing it is good or, the idea of *good occurring in a person's life* (Regan 2004). There is, in other words, no distinctive normative property beside that of goodness, in conjunction with the fact that it occurs in someone's life. It would be an error to postulate the existence of a property such as *being good for P*.

In the eyes of those who defend the irreducibility of well-being, however, the Moorean proposal misses the point. It is not enough, they will say, that something of value occurs in a subject's life in order for her to be benefitted by it. It may well be that all sorts of good things occur in her life but, as it happens, she is continuously asleep or unconscious, or that she finds these good things uninteresting, meaningless, or even alienating. How would she benefit from these occurrences? The problem is that on the Moorean analysis, the goodness of those things that are supposed to benefit a subject is determined in the absence of any reference to features of the subject or class of subjects for which these things are supposed to be good.

Note that reference to the subject here is *not* necessarily to be understood as a reference to a particular individual with a specific (to her) conative and/or affective profile, but rather more generally, as a member of a community characterized by community-specific biological and psychological features. At this stage, then, the point against the Moorean analysis is not made from a subjectivist stance. It is rather an invitation to consider analyses of "good for" that articulate this concept in terms of what is *suitable* or *fitting* to a certain class of subjects. Suitability and fittingness are *relational* notions: something is fitting or suitable always to someone or something. On the analysis sketched here, then, well-being is a relational good.

The fundamental idea of the analysis is nicely captured by Railton (1986a: 9) who takes relational goodness to have:

> a place in the scheme of things only in virtue of facts about what matters, or could matter, to beings for whom it is possible that something matter. [It] would have no place within a universe consisting only of stones, for nothing matters to stones. Introduce some people, and you will have introduced the possibility of [relational] value as well. It *will* matter to people how things go in their rock-strewn world. Of course, what in particular will matter, or could matter, to these people will depend upon what they are like.

The idea of fittingness or suitability at issue here ought to be qualified in two important ways. First, as mentioned above, relationalism does not entail subjectivism. While reference to a group characterized by some distinctive (biological, psychological, etc.) features is essential, the reference need not track the pro-attitudes of the single individual. Relationalism is hence compatible with objective theories of well-being.[9] Whether such theories can capture the particular individual's perspective or stance sufficiently well is, of course, another matter.

Second, relationalism abandons the Moorean idea of an absolute, monadic goodness property, which is then relativized to an individual in order to account for *his* good. Rather, we are from the start dealing with a distinct, relational value property.[10] The upshot is that we are no longer prompted, as were the Mooreans, to interpret "X is good for P" as necessarily involving agent-relativity.

In short, the claim that well-being is a relational good is, as such, a modest or unassuming claim to be contrasted with absolutist approaches to value such as Moore's. In particular, while it leaves room for analyses that define well-being as subjective and/or agent-relative, it does not exclude objective and agent-neutral accounts, as well as mentalist and non-mentalist accounts. Relationalism should be seen as a first step of any sui generis analysis of well-being understood as a kind of value resistant to the reductive challenge put by Moorean sceptics. With the exception of some versions of the *Objective List* theory, all of

9 Aristotelian *eudaimonia* should be understood as relational in the sense I have in mind without being subjectivist (see Kraut 2007). The relevant *relata* are individuals *qua* human beings, and not *qua* particulars with individualized conative profiles.

10 We should understand "X is good for P" *not* as taking the logical form *(X is good) for P* but rather $x\ G\ p$, where "G" expresses the relation *is good for* between *relata* x and p (Rosati 2008: 329, note 43).

the theories of well-being discussed in this chapter can and should be seen as theories of relational well-being.

Theories of well-being

Hedonism

At the substantive level, hedonism is understood as the claim that pleasure is the only prudential value and pain the only prudential disvalue. At the formal level, hedonism consists in the claim that pleasantness and painfulness are, respectively, the only prudential value- and disvalue-makers. Traditionally, when referring to hedonism, one conjointly refers to, both, the formal and substantive claims (e.g., pleasurable states are the only prudential goods because pleasantness is the only prudential value-maker). Hedonists go on to claim that well-being is the greatest positive balance of pleasure over pain.

The philosophical fortunes of hedonism have tended to wax and wane through the ages.[11] In the nineteenth and twentieth centuries, it came more prominently to the foreground through the work of Jeremy Bentham (1789) and, in different forms, the other famous classical utilitarian thinkers, J.S. Mill (1861) and Henry Sidgwick (1907). Note that at least in Bentham and Mill, well-being is equated to happiness, where the latter is understood hedonistically in terms of pleasure and the absence of pain. As we shall see, however, both, the equation of happiness and well-being and the hedonistic analysis of happiness have been contested in the recent debate. While in the latter part of the twentieth century hedonism was thought to have received a fatal blow at the hands of Nozick (1974), its prospects seem rosier today through some revived efforts in both philosophy (Crisp 2006; Feldman 2004) and psychology (Kahnemann 1999).

In order to assess the plausibility of hedonism as a prudential theory, one should first understand the way in which the central notions of pleasure and pain are understood. There are at least two models or conceptions. On the *sensation model*, operative in Bentham, pleasure and pain are sui generis sensations, readily discriminable in our experience from other sensory perceptions and from each other, and susceptible of no definitions other than ostensive ones (Sumner 1996: 88). Bentham (1789: ch.5) thought of pleasure as embracing experiences such as bodily pleasures, as well as all forms of gratification, enjoyment, satisfaction, fulfillment, etc. What these experiences all have in common is their positive tone: "an intrinsic, unanalyzable quality of pleasantness which is present to a greater or lesser degree in all of them." (Sumner 1996: 88) On the sensation model, then, pleasurable and painful experiences are homogenous or uniform in their quality, and heterogeneous in their sources or causes. In fact, more specifically, pleasurable (and painful) experiences are uniform in quality, while varying in intensity, duration, and their causes.

The *attitude* model acknowledges that pleasurable and painful experiences may be quite heterogeneous and thus cannot be placed under the label pleasure and pain simply on the basis of their phenomenal character. This is rather to be done by taking into

---

[11] See Plato (360 BCE; 380 BCE) for early discussions.

account the attitudes that accompany such sensations as, for example, our liking, seeking, or wanting these experiences to continue or our disliking, avoiding, or wanting these experiences to cease.

Let us now assess hedonism as based, in turn, on the *sensation* and on the *attitude* models of pleasure. The first criticism against *sensation hedonism* is that it fails properly to reflect the structure of our prudential choices. Griffin (1986: 8) may be taken to make this point through the example of Freud who, at the very end of his life, ill and in pain, refused drugs except aspirin, claiming to prefer thinking in torment to not being able to think clearly. Griffin argues that we cannot find a single pleasurable feeling or mental state in both of Freud's options in virtue of which he ranked them as he did. The hedonist would have to reply that Freud was making an evaluative mistake.

A second criticism may be put forth by those with subjectivist leanings (Sumner 1996: 93). On the sensation model, pleasurable experiences are to determine an individual's well-being irrespective of the way in which the individual relates to them, even after reflection. On this model, whether a subject actually desires or endorses his pleasurable experiences is irrelevant to the prudential value of his life (or only relevant to the extent to which failing to desire or endorse these experiences is itself unpleasant).

The third and final criticism comes across through another classic example (Crisp 1997: 24–25). Consider two lives: that of a brilliant musician who composed wonderful music, influenced the evolution of the symphony, was met with success and honor in his own lifetime, was cheerful and popular, travelled and gained much enjoyment from field sports but died at the age of seventy-seven; or the *eternal* life of an oyster that enjoyed only mild sensual pleasure rather like that experienced by a human when floating very drunk in a warm bath. Now if pleasure is homogenous and is to be measured only in accordance to its intensity and duration, even granting that the first life involves more intense pleasures, the oyster's life will in the end have lasted long enough to have accumulated a greater quantity of pleasure. That, then, should be the option we should prudentially prefer on this type of hedonism. Many, however, would judge the musician's life better in welfare terms, no matter how long the oyster's life.

One could at this point argue along with J. S. Mill (1861) that pleasures are heterogeneous and that some "higher" pleasures are more valuable than "lower" ones, no matter the amount of the latter. This move would clearly solve cases such as the musician's: his life will always be better for him than an oyster's life, no matter how extended a life. The question, however, is whether the move is open to sensation hedonists or, for that matter, to hedonists in general. A position such as Mill's seems to face a dilemma: either return to a homogenous view of pleasure where pleasurable experiences are to be compared only in terms of their intensity and duration, or renounce sensation hedonism.

To see this point, consider two pleasurable experiences: a "higher" and a "lower" one. On the one hand, if pleasantness were the only prudential value-maker, it is hard to see how increasing the intensity or duration of the "lower" experience would not at some point generate enough pleasure as that contained by the "higher" experience. In this instance, no case can be made for the discontinuity in pleasurable experiences imagined by Mill, and hence the distinction between "lower" and "higher" pleasures would fall. On the other hand, if the two experiences were not to be commensurable in this way, then what makes higher "pleasures" more valuable must be something other than their pleasantness.[12]

In order to preserve hedonism, while at the same time providing an answer to the musician's case, some have moved to *attitude hedonism*,[13] which easily allows discontinuities in our attitudes toward various experiences such that, for example, we would always enjoy something more than something else we also enjoy, no matter the amount of the latter. *Attitude hedonism* would also clearly be more palatable to those who favor subjectivist views of well-being.

Desires have historically occupied an important role as the relevant pleasure-defining attitudes within *attitude hedonism*.[14] Mill (1861: IV10), for example, writes that "to desire anything, except in proportion as the idea of it as peasant, is a physical and metaphysical impossibility." This claim, however, seems false as Nozick (1974: 42–43) argues through his famous thought experiment. Suppose you could plug into an experience machine that would give you any experience you wanted: climbing Mount Everest, saving someone's life, or being a famous actor. All the time you would be floating in a tank, with electrodes attached to your brain. Would you plug in? Nozick (1974: 43) wants to argue that various things matter to us in addition to pleasurable experiences. In particular, (1) we want to *do* certain things, rather than merely having the experience of doing them; (2) we want to *be* a certain kind of person; and (3) we want to be able to make contact with a reality deeper than one that is entirely man-made. We can call the objects of desires such as these, respectively, accomplishment, personhood, and knowledge and understanding.

Along with desires for pleasure, we do seem to have desires such as these. Perhaps, then, attitude hedonism should pick a pro-attitude other than desires, whose scope now seems too broad for substantive hedonism. What Nozick's argument allegedly brings to the fore, however, is that even if we could find a pro-attitude that successfully tracked pleasure and only pleasure, a problem would remain: accomplishment, personhood, and knowledge do seem to matter to us in a way that prudential theories should account for and substantive hedonism fails to account for that.[15]

Desire theories

Theories in this group were originally developed by welfare economists with utilitarian credentials who were confronted with the resistance of pain and pleasure to reliable, public

[12] Crisp (2006) attempts to account for discontinuities while retaining the sensation model. He does this by claiming that the value of a pleasure depends on its intensity and duration *as well as* on its *quality*.

[13] Crisp (2006: 11–117) reinterprets Mill in this direction, where the relevant attitude is enjoyment.

[14] Katz (2006) offers a nice review of other attitude theories of pleasure. Feldman (2004) is a recent good example, as pleasure is defined not simply in terms of an attitude but in terms of a *propositional* attitude.

[15] Crisp (2006: 117–125) argues that substantive hedonism can account for the prudential value of these things in an indirect way.

measurement.[16] Desire theories owe their current dominance in large part to the emergence of welfare economics.

Philosophically, we should see desire theories mainly as formal theories stating, in their simplest form, that what makes someone better off is the extent that their current desires are fulfilled. On such *present desire* theory, substantively, an individual's well-being consists in the obtaining of the objects of her current desires, whatever they may be.[17] In philosophy, however, this view is not very popular, as it is open to one simple objection: we do happen to desire or prefer things that are clearly not in our interest or good for us and, in fact, things that are positively bad for us.[18]

In the contemporary debate, the type of desire theory that has by far drawn the largest amount of support goes under a number of different appellations, to wit, *informed desire, full information*, or *ideal preference* accounts of well-being. Spurred by early and incisive efforts made by Henry Sidgwick (1907: 111–112), the account comes today in various shades (Brandt 1979: ch. 6–7; Griffin 1986: ch. 1–2; Harsany 1982; Rawls 1971: 417 ff.). The common idea behind them all is that well-being is to be characterized by starting with a desire (or with a preference or with contentment) that is idealized by attaching some condition C, be it avoidance of the influence of mistaken belief and of ignorance of material facts, etc.[19] One example would be the following:

> *g* is an ingredient of *x*'s well-being if, and only if, *g* is what *x* would desire if *x*'s rationality could not be faulted and *x* was equipped with all relevant information.

Robert Shope (1978a, b) subjected this account to an objection known as the *conditional fallacy*: idealization, he claimed, may well lead to fairly counterintuitive and arbitrary results. Suppose that something is good just in case an agent would choose it, if she were fully deliberatively rational. Suppose now that a troubled person is considering whether to go to psychotherapy. Now if this person were fully rational she would not choose to go to psychotherapy, for, as someone who is fully rational, she would not need to. But on the account at hand, this means that it would not be good for the troubled person in the actual world to go to psychotherapy.[20]

[16] See Little (1950) for the evolution of modern utility theory at the hands of economists and Sumner (1996: 113–122) for a very short introduction to revealed preference theory that connects it to its classical utilitarian roots.

[17] Note, however, that there may logically be substantive versions of desire theories according to which what has final prudential value is the circumstance that an (intrinsic) desire is satisfied (as opposed to the states that are the objects of our desire) (Brülde 2007a: 7).

[18] See Parfit (1984: 496–499) for *summative* and *global* versions of desire theories (where the former claim that the more desire-fulfilment in a life the better, and the latter claim that desires about the shape and content of a part or of the entirety of one's life are given priority).

[19] Brandt, for example, defines as rational the intrinsic desires that would survive the idealized scrutiny that he describes under the notion of "cognitive psychotherapy": an intrinsic desire is rational if a person would still have it after repeated representation of all relevant scientifically available information, in an ideally vivid way, at appropriate times.

[20] Hubin (1966) and Gibbard (1990: 20) have further developed this type of objection.

To avoid this kind of objection, Railton (1986a, b) has developed another, more sophisticated version of the informed desire account:

> [A]n individual's good consists in what he would want himself to want, or to pursue, were he to contemplate his present situation from a standpoint fully and vividly informed about himself and his circumstances, and entirely free of cognitive error or lapses of instrumental rationality.
>
> (Railton 1986a: 16)

This type of analysis is often referred to as an *ideal advisor account* of an individual's good, as the latter is defined in terms of what a cognitively idealized version of the self would advise the actual self to want and pursue.

Informed desire or *ideal advisor* kinds of account have also received other criticisms. Perhaps the most fundamental one comes from those who find them too subjective. Rawls (1971: 432) gives a good illustration of the tension at play here through a famous example: a brilliant mathematician, fully informed about the options available to her, develops a desire to spend much of her life counting blades of grass. Thoroughgoing subjectivists will accept that if she really is informed and not suffering from some psychic condition, then the life of grass-counting will be best for her. Others will find this conclusion too unpalatable.

Yet other criticisms appeal to one or more of the following issues: (1) the incoherency of the notion of a fully informed agent;[21] (2) the failure of such accounts to account for the autonomous features of agency (Rosati 2000); (3) their lack of normative force; and (4) their susceptibility to the scope problem. Two important criticisms are worth mentioning here.

The first covers points (1) and (3). If a person is to appreciate information, argues Rosati (1995), she must be capable of receiving it. What kind of information a given individual takes as informing (can receive) is a function of this individual's personality at a time, it is a function of who she is at that time. Given an individual's personality, some information is such that the individual would have to change her personality quite dramatically in order to be able to receive it. To illustrate: if the extremely cautious individual wants to know whether it would be good for her to become an adventurous person, she should not appreciate adventurous lives only from the perspective of her actual cautious self, but also from the perspective of more adventurous selves.

> At the end of the process of imaginatively surveying her possible lives in all their permutations, she must have . . . traits that enable her to appreciate what each experience was like, rather than traits that enable her to appreciate only some experiences while not appreciating others. Even if we assume that we are still imagining a person at the end of this process, it is surely a person radically different from (albeit continuous with) the person who underwent idealization.
>
> (Rosati 1995: 310)

This difference, however, results in a failure of identification between the person who occupies the ideal standpoint and the person who is being idealized, which in turn results in the latter failing to take the responses of the former as authoritative and motivating.

---

[21] Rosati 1995; Sobel 1994; Velleman 1988. For replies see: Miller 2003: 208–217; Zimmerman 2003.

The final criticism covers the so-called scope problem. As discussed in the "Language of well-being" section, the limits of the concept of well-being are drawn with the help of the concept of self-sacrifice. An account that classifies under the idea of well-being, states or actions that are clearly self-sacrificial has too wide a scope. Many (Darwall 2002: 25–31; Griffin 1986: 16–17; Sumner 1996: 124–128) believe desire accounts to be susceptible to this problem. The problem is so acute that it can be spotted even without an appeal to self-sacrifice. As Scanlon (1998: 115) puts it:

> ... the objects of a person's informed desires are likely to include many things that are not related to the quality of the desirer's own life, intuitively understood. Suppose, for example, that I very much admire a certain person, and therefore desire that her struggle and sacrifice will be crowned with success and happiness. This may be a rational desire as well as an informed one; it might, quite properly, be strengthened by fuller knowledge of the person's life and character. Even if this is so, however, if I have no connection with her beyond my admiration and this desire, then the quality of my life is not affected one way or the other by her fate.[22]

Some informed desire theorists accept that the type of account they defend has too wide a scope. They, therefore, adopt a strategy that consists in restricting the scope by selecting only those desires that pertain to the subject's own life. Overvold (1982: 90), for one, proposes an account in terms of only those desires whose object includes states of affairs, the obtaining of which requires the existence of the subject.[23] Consider Scanlon's example. My desire that the person reaches success does not at all fulfill this requirement, for it is not logically required that I exist in order for the admired person to reach success. Overvold would agree with Scanlon, then, that the satisfaction of this desire would not count toward a person's well-being and his account would have a principled way of showing why this is so.

Overvold's analysis, however, is still too restrictive in some respects and not restrictive enough in others. The latter is the case insofar as, for example, the analysis allows me to have an informed desire to do my duty that requires my existence but that is clearly not to my advantage. Yet, the account seems too restrictive insofar as it excludes informed desires the fulfillment of which does not necessarily entail my existence but which are potentially good for me such as; for example, my desire that one of my projects, e.g., saving Venice, succeeds after my death.

Finally, other (individual or cumulative) strategies would consist (1) in expanding the idea of a person's good as idealists have suggested (Skorupski 2006); (2) in discussing more substantive and affective accounts of the notion of desire (De Sousa 1987: 167–69; Skorupski 1999: 130–133); or (3) in attempting to deflate the problematic nature of the scope "problem" by showing that well-being and self-sacrifice do not stand in a straightforward exclusionary relation (Raz 2000; Rosati 2009b).

---

22 Scanlon elaborates here a point and an example originally made by Parfit (1984: 494). See also Kagan (1992)

23 Griffin (1986: 21–23) offers another account that acknowledges the scope problem while attempting to address it by restricting the scope.

Happiness theories

What we call here *happiness theories* are fairly recent additions to theories of well-being, with only two major exponents or theories, namely, Haybron's (2008) *Psychic Flourishing* and Sumner's (1996) *Authentic Happiness*. Both accounts consist of two parts: first, a psychological account of happiness and, second, a specification of the role of happiness within a theory of well-being. At the psychological level, both theories react to the classical utilitarian hedonic understanding of happiness, yet propose rather different views of happiness as alternatives. At the level of their theories of well-being, both accounts allot happiness a central role (hence their denomination as *happiness theories*). Yet, while on one account happiness is considered as a central *substantive* good (Haybron 2008), on the other it is the sole formal good or prudential value-maker (Sumner 1996). Let us say a few more words about each account, beginning with Sumner's *Authentic Happiness*.[24]

On this view, psychologically, happiness is understood as a disposition involving both a cognitive and an affective component:

> The cognitive aspect of happiness consists in a positive evaluation of the conditions of your life, a judgement that, at least on balance, it measures up favourably against your standards or expectations. . . . It represents an affirmation or endorsement of (some or all of) the conditions or circumstances of your life, a judgement that, on balance and taking everything into account, your life is going well for you. . . . However, there is more involved in being happy than being disposed to think that your life is going (or has gone) well. The affective side of happiness consists in what we commonly call a sense of well-being: finding your life enriching or rewarding, or feeling satisfied or fulfilled by it.
>
> (Sumner 1996: 146–147)

From a psychological perspective, then, happiness is a retrospective evaluative attitude or disposition with, both, a cognitive and an affective component. Let us call this view of happiness *Life Satisfaction* as this idea captures, both, the evaluative idea that one's life satisfies one's goals, and the more hedonic idea of one's sense of satisfaction, gratification, and the like.

What role does happiness so understood play in this theory of well-being? As characterized so far, happiness cannot yet play its role as prudential value-maker because a person's happiness may either rest on a mistake, as when, for example, the person is misinformed about the facts, or be less than fully autonomous, as when, for example, the person's life experiences have affected her ability to reflect critically on her situation. Sumner, therefore, introduces the notion of *Authentic Happiness* as a shortcut for "factually informed and autonomous happiness." With this notion in hand, Sumner (1996: 172–173) introduces his theory of well-being:

> [S]ome condition of a subject's life is (directly or intrinsically) beneficial for him just in case he authentically endorses it, or experiences it as satisfying, for its own sake. The intrinsic sources of welfare will be whatever conditions of subjects' lives elicit this response.

---

[24] See Brülde (2007b) for a systematic and in-depth review of happiness theories, as well as a defence of another version of them.

The authentic happiness view looks very much like a formal, informed desire theory of well-being, with authentic happiness playing a role analogous to informed desire. Like informed desire views, the happiness view is supposed to be thoroughly subjective: nothing can count as beneficial for someone unless the subject has, or is disposed to have, the relevant attitude. As in informed desire theories, the level of subjectivity may be too much for some. Hence, for example, on this theory "one cannot assume *a priori* that the happy slave has a bad life, or that a life of servility and subservience (a life which we regard as trivial or demeaning or depraved) cannot be prudentially valuable for its subject." (Brülde 2007b: 44) As Sumner (1996: 182) would retort, however, we can have pretty good empirical reasons for thinking that such a life is rarely embraced under conditions of full autonomy, and therefore not likely to be a good life.

Similarly, those who worry that informed desires views have too wide a scope, should harbor a similar worry with regard to the authentic happiness view. Even though (authentic) happiness is supposed to be elicited in connection with standards that apply to the subject's own life, the standards in question may well refer to projects, such as saving Venice or eradicating poverty, the accomplishment of which may work against an intuitive understanding of the subject's well-being.

A connected worry with scope arises when we look at the way in which people answer questions concerning how happy or satisfied they are with their life. As Haybron (2008: 92) puts it:

> Life satisfaction attitudes are governed by norms that make systematic, often radical, deviations from well-being—by *any* sane measure—both expectable and utterly reasonable. You might, for instance, be satisfied with your life, not because you think things are going well for you, but because that seems to you the most fitting or appropriate way to respond to the life you have.

Hence someone in a predicament may still express satisfaction with life, if her attitudes embody norms such as gratitude, fortitude, ambition, pride, and the like.

Finally, there are also worries with regard to Sumner's psychological view of happiness. In a sustained critique of this view, Haybron (2008: 79–103) argues among others that this attitude is not psychologically robust. Part of the argument turns around the alleged cognitive *and* affective nature of *Life Satisfaction*. Now this view would be put under some strain by findings that confirm cognitive-affective divergence, i.e., cases in which a person displays, say, the cognitive element of the happiness evaluation without displaying the affective element. And sure enough there is solid evidence to that effect (Haybron 2009: 84–86).

Let us now move on to Haybron's substantive happiness account (2008: 105–151). This view rests on quite a different psychological account of happiness. Instead of identifying happiness with pleasurable experience, as in classical utilitarianism, or with *Life Satisfaction* as Sumner's does, happiness here consists in a subject's emotional condition as a whole. This includes non-experiential aspects of emotions and moods (or perhaps just moods), and excludes pleasures that don't directly involve the individual's emotional state. It might also include a person's propensity for experiencing various moods, which can vary over time. Happiness on such view is more nearly the opposite of depression or anxiety, whereas hedonistic happiness is simply opposed to unpleasantness. Finally, on Haybron's view, emotional state happiness involves three broad categories of affective state, including "endorsement" states like joy versus sadness, "engagement" states like flow or a sense of vitality, and "attunement" states like tranquility, emotional expansiveness versus compression, and confidence. Haybron calls this view *psychic flourishing*.

Haybron argues that happiness understood in this sense plays a central substantive role in a theory of well-being. A theory of well-being such as this can only be fully assessed when one also knows what other goods the theory includes and what importance such goods have relative to happiness and to each other. This point notwithstanding, another fundamental challenge stands in the way of any theory of well-being that takes happiness to be a central, substantive good. Some may fail to be swayed by the claim that psychic happiness is a final prudential good and a central one at that. Just as many would be inclined to think that depression and anxiety, the opposite of happiness on Haybron's account, are reliable *indicators* that a person is doing bad, being in the positive emotional state described by Haybron may be taken as an *indicator* that we are doing well. The suggestion here is analogous to one made by many psychologists and philosophers of emotion: just as emotions serve the evaluative function of indicating how we are faring in our environment, the affective states that constitute psychic flourishing serve the evaluative function of indicating whether our lives contain those things that, themselves, are ultimately good for us (Rodogno 2014b).

Objective list and perfectionist theories

Like hedonism, objective list theories can be understood either as substantive, or as, both, formal and substantive theories of well-being. In either case, the substantive claim these theories make is that there is an irreducible *plurality*, a list, of prudential goods such as pleasure and the absence of pain, achievement, friendship and other deep personal relations, autonomy, virtue, knowledge, etc. This is a feature of these views traditionally asserted contra hedonism, which, as we saw, is a substantively monistic view. The list, however, is also supposed to be an objective one. This is a formal feature generally common to this family of theories to the effect that the subject's pro-attitudes are not necessary prudential value-makers.[25] In this respect, objective list theories are unlike desire theories or *Authentic Happiness*.

There is, however, disagreement with regard to what other formal claims are true of objective list theories. One possible position reflects the structure of classical hedonism quite closely. Just as for the latter there is one substantive good, i.e., pleasurable experience, and one value-maker, i.e., pleasantness, objective list theorists would claim that there is a plurality of substantive goods each accompanied by its respective value-maker. This is a commitment incurred by philosophers, such as John Finnis (2011), who provide a list of basic human goods (life, knowledge, play, esthetic experience, friendship, practical

[25] "Generally" because, as we shall see in this chapter, some theories within this family may indeed claim that some, if not all, the goods they list necessarily involve some pro-attitude. We shall discuss the objectivist credentials of such theories in this chapter.

reasonableness, and religion), that are (1) basic aspects of one's well-being and final ends; (2) known by practical reason (or self-evident); and (3) not grounded in any metaphysics or anthropology.

Another possibility, however, is that one finds unity at the formal level precisely via an appeal to metaphysics or anthropology. This, for example, is the aim of perfectionist theories, according to which what makes something a component of well-being (an entry on the substantive list) is their role in perfecting human nature. Aristotle, for example, famously thought that human nature has a specific *telos* or function and that whatever activity contributed to developing or perfecting this function would by necessity be part of one's well-being.[26] Not all varieties of perfectionism, however, are, as Aristotle's, grounded on *human nature*. According to Haybron (2008: 177–196), for example, we should perfect or fulfill the self, and, in particular, what he calls the emotional self.

One objection posed to objective list views such as Finnis' is that they are based on a number of unsystematic intuitions. Reliance on intuitions, however, is not uncommon to this area of philosophy. Hedonism does after all rely on intuitions about pleasurable experience and pleasantness. Arguably, one could similarly take perfectionism to rely on the intuition that whatever fulfills one's nature is of prudential value.[27]

Consider now perfectionist versions of the objective list theory. One objection often posed to them denies as conceptually confused their fundamental intuition: perfectionism mistakes prudential value for perfectionist value (Glassen 1957: 320). Consider our Harvard grass-counting mathematician once again. Suppose that exercising and perfecting her mathematical skills would have perfectionist value, would make her a more perfect exemplar of her kind. Why think at the same time that this would be prudentially better than any option, such as counting grass all day, which did not develop her human nature as much? As Sumner (1996: 24) puts it: "there is no logical guarantee that the most developed specimen will also be the best off, or that their undeveloped rivals would not be faring better." Then again, perfectionists may well agree that perfectionist and prudential values are conceptually distinct, while at the same time making the claim that they are substantively overlapping in some cases.

Finally, the most fundamental objection to objective list theories (in any guise) is inspired precisely by their alleged objective nature, i.e., that a prudential good may be what it is irrespective of the subject's pro-attitudes toward it. As Railton (1986a: 47) writes:

> It would be an intolerably alienated conception of someone's good to imagine that it might fail in any way to engage him.

---

[26] See Hurka (1993) for a contemporary version of perfectionism. Note, however, that like Moore (1903), Hurka is sceptical about prudential value and hence his perfectionism is intended as a full-fledged moral theory: the good life is that which develops human nature and the development of human nature is ultimately (as opposed to merely prudentially) good.

[27] Dorsey (2010) argues that all other kinds of arguments in favor of perfectionism, i.e., Hurka's (1993) *essence argument* and Brink's (2008) *agency argument*, ultimately rest on this intuition, which, he argues cannot support perfectionism on its own.

A possible line of reply consists in accepting the charge, while refusing that *all* lists of goods need be alienating. Fletcher (2013: 215–216), for example, endorses a list comprising of goods that have pro-attitudes as *necessary* components. Hence goods such achievement, friendship, happiness, pleasure, self-respect, and virtue would allegedly involve the person's engagement through her holding various kinds of pro-attitudes such as endorsement, desires, and affection. If one is experiencing these kinds of states of engagement, one is doing well. On this view, however, it looks like the pro-attitudes at issue are internal or constitutive of the various goods at hand rather than pro-attitudes about them. Now, we can all agree that friendship involves the pro-attitudes of desiring to spend time and engaging with one's friend. What's crucial to respond to the alienation charge, however, is whether one should have a pro-attitude toward friendship relations (and the pro-attitudes *they* involve). Suppose an individual lacked such pro-attitude. Would friendship be on her list of goods anyways? If so, the view proposed here does not answer the alienation challenge.

Another line of reply is to read objective list views such as Hursthouse (1999) and Nussbaum (2000: 78, 160) as involving the requirement that each of the goods on the list be thought important by the actual subjects.[28] Far from being an objective list theory, however, this would be a subjective theory, where the subject's relevant pro-attitude is *thinking that thing important* as opposed to, say, desiring it.

Well-being in psychology

Work on the psychology of happiness and well-being seems largely unconcerned with the formal and substantive theories that entice philosophers and are more concerned with operationalizing and measuring some conception or other of happiness or well-being and, more importantly, with uncovering the correlations and causal relations that stand between the view of well-being at hand and various activities and state of affairs (being married, being unemployed, level of income, physical and mental health, etc.). Overviews of the recent psychological literature (Tiberius 2006, 2007) suggest that researchers in this field work with three conceptions of happiness and/or well-being: *Objective Happiness, Subjective Well-being, and Eudaimonism*. I shall follow this categorization and present these conceptions in turn. The focus will be on relating them to their respective philosophical counterparts and, by so doing, on bringing philosophical thinking to bear on psychological research.[29]

Objective happiness

Objective Happiness is the name that Kahneman (1999) has chosen for the approach he and his affiliates have developed. The approach is thoroughly Benthamian in at least three

---

[28] Tiberius (2007: 380–381) suggests this reading of Nussbaum and Hursthouse.

[29] I shall avoid focusing on the substantive results, i.e., the correlations and causal relations, uncovered by research conducted within each paradigm. The interested reader will find it useful to read Kahneman and Krueger (2006); Diener and Seligman (2004); and Ryan et al. (2008).

ways: (1) psychologically, happiness is here understood in hedonistic terms as pleasure and the absence of pain (as opposed to *psychic flourishing* or *life satisfaction*); (2) prudentially, substantive hedonism is also taken to be the case, i.e., pleasure is the only value and pain the only disvalue; and, finally, (3) pleasure is to be understood as on the sensation model, i.e., pleasurable experiences are homogenous, varying only in their intensity and duration.[30]

The idea of objectivity in *Objective Happiness* is largely in line with that discussed above, as it involves a denial of the subject's pro-attitudes in the determination of his or her well-being. To be more precise, objective happiness denies a role to *retrospective evaluations of one's experiences and life* such as those constituting *life satisfaction*. The reasons for this denial are both ontological and methodological. Ontologically, as we saw, happiness amounts to the positive balance of pleasure over pain, which, in this context, involves the integrated durations and intensities of all pleasures minus the integrated durations and intensities of all pains. Now as a number of experiments have shown (Kahneman 1999), retrospective evaluations of one's experiences introduce all sorts of biases in our evaluations of pleasures and pains. They are, therefore, methodologically or epistemologically, the wrong kind of tool for the measurement of (objective) happiness. It is for this reason that Kahneman (1999) proposes a bottom-up methodology aimed at constructing measures of happiness that aggregate moment-by-moment measurements and that avoid reliance on retrospective evaluations. The whole argument, however, is grounded in the undefended assumption that *Objective Happiness* involves the right views of, both, happiness and well-being. Without this premise the idea that retrospective evaluations introduce biases is entirely unsupported. As we saw in the "Language of well-being" section, however, hedonism does have its critics.

Specific versions of these criticisms can be observed in the way in which Kahneman and affiliates operationalize happiness. Remember, for example, the exchange between quantitative and qualitative hedonists discussed above, the latter endorsing heterogeneity in the quality of pleasure, the former, like Kahneman, denying it. In fact, on a closer reading, Kahneman may seem less firm on this point than previously stated, as he does also claim (1999: 6–7) that beside the hedonic quality of current sensory experience, his notion of instant utility should include the pleasures and pains associated with anticipation of future experience and with remembering the past; other pleasures of the mind such as states of "flow" in which one is so involved in an experience or activity where hedonic value fades into the background of experience; mood; activities that have a promotion focus or a prevention focus, and situations that vary in the extent of personal control. The question, here, is whether we can call in the appropriate hedonic sense "pleasures of the mind" experiences for which "the hedonic value fades into the background" and similarly with activities with a promotion as opposed to an aversion focus, or situations that vary in the extent of personal control.

[30] These claims are for the most part based on Kahnemann (1999). See also the other contributions in Kahneman et al. (1999).

Granting that all these items are indeed hedonic in the relevant sense, Kahneman faces an important operationalization challenge. As he is well aware (1999: 7), it may be an intractable task to measure all these items on the same bipolar scale with a zero point at the center, displeasure at one end, and pleasure at the other, what he calls the *Good/Bad Scale*. He also claims, however, that the study of objective happiness can be pursued usefully on such a scale with much weaker measurements of instant utility, as it is not particularly difficult to distinguish good, bad, and neutral moments. As "a first approximation," he writes, we could call someone objectively happy if, during a set period of time, she spent most of her time engaged in activities "that she would rather have continued than stopped, little time in situations she wished to escape, and—very important because life is short—not too much time in a neutral state in which she would not care either way" (Kahneman 1999: 7).

In short, desires and aversions for specific activities and experiences are to measure instant utility. Perhaps they do in some sense of "utility." The question, however, is once again whether this appeal to desires and aversions maintains a strong enough connection to utility understood hedonically. Pace Mill (1861: IV10), it is not clear that there is a one-to-one physical (and a fortiori conceptual or metaphysical) connection between desire and pleasure, on the one hand, and aversion and pain, on the other.[31] We may, in other words, desire things in virtue of properties other than their pleasantness. If this is true, there would be little reason to believe that the good/bad scale is a hedonic scale and, hence, that it is a unitary bipolar scale.

Friends of *Objective Happiness* seem to be undeterred by such worries, thinking perhaps that, all in all, desire and approach behavior is robustly connected to pleasure and aversion and avoidance behavior to pain. Even if one granted this much, however, there is reason to be skeptical with regard to the idea that hedonic tone is a consistent feature of the affective realm measurable on a bipolar scale. If positive and negative affective states are to be a sound measure rod, their actual occurrences qua groups should be inversely correlated, for if they weren't the occurrence of, say, a negative state may well be accompanied by the occurrence of a positive state. And if that were the case, it would be meaningless to measure well-being by subtracting occurrences of negative emotions from occurrences of positive ones, for a negative emotion may well tend to be accompanied by a positive one. Yet, various correlation studies (de Boer 2013: 9–12) show that the negative correlation between positive affect and negative affect is invariably low, not only between subjects, but also within them. These results strongly suggest that there is no bipolar scale.

Finally, we should expect opposition to *Objective Happiness* to arise from two of its defining features. First, from the fact that it focuses on happiness understood as the mere aggregate of many moments thus failing to take a more holistic perspective on lives. As Haybron (2008: 83) puts it:

> What matters to us, arguably, is not just having a plurality of good moments, but having a good *life*. And we see our lives as more than just the sum of their parts. Thus the pains suffered in boot camp,

[31] Simplifying very much, the work of neuroscientist Berridge (2009) shows that while hedonic "liking" is often connected to what he calls "wanting," the latter is not as likely to be connected with the former.

> in pursuit of some other achievement, might be seen as a good thing in the context of one's life as a whole. They will at least take on a different significance from the pains considered in isolation, as mere pains.[32]

Second, resistance to *Objective Happiness* is likely to arise from its objectivism: what if subjects harbor retrospective negative (perhaps second-order) attitudes toward some of their moments of pleasure?

Subjective well-being

Subjective well-being may be conceived as an approach that affords precisely the subjectivist and holistic perspective missing in *Objective Happiness*. At the core of this approach is the idea that an individual's well-being is to be determined by her subjective evaluations, which comprise both cognitive judgements of satisfaction and affective appraisals of moods and emotions. More in particular:

> It would be accurate to conceptualize subjective well-being as an umbrella term, consisting of a number of interrelated yet separable components, such as life satisfaction (global judgements of one's life), satisfaction with important life domains (e.g. marriage or work satisfaction), positive affect (prevalence of positive emotions and moods), and low levels of negative affect (prevalence of unpleasant emotions and moods).
>
> (Kesebir and Diener 2008: 66–67)

The cognitive component is typically measured with the help of self-report tools such as the *Satisfaction with Life Scale*, a five-item instrument that asks subjects to indicate their level of agreement on a seven-point Likert scale with the following five items:

- In most ways my life is close to my ideal.
- The conditions of my life are excellent.
- I am satisfied with my life.
- So far I have gotten the important things I want in life.
- If I could live my life over, I would change almost nothing.

The positive and negative affect components are measured separately as they can be somewhat independent and have different correlates. They are typically measured through retrospective self-reports, though peer-informant reports and instant measures of the kind preferred by *Objective Happiness* theorists are occasionally used.

The *Subjective Well-being* paradigm has a lot of ground in common with Sumner's (1996) *Authentic Happiness* theory. In both cases well-being is determined by subjective satisfaction evaluations that comprise a cognitive and an affective component. The difference resides in the fact that on Sumner's theory the evaluations have to be informed and autonomous. Given the nature of the overlap between the two approaches, the criticisms made against Sumner's theory in the "Well-being in philosophy" section, should be taken to apply pari passu to *Subjective Well-being*.

---

32 Friends of *Objective Happiness* may accept this criticism, if they were allowed to refer to later pleasures.

A couple of problems, however, are worth mentioning again here. First, consider the context sensitivity of life-satisfaction attitudes (Schwarz and Strack 1999) discussed in the "Well-being in philosophy" section. In the eyes of critics, this feature undermines the credibility of these attitudes as attitudes that are sufficiently robust to identify well-being. Friends of *Subjective Well-being*, however, see the problem differently. While they generally acknowledge context sensitivity, they seem to be more inclined to consider it as evidence of measurement problems than as evidence of a lack of the relevant stable *life satisfaction* disposition. That is, despite the transitory influences of moods and other distractions, subjective well-being is moderately stable across situations and across the lifespan (Diener and Lucas 1999: 214). This, they claim, is also corroborated by a strong correlation between overall life satisfaction and domain satisfaction, with high test–retest stability (Schimmack and Oishi 2005).

Second, consider once again the charge that *Subjective Well-being* is deficient because it is too subjectivist. As claimed above, well-being is a normative (as well as a descriptive) concept. We appeal to well-being and its synonyms when, for example, (self-)criticizing an agent's choices not only as instrumentally bad, but also, in some cases, as proceeding from imprudent goals and values. That is, we appeal to the agent's own well-being in order to invite her to revise her own goals and values. The problem with *Subjective Well-being* is that it seems to restrict the possibility of such (self-)criticism. To illustrate this, consider the case of someone who is quite unsatisfied with her life because she has values and goals that she simply cannot fulfill. On this theory, unless the agent adopts the goal of reaching a high level of satisfaction with her life, no one can coherently make an appeal to her well-being in order to invite her to reconsider her goals and values. Yet, it is precisely out of consideration for her well-being that a friend would invite her to revise her goals and values.

Eudaimonism

Two of the most prominent eudaimonistic paradigms in psychology are Ryan and Deci's (2000, 2008) self-determination theory of well-being and Ryff and Singer's multidimensional account. What is common to both approaches is their opposition to conceptions of well-being focused on assessments of feeling good, contentment, and life satisfaction, conceptions referred to under the heading of hedonia. Now hedonia and eudaimonia are claimed to be distinct; the latter, not the former, provides the correct basis for conceptualizing well-being. More positively, as Ryan, Huta and Deci put it (2008: 139), while hedonic approaches "focus on the outcome of happiness or pleasure," eudaimonic approaches focus "on the process of living well." Now while for Ryff and Singer (1998) living well consists in actualizing six human potentialities—autonomy, personal growth, self-acceptance, life purpose, mastery, and positive relatedness—for Ryan, Huta, and Deci (2008: 139) it consists in: (1) pursuing intrinsic goals and values for their own sake, including personal growth, relationships, community, and health, rather than extrinsic goals and values, such as wealth, fame, image, and power; (2) behaving in autonomous, volitional, or consensual ways, rather than heteronomous or controlled ways; (3) being mindful and acting with a sense of awareness; and (4) behaving in ways that satisfy basic psychological needs for competence, relatedness, and autonomy. In fact, they theorize that the first three of these aspects of eudaimonic living have their positive effects of psychological and physical wellness because they facilitate satisfaction of these basic, universal psychological needs.

Eudaimonist theories in psychology make explicit reference to Aristotelian *perfectionism* (Ryff and Singer 2008: 15–18; Ryan et al. 2008: 142–145) and to the extent to which they do, they are open to the same kind of criticisms. The charge of alienation is perhaps the most relevant here: Should I pursue friendship if such pursuit leaves me utterly cold? And what if fame, image, and power just did it for me? In fact these questions become particularly pressing when the relevant results in psychology not only inspire self-understanding and prudential self-regulation at the individual level but also influence public policy, as they increasingly seem to be doing.

Conclusion

Returning to Kim's questions, what we now can say is that these questions are in large part asked from an evaluative standpoint that is sui generis or irreducible to other evaluative standpoints. Moorean analyses that conceptualize prudential value in terms of absolute value occurring in a person's life miss an important point. They lack a relational element that is essential to the correct understanding of well-being: prudential goods are such only to the extent to which they are fitting or suitable *to someone*.

Relationality, however, is not to be confused with subjectivity and leaves conceptual room to objectivist theories of well-being that do not take the pro-attitudes peculiar to the individual to determine well-being. From the perspective of such objectivist theories, one could advise Kim without much in the way of reference to the conative and/or affective profile peculiar to him or her. These theories, however, will have to rely on a specific theory of human nature, or of theories of the self that give pride of place to emotional happiness, or otherwise heavily rely on some intuitions about what the human good substantively consists in. Alternatively, we may opt for a more subjectivist approach. Kim's pro-attitudes, idealized or otherwise, will at that point be an essential determinant of any answer to his or her questions.

Disagreement between subjectivist and objectivist theories of well-being is indeed a fundamental and persistent feature of the philosophy of well-being that carries over to psychological research. Another fundamental disagreement is likely to take center stage due to the recent surge in interest in both philosophy and psychology of both psychological theories of happiness and eudaimonistic approaches to well-being. What is at issue here is whether happiness in any of its hedonic, life satisfaction, or emotional guises is formally or substantively central to well-being, or whether it is at best a central indicator of other states, processes, or activities that are themselves ultimate constituents of well-being.

Acknowledgments

Many thanks to Roger Crisp, Julien Deonna, Johanna Seibt, and Fabrice Teroni for their precious comments.

References

Arneson, R. (1999). Human flourishing versus desire satisfaction. *Social Philosophy and Policy*, **16**, 113–142.

Bentham, J. (1789). *An Introduction to the Principles of Morals and Legislation*, J. Burns and H. L. A. Hart (eds) (1996). Oxford: Clarendon Press.

Berridge, K. (2009). Wanting and liking: observation from the neuroscience and psychology laboratory. *Inquiry: An Interdisciplinary Journal of Philosophy*, **52**, 378–398.

Brandt, R. B. (1979). *A Theory of the Good and the Right*. Oxford: Clarendon Press.

Brink, D. O. (2008). The significance of desire. In: R. Shafer-Landau (ed.) (2008). *Oxford Studies in Metaethics* vol. 3. Oxford: Oxford University Press, pp.5–46.

Brülde, B. (2007a). Happiness and the good life: introduction and conceptual work. *Journal of Happiness Studies*, **8**, 1–14.

Brülde, B. (2007b). Happiness theories of the good life. *Journal of Happiness Studies*, **8**, 15–49.

Crisp, R. 1997. *Mill on Utilitarianism*. London: Routledge.

Crisp, R. 2006. *Reasons and the Good*. Oxford: Oxford University Press.

Darwall, S. (2002). *Welfare and Rational Care*. Princeton, NJ: Princeton University Press

De Boer, J. 2013. Scaling happiness. *Philosophical Psychology*, Online First, 1–16.

De Sousa, R. 1987. *The Rationality of Emotion* Cambridge, MA: MIT Press.

Diener, E. and Lucas, R. (1999). Personality and subjective well-being. In: D. Kahneman, E. Diener, and N. Schwarz (eds) (1999) pp. 213–229.

Diener, E. and Seligman, M. E. P. (2004). Beyond money: toward an economy of well-being. *Psychological Science in the Public Interest*, **5**, 1–31.

Dorsey, D. (2010). Three arguments for perfectionism. *Noûs*, **44**, 59–79.

Feldman, F. (2004). *Pleasure and the Good Life*. Oxford: Clarendon Press.

Finnis, J. (2011). *Natural Law and Natural Rights*, 2nd edition. Oxford: Clarendon Press.

Fletcher, G. (2013). A fresh start for the objective list of well-being. *Utilitas* **25**, 206–220.

Frankena, W. K. (1973). *Ethics*, 2nd edition. XX Prentice-Hall.

Gibbard, A. (1990). *Wise Choice, Apt Feelings: A Theory of Normative Judgment*. Cambridge, MA: Harvard University Press.

Glassen, P. (1957). A fallacy in Aristotle's argument about the good. *Philosophical Quarterly* **29**, 319–322.

Griffin, J. (1986). *Well-Being: Its Meaning, Measurement, and Moral Importance*. Oxford: Clarendon Press.

Harsany, J. C. (1982). Morality and the theory of rational behaviour. In: A. Sen and B. Williams (ed.). *Utilitarianism and Beyond*. Cambridge: Cambridge University Press, pp.39–62.

Haybron, D. 2008. *The Pursuit of Unhappiness*. New York: Oxford University Press.

Hubin, D. (1996). Hypothetical Motivation. *Nous*, **30**, 31–54

Hurka, T. (1987). "Good" and "good for." *Mind*, **96**, 71–73

Hurka, T. (1993). *Perfectionism*. Oxford: Oxford University Press.

Hursthouse, R. (1999). *On Virtue Ethics*. Oxford: Oxford University Press.

Kagan, S. (1992). The limits of well-being. *Social Philosophy and Policy*, **9**, 169–189.

Kahneman, D. (1999). Objective happiness. In: Kahneman, D., Diener, E., and Schwarz, N. (eds) (1999). *Well-Being: The Foundations of Hedonic Psychology*. New York: The Russell Sage Foundation, pp.3–25.

Kahneman, D. and Krueger, A. B. (2006). Developments in the measurement of subjective well-being. *Journal of Economic Perspectives*, **20**, 3–24.

Kahneman, D., Diener, E., and Schwarz, N. (eds) (1999). *Well-Being: The Foundations of Hedonic Psychology*. New York: The Russell Sage Foundation.

Katz, L. (2006). Pleasure. In: E. N. Zalta (ed.) (2014). *The Stanford Encyclopedia of Philosophy* Available at: http://plato.stanford.edu/archives/spr2014/entries/pleasure/ [Accessed 28 March 2014]

Kesebir, P. and Diener E. (2008). In defense of happiness: why policymakers should care about subjective well- being. In: L. Bruni, F. Comim, and M. Pugno (eds) (2008). *Capabilities and Happiness*. New York: Oxford University Press, pp.60–80.

Kraut, R. (2007). *What is Good and Why: The Ethics of Well-Being*. Cambridge, MA: Harvard University Press

Little, I. M. D. (1950). *A Critique of Welfare Economics*. Oxford: Oxford University Press.

Mill, J. S. (1861). *Utilitarianism*. R. Crisp (ed.) (1998). Oxford: Oxford University Press.

Miller, A. (2003). *An Introduction to Contemporary Metaethics*. Cambridge: Polity Press.

Moore, G. E. (1903/1993). *Principia Ethica*, revised edition. Baldwin, T. (ed.). Cambridge: Cambridge University Press.

Moore, A. and Crisp, R. (1996). Welfarism in moral theory. *Australasian Journal of Philosophy*, **74**, 598–613

Nozick, R. (1974). *Anarchy, State, and Utopia*, Oxford: Basil Blackwell.

Nussbaum, M. (2000). *Women and Human Development: The Capabilities Approach*. Cambridge: Cambridge University Press.

Overvold, M. C. (1982). Self-interest and getting what you want. In: H. Miller and W. Williams (eds) (1982). *The Limits of Utilitarianism*. Minneapolis: University of Minnesota Press, pp.185–194

Parfit, D. (1984). *Reasons and Persons*. Oxford: Clarendon Press.

Plato (360 BCE). *Philebus*. J. M. Cooper (ed.) 1997. *Plato: Complete Works*. Indianapolis: Hackett.

Plato (380 BCE). *Protagoras*. J. M. Cooper (ed.) 1997. *Plato: Complete Works*. Indianapolis: Hackett.

Railton, P. (1986a). Facts and values. *Philosophical Topics*, **14**, 5–31

Railton, P. (1986b). Moral realism. *Philosophical Review* **95**, 163–207

Rawls, J. (1971). *A Theory of Justice*. Cambridge, MA: Belknap Press of Harvard University Press.

Raz, J. (1986). *The Morality of Freedom*. New York: Oxford University Press.

Raz, J. (2000). The central conflict: morality and self-interest. In: R. Crisp and B. Hooker (eds) (2000). *Well-Being and Morality: Essays in Honour of James Griffin*. New York: Oxford University Press, pp.209–238.

Regan, D. (2004). Why am i my brother's keeper? In: R. J. Wallace, P. Pettit, S. Scheffler, et al. (eds) (2004). *Reason and Value: Themes from the Moral Philosophy of Joseph Raz*. Oxford: Oxford University Press, pp.202–230.

Rodogno, R. (2008). On the importance of well-being. *Ethical Theory and Moral Practice*, **11**, 197–212

Rodogno, R. (2010). Sentientism, well-being, and environmentalism. *Journal of Applied Philosophy*, **27**, 84–99.

Rodogno, R. (2014a). Well-being between science and philosophy. In: J. H. Søraker, P. Wong, J. Boer, J. De Rijt, and P. Brey (eds) (2014). *Well-Being in Contemporary Society*. Springer: Berlin.

Rodogno, R. (2014b). Happiness and well-being: shifting the focus of the current debate. *South African Journal of Philosophy*, **33**, 433–446

Rosati, C. S. (1995). Persons, perspectives, and full information accounts of the good. *Ethics*, **105**, 296–325.

Rosati, C.S. (2000). Brandt's notion of therapeutic agency. *Ethics*, **110**, 780–811.

Rosati, C.S. (2006). Personal good. In: T. Horgan and M. Timmons (eds) (2006). *Metaethics After Moore*. Oxford: Oxford University Press, pp.107–132.

Rosati, C. S. (2008). Objectivism and relational good. *Social Philosophy and Policy*, **25**, 314–349.

Rosati, C.S. (2009a). Relational good and the multiplicity problem. *Philosophical Issues*, **19**, 205–234.

Rosati, C. S. (2009b). Self-interest and self-sacrifice. *Proceedings of the Aristotelian Society*, **109**, 311–325.

Ryan, R. and Deci, E. (2000). The "what" and "why" of goal pursuits: human needs and the self determination of behavior. *Psychological Inquiry*, **11**, 227–268.

Ryan, R., Huta, V., and Deci, E. (2008). Living well: a self-determination theory perspective on eudamonia. *Journal of Happiness Studies*, **9**, 139–170.

Ryff, C. and Singer, B. (1998). The contours of positive human health. *Psychological Inquiry*, **9**, 1–28.

Ryff, C. and Singer, B. (2008). Know thyself and become what you are: a eudaimonic approach to psychological well-being. *Journal of Happiness Studies*, **9**, 13–39.

Sandvik, E.,Diener, E., and Seidlitz, L. (1993). Subjective well-being: the convergence and stability of self-report and non-self-report measures. *Journal of Personality*, **61**, 317–42.

Scanlon, T. (1998). *What We Owe to Each Other*. Cambridge, Mass., London: Belknap Press of Harvard University Press.

Schimmack, U. and Oishi, S. (2005). Chronically accessible versus temporarily accessible sources of life satisfaction judgments. *Journal of Personality and Social Psychology*, **89**, 395–406.

Shope, R. (1978a). The Conditional Fallacy in Contemporary Philosophy *Journal of Philosophy*, **75**. 397–413.

Shope, R. (1978b). Rawls, Brandt, and the Definition of Rational Desires. *Canadian Journal of Philosophy*, **8**, 329–340.

Schwarz, N. and Strack, F. (1999). Reports of subjective well-being: judgmental processes and their methodological implications. In: Kahneman, D., Diener, E., and Schwarz, N. (eds) (1999). *Well-Being: The Foundations of Hedonic Psychology*. New York: The Russell Sage Foundation, 61–84.

Sidgwick, H. (1907). *The Methods of Ethics*, 7th edition. London: Macmillan.

Skorupski, J. (1999). *Ethical Explorations*. Oxford: Oxford University Press.

Skorupski, J. (2006). Green and the idealist conception of a person's good. In: M. Dimova-Cookson and W. J. Mander (eds) (2006). *T.H. Green: Ethics, Metaphysics, and Political Philosophy*. Oxford University Press, pp.47–75.

Sobel, D. (1994). Full informtion accounts of well-being. *Ethics*, **104**, 784–810.

Sumner, W. L. (1996). *Welfare, Happiness, and Ethics*. Oxford: Oxford University Press.

Tiberius, V. (2006). Well-being: psychological research for philosophers. *Philosophy Compass*, **1**, 493–505.

Tiberius, V. (2007). Substance and procedure in theories of prudential value. *Australasian Journal of Philosophy*, **85**, 373–391.

Tiberius, V., and Plakias, A. (2010). Well-being. In: J. M. Doris (ed.) (2010). *The Moral Psychology Handbook*. New York: Oxford University Press, pp. 402–432.

Velleman, J. D. (1988). Brandt's definition of "good." *Philosophical Review*, **97**, 353–371.

Zimmerman, D. 2003. Why Richard Brandt does not need cognitive psychotherapy, and other glad news about idealized preference theories in meta-ethics. *Journal of Value Inquiry*, **37, 373–394.**

Chapter 15

Musical value

Jerrold Levinson

Introduction

In this article I survey the kinds of value that music can possess, or perhaps equivalently, the variety of ways in which music may reasonably be valued. For that music is multiply valuable is the central theme of this essay. (On the general subject of musical value see: Budd 1995; Davies 2007; Goldman 1995, 2011; Kivy 2002; Levinson 2006b, 2011b; Ridley 2004; Scruton 1997; Sharpe 2004; Storr 1992.)

It is not uncommon for those who reflect on the value of the arts, from the perspective of either art makers or art appreciators, to propose that art is useless, and that it is precisely in being useless, or not satisfying any practical objective, that it is both most true to its nature and of greatest worth. It is not hard to understand the motivation of such an attitude toward art, sometimes described as "estheticist" or "art for art's sake." At bottom is the concern that art not be viewed in utilitarian terms, that it not be bound to the marketplace, that it not be rudely harnessed to social or political goals. For to treat art in such fashion would be at odds with the formal and expressive freedom that art must arguably be accorded if it is to achieve all that it might in artistic terms.

But regarded soberly, the claim that art is useless is hyperbolic. It is true only in the limited sense in which usefulness is equated with the achieving of narrowly practical ends. But the arts, and music among them, are certainly not, in the broad sense, useless. The arts answer to certain interests we possess, certain goals we entertain, and certain purposes that we embrace. They answer, perhaps, even to certain needs that we have, in the sense of goods without which our lives cannot fully flourish, even if we are not likely to actually perish without those goods.

Consider in this connection the well-known remark of Friedrich Nietzsche: "Without music, human life would be a mistake." This can, of course, like the claim that art is useless, seem somewhat exaggerated. For if Nietzsche's affirmation is valid, then why not, "Without flowers, human life would be a mistake?" Or "Without tennis, human life would be a mistake?" Or even, "Without Coca-Cola, human life would be a mistake?" Clearly, music, flowers, tennis, and carbonated beverages are all, in their different ways, good things, but is there really something special about music, such that its absence from our lives would be almost tragic, whereas that would perhaps not be so were those other good things to be absent? I return to that question throughout this essay.

Preliminary distinctions

Certain preliminary distinctions regarding the value of music are in order at the outset of our inquiry. First, we can distinguish the *intrinsic* value of music from the *instrumental* value of music, where the former can be understood as the value of engagement with music for its own sake, without any further end, while the latter can be understood as the value of music as a means to some good other than that residing in the engagement with music for its own sake. Second, we can distinguish the *artistic* value of music, which includes music's intrinsic value but arguably also some of its instrumental value, from its *non-artistic* value, which is entirely instrumental. Third, we can distinguish the *artistic* value of music from its *esthetic* value, where the former includes the latter as its core but is not exhausted by it.

Fourth, we can distinguish the value of music for an individual from the value of music for a given community, or even more broadly, for all of humankind. Fifth, within the value of music for an individual we can distinguish between its value for someone as a listener, its value for someone as a performer, and its value for someone as a composer (see: Levinson 2006b; Sessions 1950). Sixth and last, we can distinguish between the value of music or the practice of music as a whole, and the value of individual pieces or occasions of music.

Corresponding to that last distinction are two questions that might naturally be posed about musical value. One, what makes music or the practice of music as a whole a good, or something that contributes to human flourishing? Two, what makes a given piece or occasion of music good, or good compared to other such pieces or occasions of music? Let us dwell on these questions for a moment.

Could music as a whole be valuable if no individual pieces or occasions of music were valuable? That is hard to envisage, for the value of music as a whole seems to depend on the value of at least some such individual pieces or occasions. Could an individual piece or occasion of music be valuable even though music as a whole was not? That seems slightly easier to envisage, if still highly improbable, for the existence of even one valuable instance of music would surely point the way to others.

To frame the question somewhat differently: Is music in general valuable because specific instances of music are valuable, or are specific instances of music valuable because music in general is valuable? At this point we may begin to suspect that there is something unhappy about the very question, but if forced to choose it looks as if the first option is the better one, holding that the value of music in general must somehow derive from the value of specific instances of music.

Perhaps the best thing to say is this: that music *as a whole* is valuable insofar as it is *possible* for there to be valuable instances of music or occasions of music-making, where such instances or occasions may be valuable in different ways, and that a given *genre* of music will be valuable to the degree that valuable instances of music or occasions of music-making are possible *within* that genre.

At any rate, I will here be primarily concerned with the value attaching to music or the practice of music *generally*, rather than with the value of *individual* pieces of music or genres of music. That means that my discussion of the values of music will often situate itself at a fairly abstract level, seeking those musical values that are to be found, though of course to varying degrees, in music of just about any sort.

The *social* value of music provides a clear example of the divergence between a value of music in general and the value, inherently comparative, of an individual piece of music. Let us understand the social value of music as consisting centrally in the opportunity that music affords to bring people together in a public context for shared experience, interaction, coordination, and mutual affirmation. So understood, social value does not serve to any extent as a differentiating value of individual pieces or occasions of music, since it is possessed by virtually all pieces or occasions of music, and yet remains a value of music generally (see: Bigand 2010; Higgins 1991; McNeil 1995).

Music's value for listener, performer, composer

It is helpful at this point to distinguish music's value to listeners from music's value to performers from music's value to composers. These are, of course, different in theory, so it is hardly surprising that in practice they only partly overlap (see: Sessions 1950).

Music can be more rewarding to listen to than it is to perform—perhaps it is technically too easy to challenge a player and yet manages to be melodically ravishing. An example that comes to mind is the Rodgers and Hart standard *You Are Too Beautiful*. Music can be more rewarding to compose than it is to listen to—perhaps involving ingenious solutions to problems in counterpoint that are difficult to relish audibly. An example might be Ferruccio Busoni's gargantuan work for piano, *Fantasia contrappuntistic*a. And music might be more rewarding to perform than it is either to listen to or to compose—perhaps interestingly challenging the performer without either calling forth anything new from the composer or especially captivating the listener. An example might be Max Bruch's *Scottish Fantasy* for violin and orchestra, which despite many virtuosic turns for the soloist, features thematic material that is far from enthralling, and works its folksy closing theme to death (see: Levinson 2011b).

So a given piece of music can differ in value according to the role in the musical situation that is focused on—whether that of listener, performer, or composer. Still, it seems as if the first of those, that of the listener, appropriately takes priority over the others. Why? The reason is that making music the heard experience of which is rewarding is the fundamental *raison d'être* of the musical enterprise, that by which success in composing and success in performing is ultimately to be judged. Basically, someone composes well if they compose music that rewards listening, and performs well if they perform in a manner that rewards listening, whatever satisfactions may or may not accrue to the composer or the performer in the activities of composing and performing themselves.

Another reason, often noted, is that composers and performers are always perforce listeners as well as composers and performers, and that their listening responses, at least in imagination, are integral to the successful pursuit of their composing and performing activities. The satisfaction that a performer takes in performing or that a composer takes in composing may be, in part, a matter of challenges met or problems solved in their respective arts, but in virtually all cases, spelling out what that amounts to will acknowledge the goal of a *good-sounding* performance or composition; that is, one that appeals above all to the ear of the listener, and not only the mind of the composer or the body of the performer.

Manners of musical value

It will be useful now to distinguish different *manners* in which music can be valuable in regard to a given desirable end. Doing so is essential if we hope to justify in some measure Nietzsche's rather hyperbolic pronouncement about music's importance.

The different manners I have in mind are as follows. First, music might be valuable *as one among many* other things conducive to some desirable end. Second, music might be *particularly* conducive to a desirable end, despite there being a number of other things conducive to that end as well. Third, music might be valuable as *distinctively* conducive to some desirable end, unlike almost anything else. And fourth, music might be valuable as *uniquely* conducive to some desirable end, unlike anything else at all.

Clearly, the more values of music we can identify that are valuable in the second, third, and fourth ways of being valuable, the better position we will be in to justify the judgment that a world without music would be a vastly regrettable thing, which in more sober guise is the force of Nietzsche's remark. I will be particularly attentive in what follows to values in the third and fourth categories sketched above; that is, ones that are arguably either distinctive of music or else unique to music. But even those values of music that fall under the first and second of the above categories may enter into that justification, if substantial enough.

The centrality of music in human life

In a recent survey of the philosophy of music, the esthetician Peter Kivy nicely poses a version of Nietzsche's remark, though in the form of a question: "Does music strike deep enough into human bedrock that it can be seen as partly defining our lives?" (Kivy 2002: 8). Kivy is pretty sure that it does, going on to observe that there has never been, anywhere, a culture without music.

The fact that music is ubiquitous in human societies is a striking one, and indeed suggests that music answers to some deep need or interest that we have, apart from those for food, drink, sex, shelter, companionship, and the like. But noting music's ubiquity does not of itself tell us what that need or interest is. Moreover, music is not only ubiquitous, but appears to play an irreplaceable role in the lives of most of us. It pervades our existence to such an extent that its disappearance would be immediately remarked, and with considerable consternation. But the irreplaceability of music, like its ubiquity, is again at best a symptom of music's importance, and neither an explanation of nor a reason for that importance.

We could do worse at this point than quickly pass in review some well-known proposals regarding music's special value that have been offered in the course of the last two centuries of philosophical reflection on that noble art. I have in mind those associated with the names of Eduard Hanslick, Edmund Gurney, Arthur Schopenhauer, Susanne Langer, James Sullivan, and Leonard Meyer.

The idea of a specifically musical beauty championed by Hanslick, that of a deep-rooted and non-rule-governed musical impressiveness emphasized by Gurney, that of music as a supremely adequate mirror of emotional life advanced by Schopenhauer and Langer, that of music as a revealer of novel or unprecedented states of mind proposed by Sullivan, and that of music as a potential developer of personal character offered by Meyer, are all of substantial merit (see the Appendix for elaboration). Those ideas no doubt point to values that are either distinctive of, or even unique to, music. But instead of assessing those ideas as such I am going to explore, in my own fashion, a number of suggestions regarding the special value of music, though ones in which can surely be heard echoes of the ideas just canvassed.

The esthetic value of music: first pass

As stated at the outset, the central theme of this article is how many and how various are the values that music possesses or that music can have for us. But that is not to say that those values are all on a par. There are, rather, priorities and asymmetries among them. Some musical values are more important than others, and some musical values presuppose and depend on others.

Among the values that music possesses, pride of place must be given to what one can label music's *musical* value, or the value of music *as music*. Since music is, in the primary sense, an art, the musical value of a piece of music is thus a species of *artistic* value. Now what exactly artistic value comprises is a difficult question, which I will pursue in the following section. Nonetheless, it will probably be agreed at the outset that a major part of music's artistic value is what we can label music's *esthetic* value, or the value that music has as an object of esthetic appreciation.

But what is *esthetic appreciation*? Let us say that esthetic appreciation of an object is a perceptual-imaginative engagement with it in which its manifest properties, including formal and esthetic ones, and the relations among them, including relations of dependence between lower level and higher level properties, are registered and savored in their full individuality, and for their own sake. The esthetic value of music would then be the value that it affords a listener when attended to in that way, that is to say, when appreciated esthetically (see: Levinson 2009).

I have just characterized the engagement involved in esthetic appreciation of an object, whether an artwork or not, as *perceptual-imaginative*, rather than simply *perceptual*, and there are at least two reasons for that. A first reason is that grasp of most esthetic properties recruits the imagination in one way or another, often through a kind of metaphorical seeing or hearing or construing. Our typical esthetic interactions with absolute music, abstract paintings, rock formations, and fluffy clouds are clear illustrations of this, as it is unlikely we could find such things cheerful, anguished, desolate, elegant, or oppressive if no imaginative or metaphorical processes were in play. A second, closely related, reason is that the possibility of emotional or affective response to objects, and especially works of art, seems to require an imaginative involvement with their expressive aspects going beyond the mere perceptual recognition of such aspects. And a third reason is that in the case of a verbal art form, such as that of the novel, the purely perceptual element of the experience—the visual apprehension of the sentences of the text—is only a means to the esthetic experience the novel provides on an imaginative and contemplative plane.

So much for the general characterization of esthetic appreciation, aimed at being adequate to such appreciation whether focused on works of art or objects of other sorts, such as persons or portions of nature. We can be somewhat more specific in characterizing the esthetic appreciation of *music* if we allow ourselves an assumption about what listening to music with understanding centrally involves, namely, a kind of close tracking of music as it evolves in time, what we often call *following* music. Then we can say that the esthetic value of a piece of music is given roughly by the value of the perceptual-imaginative experience that the piece is capable of affording a prepared listener when the listener tracks or follows the music attentively and responds appropriately to its formal and expressive features (see: Levinson 1997, 2006a, 2006b; for contrasting perspectives, see: Kivy 1991; Davies 2011).

So conceived, the esthetic value of a piece of music is thus inescapably a kind of *experiential* value. Moreover, since the idea of appreciation implies finding something experientially *rewarding*, and since this often, if not always, amounts to *enjoying* that something, it is only a small step from that to affirm that music's esthetic value is typically reflected in the *pleasure* that it gives us when we attend to it esthetically. Or in other words, that the esthetic value of music is not only an experiential value, but often, quite plainly, a *hedonic* value.

Music is perhaps above all something designed to give pleasure, although of a special sort, to those who engage with it esthetically. And that has been taken as a reason, by those adhering to an "art for art's sake" perspective on music, for declaring music, in company with all the other arts, to be in effect useless, or of no practical utility. But something that is a source of non-injurious, non-ruinous, and highly repeatable pleasure cannot reasonably be thought of as useless. If one adds further that music, in the course of giving us harmless pleasure, profitably exercises our perceptual, cognitive, affective, and imaginative faculties, the charge of music's uselessness appears even less well-founded.

Exactly what psychological benefits accrue to individuals who actively engage with music, especially, though not exclusively, in virtue of learning to sing or play music, is currently a lively area of research in the cognitive psychology of music. It is clear that there are some such benefits, consisting most likely in the enlivening and sharpening of various of our mental faculties, such as those involved in spatial reasoning, arithmetical calculation, anticipating the future, remembering the past, coordinating motor activity, and empathizing with others (see: Bigand 2010; Huron 2006). There also appears to be synergy between regular engagement in musical activity and ease of foreign language acquisition, and between such engagement and the forestalling of various dementias that threaten as we age.

However, instrumental benefits of an engagement with music, such as those just mentioned, are mostly of a delayed and indirect sort, as opposed to benefits one currently enjoys or realizes. By contrast, the psychological benefits of musical engagement I highlight later on in this essay are for the most part quite different, involving manifest and immediately experienced positive goods.

Finally, the case can also be made that engaging in musical activity proved directly adaptive for humankind in its prehistory, most notably by facilitating collective action, apart from any benefits that accrue to individuals now through such engagement (see: Hauser and McDermott 2003; Huron 2006; Levitin 2006). But apart from the fact that the jury is still out on the validity of evolutionary explanations of music's origins, whether or not such explanations are valid is orthogonal to the concerns of this essay, which is restricted to values that music incontestably possesses for us here and now.

The artistic value of music

I return to the issue of the *artistic* value of music, or the value of music *as art*, which includes music's *esthetic* value but extends beyond that. So how might the artistic value of music be delimited? Even if music's artistic value outruns its esthetic value, not *all* the value that engagement with music can have for us is properly regarded as entering into its artistic value, or value as art, and detachable long-term psychological benefits of the sort invoked above perhaps furnish a clear example of undeniable yet non-artistic values of music.

We must first put in evidence some values that music *as art* can possess, and which are thus *artistic* values of music, but which do not belong to its esthetic value. Some plausible candidates are these: the *accomplishment* in a medium that a piece of music can represent, the *originality* of invention that a piece of music can display, and the positive *influence* on the course of future compositions that a piece of music can exert (see: Levinson 2006b). These seem clearly to be *artistic* values of music, ones internal to the musical enterprise, and not simply external fruits or side-benefits of musical activity, such as a possible improvement in memory capacity. And yet they are not *esthetic* values in the sense earlier specified, since they are not as such *experiential* values, whereby music is of esthetic value just insofar as it affords a listener who properly attends to the music an intrinsically rewarding perceptual-imaginative experience. The values of artistic originality, artistic accomplishment, and artistic influence—what we can collectively label *achievement* values—do not primarily reside in the experience of those things. And that is so even if, as I argue elsewhere, they must themselves ultimately be *grounded* in valuable appreciative experiences that they make possible (see: Levinson 2014 forthcoming).

Grant, then, that music's *artistic* value has as its core music's *esthetic* value but is not exhausted by that, as the example of achievement values illustrates. The question still remains of how music's artistic value can be circumscribed *generally*. One way would be to conceive such value as residing in the capacity that music has to fulfill objectives or answer to purposes that are proper to music *as an art*. But what objectives or purposes are those? We might be tempted at this point to offer a historical answer. That is, we might simply look to the objectives or purposes that music, practiced as an art, has traditionally aimed to fulfill. These would surely include such as the exploration of form, the expression of emotion, the exercise of imagination, the creation of tonal beauty, the elevation of the soul, the embodiment of ideas in sensuous form, the heightening of a sense of occasion, and so on.

The historical answer is good as far as it goes, but it seems both possible and desirable to supply another, more principled one. The issue, recall, is what is to count as an *artistic* objective or purpose of music. Why do the objectives just mentioned qualify as artistic—exploration of form, expression of emotion, attainment of tonal beauty—whereas other objectives, such as the production of economic worth, the obtaining of medical benefit, the acquisition of prestige, and so on, which might well result from musical activity, seem not to qualify?

A short answer is that something is an artistic objective of music when accessing the associated value requires *adequate* engagement with the music as music, that is, engagement in which the music is *understood*, its distinctive forms, qualities and meanings acknowledged and appreciated for what they are (see: Budd 1995). A musical work's esthetic value, most obviously, but also its influence value, originality value, and accomplishment value, is inaccessible to someone who lacks an understanding engagement with the work, whereas its economic or medicinal or prestige value, by contrast, are arguably accessible without such engagement. In other words, it may suffice, to harvest the economic value, to just own the rights to some music; to receive the medical value, to audit it inattentively; to reap the prestige value, to simply have sponsored its composition.

The esthetic value of music: second pass

I now return to the most important of music's artistic values, namely music's *esthetic* value. This, arguably the fundamental value of music as such, is the value of experiencing music's forms and qualities for their own sakes, a value accessed when we appreciate a piece of music for the distinct individual it is, formally and expressively, and for the fusion of form and expression that it presents (see: Levinson 2009).

Schematically, we might say that with any music there is, first, how it very concretely *goes*—how sound follows sound, note follows note, chord follows chord, phrase follows phrase, and so on; then, second, what it variously *conveys*—movements, gestures, attitudes, and emotions; and, third, what it conveys *in relation to* and *as embodied in* how it precisely goes. It is that third thing, that specific complex of motion and meaning, that is likely most distinctive of a piece of music, and that it is perhaps most rewarding to focus attention on (see: Levinson 2006b).

Great music, especially, stands as an exemplar of the most concrete and indissoluble union of form and content, something absolutely wonderful in its unparaphrasability—more unparaphrasable even than great poetry, where poem and paraphrase are at least in the same medium. I recall here Mendelssohn's celebrated remark that what music conveys, in its own fashion, is not too vague for words, but too specific for them; and Beethoven's response to a listener who, having just heard him perform one of his piano sonatas, asked him what it meant, Beethoven's response being to simply play the piece again. This, of course, is not far from what both Hanslick and Gurney proposed as most distinctively valuable about music.

The music theorist William Benjamin has offered a conjecture about the distinctive pleasure listeners take in following the unfolding of music, which goes beyond what I have said so far, where the emphasis was put on the indissoluble union of form and content in music and the consequent unparaphrasability of what it conveys. Benjamin's conjecture is as follows: "We find intensely pleasurable a power that we experience, the power to remember the sound of small sections of music and to reproduce them in our imaginations . . . because as we engage that power, we feel as if the music is emerging from within us, as if we were its virtual source" (Benjamin 2006).

Elaborating on Benjamin's conjecture, we might suggest that part of the distinctive value of music is the ease with which it is internalized by us, so that we in effect possess it in auditing it attentively. Music enters into us and pervades us like no other artistic offering, whether film, novel, painting, or sculpture, which always remain to some extent outside us and at a distance from us. Music is in effect recreated within us each time we listen, by seconding its movement, for the most part without conscious intent, in our aural imaginations, often anticipating each gesture of the music as if it were our own, as if coming from within us instead of from without.

Music's extra-artistic value

So much for music's esthetic value and, more encompassingly, its artistic value. It is time to state squarely that music has considerable value beyond its artistic value. Most patently, as recalled above in passing, music clearly also has *economic* value, whether as a commodity, a service, or a skill. Many people earn their living in whole or in part from music, and from many angles: some from composing it, some from performing it, some from publicizing it, some from marketing it, some from promoting it, some from criticizing it, some from engineering it, some from recording it, some from teaching it, some from analyzing it, and some, even, from theorizing and lecturing about it.

More generally, music has various sorts of *practical* value. Notable among practical values of music, in addition to economic value, would be social value, entertainment value, distraction value, relaxation value, therapeutic value, memory-improvement value, mobility-enhancing value, seduction-facilitating value, and so on. Music's practical values constitute a fairly open-ended set, and I am by no means the first to attempt to catalog them. The practical uses and virtues of music have been systematically surveyed since at least the beginning of the Renaissance, as the treatises of Johannes Tinctoris (1435–1511), Giulio Caccini (1551–1618), and Marin Mersenne (1588–1648), among others, clearly attest.

There are some further sorts of value that music might possess that are perhaps not purely practical. I have in mind such as *cognitive* value and *moral* value. The former would consist in the potential of music to convey knowledge about important aspects of human life, while the latter would consist in the potential of music to morally improve those who engage with it seriously. Since skepticism about values of music such as these is surely appropriate, we cannot uncontentiously range them among music's artistic values, though it is possible to mount arguments for so ranging them. The existence and the status of moral and cognitive values in art is currently a lively topic of debate in esthetics (see: Gaut 2003; Kieran 2003; Kivy 2008; Levinson 2006b; Savile 1993).

In what follows, I highlight some distinctive values of music deserving of special notice. Some are clearly artistic values, in that they presuppose an engagement with music in which the music is properly understood, and not simply heard or registered, and some are clearly extra-artistic values, because not presupposing such understanding. But for at least one of the values described below, music's idiosyncratic value, it is unclear whether or not the value in question counts as artistic.

Music's symbolic value

It has often been observed that music serves to model in audible form myriad of ways of being, of moving, of developing, of unfolding, of progressing, which modeling would seem to qualify as an artistic value of music (see: Beardsley 1981). Its capacity to do so is clearly rooted in its being a temporal art, but unlike, say, dance or film, which are equally temporal in nature, the abstractness of music imparts to such modeling a reach and a power beyond what those other arts can attain. Music, through the virtual movement that it delineates and the real movement that it induces, introduces us to possibilities of movement that would otherwise have remained closed to us, and to ways of inhabiting our bodies, that we may never have suspected. Music provides, in its sounding form, a paragon and practicum of how to move, how to grow, how to evolve—of how to go on (see: Levinson 2006b).

The medium of music is unparalleled for the virtually unlimited possibilities that it exemplifies, and that on at least three levels. First, in a purely formal sense, presenting a limitless variety of ways that *sounds* can be combined in time; second, in terms of how many kinds of virtual *movement* and virtual *gesture* are generated by those sonic combinations; and third, in how many *emotions, moods, attitudes* and other states of mind or spirit are mirrored in those limitless sonic combinations and the manifold musical gestures they generate. (see Kivy 1989, Ridley 1995).

That third level, of course, constitutes the *expressive* dimension of music, the most important part of its symbolic import. Furthermore, recognizing and then inhabiting in imagination those virtual movements and gestures when attending closely to expressive music can perhaps allow us to enter into, and grasp, the states of mind or spirit thereby expressed more fully or more vividly than we are able to in our lives outside of music (see: Bicknell 2009; Levinson 2011a). This recalls, in some measure, what Langer and Sullivan thought worth underlining about the special value of music.

Music's self-affirmation value

Music has manifest value as a reflector of self and a definer of identity, a value that seems likely to also qualify as artistic. This works differently, of course, for composers than for performers, for performers than for listeners, but it does work for them all, in one way or another. One's involvement with music has the potential to be almost as absorbing and challenging as a relationship, amorous or otherwise, with another person, often leading to the same sorts of constructive self-questioning. Musical works arguably help to crystallize or constitute the self that attends to them, internalizes them, and identifies with them.

Moreover, the musical tastes of a listener are often taken to be a clear barometer of his or her personality, the sensibility of a performer is manifest not only in how he or she performs but in what he or she chooses to perform, and composers are often said to live in and through their music. One has the sense of Gustav Mahler the person, for example, more fully and vividly through his ten symphonies and five song cycles than through the most detailed biography that might be devoted to him, and one suspects that the sense of the personality of Sviatoslav Richter emanating from his performances—one of massive strength, solidity, and self-reliance—is truer than what might be gleaned from newspaper or radio interviews with him. Moreover, there is probably no surer indicator of spiritual kinship between two persons than their sharing musical preferences and predilections.

That last point reminds us that music serves as a powerful source of group, and not just individual, identity. What music you favor often allies you with a given group, affirming your identification with it. As we all know, the musically inclined are not simply generic music lovers, but aficionados, variously, of Beethoven, the Stones, Bob Dylan, Baroque opera, Swedish fiddling, Arvo Part, punk rock, bebop, heavy metal, hip-hop, Javanese gamelan, and so on. Almost every genre of music spawns a community of appreciators of it who find in its sounds a special charm that makes that music—and by extension, them—stand out from the usual run of music and persons.

Music's social value

I come now to music's *social* value, probably the most important of its extra-artistic values. Music is of undeniable value as a sort of social glue and agent of solidarity, helping to create, maintain, and strengthen a sense of community. Music is notably more effective in this regard than almost any other art form. But why is that the case? Comparing music with literature, painting, and film will bring out part of the reason.

The experience of a concert, of publicly performed music, is an especially communal one, with many people focused on, and enjoying, the same thing, in full awareness of the participation of others. Concert attending is rather unlike film viewing, which is communal but solitary and isolating, or painting viewing, which does not lend itself to being communal, or most obviously, to the consumption of literature, normally a wholly private activity. Even a theatrical performance, though as communal an event as a concert, seems not quite as effective as a binder of persons as a musical performance, though that may just be due to the fact that in our culture audience response is normally a smaller part of theatre events than it is of musical events. And if we shift our focus from the context of the modern concert, whether of rock, jazz, or classical music, to how music manifests itself in tribal and traditional cultures, the social affirmation-interaction aspect of music is all the more salient. We should also not fail to note, as part of music's social value, occasions of public music as facilitators of human intercourse in the most ordinary sense, the conversing, gesturing, acknowledging, and exchanging that are the very fabric of social life.

A more specific aspect of music's social value, and one that perhaps deserves its own designation, ecumenical power, is the ability of music to transcend cultural barriers, to disarm prejudices, to unite people simply as human beings, regardless of linguistic, religious, or ethnic affiliations. Of course its power to do this is not unlimited, and may be greater for some genres rather than others, but it is noticeably greater than that of other artistic manifestations, which often struggle to export themselves outside of their culture of origin. This no doubt owes in part to the abstract, non-verbal nature of music, but perhaps also to its greater capacity to enter into us, to take hold of us, to set out bodies and souls in motion, almost without the participation of our wills (see: Bicknell 2009).

Music's idiosyncratic value

I here acknowledge what one might call the *idiosyncratic* value of music, a value hard to classify as either artistic or extra-artistic. Music can have value for a given listener that need not be shared, or even shareable, with others. Music's idiosyncratic value is a matter of the way some music speaks to someone in a completely individual way, resonating with his or her specific memories, associations, history, and physiology.

Of course what I am calling idiosyncratic value, which is a cousin of *sentimental* value though not quite identical to it, can attach to anything—a dilapidated wall in one's neighborhood, a piece of bottle glass found on the beach, the way one's sister shakes her head—but music seems to have a particularly strong propensity to take on such value for us. This is the phenomenon of "just something about it" or "*je ne sais quoi*," that strange appeal that resists explanation. Think of the ineffable charm that the "little phrase" in Vinteuil's sonata in Proust's *Remembrance of Things Past* has for Charles Swann, whose model was possibly Gabriel Faure's Violin Sonata in A major, the soaring main theme of which, consisting of a series of five-note motifs, squares well with Proust's description of the Vinteuil.

I suspect that music's unusual capacity to take on idiosyncratic value of this sort has something to do with music's so often striking us as a sort of veiled speech or opaque utterance, in which something is being said, something of significance, but which one nevertheless cannot quite make out or pin down.

Music's mood-enhancement value

Consider next music's undeniable value as an improver of mood and lifter of spirits. When one is down, there is almost nothing that works as well to bring one up again, or at least part of the way, as suitably chosen music. Even if the cheering effect of such music is transient, and cannot alone transmute unhappiness into its opposite, the effect, however temporary, is undeniably real.

Mood-enhancement value is an extra-artistic value of music in general, a marked potential that music possesses for quickly bringing about a lightening of spirits. But of course not *all* music exhibits that potential. However, contrary to what one might at first think, it is not only music that is expressive of *positive* emotion that can serve to brighten one's mood or alter one's outlook for the better. For to hear one's sadness mirrored exquisitely in sad music can be psychologically beneficial, affording the sense of being intimately understood and virtually empathized with that such music can impart (see: Bicknell 2009; Levinson 2011a).

On the other hand, the possible effect of truly depressive music should not be overlooked, especially when coupled with a suitably pessimistic text. According to urban legend a song recorded by Billie Holiday in 1941 called *Gloomy Sunday*, based on a Hungarian original entitled *The End of the World*, was so convincingly despairing that it was credited with prompting hundreds of suicides, and earned the song the nickname "the Hungarian suicide song." It was also banned from broadcast by the BBC for sixty years.

Music's accompaniment value

I lastly underline music's familiar yet crucial extra-artistic value as an accompaniment to, and facilitator of, other activities, such as religious ritual, military parade, factory work, aerobic exercise, and most obviously, dance in all its forms. With regard in particular to the last of those activities, music is valuable for the spur and guide it affords to bodily movement of an organized, rhythmic, and fluid sort, the sort of movement that is experienced by almost everyone as unusually liberating, even those whose talent for dance is quite modest.

Music is, in fact, supremely fitted to accompany almost all the activities of life, rendering them more pleasant, more fruitful, more engaging, or just, in some cases, more bearable or tolerable. The range of such activities is vast: not only marching and dancing and wooing, but dining, cooking, gardening, raking, washing, socializing, strolling, giving birth, making love, and so on. The products of other arts, such as painting, poetry, sculpture, and film, do not lend themselves so well, if at all, to the accompanying role that music so effortlessly plays, for reasons too obvious to underline.

But music is not only an ideal accompaniment to so many of life's activities, and in the case of some, an alleviator of the discomfort or distress involved in such activities. It is in addition, for many of us, a kind of companion to life itself, without which we would often feel more isolated, more at odds with our surroundings, more shut up within ourselves. Yet music does more even than accompany so well so many of our daily activities, and more even than offer companionship of a sort in what may sometimes seem an indifferent world. Music also energizes our lives and renders them more beautiful, investing them, if only in passing, with vitality, depth, and significance.

Appendix

Some notable proposals on the special value of music

Eduard Hanslick, nineteenth-century Austrian music critic: music presents tonally moving forms ("*tonend bewegte Formen*") in which its beauty consists, apart from any emotional quality or representational content that such forms may possess. So music's special value resides in its offering us a kind of beauty irreducible to any other, and unrelated to ordinary life (see: Hanslick 1986).

Edmund Gurney, nineteenth-century British psychologist and musician: music presents an absolute specificity of content, whereby every satisfying musical passage possesses a melodic quality inseparable from its individual form, so that even the slightest change in that form, whether in pitch or rhythm, is liable to yield a wholly different, and usually inferior, melodic quality. Music's special value, then, in a spirit not too far removed from Hanslick, is for Gurney to be found in its ultimately inexplicable *impressiveness*, Gurney's term for musical beauty (see: Gurney 1966).

Arthur Schopenhauer, nineteenth-century German romantic philosopher: music transparently mirrors the inmost nature of the world, revealing it to be fundamentally *will*, a kind of blind striving, which manifests itself in a multitude of phenomenal forms, of which music is the most direct and most affecting. Music's special value thus lies in its metaphysical significance, the fact that it speaks to us of the underlying irrational nature of things, distressing as that nature might be to acknowledge (see: Schopenhauer 1966).

Susanne Langer, twentieth-century American philosopher and student of Ernst Cassirer: music, through its temporal form, mirrors and reveals the inner nature of emotions, their shape, rhythm, and tempo. Music thus provides a uniquely faithful, as well as particularly lucid, image of the inner life (see: Langer 1942).

J. W. N. Sullivan, early twentieth-century British journalist and critic: music is capable of expressing emotions, attitudes and states of mind that are not encountered in ordinary life, and thus contributes to the enlargement of human experience. This is the greatest and most distinctive contribution music can make to our lives, and is singularly exemplified in the music of Beethoven's late period, his last piano sonatas and string quartets (see: Sullivan 1960).

Leonard Meyer, twentieth-century American music theorist: classical music presents a rich field for the play of expectations, in which fulfillment and frustration alternate in complex ways, allowing suitably constructed music to serve as a beneficial shaper of character through the challenges that its appreciation presents (see: Meyer 1967).

References

Beardsley, Monroe (1981). "Understanding music," in K. Price, ed., *On Criticizing Music*, Baltimore: Johns Hopkins University Press, 55–73.

Benjamin, William (2006). "Music through a narrow aperture: a partial defense of concatenationism," *Revue Internationale de Philosophie* **60**: 515–522.

Bicknell, Jeanette (2009). *Why Music Moves Us*, London: Palgrave/Macmillan.

Bigand, Emmanuel (2010). "La musique rend-elle intelligent?," *L'Essentiel, Cerveau Psycho*, No. **4**, November: 38–42.

Budd, Malcolm (1995). *Values of Art*, London: Penguin.

Davies, Stephen (2007). "The evaluation of music," in *Themes in the Philosophy of Music*, Oxford: Oxford University Press, 88–128 [Orig. pub. 1987.]

Davies, Stephen (2011). "Musical understandings," in *Musical Understandings and Other Essays on the Philosophy of Music*, Oxford: Oxford University Press.

Gaut, Berys (2003). "Art and Knowledge," in *Oxford Handbook of Aesthetics*, Oxford: Oxford University Press, 436–450

Goldman, Alan (1995). *Aesthetic Value*, Boulder, CO: Westview Press.

Goldman, Alan (2011). "Value," in T. Gracyk and A. Kania, eds, *Routledge Companion to Philosophy and Music*, London: Routledge, 155–164

Gurney, Edmund (1966). *The Power of Sound*, New York: Basic Books. [Orig. pub. 1880.]

Hanslick, Eduard(1986). *On the Musically Beautiful*, Cambridge, MA: Hackett Publishing. [Orig. pub., in German, in 1854.]

Hauser, Mark and McDermott, Josh (2003). "The evolution of the music faculty: a comparative perspective," *Nature Neuroscience* **6**: 663–668.

Higgins, Kathleen (1991). *The Music of Our Lives*, Philadelphia: Temple University Press.

Huron, David (2001). "Is music an evolutionary adaptation?" *Annals of the New York Academy of Sciences* Vol. 930, 43–61.

Kieran, Matthew (2003). "Art and morality," in *Oxford Handbook of Aesthetics*, ed. Jerrold Levinson, Oxford: Oxford University Press.

Kivy, Peter (1989). *Sound Sentiment*, Philadelphia: Temple University Press.

Kivy, Peter (1991). *Music Alone*, Ithaca, NY: Cornell University Press.

Kivy, Peter (2002). *Introduction to a Philosophy of Music*, Oxford: Oxford University Press.

Kivy, Peter (2008). "Musical morality," *Revue Internationale de Philosophie* **62**: 397–412.

Langer, Suzanne (1942). *Philosophy in a New Key*. Cambridge, MA: Harvard University Press.

Levinson, Jerrold (1997). *Music in the Moment*, Ithaca, NY: Cornell University Press.

Levinson, Jerrold (2006a). "Concatenationism, architectonicism, and the appreciation of music," *Revue Internationale de Philosophie* **60**: 505–514.

Levinson, Jerrold (2006b). "Evaluating music," in *Contemplating Art*, Oxford: Oxford University Press, 184–208 [Orig. pub. 1998.]

Levinson, Jerrold (2009). "The aesthetic appreciation of music," *British Journal of Aesthetics* **49**: 415–425.

Levinson, Jerrold (2011a). "Music and negative emotion," in *Music, Art, and Metaphysics*, 2nd edn, Oxford: Oxford University Press, 306–335 [Orig. pub. 1982.]

Levinson, Jerrold (2011b). "Evaluating musical performance," in *Music, Art, and Metaphysics*, 2nd edn, Oxford: Oxford University Press, 376–392 [Orig. pub. 1987.]

Levinson, Jerrold (2016). "Artistic achievement and artistic value," in *Aesthetic Pursuits*, Oxford: Oxford University Press, forthcoming 2016.

Levitin, Daniel (2006). *This Is Your Brain On Music*, New York: Penguin.

McNeil, William (1995). *Keeping Together in Time: Dance and Drill in Human History*, Cambridge, MA: Harvard University Press.

Meyer, Leonard (1967). "Some remarks on value and greatness in music," in *Music, the Arts, and Ideas*, Chicago: University of Chicago Press, 22–41.

Ridley, Aaron (1995). *Music, Value, and the Passions*, Ithaca, NY: Cornell University Press.

Ridley, Aaron (2004). *The Philosophy of Music*, Edinburgh: Edinburgh University Press.

Savile, Anthony (1993). *Kantian Aesthetics Pursued*, Edinburgh: Edinburgh University Press.

Schopenhauer, Arthur (1966). *The World as Will and Representation*, Volumes I and II, New York: Dover Publications. [Orig. pub., in German, in 1844.]

Scruton, Roger (1997). *The Aesthetics of Music*, Oxford: Oxford University Press.

Sessions, Roger (1950). *The Musical Experience of Composer, Performer, Listener*, Princeton, NJ: Princeton University Press.

Sharpe, Robert (2004). *Philosophy of Music: An Introduction*, London: Acumen Publishers.

Storr, Anthony (1992). *Music and the Mind*, London: Macmillan.

Sullivan, J. W. N. (1960). *Beethoven: His Spiritual Development*, New York: Vintage. [Orig. pub. 1927.]

Chapter 16

Environmental value

Thomas Dietz

Introduction

Why do some people buy hybrid or all-electric vehicles? Why do some people adhere to a vegan or vegetarian diet? Why are some nations eliminating nuclear power from their energy portfolios? Why are some fisheries harvested in a sustainable way? Why do some companies embrace sustainability as a corporate goal?

Values are often invoked as an explanation for such environmentally consequential decisions. "Changing people's values" has been a prescription for solving environmental problems for decades but usually without reference to the scholarship on values and environmental decision-making. This is unfortunate because the robust tradition of research on environmental values could advance understanding and provide guidance for public and private policy.

This chapter examines the current state of research on environmental values. I begin the next section with a brief review of how the concept of values is used in philosophy and economics to clarify the distinction between those approaches and the study of values in environmental decision-making. The third section discusses environmental decision-making. In the fourth section I turn to the special role that altruism and self-interest play in governing the commons and other forms of collective action. The fifth section examines other values that may influence environmental decisions, while the sixth examines how environmental values are conceptualized and measured. The seventh section places environmental values in the context of an integrative approach to environmental decision-making, the Values–Beliefs–Norms theory. The eighth section examines the relationship between values and other influences on environmental decision-making. The conclusion summarizes and proposes areas for further research.

Several recent reviews complement this chapter. Dietz et al. (Dietz et al. 2005) overview environmental values research for the general environmental science audience. Steg and De Groot (Steg and De Groot 2012) provide a thorough review of values in the context of environmental and conservation psychology. Corner et al. (Corner et al. 2014) review research on values, public engagement, and climate change. The goal here is somewhat different—to communicate work on environmental values to the community of values researchers.

Values in environmental ethics and environmental economics

Values in environmental ethics

The broadest compass for the use of the term "environmental values" comes in environmental philosophy and especially environmental ethics. Environmental philosophy has been defined as the study of "the moral relationship of human beings to, and also the value and moral status of, the environment and its nonhuman contents" (Brennan and Lo 2011, n.p.). The idea of values is so central to environmental philosophy that one of the major journals in the field is titled *Environmental Values*.

Environmental ethicists examine ways to make decisions when those decisions have consequences for the environment, other species, and for the biosphere itself. They try to provide guidance as to how we ought to make environmentally consequential decisions. Such decisions nearly always involve tradeoffs. A hybrid or electric vehicle may protect the environment and save money in the long run but it may be smaller and have higher up-front costs than a conventional vehicle. How much value should be assigned to the size of the car, to up-front versus long-range costs and to pollution generated by driving? Acting to protect the environment may reduce a company's profits or reduce the availability of jobs in a community. In selecting a corporate strategy how much value should be given to the environment, to profits, to jobs? Environmental ethics deploys a rich range of ethical traditions to understand how to make such value tradeoffs (Brennan and Lo 2011; U.S. National Research Council 1999). A central debate in these discussions is whether decisions should take into account only instrumental values of the environment or also consider intrinsic values. The instrumental value of environmental change, such as the loss of a species, is its merit or worth as a means to human ends. Instrumental value is thus inherently anthropocentric—the environment is assigned value only through the lens of human needs and desires. In contrast, intrinsic value assigns worth to aspects of the environment without regard for human use or appreciation of them.

Values in environmental economics

Valuation of environmental change is at the heart of economic analysis of environmental policies and one of the most active areas of research in environmental economics (Barbier 2011; Kling et al. 2012). Economic policy analysis quantifies the effect of changes in the environment on aggregate human well-being and assesses the relative merit of alternative actions based on those changes. Almost without exception, economists use a utilitarian approach. Changes in the production of goods and services by ecosystems are valued in terms of human preferences, with "the greatest good to the greatest number" as the criterion for comparing alternative actions. Thus valuation in environmental economics sits squarely in the instrumental approach to environmental ethics—there is no mechanism for taking account of intrinsic value independent of human preferences.

The dominance of a utilitarian framework and of instrumental values often places environmental economics in conflict with environmental ethics, where non-utilitarian criteria for decisions and intrinsic values are part of the discussion. However, most environmental economists include "passive use" and "existence value" in their analyses—the worth humans assign to aspects of the environment for spiritual, philosophical, or other reasons that don't depend on direct use. A standard classification of the value of ecosystems considers four kinds of services: provisioning (supplying food, fiber, fuel, and other materials), regulating (controlling biogeochemical processes, the climate, etc.), supporting (provision of pollinators, recharge of groundwater), and cultural (which captures passive use values such as the existence of sacred places as well as more active uses such as recreation) (Reid et al. 2005).

Standard economic practice takes market prices as measures of social value and uses those prices in assessing tradeoffs. But many markets for environmental goods and services deviate substantially from the ideal conditions that allow prices to be treated as social values, and many important ecosystem goods and services are not priced in a market at all—the cultural value of the existence of a remote wilderness, for example. In "contingent valuation" people are asked to indicate how much they would be willing to pay for a change in ecosystem services, which allows an estimate of social value without using market prices. A growing consensus holds that, when done carefully, contingent valuation studies yield a value for environmental change that is useful for decision-making (Kling et al. 2012). Incorporating non-market values is important for policy analysis because for many environmental changes, existence values can be 10, 100 or even 1000 times greater than the values that flow from direct use. Thus existence values often dominate economic analyses of environmental decisions.

What is environmental decision-making?

Values are assumed to influence environmental decision-making. But what do we mean by environmental decision-making? First, we have to delineate the kinds of action that might be influenced by values (Stern et al. 1999; Stern 2000). We may act as consumers in choosing environmentally friendly over environmentally damaging products. We may act as citizens through voting, signing petitions, and expressing views on surveys. We may act as relatively passive movement supporters by joining environmental organizations and donating money to them, or we may become active members, participating in meetings, demonstrations, and other forms of action.

Second, how do people make decisions, whether as consumers, citizens, or activists? The environmental values literature has mostly assumed that individuals consider how alternative courses of action will influence things that matter to them, where what matters is shaped by their values, and thus values are the basis for making tradeoffs (Dewey 1939; see also Hechter 1992). This approach is similar to the rational actor model that has dominated economics and that is highly influential throughout the social sciences (Dietz 1994; Jaeger et al. 2001; Rosa et al. 2013). However, the environmental values literature gives central importance to altruism, while the classic rational actor model assumes narrow self-interest. In addition, environmental values scholarship acknowledges that the careful calculations of costs, benefits, and probabilities, called for under that rational actor model, do not apply to all environmentally consequential decisions. At least three influences can cause such decisions to differ from what is expected under the rational actor model, and can also cause a disjuncture between decisions and behavior.

First, new environmental issues are novel stimulae to most people. A few decades ago hydrological fracturing (fracking) was unknown to most of the public. Concerns with ocean acidification and geoengineering of climate are only beginning to be raised in public discourse. When a new issue is posed to a member of the public in news coverage, in a conversation, or in a survey, she or he will have no pre-existing attitude, preference, or position to be referenced. People respond quickly when they first hear about a new issue, whether in casual conversation, in browsing the web, or in being asked a question on a survey. In Kahneman's terms, they are using "fast" processing (Kahneman 2011). Values may be important in the "on the fly" construction of views about a new attitude object (Stern et al. 1995b). In offering an opinion, individuals may look for clues about how their values might be affected and do a quick mapping between their values and the novel stimulus. Thus framing of the issue in terms of values may be of great importance in the initial reaction to it. For example, framing a consumer choice in ways that highlight some values over others seems to influence decision-making but only among those for whom the value emphasized is already important (Gromet et al. 2013; Verplanken and Holland 2002).

Second, many environmentally consequential actions are the result of habits and not a reasoned weighing of tradeoffs. For example, a great deal of energy is wasted by unnecessarily long idling of cars, but for most people this is not a decision, it is just a habit not given conscious thought (Carrico et al. 2009). Such habits are probably not much influenced by values. A further complication is that members of the public may have inaccurate views regarding the environmental impacts of the decisions they make, which will also attenuate the influence of values—people may be trying to make decisions that are congruent with their values but their lack of understanding of the impacts of consumer choices introduces error (Attari et al. 2010; Attari 2014; Dietz 2014).

Finally, the influence of values on environmental decision-making is often constrained by what is practical (Guagnano et al. 1995). Values may have the most influence when the difficulty of an action is moderate rather than when actions are very difficult or very easy. For example, renters usually cannot weatherize their dwellings and often have little choice regarding the appliances installed. So we can expect their values might influence thermostat settings but other key aspects of home energy use are beyond their control. On the other hand, if the apartment has a "smart" thermostat that automatically does time-of-day adjustments to room temperature, then thermostat settings become so easy to carry out that again, values may have little influence.

There is some tension between the view that values are the basis for slow and rational decision-making and the view that values are used in fast, on-the-fly social construction of views around a new issue. These views are not necessarily contradictory—the same values could be used in both fast and in slow decision-making processes. Most research on the influence of values on environmental decision-making does not carefully assess the decision-making process, so reconciling the role of values in careful slow processes and more ad hoc fast processes remains an open area for further work.

Altruism and self-interest

The insertion of values into the study of environmental decision-making was motivated by the theoretical question of altruism. Many environmental issues can be framed as the governance of common pool resources, an important form of the collective action problem (Dietz et al. 2003; Ostrom 1990, Ostrom et al. 2002). A common pool resource is one where use is "non-excludable"—it is difficult to prevent the use of the resource—and "rival"—the use by one person diminishes the quality of the resources for all. Examples abound: the planetary atmosphere as a "dump" for pollution, including heat-trapping greenhouse gases; bodies of water that end up as sinks for polluting runoff; a fishery, rangeland, or forest held as common property by a community; groundwater pumped for irrigation. Such shared resources are at risk of being degraded by too much use. If individuals act only from narrow self-interest, each will realize that the resource may be degraded even if they limit their use. Someone motivated purely by self-interest will proceed to use the resource at the level that is most beneficial to him or her without regard to the larger consequences. If all individuals follow this course of action, then the resource is degraded, a so-called "tragedy of the commons." But if individuals act with some degree of altruism directed toward other resource users or toward other species or the biosphere itself, it is easier to govern the resource sustainably.

But will individuals be altruistic? If behavior is determined wholly by genes, a long line of theoretical argument suggests that it can be difficult, although not impossible, to establish altruistic behavior (Sober and Wilson 1998). Such dominance of self-interest is a central feature of the rational actor model (Becker 1976). As Adam Smith put it: "We are not ready to suspect any person of being defective in selfishness" (Smith 1976 [1804]: 446). However, if rules shaped by cultural evolution have strong influence on behavior, as is surely the case for humans, then altruism, while not automatic, will also not be rare (Richerson and Boyd 2005). Schwartz and Bardi's argument that altruistic values (called universalism in their framework) are among the most important values in many cultures is consistent with the cultural evolutionary argument for altruism (Schwartz and Bardi 2001). Of course the degree of self-interest and the degree of altruism will vary across individuals and within an individual across situations and can be influenced by framing effects (Dietz 2005).

Concern with altruistic behavior first entered the study of environmental decision-making through Schwartz's "norm-activation" model (Schwartz 1968, 1977). Black, Dunlap, Heberlein, Stern, Van Liere, and others adopted Schwartz's theory to the study of pro-environmental behavior (Black et al. 1985; Heberlein, 1977; Sternet al. 1983; Van Liere and Dunlap 1978). However, the norm-activation model as originally developed applies only to concerns with the welfare of other humans. The argument for a scope of concern that extends beyond humans was notably articulated in Leopold's *The Land Ethic* (Leopold 1987[1949]; see also Merchant 1992). Altruism that extended beyond other humans was introduced into social psychology in a debate between Dunlap and Van Liere on the one hand and Heberlein on the other (Dunlap and Van Liere 1977; Heberlein1977, 1972).

Starting in the early 1990s, a growing literature examined the influence of three values on environmental decision-making: self-interest, altruism toward other humans, and biospheric altruism. The earliest formulation assessed the contribution of these three values indirectly. The influence of values was represented by the weight given in decision-making to beliefs about how environmental change would affect the respondent and her or his family, other humans, and other species and the biosphere (Stern et al. 1993; see also Gärling et al. 2003). The regression coefficients that linked the beliefs to behavioral intentions were interpreted as measures of the importance of each domain of concern, and thus of values assigned to that domain.

However, the literature (i.e. Stern and Dietz 1994) quickly adopted the Rokeach/Schwartz approach of measuring values directly by asking respondents how important various short statements of value were "as a guiding principle" in their lives (Rokeach 1968, 1973, 1979; Schwartz and Bilsky 1987, 1990). The direct approach using value scales has the compelling advantages of linking to the larger research literature on values and deploying simpler statistical procedures than the earlier approach.

Traditional values, openness to change, and hedonism

Schwartz conceptualizes values as a circumplex with two polar axes (see Schwartz, this volume). One axis corresponds to the key concept in the environmental values literature, self-interest versus altruism, which Schwartz labels self-enhancement versus self-transcendence (Schwartz 1994). The other major axis differentiates openness to change from what Schwartz labels conservation but is often called "traditional" in the environmental values literature. Following this convention, I will refer to Schwartz's "conservation" values as traditional values hereafter.

Both traditionalism and openness to change may influence environmental decision-making. Political conservatism tends to align with the values in the traditional complex (Caprara et al. 2006, 2009; Dirilen-Gümüş et al. 2012; Schwartz et al. 2013; Vecchione et al. 2013, 2014). In the U.S. and most developed nations at least since the 1980s political conservatism has been critical of environmentalism (McCright and Dunlap 2010, 2011; McCright et al. 2014). Thus it is plausible that Schwartz's traditional values might capture and indeed underpin some of the effects of political ideology on environmental concern. Pro-environmental behaviors can involve adopting novel technologies (hybrid cars, residential solar systems, organic and free-range foods, etc.) or changing lifestyles (reducing commuting by car, shifting away from an animal-based diet). So it seems plausible that the values Schwartz labels "openness to change" might facilitate a willingness to be an earlier adopter of pro-environmental behaviors.

Recently, Steg and collaborators (Steg et al. 2014) argued that hedonic values also may be important drivers of environmental decision-making. Hedonic values assign importance to pleasure and comfort. In Schwartz's schema they are closely related to both self-enhancement and to openness to change value types, and Steg and De Groot consider them a form of self-enhancement (Steg and De Groot 2012). But the self-enhancement items used to measure self-interest in environmental values research focus on improving the resources one controls, such as money, influence, and power. The hedonic items tap more immediate rewards such as pleasure or comfort. Because many pro-environmental behaviors may be perceived to require changes in lifestyle and the loss of some comfort, convenience, or pleasurable experiences, individuals who give substantial importance to pleasure and comfort may be reluctant to undertake them.

To summarize, six values are theorized to influence environmental decision-making. The best-established empirically is altruism toward other species and the biosphere itself, often called just biospheric values. Altruism toward other humans, often called simply altruism, is also a relatively consistent influence on environmental decisions. Schwartz labels both of these together "self-transcendence." The polar opposite, self-interest, or in Schwartz's terms self-enhancement, has somewhat less empirical support. Traditional values (Schwartz's conservation) may capture some aspects of environmental politics, and its opposite, openness to change, may be related to adoption of new environmental friendly lifestyles and technologies, but the empirical support for the influence of these two values is less consistent than for the two forms of altruism and self-interest. Finally, it will be useful to examine further hedonism as a sixth value influence on environmental decision-making, as so far few studies have considered it.

Measuring values

Looking at the most common ways these six values are measured will give a better sense of how they are conceptualized. Table 16.1 displays a commonly used set of environmental values items, a recent update of that set by Steg and colleagues, and the Schwartz value types from which the items were drawn (Schwartz 1994; Steg et al. 2014; Stern, P. C. et al. 1998; see also Schwartz, this volume). In the Stern et al. 1998 study, biospheric values are measured by two items from the Universalism value type and one new item not included in Schwartz's 1994 analysis. Altruistic values directed at other humans are measured by three items also from the Universalism type. Traditional/Conservation values are measured by two items from the Conformity value type and one from the Security type. Self-interest/Self-enhancement/Egoistic values are measured by two items from the Power type and one from the Achievement type. Openness to change values are captured with two items from the Stimulation and one from the Self-direction value types.

The full array of Schwartz value items, or a substantial subset of them, has been used in many samples, using a wide array of methodologies. While details vary, there seems to be broad consensus that 4–5 values emerge (for a review see Steg and De Groot 2012). For example, Schultz et al. find consistent patterns of response in studies spanning more than seventeen nations (Schultz et al. 2005; Schultz and Zelezny 1998, 1999a; Schultz 2001). Results from the environmental values literature are consistent with the larger literature examining Schwartz's approach to measuring values—the two polar dimensions

Table 16.1 Scales to measure environmental values

Stern, Dietz, and Guagnano 1998*	Steg, Perlaviciute, van der Werff, and Lurvink 2014**	Schwartz value type***
Biospheric altruism	Biospheric altruism	
Protecting the environment, preserving nature	Protecting the environment	Universalism
Unity with nature, fitting into nature	Unity with nature	Universalism
Respecting the earth, harmony with other species	Respecting the earth	New
—	Preventing pollution	—
Humanistic altruism		
A world at peace, free from war or conflict	A world at peace	Universalism
Social justice, correcting injustice, care for the weak	Social justice	Universalism
Equality, equal opportunity for all	Equality	Universalism
—	Helpful	Benevolence
Traditional (Conservation)		
Honoring parents and elders, showing respect	—	Conformity
Family security, safety for loved ones	—	Security
Self-discipline, self-restraint, resistance to temptation	—	Conformity
Self-interest (Egoistic or Self-enhancement)		
Authority, the right to lead or command	Authority	Power
Influential, having an impact on people and events	Influential	Achievement
Wealth, materials possessions, money	Wealth	Power
—	Social power	Power
—	Ambitious	Achievement
Openness to Change		
A varied life, filled with challenges, novelty and change	—	Stimulation
An exciting life, stimulating experiences	—	Stimulation
Curious, interested in everything, exploring	—	Self-direction

Table 16.1 (continued) Scales to measure environmental values

Stern, Dietz, and Guagnano 1998*	Steg, Perlaviciute, van der Werff, and Lurvink 2014**	Schwartz value type***
Hedonic values		
	Pleasure	Hedonism
	Enjoying life	Hedonism
	Gratification for oneself	—

*Stern, P. C., Dietz, T., and Guagnano, G. A. (1998). A brief inventory of values. *Educational and Psychological Measurement*, 58, 884–1001.

**Steg, L., Perlaviciute, G., Van Der Werff, E., and Lurvink, J. (2014). The significance of hedonic values for environmentally relevant attitudes, preferences, and actions. *Environment and Behavior*, 46, 163–192.

***Schwartz, S. H. (1994). Are there universal aspects in the structure and contents of human values? *Journal of Social Issues*, 50, 19–45, figure 2.

of Conservation/Openness to change and of Self-enhancement/Self-transcendence are a very robust feature across many studies. In recent work, Schwartz and colleagues have also identified the distinction between biospheric values and altruism toward other humans (Cieciuch and Schwartz 2012; Schwartz and Boehnke 2004). In addition to this quantitative body of work, several qualitative studies also have demonstrated that biospheric and humanistic values emerge in how people think about environmental issues (Kempton et al. 1995; Satterfield et al. 2000).

The items used by Steg et al. to measure altruism, biospheric values, self-enhancement, and hedonism in 2014 are quite similar to those in the 1998 study (Steg et al. 2014). (They did not include measures of openness to change or traditional values, which are less often found to be a useful predictor of environmental decision-making.) The new measure of biospheric altruism adds "preventing pollution" to the earlier list. The measure for altruism toward other humans adds "helpful" from Schwartz's Benevolence type. Self-interest adds "social power" and "ambitious" from the Power and Achievement values types, respectively. More than twenty years and many dozens of studies on environmental values separate this recent effort from the first use of Schwartz items to understand environmental decisions (Stern and Dietz 1994). The remarkable stability in the measures used speaks to the strength of the approach to measuring values first developed by Rokeach and advanced by Schwartz and his collaborators.

Values–Beliefs–Norms Theory

Values have never been assumed to be the sole influence on environmental decision-making. Most environmental values research embeds values in a causal chain that assesses both their direct effects and their indirect effects via other constructs, including beliefs, norms, identity, and attitudes (Dietz et al. 2005; Hitlin 2011). Perhaps the most influential

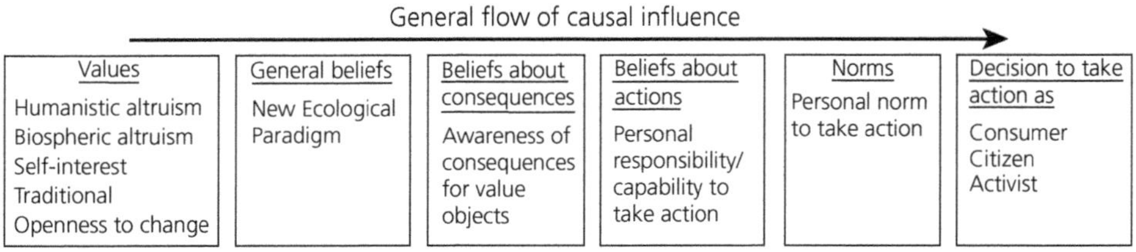

Fig. 16.1 Values–Beliefs–Norms Theory.

Dietz, T., FitzGerald, A., Shwom, R., Environmental values, modified with permission from the Annual Review of Environment and Resources, 30, pp. 335–372 © 2005 by Annual Reviews, http://www.annualreviews.org

such approach is the Values–Beliefs–Norms (VBN) theory (Stern and Dietz 1994; Stern et al. 1999). (VBN theory is very similar to the Advocacy Coalition Framework developed in political science to explain the actions of those active in policy systems (Henry and Dietz 2012).) A stylized version of the VBN theory is sketched in Fig. 16.1.

Given the potential importance of altruism in environmental decision-making, it is not surprising that VBN theory draws heavily on Schwartz's norm activation theory of altruistic behavior. Values are seen as the most stable element in decision-making and thus are usually treated as exogenous to all other social psychological variables in the model. At the next stage are generalized beliefs about the consequences of human actions—beliefs that human actions can and are causing harm to the environment. In many applications of the theory these are captured with a modification of the New Ecological Paradigm scale (Dunlap 2008; Stern et al. 1995a). In some applications, beliefs about specific environmental changes or technologies are measured, such as concern about climate change or perceptions of the risks from nuclear power. In the language of the norm activation model, both generalized beliefs and specific beliefs are measures of awareness of consequences—that human actions may harm the environment leading to deleterious effects on things valued, including the environment itself.

At the next stage in the model are beliefs about actions that might be taken to alleviate harm to the environment. Often this is operationalized as ascription of responsibility for taking action and in particular ascription of responsibility to oneself. However, in the case of environmental problems it may be reasonable to ascribe responsibility to institutional actors such as governments or corporations (Stern et al. 1986). Norms are the last link before decision-making and are usually conceptualized as a personal norm that one should take action as a consumer, as a citizen, and/or as an activist.

Other influences on environmental decisions

Theory of Planned Behavior (TPB)

The Theory of Planned Behavior (TPB) is a commonly used framework for predicting behavior, so it is natural that it would be compared to values and the VBN theory. TPB suggests that behaviors can be predicted by attitudes toward the behavior; perceived social pressure to perform the behavior, which is a form of norm; and perceived ability to perform the behavior, which is a form of locus of control focused on the behavior under consideration and thus closely related to ascription of responsibility (Ajzen 1991, 1985). In application the measures used are very precisely targeted at a specific behavior. In Ajzen's terms, TPB has high fidelity and predictive accuracy (Ajzen 2012). But this at the cost of "bandwidth"—the items used to predict one behavior, say recycling, may have little or no impact on a different behavior, say home weatherization or support for political candidates. In contrast, values have high bandwidth (in that the same values are predictive of a broad suite of behaviors) but have less predictive ability than a group of items designed around a specific behavior. As Ajzen puts it: "General attitudes and values can help explain a broad range of behaviors, but they account for relatively little variance in any one behavior; whereas behavior specific measures of attitudes, subjective norms, perceptions of control, and intentions can explain a great deal of variance, but only for the particular behavior of interest" (Ajzen 2012: 36–37).

Using the TPB to change behavior is likely to influence only the targeted behavior, while appeals to environmental values might impact multiple decisions, although admittedly little is known about "spillover" effects from one environmentally significant action to another (but see Evans et al. 2013; Thøgersen and Crompton 2009; Thøgersen and Ölander 2003, 2006). In any event, the two theories are best seen as complementary rather than as rivals. In a meta-analysis of fifty-six previous studies, Klöckner found support for both theories and for a causal chain linking them (Klöckner 2013). These results lend support to the argument that values have broad bandwidth, and effect environmental decisions primarily through the VBN chain rather than directly.

Post-materialist values

Most work on environmental values has focused on the contrast between self-interest and two forms of altruism, and is thus embedded in Schwartz's continued work on what Rokeach considered "terminal values." (Schwartz does not find the terminal/instrumental distinction useful (Schwartz and Bilsky 1990).) In contrast, Inglehart has drawn on Rokeach's instrumental values and argued that many differences across contemporary societies and within societies over time can be attributed to the difference between materialist and post-materialist values (Inglehart 1977, 1990). Materialist values are measured with items such as "Maintaining order in the nation," "Fighting rising prices," and "Making sure this country has strong defense forces." Post-materialist values are tapped with items such as "Giving people more say in government decisions," "Protecting freedom of speech," and "Trying to make our cities and countryside more beautiful." Inglehart argued that differences in the relative strength of materialist versus post-materialist values drive environmental concerns, which he sees as a post-materialist interest (Inglehart 1995). This logic applies to both the individual—post-materialists will be more likely to make pro-environmental decisions than materialists—and to the national levels—nations with a high proportion of post-materialists will be more likely to make pro-environmental decisions than nations where materialists dominate. His theory is very similar to environmental Kuznets theory in environmental economics (Grossman and Krueger 1995) and ecological modernization theory in environmental sociology (Spaargaren and Mol 1992), both of which argue that increasing affluence leads to increasing concern for the environment (for a comparison of the three theories see Dietz et al. 2010).

As Steg and De Groot (2012: 13) note in reference to Inglehart, these theories imply "that biospheric values will only emerge when basic needs are fulfilled, and that biospheric values are more likely to emerge in Western industrialized societies where affluent levels are high, while poor people can probably not afford to support biospheric values since their basic levels of subsistence are not fulfilled." However, many studies have demonstrated that biospheric values are not rare in developing societies (Schultz and Zelezny 1998, 1999b), a finding contrary to this implication of the modernization theories. In addition, a substantial literature has examined Inglehart's thesis at both the individual and the national levels, and especially with multi-level models that link the individual and national levels (Brechin 2005; Brechin and Kempton 1994; Dunlap and Mertig 1997; Fairbrother 2012; Givens and Jorgenson 2011; Knight and Messer 2012; Marquart-Pyatt 2012, 2013–2014; Stern et al. 1999). The support for the post-materialist thesis in this literature is modest at best.

Identity

Theories of values stretching from Meade and Dewey to Rokeach have emphasized the strong tie between values and personal identity (Hitlin 2011). In turn, identity is a key concept in understanding public support for, and the dynamics of, social movements, including the environmental movement (Dunlap and McCright 2008; McCright and Dunlap 2008, McCright2014). Some work has examined the relationship between values and environmental identity. Schultz has shown a close link between values and feelings of connection with nature (Schultz 2000, 2002; Schultz et al. 2004). In several recent studies, Van der Werff and colleagues (2013a, b, 2014) found that biospheric values were closely linked to identity as an environmentalist. In turn environmentalist identity was a strong predictor of environmental decisions, and when identity was controlled, values had no influence.

How well do values perform?

While there are strong theoretical arguments for values as an important influence on environmental decision-making, how well do they actually perform in explaining behavior? The answer to this question must be somewhat nuanced. Since theorists see values as one of several factors that may influence environmental decisions, it is entirely consistent to view values as important influences and yet to see their effects much reduced when factors more proximate to decision-making are controlled. That is, values are expected to have indirect effects that are mediated by other factors (Grob 1995; Milfont et al. 2010a, b; Vaske and Donnelly 1999). When strong mediating effects are found, it does not imply that values are not important, rather it specifies their impact as indirect, acting through beliefs, norms, and other influences on decision-making. Hansla et al. note that the degree to which other variables alter the effects of values will depend on the environmental decision being considered—the causal model for one environmental issue or type of decision will differ from the causal model from another, even though all may find an important role for values (Hansla et al. 2013). Nonetheless a substantial number of studies find net effects of values even when other social psychological constructs are controlled (reviewed in Steg and De Groot 2012).

A review of both direct and indirect effects of values on decision-making would have to take account of which values are included; what other factors were controlled; what decisions were predicted; whether the dependent variable was a behavioral intention, a self-reported behavior, or an observed behavior; and what populations were sampled. Such a review will be as complex as it is useful and is beyond the scope of this chapter. However, the generality of the theory that argues that values are important implies they will be important in explaining many specific environmental decisions, as well as general environmental concern or willingness to sacrifice. The empirical literature includes evidence for the influence of values on car choice (De Groot and Steg 2010), support for climate policies (Dietz, et al. 2007; Nilsson et al. 2004), donation to environmental organizations (De Groot and Steg 2010; Clements et al. 2015), attitudes about GMO food (Honkanen and Verplanken 2004), household energy use (Poortinga et al. 2004), environmental risk perceptions among citizens and environmental professionals (Slimak and Dietz 2006), support for nuclear power (De Groot et al. 2013, Prati and Zani 2013; Whitfield et al. 2009), purchase of organic foods (Thøgersen 2011), support for reduced street lighting (Boomsa and Steg 2014), choice of a vegetarian diet (Dietz et al. 1995; Kalof et al. 1999), and wildland protection (Vaske and Donnelly 1999), among others. Overall the diversity of environmental issues and decisions examined reinforces the idea that values have broad bandwidth.

In addition to asking how well values predict environmental decisions, it is also reasonable to ask how certain we can be that values are causally prior to decisions and to other social psychological constructs. Most theories that invoke values assume that individual values are more a cause of other variables, including decision-making, than a consequence of them. Put differently, values are expected to be relatively stable over the life course, influenced primarily by socialization and position in the social structure, but influencing other factors such as beliefs, norms, and decisions. This implies that values will be difficult to manipulate in experiments. And since most of the literature is based on cross-sectional samples, most studies have no way to test the assumption that causality runs from values to other influences on decisions and to the decisions themselves. In one of the few panel analyses conducted, Thøgersen and Ölander (2002) demonstrated that causal direction flows from values to environmental behavior, rather than vice versa. Prati and Zani, in a pre-post analysis, argue that the Fukushima nuclear power plant accident led to a small increase in altruism and a larger increase in the New Ecological Paradigm—a measure of beliefs about the fragility of nature (Prati and Zani 2013). These results are consistent with the idea that values are more stable than other aspects of environmental cognition. Several experiments show the ability of values to predict altruistic and self-interested behavior, bolstering the evidence that values have a causal influence in decision-making (Bolderdijk et al. 2013; Sagiv et al. 2010; Schwartz 1996; Verplanken and Holland 2002).

To say that values are relatively stable still allows for framing effects and contextual cues to activate some values over others. When asked to make a quick judgment about something unfamiliar, contextual cues provide a quick link to personal values, which then allow an attitude to be formed (Dietz and Stern 1995; Stern et al. 1995b). The logic is that the values of an individual are not completely labile. But the context can shift somewhat the weight given to one value over another. Howes and Gifford (2009) found that the nature of the decision situation posed can interact with previously measured values and, in particular, strong altruists (measured as Schwartz's universalism) were less influenced by context than others.

Conclusion

Research on environmental values emerged from questions about the relative importance of altruism and self-interest in environmental decision-making, inspired by the literature on commons' dilemmas and collective action. From the start, theorists explored the difference between altruism directed at other humans and altruism directed at other species or the biosphere itself, a distinction that emerged from the literature on environmental ethics. This framework was developed before the move to the Rokeach/Schwartz approach to measuring values. Still, it is not surprising that most of the work on environmental values has drawn heavily on the Rokeach/Schwartz tradition. The rich empirical literature on values measurement, and in particular the emphasis on samples from multiple nations, facilitated methodological progress in measuring environmental values in a fairly robust way. The Schwartz framework needed only slight modification to capture the key dimensions that underpin theoretical thinking about environmental decision-making.

Still, however successful the program of research on environmental values has been to date, there are at least two of areas that warrant further theoretical development and empirical exploration:

- *Measuring behavior and assessing causality.* Relatively few studies in the environmental values literature use measures of actual behavior rather than behavioral intentions or self-reports, and fewer still use panel data that could disentangle causality among the multiple variables invoked by most theories. This limits our ability to advance basic understanding. Given the potential importance of the decisions individuals make as consumers, citizens, and activists, it also squanders opportunities to substantially reduce human impacts on the environment (Dietz et al. 2009). The implementation of policies and programs to reduce environmental impact (for example, by reducing energy and water consumption) provides excellent opportunities for studies that allow strong inference regarding causation. Investment in theoretically driven research to evaluate such programs has the potential to advance basic scientific understanding even as it provides practical information to policy makers.
- *Values and deliberation.* Deliberative processes—the use of structured, open and balanced discussion—have become prominent in environmental decision-making (U.S.

National Research Council 2008). One of the rationales for such processes is that they may allow for reasoned discussion of value differences, aid in identification of differences based on facts versus those based on values, and facilitate compromise and value change (Dietz 2013a, b). But realizing that potential will require a better understanding of how values influence and are influenced by deliberation. A few initial studies are promising starting points, but much further work is needed (Corner et al. 2014 provide a review).

Over the last two decades, substantial progress has been made in understanding how environmental values influence decision-making and ultimately environmentally significant behavior. Much of that progress has come from an interdisciplinary approach, drawing on theoretical arguments from the literature on commons and collective action and on measurement approaches from the study of values in social psychology. Our understanding of values is capable of informing the design of policy and programs to protect the environment. And it will likely advance by continuing to engage with the broader body of scholarship on values within the social sciences and beyond.

Acknowledgements

I thank Riley Dunlap, Linda Kalof, Sandra Marquart-Pyatt, Aaron McCright, Wes Schultz, Linda Steg, and Paul Stern for conversations on these matters; Aaron McCright and Linda Kalof for comments on the draft; and Rachel Kelly for able assistance in preparing the manuscript. My work was supported in part by Michigan AgBio Research. Errors and omissions are of course my responsibility.

References

Ajzen, I. (1985). From intentions to actions: a theory of planned behavior. *In:* Kuhl, J. and Beckmann, J. (eds) *Action Control.* (pp. 11–39) Berlin, Heidelberg: Springer.

Ajzen, I. (1991). The theory of planned behavior. *Organizational Behavior and Human Decision Processes*, **50**, 172–211.

Ajzen, I. (2012). Values, attitudes, and behavior. *In:* Salzborn, S., Davidov, E., and Reinecke, J. (eds) *Methods, Theories, and Empirical Applications in the Social Sciences: Festschrift for Peter Schmidt.* (pp. 13–38) Weisbaden: Springer.

Attari, S. Z. (2014). Perceptions of water use. *Proceedings of the National Academy of Sciences.* **111**, 5129–5134.

Attari, S. Z., Dekay, M. L., Davidson, C. I., and De Bruien, W. B. (2010). Public perceptions of energy consumption and savings. *Proceedings of the National Academy of Sciences, USA*, **107**, 16054–16059.

Barbier, E. B. (2011). Pricing nature. *Annual Review of Resource Economics*, **3**, 337–353.

Becker, G. (1976). Altruism, egoism and genetic fitness: economics and sociobiology. *Journal of Economic Literature*, **14**, 817–826.

Black, J. S., Stern, P. C., and Elsworth, J. T. (1985). Personal and contextual influences on household energy adaptations. *Journal of Applied Psychology*, **70**, 3–21.

Bolderdijk, J. W., Steg, L., Geller, E. S., Lehman, P. K., and Postmes, T. (2013). Comparing the effectiveness of monetary versus moral motives in environmental campaigning. *Nature Climate Change*, **3**, 413–416.

Boomsa, C. and Steg, L. (2014). The effect of information and values on acceptability of reduced street lighting. *Journal of Environmental Psychology*, **39**, 22–31.

Brechin, S. R. (2005). Evaluating the postmaterialist argument and challenging a new explanation. *Sustainability*, **4**, 30.

Brechin, S. R. and Kempton, W. (1994). Global environmentalism: a challenge to the postmaterialism thesis? *Social Science Quarterly*, **75**, 245–269.

Brennan, A. and Lo, Y.-S. (2011). Environmental ethics. *In:* Zalta, E. N. (ed.) *The Stanford Encyclopedia of Philosophy (fall 2011 edition)* http://plato.stanford.edu/archives/fall2011/entries/ethics-environmental/.Date accessed: 12 May 2015.

Caprara, G. V., Schwartz, S., Capanna, C., Vecchione, M., and Barbaranelli, C. (2006). Personality and politics: values, traits, and political choice. *Political Psychology*, **27**, 1–28.

Caprara, G. V., Vecchione, M., and Schwartz, S. H. (2009). Mediational role of values in linking personality traits to political orientation. *Asian Journal of Social Psychology*, **12**, 82–94. DOI: 10.1111/j.1467-1839X.2009.01274.x.

Carrico, A. R., Padgett, P., Vandenbergh, M. P., Gilligan, J., and Wallston, K. A. (2009). Costly myths: an analysis of idling beliefs and behavior in personal motor vehicles *Energy Policy*, **37**, 2881–2888.

Cieciuch, J. and Schwartz, S. H. (2012). The number of distinct basic values and their structure assessed by PVQ-40. *Journal of Personality Assessment*, **94**, 321–328.

Clements, J.M., McCright, A.M., Dietz, T. and Marquart-Pyatt, S.T. (2015) A behavioral measure of environmental decision-making for social surveys. *Environmental Sociology*, **1**, 27–27.

Corner, A., Markowitz, E., and Pidgeon, N. (2014). Public engagement with climate change: the role of human values. *WIREs Climate Change* **5**: 411–422.

De Groot, J. I. M. and Steg, L. (2010). Relationships between value orientations, self-determined motivational types and pro-environmental behavioural intentions. *Journal of Environmental Psychology*, **30**, 368–378.

De Groot, J. I. M., Steg, L., and Poortinga, W. (2013). Values, perceived risks and benefits, and acceptability of nuclear energy. *Risk Analysis*, **33**, 307–317.

Dewey, J. (1939/1988). Theory of Valuation. *Later Works*. Illinois: Carbondale.

Dietz, T. (1994). "What should we do?" Human ecology and collective decision making. *Human Ecology Review*, **1**, 301–309.

Dietz, T. (2005). The Darwinian trope in the drama of the commons: variations on some themes by the Ostroms. *Journal of Economic Behavior and Organization*, **57**, 205–225.

Dietz, T. (2013a). Bringing values and deliberation to science communication. *Proceedings of the National Academy of Sciences*, **110**, 14081–14087.

Dietz, T. (2013b). Epistemology, ontology, and the practice of structural human ecology. *In:* Dietz, T. and Jorgenson, A. K. (eds) *Structural Human Ecology: Essays in Risk, Energy, and Sustainability*. (pp. 31–52) Pullman, Washington: WSU Press.

Dietz, T. (2014). Understanding environmentally significant consumption. *Proceedings of the National Academy of Sciences*, **111**, 5067–5068. DOI: www.pnas.org/cgi/doi/10.1073/pnas.1403169111.

Dietz, T. and Stern, P. C. (1995). Toward a theory of choice: socially embedded preference construction. *Journal of Socio-Economics*, **24**, 261–279.

Dietz, T., Frisch, A. S., Kalof, L., and Guagnano, G. A. (1995). Values and vegetarianism: an exploratory analysis. *Rural Sociology*, **60**, 533–542.

Dietz, T., Ostrom, E., and Stern, P. C. (2003). The struggle to govern the commons. *Science*, **301**, 1907–1912.

Dietz, T., FitzGerald, A., and Shwom, R. (2005). Environmental values. *Annual Review of Environment and Resources*, **30**, 335–372.

Dietz, T., Dan, A., and Shwom, R. (2007). Support for climate change policy: social psychological and social structural influences. *Rural Sociology*, **72**, 185–214.

Dietz, T., Gardner, G. T., Gilligan, J., Stern, P. C., and Vandenbergh, M. P. (2009). Household actions can provide a behavioral wedge to rapidly reduce U.S. carbon emissions. *Proceedings of the National Academy of Sciences*, **106**, 18452–18456.

Dietz, T., Rosa, E. A., and York, R. (2010). Human driving forces of global change: examining current theories. *In:* Rosa, E. A., Diekmann, A., Dietz, T., and Jaeger, C. (eds) *Human Footprints on the Global Environment: Threats to Sustainability*. (pp. 83–134) Cambridge, Massachusetts: MIT Press.

Dirilen-Gümüş, Ö., Cross, S. E., and Dönmez, A. (2012). Who voted for whom? Comparing supporters of Obama and McCain on value types and personality traits. *Journal of Applied Social Psychology*, **42**, 2879–2900.

Dunlap, R. E. (2008). The new environmental paradigm scale: from marginality to worldwide use. *The Journal of Environmental Education*, **40**, 3–18.

Dunlap, R. E. and McCright, A. M. (2008). Social movement identity: validating a measure of identification with the environmental movement. *Social Science Quarterly*, **89**, 1045–1065.

Dunlap, R. E. and Mertig, A. G. (1997). Global environmental concern: an anomoly for postmaterialism. *Social Science Quarterly*, **78**, 24–29.

Dunlap, R. E. and Van Liere, K. D. (1977). Land ethic or golden rule. *Journal of Social Issues*, **33**, 200–207.

Evans, L., Maio, G. R., Corner, A. et al. (2013). Self-interest and pro-environmental behaviour. *Nature Climate Change*, **3**, 122–125.

Fairbrother, M. (2012). Rich people, poor people, and environmental concern: evidence across nations and time. *European Sociological Review*. DOI: 10.1093/esr/jcs068.

Gärling, T., Fujii, S., Gärling, A. and Jakobsson, C. (2003). Moderating effects of social value orientation on determinants of proenvironmental behavior intention. *Journal of Environmental Psychology*, **23**, 1–9.

Givens, J. E. and Jorgenson, A. K. (2011). The effects of affluence, economic development, and environmental degradation on environmental concern: a multilevel analysis. *Organization and Environment*, **24**, 74–91.

Grob, A. (1995). A structural model of environmental attitudes and behavior. *Journal of Environmental Psychology*, **15**, 209–220.

Gromet, D. M., Kunreuther, H., and Larrick, R. P. (2013). Political ideology affects energy efficiency attitudes and choices. *Proceedings of the National Academy of Sciences*, **110**, 9314–9319.

Grossman, G. and Krueger, A. (1995). Economic growth and the environment. *Quarterly Journal of Economics*, **110**, 353–377.

Guagnano, G. A., Stern, P. C., and Dietz, T. (1995). Influences on attitude-behavior relationships: a natural experiment with curbside recycling. *Environment and Behavior*, **27**, 699–718.

Hansla, A., Gärling, T., and Biel, A. (2013). Attitude toward environmental policy measures related to value orientation. *Journal of Applied Social Psychology*, **43**, 582–590.

Heberlein, T. A. (1972). The land ethic realized: some social psychological explanations for changing environmental attitudes. *Journal of Social Issues*, **28**, 79–87.

Heberlein, T. A. (1977). Norm activation and environmental action. *Journal of Social Issues*, **33**, 79–87.

Hechter, M. (1992). Should values be written out of the social scientists' lexicon? *Sociological Theory*, **10**, 214–230.

Henry, A. D. and Dietz, T. (2012). Understanding environmental cognition. *Organization and Environment*, **25**, 238–258.

Hitlin, S. (2011). Values, personal identity, and the moral self. *In:* Schwartz, S. J., Luyclx, K., and Vignoles, V. L. (eds) *Handbook of Identity Theory and Research*. (pp. 515–529) New York: Springer.

Honkanen, P. and Verplanken, B. (2004). Understanding attitudes toward genetically modified food: the role of values and attitude strength. *Journal of Consumer Policy*, **27**, 401–420.

Howes, Y. and Gifford, R. (2009). Stable or dynamic value importance? The interaction between value endorsement level and situational differences on decision-making in environmental issues. *Environment and Behavior*, **41**, 549–582.

Inglehart, R. (1977). *The Silent Revolution: Changing Values and Political Styles among Western Publics.* Princeton, New Jersey: Princeton University Press.

Inglehart, R. (1990). *Culture Shift in Advanced Industrial Society.* Princeton, New Jersey: Princeton University Press.

Inglehart, R. (1995). Public support for environmental protection: objective problems and subjective values in 43 societies. *PS: Political Science and Politics*, **15**, 57–71.

Jaeger, C., Renn, O., Rosa, E. A., and Webler, T. (2001). *Risk, Uncertainly and Rational Action.* London: Earthscan.

Kahneman, D. (2011). *Thinking Fast and Slow.* New York: Farrar, Straus and Giroux.

Kalof, L., Dietz, T., Stern, P. C., and Guagnano, G. A. (1999). Social psychological and structural influences on vegetarian beliefs. *Rural Sociology*, **64**, 500–511.

Kempton, W., Boster, J. S., and Hartley, J. A. (1995). *Environmental Values in American Culture.* Cambridge, Massachusetts: The MIT Press.

Kling, C. L., Phaneuf, D. J., and Zhao, J. (2012). From Exxon to BP: has some number become better than no number? *Journal of Economic Perspectives*, **26**, 3–26.

Klöckner, C. A. (2013). A comprehensive model of the psychology of environmental behaviour—a meta-analysis. *Global Environmental Change*, **23**, 1028–1038.

Knight, K. W. and Messer, B. L. (2012). Environmental concern in cross-national perspective: the effects of affluence, environmental degradation, and world society. *Social Science Quarterly*, **93**, 521–537.

Leopold, A. (1987[1949]). *A Sand County Almanac and Sketches Here and There.* New York: Oxford University Press.

Marquart-Pyatt, S. T. (2012). Contextual influences on environmental concern cross-nationally: a multilevel investigation. *Social Science Research*, **41**, 1085–1099.

Marquart-Pyatt, S. T. (2013–2014). Environmental concern in international and cross-national context: insights and challenges for future research. *International Journal of Sociology*, **43**, 1–36.

McCright, A. M. and Dunlap, R. E. (2008). Social movement identity and belief systems: an examination of beliefs about environmental problems within the American public. *Public Opinion Quarterly*, **72**, 651–676. DOI: 10.1093/poq/nfn051.

McCright, A. M. and Dunlap, R. E. (2010). Anti-reflexivity: the American conservative movement's success in undermining climate science and policy. *Theory, Culture, and Society*, **27**, 100–133.

McCright, A. M. and Dunlap, R. E. (2011). The politicization of climate change and polarization in the American public's views of global warming, 2001–2010. *Sociological Quarterly*, **52**, 155–194.

McCright, A. M. and Dunlap, R. E. (2015). Comparing two measures of social movement identity: the environmental movement as example. *Social Science Quarterly*, in press.

McCright, A. M., Xiao, C. and Dunlap, R. E. (2014). Political polarization on support for government spending on environmental protection in the USA, 1974–2012. *Social Science Research*, **48**, 251–260.

Merchant, C. (1992). *Radical Ecology: The Search for a Liveable World.* New York: Routledge.

Milfont, T. L., Duckitt, J., and Wagner, C. (2010a). A cross-cultural test of the value–attitude–behavior hierarchy. *Journal of Applied Social Psychology*, **40**, 2791–2813. DOI: 10.1111/j.1559-1816.2010.00681.x.

Milfont, T. L., Sibley, C. G., and Duckitt, J. (2010b). Testing the moderating role of the components of norm activation on the relationship between values and environmental behavior. *Journal of Cross-Cultural Psychology*, **41**, 124–131. DOI: 10.1177/0022022109350506.

Nilsson, A., Von Borgstede, C., and Biel, A. (2004). Willingness to accept climate change policy measures: The effect of values and norms. *Journal of Environmental Psychology*, **24**, 267–277.

Ostrom, E. (1990). *Governing the Commons: The Evolution of Institutions for Collective Action.* New York: Cambridge University Press.

Ostrom, E., Dietz, T., Dolsak, N. et al. (eds) (2002). *The Drama of the Commons.* Washington, D.C.: National Academy Press.

Poortinga, W., Steg, L., and Vleck, C. (2004). Values, environmental concern and environmental behavior: a study into household energy use. *Environment and Behavior*, **36**, 70–93.

Prati, G. and Zani, B. (2013). The effect of the Fukushima nuclear accident on risk perception, antinuclear behavioral intentions, attitude, trust, environmental beliefs, and values. *Environment and Behavior*, **45**, 782–798.

Reid, W. V., Mooney, H. A., Cropper, A. et al. (2005). *Ecosystems and Human Well-Being: Synthesis.* Washington, D.C.: Island Press.

Richerson, P. J. and Boyd, R. (2005). *Not by Genes Alone: How Culture Transformed Human Evolution.* Chicago, Illinois: University of Chicago Press.

Rokeach, M. (1968). *Beliefs, Attitudes and Values: A Theory of Organization and Change.* San Francisco: Jossey-Bass.

Rokeach, M. (1973). *The Nature of Human Values.* New York: Free Press.

Rokeach, M. (1979). *Understanding Human Values: Individual and Societal.* New York: The Free Press.

Rosa, E. A., McCright, A., and Renn, O. (2013). *The Risk Society Revisited: Social Theory and Governance.* Philadelphia: Temple University Press.

Sagiv, L., Sverdlik, N., and Schwartz, N. (2010). To compete or to cooperate? Values' impact on perception and action in social dilemma games. *European Journal of Social Psychology*, **41**, 64–77.

Satterfield, T., Slovic, P., and Gregory, R. (2000). Narrative valuation in a policy judgement context. *Ecological Economics*, **34**, 315–331.

Schmuck, P and Schultz, P.W Schultz, P. S.a. P. W. (ed.) *The Psychology of Sustainable Development.* (pp. 61–78) New York: Kluwer.

Schultz, P. W. (2000). Empathizing with nature: the effects of perspective taking of concern for environmental issues. *Journal of Social Issues*, **56**, 391–406.

Schultz, P. W. (2001). The structure of environmental concern: concern for self, other people, and the biosphere. *Journal of Environmental Psychology*, **21**, 327–339.

Schultz, P. W. (2002). Inclusion with nature: the psychology of human-nature relations. *In:*

Schultz, P. W. and Zelezny, L. C. (1998). Values and proenvironmental behavior: a five-country study. *Journal of Cross-Cultural Psychology*, **29**, 540–558.

Schultz, P. W. and Zelezny, L. C. (1999a). Values as predictors of environmental attitudes: evidence for consistency across 14 countries. *Journal of Environmental Pyschology*, **19**, 255–265.

Schultz, P. W. and Zelezny, L. C. (1999b). Values as predictors of environmental attitudes: evidence for consistency across 14 countries. *Journal of Environmental Psychology*, **19**, 255–265.

Schultz, P. W., Shriver, C., Tabanico, J. J., and Khazian, A. M. (2004). Implicit connections with nature. *Journal of Environmental Psychology*, **24**, 31–42.

Schultz, P. W., Gouveia, V. V., Cameron, L. et al. (2005). Values and their relationship to environmental concern and conservation behavior. *Journal of Cross-Cultural Psychology*, **36**, 457–475.

Schwartz, S. H. (1968). Awareness of consequences and the influence of moral norms on interpersonal behavior. *Sociometry*, **31**, 355–369.

Schwartz, S. H. (1977). Normative influences on altruism. *In:* Berkowitz, L. (ed.) *Advances in Experimental Social Psychology.* Advances in Experimental Social Psychology **10**, 221–279.

Schwartz, S. H. (1994). Are there universal aspects in the structure and contents of human values? *Journal of Social Issues*, **50**, 19–45.

Schwartz, S. (1996). Value priorities and behavior: applying a theory of integrated value systems. *In:* Seligman, C., Olson, J. M. and Zanna, M. P. (eds) *The Psychology of Values*. (pp. 1–24) Mahwah, New Jersey: Lawrence Erlbaum Associates.

Schwartz, S. H. and Bardi, A. (2001). Value hierarchies across cultures: taking a similarities perspective. *Journal of Cross-Cultural Psychology*, **32**, 268–290.

Schwartz, S. H. and Bilsky, W. (1987). Toward a universal psychological structure of human values. *Journal of Personality and Social Psychology*, **53**, 550–562.

Schwartz, S. H. and Bilsky, W. (1990). Toward a theory of the universal content and structure of values: extensions and cross-cultural replications. *Journal of Personality and Social Psychology*, **58**, 878–891.

Schwartz, S. H. and Boehnke, K. (2004). Evaluating the structure of human values with confirmatory factor analysis. *Journal of Research in Personality*, **38**, 230–255.

Schwartz, S. H., Caprara, G. V., Vecchione, M. et al. (2013). Basic personal values underlie and give coherence to political values: a cross national study in 15 countries. *Political Behavior*, 1–32. DOI: 10.1007/s11109-11013-9255-z.

Slimak, M. W. and Dietz, T. (2006). Personal values, beliefs and ecological risk perception. *Risk Analysis*, **26**, 1689–1705.

Smith, A. (1976 [1804]). *A Theory of Moral Sentiments*. New York: Oxford University Press.

Sober, E. and Wilson, D. S. (1998). *Unto Others: The Evolution and Psychology of Unselfish Behavior*. Cambridge, Massachusetts: Harvard University Press.

Spaargaren, G. and Mol, A. P. J. (1992). Sociology, environment and modernity: ecological modernization as a theory of social change. *Society and Natural Resources*, **5**, 323–344.

Steg, L. and De Groot, J. I. M. (2012). Environmental values. *In:* Clayton, S. (ed.) *The Oxford Handbook of Environmental and Conservation Psychology*. (pp. 81–92) New York: Oxford University Press.

Steg, L., Perlaviciute, G., Van Der Werff, E., and Lurvink, J. (2014). The significance of hedonic values for environmentally relevant attitudes, preferences, and actions. *Environment and Behavior*, **46**, 163–192.

Stern, P. C. (2000). Toward a coherent theory of environmentally significant behavior. *Journal of Social Issues*, **56**, 407–424.

Stern, P. C. and Dietz, T. (1994). The value basis of environmental concern. *Journal of Social Issues*, **50**, 65–84.

Stern, P. C., Black, J. S., and Elsworth, J. T. (1983). Adaptations to changing energy conditions among Massachusetts households. *Energy*, **12**, 339–353.

Stern, P. C., Dietz, T., and Black, J. S. (1986). Support for environmental protection: the role of moral norms. *Population and Environment*, **8**, 204–222.

Stern, P. C., Dietz, T. and Kalof, L. (1993). Value orientations, gender and environmental concern. *Environment and Behavior*, **25**, 322–348.

Stern, P. C., Dietz, T., and Guagnano, G. A. (1995a). The new environmental paradigm in social psychological perspective. *Environment and Behavior*, **27**, 723–745.

Stern, P. C., Dietz, T., Kalof, L. and Guagnano, G. (1995b). Values, beliefs and proenvironmental action: attitude formation toward emergent attitude objects. *Journal of Applied Social Psychology*, **25**, 1611–1636.

Stern, P. C., Dietz, T. and Guagnano, G. A. (1998). A brief inventory of values. *Educational and Psychological Measurement*, **58**, 884–1001.

Stern, P. C., Dietz, T., Abel, T., Guagnano, G. A., and Kalof, L. (1999). A social psychological theory of support for social movements: the case of environmentalism. *Human Ecology Review*, **6**, 81–97.

Thøgersen, J. (2011). Green shopping: for selfish reasons or the common good? *American Behavioral Scientist*, **55**, 1052–1076.

Thøgersen, J. and Crompton, T. (2009). Simple and painless? The limitations of spillover in environmental campaigning. *Journal of Consumer Policy*, **32**, 141–163.

Thøgersen, J. and Ölander, F. (2002). Human values and the emergence of a sustainable consumption pattern: A panel study. *Journal of Economic Psychology*, **23**, 605–630.

Thøgersen, J. and Ölander, F. (2003). Spillover of environment-friendly consumer behavior. *Journal of Environmental Psychology*, **23**, 225–236.

Thøgersen, J. and Ölander, F. (2006). To what degree are environmentally beneficial choices reflective of a general conservation stance? *Environment and Behavior*, **38**, 550–569.

U.S. National Research Council (1999). *Perspectives on Biodiversity: Valuing Its Role in an Everchanging World.* Washington, D.C.: National Academy Press.

U.S. National Research Council (2008). *Public Participation in Environmental Assessment and Decision Making.* Washington, D.C.: National Academy Press.

Van Der Werff, E., Steg, L. and Keizer, K. (2013a). I am what I am, by looking past the present: the influence of biospheric values and past behavior on environmental self-identity. *Environment and Behavior*, **46**, 626–657.

Van Der Werff, E., Steg, L. and Keizer, K. (2013b). It is a moral issue: the relationship between environmental self-identity, obligation-based intrinsic motivation and pro-environmental behaviour. *Global Environmental Change*, **23**, 1258–1265.

Van Der Werff, E., Steg, L. and Keizer, K. (2013c). The value of environmental self-identity: the relationship between biospheric values, environmental self-identity and environmental preferences, intentions and behaviour. *Journal of Environmental Psychology*, **34**, 55–63.

Van Liere, K. D. and Dunlap, R. E. (1978). Moral norms and environmental behavior: an application of Schwartz's norm-activation model to yard burning. *Journal of Applied Social Psychology*, **8**, 174–188.

Vaske, J. J. and Donnelly, M. (1999). A value-attitude-behavior model predicting wildland preservation voting intentions. *Society and Natural Resources*, **12**, 523–537.

Vecchione, M., Caprara, G., Dentale, F., and Schwartz, S. H. (2013). Voting and values: reciprocal effects over time. *Political Psychology*, **34**, 465–485. DOI: 10.1111/pops.12011.

Vecchione, M., Schwartz, S. H., Caprara, G. V. et al. (2014). Personal values and political activism: a cross-national study. *British Journal of Psychology*, **106**, 84–106.

Verplanken, B. and Holland, R. W. (2002). Motivated decision-making: effects of activation and self-centrality of values on choices and behaviour. *Journal of Personality and Social Psychology*, **82**, 434–447.

Whitfield, S., Rosa, E. A., Dietz, T. and Dan, A. (2009). The future of nuclear power: value orientations and risk perceptions. *Risk Analysis*, **29**, 425–437.

Chapter 17

The place of values in a world of politics: personality, motivation, and ideology

John T. Jost, Elvira Basevich, Eric S. Dickson, and Sharareh Noorbaloochi

"Personal values are the dominating force in life, and all of a person's activity is directed toward the realization of his values. And so the focus for understanding is the other's value-orientation—or, we might say, his philosophy of life."
Gordon Allport (1961: 543)

Introduction

The study of human values as a matter of subjective concern and motivational priority is nearly as old as the science of psychology. Conceptions of value played central roles in the theorizing of Freud (1922), Murray (1938), Newcomb (1943), Maslow (1954), Allport (1961), Kelman (1961), Rokeach (1973), and many of their intellectual descendants (e.g., Braithwaite 1994; Feather 1975; Fiske 1992; Inglehart 1977, 1990; Schwartz 1992; Smith 1969; Tetlock 1986). The fact that these theorists' conceptions bear little resemblance to one another illustrates the depth of the challenges facing social and behavioral scientists who seek empirical traction on questions of value. How many basic or fundamental dimensions of value are there in human affairs, and how do we describe those dimensions? Indeed, we may ask an even more basic question: How should psychologists and others go about developing a general approach to the study of human values, given that individuals, groups, and societies differ—sometimes vastly—in the values they prize?

There are similarly daunting questions of a political or philosophical nature. If it is the case that value pluralism—if not outright conflict—is inevitable, what are the implications for democratic and related forms of governance? How might political institutions be designed so that citizens and policy makers alike will be able to absorb and tolerate ideological and other sources of conflicts without perpetually devolving into stalemate situations? Presumably, a healthy, well-functioning, democratic society needs institutional mechanisms to determine which value priorities should trump others when critical decisions must be made.

Brosch and Sander (2013) have rightly noted that discoveries in neuroscience—especially when it comes to the activation of brain regions such as the ventral striatum, ventromedial prefrontal cortex (VMPFC), and posterior cingulate cortex—may provide the key to understanding the connection between universal and culturally specific values. They hint at the possibility of a "common currency" when it comes to assessing the subjective valuation of very different objects, outcomes, and experiences. At the same time, these authors underscore the notion that neuroscientists, economists, philosophers, and others would do well to integrate research in social, personality, and political psychology. They stress the importance of "core value systems," which are defined as "stable motivational constructs or beliefs about desirable end states that transcend specific situations and guide the selection or evaluation of behaviors and events" (Brosch and Sander 2013: 3). In other words, it will require an ambitious, interdisciplinary effort to "determine the true hierarchy of values," as Friedrich Nietzsche put it. With this chapter, we wish to join that effort, albeit modestly, by seeking to synthesize, from a theoretical point of view, a few key considerations about human values arising from philosophy, psychology, neuroscience, and politics.

Equality vs. tradition: political values as motivated social cognition

Our approach is derived, at least in part, from a general theoretical model of political ideology as motivated social cognition (Jost et al. 2003a, b). This model belongs to a genealogical lineage of "functional" approaches to the study of social and political attitudes. Such approaches assume that individuals hold the beliefs, opinions, and values they do because they address one or more psychological needs or interests, such as those related to self-esteem maintenance, group cohesion, or rationalization of the social order (e.g., Adorno et al. 1950; Allport 1954; Eagly and Chaiken 1993; Katz 1960; Kelman 1961; Smith et al. 1956). This implies a relatively close connection between an individual's *personality*, which Allport (1961) defined as "the dynamic organization within the individual of those psychophysical systems that determine his [or her] characteristic behavior" (p. 28) and beliefs, opinions, and values—that is, the elements of an ideology or "philosophy of life."

The model we espouse takes additional inspiration from Max Weber's theoretical analysis of the "selective process" by which "ideas and their publics . . . find their [elective] affinities" (Gerth and Mills 1948/1970: 63). In other words, people may be said to adopt certain ideas and values because of forces of natural attraction that may be invisible to them, but there is also a reciprocal sense in which a given constellation of ideas and values may "choose" certain individuals and groups rather than others. For example, political discourse that emphasizes certain values may—for social and psychological reasons—fall on deaf ears in some cases but land on especially eager ones in other cases (see also Jost et al. 2009). The analysis by Jost et al. (2003a, b) focused on two core dimensions of value that have distinguished the left and the right since at least the time of the French Revolution, namely *equality* and *tradition* (see also Scheffler 2010). To bring about greater social, economic, and political equality, liberals and leftists have frequently advocated protest and social change (and the upending of traditional arrangements). By contrast, conservatives and rightists in the mold of Edmund Burke (1890) have sought to maintain tradition, and this has often led them to resist social change and to defend existing forms of hierarchy and inequality as necessary or just (see Lipset et al. 1954/1962: 1135).

These political or ideological differences, in turn, are linked to psychological and perhaps even physiological differences. At the level of individual needs and goals, conservatives tend to be more focused on the management of uncertainty and threat, in comparison with liberals (e.g., Jost et al. 2003a, b; Wilson 1973). Presumably, this is because the maintenance of hierarchy and tradition serves the epistemic and existential functions of fostering a subjective sense of certainty, order, safety, and control (see also: Friesen et al. 2014; Hennes et al. 2012). At the level of personality traits, conservatives tend to be more *conscientious* (especially in terms of duty, order, and obligation), whereas liberals tend to be more *open to new experiences* (Carney et al. 2008). Many of these behavioral differences between liberals and conservatives appear to be instantiated at the level of neurocognitive structure and function, especially when it comes to the anterior cingulate cortex and the amygdala (e.g., see Amodio et al. 2007; Kanai et al. 2011). Upon reflection, this fact is less surprising than it might seem at first blush. It is worth recalling Allport's (1961) declaration that the organization of personality is mental *and* physical; it "entails the functioning of both 'mind' and 'body' in some inextricable unity" (p. 28).

Putting all of this together, an "elective affinities" model would suggest that, by dint of nature as well as nurture, individuals develop "pre-political" dispositions, such as general physiological and psychological orientations toward environmental stimuli (such as uncertainty and threat), as well as personality characteristics (such as openness and conscientiousness), and that these, in turn, lead people to gravitate toward ideas of the political left or right, assuming that they are exposed to some fairly wide range of ideological "menu" options (see Jost et al. 2009). However, what is missing from previous treatments of political ideology as motivated social cognition is any satisfying account of the role of *values* in mediating the relationship between personality and ideology. This omission is significant because of the fact that values "function as important guiding principles" that are more general than individual attitudes or evaluations but less abstract than ideologies (Maio et al. 2003: 284). As Higgins (2007) put it, "value is a *motivational* experience," a compelling psychological force that fosters attraction or repulsion (p. 466).

In the remainder of this chapter, we first review several of the most popular taxonomies of values that psychologists have proposed and note that these values have been linked, both theoretically and empirically, to personality characteristics and ideological preferences. Some (but perhaps not all) of the ideological differences that have been observed with respect to the prioritization of values may be understood in terms of our "elective affinities" model of political ideology as motivated social cognition. The possibility that values mediate the relationship between personality and ideology has been touched upon, but not adequately investigated, in the research literature to date. We provide some evidence that helps to fill in existing gaps. Finally, we conclude by pondering a few of the normative implications for political philosophy of pluralistic value conflict that arises, perhaps inevitably, from dispositional and ideological variability.

The nature of human values: taxonomic approaches in psychology

One of the more distinctive aspects of human values is that they carry prescriptive (and proscriptive) force. Thus, we may accept the definition of *value* that Milton Rokeach (1973) offered in *The nature of human values*: "an enduring belief that a specific mode of conduct or end-state of existence is personally or socially preferable to an opposite or converse mode of conduct or end-state of existence" (p. 5). On such a broad definition, there are a great many viable candidates. Henry Murray (1938) generated a list of twenty-eight specific needs, but these can be classified according to six superordinate domains of value (see Table 17.1). Specifically, Murray proposed that people value ambition, information exchange, interpersonal affection, material possessions, power, and status in the eyes of others. Although Murray did not explore the connections between personal values and political life, it is easy to see that different ways of prioritizing these values would be associated with quite different ideological profiles.

Rokeach (1973) introduced a pivotal distinction between instrumental values, which pertain to "desirable modes of conduct," and terminal values, which pertain to "desirable end-states of existence." He identified numerous examples of both types of values (see Table 17.2). For the most part, instrumental values are personal in nature and largely confined to what philosophers would describe as the "private" domain (e.g., Nagel 1991; Scanlon 1998). By comparison, many of Rokeach's terminal values are social or collective in nature, and their significance is frequently debated in public discourse. Insofar as political ideologies

Table 17.1 Henry Murray's (1938) taxonomy of human needs and values

	Achievement, Accomplishment
Ambition	Exhibition, Impress Others, Recognition
Information Exchange	Cognizance, Understanding, Exposition, Sentience, Experience
Interpersonal Affection	Affiliation, Loyalty, Being Loved, Consoled, Nurturing Others, Rejection, Distancing, Sexual Gratification
Materialism	Acquisition, Possession, Construction, Creation, Order, Organization, Retention
Power	Abasement, Surrender, Aggression, Revenge, Autonomy, Independence, Avoidance of Blame, Deference, Admiration, Dominance, Control, Harm Avoidance, Humiliation, Avoidance, Opposition, Contrariance
Status Defense	Counteraction, Persistence, Concealing Shortcomings, Explanation, Excuse

Data from *Explorations in personality* by Henry A. Murray, Oxford University Press, USA, 1938.

specify "the proper goals of society and how they should be achieved" (Tedin 1987: 65), they should be linked intimately to the endorsement of specific terminal values. Rokeach was especially driven to understand ideological differences in value priorities, and came to emphasize two values in particular: *equality* and *freedom*. He suggested that the four major social systems of the twentieth century—and their ideological underpinnings—could be understood in terms of the values they placed on freedom and equality.

Specifically, Rokeach argued that Capitalists value freedom but not equality; Communists value equality but not freedom; Liberal Socialists value both; and Fascists value neither freedom nor equality. Thus, ideologues tend to prioritize values that are consistent with the social systems they hold out as ideal, and they deprioritize values that are inconsistent with those social systems. It is perhaps worthy of note that—more than forty years ago—Rokeach (1973: 83–85) observed little or no disagreement among Democrats, Republicans, and Independents in the U.S. with respect to the perceived importance of freedom, equality, and other terminal values. He did find, however, that supporters of John F. Kennedy and Lyndon Johnson in the 1968 primary election were quite a bit more likely to prioritize equality than were supporters of Richard Nixon, Ronald Reagan, or George Wallace. Rokeach observed no partisan or ideological differences when it came to the prioritization of freedom. From our point of view, it is a significant omission that Rokeach failed to explore left–right differences in the prioritization of tradition.

Cochrane, Billig, and Hogg (1979) conducted an empirical investigation of Rokeach's framework in the context of Great Britain. They surveyed residents of working-class and middle-class neighborhoods and reported that—much as Rokeach supposed—supporters of Labour (Socialist) and Communist parties placed a very high priority on equality, whereas supporters of Tory (Conservative) and National Front (Fascist) parties did not. At the same time, there was relatively little ideological variability in the value ostensibly placed on freedom. Cochrane and colleagues argued that this was because Communists and Fascists tended to endorse the value of freedom at an abstract level but subscribed to quite divergent conceptions of freedom at a concrete level. This result is consistent with philosophical observations that there are often widely divergent interpretations of the *same* political value—as illustrated, for instance, in debates over competing conceptions of freedom (e.g.,

Table 17.2 Milton Rokeach's (1973) taxonomy of instrumental and terminal values

Instrumental Values	Ambitious, Broadminded, Capable, Cheerful, Clean, Courageous, Forgiving, Helpful, Honest, Imaginative, Independent, Intellectual, Logical, Loving, Obedient, Polite, Responsible, Self-Controlled
Terminal Values	A comfortable life, An exciting life, A sense of accomplishment, A world at peace, A world of beauty, Equality, Family security, Freedom, Happiness, Inner harmony, Mature love, National security, Pleasure, Salvation, Self-respect, Social recognition, True friendship, Wisdom

Data from Milton Rokeach, *The nature of human values,* Free Press, New York, 1973.

Berlin 1958/1969; Nozick 1974/2001; Rawls 1971/1999) and equality (e.g., Nagel 1991; Pojman and Westmoreland 1997).

The study by Cochrane and colleagues was useful also because it revealed that leftists (Socialists and Communists) were more likely than rightists (Conservatives and Fascists) to prioritize "a world at peace," whereas rightists were slightly more likely than leftists to prioritize personal happiness and family security. These results have been replicated and extended in a number of ways, as we will show. To distill a core set of human value priorities that have been theorized—and, indeed, observed—to distinguish the priorities of liberals (or leftists) and conservatives (or rightists), we have summarized in Table 17.3 the values that have figured most prominently in research bearing on political psychology. The result is a fairly long (and only partially overlapping) list of values that appear to share some degree of affinity with ideological preferences for the left or the right.

Braithwaite (1994) proposed another two-dimensional model of political values that she regarded as similar to—but perhaps broader than—Rokeach's (1973) model, which focused on freedom and equality. In studies involving Australian respondents, Braithwaite (1997, 1998) observed that the endorsement of values pertaining to *security*—including the prioritization of social order, national strength, propriety in dress and manners, and desire for social standing—was associated with conservative attitudes, an unwillingness to engage in protest, and a tendency to vote for rightist political parties. By contrast, the endorsement of values pertaining to *harmony*—including the prioritization of equality, a world at peace, humanism, and personal growth and expression—was associated with liberal attitudes, willingness to protest, and a tendency to vote for leftist political parties. From the perspective of political psychology, these are important observations, insofar as they help to flesh out the goals and motives of leftists and rightists. At the same time, it is not entirely clear that "propriety in dress and manners" and the "desire for social standing" are related to "security" concerns in the same sense that social order and national strength are. Likewise, the valuation of "personal growth and expression" may pertain to intrapersonal harmony, whereas commitments to peace and equality may have more to do with interpersonal and intergroup harmony. Given that these various concerns are clearly distinguished in other taxonomies—such as those of Murray (1938) and Rokeach (1973)—we suggest that there may be some utility in treating them as separate or independent values (see Table 17.3).

Tetlock (1986) proposed a "value pluralism model" of ideological reasoning that, like Braithwaite's (1994) model, drew heavily upon Rokeach's (1973) work. Tetlock argued that an individual's ideology reflects priorities among various terminal values, such as freedom, equality, national security, economic prosperity, personal privacy, and environmental protection. Clearly, liberals (or leftists) and conservatives (or rightists) disagree when it comes to reconciling different values and resolving potential conflicts or tradeoffs among them. Conservatives are, generally speaking, more likely than liberals to opt for economic prosperity over environmental protection and national security over civil liberties, whereas liberals are more likely than conservatives to choose equality and environmental sustainability over personal comfort and prosperity (e.g., Davis and Silver 2004; Jacquet et al.

Table 17.3 Human values associated with liberal (or leftist) and conservative (or rightist) political orientation

Liberal/Leftist	**Conservative/Rightist**
Equality [1, 2, 3, 4, 11, 15]	Personal Happiness [2]
A World at Peace [2, 3]	Family Security [2]
Harmony (Humanism, Personal Growth) [3]	Security (Social Order, National Strength) [3, 4, 5, 7 8, 9, 10]
Environmental Protection [4]	Economic Prosperity [4]
Universalism [5, 6, 7, 8, 9, 10]	Conformity [5, 6, 7, 8, 9, 10]
Benevolence [7, 8, 9, 10]	Traditionalism (Resistance to Change) [6, 7, 8, 9, 10, 11, 15]
Self-Direction [7, 8, 9]	Power [5, 6, 7, 8, 9, 10]
Social Change (Progress, Innovation) [11, 15]	Achievement [7, 8, 9]
Fairness (Social Justice) [12, 13]	Hierarchy (Inequality) [11, 15]
Harm Avoidance [12, 13]	Obedience to Authority [12, 13]
Prosociality (Cooperation) [14]	Ingroup Loyalty [12, 13]
	Purity (Divinity) [12, 13]
	Competition [14]
	Individualism (Self-Interest) [14]

Sources: [1] Rokeach (1973); [2] Cochrane et al. (1979); [3] Braithwaite (1994); [4] Tetlock (1986); [5] Devos et al. (2002); [6] Jost and Gosling (unpublished data, 2013); [7] Caprara et al. (2006); [8] Schwartz et al. (2010); [9] Vecchione et al. (2013); [10] Piurko et al. (2011); [11] Jost et al. (2003); [12] Graham et al. (2009); [13] Kugler et al. (2014); [14] Van Lange et al. (2011); [15] Kandler et al. (2012).

2014; Napier and Jost 2008; Swami et al. 2012). For instance, a study of 249 Chief Executive Officers in the United States revealed that—in good economic times as well as bad—corporations led by liberals were more likely than those led by conservatives to engage in voluntary forms of corporate social responsibility with respect to human rights, environmental sustainability, employee relations, product quality, diversity initiatives, and community support (Chin et al. 2013).

An additional implication of Tetlock's model is that adherents of liberal and moderate ideologies—who tend to regard all of the values we have mentioned thus far (including freedom and equality) as at least somewhat important—are more likely to engage in integrative complexity and to be open to potential tradeoffs among these values, in comparison with adherents of illiberal or absolutist ideologies of the extreme left or right. The research literature as a whole suggests that there are indeed two distinct effects that are present in combination (Jost et al. 2003b). First, there is a linear tendency for liberals (or leftists) to score higher than conservatives (or rightists) on measures of cognitive complexity. Second, there is also a nonlinear tendency for moderates to be higher in cognitive complexity than extremists of the left and right. Thus, a textual analysis of speeches made by members of the British House of Commons demonstrated that the most complex rhetoric was offered by moderate socialists, who were significantly more complex than extreme socialists, moderate conservatives, and extreme conservatives—who were lowest in integrative complexity (Tetlock 1984).

Haidt and Graham (2007) adopt the language of "moral foundations" rather than "values" to underscore what they deem to be the *evolutionary* origins of moral intuitions or preferences (see Suhler and Churchland 2011, for a critique of their evolutionary assumptions). Nevertheless, what this research program documents is liberal–conservative divergence in the subjective prioritization of five values. More specifically, Graham, Haidt, and Nosek (2009) demonstrated that liberals place greater subjective value than conservatives on issues of *fairness* and the *avoidance of harm*, whereas conservatives place greater subjective value than liberals on *ingroup loyalty, obedience to authority*, and *purity* (or *divinity*). Moral foundations theorists refer to the former set of values as "individualizing foundations" and the latter as "binding foundations." Janoff-Bulman and Carnes (2013) pointed out that this distinction is potentially misleading insofar as fairness and harm concerns apply just as well to groups and communities as to individuals. In any case, subsequent work has confirmed that ideological cleavages do indeed exist with respect to the endorsement of these specific values but suggests that—consistent with the analysis of political ideology as motivated social cognition (Jost et al. 2003a, b)—these cleavages may be attributable to differences in personality characteristics such as "right-wing authoritarianism" and "social dominance orientation" (Federico et al. 2013; Kugler et al. 2014; Milojev et al. 2014), which are themselves linked to underlying motivational structures associated with needs to reduce uncertainty and threat (Duckitt and Sibley 2009; Jost et al. 2003a; Van Leeuwen and Park 2009).

Studies of "social value orientation" distinguish between three types of value orientations that have implications for the allocation of resources and behavior in mixed motive games (that is, games that have both cooperative and competitive elements). Actors with a "prosocial" orientation enhance others' outcomes as well as their own (and maintain relative equality), whereas actors with an "individualistic" orientation enhance their own outcomes and appear to be indifferent to others' outcomes, and actors with a "competitive" orientation seek to increase the difference between their own outcomes and those of others. Casting further doubt on Graham et al.'s (2009) notion that liberals embrace "individualizing" foundations for morality, a series of studies conducted in Italy and the Netherlands demonstrated that conservatives were more likely than liberals to adopt *competitive* and *individualistic* value orientations, whereas liberals were more likely than conservatives to adopt a *prosocial* value orientation (Van Lange et al. 2012).

In social and personality psychology today, the dominant taxonomic approach to human values is that of Shalom Schwartz (1992, 2012, this volume, ch. 4; see also: Brosch and Sander 2013). It identifies ten themes (or values) that are said to be culturally universal and that individuals draw from in constructing their own personal hierarchies of values, namely: power, achievement, hedonism, stimulation, self-direction, universalism, benevolence, tradition, conformity, and security. The ten values are organized according to a spatial scheme that revolves around two axes (or dimensions), which are referred to as openness to change (stimulation, self-direction) versus conservation (conformity, security, and tradition) and self-transcendence (universalism, benevolence) vs. self-enhancement (power, achievement, hedonism; see fig. 1 in

Schwartz, this volume, ch. 4). Schwartz (2012) notes that: "the circular arrangement of the values represents a motivational continuum. The closer any two values in either direction around the circle, the more similar their underlying motivations; the more distant, the more antagonistic their motivations" (p. 10). For instance, a motivational commitment to universalism facilitates neighboring values such as self-direction and benevolence, whereas a motivational commitment to conformity facilitates values such as tradition and security. This formulation, which emphasizes the conflicting nature of opposing values, renders Schwartz's taxonomy of human values highly pertinent to the study of personality and political ideology and especially the relationship between personality and ideology (see also: Feldman 2003).

Personality differences in value priorities and political ideology

In recent decades, the most prominent model of personality characteristics has emphasized five major factors (or dimensions), namely: Openness to New Experiences, Conscientiousness, Extraversion, Agreeableness, and Neuroticism (or Emotional Stability). These five emerge consistently as independent, non-overlapping factors used in judgments of self- and other-related personality characteristics in studies carried out over several decades in a wide variety of languages and cultural contexts (McCrae and Costa 1999). To elucidate the relationship between individual differences in personality and personal values, researchers have often explored the correlations between "Big Five" traits and the prioritization of Schwartz's ten values.

For instance, Roccas, Sagiv, Schwartz, and Knafo (2002) conducted a study involving 246 university students in Israel and observed that, as hypothesized, Openness was positively associated with universalism, self-direction, and stimulation but negatively associated with security, conformity, and tradition. They also found that Conscientiousness was positively associated with achievement and conformity, whereas Agreeableness was positively associated with benevolence, conformity, and tradition and negatively associated with power. Extraversion was positively associated with hedonism, stimulation, and achievement, and negatively associated with conformity and tradition. Emotional stability was unrelated to value prioritization. A cumulative, meta-analytic synthesis of more than fifty studies reproduced—to a remarkably high degree—these same patterns of association between Big Five personality characteristics and Schwartz's value priorities (Parks-Leduc et al. 2014: 12–14).

Openness and Conscientiousness are the two "Big Five" personality dimensions that are most strongly correlated with political ideology. More specifically, Openness is positively associated with liberalism, whereas Conscientiousness (especially the facet of orderliness) is positively associated with conservatism (e.g., Carney et al. 2008). With respect to Agreeableness, one facet (compassion) seems to be associated with liberalism and egalitarianism, whereas another facet (politeness) is associated with conservatism and traditionalism (Hirsh et al. 2010). Studies conducted in Italy suggest a correlation between Extraversion (or perhaps "Energy") and right-wing orientation (Caprara et al. 1999), but no consistent correlation between Extraversion and ideology has been observed in the U.S. (e.g., Carney et al. 2008; Gerber et al. 2010; Mondak 2010).

Taken as a whole, the evidence linking specific personality characteristics to the endorsement of values and ideologies is highly consistent with an "elective affinities" framework, which suggests that—for both situational and dispositional reasons—people are drawn to beliefs, opinions, and values that fit with their particular psychological needs and proclivities. Or, as Adorno et al. (1950) put it, "The individual's pattern of thought, whatever its content, reflects his personality and is not merely an aggregate of opinions picked up helter-skelter from the ideological environment" (p. 176).

Ideological differences in value priorities

The research literature also reveals that there is a remarkable degree of stability and consistency when it comes to correlations between the endorsement of values identified by Schwartz (1992) and left–right ideological preferences. For instance, a study of 265 university students in Switzerland found that supporters of rightist political parties in 1996 were more likely to endorse values of *conformity, security*, and *power*, whereas supporters of leftist political parties were more likely to endorse the value of *universalism* (Devos et al. 2002). Seventeen years later and five thousand miles away, we observed similar results in a sample of 259 American-born students at the University of Texas in 2013. Students who identified themselves as more conservative prioritized *conformity* ($r = 0.31$), *tradition* ($r = 0.40$), *achievement* ($r = 0.13$), and *power* ($r = 0.12$), whereas those who identified themselves as more liberal prioritized *universalism* ($r = 0.29$) and *self-direction* ($r = 0.12$).

Nearly identical results have been obtained with adult samples from many other countries. For example, a series of studies involving fairly large samples of Italian adults who were surveyed prior to the holding of national elections in 2001, 2006, and 2008 demonstrated that supporters of rightist political parties were more likely than others to endorse values of *conformity, security, tradition, power*, and (to a weaker extent) *achievement*, whereas supporters of leftist political parties were more likely than others to endorse values of *universalism, benevolence*, and *self-direction* (Caprara et al. 2006; Schwartz et al. 2010; Vecchione et al. 2013).

In an even more comprehensive investigation involving nationally representative samples from twenty countries included in the 2002–03 European Social Survey, right-wing ideological self-placement was associated (with few exceptions) with the endorsement of *conformity, security, tradition*, and *power* in at least fourteen countries, namely: Austria, Belgium, Denmark, Finland, France, Germany, Greece, Ireland, Israel, Netherlands, Portugal, Spain, Switzerland, and the United Kingdom. Furthermore, left-wing ideological self-placement was associated with the endorsement of *universalism* and (to a lesser extent) *benevolence* in nearly all of these countries (Piurko et al. 2011).[1]

[1] Notable exceptions to these patterns emerged in post-Communist countries. In Hungary, Poland, and Slovenia, right-wing orientation was associated with the endorsement of tradition, but there were no other stable correspondences between political orientation and value priorities (see also Thorisdottir, Jost, Liviatan, and Shrout, 2007).

These findings from North America, Western Europe, and Israel are readily interpretable in terms of Jost et al.'s (2003a, b) framework for understanding political ideology as a case of motivated social cognition. Insofar as leftists are motivated to push for social change in order to achieve greater social, economic, and political equality, it follows that they would deprioritize tradition, conformity, and power while prioritizing the values of universalism and benevolence. Likewise, to the extent that rightists are motivated to maintain the status quo—even if doing so entails defending existing forms of hierarchy and inequality, they should deprioritize universalism and benevolence while prioritizing tradition, conformity, security, and power.

Consistent with our analysis in terms of core dimensions of left–right ideology, Schwartz et al. (2010) observed, in research conducted in Italy, that the prioritization of conformity, security, and tradition was positively associated with *resistance to change* (e.g., traditional morality, support for law and order, rejection of immigrants) and *acceptance of inequality* (e.g., support for free enterprise, rejection of civil liberties) and that—through statistical tests of mediation—these associations helped to explain *why* conformity, security, and tradition were associated with right-wing orientation. By the same token, the prioritization of universalism, benevolence, and self-direction was associated with openness to social change (e.g., support for immigration, decreased commitment to law and order and traditional forms of morality) and a rejection of inequality (e.g., support for equality and civil liberties, skepticism about free enterprise), and this helped to explain why universalism, benevolence, and self-direction were associated with a left-wing orientation.

In an even more direct exploration of these same underlying ideological patterns, Aspelund, Lindeman, and Verkasalo (2013) analyzed public opinion data from fifteen Western European and thirteen Central/Eastern European countries included in the European Social Survey in 2006 and 2008. They observed that *resistance to change* was significantly correlated with right-wing orientation in *all* of the Western European countries they investigated, namely: Austria, Belgium, Denmark, Finland, France, Germany, Greece, Ireland, Netherlands, Norway, Portugal, Spain, Sweden, Switzerland, and the U.K. Furthermore, *acceptance of inequality* was significantly correlated with right-wing orientation in thirteen of these fifteen countries; the only exceptions were Ireland and Portugal. The results from Western Europe, then, were extraordinarily supportive of Jost et al.'s (2003a, b) analysis.

At the same time, there was no discernable pattern in the data from Central and Eastern European countries. In three of these countries (Croatia, Poland, and Slovekia) there was a positive correlation between resistance to change and right-wing orientation, but in five others (Bulgaria, Czech Republic, Estonia, Romania, Slovakia) there was a negative correlation—suggesting that some citizens in these countries may have maintained a nostalgic connection to the socialist system prior to the 1990s (see also: Cichocka and Jost 2014). No correlation was observed between resistance to change and political orientation in the other five countries. Acceptance of inequality was positively correlated with right-wing orientation in seven of the Central/Eastern European countries, namely Bulgaria, Czech Republic, Hungary, Russia, Slovakia, Slovenia, and Ukraine. The correlation was reversed in three countries (Latvia, Lithuania, and Poland) and non-significant in three others (Croatia, Estonia, and Romania).

Taken as a whole, these results suggest that the "elective affinities" model applies better to Western-style democracies in which citizens have been relatively free—historically speaking—to "choose" parties and candidates that match their psychological needs, interests, and motives, as opposed to other forms of government where menu options are (or until fairly recently were) highly constrained by the social and political system. But where do these needs, interests, and motives come from in the first place? In an effort to disentangle the effects of genetic heritability and political socialization on personality, resistance to change, acceptance of inequality, and left–right political orientation, Kandler, Bleidorn, and Riemann (2012) used an extended twin family design involving nearly 2,000 German citizens, including 224 monozygotic and 166 dizygotic twin pairs, 92 unmatched twins, 530 spouses of twins, and 590 parents of twins. Consistent with the theoretical model proposed by Jost et al. (2003a, b), the research team observed that individuals' scores on the two subscales used to measure resistance to change and acceptance of inequality were positively inter-correlated and that each of the two subscale scores were indeed associated with left–right orientation.

More importantly, Kandler et al. (2012) discovered that—with respect to both resistance to change and acceptance of inequality—correlations between monozygotic twins exceeded correlations between dizygotic twins, indicating the presence of genetic influences on values and ideology. A significant proportion of the genetic variance was attributable to the heritability of general personal traits, such as those identified with the Five-Factor model of personality. In addition, the researchers observed that dizygotic twin correlations were greater than parent–offspring correlations, suggesting either shared environmental effects or non-additive genetic effects. Finally, positive correlations between spouses with respect to traditionalism (or resistance to change) revealed that people seemed to be engaged in non-random, assortative mating behavior. Kandler and colleagues concluded that:

> The presence of genetic variance in political dimensions indicates that people choose different political positions at least partly on the basis of their genetic makeup. In addition, the presence of genotypic assortative mating as a special form of gene–environment correlation (spouses can be considered a social environment factor) indicates that genetic factors also contribute to the likely reciprocal effect in which political positions "choose" people (Jost et al. 2009). That is, people who choose a specific political position also choose partners with similar attitudes, who in turn could further intensify or deepen these particular attitudes.
>
> (Kandler et al. 2012: 639–640)

In summary, then, it appears that there are both "top-down" political, cultural, and interpersonal processes as well as "bottom-up" genetic and personality predispositions that together shape the individual's political orientation as well as his or her prioritization of potentially conflicting political values such as tradition vs. progress and equality vs. hierarchy.

Putting it all together: do values mediate the effects of personality on ideology, and does ideology mediate the effects of personality on values?

As Hochschild (2001) pointed out, there are at least two different ways of conceptualizing values, and these have theoretical and practical implications for how to understand the role of values in relation to other constructs of interest, such as personality characteristics and political ideology. On one hand, values may be treated as "deep-seated predispositions or fundamental constructs that stem from childhood socialization, community ties or searing personal experiences" (pp. 321–322). On the other hand, values may also be conceptualized as "broad statements of principle—often mutually contradictory—about how to prioritize interests" (p. 322). The former conceptualization would suggest that values mediate the effects of personality characteristics on political ideology, whereas the latter conceptualization might suggest that ideology would mediate the effects of personality on value priorities. We considered both possibilities in constructing path models using data obtained from a sample of 259 University of Texas undergraduates (mentioned previously).

In Model 1, we investigated the direct and indirect effects of the "Big Five" personality characteristics on political ideology, with value priorities entered as potential mediators. After trimming non-significant paths ($p > 0.1$) from the original (i.e., saturated) model, the resulting model exhibited good fit (X^2 (26) = 29.32, $p = 0.29$, CFI = 0.99, TLI = 0.98, RMSEA = 0.02, SRMR = 0.032). This model is illustrated in Fig. 17.1; covariance arrows are omitted for the sake of visual clarity. Most of the correlations between personality characteristics and value priorities (and between value priorities and political ideology) that were anticipated on the basis of past research were indeed observed. Direct and indirect (i.e., mediated) effects are listed in Table 17.4. We see that the relationship between Openness to New Experiences and political liberalism was mediated by universalism, conformity, and achievement. That is, students who were more open-minded tended to value universalism and to devalue conformity and achievement, and these axiological priorities helped to explain (in a statistical sense) why they were more liberal. In addition, those who were more Extraverted tended to devalue universalism and to value achievement, and these priorities partially explained why they tended to be more conservative in this sample (see also: Caprara et al. 1999). The effect of Agreeableness on political ideology was mediated by values in a fairly complex manner, consistent with the findings of Hirsh et al. (2010). More agreeable students tended to prioritize universalism, which was associated with greater liberalism, but they also prioritized conformity and tradition, both of which were associated with greater conservatism. Thus, we obtained evidence that values mediated at least some of the effects of personality characteristics on political ideology.

In Model 2, we investigated the effects of the "Big Five" personality characteristics on value priorities, with political ideology entered as a potential mediator. After trimming non-significant paths, the model illustrated in Fig. 17.2 exhibited good fit (X^2 (2) = 0.12, $p = 0.94$, CFI = 1.00, TLI = 1.135, RMSEA = 0.00, SRMR = 0.002). Direct and indirect

Table 17.4 Direct and indirect effects of "big five" personality characteristics on political ideology

	Universalism		Stimulation		Self-direction		Benevolence		Conformity	
Direct Effects	***b***	***β***	***b***	***β***	***b***	***β***	***b***	***β***	***b***	***β***
Openness → Value	.27**	.15**	.31**	.15**	.72***	.42***	—	—	–.42***	–.21***
Conscientiousness → Value	—	—	–.35**	–.19**	—	—	–.21**	–.14**	—	—
Extraversion → Value	–.16†	–.13†	.50***	.33***	—	—	.15*	.12*	.11	.08
Agreeableness → Value	.35***	.22***	—	—	—	—	.84***	.55***	.68***	.38***
Neuroticism → Value	—	—	–.26**	–.16**	—	—	.22**	.17**	.17†	.12†
Openness → Liberalism	.00	.00	.00	.00	.00	.00	.00	.00	.00	.00
Conscientiousness → Liberalism	–.02	–.01	–.02	–.01	–.02	–.01	–.02	–.01	–.02	–.01
Extraversion → Liberalism	–.18*	–.15*	–.18*	–.15*	–.18*	–.15*	–.18*	–.15*	–.18*	–.15*
Agreeableness → Liberalism	–.10	–.07	–.10	–.07	–.10	–.07	–.10	–.07	–.10	–.07
Neuroticism → Liberalism	.08	.06	.08	.06	.08	.06	.08	.06	.08	.06
Value → Liberalism	.28***	.29***	.04	.04	.05	.05	–.06	–.06	–.09†	–.11†
Indirect Effects										
Openness → Value → Liberalism	**{0.029, 0.135}**		{–0.015, 0.049}		{–0.039, 0.111}		—		**{0.008, 0.088}**	
Conscientiousness → Value → Liberalism	—		{–0.056, 0.016}		—		{–0.012, 0.044}		—	
Extraversion → Value → Liberalism	**{–0.093, –0.007}**		{–0.031, 0.067}		—		{–0.040, 0.006}		{–0.038, 0.001}	
Agreeableness → Value → Liberalism	**{0.052, 0.163}**		—		—		{–0.148, 0.061}		**{–0.133,–0.010}**	
Neuroticism → Value → Liberalism	—		{–0.039, 0.012}		—		{–0.048, 0.010}		**{–0.050,–0.001}**	
R^2	8.4%		20.3%		17.4%		26.3%		17.0%	

Table 17.4 (continued) Direct and indirect effects of "big five" personality characteristics on political ideology

	Tradition		Security		Power		Achievement		Hedonism	
Direct Effects	***b***	***β***	***b***	***β***	***b***	***β***	***b***	***β***	***b***	***β***
Openness → Value	—	—	—	—	—	—	−.39***	−.19**	—	—
Conscientiousness → Value	—	—	.91***	.44***	—	—	—	—	−.40***	−.23***
Extraversion → Value	—	—	—	—	.61***	.36***	.27**	.18**	.49***	.33***
Agreeableness → Value	.66***	.24***	—	—	−.56***	−.27***	—	—	—	—
Neuroticism → Value	—	—	—	—	—	—	—	—	—	—
Openness → Liberalism	.00	.00	.00	.00	.00	.00	.00	.00	.00	.00
Conscientiousness → Liberalism	−.02	−.01	−.02	−.01	−.02	−.01	−.02	−.01	−.02	−.01
Extraversion → Liberalism	−.18*	−.15*	−.18*	−.15*	−.18*	−.15*	−.18*	−.15*	−.18*	−.15*
Agreeableness → Liberalism	−.10	−.07	−.10	−.07	−.10	−.07	−.10	−.07	−.10	−.07
Neuroticism → Liberalism	.08	.06	.08	.06	.08	.06	.08	.06	.08	.06
Value → Liberalism	−.17***	−.30***	.02	.02	.02	.02	−.14**	−.17**	.01	.01
Indirect Effects										
Openness → Value→ Liberalism	—		—		—		{0.019, 0.106}		—	
Conscientiousness → Value→ iberalism	—		{−0.061, 0.094}		—		—		{−0.042, 0.031}	
Extraversion → Value→ Liberalism	—		—		{−0.038, 0.057}		{−0.077,−0.012}		{−0.038, 0.049}	
Agreeableness → Value→ Liberalism	{−0.187, −0.056}		—		{−0.054, 0.035}		—		—	
Neuroticism → Value→ Liberalism	—		—		—		—		—	
R^2	5.5%		19.7%		17.9%		6.2%		13.2%	

Note. R^2 signifies the proportion of variance in endorsement of Schwartz' values explained by the trimmed model.

The model explains 31.3% of variance observed in political ideology.

†$p<.1$, *$p<.05$, **$p<.01$, ***$p<.001$

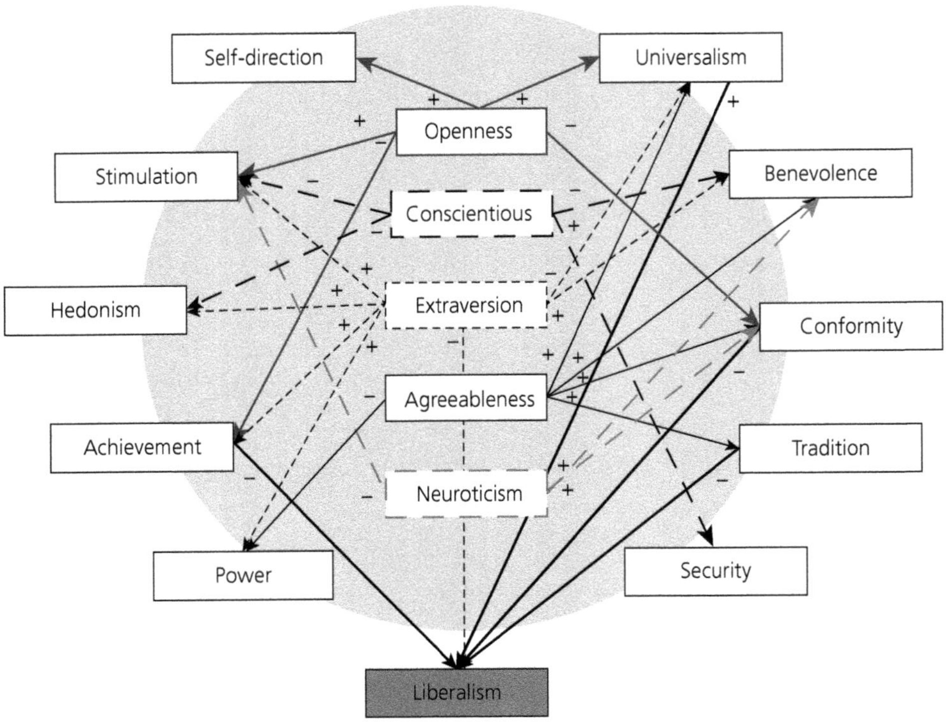

Fig. 17.1 Path model illustrating the direct and indirect effects of "big five" personality characteristics on political ideology. (See Plate 10.)

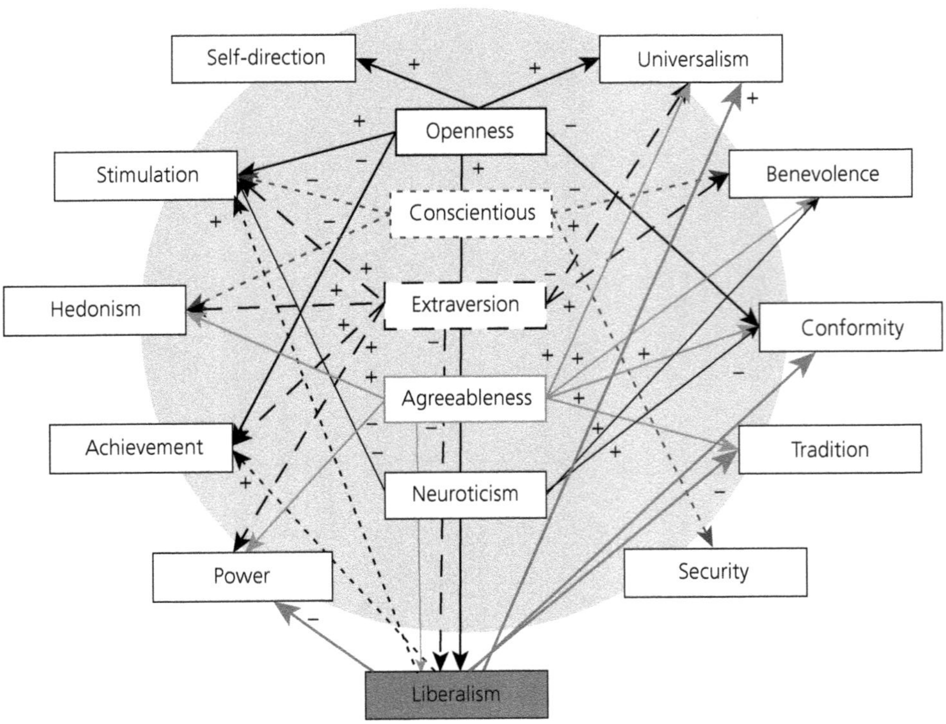

Fig. 17.2 Path model illustrating the direct and indirect effects of "big five" personality characteristics on political orientation and value endorsement. (See Plate 11.)

Table 17.5 Direct and indirect effects of "big five" personality characteristics on political ideology

	Universalism		Stimulation		Self–direction		Benevolence		Conformity	
Direct Effects	***b***	***β***	***b***	***β***	***b***	***β***	***b***	***β***	***b***	***β***
Openness → Liberalism	.25**	.15**	.25**	.15**	.25**	.15**	.25**	.15**	.25**	.15**
Conscientiousness → Liberalism	—	—	—	—	—	—	—	—	—	—
Extraversion → Liberalism	–.30***	–.24***	–.30***	–.24***	–.30***	–.24***	–.30***	–.24***	–.30***	–.24***
Agreeableness → Liberalism	–.23*	–.14*	–.23*	–.14*	–.23*	–.14*	–.23*	–.14*	–.23*	–.14*
Neuroticism → Liberalism	—	—	—	—	—	—	—	—	—	—
Liberalism → Value	.31***	.30***	.11	.08	.08	.08	.00	.00	–.25***	–.22***
Openness → Value	.23*	.13*	.35**	.16**	.73***	.42***	.03	.02	–.39**	–.20**
Conscientiousness → Value	.05	.03	–.35**	–.18**	.01	.01	–.15†	–.10†	.07	.04
Extraversion → Value	–.07	–.05	.55***	.35***	.11	.09	.17*	.14*	.09	.07
Agreeableness → Value	.40***	.25***	.03	.02	–.10	–.07	.78***	.52***	.58***	.33***
Neuroticism → Value	.03	.02	–.29**	–.18**	–.06	–.05	.23*	.19*	.22*	.15*
Indirect Effects										
Openness → Liberalism→ Value	**{0.031, 0.139}**		{–0.001, 0.073}		{0.000, 0.057}		{–0.022,0.024}		**{–0.116, –0.026}**	
Conscientiousness → Liberalism → Value	—		—		—		—		—	
Extraversion → Liberalism → Value	**{–0.154, –0.050}**		{–0.073, 0.001}		{–0.063, 0.002}		{–0.027, 0.026}		**{0.042, 0.125}**	
Agreeableness → Liberalism → Value	**{–0.134, –0.026}**		**{–0.069, –0.001}**		{–0.055, 0.000}		{–0.024, 0.018}		**{0.020, 0.117}**	
Neuroticism → Liberalism → Value	—		—		—		—		—	
R^2	16.9%		23.2%		20.7%		24.5%		22.4%	

Table 17.5 (continued) Direct and indirect effects of "big five" personality characteristics on political ideology

	Tradition		Security		Power		Achievement		Hedonism	
Direct Effects	***b***	***β***	***b***	***β***	***b***	***β***	***b***	***β***	***b***	***β***
Openness → Liberalism	.25**	.15**	.25**	.15**	.25**	.15**	.25**	.15**	.25**	.15**
Conscientiousness → Liberalism	—	—	—	—	—	—	—	—	—	—
Extraversion → Liberalism	−.30***	−.24***	−.30***	−.24***	−.30***	−.24***	−.30***	−.24***	−.30***	−.24***
Agreeableness → Liberalism	−.23*	−.14*	−.23*	−.14*	−.23*	−.14*	−.23*	−.14*	−.23*	−.14*
Neuroticism → Liberalism	—	—	—	—	—	—	—	—	—	—
Liberalism → Value	−.66***	−.36***	−.07	−.05	−.13†	−.10†	−.11	−.10	.07	.06
Openness → Value	−.01	−.00	−.08	−.04	.10	.04	−.30**	−.15**	.15	.07
Conscientiousness → Value	.21	.08	1.02***	.49***	.14	.07	.01	.01	−.47***	−.26***
Extraversion → Value	.05	.02	−.06	−.03	.56***	.33***	.26**	.18**	−.47***	−.32***
Agreeableness → Value	.42*	.15*	−.08	−.04	−.65***	−.31***	−.11	−.06	.19†	.10†
Neuroticism → Value	.07	.03	.21	.12	.05	.03	.15	.10	−.05	−.03
Indirect Effects										
Openness → Liberalism → Value	**{−0.291, −0.066}**		{−0.062, 0.013}		**{−0.084,−0.005}**		{−0.079, 0.000}		{−0.006, 0.057}	
Conscientiousness → Liberalism → Value	—		—		—		—		—	
Extraversion → Liberalism → Value	**{0.111, 0.312}**		{−0.019, 0.066}		**{0.006, 0.089}**		{−0.003, 0.080}		{−0.066, 0.009}	
Agreeableness → Liberalism → Value	**{0.059, 0.267}**		{−0.009, 0.059}		**{0.005, 0.078}**		**{0.001, 0.073}**		{−0.055, 0.004}	
Neuroticism → Liberalism → Value	—		—		—		—		—	
R^2	18.9%		23.2%		20.1%		7.0%		15.6%	

Note. R^2 signifies the proportion of variance in endorsement of Schwartz' values explained by the trimmed model.

The model explains 9.6% of variance observed in political ideology.

†$p<.1$, *$p<.05$, **$p<.01$, ***$p<.001$

effects are listed in Table 17.5. We observed that Openness was positively associated with the endorsement of universalism and negatively associated with the endorsement of conformity, and both of these effects were mediated by ideology. There were no direct effects of Openness on the prioritization of power or tradition, but there were indirect effects through ideology; to the extent that more open-minded individuals were more liberal, they tended to deprioritize these values. Agreeableness was associated with the prioritization of conformity, tradition, and universalism as well as the deprioritization of power; these effects were mediated (sometimes in opposing fashion) by ideology. Extraversion, as already noted, was associated with greater conservatism, which was, in turn, associated with the prioritization of conformity, tradition, and power and the deprioritization of universalism. Thus, we obtained some evidence that ideological proclivities mediate the effects of personality characteristics on value prioritization. Future research—especially longitudinal and experimental research—is needed to draw any conclusions about causal pathways, including developmental and neurological mechanisms, that are responsible for the "elective affinities" we have observed among personality characteristics, value priorities, and political ideologies.

Implications of value pluralism and conflict for normative theories in political philosophy

When Aristotle famously declared that "man is by nature a political animal," he adopted a naturalistic stance to the study of political science and philosophy and argued that the human tendency to form political associations arises from biological inclinations, so the emergence of the state is itself a natural consequence (*Politics* 1.2.1253a1–38). Political institutions, including the state, are the realization of what it means to be a human animal—a type of animal that is fundamentally social and one that is capable of formulating *normative* concepts, such as "right" and "wrong," "good" and "bad," "citizen" and "foreigner." In this context, political values, such as those pertaining to equality, freedom, tradition, progress, universalism, and benevolence, are normative concepts that specify how citizens *ought* to behave and relate to one another in society.

Modern philosophers tend to agree with Aristotle that political values are normative concepts that extend to the state and set expectations for the behavior of citizens, and some philosophers aspire to *legitimize* a specific set of these values, such as equality and tradition (e.g., Scheffler 2010). In writing for a relatively homogenous population, Aristotle did not attempt to legitimize specific political values because he assumed (more or less correctly) that his fellow citizens already possessed a shared set of values. In a contemporary pluralistic state, however, diverse sets of religious, cultural, and ideological backgrounds have brought into politics a cacophony of moral and political values. When these are taken together, they are not only inconsistent but often contradictory, as in Schwartz's (2012) model. Establishing which values are legitimate and thus deserving of official recognition in public life is a difficult but crucial task for political philosophers (e.g., Nagel 1991;

Scanlon 1998)—and a task about which social and behavioral scientists should have something useful to say (see: Jost and Kay 2010).

It follows from the theoretical perspective we have adopted in this chapter that value pluralism will result—perhaps inevitably—from dispositional and situational variability in social, cognitive, and motivational needs, interests, and tendencies. And if we are correct that individual and ideological differences in value prioritization are embedded in psychological (and perhaps even physiological) differences, this poses a supreme challenge for the philosophy and practice of politics. Are democratic institutions and mechanisms up to the task of addressing and reconciling not only conflicts at the level of value priorities, but also underlying conflicts at the level of individual and social psychology? It would be ambitious enough for a political system (or philosophical scheme) to determine reliably—on the basis of facts and not just opinions divorced from fact—how to overcome inaction and to resolve controversial tradeoffs between values, such as values of economic stability and environmental stewardship, to take just one timely and troubling conflict (for example, see: Gardiner 2011; Jamieson 2014).

Insofar as those who disagree (more often than not aggressively) about which values should trump others are intensely motivated by largely non-overlapping webs of beliefs, opinions, and values and, at a deeper level, divergent psychological needs, interests, and proclivities, it is difficult, if not impossible, to envision political institutions that will consistently yield optimal solutions from a normative point of view. Here we have in mind solutions that are driven primarily by forces of objectivity, rationality, and "reasonableness," which involves (among other things) a commitment to updating one's opinions on the basis of logic and scientific evidence (Broome 2013; Dworkin 1996; O'Neill 1997; Rawls 1993; Scanlon 2014). We would also stress the importance of procedural justice (Tyler 2007) and non-coercive forms of communication and deliberation—as opposed to the ruthless exercise of political or economic power (e.g., Habermas 1987). What would seem to be required is nothing less than this: a political system that will resolve conflicts arising from personality, ideology, and a high degree of value pluralism, so that difficult tradeoffs are made—and the overriding interests of society are not only revealed and expressed but actually enacted. One can only hope that it is in the nature of humanity to devise such a system and to live by it.

Acknowledgments

We wish to thank Tobias Brosch, Dan Relihan Johnson, Lawrence J. Jost, Melanie Langer, Joanna Sterling, and Chadly Stern for helpful comments on an earlier draft. And we are especially grateful to Sam Gosling and Jamie Pennebaker for making data from the University of Texas study available to us for statistical analysis.

References

Adorno, T.W., Frankel-Brunswick, E., Levinson, D.J., and Sanford, R.N. (1950). *The authoritarian personality*. New York: Harper and Row.

Allport, G.W. (1954). *The nature of prejudice*. Cambridge, MA: Addison-Wesley.

Allport, G.W. (1961). *Pattern and growth in personality*. New York: Holt, Rinehart, and Winston.

Amodio, D.M., Jost, J.T., Master, S.L., and Yee, C.M. (2007). Neurocognitive correlates of liberalism and conservatism. *Nature Neuroscience*, **10**(10), 1246–1247.

Aspelund, A., Lindeman, M., and Verkasalo, M. (2013). Political conservatism and left-right orientation in 28 Eastern and Western European countries. *Political Psychology*, **34**, 409–417.

Berlin, I. (1958/1969). Two concepts of liberty. In I. Berlin (ed.), *Four essays on liberty*. Oxford, UK: Oxford University Press.

Braithwaite, V. (1994). Beyond Rokeach's equality-freedom model: two dimensional values in a one dimensional world. *Journal of Social Issues*, **50**, 67–94.

Braithwaite, V. (1997). Harmony and security value orientations in political evaluation. *Personality and Social Psychology Bulletin*, **23**, 401–414.

Braithwaite, V. (1998). The value orientations underlying liberalism-conservatism. *Personality and Individual Differences*, **25**, 575–589.

Broome, J. (2013). *Rationality through reasoning*. New York: Wiley.

Brosch, T. and Sander, D. (2013). Neurocognitive mechanisms underlying value-based decision-making: from core values to economic value. *Frontiers in Human Neuroscience*, **7**, 398.

Burke, E. (1890). *Reflections on the revolution in France*. New York: Macmillan.

Caprara, G.V., Barbaranelli, C., and Zimbardo, P.G. (1999). Personality profiles and political parties. *Political Psychology*, **20**, 175–197.

Caprara, G.V., Schwartz, S., Capanna, C., Vecchione, M., and Barbaranelli, C. (2006). Personality and politics: values, traits, and political choice. *Political Psychology*, **27**, 1–28.

Carney, D.R., Jost, J.T., Gosling, S.D., and Potter, J. (2008). The secret lives of liberals and conservatives: personality profiles, interaction styles, and the things they leave behind. *Political Psychology*, **29**(6), 807–840.

Chin, M.K., Hambrick, D.C., and Treviño, L.K. (2013). Political ideologies of CEOs: illustrative evidence of the influence of executive values on corporate social responsibility. *Administrative Science Quarterly*, **58**, 197–232.

Cichocka, A. and Jost, J.T. (2014). Stripped of illusions? Exploring system justification processes in capitalist and post-Communist societies. *International Journal of Psychology*, **49**, 6–29.

Cochrane, R., Billig, M., and Hogg, M. (1979). Politics and values in Britain: a test of Rokeach's two-value model. *British Journal of Social and Clinical Psychology*, **18**, 159–167.

Davis, D.W. and Silver, B.D. (2004). Civil liberties vs. security: public opinion in the context of the terrorist attacks on America. *American Journal of Political Science*, **48**(1), 28–46.

Devos, T., Spini, D., and Schwartz, S. H. (2002). Conflicts among human values and trust in institutions. *British Journal of Social Psychology*, **41**, 481–494.

Duckitt, J. and Sibley, C.G. (2009). A dual process motivational model of ideological attitudes and system justification. In J.T. Jost, A. C. Kay, and H. Thorisdottir (eds), *Social and psychological bases of ideology and system justification* (pp. 292–313). New York: Oxford University Press.

Dworkin, R. (1996). Objectivity and truth: you'd better believe it. *Philosophy and Public Affairs*, **25**, 87–139.

Eagly, A.H. and Chaiken, S. (1993). *The psychology of attitudes*. Harcourt Brace Jovanovich College Publishers.

Feather, N.T. (1975). *Values in education and society*. New York: Free Press.

Federico, C.M., Weber, C.R., Ergun. D., and Hunt, C. (2013). Mapping the connections between politics and morality: the multiple sociopolitical orientations involved in moral intuition. *Political Psychology*, **34**, 589–610.

Feldman, S. (2003). Values, ideology, and the structure of political attitudes. In D.O. Sears, L. Huddy, and R. Jervis (eds), *Oxford handbook of political psychology*. New York: Oxford University Press.

Fiske, A.P. (1992). The four elementary forms of sociality: framework for a unified theory of social relations. *Psychological Review*, **99**, 689–723.

Freud, S. (1922). *Beyond the pleasure principle*. London: Hogarth Press.

Friesen, J.P., Kay, A.C., Eibach, R.P., and Galinsky, A.D. (2014). Seeking structure in social organization: Compensatory control and the psychological advantages of hierarchy. *Journal of Personality and Social Psychology*, **106**, 590–609.

Gardiner, S.M. (2011). *A perfect moral storm: the ethical tragedy of climate change*. New York: Oxford University Press.

Gerber, A.S., Huber, G.A., Doherty, D., Dowling, C.M., and Ha, S.E. (2010). Personality and political attitudes: relationships across issue domains and political contexts. *American Political Science Review*, **104**, 111–133.

Gerth H.H. and Mills C.W. (1948/1970). *Essays from Max Weber*. London: Routledge and Kegan Paul.

Graham, J., Haidt, J., and Nosek, B. (2009). Liberals and conservatives rely on different sets of moral foundations. *Journal of Personality and Social Psychology*, **96**, 1029–1046.

Habermas, J. (1987). *The theory of communicative action* (2 vols). Boston, MA: Beacon Press.

Haidt, J. and Graham, J. (2007). When morality opposes justice: conservatives have moral intuitions that liberals may not recognize. *Social Justice Research*, **20**, 98–116.

Hennes, E.P., Nam, H.H., Stern, C., and Jost, J.T. (2012). Not all ideologies are created equal: Epistemic, existential, and relational needs predict system-justifying attitudes. *Social Cognition*, **30**, 669–688.

Higgins, E.T. (2007). Value. In A.W. Kruglanski and E.T. Higgins (eds), *Social psychology: Handbook of basic principles* (2nd edn, pp. 454–472). New York: Guilford.

Hirsh, J.B., DeYoung, C.G., Xu, X., and Peterson, J.B. (2010). Compassionate liberals and polite conservatives: associations of agreeableness with political ideology and moral values. *Personality and Social Psychology Bulletin*, **36**, 655–664.

Hochschild, J.L. (2001). Where you stand depends on what you see: Connections among values, perceptions of fact, and political prescriptions. In J.H. Kuklinski (ed.), *Citizens and politics: perspectives from political psychology* (pp. 313–340). Cambridge, UK: Cambridge University Press,

Inglehart, R. (1977). *The silent revolution: changing values and political styles among Western publics*. Princeton, NJ: Princeton University Press.

Inglehart, R. (1990). *Culture shift in advanced industrial society*. Princeton, NJ: Princeton University Press.

Jacquet, J., Dietrich, M., and Jost, J.T. (2014). The ideological divide and climate change opinion: "top-down" and "bottom-up" approaches. *Frontiers in Psychology*, **5**.

Jamieson, D. (2014). *Reason in a dark time: why the struggle against climate change failed—and what it means for our future*. New York: Oxford University Press.

Janoff-Bulman, R. and Carnes, N.C. (2013). Surveying the moral landscape: moral motives and group-based moralities. *Personality and Social Psychology Review*, **17**, 219–236.

Jost, J.T. and Kay, A.C. (2010). Social justice: History, theory, and research. In S.T. Fiske, D. Gilbert, and G. Lindzey (eds), *Handbook of social psychology* (5th edn, Vol. 2, pp. 1122–1165). Hoboken, NJ: Wiley.

Jost, J.T., Glaser, J., Kruglanski, A.W., and Sulloway, F. (2003a). Political conservatism as motivated social cognition. *Psychological Bulletin*, **129**, 339–375.

Jost, J.T., Glaser, J., Kruglanski, A.W., and Sulloway, F. (2003b). Exceptions that prove the rule—using a theory of motivated social cognition to account for ideological incongruities and political anomalies: reply to Greenberg and Jonas (2003). *Psychological Bulletin*, **129**, 383–393.

Jost, J.T., Nosek, B.A., and Gosling, S.D. (2008). Ideology: its resurgence in social, personality, and political psychology. *Perspectives on Psychological Science*, **3**, 126–136.

Jost, J.T., Federico, C.M., and Napier, J.L. (2009). Political ideology: its structure, functions, and elective affinities. *Annual Review of Psychology*, **60**, 307–337.

Kanai, R., Feilden, T., Firth, C., and Rees, G. (2011). Political orientations are correlated with brain structure in young adults. *Current Biology*, **21**(8), 677–680.

Kandler, C., Bleidorn, W., and Riemann, R. (2012). Left or right? Sources of political orientation: The roles of genetic factors, cultural transmission, assortative mating, and personality. *Journal of Personality and Social Psychology*, **102**, 633–645.

Katz, D. (1960). The functional approach to the study of attitudes. *Public Opinion Quarterly*, **24**, 163–204.

Kelman, H.C. (1961). Processes of opinion change. *Public Opinion Quarterly*, **25**, 57–78.

Kugler, M., Jost, J. T., and Noorbaloochi, S. (2014). Another look at moral foundations theory: do authoritarianism and social dominance orientation explain liberal-conservative differences in "moral" intuitions? *Social Justice Research*, **27**, 413–431.

Lipset, S.M., Lazarsfeld, P., Barton, A., and Linz, J. (1954/1962). The psychology of voting: an analysis of political behavior. In G. Lindzey (ed.), *Handbook of social psychology* (pp. 1124–1175). Reading, MA: Addison-Wesley.

Maio, G.R., Olson, J.M., Bernard, M.M., and Luke, M.A. (2003). Ideologies, values, attitudes, and behavior. In J. Delamater (ed.), *Handbook of social psychology* (pp. 283–308). New York: Kluwer-Plenum.

Maslow, A.H. (1954). *Motivation and personality*. New York: Harper.

McCrae, R.R. and Costa, P.T., Jr. (1999). A five-factor theory of personality (pp. 139–153). In L.A. Pervin and O.P. John (eds) *Handbook of personality: theory and research* (2nd edn). New York: Guilford.

Milojev, P., Osborne, D., Greaves, L.M., Bulbulia, J., Wilson, M.S., Davies, C.L., Liu, J.H., and Sibley, C.G. (2014). Right-wing authoritarianism and social dominance orientation predict different moral signatures. *Social Justice Research*, **27**, 149–174.

Mondak, J.J. (2010). *Personality and the foundations of political behavior*. New York: Cambridge University Press.

Murray, H.A. (1938). *Explorations in personality*. New York: Oxford University Press.

Nagel, T. (1991). *Equality and partiality*. New York: Oxford University Press.

Napier, J.L., and Jost, J.T. (2008). Why are conservatives happier than liberals? *Psychological Science*, **19**, 565–572.

Newcomb, T. (1943). *Personality and social change*. New York: Dryden.

Nozick, R. (1974/2001). *Anarchy, state and utopia*. Oxford: Blackwell.

O'Neill, O. (1997). Political liberalism and public reason: a critical notice of John Rawls, *Political Liberalism*. *The Philosophical Review*, **106**, 411–428.

Parks-Leduc, L., Feldman, G., and Bardi, A. (2014). Personality traits and personal values: a meta-analysis. *Personality and Social Psychology Review*, online first.

Piurko, Y., Schwartz, S.H., and Davidov, E. (2011). Basic personal values and the meaning of left-right political orientations in 20 countries. *Political Psychology*, **32**, 537–561.

Pojman, L.P. and Westmoreland, R. (eds) (1997). *Equality: selected readings*. New York: Oxford University Press.

Rawls, J. (1971/1999). *A theory of justice*. Oxford, UK: Oxford University Press.

Rawls, J. (1993). *Political liberalism*. New York: Columbia University Press.

Roccas, S., Sagiv, L., Schwartz, S.H., and Knafo, A. (2002). The big five personality factors and personal values. *Personality and Social Psychology Bulletin*, **28**, 789–801.

Rokeach, M. (1973). *The nature of human values*. New York: Free Press.

Scanlon, T. M. (1998). *What we owe to each other*. Cambridge, MA: Belknap Press.

Scanlon, T. M. (2014). *Being realistic about reasons*. Oxford, UK: Oxford University Press.

Scheffler, S. (2010). *Equality and tradition: questions of value in moral and political theory*. New York: Oxford University Press.

Schwartz, S.H. (1992). Universals in the content and structure of values: theoretical advances and empirical tests in 20 countries. *Advances in Experimental Social Psychology*, **25**, 1–65.

Schwartz, S.H. (2012). An overview of the Schwartz theory of basic values. *Online Readings in Psychology and Culture, 2*, 1–11. May be downloaded here: http://scholarworks.gvsu.edu/cgi/viewcontent.cgi?article=1116&context=orpc (last accessed: May 6, 2015).

Schwartz, S.H., Caprara, G.V., and Vecchione, M. (2010). Basic personal values, core political values, and voting: A longitudinal analysis. *Political Psychology*, **31**, 421–452.

Smith, M.B. (1969). *Social psychology and human values*. Chicago: Aldine.

Smith, M.B., Bruner, J.S., and White, R.W. (1956). *Opinions and personality*. Oxford: Wiley.

Suhler, C.L. and Churchland, P. (2011). Can innate, modular "foundations" explain morality? Challenges for Haidt's moral foundations theory. *Journal of Cognitive Neuroscience*, **23**(9), 2103–2116.

Swami, V., Nader, I.W., Pietschnig, J., Stieger, S., Tran, U.S., and Voracek, M. (2012). Personality and individual difference correlates of attitudes toward human rights and civil liberties. *Personality and Individual Differences*, **53**, 443–447.

Tedin, K.L. (1987). Political ideology and the vote. *Research in Micropolitics*, **2**, 63–94.

Tetlock, P.E. (1984). Cognitive style and political belief systems in the British House of Commons. *Journal of Personality and Social Psychology*, **46**, 365–375.

Tetlock, P.E. (1986). A value pluralism model of ideological reasoning. *Journal of Personality and Social Psychology*, **50**, 819–827.

Thorisdottir, H., Jost, J.T., Liviatan, I., and Shrout, P. (2007). Psychological needs and values underlying left-right political orientation: Cross-national evidence from Eastern and Western Europe. *Public Opinion Quarterly*, **71**, 175–203.

Tyler, T.R. (2007). *Psychology and the design of legal institutions*. Nijmegen, Netherlands: Wolf.

Van Lange, P.A., Bekkers, R., Chirumbolo, A., and Leone, L. (2012). Are conservatives less likely to be prosocial than liberals? From games to ideology, political preferences and voting. *European Journal of Personality*, **26**(5), 461–473.

Van Leeuwen, F. and Park, J. H. (2009). Perceptions of social dangers, moral foundations, and political orientation. *Personality and Individual Differences*, **47**(3), 169–173.

Vecchione, M., Caprara, G., Dentale, F., and Schwartz, S. H. (2013). Voting and values: Reciprocal effects over time. *Political Psychology*, **34**, 465–485.

Wilson. G.D. (ed.) (1973). *The psychology of conservatism*. New York: Academic Press.

Chapter 18

Religious value and moral psychology

Adam C. Pelser and Robert C. Roberts

Introduction

While the term "religious value" and its plural are widely used in academic literature and popular discourse, seldom is much attention given to specifying what the term means. We aim here to clarify the nature of religious value and explore its connection to moral psychology. We begin, in the first section, by offering an account of the concept. We distinguish two senses of "religious value" and distinguish religious value from various related concepts, including moral value, the pragmatic value of religion, and the epistemic value of religious beliefs. We then turn our attention, in the next section, to a consideration of one recent evolutionary account of the psychological origins of religious values and explore some of the ways religion and religions influence the development of religious values. In the final section, we draw on our discussion of the psychological sources of religious values to argue briefly that any adequate moral psychology ought to encourage the cultivation of religious values and that the natural human religious sensitivities that give rise to religious values can serve as evidence in favor of religious truth.

What religious value is: a sketch

Two senses of religious value

When considering the nature of religious value, we must first distinguish two senses of "value." In one sense, "value" refers to some goodness, excellence, or worth of a thing, whether that worth be intrinsic to the thing or merely instrumental. Human beings are sometimes said to have intrinsic value, just by virtue of their nature as rational beings, but a person can also have instrumental value, for example, as a member of a scientific team. In both these cases, the value resides in the thing assessed. In a second sense, values are attitudes held by persons and are psychological dispositions, as when we say that we want to rear our children to have good values (we want them to love justice and hate the suffering of others). This kind of value resides not in the thing assessed, but in the assessor and makes the value of the thing assessed evident to the assessor.

There appear to be various kinds of value in the first sense, each of which corresponds to some significant facet of human life. We thus speak of the economic or monetary value of property and investments, the political value of democracy and a balance of federal powers, the esthetic value of Beethoven's *9th Symphony* and Monet's *Water Lilies*, the literary value of Tolstoy's *Anna Karenina* and Austen's *Pride and Prejudice*, the moral value of integrity and of doing one's duty, and the intellectual or epistemic value of knowledge and understanding. While these various kinds overlap and intersect, they are distinct, as we can see by the fact that a thing can possess or exhibit one kind of value without possessing or exhibiting some of the other kinds.

Since religion is a significant facet of human life, distinct from, though importantly related to, the other aspects of human life that admit of special kinds of value, it seems prima facie plausible that there is distinctively religious value—i.e., distinctively religious goodness, excellence, or worth. We can make some progress toward understanding what such religious value might be like by first identifying the objects that are thought to have such value paradigmatically. Here, it seems that we ought first to look to the proper objects or ends of religion, as opposed to religious institutions or practices. By way of analogy, it seems wrong to say that esthetic value is paradigmatically instantiated in the *production* of excellent art—say, in the processes employed in painting, or in the techniques used by a composer of music; rather, the art product itself has the basic value. Similarly, religious value would not be instantiated paradigmatically in a religion—the rituals, the scriptures, the institutions—but rather in the goods toward which these things point, the goods the religion is "for" in the sense made current by Robert Adams.[1] If there is a special kind of religious value, therefore, we might think that the most obvious candidates for possession of such value are ultimate spiritual or "transcendent" realities such as Nirvana or God. Most religions posit an Ultimate Reality that transcends human moral, economic, and political systems in the sense that it is ontologically more fundamental than those systems and its value is not measurable purely in terms of those systems, but rather by reference to what they subserve.[2] Insofar as religious value is understood to refer to the special value of Ultimate Reality, therefore, we might treat "religious value" as roughly synonymous with "transcendent value."

In addition to being exemplified by Ultimate Reality itself, religious value, so understood, might also be manifest in objects (broadly construed) that participate in or reflect the "transcendent" value of Ultimate Reality. Such objects might include first the saints and institutions (for example, the Church), and, second, the shrines, statues or other icons, relics, symbols, music, and sacramental elements like the bread and wine of the Christian Eucharist or the water of baptism. Thus it might be possible for humans to exemplify religious value. For example, M. M. Sharif explains that in Islam all ultimate values are

1 *Finite and Infinite Goods: A Framework for Ethics*. Oxford: Oxford University Press, 1999.

2 Robert Adams identifies God with the Good and argues that "The Good is transcendent in the sense that it vastly surpasses all other good things, and all our conceptions of the good. They are profoundly imperfect in comparison with the Good itself." *Finite and Infinite Goods*, p. 50.

transcendent or "spiritual" and that the goal of human life is to share in ultimate spiritual values by growing in likeness to God:

> The sole aim of man is, therefore, a progressive achievement of life divine, which consists in the gradual acquisition of all divine attributes—all intrinsic values. These divine attributes or intrinsic values are connoted by the different names of God, but they can all be summarized under a few essential heads: life, unity, power, truth, beauty, justice, love, and goodness. God is one. He is a free creative activity, which is living, all-powerful, all-knowing, all-beauty, most just, most loving, and all-good. These attributes are our ultimate goals. The unrestricted achievement of these goals for a long time gives a value-tone to the whole of personality. This value-tone is called peace, bliss, or happiness.[3]

The idea of the spiritual development of humanity into the likeness of God that Sharif describes bears a close resemblance to the Eastern Orthodox Christian doctrine of *theosis*. Other major religious traditions similarly identify the goal of human existence as some kind of valuable participation in, loving union with, or reflection of Ultimate Reality. Insofar as the purpose of a religion is to connect people in one valuable way or another to Ultimate Reality, religious value, in the sense we have been discussing, might also be manifest in anything that helps to accomplish that purpose. To return to our analogy with esthetic value, it seems that just as the ways of producing excellent art can exemplify a derivative esthetic value, so religious practices and institutions might exemplify derivative religious value, value derived from the ultimate ends or goods that the religion in question facilitates. Here we might think of religious practices (e.g., prayer, meditation, reading scripture, pilgrimage, communal worship, proselytizing, acts of service, dressing in sacred clothing, ceremonial washing and sacrifices), moral or otherwise life-guiding principles (e.g., the Ten Commandments, the "Golden Rule," the Eightfold Path), religious experiences, and religious beliefs. Just as in performance arts, where some aspects of the production of the art are constitutive of the artistic product itself, so too we might think that the religious life (beliefs, practices, and communal relationships) is not merely instrumentally or derivatively valuable, but rather partially constitutive of the valuable ends of a religion.

Turn now to the second sense of religious value. Often when people speak of "values," especially "religious values" (note the plural), they refer not to a distinctive kind of excellence or worth, but to an attitude held by some person or group. Understood in this way, for a person to have a religious value is not for her to manifest some distinctively religious or "transcendent" excellence, but rather for her to be committed to, to appreciate, or to have a concern for something, where her commitment, appreciation, or concern is informed by her religious beliefs, experiences, practices, or membership. Here, "religious values" is colloquial shorthand for what we might call "religiously-informed valuings." For a person to have a religious value, in this sense, is for her to be *for* something, where her *being for* the thing in question is significantly informed by her religion and partly constitutive of her religious life. As Adams explains, we can be for a thing in several different ways, including "loving it, liking it, respecting it, wanting it, wishing for it, appreciating it, thinking highly

3 M. M. Sharif, "Islam and spiritual values," *Philosophy East and West* 9 (1959): 42.

of it, speaking in favor of it and otherwise intentionally standing for it symbolically, acting to promote or protect it, and being disposed to do such things."[4]

We might also think about this second sense of religious values in terms of evaluative outlooks. Most human adults have an evaluative outlook that is comprised of our evaluative commitments, concerns, emotion-dispositions, dispositions to judge, and perceptual sensitivities.[5] From the fundamental values of, say, Christianity, an individual's outlook might include a belief that racism is wicked, a concern for the advancement of racial diversity and equality in schools and businesses, a keen attunement to situations involving racial injustice, a disposition to experience indignation, sadness, guilt, joy, and gratitude in response to situations involving racial injustice and justice, and a disposition to act so as to bring about states of affairs that exemplify racial justice. These various features of the evaluative outlook in question are all ways of being for racial equality and justice. We might call the underlying value respect for human dignity and equality or, more specifically, the value of racial justice. Religious values like respect for human dignity are constitutive aspects of the evaluative outlooks of religious individuals.

We have thus identified two senses of "religious value." We might call them ontological and psychological religious value. Ontological religious value is "transcendent" excellence or worth such as God's goodness and love and objective values that derive from them such as human dignity. A psychological religious value is an attitudinal or dispositional valu*ing* of some object that is importantly informed by or otherwise integrally connected with one's religion.

These two senses of religious value are related in the following important way: a person with a psychological religious value takes the object or principle he values to have ontological religious value. For example, to exemplify the religious value expressed in the judgment that fetuses should not be aborted because they have a sacred status as creatures beloved of God is to be disposed to construe fetuses, with heartfelt appreciation, as being sacred in that way. Psychological religious values are thus accurate to the degree that they get ontological religious value right. So, the religious value expressed in the judgment that fetuses should not be aborted due to their sacred status will be an accurate one just in case fetuses actually have a sacred status.

As this example reveals, psychological religious values overlap with moral values, but they are more than simply moral values that happen to be shared within and encouraged by a religious tradition or community. This distinction is blurred by the fact that sometimes a person holds an apparent religious value without construing what he values as having ontological religious value. He might, for example, believe it's morally wrong to abort a fetus and hold this belief largely, if not wholly, as a result of the influence of his religious

[4] Robert Merrihew Adams, *A Theory of Virtue: Excellence in Being* for *the Good* (Oxford: Oxford University Press, 2006), pp. 15–16.

[5] Robert C. Roberts uses the concept of an evaluative outlook in his *Emotions in the Moral Life* (Cambridge: Cambridge University Press, 2013).

community, but without actually seeing the fetus as sacred or feeling the principle against aborting it to be, say, a divine command. In the ideal case, the integration of the individual's moral and religious values is a process of "sanctification" in which his dispositional consciousness is tied together and lighted up by the ontological values that he affirms.

The integration of religious with other values

Thomas Nagel has flagged a different problem of integration, which he calls "the fragmentation of value."[6] He is worried that the various kinds of value—moral, esthetic, political, economic, and so on—are ultimately incommensurable, having no hierarchical order. Without such a ranking we would have no way to decide which type of value ought to prevail when values of various kinds conflict. Given the connection of religious value to ontologically fundamental Ultimate Reality, we might make a start at solving the fragmentation problem by subsuming all other kinds of value under religious value. On this view, one should always choose what is religiously valuable over what is merely morally, esthetically, politically, or economically valuable. As Adams points out, however, we cannot solve the fragmentation problem simply by positing religious (or moral) value as the most fundamental kind of value. Adams defends a theistic moral outlook according to which God is the Good (i.e., the ultimate ontological value) and love for God is the central psychological value, and thus central to the moral life. He relates the problem of the fragmentation of value to his specifically theistic account of value:

> Contemporary support for the fragmentation of value is rooted largely in reaction against what might be called "excessive high-mindedness"—that is, against moral and religious ideals that seem to many to leave too little room for interests not obviously and narrowly moral or religious. I am sympathetic with this reaction, but it confronts me with an obvious challenge. Can love for God provide an integrating principle for our motives and values without an oppressive excess of high-mindedness?[7]

Adams' proposed solution, which seems unavailable to someone who thinks of the ultimate ontological religious value as impersonal, is to suggest that loving God involves loving and appreciating for their own sake those values that *God loves and appreciates*. He explains,

> God should be conceived as appreciating the values that are the objects of intellectual and esthetic interests, as caring about them for their own sake—and even as loving strange things that we do not begin to understand how to care about . . . . With an adequately large conception of God's interests, it should be possible to unite devotion to God with an interest in any good thing for its own sake (p. 181).

Adams thus integrates our loves and appreciations for all goods (i.e., our values in the psychological sense) by including them as aspects or manifestations of our love for the Good, which he identifies with God.

---

6 Thomas Nagel, *Mortal Questions* (Cambridge: Cambridge University Press, 1979), chapter 9.

7 *Finite and Infinite Goods*, p. 180.

While Adams' theistic integration of values goes some way toward resolving the fragmentation of value problem, a worry remains about cases in which values come into conflict. Sometimes we must sacrifice or fail to promote something that is intrinsically good, to preserve or promote something else that is intrinsically good. In such cases, how are we to decide which value to promote? Adams suggests that the answer lies in the fact that love for some goods (for example, the good of other persons) is more essential to fostering social alliances than love for other goods (for example, esthetic goods). Since the proper end of humans is to be united with the Good and with others in love for the Good, he argues, those goods the love of which is essential to social unification are to be preferred over those the love of which is not essential to social unification.[8] Adams' orientation here is the biblical affirmation that the first great commandment is to love God above all things, and the second is to love one's neighbor as oneself. Other values, such as esthetic ones, come in farther down the hierarchy. Adams' account is valuable for our purposes because it suggests one way of integrating religious value with other kinds of value without reducing religious value to those other kinds of value and without making non-religious values merely instrumentally valuable as means to the achievement of religious value.

The epistemic and pragmatic value of religion

Another way to understand the relationship between religious value and other kinds of value is to conceive of religion as merely pragmatically or instrumentally valuable, i.e., as a means to some higher psychological or social good. At the turn of the twentieth century, Cambridge philosopher G. E. Moore took up the question of the value of religion, writing:

> [M]y question is whether it is good to believe, as most religious persons do believe, that a God possessing at least these qualities [perfect wisdom, power, and goodness], however many more he may possess, however much he may transcend anthropomorphic notions, does actually exist? Is it good to believe that such a God exists? Ought we to believe that he exists? What is the value of such a belief? This is an ethical question, and for that reason I believe it covers more completely than any other the whole ground of controversy between the believer and the unbeliever.[9]

Moore is careful to distinguish the epistemic from the pragmatic value of religion. Concerning the epistemic value of religious belief, he explains, "For I admit or assume, whichever you please, that if it is true that God exists, if he really does exist, then it is good to believe that fact. It may not be much good, but it is *pro tanto* good to know the truth"

8 *Finite and Infinite Goods*, pp. 183–185. In his chapter on "Vocation" (pp. 292–317), Adams argues further that there might be cases in which the weight one ought to put on the various goods one loves can be at least partially determined by whether one has a sense of divine calling to pursue one good or the other and that this can differ from person to person.

9 G. E. Moore, "The value of religion," *International Journal of Ethics* 12, 1 (1901): 85.

(p. 85). Moore does not think we ought to treat the question of the pragmatic (or moral) value of religion in isolation from the question of the epistemic value of religious belief:

> What I have called the factual inquiry into the truth of religious belief must be kept quite distinct from the moral inquiry into the worth of its effects. But at the same time the factual inquiry is necessary before we can decide upon the value of religion; because the truth of a belief, although it cannot alter its effects, has in itself some ethical importance (p. 87).

Moore proceeds to argue that we in fact have no good grounds for believing in the existence of God and that while religion might have some good psychological and social side-effects, we can get all that is valuable out of religion without it, or at least without believing that religious claims are true (p. 98). He thus recommends abandoning religious beliefs, since they are epistemically (and, hence, morally) disvaluable and pragmatically unnecessary.

Recent years have seen much heated argument, largely instigated by a group of scholars and popular writers whose views represent the New Atheism, over whether religion is valuable for human psychology or for the health and flourishing of human society. The so-called New Atheists have argued vehemently not only that there is good (evidential) reason to reject religious truth claims, but also that the negative impacts of religion on human psychology and society far outweigh any positive value it might be thought to have.[10] Religion, according to these writers, has negative pragmatic value.

In his recent book, *The Righteous Mind*, Jonathan Haidt offers a reply to the New Atheism in which he argues that religion is on the whole beneficial for human psychology and society. Haidt acknowledges that religious experiences and emotions have the effect of binding groups together, but he rejects the assumption that religious group-binding is always bad; rather, he suggests that religion makes groups more cohesive and cooperative, in part by helping them to create moral communities.[11] He explains, "Gods and religions . . . are group-level adaptations for producing cohesiveness and trust. Like maypoles and bee-hives, they are created by the members of the group, and they then organize the activity of the group" (p. 306). So, even if the New Atheists are right that religious practices are biologically inefficient and religious beliefs irrational, religious practices and beliefs still might be of some practical value (i.e., for cultural evolution)—"Gods really do help groups cohere, succeed, and outcompete other groups" (p. 299).

We will say more about Haidt's account of the psychological origins of religion in the following sections. Here, our primary aim is simply to distinguish what we have been calling religious value from what might be called the value of religion. As our discussion up to this point reveals, the value of religion has at least two dimensions. The first is the epistemic (or alethic) value of religious beliefs. If religious beliefs are demonstrably false,

[10] See, e.g., Richard Dawkins, *The God Delusion* (Boston: Houghton Mifflin, 2006); Sam Harris, *Letter to a Christian Nation* (New York: Knopf, 2006).

[11] Jonathan Haidt, *The Righteous Mind: Why Good People are Divided by Politics and Religion* (New York: Pantheon Books, 2012), p. 296.

then religion lacks value in at least one sense—i.e., its claims about the way the world is are false and insofar as its practices are based on those claims, they are misguided, if not practically irrational. Yet, even if religious beliefs are false, they and their associated practices might have some pragmatic psychological or social value. Indeed, this is Haidt's view. While Haidt leaves open the question whether any particular religious beliefs are true or justified (i.e., whether they have positive epistemic value), he argues that religiously based morality plays a valuable evolutionary role in the binding of communities (p. 315).

Setting aside the question of the pragmatic value of religion, if the New Atheists and Moore are right that we have no good reason to believe any religion's claims about ultimate reality, it follows that we have no good reason to believe that religion is valuable as a means of participating in, or reflecting, transcendent ontological religious value. Indeed, if no transcendent religious entity exists, then no transcendent ontological religious value exists. And if no ontological religious value exists, then psychological religious values are all false, whatever else we might say to commend them, since they involve taking an object to have ontological religious value. Conversely, if we have reason to think that the faculties and processes that give rise to psychological religious values are capable of tracking the truth, then perhaps the natural human propensity toward psychological religious values can serve as evidence in favor of the existence of ontological religious value. In an effort to determine whether the faculties and processes that give rise to psychological religious values are at all trustworthy guides to the nature of ontological religious value, it will be helpful to consider just what those faculties and processes might be.

The sources of psychological religious values

Haidt on the evolutionary origins of religious psychology

In *The Righteous Mind* Haidt offers a complex evolutionary account of the origin of moral and religious values, which might help us begin to think about their psychological sources. He begins by offering compelling empirical evidence that moral judgments are sometimes made on the basis of emotional intuitions (gut reactions), rather than deliberative reasoning. For example, he notes that even if subjects' explicit moral reasoning is dominated by deference to something like a utilitarian harm principle (i.e., harm, and only harm, is morally wrong), they nevertheless deem it morally wrong and disgusting for a family privately to eat their dog that has just been killed by a car. If asked to say why they think so, subjects have great difficulty identifying any victim of harm in the case. (The dog has, of course, been harmed, but not by anything the family did.) In fact, Haidt notes that many subjects try to "invent" victims to justify their emotional judgments using the harm principle. He concludes, "These subjects were reasoning. They were working quite hard at reasoning. But it was not reasoning in search of truth; it was reasoning in support of their emotional reactions" (p. 29). On the basis of this research, Haidt concludes that most of our moral judgments are not rooted in deliberative moral reasoning from a single moral principle like the utilitarian harm principle or Immanuel Kant's categorical imperative; rather, they are caused by our intuitive moral leanings, which are culturally-shaped manifestations of a foundational set of emotion-based evaluative dispositions ("taste receptors") that have become ubiquitous over the course of human history due to their value for biological and cultural survival. As a caution to those who would draw a sharp distinction between emotion and cognition, Haidt explains that "intuitions (including emotional responses) are a kind of cognition. They're just not a kind of reasoning" (p. 56). Even people whose moral reasoning is limited to considerations of just two out of the six innate foundations (harm and fairness), as are most educated Westerners, have intuitions that arise from the other four.[12]

The six emotional foundations or innate human moral-psychological triggers are: (1) the care/harm foundation, which is the basic source of utilitarian thinking, (2) the fairness/cheating foundation, which is the source of moral theories that center on the concept of justice, such as those of Kant and Rawls, (3) the loyalty/betrayal foundation, which is the ground of such virtues as patriotism and (military) loyalty to members of one's fighting unit, (4) the authority/subversion foundation, on which is built the human tendency to respect and obey persons in authority and to feel comfortable in chains of command, (5) the sanctity/degradation foundation, which explains such virtues as cleanliness, chastity, reverence for Nature, and temperance, and (6) the liberty/oppression foundation, which explains our hatred of tyrants and bullies and others who threaten to dominate us, and the virtue of autonomy.[13]

Of particular relevance for our discussion of religious values is Haidt's discussion of the sanctity/degradation moral foundation, which he takes to arise out of our biologically valuable emotion of disgust. He argues that a disgust disposition, tempered by a cautious openness toward unfamiliar features of the environment, had great survival value in the evolutionary environment because it protected its possessors from eating poisonous or rotten foods and from contracting infectious diseases. He hypothesizes that as humans began to form societies, this sense of disgust gave rise to aversion toward out-groups and thus had a kind of group-binding effect, since "Plagues, epidemics, and new diseases are usually brought in by foreigners" (p. 173).[14] He then argues that this primitive sense of disgust ultimately gave rise to a more morally significant sense of sacredness and desecration:

> The Sanctity foundation makes it easy for us to regard some things as "untouchable," both in a bad way (because something is so dirty or polluted we want to stay away) and in a good way (because something is so hallowed, so sacred, that we want to protect it from desecration). If we had no sense of disgust, I believe we would also have no sense of the sacred. And if you think, as I do, that one of the greatest unsolved mysteries is how people ever came together to form large cooperative

[12] See Haidt, pp. 146, 178–179 for a summary of the first five "moral foundations" and p. 197f for his discussion of the liberty/oppression foundation.

[13] For a discussion of the virtue of autonomy, especially in its intellectual dimension, in its dialectical connection to respect for authority, see Robert C. Roberts and W. Jay Wood, *Intellectual Virtues: An Essay in Regulative Epistemology* (Oxford: Oxford University Press, 2007), chapter 10.

[14] It seems to us that the loyalty foundation would also be at work here. The authority foundation also seems relevant, at least for religions whose theology makes God a commander.

> societies, then you might take a special interest in the psychology of sacredness. . . . Whatever its origins, the psychology of sacredness helps bind individuals into moral communities. . . . Whether or not God exists, people feel that some things, actions, and people are noble, pure, and elevated; others are base, polluted, and degraded (pp. 173–174).

Even if we grant Haidt's explanation of the psychological origins of our sense of the sacred, it is not yet an explanation of the psychological origins of full-fledged religious values. To have psychological religious values we must have religion, which is surely more than a communal moral system informed by a shared sense of sacredness.

To account for the psychological origins of religion, Haidt follows Emile Durkheim in identifying two sets of "social emotions"—one set that binds individuals together with other individuals within their society (e.g., honor, respect, affection, fear) and one that "pull[s] humans fully but temporarily into the higher of our two realms, the realm of the sacred, where the self disappears and collective interests predominate" (p. 262). Haidt argues that the latter set of "collective emotions" is effectively induced by religious practices of communal worship, chanting, singing, and dancing. He hypothesizes that these practices give rise to feelings of oneness and belonging by increasing levels of the hormone oxytocin, which has been shown to facilitate pair-bonding in mammals, and by activating mirror neurons, by which people undergo neural activity similar to that of those with whom they are interacting, thus enabling them to understand and empathize with the feelings and thoughts of others. Haidt locates the evolutionary value of religion in the evocation of group-binding emotions, whatever may be the underlying biological cause(s). Some societies function better than others because their members are willing to invest their time, energy, and effort in cooperative activities that are not in their direct individual (or familial) interest.

Responding to the New Atheists' charge that religious practices are biologically inefficient and irrational, Haidt writes:

> *the very ritual practices that the New Atheists dismiss as costly, inefficient, and irrational turn out to be a solution to one of the hardest problems humans face: cooperation without kinship.* Irrational beliefs can sometimes help the group function more rationally, particularly when those beliefs rest upon the Sanctity foundation. Sacredness binds people together, and then blinds them to the arbitrariness of the practice. . . . Gods really do help groups cohere, succeed, and outcompete other groups (p. 299, italics original).

Haidt's account of the evolutionary value of religion thus goes something like this: religious beliefs (however irrational or evidentially unwarranted) encourage religious practices (however inefficient at the individual level), which in turn evoke "collective emotions" that give people a sense of belonging and oneness with the group, and this sense of belonging or oneness in turn helps to motivate cooperative individual investments of time, energy, and resources for the sake of the group. He rejects the New Atheists' claim that religion is an inherently "pernicious delusion,"[15] since he thinks that religion's primary effect is to

[15] Dawkins, *The God Delusion*, p. 31.

cause people to pursue the well-being of their group's members, not to pursue harm toward outsiders.

However, he also rejects the assumption that religion causes people to be indiscriminately altruistic. Rather, he argues that religion causes people to be "parochial altruists" who seek the good of others within their group, and the good of their group as a whole, but who are no more altruistic toward outsiders than non-religious individuals. As evidence for this thesis, Haidt cites studies that indicate that:

> people in the least religious fifth of the population give just 1.5 percent of their money to charity. People in the most religious fifth (based on church attendance, not belief) give a whopping 7 percent of their income to charity, and the majority of the giving is to religious organizations. It's the same story for volunteer work: religious people do far more than secular folk, and the bulk of the work is done for, or at least through, their religious organizations (p. 308).

We cannot offer a thorough critique of Haidt's account of the evolution of religious values, but will here offer a couple of brief critical remarks before moving on to explore some of the particular ways that religious teachings and practices, informed as they are by religious beliefs and community membership, inform and shape our evaluative outlooks, thereby giving rise to (psychological) religious values.

The first thing to note in response to Haidt's account is that even if he is right that most peoples' moral judgments are based in their emotional reactions, as opposed to deliberative moral reasoning, it does not follow that their post hoc moral reasoning is "not reasoning in search of truth" (p. 29). The emotional reactions in question may well be properly tracking and responding to the moral value (or disvalue) of the cases Haidt describes. And the subjects' attempts to justify their moral judgments by reasoning may be read as their efforts to understand their perceptions by articulating reasons. The misguided effort to do this by reference to something like a utilitarian harm principle may be rooted, in part, in the poverty of their culture's ethical vocabulary. Perhaps they need a religion that affords the conceptual resources to make sense of their intuitions. Perhaps the subjects' inability to articulate plausible harm-based reasons in favor of their moral judgments should be interpreted as evidence against the truth of their practical assumption that all moral wrongness reduces to harm, rather than as evidence against the truth of their particular emotion-based moral judgments (more on this in the final section).

Second, we contend that Haidt's pessimism about the altruism of religious individuals toward those outside their religious communities is unwarranted. He cites the research of sociologists Robert Putnam and David Campbell that religious people do "the bulk" of their volunteer work "for, or at least through, their religious organizations." In reply, we note that a great deal of volunteer work done *through* religious organizations is not done *for* members of those religious organizations, but rather for people in need outside of the religious community. That the members of religious communities work together in cooperative volunteer efforts, with the encouragement or organizational support of their religious institutions, is no evidence at all that they are more interested in promoting the welfare of their fellow group members than that of outsiders. It is consistent with Haidt's suggestion that religious group binding enhances cooperative group projects and group cohesion that those projects be directed at improving the lot of people outside the group.

In fact, while the Putnam and Campbell research does indicate that the majority of religious individuals' charitable giving and volunteer work is done for, and through, religious organizations, it also reveals that religious individuals (measured in terms of regular church attendance, not doctrinal adherence) are more likely than non-religious individuals to volunteer for *secular* causes. As they explain:

> It is not surprising in the slightest that churchgoers have a higher rate of religious volunteering than nonchurchgoers. Nonchurchgoers rarely turn up as church ushers. . . . However, religion boosts total volunteering so substantially that in addition to their higher rate of religious volunteering, regular churchgoers are also much more likely to volunteer for secular causes. Though religion channels volunteering toward religious institutions, that religious volunteering does not crowd out secular volunteering.[16]

These findings thus seem to undermine, not support, Haidt's thesis that human altruism is parochial. While the research of Putnam and Campbell leaves open many questions about the nature and value of religious peoples' motives for volunteering, it provides at least some evidence that a concern for the welfare of others, including those who don't belong to one's own religious group, is a common religious value, understood as an aspect of an evaluative outlook that has been largely caused or informed by one's religion. This phenomenon seems difficult to explain on an adaptationist account of the psychological origins of religion, and better explained by the religious belief that their God is concerned about the wellbeing of all people, and not just the members of their religious group.

How religion shapes evaluative outlooks

We now turn our attention to some of the ways religion informs evaluative outlooks, giving rise to religious values like the religiously informed altruism suggested by Putnam and Campbell's research. One of the primary ways religions shape the evaluative outlooks of their members is through narratives.[17] In Jewish and Christian teaching, for example, the narratives of Creation, the Fall, the Flood, and God's deliverance of the people of Israel out of Egyptian slavery into the Promised Land are told and retold to impress on the community a sense of God's sovereignty over nature, the severity of human sinfulness, and God's faithfulness to save and redeem his people. Jesus often taught in parabolic narratives that employ common this-worldly illustrations of moral and spiritual truths. One of Jesus' most famous parables is The Good Samaritan in which a man who has been mugged and

[16] Robert D. Putnam and David E. Campbell, *American Grace: How Religion Divides and Unites Us* (New York: Simon and Schuster, 2010), p. 445. For further discussion of research indicating that religious participation and membership enhances pro-social and generous actions, see Rodney Stark, *America's Blessings: How Religion Benefits Everyone, Including Atheists* (West Conshohocken, PA: Templeton Press, 2012).

[17] For a brilliant discussion of the diversity and moral power of narratives, see Christian Smith, *Moral, Believing Animals* (Oxford: Oxford University Press, 2003), chapter 4.

severely beaten is passed without help by two religious authorities, only then to be aided by an unlikely hero—a compassionate Samaritan (to Jews of Jesus' day Samaritans were social and religious outcasts due to their mixed racial heritage). The narrative is meant to communicate memorably the morality of being a neighbor to others, regardless of their ethnicity, while simultaneously subverting the view that one's ethnic heritage could qualify or disqualify one from true spiritual righteousness and belonging to God. Jesus' parable thus challenges the parochial character of the altruism that Haidt takes to be the main pragmatic value of religion.

Of course, many people hear and even teach religious narratives like the parable of the Good Samaritan without the narrative's affecting their evaluative outlook in the intended way. In a now famous experiment conducted by John Darley and Daniel Batson,[18] some Princeton seminarians were instructed to give a talk on the Good Samaritan while others were told to give a talk on job prospects for seminarians. Some of the subjects from each group were told that they had ample time to walk to the building where their audience would be waiting, while others were told that they were going to be late and had to hurry. Along the way, the seminarians all had to pass by a man wearing shabby clothes, slumped in an alley doorway. Of those who believed they were on time for their talk 63% stopped to help the man, while only 10% of those in a hurry stopped to help or even to check on the man. The content of the talk, by contrast, did not have a statistically significant impact on whether the seminarians stopped to help.

This study might appear initially to undermine the claim that religious narratives can have a profound impact on evaluative outlooks. It might be thought, in other words, that the motivational influence of a subtle situational variable (whether one is in a hurry) is stronger than the motivational influence of the narrative, even when one has the narrative almost directly before one's mind. After all, 90% of the hurried seminarians who had just been preparing a talk on the Good Samaritan didn't stop to help the man. Before drawing such a conclusion, however, note the inherent ambiguity of the case. The authors explain that the "victim should appear somewhat ambiguous—ill-dressed, possibly in need of help, but also possibly drunk or even potentially dangerous."[19] It is possible, therefore, that some of the seminarians' evaluative outlooks had been influenced over time by the parable of the Good Samaritan to include a concern to help those in need, but they simply did not perceive the man as needing help. It is also possible that some of the seminarians who did not stop simply judged that they had a moral obligation to arrive for their talk on time (or as close to on time as possible) and that that obligation was weightier in this case than any obligation they might have to help the ambiguously distressed man.

Of course, less heartening explanations of the seminarians' behavior are available. After all, simply having a moral-religious narrative before your mind is not the same thing as

[18] John Darley and C. Daniel Batson, "From Jerusalem to Jericho: a study of situational and dispositional variables in helping behavior," *Journal of Personality and Social Psychology* 27 (1973): 100–108.

[19] Darley and Batson, p. 102.

having so internalized the narrative that it transforms your evaluative outlook and motivates your behavior. Whatever objections might be raised to the set-up of Darley and Batson's experiment, it seems reasonable to conclude that having the parable of the Good Samaritan before their minds should have encouraged the seminarians to help, or at least attempt to help, or investigate whether help was needed, more than they did. Søren Kierkegaard argues for a difference between the kind of understanding that grounds academic success and the kind of understanding that essentially involves a will-engaging appreciation of the significance for one's life of that which is understood. Such appreciative understanding contrasts sharply with the mere verbal understanding of one who professes the truth, but fails to see, feel, and act in accordance with it. Indeed, he concludes, "to understand and to understand are two things."[20] It thus can happen that one thinks one has a religious value, but in fact lacks it, because the value has not been sufficiently integrated into one's character.

One way religions attempt to move their members beyond mere verbal understanding to the kind of life-guiding, appreciative understanding that Kierkegaard has in view is by encouraging regular participation in actions that accord with, and express, religious beliefs. Regularly serving in a soup kitchen, caring for orphans, and visiting the elderly in convalescent homes, for example, can reinforce a person's religious value of caring for the needs of others and treating others as one would like to be treated.

In an effort to take their members beyond mere verbal understanding of spiritual truths and to inculcate life-guiding appreciative understanding, religious communities also engage in various practices and symbolic rituals that evoke emotions and desires, directing them toward their proper objects, engage the body in symbolic activity, and so shape the evaluative dispositions and wills of participants. William LaFleur explores how ritual practices have helped to shape the moral outlooks of Japanese Buddhists, specifically with respect to the issue of abortion. He writes:

> Instead of logic chopping and the unconnected neat boxes produced by definitionism, ritual provides activities that fuse a wide variety of things that seem otherwise unrelated. Whole ganglia of semantic units are present in ritual—and allowed to seem coordinated on a deep level. Ritual, then, can operate with considerable effect and power in the realm of morals. It can, much more than we usually realize, be one of the odd but important pieces we can pick up and fit into that piece of bricolage that is our moral posture in the world.[21]

LaFleur goes on to explain in lucid detail the symbolic significance of a ritual performed at the Nembutsu-ji temple in Kyoto. Behind the temple in a grove beyond a cemetery sits a hexagonal sculpture with six images of the bodhisattva, a savior figure, Jizō, who is closely associated with children and who is believed to be voluntarily present in each of

[20] *The Sickness Unto Death*, ed. trans. Howard V. Hong and Edna H. Hong (Princeton, NJ: Princeton University Press, 1980), pp. 91–92.

[21] William R. LaFleur, *Liquid Life: Abortion and Buddhism in Japan* (Princeton, NJ: Princeton University Press, 1992), p. 15.

the six realms of the universe to aid those who suffer and to draw them toward Nirvana. Visitors who have had young children die, including many who have had abortions, ladle water over each of the images of Jizō in an act that symbolizes the provision of relief for their deceased children and fetuses. He suggests that this ritual practice is importantly tied to Japanese Buddhist views of abortion. Rather than viewing human life as having a definite beginning and ending point and then debating whether unborn fetuses have already crossed the threshold into life, LaFleur argues, many Japanese Buddhists have a more "fluid" conception of life according to which children become more and more solidified in their this-worldly existence as they grow older and, once having become fully formed human beings, they then begin gradually to fade back out of this-worldly existence in old age. According to this view, then, fetuses are lives in the making (i.e., in the process of becoming), but are not yet fully solidified human lives. When fetal development is interrupted by miscarriage or abortion, the fetus is believed to flow back into (or, rather, stay in) its pre-embodied—"liquid"—form of life to be born again at a later time, hopefully into better circumstances. Abortions are thus mourned as a kind of temporary postponement of the life-forming process, but are not thought of as the taking of a fully formed life. Rituals such as the one practiced at Nembutsu-ji help to give shape to this evaluative outlook and to reinforce it once it is formed. As LaFleur explains, the act of ladling water over the images of Jizō physically symbolizes that the lives of the "mizuko"—literally "children of the waters"—were never fully solidified and that they thus continue to live on in their liquid existence, hopefully to be born again at another time. As participants perform the ritual, they receive comfort from the opportunity to care symbolically for their deceased children and the physical reminder that their little ones continue to exist in a liquid form of life shapes their evaluative outlook.

Ritual plays a similar role in shaping Christian evaluative outlooks. In the Eucharist, for example, the bread and wine are taken as symbols (and in the Catholic tradition as literal instantiations) of the broken body and shed blood of Jesus, whose physical death on a Roman cross is understood to be efficacious for the forgiveness of the sins of those who place their faith in him. Eating the bread and drinking the wine remind the faithful of Jesus' self-sacrificial death. This is why the Eucharist is often observed amidst the backdrop of an environment that evokes emotions of humble gratitude and solemn joy through music, prayers of gratitude, or other means. This ritual is also a physical enactment of the unity of the Christian community—"the body of Christ"—with one another, as they find their spiritual identity in their relationship with Christ.

Similarly, in baptism Christians are either sprinkled or immersed in water to symbolize and physically enact their death to their old sin-dominated selves and their rebirth into new spiritual life in Christ, an act that at once connotes the washing away of sin, reminds them of Jesus' death and physical resurrection, and points forward to the yet future physical resurrection of the Christian. Such rituals, typically referred to in the tradition as sacraments, can have a profound influence on the evaluative outlooks of those who participate in them regularly. The Eucharist, especially when taken in community, can, for example, help a person to begin to see herself as a member of a unified communal "body."

Likewise, the gratitude evoked by the ritual can enhance and even constitute one's appreciation of the significance of Christ's gracious sacrifice for the forgiveness of sins in a way that motivates repentance from sin, joyful living, and humble forgiveness of others.

Religions influence evaluative outlooks in myriad other ways. Here we will mention just one more common way. Members of religious groups often remind themselves and each other in formal and informal ways of their shared commitment to important moral principles and spiritual truths. This helps to keep those aspects of their religious worldviews at the forefront of conscious awareness and heighten the salience of those aspects of their worldviews for moral perception and deliberation. Religious traditions have long employed such regular reminders as a part of their communal religious life and they have used art, architecture and articles of clothing in service of this practice. Tefillin, or phylacteries, for example, are small cube-shaped boxes containing texts from the Torah that are worn by Orthodox Jews across the forehead and the arm or hand as a daily reminder that the Torah is to be ever before one's mind and is to be lived out in one's actions.[22]

Recent psychological research has suggested the effectiveness of such regular reminders by demonstrating that cues that cause people to think about religion and morality significantly decrease immoral behaviors and increase morally upright behaviors. In one set of studies,[23] for example, researchers informed a group of students that they were to take a test and, when they were finished, to report the number of answers they got right. The students were allowed to take their test with them when they left the testing room, so they knew that no one would check their answers. The researchers promised that at the end of the test two randomly selected students would receive $10 per correct answer reported. The subjects were split into two groups and before beginning the test one group was asked to recall as many of the ten commandments as they could remember (with no control for religious commitment or affiliation), while the other group was asked to recall ten books they read in high school. The group that was asked to recall the ten commandments did not cheat at all, as indicated by the fact that the number of correct answers they reported was the same as the number the students got correct in a control condition, while the group that was asked to recall ten books from high school cheated to a moderate degree when given the opportunity to do so. The researchers achieved similar results by asking students to sign an honor code before taking the test. In another experiment, a different team of researchers placed an image of human eyes (as opposed to an image of flowers) above a notice to pay on an honor system for coffee and tea in the break room of the Psychology Division at the University of Newcastle.[24] They found that the ratio of donations for the drinks to volume consumed was 2.76 times higher on average during weeks when the eyes

[22] Cf., Deuteronomy 6:4–9

[23] Nina Mazar, On Amir, and Dan Ariely, "The dishonesty of honest people: a theory of self-concept maintenance," *Journal of Marketing Research* XLV (2008): 633–644.

[24] Melissa Bateson, Daniel Nettle, and Gilbert Roberts, "Cues of being watched enhance cooperation in a real world setting," *Biology Letters* (2006): 412–414.

were displayed over weeks when flowers were displayed. If such subtle reminders of moral norms or the mere quasi-perception of being watched can influence behavior so dramatically, surely repeated reminders from fellow members of one's religious community can have similar effects on behavior and evaluative outlooks.

The reality of ontological religious value

In light of evolutionary accounts of religious psychology such as Haidt's, in light of the subtle ways that religious practices can shape psychological religious values, and in light of the apparent fact that emotions play a crucial role in our epistemic access to ontological religious value, we might wonder whether it is reasonable to believe in the existence of ontological religious value. Have we any reason to think that psychological religious values might actually be epistemically appropriate responses to value that exists independently of the valuing subject? This is a large topic, but we here conclude by offering a few brief considerations in favor of the existence of ontological religious value. Let us begin with the point about the essential epistemic inadequacy of "information" derived from our emotions.

Whether God designed us to form religious beliefs and be sensitive to ontological religious value, or our religious psychology is an incidental by-product of random mutations favored and established purely by mechanisms of survival and reproduction, it seems that emotions play an important role in shaping our understanding of religious value. As Haidt observed in his study of ordinary human moral reasoning, many widespread and strongly held value judgments seem to be formed on the basis of emotions rather than discursive reasoning.

One reason that people may feel that emotions can't possibly be sources of accurate information is that they take emotions to be "non-cognitive" feelings or bodily perturbations. This is the view of William James,[25] and he has present-day followers such as Antonio Damasio[26] and Jesse Prinz.[27] Even these "non-cognitivists" have ways of explaining how emotions give rise to beliefs and judgments, but a more dominant and more elegant way of conceiving emotions as originating judgments is to think of them as a kind of perception, as ways of "seeing" the situations that have bearing on our human concerns (see also Deonna and Teroni, 2015).[28] Sense perceptions are not always reliable, especially in demanding situations such as bird-watching and scientific use of microscopes and telescopes. Without the proper conceptual training (cultivation), we may see the birds or

---

25 "What is an emotion?," *Mind* 9:18–205.

26 *Descartes' Error: Emotion, Reason, and the Human Brain* (New York: Avon, 1994).

27 *Gut Reactions* (Oxford: Oxford University Press, 2004).

28 We have both defended this kind of account of emotions. See: Robert C. Roberts, *Emotions in the Moral Life*, chapters 3 and 4; and Adam C. Pelser, "Emotion, evaluative perception, and epistemic justification," in *Emotion and Value*, ed. Sabine Roeser and Cain Todd (Oxford: Oxford University Press, 2014), pp. 106–122. An early defender of something like a perceptual view of emotions is Ronald de Sousa, *The Rationality of Emotions* (Cambridge, MA: MIT Press, 1987).

the object of scientific inquiry, and have no idea what we're seeing, or think we're seeing one thing while in fact we're seeing something else. A similar point might be made about wine tasting, refereeing fast-paced sporting events, crime scene investigation, and any number of other perceptually demanding activities. Something analogous is true of our emotions. When we're angry, we see somebody as having culpably offended against something important to us—perhaps as having done a grave injustice. Sometimes our anger is exactly right: it's an accurate perception of an injustice. But many people get angry in an undisciplined way, seeing as injustices things that aren't. A person who is rightly formed emotionally (morally) will have a strong tendency to see moral situations correctly, just as the expert bird-watcher tends to identify bird species accurately. A person with the moral virtues is a person who is rightly formed emotionally. For such a person, then, emotional perceptions are reliable (not infallible), and the fact that such a person feels anger (or guilt, or anxiety, or hope, or gratitude) can justify moral judgments because such a person tends to be accurate in his or her moral perceptions. Something analogous may be true of the religious emotions: the saint or religious sage may be so formed in her character that her religious judgments about ontological values are reliable.

But if the basic religious dispositions were formed by an evolutionary process, doesn't this suggest that they're *basically* unreliable, so that no amount of cultivation will bring it about that they reliably give access to ontological values? We think the answer is no. Evolutionary accounts of religious psychology like Haidt's are not obviously inconsistent with realism about religious values.[29] If God or some other ultimate religious entity exists, it is not improbable that an evolved cross-cultural emotional disposition, such as the one that Haidt, following Richard Shweder, designates "the ethics of divinity," might be an attuned response-type to the (ontological, transcendent) value of that reality.

It can be plausibly argued that if God, as a transcendent rational orderer, does not exist, and the rational powers of human beings are products of random genetic mutations selected from *only* by the mechanism of adaptation (survival long enough to reproduce), then we have no reason to trust those powers when they are applied to something incommensurably more complicated and difficult than mere survival, such as higher mathematics and theories in such sciences as physics, psychology, and biology. That is, if our minds evolved only to facilitate the perpetuation of our genes, we have no reason to think that our minds can be trusted to get to the truth in such matters as the theory of evolution. Thus the thesis of Alvin Plantinga's recent book is that "there is superficial conflict but deep concord between science and theistic religion, but superficial concord and deep conflict between science and naturalism."[30] Purely naturalistic theories of moral psychology seem to undercut their own claim to be adequately rational, suggesting that the theory of evolution needs to be supplemented with theism.

[29] Alvin A. Plantinga defends this consistency claim at length in chapters 5 and 6 of *Where the Conflict Really Lies: Science, Religion, and Naturalism* (Oxford: Oxford University Press, 2011).

[30] *Where the Conflict Really Lies*, p. ix, italics removed.

A moral psychologist, then, who followed Shweder[31] and Haidt in regarding the divinity–sanctity emotional–evaluative disposition as a fundamental moral feature of the human mind might naturally think that some of the deliverances of this faculty will probably have objective correlates. Haidt comments, for example, on a kind of rational response characteristic of a person whose moral culture, in contrast with that of the Western intellectual establishment, supplies him with the conceptual wherewithal to articulate this sense:

> The body is a temple, not a playground. Even if it does no harm and violates nobody's rights when a man has sex with a chicken carcass, he still shouldn't do it because *it degrades him, dishonors his creator, and violates the sacred order of the universe* (pp. 116–17, italics added).

The person who thinks (and responds emotionally) in this way about sex has a value-laden picture of his body integrated into a wider value-laden picture of the universe in which it lives. Both his body and the universe belong to a sacred order by reference to which certain actions are to be eschewed as repugnant and as violations.

Commentators like Martha Nussbaum[32] and Paul Bloom[33] stress the moral dark side of disgust as manifested in racism, homophobia, and caste divisions, and advocate its elimination, as far as possible, from our moral vocabulary and consciousness. They evaluate it from the point of view of the ethics of justice and harm, which in Haidt's psychology are equally fundamental to the human moral constitution. And they find disgust to be an emotion without redeeming value. Haidt, wishing to be less reductive and truer to fundamental human nature, needs to find a place for it, and we think that place must be in a balanced integration with our other moral dispositions. Classic moral philosophers found a place for the disgust disposition in their treatment of the virtue of temperance.[34] Virtues regulate and shape the passions, bringing it about that the person is disgusted at *truly* disgusting things, and delighted by *really* delightful things; the innate passion disposition determines only very broadly the kinds of moral objects that evoke the different responses. Innate passion dispositions are not, in themselves, adequate guides to ethics. All passions, including joy and hope and gratitude, are subject to perversion, and must be properly trained in terms of an adequate vocabulary to get their objects right.

Nevertheless, our natural inclination to perceive ontological religious value through emotional sensitivities to sacredness and degradation give us as much reason to believe in the existence of ontological religious value as our natural sensitivities to harm and fairness give us to believe in the objective value of justice. After all, we have no reason to privilege

[31] For a defense of realism about such "metaphysical realities," see: Richard Shweder, "The metaphysical realities of the unphysical sciences: or why vertical integration seems unrealistic to ontological pluralists" in *Creating Consilience: Integrating the Sciences and the Humanities*, ed. Edward Slingerland and Mark Collard (Oxford: Oxford University Press, 2012), pp. 56–73.

[32] *Political Emotions* (Cambridge, MA: Harvard University Press, 2013), chapter 9.

[33] *Just Babies* (New York: Random House, 2013), chapter 5.

[34] See Thomas Aquinas, *Summa Theologiae*, the Second Part of the Second Part, Question 144.

some of these evaluative intuitions (or psychological values) over others, since, as Thomas Reid pointed out with respect to our epistemic faculties like reason and sense perception, they came "out of the same shop" having been made "by the same artist."[35] Just as a well-developed passion for justice can be a reliable source of information about the justice and injustice of various situations, so too a well-developed disgust disposition can be a reliable source of information about the disvalue of degrading acts. The person who finds having sex with a chicken carcass disgusting and thus ruled out for the reasons that Haidt identifies may be right in an objective sense. Maybe such an action does morally pollute the person who performs it (even if it doesn't "harm" him in any other, more obvious, way) and violate the sacred order of the universe. Maybe it's contrary to God's will for persons. Maybe it's contrary to human nature, not in the sense that people can't do it and be complacent about others who do it, but that they can't do it while properly respecting themselves and the created order and being in a fully appropriate relationship with God.

What *is* the created order? What is it to respect the dignity of human bodies? We can expect only a minimum of intercultural agreement on these questions. Cultivated people who haven't been too badly spoiled by reductive moral theories may mostly agree on the chicken carcass question and on defecating in public (the ancient cynics tried to challenge ordinary moral sensibilities even on this one). But in our view the more fully elaborated conception of human nature and the moral nature of the universe must be worked out over long periods of cultural history punctuated with the aid of particularly wise individuals like Confucius, the Hebrew prophets, Socrates, and Jesus, and many lesser lights who refine and apply their insights and recall the straying generations to the traditions.

We think that an adequate moral psychology will take account of all the basic evaluative intuitions that our evolution has bequeathed to us, including at least the ones that Haidt identifies: Sanctity/Degradation, Authority/Subversion, Loyalty/Betrayal, Fairness/Cheating, Care/Harm, and Liberty/Oppression. In our view, a rational ethics must consider these as a package, and thus as balancing and qualifying one another, as far as possible. Pertinent to the matter of the present paper, such integration (particularly of Sanctity/Degradation and Authority/Subversion) will imply that an adequate moral psychology must have a religious dimension and endorse the cultivation of psychological religious values. We also propose that such cultivation be realist in the sense that the psychological values be conceived as dispositional responses to ontological religious value.[36]

35 *An Inquiry into the Human Mind on the Principles of Common Sense*, ed. Derek R. Brookes (University Park, PA: The Pennsylvania State University Press, 1997), VI xx, p. 169.

36 The views expressed in this article are those of the authors and do not necessarily reflect the official policy or position of the U.S. Air Force, the U.S. Department of Defense, or the U.S. government.

Section 4

Concluding remarks

Chapter 19

From values to valuation: an interdisciplinary approach to the study of value

Tobias Brosch and David Sander

Value matters

Value is one of the central concepts governing human life. It reflects the importance that something holds for us: what doesn't have any value is of no interest. Whether we choose between consumer goods, whether we decide whom to marry or which political candidate to elect, whether we ask ourselves what is morally right, or beautiful, or sacred, value plays a crucial role. As illustrated by the variety of contributions represented in this volume, the investigation of value is central to many disciplines studying human thinking, feeling, and behavior, including economics, neuroscience, philosophy, psychology, or sociology. Scholars from these different disciplines have advanced our understanding of issues such as: "What is value?," "Where does it come from?," or "How does it impact our emotions, choices and experiences?."

While value research is of interest to many different disciplines and academic traditions, they define the phenomenon somewhat differently and focus their investigation on different aspects. For example, many economists and neuroscientists conceptualize value as a currency that allows comparing different goods or experiences on the same scale in a choice situation. This conceptualization can be traced back, e.g., to philosopher–economists like Adam Smith (1776/1994), who defined value as the "worth of an object" that was determined by how much people would work for it or would be willing to pay for it. Moral philosophers such as Immanuel Kant (1785/2000) used the term in a different, vastly expanded sense. Here, value refers to the "importance of an action," in the context of ethical questions such as: "What is the right thing to do?" or "What is the good way to live?." This definition is reflected in contemporary research in sociology and social psychology, where value is conceptualized as a motivational construct that guides choices across situations, often framed as shared beliefs about ideal objectives with transcendental significance ("core values" such as honor, love, justice, life, civil liberties). These different conceptualizations of value obviously do not refer to one and the same thing[1]. However,

[1] As noted by one of the reviewers of our book proposal, "... the word is used in very different senses. '*Values*' usually refers to moral or ethical principles. '*Value*,' in contrast, refers to how highly one appraises a good or experience. Though the terms differ only by one letter, I believe they are very different entities, and it's not obvious that they belong in a single book."

they tap into a common core component of value, in its broadest sense "the importance of something." All value researchers have in common that they are interested in the constructs and mechanisms that people use to define what is important to them. Economists are interested in value as a construct that allows modeling choices, cognitive psychologists and neuroscientists investigate the mechanisms that explain how an individual ascribes value, sociologists and social psychologists focus on concepts of value that can be shared within a social group, philosophers address a vast array of conceptual questions concerning the properties of value at all these different stages. Thus, we hold that the different research traditions and definitions of value do not refer to completely different entities, but that all of them address critical aspects of the process of valuation, of attributing importance to something. For this reason we think that a stronger integration of the different perspectives in value research can be useful. The aim of this volume is to bring together the different perspectives, to contribute to an interdisciplinary dialogue by providing a common reference point that may serve as a resource for interdisciplinary cross-fertilization, and to "combine the forces" of the different approaches to reach a better understanding of value. In this final chapter, we briefly look back at the different contributions assembled in the preceding chapters and highlight some themes that may prove useful in order to accomplish such interdisciplinary cross-fertilization.

What is value and where does it come from?

The first part of the *Handbook* tackles the questions: "What is value?" and "Where does it come from?." We posed these questions to researchers from several different disciplines in order to bring together multiple views on this fundamental issue. Tappolet and Rossi present a philosophical perspective. They give an overview of the main concepts and debates on the philosophy of values, discussing the important definitional distinction between evaluative concepts, evaluative judgments, evaluative sentences, and evaluative facts. They then present different positions concerning the objectivity of value, i.e., whether value can exist independently of what we think and feel. They finally introduce a topic to be picked up in many of the subsequent chapters: the link between value judgments and emotions. Rabinowicz and Rønnow-Rasmussen discuss conceptual distinctions that are central to debates about value in modern philosophy, such as distinctions between non-relational value and relational value (something is "good" versus "good for someone"), and between final and non-final value (something is "good" versus "good for something"). Higgins presents a psychological perspective on the mechanisms of valuation, proposing the definition of value as "the experience of a force of attraction toward something or repulsion from something." He then addresses the topic of the determinants of value. This issue has often been framed in terms of the hedonic principle: value comes from experiencing pleasure and from not being in pain. In contrast to this view, he argues that hedonic concerns are not exclusive in determining value, and reviews evidence for the importance of factors such as knowledge and control, need satisfaction, shared beliefs, personal standards, and even adversities and obstacles in the attribution of value. Schwartz reviews one of the most influential theories in sociological and social psychological value research. Values are defined here as "beliefs about a broad motivational goal that express what is important to people." In his contribution, Schwartz presents the organization of individual value-types according to their motivational content, a structure that has been confirmed by a vast amount of cross-cultural research. He discusses mechanisms by which values can influence decisions and behaviors, such as influencing people's allocation of attention, situational interpretation, and valuation of the consequences of a given action. Levy and Glimcher present the economic and neurobiological perspective on value. In this view, value is perceived as a "converged representation of the evaluation of a choice option," a common currency that allows comparing and choosing between different options. They review a large amount of brain-imaging research, outlining the neural basis of economic valuation, pointing out the important role of a network centered on the ventromedial prefrontal cortex. Their review illustrates to what extent a better understanding of the neural mechanisms of valuation is helpful, allowing not only modeling choice behavior, but even predicting individual choices. Moll, Zahn, and de Oliveira-Souza's contribution complements the previous chapter by discussing the neural mechanisms underlying the impact of moral values, which are here defined as "trans-situational goals tied to the welfare of others." While classic economic perspectives are based on the assumption that individuals try to maximize their self-interest, here the focus is on the mechanisms of behavior that set back self-interest in favor of other-interest. The chapter reviews research illustrating how neural regions representing social concepts, emotional influences, and contextual-sequential knowledge interact to realize behavior that opposes our self-interest. Boer and Boehnke round off the first part of the *Handbook* by outlining a developmental perspective on value. Drawing on a review of central developmental theories, they illustrate the processes by which values develop and change during childhood and across the lifespan, discussing both intergenerational and intragenerational value transmission mechanisms. In the second part of their chapter, they outline mechanisms of value change within and across societies and cultures.

While an attempt to coherently integrate these various chapters would certainly be overly ambitious, we can nevertheless try to distill some insights resulting from the ensemble of contributions. Importantly, it seems as if the conceptual distance between the definitions of value that are used by the different disciplines and authors is not insurmountable. The types of value presented in the different chapters may roughly be grouped into "decision value" (referring to the worth or evaluation of an object in a concrete behavior situation; see Chapters 1, 2, 3, 5) and "core value" (referring to a cross-situational concept of worth; see Chapters 1, 2, 4, 6, 7). One of the main conceptual differences seems to be that decision value "belongs to" (or is attributed to) an evaluated object, while core value resides in the evaluator and informs or modulates the evaluation of an object. However, as already pointed out in several of the chapters, decision value and core value interact closely during the process of valuation. For example, in Schwartz's contribution, one of the mechanisms by which core value influences decision-making is by modulating the valuation of the different choice options and their consequences (i.e., decision value).

The chapters by Levy and Glimcher, as well as Moll, Zahn, and de Oliveira-Souza, illustrate that decision value and core value have separable, but partly overlapping, neural representations, indicating potential functional similarities. We will discuss this issue further below.

Values, emotions, and decision-making

For the second section of the *Handbook*, we invited our authors to address the links between value, emotion, and decision-making. The first contribution comes from the philosophical perspective, with Deonna and Teroni elaborating on the close connection between value and emotion. They discuss several aspects of this connection, including the role of emotions in elucidating the nature of value, the role of emotions in our gaining access to values, and the value of emotions. Von Scheve outlines a sociological perspective on the origins of values with a focus on the important role of affect. He discusses the function of emotion and affect in value commitment and morality, emphasizing the role of the social and cultural environment within which individuals are socialized. Sokol-Hessner and Phelps outline the neural and psychological mechanisms underlying the influence of emotion in decision-making. They review evidence illustrating that emotion and value are inherently and fundamentally intertwined. They furthermore demonstrate how emotional processes may represent and modulate decision value and may underlie core value-related influences such as concerns for fairness. Gibson, Tanner, and Wagner present the concept of protected values, referring to objects or behavioral standards that "have no price," i.e., that are thought absolute and are protected from tradeoffs. This perspective attempts to integrate the moral dimension into economic decision models. The authors discuss the implications of research on protected values for business policies and political regulation. Jiga-Boy, Maio, Haddock, and Tapper elaborate the mechanisms that link core values to decisions and behavior in several behavioral domains, such as political voting, prosocial behavior, sustainable environmental behavior, and consumer decision-making. They discuss the limits and boundary conditions of the link between core value and behavior, pointing out that the impact of core value on behavior should be considered at the level of aggregate behaviors instead of single behaviors.

This section assembles important insights concerning the role of values and valuation in decision-making and behavior, and the importance of affect and emotion in this context. In concrete decision situations, valuation processes are used to evaluate and compare different options and "tag" one of them for selection. The function of value as a common currency, as put forward by neuroeconomic approaches, emphasizes the possibility to integrate several positive and negative dimensions into one "verdict." Importantly, research on morality, prosocial behavior, protected values, and sustainable environmental behavior reviewed in this section illustrates that not only the consideration of self-interest drives valuation and decision, but also considerations about others and the group. Value representations may furthermore organize behavior even in the absence of a concrete choice situation. For example, a person with pronounced prosocial values may make efforts to select environments in which concrete altruistic behaviors can be realized. Furthermore, value representations can be used to promote and distribute conceptions of importance and to influence the implicit and explicit rules that guide the functioning of social groups in the political process.

To move toward an integration of decision value and core value, it may be helpful to revisit the notion of value as a force of attraction toward something or repulsion from something (see the contribution by Higgins, this volume; see also: Lewin 1951). Valuation can thus be considered as the result of a "value field" with different zones of attraction and repulsion that define the decision value of different choice options (see Fig. 19.1). Core value differences may thus represent differences in the shape of this force field, which determine the decision value of an option and allow accounting for individual differences in the decision value of one option. For example, the option to donate a portion of one's income in order to save a part of the rainforest may seem highly attractive to a person with pronounced environmental core values, who may thus be motivated to seek out opportunities to do so. The same behavior may be evaluated as neutral or even repulsive by another person with a different "value landscape."

In this framework, economists would mainly be interested in the "read-out" of the decision value for different options that are situated in the field, cognitive and moral psychologists, as well as neuroscientists, would additionally investigate the structure of the field and the mechanisms that generate the "hills and troughs," sociologists would furthermore be interested in the structure and effects of inter-individual "landscape differences." While far from being a formal framework for decision value and core value, this perspective may point toward avenues for integrating concepts and research findings in value research.

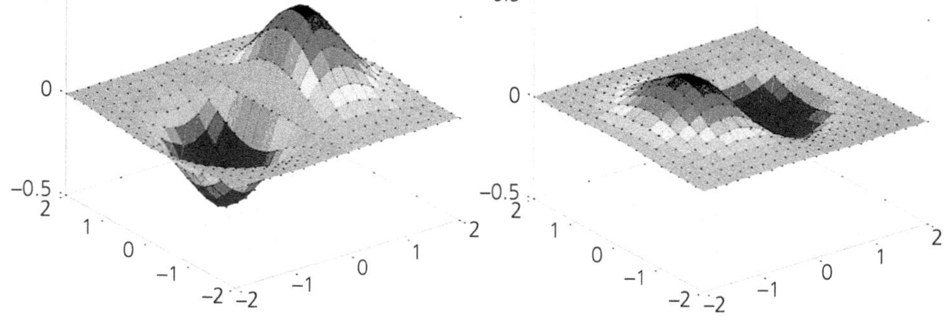

Fig. 19.1 Two different "value fields" with zones of attraction and repulsion that define the "decision value" of different choice options located at specific positions within the field. Differences in the overall "value landscape" of two individuals may represent individual "core value" differences. (See Plate 12.)

Another central theme of this section is the important role of emotion and affective processes in valuation and decision processes. The interaction of emotion and cognition has been the topic of enormous research interest over the last two decades. The role of emotion has been revised from an irrational bias to a source of information that helps individuals to interact with their environment in a more adaptive manner. The chapters presented in this section illustrate that the importance of affective processes also extends to the domain of valuation. Affect and value are strongly intertwined. More specifically, affective processes have been shown to represent both decision value and core value. This suggests strongly that value cannot be studied without studying emotion, and that emotion cannot be studied without studying value.

Varieties of value

The final section of the *Handbook* illustrates the "variety of value." Intended as a series of case studies that illustrates different approaches in value research, these contributions focus on selected aspects of different values, including their underlying mechanisms and their application potential in different domains. Ellingsen, Leknes, and Kringelbach review current research on the biological basis of hedonic value, the processing of pleasure and displeasure, and its influence on our behavior. A large amount of neuroscientific evidence on the determinants of hedonic value supports a separation of hedonic processing into several dissociable components related to wanting, liking, and learning. Rodogno addresses the topic of prudential value, which is concerned with the issue of "living a good life." He outlines the different philosophical and psychological perspectives that have been proposed with regard to this question, including approaches centered on hedonism, desire, happiness, and eudaimonia. He then discusses whether either subjective or objective approaches are most appropriate to tackle the question of the determinants of "a good life." Levinson discusses musical values, i.e. the different kinds of value that music can have (such as esthetic or artistic value, economic value, or practical value), and the relationships and correlations among these values or valuations. Dietz reviews the role of core value in the context of environmental behaviors and decisions, emphasizing the role of self-interest, altruism toward other humans, and altruism toward other species and the biosphere. Jost, Basevich, Dickson, and Noorbaloochi discuss the role of values in the political domain. They review a large body of research addressing the link between personality characteristics, value priorities, and political ideology. They argue that value pluralism in society results from variability in social, cognitive, and motivational factors, and discuss some of the implications for philosophical and political systems. Finally, Pelser and Roberts address the topic of religious value, differentiating between the ontological value of having a God and the psychological values that are informed by ones' religion. They move on to discuss the adaptive advantages of psychological values of religion independent of ontological questions in the context of recent findings in moral psychology.

From values to valuation: toward more interdisciplinary dialogue in value research

As outlined before, the aim of this volume is not to provide a comprehensive summary and integration of all value research, but rather to provide a common reference point that may serve as a resource for interdisciplinary dialogue and collaboration between researchers focused on decision value and researchers focused on core value. To illustrate the potential of such an approach, we will briefly review some recent neuroimaging research that is trying to bridge decision value and core value, focusing on the mechanisms underlying the conflict between self-interest and altruism (see also: Brosch and Sander 2013). This research investigates at the neurocognitive level how decision value is represented and modulated by core value during charitable donations. The first neuroimaging studies in this domain found increased activation of neural reward regions, including the striatum and the ventromedial prefrontal cortex, both when participants received money for themselves and when they decided to donate for a good cause (Hare et al. 2010; Moll et al. 2006), suggesting that both behaviors are based on a shared anatomical system of value representation. These valuations have been shown to be modulated by individual differences in core value hierarchies (Brosch et al. 2011). Charitable choices have furthermore been shown to be associated with increased recruitment of social cognition regions, such as dorsomedial prefrontal cortex (Brosch et al. 2011) and temporo-parietal junction (Morishima et al. 2012), which are involved in perspective-taking and thinking about the needs and goals of others. During charitable choices, social cognition regions show increased connectivity with regions representing economic value (Hare et al., 2010), and may thus increase the decision value of selfless actions. Thus, in addition to relatively indirect effects of core value on the beliefs and norms of an individual, which then result in behavioral consequences, core value may also directly modulate the decision value of behavioral options (see also Schwartz, this volume), potentially changing the "value landscape" outlined in Fig. 19.1.

However, this kind of research is only at the beginning, and many more efforts are needed. We hope that the collection of excellent chapters assembled in this volume will be helpful in this context, will encourage scholars to make new conceptual connections, to develop new and exciting research questions, to build interdisciplinary bridges, and to expand the boundaries of what they have previously considered as belonging to the field of value research.

References

Brosch, T. and Sander, D. (2013). Neurocognitive mechanisms underlying value-based decision-making: from core values to economic value. *Frontiers in Human Neuroscience*, **7**, 398.

Brosch, T., Coppin, G., Scherer, K. R., Schwartz, S., and Sander, D. (2011). Generating value(s): psychological value hierarchies reflect context-dependent sensitivity of the reward system. *Social Neuroscience*, **6**, 198–208.

Hare, T. A., Camerer, C. F., Knoepfle, D. T., O'Doherty, J., and Rangel, A. (2010). Value computations in ventral medial prefrontal cortex during charitable decision making incorporate input from regions involved in social cognition. *Journal of Neuroscience*, **30**, 583–590.

Kant, I. (1785/2000). *Grundlegung zur Metaphysik der Sitten*. Berlin: Suhrkamp.

Lewin, K. (1951). *Field theory in social science*. New York: Harper.

Moll, J., Krueger, F., Zahn, R., Pardini, M., de Oliveira-Souza, R., and Grafman, J. (2006). Human fronto-mesolimbic networks guide decisions about charitable donation. *Proceedings of the National Academy of Sciences*, **103**, 15623–15628.

Morishima, Y., Schunk, D., Bruhin, A., Ruff, C. C., and Fehr, E. (2012). Linking brain structure and activation in temporoparietal junction to explain the neurobiology of human altruism. *Neuron*, **75**, 73–79.

Smith, A. (1776/1994). *The wealth of nations*. New York: Modern Library.

Author index

f indicates footnotes

Subject index

f indicates footnotes

F